Patterns for a Purpose

A Rhetorical Reader

Canadian Edition

Barbara Fine Clouse / Kathleen Wall
University of Regina

**McGraw-Hill
Ryerson**

Toronto   Montréal   Boston   Burr Ridge, IL   Dubuque, IA   Madison, WI   New York
San Francisco   St. Louis   Bangkok   Bogotá   Caracas   Kuala Lumpur   Lisbon   London
Madrid   Mexico City   Milan   New Delhi   Santiago   Seoul   Singapore   Sydney   Taipei

McGraw-Hill Ryerson

ISBN-13: 978-0-07-098457-8
ISBN-10: 0-07-098457-3

1 2 3 4 5 6 7 8 9 10 TCP 1 9 8 7 6 5 4 3 2 1 0

Printed and bound in Canada.

Vice President and Editor-in-Chief: Joanna Cotton
Publisher: Cara Yarzab
Sponsoring Editor: Lisa Rahn
Marketing Manager: Michele Peach
Developmental Editors: Sara Braithwaite, Jennifer Oliver
Editorial Associate: Marina Seguin
Senior Supervising Editor: Joanne Limebeer
Copy Editor: Lisa Berland
Team Lead, Production: Paula Brown
Cover Design: Brett J. Miller, BJM Graphic Design & Communications
Cover Image: Burazin/Getty Images
Interior Design: Brett J. Miller, BJM Graphic Design & Communications
Page Layout: Bookman Typesetting Co. Inc.
Printer: Transcontinental Printing Group

Library and Archives Canada Cataloguing in Publication Data

Clouse, Barbara Fine
   Patterns for a purpose: a rhetorical reader / Barbara Fine Clouse, Kathleen Wall. — Canadian ed.

Includes bibliographical references and index.
ISBN 978-0-07-098457-8

   1. College readers.   2. English language—Rhetoric—Problems, exercises, etc.   3. Report writing—Problems, exercises, etc.   I. Wall, Kathleen, 1950–   II. Title.

PE1417.C6314 2009   808'.0427   C2009-903665-7

Brief Contents

Contents

Chapter 9

COMPARISON AND CONTRAST

Chapter 10

CAUSE-AND-EFFECT ANALYSIS

Chapter 11

CLASSIFICATION AND DIVISION

works to persuade his audience that the non-violent way is the best, using cause-and-effect analysis and definition.

Chapter 12

A CASEBOOK FOR ARGUMENTATION AND PERSUASION

Grady attempts to persuade us by describing the rewards of walking, using examples of famous walkers to illustrate how walking affects our experience of nature and time, and encourages us to create a new relationship with the natural world—a crucial step in respecting and becoming stewards of that world.

Mason uses examples of institutions, cities, and countries that have addressed their need to conserve energy in order to persuade us that we can reduce our carbon footprint by thinking small, not big.

Falconer uses narrative and cause and effect to consider how the car has become so important in our culture and to reveal its impact on our cities and our environment.

Dr. Maté uses cause and effect and description to encourage us to see drug addiction as a response to brain chemistry gone awry, often damaged by the addict's traumatic and alienating experiences.

To consider whether addiction should be treated as a disease, the authors use contrast and comparison to examine addiction in twins to scientifically explore how individuals might be genetically predisposed to addiction.

Sullum uses examples to argue that the image of heroin addiction as a complete loss of control is false, and uses facts and statistics to point out that the number of heroin addicts is considerably smaller than the number of people who have used heroin, leading him to argue that heroin users have control over their drug use.

After 40 years, White returns to a family vacation spot with his son and comes to a startling conclusion. To express his feelings and relate his experience, White combines description with narration and comparison-contrast.

Thematic Contents

Places with Special Meaning

Childhood, Adolescence, Adulthood, and Death

Technology

Relationships between Humans and Animals

The Environment

Race

Preface

How do we teach students to write in an age of MSN® Messenger? At a recent meeting to talk about the University of Regina's first-year English classes, the associate deans observed that employers most value the ability to write well, yet acquiring this skill seems unimportant to the average undergraduate who communicates perfectly well with LOL and ;).

We teach students to write by challenging them to engage with some of the most important questions of our time—of any time. This rhetorical reader, as a result, contains some challenging essays: Mark Kingwell's "What Is the Good Life?" challenges students as it thinks through one of the oldest philosophical questions. Who doesn't want to decide for themselves what the good life really is? This reader also includes some controversial essays, such as J. M. Kearns' "How Men Choose Women." How many undergraduates are not interested in examining the gender stereotypes at play amongst people of their generation—if only to get the right boy or girl?

Any art, whether painting or composing or writing, involves ideas and a form for those ideas, the craft to express oneself, and the vision that deserves and needs to be expressed because it provides its authors and readers with a new perspective. So we teach students to write by engaging them in the conversation about the ideas central to Canadian and contemporary culture, while using and reflecting on models of writing that illustrate effective use of form and the writer's craft. We feel in a rush to bridge the gap between the high school opinion piece (which is as likely to be a poster or a poem as it is an essay) and the research paper students are going to need to write for their classes. But more than ever we need to help them develop the reflective and articulate voice that reaches out toward a diverse audience. (There's a very limited audience for—and not much nuance in—LOL.) The essays here are chosen to do precisely that.

Patterns for a Purpose is different from other rhetorical readers in two ways: it emphasizes the way that we can *think* through a writing task by using the patterns of development, and it acknowledges that many of the real-world writing tasks we undertake are ill-served by the rhetorical patterns in their purest form. For a Canadian history research paper, students are likely to use narration and description to provide a historical context, cause and effect to consider the impact of an event, and comparison and contrast to look at ways history affects the present. *Patterns* emphasizes the way writers can use and combine two or more rhetorical patterns. Every chapter provides a straight-forward example of the rhetorical mode, followed by essays that combine that pattern with others.

The Canadian essays in this edition reflect the variety of our voices. From Mark Kingwell's wrestling with ideas of the good life to Thomas King's thoughts about how our narratives shape our lives; from Carol Shields' musings on the delights and challenges of travelling to June Callwood's thoughts about forgiveness; from Brian Payton's startling evocation of a grizzly bear preserve and the nature of "bear-ness" to Wayne Grady's discussion of walking—these Canadian essays portray a particularly Canadian penchant for reflecting on and interrogating our culture.

Thorough pedagogy follows each essay. *Reading Closely and Thinking Critically* questions encourage students to think critically about the relationship between the essay and the world they live in, acknowledging that readers' experience and knowledge is their entry point into a piece of writing. In encouraging students to examine *Structure and Strategy* as well as consider *Language and Style,* the questions move readers beyond the content of the essay to consider the writer's craft; these questions enable students to discover the writing strategies that will work for them. Finally, the many writing assignments that range from journal entries to research papers help professors keep students writing in a variety of contexts.

A Note from Kathleen Wall

It was the remarkable and exciting quality of Canadian non-fiction that provided my inspiration for this adaptation of Barbara Fine Clouse's *Patterns for a Purpose*. I have included some difficult essays: Gabor Maté's "The Keys of Paradise" certainly challenges students as it examines the roots and nature of addiction. I have also included some controversial essays; several reviewers of the draft manuscript found J. M. Kearns' essay "How Men Choose Women" to be demeaning to men—a perception I don't share (or I wouldn't have included the essay in the first place). But clearly the manuscript reviewers' response suggests that Kearns examines an aspect of masculinity that these readers found uncomfortable.

A number of the readers of the draft manuscript hoped I would be able to incorporate engaging but fairly accessible academic essays. While I will certainly be searching for examples of academic writing as I think about a second edition, such essays are rare. Scholarly essays almost always assume some level of knowledge or expertise on the part of the reader—we simply can't know whether students have the background in sociology, psychology, or history, for example, to benefit from academic essays. Instead, I have chosen a couple of themes for more academic examples throughout the chapters—such as gender and the urban environment—that I believe students have experienced in their daily lives and can thus reflect on. In the chapter on definition, students are given R. W. Connell's definition of hegemonic masculinity; in the chapter on cause and effect, students are asked to consider how the shape of their cities influences their daily lives and their ability to respond to climate change. In this latter case, this issue is again introduced in the Chapter 12 casebook, in Tim Flannery's essay on cars in Toronto. The writing assignments at the end of each chapter give students the opportunity to write about disciplines they are more familiar with. Finally, the essays themselves are occasions for analysis; professors wanting to emphasize student engagement with ideas might find the *Connecting the Readings* questions in the pedagogy following each essay will stretch their students' analytical skills.

I admired Barbara Fine Clouse's use of a "casebook" to teach argument and persuasion. I decided to focus on two issues. The first set of essays picks up on a theme that considers our relationship to an environment being threatened by climate change. I selected these essays because, unlike those on substance abuse that follow, they address the issue from widely different vantage points. The three essays on substance abuse implicitly consider whether the Canadian "law and order" strategy is effective by examining the causes of substance abuse and asking whether the current practices adequately and accurately acknowledge those complex causes.

FEATURES OF THE CANADIAN EDITION

- **Showcases professional and student essays**: 42 lively essays, 32 written by professional writers, and 10 penned by student writers, provide excellent models.
- **Encourages critical reading through an analogy of a crime scene**: Using a crime scene investigator as a model, Chapter 1 harnesses a popular television concept to help students remember the stages of critical reading. This analogy suggests that students thoroughly examine the crime scene (the reading), and then ask questions about the crime (the author's logic). Next students should turn to their own knowledge of the wider world to provide the context that illuminates the reading in the same way an investigator examines the life of the victim to help make sense of the crime.
- **Reviews the writing process**: Chapters 2 and 3 explain the procedures for planning an essay, developing a thesis, drafting, revising, and editing.

Progressive drafts of an annotated essay in Chapters 2 and 3 exemplify the writing process.

- **Emphasizes the importance of a well-written thesis statement**: *Patterns* emphasizes that a thesis statement must be both arguable and significant, and illustrates how drafting and revising a thesis statement can be useful for writers as well as for readers. This edition of *Patterns for a Purpose* encourages writers to use the thesis statement to consider, before drafting, the most effective order in which to make their points and to ensure they have sufficient evidence to support their statement. The text offers academic thesis statements in examples throughout the text.

- **Provides extensive apparatus that supports reading and writing**: Headnotes precede every professional essay; each essay is followed by critical reading and thinking questions as well as questions that focus attention on structure, strategy, language, and style, discussion questions, and writing prompts.

- **Illustrates the structure of essays through annotated student examples**: Each rhetorical mode chapter presents a student's final paper with annotations that show its organization and layout.

- **Describes the uses for each rhetorical mode**: The "[Pattern] for a Purpose" sections describe how to employ each pattern to persuade, to inform, to relate experiences, to express feelings, and to entertain.

- **Demonstrates how to apply patterns for a *variety* of purposes**: The "[Pattern] at School, at Work, and in the Community" sections for each rhetorical mode explain how to use each pattern for writing in a variety of contexts.

- **Examines how to blend patterns**: Chapter 13 explains how to combine two or more patterns to achieve a writing purpose. Additionally, "Process Guidelines" boxes offer practical strategies for using and combining patterns of development, while "Combining Patterns for a Purpose" sections demonstrate how professional writers blend the modes to achieve a range of writing purposes.

- **Explores argumentation and persuasion in depth**: Chapter 12, *A Casebook for Argumentation and Persuasion*, is an in-depth study of this mode that includes six essays on two issues: the environment and substance abuse. Requiring students to apply their critical thinking and reading skills to synthesize and evaluate multiple perspectives on these two topics, this chapter's contents and essays provide a tremendous grounding for using this pattern.

- **Equips students with the tools to research and cite sources**: Chapter 14 provides clear guidelines for locating and evaluating sources as well as quoting, paraphrasing, and summarizing, and also explains that students need to respect and acknowledge the voices of others in their own writing.

SUPPLEMENTS

  ## For Professors

The following teaching tools are available for download from the Instructor Edition of the Online Learning Centre at **www.mcgrawhill.ca/olc/clouse**:

- Instructor's Manual
- PowerPoint slides

 Connect Composition, available at **www.connect english.ca**, can be used for student practice, homework, quizzes, and cumulative tests. Detailed grade reports enable instructors to see how each student performs on an assignment, and in the context of the overall class. The **Connect Composition** grade reports can be easily integrated with WebCT and Blackboard. With a single access code, students can read instructional material, work through practice problems, do homework, and take tests.

For Students

The Student Edition of the Online Learning Centre at **www.mcgrawhill.ca/ olc/clouse** offers various learning and study resources, including Web links to Internet research sources.

Connect Composition, available at **www.connect english.ca**, is a web-based assignment platform that helps professors *connect* their students to coursework and to success beyond the writing course.

For students, this innovative tool helps them to improve and to master writing and grammar skills through instructional video and animations, practice exercises and editing quizzes, and individualized feedback. Diagnostics point students to skill areas that require development. Making learning more efficient, **Connect Composition** allows students to create their own personalized study plan. Making learning accessible, students can engage with their coursework anytime and anywhere, making the learning process accessible.

For professors, **Connect Composition**'s easy-to-use course management tools mean that less time will be spent administering the course and more time can be spent teaching the course.

Connect Composition offers the best, most convenient way to learn, interact, and succeed!

(Note that *Connect Composition* is not automatically included with the textbook. Please speak with your *i*Learning Sales Specialist for details.)

ACKNOWLEDGMENTS

I owe a debt of gratitude to the following reviewers:

Jason Bermiller, Thompson Rivers University
Tim Chamberlain, Camosun College
Paula Crooks, Conestoga College
Arlene Davies-Fuhr, Grant MacEwan College
Christopher Gordon-Craig, University of Alberta
Dr. Nathan M. Greenfield, Algonquin College
Avrille E. Headley, George Brown College
Henry M. Heggie, Cambrian College
Joyce Hall, Seneca College
Carolyn Ives, Grant MacEwan College
Marcela Jonas, University of the Fraser Valley
Raj Mehta, Camosun College
Kathleen Moran, Conestoga College
Dr. Dennis Nighswonger, Lakehead University
Ken Paradis, Wilfrid Laurier University
Dr. K. B. Patterson, University of British Columbia
Alex Pierce, Cape Breton University
Barry Reynolds, John Abbott College
Melanie A. Rubens, Seneca College
Jonathan Singer, Seneca College
JJ Sudlow, Seneca College
Gail L. Tucker, University of New Brunswick

Thanks to my developmental editors at McGraw Hill Ryerson, Jennifer Oliver and Sara Braithwaite, both of whom were gracious and encouraging—as well as very helpful. Jennifer Oliver's summaries of the reviewers' comments made my revision infinitely easier and ensured that the people who took time to respond to the text were heard. My copy editor, Lisa Berland, brought her enthusiasm for precision to the text; I am grateful for her "fussy" ways. Joanne Limebeer ensured that the production process proceeded smoothly. This adaptation is entirely the fault of Lisa Rahn, my sponsoring editor at McGraw-Hill Ryerson. Her positive voice provided the support that I sometimes required. Finally, I thank Larry McDonald, University of Regina reference librarian extraordinaire, for all of his help.

Chapter 1

Reading Critically

We read to know we're not alone.

— C.S. Lewis

To admit authorities, however heavily furred and gowned, into our libraries and let them tell us how to read, what to read, what value to place upon what we read, is to destroy the spirit of freedom which is the breath of those sanctuaries. Everywhere else we may be bound by laws and conventions—there we have none.

— Virginia Woolf, "How Should One Read a Book?"

Much of your life thus far has involved reading. It's quite possible that you can barely begin your day without an accurate reading of your parent's or your roommate's moods. As you stumble into the kitchen after a late night (necessitated by your classes, of course), your eyes will sweep over whomever you find there. Do you see someone whose posture is rigid with defensiveness that says no even before you ask? Or someone bent with exhaustion like yours, practically wrapped around her cup of coffee, defending it against any interlopers? Or can you see someone cheerfully relaxed who might make you toast rather than forcing you to stumble around like the undead? If you negotiate this situation successfully, knowing when you can ask for favours or when you had better make your own toast, you're a skilful reader.

You read text messages, a language your parents can't quite decipher. (Clearly, you can pick up new vocabulary.) You read T-shirts at parties and infer whether the guy with "Your mother's worst nightmare" printed on his chest is self-ironic or rather mistakenly proud of himself. (You are sensitive to a writer's tone and can make inferences about the relationship between what someone says and what his tone suggests he means.) You read the status updates on your Facebook page; eventually you create a mental collage of your friends' lives. (You can synthesize.)

So you're ready to read critically. That doesn't mean your job is to criticize everything you read. Rather, it means that you need to learn, in an academic context, how to look beyond what is readily apparent in the text, to see beneath the surface and outside the boundaries. Reading critically includes evaluating the quality and reliability of a piece, drawing conclusions about the significance of the author's ideas and the meaning of the points he or she is making, and discovering connections between these new ideas and the knowledge base you are building through your experiences, observations, your classes, and your reading. In short, critical reading is *thoughtful* reading. It involves evaluating and assimilating the ideas you read, whether they are in textbooks, in journals, in newspapers, or on the Internet.

When you read material for your college or university classes, you are like a crime scene investigator. You know how they work. First they gather evidence. Their basic job is to be curious and observant. They attend to detail. Similarly, the first time you read something, your task is to focus in detail on the text at hand: What is the writer's purpose and tone? What is the basic argument? What facts are brought to bear to support that argument? Are these facts used responsibly? Just as a crime scene investigator needs to gather and label everything that might be evidence, you need to identify and collect the ideas in the pages you are reading. Crime scene investigators take careful photographs to establish the location and context of the evidence they're collecting so they can come to understand how it all fits together; similarly you might underline the major ideas in the chapter or essay to clarify the shape and direction of the argument. In their collecting mode, crime scene investigators are willing to consider anything. If two people offer eyewitness accounts, they're not going to say no.

But once the crime scene investigators have as much evidence as possible from the scene, they turn their attention elsewhere. They know that the enclosed space of the crime scene and the seconds it took to commit the crime are merely the centre of the whirlpool that was the victim's life. They spread out, visiting other places, collecting more evidence, talking to people from the victim's past, and trying to find the connection between what happened in those moments in that confined space and what's going on in the wider world. Similarly, once you are familiar with the chapter or essay, you need to uncover how this particular argument is in sync with the bigger picture that is the world you live in. Is the author (your equivalent of the eyewitness) reliable and unbiased? What is the author's purpose—his or her motives—for offering you the account you have just read? Has the writer offered you facts or opinions? Does the essay's argument conform to your experience? What have other people—other eyewitnesses—thought about this issue or problem?

This is how we're going to talk about critical reading in this chapter: It's a two-stage process. The first stage involves mastering the evidence and the argument in a chapter, essay, or article—collecting your evidence. The second step involves taking that evidence and argument into the larger world that is both the academy and the world you live in, making sure this argument and evidence offer a real-world explanation.

STRATEGIES FOR CRITICAL READING

Preview the Material

Previewing the material helps you form preliminary impressions and create a context for your more studied reading, which is to come. To preview, gather some initial evidence about the essay—your crime scene.

- **Consider the author**. Do you know the author's politics or usual subject matter? Is the author a newspaper columnist, a humorist, or a political commentator?
- **Check out the publication information.** In this book, publication information is part of the headnote that tells you something about the author's background and publications, the place the selection first appeared, and the content of the selection. This information can help you draw conclusions and evaluate the reading. But as you read for your other classes you might consider whether the reading comes from a textbook your instructor has chosen, in which case, you will already know something about the attitudes of the person who thought you could benefit from reading it. If it's from an anthology, see what other writers have been collected there and look at the titles of the other chapters. Can you infer anything from the other topics that are covered? See if you can find out when and where the essay or chapter was first published, which will suggest how current the information is and who the original audience was. If the reading comes from a journal, do a quick Google search to see what you can tell about that journal's editorial policy and leanings. Evaluating Internet sites is even trickier; you will find information on how to do that in Chapter 14.
- **Read the first paragraph or two and the first sentence of other paragraphs** to learn a little about the tone, subject matter, and organization of the selection.

Do a First Reading

After previewing the reading, you will have a first impression and some expectations about the material—an impression and expectations that may or may not be borne out as you read more closely. To begin that closer examination, read the material through in one sitting, without pausing or labouring over anything. If you encounter unfamiliar words, try to figure them out from their context, or circle them to look up later. If you do not understand a point, push on, knowing that you will come back to that idea later and wrestle with it. If the piece is too long to read in one sitting, break it into sections and do separate first readings.

Reread and Study

After your first reading, return to the essay and study it more closely to discover as much as you can. Shorter, simpler pieces may require only one rereading, but you may have to return to longer, more complex selections a couple of times. Keep a pencil or pen in your hand so you can make notes in the margin and underline key passages. You may be accustomed to using a yellow or blue marker to highlight important sections; this technique is more useful for marking important textbook passages to study. For most other materials, critical reading goes better when you can make notes about why certain elements are significant. If you do not own the reading or prefer not to mark the text for other reasons, write your annotations on a separate sheet or in a computer file. Or use removable sticky notes and attach your reactions to the appropriate sections of the text. As you reread and study, the following procedures can be helpful.

- **Look up words** that you circled during your first reading and any other vocabulary you are unsure of. You can write the meanings in the margins as a study aid.
- **Identify the thesis (the main or central point).** If it is stated, place brackets around it or underline it. If the thesis is implied rather than stated, write it out in your own words in the margin or at the end of the reading.
- **Identify the purpose.** Most of the time you cannot ask the author about the purpose of a reading, but clues in the selection will tell you whether the author aims to express feelings, relate experience, entertain the reader, inform the reader, or convince the reader to think or act in a particular way. These elements of the writer's purpose affect the writer's tone and style—the relationship to the reader the writer wants to create. In addition, however, each writer has a distinctive purpose that is more closely related to content. Writers want to articulate an idea or a point of view that only they can see because their particular experience has led them to a perspective and to a vision of the world that they want to share with the reader. Write out the purpose or combination of purposes in the margin or at the end of the

reading. Then note how well you think the reading achieves the author's purpose. (For a discussion of a writer's purpose, see p. 35.)

- **Underline major points.** As you encounter important ideas that support the thesis, note them for special consideration. However, be careful not to underline too much or the selection will have more words underlined than not. Just mark the major points; leave the examples, clarifying description, and other explanations as they are unless you have a reason to highlight a particular item.

- **Reconsider any material you did not understand earlier.** If necessary, make a list of questions to ask other readers or your instructor. Consider researching in the library or on the Internet.

Troubleshooting Guide

Reading Critically

As you reread, consider the following questions:

- What is the source of the author's ideas: experience, observation, considered opinion, or research?

- Is the author expressing facts, opinion, or both?

- Is the author's detail adequate and convincing? Does the author support generalizations by showing and not just telling?

- What is the author's purpose? Tone? Intended audience? Role? (See the discussion of the writer's context beginning on page 35.)

- What is this author trying to contribute to our knowledge about or attitudes toward the world we live in?

Let's return to our crime scene analogy. Just as the crime scene investigator needs to study the detail of the scene of the crime, you need to be comfortable and familiar with what you've read. The investigator takes photographs to create a visual map of the scene so he or she can create some hypotheses about how events unfolded just before and after the crime. Similarly, you need to understand how the essay or chapter can be "mapped," so you understand how the writer's purpose or argument unfolds. If the writer is asking you to follow her through the exploration of her experience or feelings, what route is she taking? If the writer is giving you information, how does the network of ideas fit together? If the writer is making an argument, what order has the writer given to the ideas and how is that order shaping your perception?

READING CRITICALLY

Once you know, in effect, how an essay works, you can move beyond its confines to explore how it fits into the wider context of the human experience and our knowledge about the world. This is where the real down and dirty critical reading begins. Just as the crime scene investigator must be relentlessly sceptical, trying to force witnesses and suspects to tell the truth, so must you.

Distinguishing Facts from Opinions

People often assume that anything that appears in print is a fact, but the words on a page or computer screen can represent the writer's opinion instead. **Facts** can be proven or have been proven, but **opinions** are the writer's judgments, interpretations, or beliefs. For example, it is a *fact* that electricity can power automobiles, but it is an *opinion* that electrically powered cars will be commonplace in 10 years. As a critical reader, you must distinguish between facts and opinions and determine whether or not the opinions a writer asserts are well founded and well supported.

Sometimes people think that facts are better than opinions, but they both have their place and importance. For example, scientists seeking to prove a theory must be able to support their case with facts. Opinion is equally important, however, especially once a theory has been established. For what benefit can the theory be applied? How does the theory affect subsequent research? How should the theory influence public policy? The answers to questions such as these are matters of opinion, but the answers are nonetheless important because they can guide the course of future research and the application of the established theory.

Much of the reading you encounter in college and university will include both facts and opinions. For example, consider this paragraph from the introductory business textbook *Understanding Canadian Business* by William Nickels, James McHugh, Susan McHugh, and Rita Cossa:

> Businesses need to be aware of the laws that are in place (or may be passed) that will affect their business. For example, a government can keep taxes and regulations to a minimum, thereby encouraging entrepreneurship and increasing wealth. Entrepreneurs are looking for a high return on investment (ROI), including the investment of their time. If the government takes away much of what the business earns through high taxes, ROI may no longer be worth the risk. Provinces and territories that have high taxes and restrictive regulations tend to drive entrepreneurs out, while areas with low taxes and less restrictive regulations attract entrepreneurs.

Look again at the paragraph. This time the sentences in brackets point out places where fact and opinion are blended.

> Businesses need to be aware of the laws that are in place (or may be passed) that will affect their business. For example, a government can keep taxes and regulations to a minimum, thereby encouraging entrepreneurship and increasing wealth. (*In this statement, the authors are overgeneralizing [see page 9 for errors in logic]. By doing so, they are turning what might be a fact into an opinion. What is meant by "a minimum"? What kind of wealth is the writer talking about? In the fall of 2008, the failures of banks and other lending institutions in the U.S. and Europe occurred because bank regulations had lessened the amount of equity a bank had to keep on hand to cover its loans. There were fewer problems in Canada because we have more stringent banking regulations. Regulations, then, aren't always bad.*) Entrepreneurs are looking for a high return on investment (ROI), including the investment of their time. If the government takes away much of what the business earns through high taxes, ROI may no longer be worth the risk. (*What is "much of what the business earns"? What are* high *taxes? Again, such generalizations have the effect of opinion.*) Provinces and territories that have high taxes and restrictive regulations tend to drive entrepreneurs out, while areas with low taxes and less restrictive regulations attract entrepreneurs. (*In other passages in this text, the authors admit that regulations designed to maintain and create a clean environment benefit a business's workers, and hence the business itself. "Regulations" here are too broadly defined to reflect facts.*)

Critical readers must do more than distinguish between facts and opinions. They must also evaluate the *quality* of the opinions they identify. Some opinions are more valuable than others. Valuable opinions—ones to take seriously—are offered by knowledgeable people, are backed up by solid support, or both. Less valuable opinions—ones to be wary of—are unsupported beliefs or are offered by people with little relevant knowledge or experience.

Making Inferences

Critical readers make inferences. An **inference** is a conclusion drawn on the basis of what a speaker's or writer's information "suggests" rather than "states." Think of making inferences as "reading between the lines." For example, consider this paragraph from "What Is behind the Growth of Violence on College Campuses?"—an essay that examines the causes of campus violence:

> The same students who sponsor night walks to check the lighting and grounds to increase safety will hold the door open for a stranger entering their residence hall. Despite frequent warnings, students—and even faculty, administrators, and other campus personnel—act less judiciously than they would elsewhere.

In this paragraph, the author *says* that students and campus employees are not as careful on campus as they are in other places. However, readers can *infer* that the author believes that this lack of caution contributes to campus crime, even though that point is not specifically made.

Making inferences is an important part of critical reading. However, conclusions you draw—your reading between the lines—must be supported by evidence. Thus, you cannot infer from the above paragraph that the author believes victims of campus crime get what they deserve because they are not sufficiently careful. As a reader, *you* might feel that way, but you cannot ascribe that idea to the author, based on the evidence in the paragraph.

Synthesizing Information

Synthesis is the process of connecting new information to what you already know. Thus, synthesis involves fitting new information into the larger scheme of your knowledge. When you read or hear a lecture, you can synthesize the information by noting how it supports, refutes, clarifies, illustrates, or calls into question other ideas, observations, or experiences. Say, for example, that you are reading a newspaper article that mentions the shortage of male teachers in elementary schools. If you heard an education professor comment that male elementary school teachers get little respect, you can synthesize your reading with your instructor's lecture by assuming that there may be a cause-and-effect relationship: One reason for the shortage of male elementary school teachers might be that males do not want to teach elementary school because they do not get enough respect for doing so.

In college and university classes, you will synthesize by relating new ideas to information you have already learned. Thus, your history teacher might ask you to compare some aspect of the Charter of Rights and Freedoms (which you just read about) with some aspect of the Magna Carta (which you studied last term). Even though in your university classes you will usually synthesize by relating new classroom learning to earlier classroom learning, do not hesitate to synthesize ideas in a more personal way as well. For example, if your education instructor lectures on bilingual education and you are an international student, you can relate your instructor's points to your own school experience using English as a second language.

Evaluating Quality

People often think that if something is in print, it must be accurate and it must be good, but this assumption is not true. A great deal of material of dubious quality and questionable truth makes its way into print and onto the

Internet. For this reason, critical readers must evaluate the quality of their reading material. As a student, you may feel uncomfortable judging what you read. Perhaps you feel that you do not know enough or are not high enough in the academic "pecking order" to make such judgments. In fact, as a student you should practise critical reading at every opportunity. You are entitled to your opinion, as long as you back it up with evidence for your view. Answering the following questions about reading material can help you form a reasonable judgment.

- **Are the "facts" really facts, or are they opinions?** A point is not a fact just because a writer calls it one. The statement could be an opinion dressed up as a fact. Consider this example: "The fact that science is poorly taught in elementary school helps explain our nation's lack of scientific literacy." *Is* it a fact that science is poorly taught in elementary school? *Is* it a fact that we lack scientific literacy? No, these are opinions, and calling them facts does not make them so.
- **Are the opinions adequately supported?** Opinions backed up by sound reasoning and solid evidence are valuable; opinions offered without any support may not be. For example, an author may offer the opinion that Canada should increase spending for space exploration, but without reasons for doing so, this opinion is not worth much.
- **Is the material current or dated?** If you are reading a biography of Wilfrid Laurier, Canada's prime minister between 1896 and 1911, the fact that it was written 20 years ago may not be a problem (unless historians have recently made important new discoveries about Laurier's life). However, if you are reading about population trends in rural areas, an essay with Statistics Canada information from 1980 will not be as relevant as a piece with StatsCan information from 2000.
- **Are the source and author trustworthy?** Consider the author's credentials and possible biases. If you are looking for a balanced view of the issues surrounding handgun control, for instance, the National Firearms Association's Web site or an essay written by the mother of a student killed in a school shooting may not be the best sources.
- **Is the reasoning logical?** A critical reader discounts material that contains faulty reasoning. The next section will help you recognize errors in logic when you read and avoid them when you write.

Detecting Errors in Logic

You should always be on the lookout for errors in logic. An **error in logic** is a form of faulty reasoning that can lead a person to a false conclusion.

Unethical writers use errors in logic intentionally, to mislead or manipulate a reader. However, many writers do not intend to deceive; they use flawed logic without meaning to. In either case, as a critical reader, you should be wary of material that includes errors in logic. As a writer, you should avoid such errors in your own work. Some of the most common errors in logic are explained here.

1.   Overgeneralizing. Very little is true all of the time, so be careful of sweeping statements.

> EXAMPLE   The only reason teenagers quit school is to avoid the work. (This may be true for some, but not for all.)

2.   Oversimplifying. Most issues worth arguing are complex, so be wary of "quick fix" explanations or solutions.

> EXAMPLE   If women would just stay home to care for their children, we would have no daycare problem in this country. (The issue is not that simple. Many women must work in order to feed their children.)

3.   Begging the question. "Begging the question" is basing an argument or conclusion on the truth of a point that has not been proven.

> EXAMPLE   Immature couples who live together do not deserve spousal rights. (Where is the proof that couples who live together are "immature"? To assume they are is to beg the question.)

4.   Name calling. Also called an *ad hominem* ("to the man") attack or *mudslinging*, this fallacy involves attacking the people who believe something instead of criticizing their ideas or sticking with issues.

> EXAMPLE   People who oppose mandatory sentences are bleeding-heart liberals who will destroy this country. (The pros and cons of mandatory sentences are unrelated to the people who oppose or favour them.)

5.   Either–or reasoning. With complex issues, more than two alternatives usually exist.

> EXAMPLE   If we do not ban hand guns, we will have a social crisis on our hands. (What about other alternatives, such as limited gun control or mandatory jail sentences?)

6.   Assuming an earlier event caused a later event. This fallacy is also called *post hoc, ergo propter hoc,* which means "after this, therefore because of this." The fact that one event occurred before another does not prove that the first event caused the second.

EXAMPLE   After homosexual characters began to be featured in television and movies, more people began considering homosexual marriage. (The first event did not necessarily cause the second.)

7.   Attacking or defending an issue on the basis of what was believed or done in the past. This kind of fallacy would have kept women from getting the vote.

EXAMPLE   If our grandparents managed without federally subsidized health care, so can we. (Our grandparents lived in a different world.)

8.   Assuming that what is true for one person is true for everybody.

EXAMPLE   My cousin and his girlfriend live together without benefit of marriage, and they are just fine. Obviously, marriage is not that important. (What is true for the cousin may not be true for others.)

9.   Playing to general sentiments. Also called *ad populum,* which means "to the crowd," this fallacy involves winning people over by calling upon commonly held feelings such as patriotism, fear of war, and religious fervour rather than discussing issues.

EXAMPLE   I would make an excellent MP because I come from humble beginnings and know what it means to work for a living. (This argument appeals to our respect for those who work hard to improve their circumstances. It says nothing about the speaker's political qualifications.)

10. Falsely indicating that one point follows conclusively from another. This fallacy is also called *non sequitur,* which means "it does not follow."

EXAMPLE   Fewer Aboriginal students are attending our university this year. Apparently, Aboriginals are losing interest in higher education. (The conclusion does not follow from the first statement. There may be many causes for the decline in enrolment, including the fact that many Aboriginal students are attending other post-secondary institutions.)

11. Using the "as any fool can see" approach. Because this approach insults those who disagree, it can alienate readers.

EXAMPLE   It is apparent to everyone that deer hunting solves many problems. (No, it is not apparent to everyone, or your essay would not be necessary.)

EXAMPLE   As any reasonable person can see, prison reform is necessary. (Those who disagree are cast as "unreasonable," which is both unfair and likely to alienate some readers.)

12. Alluding to but not naming authorities. Careful readers distrust phrases such as "experts agree" or "research shows" because they suggest authority or evidence without naming that authority or evidence.

EXAMPLE   Studies show that most Canadians distrust politicians. (What studies?)

A Sample Marked Essay

Obviously you can't keep all your questions and challenges in your head. The most effective way to read critically is to write your queries and comments in the margin. To see what a marked essay can look like, review the following selection marked by a student.

Well. Her opinion on this is clear.

What does she mean by this? How does masculinity change?

The Men from the Boys: Bull Riding Is Dangerous, Irrelevant, and a Rare Expression of Old-Style Masculinity

Joanne Byfield

1   Bull riding has been called the most thrilling eight seconds in sports. But spectators at the Canadian Finals Rodeo in Edmonton in mid-November experienced a far different emotion seconds after Greg Whitlow came flying out of the chute atop a 1,300-pound mountain of raging muscle called Lights Out. That feeling was horror. The beast knocked the 26-year-old cowboy unconscious, threw him to the ground, stomped on him and gored him before rodeo clowns could intervene.

2   By week's end, Whitlow, whose left eye was gouged out by a bull two years ago, remained in an intensive care ward in hospital, but was responding to family and doctors. His prognosis was good and one friend predicted he was "100% sure Greg will ride bulls again." But that prediction invites an obvious question: why would any sane person ride a bull?

This question is the closest thing to a thesis. Why pose it as a question?

3   Bull riding is the most dangerous of the rodeo sports. The challenge is to remain for eight seconds atop an animal specially bred for its bucking ability and sheer meanness. Other rodeo events, like saddle bronc riding and calf roping, are actual cowboy activities, but working cowboys never rode bulls. The event was created for rodeo, and now has its own professional circuit. But the rewards are low and the risks high; the average pro makes only $30,000 a year, and has endured at least one broken bone, concussion or lost tooth. Albertans Glen Keeley and Chris Self died earlier this year while bull riding.

Evidence?

4   So why do they do it? Paul Nathanson, a researcher and co-author with Katherine Young of *Spreading* (Misandry:) *The Teaching of Contempt for Men in Popular Culture,* points out that risk-taking is one of the primary social skills men had to develop ages ago to hunt and protect their families. Later, about 10,000 years ago, agricultural societies required men for war. Rodeo, he says, is a kind of ritualized combat, much like bull fighting or the famous running of the bulls in Pamplona, Spain. Nevertheless, such behaviours are increasingly irrelevant. "It asserts that we are men," Mr. Nathanson says. "It's an ego trip."

Hatred of men; hatred of men as a sex.

Makes sense. But we're not living 10,000 years ago.

So these aren't published yet. Should I believe them?

5   In (forthcoming books,) authors Nathanson and Young will examine men's traditional roles, those of provider, protector and progenitor, and how these are being stripped away by modern culture. Rodeo culture is certainly masculine, Mr. Nathanson adds, but it is also self-destructive.

Examples? What about Bruce Willis movies? Or superhero flicks?

If cowboys never had to ride bulls in their work, you do have to ask about their motives.

6   Karson Legault, a friend of rider Whitlow, is a bull rider himself because "that's the profession I chose." The appeal, he says, "is being able to put the fear aside and go with that bull. It's mind over matter and the strongest mind comes out on top." He is not persuaded by Mr. Nathanson's war analogy but he says bull riding is "sure a challenge."

This sounds so human.

We believe in mind over matter. Because we want a sense of control? How do we know?

7   Rider Kelly Armstrong must agree. Upon learning of the Whitlow accident, Armstrong told *Edmonton Sun* columnist Dick Chubey, "This just makes me want to spur harder, ride better and kick them bulls' ass one time instead of us getting the worst end of it."

I think it's unfair to end here. The writer is letting Armstrong sound a bit like a fool.

Answers to Questions about "The Men from the Boys: Bull Riding Is Dangerous, Irrelevant and a Rare Expression of Old-Style Masculinity"

1. What is the source of the author's ideas: experience, observation, or research? *The author observed Greg Whitlow's injuries during the Stampede, which led her to question why people ride bulls. She turned to research on masculinity to explain the behaviour.*

2. Is the author expressing facts, opinions, or both? *Both. There are facts in the piece about the injuries and deaths of bull riders, as well as about their relatively poor salaries. But she uses experts on masculinity to make the argument that they ride bulls to prove they're masculine. The bull riders themselves don't think this is the reason they ride bulls.*

3. Is the author's detail adequate and convincing? Does the author support generalizations by showing and not just telling? *There are a couple of points where Byfield needs to give more detail to support her argument. One is the assertion that bull riding is the most dangerous rodeo sport. The second is that modern culture is stripping away the traditional ideas of masculinity. She at least needs some evidence of this; better yet, she should consider what ideals are now common.*

4. What are the author's purpose, tone, intended audience, and role? *The author clearly wants us to think about what it means to be masculine; otherwise, why pose her thesis as a question? Sometimes her tone is matter-of-fact, as if she's just stating the facts. But this is contradicted by the fact that she plays naive bull riders off against academic experts, leaving the bull riders to look as if they don't know what they're doing or why they're doing it. Her intended audience clearly isn't bull riders. Perhaps it's urban, educated males who can think more critically and who also think they're smarter than cowboys.*

5. Do you agree or disagree with the author? Do you like or dislike the selection? *What does it make you think of? Does it arouse any strong feelings? I agree that masculinity is changing, and for the most part, I think this is good. It's hard work being Bruce Willis or John Wayne, and not very emotionally satisfying. But I don't quite think Byfield plays fair with the men she quotes.*

6. What is the significance of the selection? *Like a recent essay in* The Globe and Mail *about male friendship, this article illustrates the fact that we're asking questions about masculinity. It seems so invisible and natural, but it's really a role.*

SUMMARIZING

When you write a **summary,** you restate the selection's major ideas using your own style and your own words. A summary should faithfully reflect the original, so you should not add points, interpret or evaluate the author's ideas, or change the original meaning. Think of a summary as a distillation of the author's most important points. Because a summary includes only the most important points, it is shorter than the original selection.

The Purpose of Summaries

You will have many opportunities to summarize in university and college. For one thing, summarizing is a valuable study technique because writing out the major points of a reading selection gives you a study guide for that material and helps you learn information.

You may also write summaries for a grade. For example, instructors may ask you to summarize material so they can determine if you have read and understood assignments. On mid-terms and finals, they may also ask you to summarize reading assignments so they can check your comprehension and retention.

In addition, summaries are frequent components of other kinds of writing. If you are writing a research paper, for example, you will need to summarize information you discover in the library or on the Internet. If you are writing an argumentation essay, you can summarize the major points of an article that states a position you oppose and go on to disagree with those points. If you read something that helps explain a point you want to make in an essay, you can summarize what you read and use it as one of your supporting details. (For help with documenting materials from other sources, see p. 514.)

Suggestions for Writing a Summary

Step 1. Read the material over as many times as necessary in order to understand it. Look up unfamiliar words and get help with any passages you do not understand. (You cannot summarize material you do not understand.)

Step 2. Identify the major points and underline them in the text or list them on a piece of paper. You can omit examples, description, repetition, or explanations that support major points, unless these are necessary for clarification.

Step 3. Draft an opening sentence that mentions the author's name, the title of the piece you are summarizing, and one, two, or three of the following: the thesis, the author's purpose, the author's point of view. Here are some examples:

AUTHOR, TITLE, AND THESIS
In "The Men from the Boys; Bull Riding Is Dangerous, Irrelevant and a Rare Expression of Old-Style Masculinity," Joanne Byfield suggests that undertaking unnecessary and dangerous tasks, like riding bulls, is an expression of masculinity.

AUTHOR, TITLE, AND PURPOSE
In "The Men from the Boys; Bull Riding Is Dangerous, Irrelevant and a Rare Expression of Old-Style Masculinity," Joanne Byfield wants the reader to see how some expressions of masculinity, like bull riding, are no longer necessary, but are self-destructive.

AUTHOR, TITLE, POINT OF VIEW
In "The Men from the Boys; Bull Riding Is Dangerous, Irrelevant and a Rare Expression of Old-Style Masculinity," Joanne Byfield argues that when men engage in dangerous and unnecessary activities like riding bulls, they're trying to prove they're still men.

Use present tense verbs with the author's name because the words of the text "live on" in the present: Joanne Byfield *explains, notes, says, expresses, examines, believes,* and so forth (not *explained, noted, said, expressed, examined, believed*).

Step 4. Following your opening statement, draft your summary by writing out the major points you underlined or listed. Be sure to express these points in your own distinctive style by using your own wording and sentence structure. If you have trouble rewording a phrase or sentence, you can use the original if you place the borrowed words in quotation marks. Just be careful to use quotations sparingly.

To keep your summary flowing smoothly, use transitions to show how ideas relate to each other. In addition, repeat the author's name with a present tense verb as a transitional device, like this:

Smith explains
Smith further believes
The author goes on to note

Troubleshooting Guide

Summarizing
If you have trouble expressing all or part of a passage in a different way, imagine yourself talking to a friend and explaining the ideas you just read. Then write the explanation in the words you use to explain the passage. If necessary, you can revise the material later to make it less like speech and more like writing.

A Sample Summary

The following is a sample summary of "The Men from the Boys; Bull Riding Is Dangerous, Irrelevant and a Rare Expression of Old-Style Masculinity," which appears on page 12. The annotations in the margin call your attention to some of the summary's key features. Notice that the summary is a single paragraph. Because summaries are condensed versions of readings, they are brief. However, summaries of longer selections or those with many main ideas can be two or more paragraphs.

Summary of "The Men from the Boys; Bull Riding Is Dangerous, Irrelevant and a Rare Expression of Old-Style Masculinity"

In "The Men from the Boys," Joanne Byfield shows that bull riding is extremely dangerous, while also suggesting that men's reasons for trying to stay on a bull for eight seconds are absurd and self-destructive.[1] Most bull riders have broken at least one bone; two Albertans died this year.[2] Given that the original cowboys didn't ride bulls—that this is a skill not needed by ranchers—Byfield wonders[3] why they do it. For an explanation, she turns to the authors of a book on masculinity and popular culture. These authors argue that men developed the willingness to take risks initially to protect their families from threats and then to fight in wars.[4] If men no longer need to take such risks to protect and support their families, they may find ways of ritualizing the taking of risks in order to prove that they are still men.[5] Bull riders disagree, asserting that [6]"it's mind over matter and the strongest mind comes out on top." By ending with the words of a bull rider, Byfield suggests that some men remain unreflective about their expressions of masculinity and do not question them.

[1]Summary opens with a statement that gives the author, title, and thesis of material summarized.

[2]First cluster of facts

[3]This verb, like all the verbs describing Byfield's facts and opinions, is in the present tense

[4]Second cluster of facts.

[5]This summarizes the contribution of Byfield's authorities on masculinity and risk-taking.

[6]Quotation marks indicate quoted words.

SYNTHESIZING

To **synthesize,** use your critical reading strategies to integrate material from two or more sources with each other and with your own ideas. Synthesis involves recording, evaluating, and drawing conclusions about material from multiple sources. For example, if you were writing an essay about addiction, you would be using synthesis if you incorporated ideas from "Predicting Addiction" (page 435) and from "The Surprising Truth about Heroin and Addiction" (page 446) about whether addictions have biological causes or whether individuals can completely control their responses to addictive substances. You would also be synthesizing if you explained the ideas in two or more essays and went on to argue that the ideas in one of the essays are more valid than the ideas in the other, or if you explained why you disagreed with one or more ideas in the essays. In other words, when you synthesize, you bring material together from multiple sources, but you do more than record what you read (which is summarizing)—you go on to think critically about that material and draw conclusions, see relationships, and make inferences.

The Purpose of Synthesis

Synthesis can help support a thesis. In fact, synthesis is so important to thesis support that you will use it often to inform and persuade in many types of classroom writing. For example, in a paper for a child psychology class about the effects of televised violence on preschoolers, you can inform by mentioning the effects described in several journal articles on the subject.

To stamp the material with your own conclusions, you can indicate which effects are the most significant. To persuade, you could devise a strategy for minimizing the effects of televised violence and argue for its implementation.

Suggestions for Synthesizing Information

Step 1. Be sure you understand everything in all the sources you are dealing with. If necessary, look up words and ask your instructor for clarification.

Step 2. Underline or list the major ideas in each source.

Step 3. Review all of the major ideas and determine how they relate to each other. Answering these five questions can help:

a. Do the ideas in the sources support each other or contradict each other?
b. Do the ideas in the sources form a cause-and-effect relationship?
c. Do the ideas in one source explain or exemplify the ideas in another source?
d. Do the ideas in one source pick up where the ideas in another source end?
e. Do the sources examine the same topic from different perspectives?

Step 4. Decide how you want to use the material in the sources. Answering these five questions can help:

a. Can I use the information to explain something?
b. Can I use the information to prove something?
c. Can I show how the sources contradict each other or present different perspectives?

d. Can I explain the significance of the information?

e. Can I use the information to support my own experience or observation?

Troubleshooting Guide

Avoiding Plagiarism

If you have trouble knowing whether what you write is plagiarizing—using source material dishonestly—remember these points:

- For the most part, rewrite the author's ideas in your own words—do not imitate the author's style.

- When you do use the author's words, place them in quotation marks.

- Check the accuracy of your paraphrases and quotations.

- Document your sources with introductions and citations according to the guidelines on documenting sources in Chapter 14.

Sample Synthesis

This essay synthesizes material found in Chapter 13, as well as additional resources. You'll find a bibliography at the end in both MLA and APA styles.

Radical Weather vs. Cautious Politicians

[1]Our weather is making it impossible to ignore the effects of climate change. David Phillips reports on the Canada Foundation for Innovation Web site that 1996 brought us the Saguenay flood, the first disaster in Canada with a price tag of a billion dollars. Two years later, Ontario and Quebec experienced the ice storm. Nova Scotia experienced three "50-year storms" in less than 12 months. Vancouver saw winds destroy the giant trees in Stanley Park. On the prairies, we're seeing too much rain or too little. Some of the world's leaders are saying, "Go slow. Don't mess with the economy. The sky isn't falling yet." But the weather in Canada is suggesting the sky is falling. [2]If our leaders aren't going to take the challenge of global warming seriously, corporations, cities, and individuals are going to need to take the lead in cutting greenhouse gas emissions.

[3]The science is clear about the causes and effects of climate change. In addition to extreme weather patterns, warmer summers and hurricanes like Katrina, we are seeing the melting of polar ice and of the permafrost in the north as the result of global warming. What is inexplicable is the tendency of

[1]The writer's ideas provide background and evaluation to lead in to the synthesis.

[2]The thesis.

[3]The paragraph presents the writer's ideas.

North American politicians to alternate between thinking that we really don't need to do anything *yet* and suggesting that our economy is so fragile that it cannot absorb change. The Kyoto Accord has been ratified by 183 countries, and the European Union has set in place its own goals for reducing greenhouse gas emissions. But Canada and the U.S. remain unpersuaded that something needs to be done. They are unwilling to pass the legislation that would require industry and individuals to produce less carbon dioxide.

[4]The introduction credits source. It includes the authors' full names and the title of the essay, since this is the first use of the source. See also the introduction of *Green*.

[4]In *The Hot Topic*, Gabrielle Walker and Sir David King note that industry is responsible for nearly 20 percent of greenhouse gases, securing an energy supply produces an additional 25.9 percent, while agriculture produces 13 percent and deforestation another 16 percent (98). They [5]disagree with leaders who suggest that developing and implementing environmentally friendly technologies is going to have a negative impact on the economy: [6]"In fact, far from being expensive, many of the strategies we could use to reduce carbon dioxide emissions by improving efficiency will actually save money" (97). [7]In *Green*, Jane Hoffman and Michael Hoffman observe that conserving energy or using renewable energy resources has helped the bottom line of many businesses. By using solar and wind energy and by asking producers to reduce the amount of packing material, "Wal-Mart estimates that it has prevented 667,000 metric tons of carbon dioxide ($CO2$) from entering the atmosphere—and saved 10.98 billion on the corporation's bottom line" (164). [8]The Hoffmans also report that Google hired a team of engineers to figure out how to produce a gigawatt of renewable energy—enough to provide all the power needed by San Francisco (165). [9]While it's true that wind turbines and solar panels for houses aren't cheap, we know from the drop in the prices of computers and the iPhone that the more a product is bought, the less expensive it becomes.

[5]Note the present tense introduction to the quotation.

[6]Direct quotation.

[7]Parenthetical citation to credit the source. See also the parenthetical citation for *Green*.

[8]Paraphrase from *Green*. Note present tense introductions and parenthetical citations.

[9]Writer's ideas.

Some commentators suspect that the vacuum created by the lack of leadership on the national level will lead to smaller communities and individuals taking the lead. [10]In an article in *The Globe and Mail*, Gary Mason describes the Hotel Arctic in Ilulissat, Greenland. In spite of being 250 km north of the Arctic Circle, it has found ways of using less energy and less water than conventional hotels. Similarly, the city of Delta, B.C., is considering installing solar panels on top of its facilities that would provide all the energy it needs. [11]In a similar vein, Walker and King write that all of us can have an impact on global warming. We can insulate our houses while turning down the thermostat in the winter and tolerating slightly warmer houses in the summer. We can buy energy-efficient

[10]Paraphrase from Mason's essay. Note the present tense introduction.

[11]Paraphrase from Walker and King, followed by quotation.

lighting and not leave our computers on standby. We can demand cars and appliances that are more energy efficient: "The more customers seek energy-efficient gadgets, the more pressure there will be on manufacturers to meet the demand" (101). [12]If "the economy" is the reason our leaders give for doing nothing, we can affect that economy in such a way that we send a clear message: We are committed to cutting our greenhouse gases. We can make it ethically intolerable to do nothing.

[12]Writer's analysis.

[13]Perhaps the extreme weather can help us. What influences our moods more than a brilliantly sunny day or a cloudy, windy one? What makes us feel more helpless than snow that simply won't stop falling? We talk about the weather constantly, perhaps because we feel we have no control over it. But the science suggests we do. What I propose is that we should all get out of our cars, leaving our cell phones and iPods behind, and walk more, connecting with the planet that is our responsibility. That's one way, at least, of being aware of what we stand to lose if we don't change our habits.

[13]The writer's ideas.

Works Cited—MLA style

Hoffman, Jane, and Michael Hoffman. *Green: Your Place in the New Energy Revolution.* New York: Palgrave Macmillan, 2008. Print.

Mason, Gary. "Call Me an Optimist, But if Denmark Can Go Green, Canada Can Too." *Globe and Mail* 12 August 2008: A6. Print.

Phillips, David. "Change the Climate and You Change the Weather." *InnovationCanada.ca,* 1 May 2006. Web. 3 Nov. 2008.

Walker, Gabrielle, and Sir David King. *The Hot Topic.* Toronto: Douglas and MacIntyre, 2008. Print.

Works Cited—APA Style

Hoffman, J., & Hoffman, M. (2008). *Green: Your place in the new energy revolution.* New York: Palgrave Macmillan.

Mason, G. (2008, August 12). Call me an optimist, but if Denmark can go green, Canada can too. *The Globe and Mail,* p. A6.

Phillips, D. (2006). Change the climate and you change the weather. Retrieved November 3, 2008, from www.innovationcanada.ca/en/articles/change-the-climate

Walker, G., & King, D. (2008). *The hot topic.* Toronto: Douglas and MacIntyre.

READING VISUAL MATERIAL CRITICALLY
Charts and Graphs

Charts and graphs often appear in textbooks, scholarly journals, and popular magazines. As visual representations, charts and graphs convey a great deal of information very succinctly. Line graphs are particularly good for showing how data change over time and how trends progress; pie charts and bar graphs show how items relate to each other. The bar graph "Single Parents, Canada, 1951–2006" from the 2006 census, gives information about the circumstances under which people are or become single parents. A second bar graph looks at the growth, over the last 20 years, of young adults living at home.

Not only do the graphs convey a great deal of information, but they also allow you to analyze data and draw conclusions. For example, the "Single Parents" graph suggests that in 1951, most single parents had lost husbands or wives; beginning on 1976, we see that single parents are more likely to be divorced or to have never married. The graphs also allow you to make inferences, such as noting that families are being defined differently. Graphs also encourage us to ask questions. The "Young Adults Living in the Parental Home" graph shows that an above-average number of young people in Toronto and Vancouver live at home, while a lower than average number of young people live at home in Regina and Saskatoon. If you know, for example, that apartments are expensive in Toronto and Vancouver, while they're relatively inexpensive in Regina and Saskatoon, you might hypothesize that

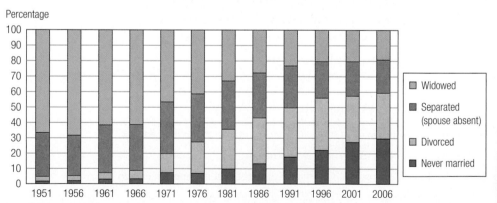

Note: Comparable historical data are not available for census years prior to 1951.

Single Parents by Marital Status, Canada, 1951–2006

Source: Statistics Canada, "More Never-Married, Fewer Widowed Lone Parents," 2006 Census, September 11, 2007, http://www12.statcan.ca/english/census06/analysis/famhouse/charts/chart3.htm (accessed January 27, 2009).

Census Metropolitan Areas

Proportion of Young Adults Aged 20 to 29 Living in the Parental Home, Census Metropolitan Areas, 2001 and 2006

Source: Statistics Canada, "Proportion of Young Adults Aged 20 to 29 Living in the Parental Home, Census Metropolitan Areas, 2001 and 2006," 2006 Census, September 11, 2007, http://www12.statcan.ca/english/census06/analysis/famhouse/tables/table16.htm (accessed January 27, 2009).

one of the reasons young adults in Saskatchewan leave home is that they can afford to. Such a hypothesis might give you a direction for your research: You can explore whether Saskatchewan has a culture that encourages young people to be independent at an early age, or whether young adults leave home because they can.

To read graphs and charts critically, study the data, captions, explanations, or other text that accompanies the image. Then be sure you can answer these questions:

- What point is the graph or chart trying to make?
- What is the source of the information—a newspaper, the government, a university, a private foundation, a corporation, an individual researcher? Is the source reliable? Does the source have a particular agenda to promote?
- What is the date of the information? Is it sufficiently current?
- Is there any attempt to mislead? For example, are important time periods or groups omitted?
- What can you infer?
- How do the data and inferences relate to the text? How do they relate to what you already know?

Photographs

Like charts and graphs, photographs have to be studied for what they can reveal. Many photographs are posed, or arranged, for a particular purpose, but even candid shots, which record a particular individual or a particular place and time, can radiate with information and meaning. Keep in mind that the photographs you will encounter in the classroom have been selected by textbook editors or by your instructor for their rich insights into the subject of your course.

Implicit in the photograph by Veronica Geminder on page 25 is the kind of variety we find in the city, particularly in older areas like Winnipeg's Exchange District. But the photographer has also captured the way the city is a kind of text. Old signs for Wilder's stomach powders and MacGregor Hosiery Mills with their "happy foot" cushioned socks and C. Turnbull's "underwear for the family" are juxtaposed to vibrant and very modern graffiti. What does that juxtaposition say about a city's history? Finally, the figure going into Albert Street Burgers is a street person whose cart of belongings is in the foreground. Contrast her track suit with the clothing you see on the Candie and Dolls Web site. What do you think the photographer is saying about city space?

To "read" a photograph, ask yourself questions like these:

Veronica Geminder, "The Exchange District," Winnipeg Manitoba, 17 April, 2008. "The Exchange District" was shot in Winnipeg by the young Canadian photographer Veronica Geminder. Her work evinces a curiosity about the variety of spaces we find in the North American city. The photograph's main subject is the two businesses that exist side by side, Candie and Dolls, a very upscale clothing boutique (you can see inside their store at www.candieanddolls.com) and Albert Street Burgers, a small indoor burger stand. The Yahoo travel site reports that Albert Streets Burgers offers "incredibly huge burger and homemade fries. Patrons have three dining options when devouring this feel good food. They can stand an eat at the lunch bar, they can take their meal across the street to the Fleet Art Gallery to enjoy the large selection of prints and frames, or they can take their fare to Old Market Square which offers a park experience in the city core."

- Who took the photograph, and why—for what organization or cause?
- Is the photograph candid or posed?
- Is the image meant to document an event or to arouse emotions? Or does it do both?
- What inferences can you make about the photograph? What message is it intended to convey?
- How does the caption help you understand the photograph?

Critical reading strategies are essential for interpreting visual images. You ask questions similar to those you ask about a written text to determine the purpose and the means by which the purpose is achieved. For contemporary photographs, you may also need to ask if they are likely to have been retouched and how authentic they are.

Advertisements

Learning to read visual material critically is an especially important skill out-side the classroom, because we are bombarded with images intended to influ-ence our thinking and behaviour. Television and print advertisements are the most prominent examples. Most often such ads try to convince us to buy a particular product. Sometimes, they try to convince us to have positive feel-ings about the company that manufactures the product or offers a service,

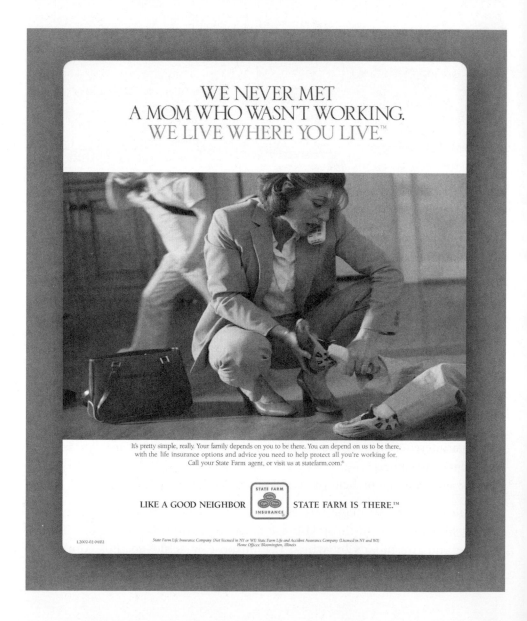

such as an energy-company ad that showcases its concern for the environment. Either way, advertisements aim to profit those who sponsor them. The only way to avoid being manipulated by the ads is to learn to read them critically.

Consider, for example, the advertisement on page 26 featuring a photograph of a young mother. Study this advertisement, both the image and the text that accompanies it. What is State Farm's purpose in running the ad? What aspects of the photograph and text help the company achieve its purpose? Notice that the young mother is wearing business clothes, indicating that the primary audience for the ad is working mothers of young children. But the text at the top of the image suggests that all moms are always working. So this ad also aims to appeal to mothers who are not paid to work outside the home. It tells women that State Farm understands their needs and can help them meet those needs.

Notice the way motion is used in the ad: The boy in the background is on the move, and the mother is talking on the phone while she puts on another child's shoe. Obviously the woman is multitasking, and as a viewer of the ad we have to admire her poise as she capably manages to do many things at once. At the same time, we might see that her life is busy, perhaps even hectic. Does the target audience see themselves in this image? State Farm certainly hopes so.

Advertisements often work by encouraging us to identify emotionally with the individual pictured in the ad. Sometimes the appeal is to an ideal we all cherish—motherhood, in this case. Notice how this ad implies that mothers are essential, always there for their families. And the text explains that just as the family depends on mothers, so mothers can depend on State Farm.

Other advertisements make emotional appeals through symbols of power, pleasure, patriotism, beauty, or sex to sell products and services, to imply, "If you buy our products or services, you, too, will be a competent mother, or a powerful executive, a fun-to-be-with friend, a patriotic Canadian, or a person with sex appeal." To avoid being too easily convinced that you can achieve your ideal by purchasing a product, learn to "read" an advertisement critically by asking yourself questions like these:

- What audience does the advertisement target? Are you in that audience? If not, do you respond favourably to the advertisement anyway?
- What is the purpose of the ad?
- Does the ad appeal more to reason or emotion?
- What does the ad imply?

- How do techniques involving colour, size, shape, texture, and lighting highlight the ad's appeal?
- How does the text work with the image to achieve the ad's purpose? Are there slogans or symbols? Testimonials by celebrities? Statistics or research findings?
- Is the ad credible? Can its claims—implied or stated directly—possibly be true?

When you apply your critical reading strategies to advertisements, you are able to take *from* them what information you need without being taken *in* by their manipulations of your emotions and your reasoning. In fact, the critical reading strategies you will practise throughout *Patterns for a Purpose* will help you assess and respond appropriately to everything you read and view—in the classroom, in your workplace, and in your community.

READING SELECTION

The following reading selection says something about critical reading. It reinforces and, in some cases, adds to points made in this chapter.

Background

Born in New York City, philosopher and writer Mortimer Adler (1902–2001) taught at the University of Chicago, where he helped develop the Great Books program and where he directed the Institute for Philosophical Research. Although a high school dropout, Adler earned a PhD, was an editor for the *Encyclopaedia Britannica,* and wrote widely on philosophy and education. He spent much of his career popularizing the great ideas of Western civilization in works such as the multi-volume *Great Books of the Western World.* (1954 and revised in 1990). He is particularly noted for *How to Read a Book: The Art of Getting a Liberal Education* (1940). The following essay first appeared in the *Saturday Review* in 1940.

Reading with a Purpose

A person cannot truly own a book without writing in it, according to Mortimer Adler, for writing in a book "is not an act of mutilation but of love." Thus, Adler explains that it does not matter how many expensive volumes a person has on display. What matters is whether a person "consumes" the books with a pen or pencil in hand. Although the essay was written over 60 years ago, it still offers sound advice to readers. As you read, try to determine why this essay has remained popular for so long.

Assignment

Read with a pencil or pen in hand, and mark the selection using the strategies for annotation found on page 4. If your instructor directs, form small groups in class and compare the ways you have marked the selection. What similarities and differences do you note? What accounts for the differences?

How to Mark a Book
Mortimer Adler

1   You know you have to read "between the lines" to get the most out of anything. I want to persuade you to do something equally important in the course of your reading. I want to persuade you to "write between the lines." Unless you do, you are not likely to do the most efficient kind of reading.

2   I contend, quite bluntly, that marking up a book is not an act of mutilation but of love.

3   You shouldn't mark up a book which isn't yours. Librarians (or your friends) who lend you books expect you to keep them clean, and you should. If you decide that I am right about the usefulness of marking books, you will have to buy them. Most of the world's great books are available today, in reprint editions, at less than a dollar.

> "Most of the world's great books are available today, in reprint editions, at less than a dollar."

4   There are two ways in which you can own a book. The first is the property right you establish by paying for it, just as you pay for clothes and furniture. But this act of purchase is only the prelude to possession. Full ownership comes only when you have made it a part of yourself, and the best way to make yourself a part of it is by writing in it. An illustration may make the point clear. You buy a beefsteak and transfer it from the butcher's icebox to your own. But you do not own the beefsteak in the most important sense until you consume it and get it into your bloodstream. I am arguing that books, too, must be absorbed in your bloodstream to do you any good.

5   Confusion about what it means to *own* a book leads people to a false reverence for paper, binding, and type—a respect for the physical thing—the craft of the printer rather than the genius of the author. They forget that it is possible for a man to acquire the idea, to possess the beauty, which a great book contains, without staking his claim by pasting his bookplate inside the cover. Having a fine library doesn't prove that its owner has a mind enriched by books; it proves nothing more than that he, his father, or his wife, was rich enough to buy them.

6   There are three kinds of book owners. The first has all the standard sets and bestsellers—unread, untouched. (This deluded individual owns wood-pulp and ink, not books.) The second has a great many books—a few of them read through, most of them dipped into, but all of them as clean and shiny as the day they were bought. (This person would probably like to make books his own, but is restrained by a false respect for their physical appearance.) The third has a few books or many—everyone of them dog-eared and dilapidated, shaken and loosened by continual use, marked and scribbled in from front to back. (This man owns books.)

7   Is it false respect, you may ask, to preserve intact and unblemished a beautifully printed book, an elegantly bound edition? Of course not. I'd no more scribble all over a first edition of *Paradise Lost* than I'd give my baby a set of crayons and an original Rembrandt! I wouldn't mark up a painting or a statue. Its soul, so to speak, is inseparable from its body. And the beauty of a rare edition or of a richly manufactured volume is like that of a painting or a statue.

8   But the soul of a book *can* be separated from its body. A book is more like the score of a piece of music than it is like a painting. No great musician confuses a symphony with the printed sheets of music. Arturo Toscanini[1] reveres Brahms, but Toscanini's score of the C-minor Symphony is so thoroughly marked up that no one but the maestro himself can read it. The reason why a great conductor makes notations on his musical scores—marks them up again and again each time he returns to study them—is the reason why you should mark your books. If your respect for magnificent binding or typography gets in the way, buy yourself a cheap edition and pay your respects to the author.

---

[1]Arturo Toscanini (1867–1957), an Italian conductor.

9   Why is marking up a book indispensable to reading? First, it keeps you awake. (And I don't mean merely conscious; I mean wide awake.) In the second place, reading, if it is active, is thinking, and thinking tends to express itself in words, spoken or written. The marked book is usually the thought-through book. Finally, writing helps you remember the thoughts you had, or the thoughts the author expressed. Let me develop these three points.

10   If reading is to accomplish anything more than passing time, it must be active. You can't let your eyes glide across the lines of a book and come up with an understanding of what you have read. Now an ordinary piece of light fiction, like say, *Gone with the Wind,* doesn't require the most active kind of reading. The books you read for pleasure can be read in a state of relaxation, and nothing is lost. But a great book, rich in ideas and beauty, a book that raises and tries to answer great fundamental questions, demands the most active reading of which you are capable. You don't absorb the ideas of John Dewey[2] the way you absorb the crooning of Mr. Vallee.[3] You have to reach for them. That you cannot do while you're asleep.

> "If reading is to accomplish anything more
> than passing time, it must be active."

11   If, when you've finished reading a book, the pages are filled with your notes, you know that you read actively. The most famous *active* reader of great books I know is President Hutchins, of the University of Chicago. He also has the hardest schedule of business activities of any man I know. He invariably reads with a pencil, and some times, when he picks up a book and pencil in the evening, he finds himself, instead of making intelligent notes, drawing what he calls "caviar factories" on the margins. When that happens, he puts the book down. He knows he's too tired to read, and he's just wasting time.

12   But, you may ask, why is writing necessary? Well, the physical act of writing, with your own hand, brings words and sentences more sharply before your mind and preserves them better in your memory. To set down your reaction to important words and sentences you have read, and the questions they have raised in your mind, is to preserve those reactions and sharpen those questions.

13   Even if you wrote on a scratch pad, and threw the paper away when you had finished writing, your grasp of the book would be surer. But you don't have to throw the paper away. The margins (top and bottom, as well as side), the end-papers, the very space between the lines, are all available. They aren't sacred. And, best of all, your marks and notes become an integral part of the book and stay there forever. You can pick up the book the following week or year, and there are all your points of

---

[2]John Dewey (1859–1952), a philosopher and educator.
[3]Rudy Vallee (1901–1986), a band leader and singer.

agreement, disagreement, doubt, and inquiry. It's like resuming an interrupted conversation with the advantage of being able to pick up where you left off.

14   And that is exactly what reading a book should be: a conversation between you and the author. Presumably he knows more about the subject than you do; naturally, you'll have the proper humility as you approach him. But don't let anybody tell you that a reader is supposed to be solely on the receiving end. Understanding is a two-way operation; learning doesn't consist in being an empty receptacle. The learner has to question himself and question the teacher. He even has to argue with the teacher, once he understands what the teacher is saying. And marking a book is literally an expression of your differences, or agreements of opinion, with the author.

"The learner has to question himself and question the teacher."

15   There are all kinds of devices for marking a book intelligently and fruitfully. Here's the way I do it:

16 **1.** *Underlining:* of major points, of important or forceful statements.

17 **2.** *Vertical lines at the margin:* to emphasize a statement already underlined.

18 **3.** *Star, asterisk, or other doo-dad at the margin:* to be used sparingly, to emphasize the ten or twenty most important statements in the book. (You may want to fold the bottom corner of each page on which you use such marks. It won't hurt the sturdy paper on which most modern books are printed, and you will be able to take the book off the shelf at any time and, by opening it at the folded-corner page, refresh your recollection of the book.)

19 **4.** *Numbers in the margin:* to indicate the sequence of points the author makes in developing a single argument.

20 **5.** *Numbers of other pages in the margin:* to indicate where else in the book the author made points relevant to the point marked; to tie up the ideas in a book, which, though they may be separated by many pages, belong together.

21 **6.** *Circling of key words or phrases.*

22 **7.** *Writing in the margin, or at the top or bottom of the page, for the sake of:* recording questions (and perhaps answers) which a passage raised in your mind; reducing a complicated discussion to a simple statement; recording the sequence of major points right through the books. I use the end-papers at the back of the book to make a personal index of the author's points in the order of their appearance.

23   The front end-papers are, to me, the most important. Some people reserve them for a fancy bookplate. I reserve them for fancy thinking. After I have finished reading the book and making my personal index on the back end-papers, I turn to the front and try to outline the book, not page by page, or point by point (I've already done that at the back), but as an integrated structure, with a basic unity and an order of parts. This outline is, to me, the measure of my understanding of the work.

24   If you're a die-hard anti-bookmarker, you may object that the margins, the space between the lines, and the end-papers don't give you room enough. All right. How about using a scratch pad slightly smaller than the page-size of the book—so that the edges of the sheets won't protrude? Make your index, outlines, and even your notes on the pad, and then insert these sheets permanently inside the front and back covers of the book.

25   Or, you may say that this business of marking books is going to slow up your reading. It probably will. That's one of the reasons for doing it. Most of us have been taken in by the notion that speed of reading is a measure of our intelligence. There is no such thing as the right speed for intelligent reading. Some things should be read quickly and effortlessly, and some should be read slowly and even laboriously. The sign of intelligence in reading is the ability to read different things differently according to their worth. In the case of good books, the point is not to see how many of them you can get through, but rather how many can get through you—how many you can make your own. A few friends are better than a thousand acquaintances. If this be your aim, as it should be, you will not be impatient if it takes more time and effort to read a great book than it does a newspaper.

"There is no such thing as the right speed for intelligent reading."

26   You may have one final objection to marking books. You can't lend them to your friends because nobody else can read them without being distracted by your notes. Furthermore, you won't want to lend them because a marked copy is a kind of intellectual diary, and lending it is almost like giving your mind away.

27   If your friend wishes to read your *Plutarch's Lives, Shakespeare,* or *The Federalist Papers,* tell him gently but firmly to buy a copy. You will lend him your car or your coat—but your books are as much a part of you as your head or your heart.

Chapter 2

Planning an Essay and Using the Patterns of Development

> Our goals can only be reached through a vehicle of a plan, in which we must fervently believe, and upon which we must vigorously act. There is no other route to success.
>
> — Stephen A. Brennan

To become a better hockey player, you play more hockey. But practice alone is not the key to improvement. You must also consider what you *do* when you play hockey, so you adjust your form, practise backchecking and penalty killing. To become a better writer, you should do much the same thing by working to improve the procedures you follow when you write. Unfortunately, no one can tell you that certain methods will guarantee successful writing. Instead, you must experiment a little to discover the procedures that work best for you. This chapter and the next can help with that experimentation. They explain what all writers must pay attention to:

The writing context (identifying purpose, audience, and role)
Generating ideas (discovering what you have to say)
Ordering ideas (determining the progression and relationship of ideas)
Drafting (writing a preliminary version of the essay)
Revising (rewriting to improve content, organization, and expression of ideas)
Editing (finding and correcting errors in grammar and usage)

In addition to explaining context, idea generation, sequencing, drafting, revising, and editing, these chapters present strategies for working on each of these areas. Sample these procedures until you find ones that work well for you, and your writing is sure to improve. Keep in mind, however, that different writers function in different ways, and the methods that work well for some of your classmates will not necessarily work well for you. Also keep in mind that different writing situations or contexts might necessitate a different approach. The purpose for which you're writing—to entertain, inform, express your feelings, or persuade your reader—might also have an impact on which strategies work for you. Your goal is to find your own effective strategies.

CONSIDERING YOUR WRITING CONTEXT

Successful writers do not plan their writing in a vacuum. Instead, they consider the *context* in which their writing occurs. The **writing context** includes the reason for writing (the writer's *purpose*), who the readers are (the *audience*), and how the writer wants to present himself or herself (the writer's *role*). Together, purpose, audience, and role affect everything the writer does—from idea generation through the final check for typos.

Purpose

Whether you are writing an email to your best friend, preparing a business report, or composing a university or college essay, you are writing for a reason—and that reason is your **purpose.** In general, the primary purposes for writing are

- To entertain the reader.
- To relate experience and/or express feelings.
- To inform the reader about something interesting or important.
- To persuade the reader to think or act a particular way.

You encounter writing that fulfills these purposes all the time. Rick Mercer's books and blog amuse you, so they *entertain*; a friend emails you to tell about the frustrations of interviewing for a job in order to *express feelings and relate experience*; the letter you receive explaining the terms of your student dental plan *informs* you about the nature of your coverage; and the newspaper editorial about a critical blood shortage tries to *persuade* you to donate blood to Canadian Blood Services.

Your purpose in writing influences your approach. Say, for example, that you are a single parent who wants to write about the shortage of child-care spaces in Canada. To entertain your reader, you can write a funny piece about what you went through the day you had to take a final exam and the babysitter cancelled. To express your feelings, you can describe how much you worry about whether your children get quality care while you are at work. To inform your reader, you can explain what the child-care options are for a single working parent of preschool children. To persuade your reader, you can argue for a federally funded child-care program. Of course, you can also combine purposes. For example, you can relate your own experiences and then go on to argue that a federally funded program would make life easier for you and others. Obviously, each essay would have a different character because the content would be shaped by your purpose.

Because purpose influences the content and character of writing so profoundly, you should be clear about your purpose at the outset. For help establishing a purpose or combination of purposes, answer these questions:

- Do I need or want to relate ideas, feelings, or experiences to my reader?
- Am I seeking to inform my reader about something?
- Am I trying to entertain my reader?
- Do I need or want to persuade my reader to think or act a particular way?

Keep in mind that once you have a general topic (daycare options or blood donations) and a purpose (to persuade or entertain), everything else you do should aim toward discovering a deeper purpose: something you want to tell your audience that no one else has seen from quite your perspective in words that belong to you alone. American essayist Annie Dillard sets the bar high when she writes,

> There is something you find interesting, for a reason hard to explain. It is hard to explain because you have never read it on any page; there you begin. You were made and set here to give voice to this, your own astonishment. Write as if you were dying. At the same time, assume you write for an audience of terminal patients. That is, after all, the case. What would you begin writing if you knew you would die soon? What could you say to a dying person that would not enrage by its triviality?

This is a profound goal. All your writing will be better if you always make the attempt to reach it, even while knowing you can do so only occasionally.

Audience

To write successfully, you must achieve your purpose. However, you cannot achieve your purpose without a clear sense of **audience**—that is, a clear sense of who the reader is and what that reader is like. Suppose you are writing an essay about the pollution in a local river. If you were writing the essay for your biology class, you might include a great deal of technical information about specific chemical pollutants. However, if the essay were for a letter to your local newspaper, such technical information might overwhelm the average reader of that paper. Now suppose that you are writing to convince your reader to support a property tax increase so the city could give more to schools. If your reader has school-age children, you could argue that the quality of their education will improve if the increase passes. However, if your reader has no children, you may do better to argue that good schools will increase the value of the reader's property.

In some writing classes, you can establish any audience (person or group of people) for your writing because your instructor will assume the role of any reader you designate. Thus, you can say that your audience consists of city council members, your housemates, a co-worker, the Minister of the Environment, the professors at your university or college, your parents, and so forth. In other writing classes, you must consider your classmates and teacher to be your audience. In either case—or in any situation in or out of the classroom—you must identify your audience and the particular characteristics and needs of that audience because this information will influence your approach, your details, your word choice, and almost every decision you make about your writing. Do you need to define a term? That depends on whether your reader is likely to know its meaning. Should you provide an example? That depends on whether your reader requires the clarification. Should you use this sophisticated word or that more common one? That depends on your reader's likely vocabulary. Which of two points will be more persuasive? That may depend on your reader's age, gender, political leanings, or economic situation.

If you need help identifying an audience for your writing, answer the following questions.

Who would enjoy reading my essay?
Who would learn something from my essay?
Who is interested in my topic?
Who should be persuaded to think or act in the way my essay recommends?
Who would find my essay important?
Who needs to hear what I have to say?

Once you have identified your audience, consider your reader's traits and needs, so you do not inadvertently bore, confuse, or annoy your audience and thereby fail to achieve your purpose. How do you assess traits and needs to avoid this outcome? Answering the following questions can help.

- **What does my reader already know about my topic?** The answer to this question can help you decide what your reader needs to know, and it can help you avoid boring your audience by providing information your reader does not need or already has. It can also help you determine the nature and number of clarifying points, such as examples and definitions, you need to provide.

- **How interested is my reader in what I have to say?** The answer to this question can help you decide how much of your writing should be devoted to capturing the reader's interest or convincing your reader that your topic is important.
- **Does my reader have strong feelings about my topic?** The answer to this question will help you determine whether you must overcome a reader's particular biases or respond to the reader's concerns.
- **How will my reader's age, gender, level of education, income, job, politics, or religion affect his or her reaction to my writing?** The answer to this question will help you decide on appropriate details and language.

When your audience is a diverse group—say, the readers of your local newspaper, the students on your campus, or the members of a large organization—your readers may not have much in common, so you may not be able to assess their needs and traits in a way that yields a single useful profile. In that case, you can identify one or two characteristics that are shared by many members of the group and let that information guide you. For example, if you are writing to working students on your campus, you can think of them as dealing with the stress of juggling courses, studying, and work.

The Writer's Role

In addition to audience and purpose, the role you assume as a writer will influence the character of your writing. Your **role** is the particular way you want to present yourself. For example, a student writing for a teacher will be careful to conform to all the terms of the assignment. An employee writing for a supervisor will adopt the appropriate respectful tone. A friend writing to another friend may be casual and use slang, but a student writing an essay as part of a scholarship competition will avoid colloquial language.

To appreciate the significance of the writer's role, consider a report on how to select the right post-secondary institution. A person in the role of a high school counsellor will provide an objective set of procedures, but a person in the role of a university admissions counsellor may slant the detail to favour his or her school. A person in the role of a student may express the frustrations that are part of the process, but a person in the role of a parent may stress financial concerns.

GENERATING IDEAS

Perhaps you think that writing is the product of inspiration and that it involves staring at a blank page or computer screen until a brilliant flash of insight sends your pen racing across the page or your fingers flying across the keys. If the inspiration does not strike, perhaps you assume that you cannot write, so you might as well pack it up and go play racquetball. If you think this way, you are not alone—but you are wrong.

Inspiration *does* strike writers on occasion, but most often it does not, and we must rely on other techniques to come up with ideas. Collectively, these other strategies are called *idea generation.* Successful writers use the idea generation techniques described in this chapter to pursue ideas in the absence of inspiration. They use these techniques to shape and develop writing topics.

Shaping a Writing Topic

Many times an instructor will specify your writing topic. In that case, your first priority is to be sure you understand the terms of the assignment so you meet your instructor's expectations. First of all, you must be sure you understand the *kind of paper* called for. Does your instructor want you to take a position and defend it? Summarize an author's ideas? Explain the meaning of a concept? Compare and contrast two essays? Consider, for example, this assignment that could be made in response to "The Men from the Boys: Bull Riding Is Dangerous, Irrelevant and a Rare Expression of Old-Style Masculinity" (p. 12).

> In what ways do movies and television influence our views of how men or women are supposed to behave?

This topic requires you to deal with only one gender; dealing with both is not called for and would result in an unwieldy paper. The topic also requires you to provide examples of specific movies and television programs to illustrate your points.

Now consider this assignment based on the same reading selection:

> Agree or disagree with Joanne Byfield's suggestion that men undertake unnecessary and dangerous tasks to prove they are men. Are there other options she's ignored?

This topic requires a different approach. First, you will have to think about real-life examples of men undertaking unnecessary and dangerous tasks. These in turn will lead you to consider why men might do them. You might also consider whether women do them as well. Alternatively, you may find that most men over the age of 30 don't do things that put their safety at risk, in which case you may want to argue with Byfield's theory or suggest that believing you're invincible is "just a phase." Finally, you must convince your reader of the validity of your point of view by using examples and arguing effectively.

In addition to understanding the kind of paper required, you must also be sure you understand the *terms of the assignment*: the length; the due date; the necessary manuscript form; the need to have a teacher conference, engage in peer review, or submit an outline; and so forth. If you have questions about the nature of an assigned topic, or if you are having difficulty fulfilling the assignment, speak to your instructor for guidance.

When you are not given a specific topic to respond to, the following idea generation techniques can help you shape a writing topic.

1.   Review the marginal notes you made during critical reading. (See Chapter 1 on critical reading.) Your comments, questions, and areas of disagreement and agreement may suggest a topic. For example, the marginal note indicating that you'd like to see more evidence of how popular culture is stripping away men's roles as provider, protector, and progenitor could lead you write an essay on the depictions of men in the movies.

2.   Use a provocative quotation as a topic source. For example, in paragraph 4, Byfield writes that that "risk-taking is one of the primary social skills men had to develop ages ago to hunt and protect their families." This might lead to an essay on young boys' dangerous joyriding.

3.   Pick a subject treated in a reading and brainstorm. To brainstorm, make a list of every idea that occurs to you and then examine the list for possible topics. For best results, you should not censor yourself. Just list everything that occurs to you without evaluating the worth of the ideas. For example, one student wrote the following list to brainstorm for topics about violence in sports.

fan violence	*why athletes are violent*
player violence	*Are athletes too violent?*
causes of violence	*Is it violence or aggression?*
effects of violence	*How can we make sports less violent?*
Is the violence justified?	*Fans love it.*
violence = part of the game	*Players think it's okay.*
It's expected.	*Are players violent off the field?*
Is society sick if it likes violence?	*fans getting hurt*
players getting hurt	

The student ultimately drew his topic from the question "Are players violent off the field?" That question prompted him to write about players being violent on the playing field and non-violent off the field.

4.   Freewrite for about 10 minutes on a subject found in a reading. Freewriting helps you stop questioning every idea you have before you even consider whether you can develop it. To freewrite, write non-stop without censoring yourself. Simply record everything that occurs to you without worrying about its quality or about spelling, grammar, or neatness. Do not stop writing for any reason. If you run out of ideas, just write anything: the alphabet, names of family members—anything. Soon new ideas will occur to you, and you can record those. If you like to use a computer, try freewriting with the screen dark. Just turn off your monitor and freewrite "blindfolded." You will have many typing errors, but the freedom that comes from not seeing what you are writing can stimulate your thinking.

The following freewriting was done in response to an assignment for a sociology class that asked students to consider the ways in which popular culture shapes our ideas of masculinity or femininity.

> Prof tells us that thinking about gender as something "natural" is letting society off the hook for putting us in boxes we call masculine and feminine. What's natural for women? Not everyone wants to have children. Women do more listening and emotional housekeeping than men, but how do we tell whether that's nature or nurture? If we don't know nature from nurture, does popular culture weigh in and try to decide for us? Is that how it works? How does popular culture decide what's nature and what's nurture? Is it simply trying to uphold the status quo? And what's this popular culture the prof is talking about? Chick lit? —Bridget Jones? Writing about "popular culture" is probably way too broad. TV advertisements still show women cleaning and cooking and partying. TV shows give women a little more wiggle room. While Calley Dukane in CSI (check spelling!) always looks gorgeous and sexy, she's no pushover. She's feminine looking and yet fascinated with guns. But TV shows depend on advertising. So do women's magazines, which are largely advertisements showing impossibly beautiful women. Glamour last month wanted me to know that Kiera Knightley cleaned, cooked, and cursed. That she conformed to some feminine stereotypes while challenging others. What's the pattern here?

The student's freewriting suggests at least three topics or problems. Note that these involve questions that the writer will need to answer. The best topics are not always the ones we can write about without thinking much; in these essays, we tend to stick to the obvious. Rather, the best topics probe a little, ask questions, force us to think beyond what is simply "common

Troubleshooting Guide

Narrowing Your Topic

If you have trouble working with your writing topic, perhaps that topic is too broad. A topic like "education reform" may seem perfect to you at first because you think there are so many problems with schools today. However, you may also find that you have *too* much to say and don't know where to begin, or that you have too much to say in the specified length. Try narrowing your topic by writing a tree diagram. Place your broad topic on top and "branch off" some ideas, like this:

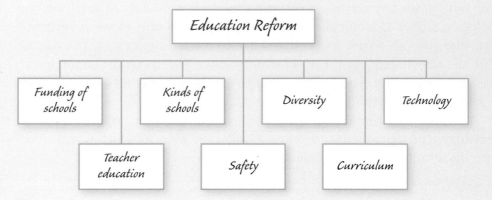

Select a branch that interests you and branch a second time, like this:

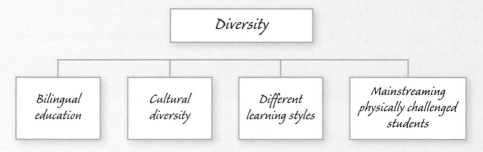

If the topics in your second branching are still too broad, branch again.

Any of these last branches could make a workable, narrow writing topic.

sense." Some of that thinking will mean being more observant of our society; some of it will require some research—help from others who have been similarly puzzled.

- We still don't know which aspects of masculinity and femininity are natural, so popular culture weighs in on the debate. Does it try to uphold gender roles or change them?
- When popular culture tries to sell us something, it's more likely to uphold common ideas about gender roles rather than question them. Why?
- Heroines from popular culture challenge some gender roles while upholding others. What determines how she conforms to expectations of femininity and which expectations she can challenge?

Your freewriting may not yield as many topics or questions, but it is likely to suggest at least one.

5. Examine the subject of a reading from different angles. Answering these questions will help:

a. Does the subject make me think of something else?
b. Why is the subject important?
c. Do I agree or disagree with the author?
d. What interests me about the subject?
e. Can I give the author's ideas a broader or different application?
f. Can I relate the subject to my own experience?

An Essay in Progress: Shaping a Topic and Identifying Context

To see how idea generation techniques can help you shape a writing topic, examine the following brainstorming list written by a student writer, Jeff, who was working to shape a writing topic based on "The Men from the Boys: Bull Riding Is Dangerous, Irrelevant and a Rare Expression of Old-Style Masculinity" (p. 12).

What's masculine or manly? According to whom?
Nature of concept of "ideal male"
When this ideal is unreasonable
Cultural conflict over gender roles
    — world scale
    — national scale
    — local scale
Are urban ideas of masculinity different from rural ideals?
Need for more realistic concept of gender roles: bravery vs. wisdom or experience

Notice that Jeff felt free to abbreviate. During idea generation, use any nota-tions that stimulate your thinking and help you push forward.

After reviewing his brainstorming, Jeff decided his topic would be the concept of the ideal male. Jeff also decided his purpose would be to inform the reader of the source of misconceptions about the idealized male. His teacher was willing to adopt the role of any reader, so he established his audi-ence as the average, general reader and his role as that of a young, concerned male.

EXERCISE 2.1

Shaping a Writing Topic and Identifying Context
(These exercises can be done individually or in small groups.)

1. Select two subjects from the following list and shape a writing topic from each. For one sub-ject, use brainstorming to shape a topic. For the other subject use freewriting.

   a. MuchMusic
   b. Education
   c. Television
   d. Automobiles

   e. The image of men or women in the media
   f. The movie rating system
   g. Friendship
   h. Technology

2. For each of the following, set up a writing context by establishing a possible purpose, audi-ence, and role. For example, using the topic the dangers of boxing, your purpose might be to persuade the reader that boxing should be banned; your audience, boxing fans; and your role, concerned citizen.

   a. Topic: a car accident you witnessed
   b. Topic: a report on the financial health of the local schools
   c. Topic: the use of pesticides on food grown in Canada
   d. Topic: the causes of the high divorce rate in Canada

3. Select one of the writing contexts you created for number 2 and change the context by altering one or more of the elements (audience, purpose, and role). How do you think the change(s) will affect the final essay?

4. Establish a writing context for the topics you generated in response to number 1. Save your work to use in a later exercise.

Discovering Ideas to Develop Your Topic

Once you have a topic, you must discover ideas for developing that topic, ideas compatible with your writing context. Some of the following proce-dures may help.

1. With the new focus provided by your freewriting, continue freewriting to discover what you know about the topic that would support your essay. This freewriting might also reveal what you don't know—what questions seem important but can't be answered by you right now. If a student were to consider the first topic that comes out of the freewriting above ("We still don't know which aspects of masculinity and femininity are natural, so popular culture weighs in on the debate. Does it try to uphold gender roles or change them?"), she would have to consider what example of popular culture she would consider. Having decided to look at women's magazines, she might freewrite on four topics:

What does science tell us about gender that's hard-wired?

What gender stereotypes can science not explain?

How do magazines for young women reinforce these stereotypes?

Why might the magazines choose to uphold certain female stereotypes?

2. Review the marginal notes you made during critical reading. They may include ideas for developing your topic. (See Chapter 1 on critical reading.)

3. Write a brainstorming list that focuses on your subject. Like brainstorming for a topic, brainstorming for ideas to develop a topic involves listing every idea that occurs to you. Remember, do not evaluate the worth of your ideas; just write down everything you can think of. Later, you can reject anything unusable. Here is an example of a brainstorming list for one of the topics that emerged from the freewriting on page 41.

Topic: how does popular culture shape our ideas of masculinity or femininity?

Advertising in my mother's Oprah at odds with magazine's purpose

Oprah herself gives us lots of articles on "self-actualization"

How to talk back. How to cope with stress. How to be ourselves

Suze Orman — managing our own money

Dr. Phil—talking back to men if necessary

The ad models are usually thin—and have way more money than I do

Emphasis on being perfectly made up.

Will this mascara really give me those eyelashes? Who are we kidding?

The underwear is great, but couldn't I buy the body too?

Oprah arranges make-overs. Who is this for?

How do we ever know changes are for us?

Oprah gets us to buy her magazine by promising to make us feel good about ourselves.

Advertisers get us to buy their stuff by making us feel awful in comparison to the perfect, skinny models.

Because brainstorming is idea generation, its results are preliminary. You need not use everything on the list, and you can add to the list at any time.

4.   Try clustering. Clustering helps you generate ideas and see how those ideas relate to each other. To cluster, first write your topic in the centre of the page and draw a circle around it. As ideas to develop your topic occur to you, write them down, circle them, and draw lines attaching them to the circled ideas they relate to. Do not censor yourself. Write down everything, regardless of its quality. The following clustering was done for an essay about violence on the playing field.

In the final version of the essay, the writer did not use all of the ideas in his clustering, though he used some ideas that do not appear in the clustering. That is fine because nothing about idea generation is set in stone. Also notice that the writer placed "split personality" in two spots on the clustering. That is also fine. If you are unsure what an idea relates to, jot it down in more than one spot and solve the problem later.

5.   Talk to other people about your topic. Your classmates, in particular, can suggest ideas for developing your topic.

Troubleshooting Guide

Using the Internet

If you have trouble generating ideas, try using the Internet.

- *Surf the Internet.* Type a subject into a search engine like one of the following, and scan the titles returned for possible writing topics or ideas for developing a topic.

  Google: www.google.com (if your essay requires some research, you might try Google Scholar as a first resource, but check with your instructor or librarian to find the databases appropriate to your discipline.)
  Yahoo: www.yahoo.com

- *Browse news sites and electronic newspapers and magazines.* Scan one of these popular sites for information on current events, health, business, and entertainment. You might get several writing ideas.

  Canadian Broadcasting Corporation: www.cbc.ca
  The Globe and Mail: www.theglobeandmail.com
  The National Post: www.nationalpost.com
  CanWest Global: www.canada.com
  Google News: news.google.com

- *Browse Web sites with links to varied content.* These two sites, in particular, may give you writing ideas:

  Science and Technology Daily: scitechdaily.com
  Arts and Letters Daily: aldaily.com

Information on the Internet, like that found in books, magazines, journals, and newspapers, still constitutes someone else's ideas, so don't plagiarize and pretend it's your own. Take down the information on the Internet site so you can include it in your Works Cited page. (See page 514 in Chapter 14. Also see page 504 for information on how to ensure that the Internet site is trustworthy.)

6. **Combine techniques.** Begin by freewriting and then try clustering. Or begin with a brainstorming list and then talk to other people. Combine idea generation strategies in any way that suits you.

An Essay in Progress: Discovering Ideas to Develop Your Topic

Student-author Jeff created the cluster on page 48 as a way to discover ideas that would help him develop the topic he generated with the brainstorming list on page 43.

Discover Ideas to Develop Your Topic

1. Select three of the following topics. For each one, generate three ideas that could be used for development. Use a different idea generation technique for each topic.

   Mandatory drug testing of university and college athletes.
   The ethical issues associated with cloning animals.
   The causes of stress among college and university students.
   The characteristics of a leader.

2. Using the idea generation techniques of your choice, discover enough ideas to write a first draft on one of the topics you established a writing context for in number 4 of Exercise 2.1.

DEVELOPING A THESIS

A successful essay has a central focus, a main idea the writer wants to convey. This central point is the **thesis,** the idea that everything else in the essay pertains to. It represents both a contract with your reader and a contract with yourself: A well-written thesis statement gives your reader a sense of what to expect in the essay, and it gives you an opportunity to see whether your essay will work before you've laboured over an entire draft.

A thesis statement should be arguable. It defines your topic, and it also indicates your particular—and carefully considered—observations, comments, or opinions about the topic. As a consequence, your thesis lets your reader know the subject of your essay and your assertion about the subject. Particularly in academic essays, it might elaborate on the particular points you intend to make. This type of thesis is also helpful for the writer. While it may take several drafts to get such a thesis right, it allows you to see the essay in a miniature version. You can make sure you aren't going to contradict yourself. You can also consider how strong each of your points is and put them in an appropriate order. In essays where you need to explain causes or effects, or to articulate exactly how the causes produce the effects or why two incidents are related by cause and effect, you can stop and evaluate your reasoning. Once you've got a thesis statement, you can also consider whether you have the evidence to support your assertions. If not, you now know what you're looking for.

A good thesis is significant and individual. It shouldn't be obvious to everybody. If it is, the essay that grows out of it will be underwhelming. Consider the brainstorming above about *Oprah Magazine*. Your thesis could be "advertising is sexist." You've got a topic—advertising. You've got your opinion—it's sexist. But consider how much more interesting the following essay might be:

> While Oprah herself tries to convince us we can be whatever we want and gives us the advice we need to make the necessary changes, the advertisements continue to reinforce gender stereotypes, particularly those that make us feel we're too fat or not beautiful enough. They're both trying to get us to buy something by making us feel we need to be "improved."

A good thesis statement is expressed in the most precise and specific language possible, which in turn ensures that your topic is manageable. If you are aiming for precise expression, revise general and unworkable thesis statements like "Our cities need a complete overhaul if they want to become sustainable" to reflect what you can actually accomplish in an essay, particularly if it isn't a lengthy research paper.

Once you've written—and rewritten—your thesis statement, spend some time considering how valid it is. Does it fully and usefully reflect the evidence you have gathered for your assertion? Then see whether it will help guide the writing process, particularly if it's going to take you several days to write your essay. You might want to revise it a few times more!

In the table below, you can see the relationship between a broad (and often unworkable) subject, the writer's assertion about the subject, and a thesis statement that is arguable and significant.

SUBJECT	WRITER'S ASSERTION(S)	THESIS
MTV	MTV airs sexually explicit material. It demeans people. Parents should limit their children's exposure to it.	Parents should limit their children's exposure to MTV because the channel airs sexually explicit material, and it demeans people.
Cellphone users	Four kinds of cellphone users: those who can't live without it because it plays a crucial role in their social lives; those who believe their next business deal is just around the corner; those who prefer to use it to text; and those who use it only for emergencies or to keep track of kids.	There are four kinds of cellphone users. Some people use it to ensure that they and their children are safe; others use it because they're indispensable at the office; others use it only to text, avoiding verbal contact with people; while some people organize their entire (and very busy) social lives around it.
Cities and sustainability—for a geography class or a class on the environment	We need to change the structure of cities to make them more sustainable.	Bit by bit, by improving the effectiveness of public transit, by creating pedestrian-friendly spaces, and by building housing in the city's core, we can make cities more sustainable and more pleasant to live in.
The 1960s—for a history class	Youth culture changed because young people had money and buying power. They were also critical of authority.	In the 1960s, teenagers had enough money to become a cultural force; as a result, their criticisms of authority had an impact on the society at large.

In scientific, technical, business, and some social science writing, thesis statements that indicate major points are fairly common. Especially when the piece of writing is long or technical, such a thesis helps the reader and the writer by laying out the architecture of the piece; if you need to write your essay over several days, your thesis will tell you exactly what you need to do next.

Location of the Thesis

Doubtless you have been taught to write a "five-paragraph special"—that is, an essay with an introduction, conclusion, and three (not always related) points. In such a brief essay, the convention is to place the thesis statement in the essay's introduction, frequently at the end of that section, as in this example in which the thesis statement is underlined.

> Have you ever received unwanted credit cards in the mail? Did a credit card company ever offer you such a big line of credit at such a low interest rate that you could not resist the offer? Yes, accepting the cards is tempting, but they come with risks the credit card companies never mention. <u>As a former credit card addict, I can assure you that the dangers of relying on credit are very serious.</u>

Writing for college and university classes requires, however, a more varied repertoire. In some essays, the thesis is placed in the final paragraph. This works well when all the detail in the essay builds cumulatively to a conclusion that is the essay's main point. In other essays, the thesis is not stated. Instead, it is strongly implied by the details in the essay. When the thesis is not stated, a critical reader must infer the thesis. In research papers and technical essays, the thesis might be found on the second or third page. This placement is effective when you need to teach your readers enough about your subject for them to understand your particular treatment of it. In other words, just as you consider your audience, purpose, the evidence, and your attitude toward it when you structure your essay, so you should also take these elements into consideration when you decide where your thesis should go.

How to Compose Your Thesis

1.   **Study the ideas and details you have generated.** Does one idea have more points than the others? Does one idea interest you more than the others? Does one idea seem more manageable than the others? The answer to one or more of these questions can lead to a thesis.

2.   **Engage in additional idea generation, if necessary.** If you cannot formulate a thesis, you may not yet have generated enough ideas and details. Try again, this time using a different idea generation technique.

3.   **Consider your writing context.** What do you already know or what can you determine about your audience, purpose, and role that can point you toward a thesis? Say you are writing about the dangers associated with the

Internet. If you cannot think of a thesis, identify an audience and go from there. For example, you could establish your audience as teenagers, which could lead you to explain how teens can avoid sexual predators in chat rooms.

4. Allow your early thesis to be preliminary. Although you are learning about the qualities of an effective thesis right now, your first version need not have all those qualities. An imperfect thesis can be revised later. Write an announcement if doing so moves you forward. Later, you can craft a more elegant thesis.

An Essay in Progress: Composing a Preliminary Thesis

Before drafting a preliminary thesis, Jeff studied his clustering, which appears on page 48. He thought he had many good ideas, but at first he had trouble seeing how the ideas in the main circles branching off his centre topic related to each other. He reflected about this and was somewhat frustrated until he considered the ideas in light of his personal dislike of the concept of the ideal male. Then he related the ideas to that dislike and found a unifying thread, which he expressed in this sentence:

The concept of the ideal male is a problem and has no basis.

He rewrote that sentence for clarity and came up with a preliminary thesis he was happy with:

The popular concept of the ideal male is unsuitable in our society.

Next, Jeff considered the thesis in light of his writing context and realized that he wanted to broaden his purpose. Rather than just inform his reader, he also wanted to convince his audience that the concept of the ideal male is misguided.

EXERCISE 2.3

Composing a Thesis

1. Explain what you can expect to find in an essay with each of the following thesis statements. Try to determine the pattern of development (p. 59) and purpose (p. 35) for each essay.

    EXAMPLE   The 12-month school year offers several advantages.

    EXPLANATION   The essay will mention and explain the effects of the 12-month school year, perhaps to persuade the reader that it is the best academic calendar.

    a. Professional athletes are often viewed as superheroes, but unlike the superheroes of movies, they have vulnerable human bodies that sooner or later fail them. Our superhero expectations of them are unfair both to them and to us.

b. Karate is an excellent sport for school-age children who need to build self-esteem.

c. Although the technology of cellphones, PDAs, and the Internet was originally intended to make us more efficient, psychologists report it has instead had the effect of interrupting us constantly, making it harder to focus and to retain what we learn; hence it makes us less efficient in the long run.

d. A good teacher has a sense of humour, a commitment to excellence, and the ability to be flexible.

e. The spring drought will create economic hardships on the prairies.

2. In the following thesis statements, underline the subject once and the writer's assertion twice. If the major points are included, place brackets around them.

a. Colleges and universities should not have physical education requirements because they delay students' progress and contribute little to students' education.

b. I was deeply moved by the prayer service held at the war memorial.

c. Paul Newman's success as a film star was a result of his wise choice of roles, his sex appeal, and his acting talent.

d. African-Canadian authors Austin Clarke and Dionne Brand have very different writing styles.

e. Oil and gas well drilling should be banned from residential areas because of the danger to the environment and the problem for homeowners.

3. Indicate whether each thesis is acceptable or unacceptable. If it is unacceptable, state what is wrong with the thesis and rewrite it to make it acceptable.

a. Regular exercise is important to a person's physical well-being.

b. *Seinfeld* is one of the most popular television comedies of all time.

c. Newspapers are a better source of information about current affairs than television news programs.

d. The following paragraph will explain why all high school students should take four years of a foreign language.

e. The current movie rating system is inadequate for a number of reasons.

f. The entertainment available to Canadians is of the poorest quality.

g. Summer camp is a good experience for children.

4. Return to the idea generation material and topic you developed for number 2 of Exercise 2.2 on page 48. Study that material and develop a thesis from it. Save your work to use in a later exercise.

ORDERING IDEAS

The order in which you present your ideas is important because a reader who cannot follow the sequence will become confused and frustrated. There are many possibilities for ordering ideas. Here are three common ones, which can be used alone or in combination.

1. **Chronological order** arranges details across time. The event that occurred first is written first; the event that occurred second is written second; and so on.
2. **Spatial order** arranges details as they appear across space—front to back, near to far, top to bottom, left to right.
3. **Progressive order** arranges details from the least to the most important, compelling, interesting, representative, surprising, and so on. A progressive order allows for a big finish because the most significant point comes at the end. A variation of progressive order is to begin with the second strongest point and sandwich everything else in the middle for the strongest possible beginning and ending.

Outlining

With a workable outline in hand, writers often find that drafting goes much more smoothly. However, many people who would benefit from outlining resist it because they are familiar only with the formal outline developed with roman numerals, letters, and numbers. The formal outline is very helpful, especially for long or complex essays. However, less formal and less detailed alternatives are available for simpler papers, and these are also explained in this chapter. You might find one of these works well for you. Choose the outline that best suits your paper: The more complicated the paper, the more detailed the outline should be.

The Scratch Outline

The scratch outline is the least detailed outline. It is simply a list of the major ideas you plan to include in your first draft, written in the order you plan to cover them. Typically, the scratch outline just covers major points with no mention of details for developing those points, so it is not well suited for complicated essays or for writers who must plan in detail before drafting. As an example, here is a scratch outline based, in part, on some of the ideas generated with the clustering on page 46.

Preliminary thesis: Even non-violent people are often violent on the playing field.

Violence is seen as okay because it's part of the game.

A player has to be violent to compete with other players.

Sports is different from the real world, so violence is justified.

Fans want the violence.

If you brainstormed at the computer, you can turn your brainstorming list into a scratch outline. First delete ideas you do not want to use and add any new ones that occur to you. Then, using your cut-and-paste functions, arrange the ideas in your list in the order you want to treat them in your draft.

The Informal Outline

The informal outline is more detailed than the scratch outline. It includes some details for developing major points and it groups related ideas together, so the writer has a sense of which details will appear together in the same paragraph. Although more detailed than the scratch outline, the informal outline may not be suitable for complex papers or writers who need a fair amount of structure before they draft. An informal outline might look like this:

> *Preliminary thesis: Even non-violent people are often violent on the playing field.*
> *Violence is okay because it's part of the game.*
> > *Use roommate as example.*
> > *Coaches only play people with killer instinct.*
> *A player has to be violent to compete with other players.*
> > *Get other guys before they get you.*
> > *If everyone else is violent, you have to be, too.*
> > *Violence is okay if you win the game.*
> *Sports is different from the real world, so violence is justified.*
> > *It's only a game and not part of reality, so it's okay to be violent.*
> > *But the injuries are real.*
> *Fans want the violence.*
> > *Fans cheer for violence.*
> > *They even act violently themselves in the stands.*

The Outline Tree

An outline tree, which can be moderately to heavily detailed, allows a writer to see how ideas relate to each other. Many writers appreciate the visual representation the tree provides. To construct an outline tree, write your preliminary thesis at the top of a page and connect ideas with "branches," as the student example on page 56 illustrates.

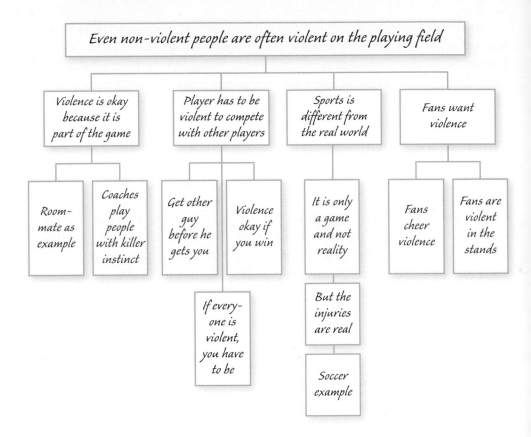

The Formal Outline

The formal outline allows you to plan your essay in considerable detail. To construct a formal outline, write your preliminary thesis at the top of the page. Then label your major points with roman numerals and your supporting details with capital letters. Details that explain or illustrate supporting details are given numbers. You are probably familiar with the formal outline, which looks something like this:

Preliminary thesis: _____

    I.

       A.

       B.

       C.

    II.

       A.

       B.

1.
2.
III.
   A.
      1.
      2.
      3.
   B.
      1.
      2.
   C.

To see how a formal outline plots a draft, review the following formal outline for an essay with this thesis: Non-violent people can be violent on the playing field.

I. *Hurting people is part of the game.*
   A. *My roommate is gentle off the basketball court and hurtful on the court.*
   B. *If he didn't hurt others, the coach would bench him.*
II. *Violence is necessary for winning.*
   A. *Players feel violence is okay if they win*
      1. *In my soccer game, an opposing player intentionally hurt one of our players.*
      2. *He did it to win.*
   B. *Players injure others so they don't get hurt themselves.*
III. *Players think violence is okay because sports are games.*
   A. *But the violence is real.*
   B. *The injuries are lasting.*
      1. *Our soccer goalie missed a month of school.*
      2. *He still has effects from a violent play.*
IV. *Fans like violence.*
   A. *Fans encourage player violence.*
   B. *Fans are violent themselves.*

If you like to compose at the computer, check your word processing program to see if it has outlining capability. If it does, you can develop a formal outline by filling in the various levels. If it does not, develop your own outline form, using roman numerals, letters, and numbers. Save the form as a file you can retrieve whenever you want to outline. To learn more about the mechanics of writing a formal outline, visit Purdue University's Online Writing Lab at owl.english.purdue.edu/handouts/general/gl_outlin.html.

> **Troubleshooting Guide**
>
> ### Writing an Outline
>
> If you have trouble outlining, these tips can help:
>
> - **Refer to your preliminary thesis.** Ideas that don't seem to fit in your outline may not be sufficiently related to your thesis. You may need to eliminate some ideas or adjust your thesis to accommodate them.
>
> - **Consider your context.** Ideas that don't seem to belong may not be appropriate for your purpose, audience, or role. Adjust your ideas or context as necessary.
>
> - **Be flexible.** The outlining process may lead you to reconsider some of your ideas or your thesis. Be ready to add and delete ideas and adjust your thesis in light of new insights.
>
> - **Return to idea generation, if necessary.** If you cannot outline, you may not yet have enough material.

An Essay in Progress: Outlining

Using his clustering as a guide (see page 48), student writer Jeff developed the following informal outline. You will notice that Jeff did not use all the ideas from his clustering and that he included ideas that do not appear in the clustering. Writers are always free to make changes as new ideas occur to them.

Preliminary thesis: The popular concept of the ideal male is unsuitable in our society.

The sources of the ideal are ridiculous.

   movie industry
      —highly unrealistic situations
   advertising
      —deceitful industry to begin with
   folktales and childhood stories
      —originated in completely different eras and societies

The admired/discouraged qualities of the ideal are out of place.

   instinctive vs. considered action
      —increasingly complex society
   self-containment vs. need for others
      —increasingly cooperative society

The idealized male's relation to women is archaic.

   protector, saviour, rescuer, dominant male
      —increasing appearance of female equality in all respects

---

EXERCISE 2.4

Ordering Ideas

1. For each preliminary thesis statement, indicate whether the order of ideas is likely to be spatial, chronological, or progressive.

    a. The university should offer a study skills seminar as part of its orientation program.
    b. Once the flood waters receded, I discovered the devastation to my apartment.
    c. The movie version of *Lord of the Rings* is better than the book version.
    d. I will always remember the day Julio won the provincial pole vault championship.
    e. You can learn to change the oil in your car and save money as a result.
    f. At sunset, the flower garden of Municipal Park offers a peaceful retreat.

2. Using the techniques of your choice, generate ideas for an essay with one of the following preliminary thesis statements:

    Canadians are too materialistic.
    Canadians are not too materialistic.

    Then write an informal outline for the essay.

3. Using the techniques of your choice, generate ideas for an essay with one of the following preliminary thesis statements:

    Our enthusiasm for computers has gone too far.
    Our enthusiasm for computers has not gone too far.

    Then write an outline tree for the essay.

4. Using the thesis and ideas you have from number 4 for Exercise 2.3, write either a formal outline or outline tree. Feel free to add or delete ideas as you see fit. Save your work to use in a later exercise.

USING THE PATTERNS OF DEVELOPMENT

As you generate ideas, compose your thesis, and organize your draft, consider how the patterns of development can help you achieve your writing purpose. As tools, the patterns of development can help you generate ideas and find an effective order for those ideas. The following patterns of development are explained and illustrated throughout this text.

- **Description** (Chapter 4)—using words to explain what something looks, sounds, feels, smells, and/or tastes like (spatial or progressive order often used)
- **Narration** (Chapter 5)—telling a story (chronological order often used)

- **Exemplification** (Chapter 6)—providing examples (progressive order often used)
- **Definition** (Chapter 7)—explaining the meaning of a term or concept (progressive order often used)
- **Process analysis** (Chapter 8)—explaining how something works or how it is made or done (chronological order often used)
- **Comparison-contrast** (Chapter 9)—explaining similarities and/or differences (block pattern or alternating pattern often used)
- **Cause-and-effect analysis** (Chapter 10)—explaining the reasons for an action and/or the results of an action (progressive order often used)
- **Classification-division** (Chapter 11)—grouping items into categories and/or breaking something down into its parts (progressive order often used)

In addition to using the strategies on pages 39 and 44, you can ask these questions related to the patterns to help shape a writing topic and generate ideas to develop that topic. (You will not be able to answer every question for every writing subject.)

a. Can I describe something related to my subject? (description)
b. Can I tell a story related to my subject? (narration)
c. Can I provide examples that illustrate my subject? (exemplification)
d. What is the meaning of my subject? Are there any terms or concepts I need to define? (definition)
e. Can I explain how my subject works or how it is made or done? (process analysis)
f. What is my subject like? What is it different from? (comparison-contrast)
g. What causes my subject? What are the effects of my subject (cause-and-effect analysis)
h. Can I classify my subject into different categories? Can I break my subject down into parts? (classification-division)

To see how considering the patterns of development can help with idea generation and organization, consider the following chart, developed to discover ideas for an essay about the need to think about the effect of cellphones on our daily lives.

How Cellphones Affect Our Daily Lives

PATTERN	IDEA	ORDER
Description	Describe a person who is addicted to his or her cellphone.	While spatial order is often used to describe people and places, progressive order might be used here.
Narration	Tell a story of how someone panicked when he or she found his or her cellphone had been forgotten—and then later realized it was a good thing.	Chronological order is likely.
Exemplification	Give examples of the kinds of anxieties people experience when they realize they don't have their cellphone. Or give examples of the way a variety of people use their cellphones.	Progressive order is possible. Examples could also be grouped by category (see Chapter 11.)
Definition	Define cellphone addiction.	Progressive order is possible if aspects of the definition are given in order of significance.
Process analysis	Describe how to wean people off excessive dependence on their cellphones.	Chronological order would be used if the steps were to be performed in a specific order, progressive order would be used if steps were arranged in order of effectiveness or difficulty.
Comparison-contrast	Compare individuals whose excessive cellphone use has a detrimental effect on the people around them with individuals who know the place of their cellphones in a rich and complex social life.	Block pattern would be used to make all the points about the addicted cellphone user and then all the points about the person who is polite about his or her cellphone use. Alternating pattern would be used if one point were made about the addicted cellphone user and then one about the polite cellphone user, until all the points were presented.
Cause-and-effect analysis	Explain the effects excessive cellphone use has on the people around the user— how they come to feel angry, hurt, and unimportant.	Progressive order is possible, with the most significant effects given last.
Classification-division	Classify the kinds of people who use cellphones—perhaps for business, for social networking, and for safety.	Grouping by category is possible if personality components are given together. This order could be combined with progressive order if components or groupings are given in order of significance.

READING SELECTION

In the following essay, Gail Godwin discusses what may be the most difficult aspect of writing: the feeling that one can't write—what some people call lack of inspiration or "writer's block." Godwin understands the problem and has recommendations for dealing with it.

Background

Born in Alabama in 1937 and raised in Asheville, North Carolina, Gail Godwin received her journalism degree from the University of North Carolina and her PhD in English from the University of Iowa, where she studied with John Irving and Kurt Vonnegut. She was a journalist and English teacher before becoming a fiction writer. She has won numerous writing awards, including the Simon Guggenheim Fellowship and the Award in Literature from the American Academy and Institute for Arts and Letters. Godwin is the author of ten novels and two collections of fiction. Three of her novels were nominated for the National Book Award: *The Odd Woman, A Mother and Two Daughters,* and *Violet Clay.* Her novels frequently appear on the *New York Times* bestseller list. Her most recent novel, *Evenings at Five,* was published in 2003. "The Watcher at the Gates" originally appeared in the *New York Times Book Review* in 1977.

Reading with a Purpose

All writers—both student and professional—experience writer's block. In "The Watcher at the Gates," Gail Godwin looks at the cause of the block— the "inner critic" that restrains writers if it is not silenced during the early stages of writing, during idea generation and drafting. Godwin explains (and you will learn in the next chapter) that writers should hold the inner critic at bay until they are ready to revise their writing. As you read, consider your own inner critic. How much of a problem is it?

Assignment

In a paragraph or two, note what Godwin says that pertains to you as a writer. If nothing pertains to you, explain why.

The Watcher at the Gates
Gail Godwin

1   I first realized I was not the only writer who had a restraining critic who lived inside me and sapped the juice from green inspirations when I was leafing through Freud's "Interpretation of Dreams" a few years ago. Ironically, it was my "inner critic" who had sent me to Freud. I was writing a novel, and my heroine was in the middle of a dream, and then I lost faith in my own invention and rushed to "an authority" to check whether she could have such a dream. In the chapter on dream interpretation, I came upon the following passage that has helped me free myself, in some measure, from my critic and has led to many pleasant and interesting exchanges with other writers.

2   Freud quotes Schiller, who is writing a letter to a friend. The friend complains of his lack of creative power. Schiller replies with an allegory. He says it is not good if the intellect examines too closely the ideas pouring in at the gates. "In isolation, an idea may be quite insignificant, and venturesome in the extreme, but it may acquire

importance from an idea which follows it . . . In the case of a creative mind, it seems to me, the intellect has withdrawn its watchers from the gates, and the ideas rush in pell-mell, and only then does it review and inspect the multitude. You are ashamed or afraid of the momentary and passing madness which is found in all real creators, the longer or shorter duration of which distinguishes the thinking artist from the dreamer . . . you reject too soon and discriminate too severely."

3   So that's what I had: a Watcher at the Gates. I decided to get to know him better. I discussed him with other writers, who told me some of the quirks and habits of their Watchers, each of whom was as individual as his host, and all of whom seemed passionately dedicated to one goal: rejecting too soon and discriminating too severely.

4   It is amazing the lengths a Watcher will go to keep you from pursuing the flow of your imagination. Watchers are notorious pencil sharpeners, ribbon changers, plant waterers, home repairers and abhorrers of messy rooms or messy pages. They are compulsive looker-uppers. They are superstitious scaredy-cats. They cultivate self-important eccentricities they think are suitable for "writers." And they'd rather die (and kill your inspiration with them) than risk making a fool of themselves.

5   My Watcher has a wasteful penchant for 20-pound bond paper above and below the carbon of the first draft. "What's the good of writing out a whole page," he whispers begrudgingly, "if you just have to write it over again later? Get it perfect the first time!" My Watcher adores stopping in the middle of a morning's work to drive down to the library to check on the name of a flower or a World War II battle or a line of metaphysical poetry. "You can't possibly go on till you've got this right!" he admonishes. I go and get the car keys.

6   Other Watchers have informed their writers that:

7   "Whenever you get a really good sentence you should stop in the middle of it and go on tomorrow. Otherwise you might run dry."

8   "Don't try and continue with your book till your dental appointment is over. When you're worried about your teeth, you can't think about art."

9   Another Watcher makes his owner pin his finished pages to a clothesline and read them through binoculars "to see how they look from a distance." Countless other Watchers demand "bribes" for taking the day off: lethal doses of caffeine, alcoholic doses of Scotch or vodka or wine.

10   There are various ways to outsmart, pacify or coexist with your Watcher. Here are some I have tried, or my writer-friends have tried, with success:

11   Look for situations when he's likely to be off-guard. Write too fast for him in an unexpected place, at an unexpected time. (Virginia Woolf captured the "diamonds in the dustheap" by writing at a "rapid haphazard gallop" in her diary.) Write when very tired. Write in purple ink on the back of a Master Charge statement. Write whatever comes into your mind while the kettle is boiling and make the steam whistle your deadline. (Deadlines are a great way to outdistance the Watcher.)

12   Disguise what you are writing. If your Watcher refuses to let you get on with your story or novel, write a "letter" instead, telling your "correspondent" what you are going to write in your story or next chapter. Dash off a "review" of your own unfinished opus. It will stand up like a bully to your Watcher the next time he throws obstacles in your path. If you write yourself a good one.

13   Get to know your Watcher. He's yours. Do a drawing of him (or her). Pin it to the wall of your study and turn it gently to the wall when necessary. Let your Watcher feel needed. Watchers are excellent critics after inspiration has been captured; they are dependable, sharp-eyed readers of things already set down. Keep your Watcher in shape and he'll have less time to keep you from shaping. If he's really ruining your whole working day sit down, as Jung did with his personal demons, and write him a letter. On a very bad day I once wrote my Watcher a letter. "Dear Watcher," I wrote, "What is it you're so afraid I'll do?" Then I held his pen for him, and he replied instantly with a candor that has kept me from truly despising him.

14   "Fail," he wrote back.

Chapter 3

Writing and Rewriting

"If our grammar is loose and shabby, our punctuation random, and our mechanics haphazard, we will lose our audience. We must put sentences together by rules, because rules describe the readers' expectations. If our language ignores these rules—if we substitute commas for periods or neglect to match parts of sentences to each other—readers will be confused and bored; they will not follow where we want to lead them, even if our ideas are profound and our information fascinating."

— Donald Hall & Sven Birkerts, *Writing Well*, 1991

Once you have a preliminary thesis and outline, you are ready to write your first draft. A **first draft** is your initial attempt to write your ideas in essay form. Because it is a first attempt, your first draft will be rough—and that is fine. In fact, first drafts are supposed to be rough, which is why they are often called *rough drafts*. Later, during **revising,** you can refine your writing.

WRITING YOUR FIRST DRAFT

Many writers expect too much of a first draft. They think they should be able to write one draft, "fix it up" by correcting spelling and punctuation, and be done. However, this is not the way writing usually goes. For most writers, the first draft produces raw material that requires shaping and polishing through multiple drafts. Thus, do not expect perfection; write your ideas the best way you can and be prepared to revise—more than once—after drafting.

Tips for Drafting

- **If you get stuck, move on.** Skip troublesome aspects and go on to sections that are easier to write. If you cannot think of an appropriate word, type three x's (which are easy to find using the Find command) and come back to it later. If you cannot come up with a suitable introduction, begin with your first major point and deal with your opening later. Don't be afraid to draft out of order. Just concentrate on what you *can* write and do not dwell on what you cannot.
- **Use your outline.** Your outline can be a guide and a support system. At the same time, depart from your outline if a better strategy or new idea occurs to you. Remember, inspiration is welcome no matter when it occurs.

- **Write from start to finish in one sitting.** Even if you skip parts, push through to the end to get as much raw material as possible.
- **Draft the way you speak.** If you have trouble getting the words down, you may be straining for an academic style. It's difficult to deal with both an unfamiliar role and unfamiliar ideas, so focus on getting your ideas down and write your draft the way you would speak it to a friend. But be aware that you will need to polish the style during revision.

ESSAY STRUCTURE

Essays are typically made up of an *introduction, body paragraphs,* and a *conclusion.* Think of the introduction as the beginning of your essay, the body paragraphs as the middle, and the conclusion as the end.

The Introduction

Because first impressions are important, a successful essay begins well. In general, that beginning is a one- or two-paragraph **introduction** aimed at stimulating the reader's interest and, many times, presenting the thesis. You can approach the introduction many ways, some of which are illustrated in the examples that follow. (Notice that the thesis, underlined in these examples, appears as the last sentence of each introduction. Student writers often find this placement convenient. However, as explained on page 51, the thesis can appear elsewhere.)

TELL A STORY (USE NARRATION)

The new boy walked into fourth-period English with his head down. He handed a slip to Mrs. Kuhlins, who announced, "Frankie is our new student, class. I trust that you will make him welcome." With that, Frankie brushed a stray hair out of his eyes and shuffled to a seat in the back. His clothes were hopelessly out of date, and his hair was a mess. But as he passed my desk, our eyes met, and I saw something there. <u>At that moment, I knew there was something special about this new kid.</u>

ESTABLISH YOURSELF AS SOMEONE KNOWLEDGEABLE ABOUT THE SUBJECT

When I was six, I joined a T-ball league and spent a glorious summer at third base. When I was ten, I began playing intramural basketball and learned the pleasures of rebounding and making foul shots. In junior high school, I began running middle distances for the track team and learned the joy of crossing the finish line in one last burst of speed. In high school, I was active in football, track, and water polo. <u>As a result of all these years of playing team sports, I have come to realize that there are three kinds of coaches.</u>

PROVIDE HELPFUL BACKGROUND INFORMATION

In the 1970s, a gas pipeline along the Mackenzie Valley, stretching from the Beaufort Sea to southern Canada, was proposed. When people argued that the pipeline would change the way of life of the people living there, the Liberal government appointed Mr. Justice Thomas Berger to conduct an inquiry that explored the potential impact of the pipeline. Berger met with Dene, Inuit, and Metis groups in tents, log cabins, and outdoors; he met with experts in Yellowknife. The title of his report, "Northern Frontier, Northern Homeland," reflected two competing visions of the north. On the one hand, those arguing that we needed this corridor to meet the energy needs of the more populated areas of Canada saw the north primarily as a frontier—a frontier to be exploited. On the other hand, the people who lived there took seriously their responsibility to protect the landscape from the infrastructure of roads, airstrips, and new towns that would have a profound impact on their way of life and on the wildlife that lived in and migrated through the area. <u>These two attitudes, which perceive the north either as a frontier to develop or as a homeland to protect, continue to permeate the contemporary discussion</u> of a pipeline from the Mackenzie Valley to the Alberta border, where it could link up with existing pipelines.

EXPLAIN WHY YOUR TOPIC IS IMPORTANT

If you are planning to buy a used car, you can make a very costly mistake. <u>For this reason, you should know what to look for when you examine and test drive an automobile.</u>

DESCRIBE SOMETHING

In Raymond Carver's short story "Cathedral," we meet a narrator who isn't happy with his work but doesn't do anything to change it; who sits up late at night, after his wife has gone to bed, and smokes marijuana in the hope of avoiding dreams that makes his heart pound. The narrator also doesn't like change, which explains why he doesn't want to meet Robert, an old friend of his wife's, because Robert is blind. The narrator has many stereotypes of blind people: they don't smoke, they don't laugh, they don't watch TV. But when Robert arrives, the narrator finds all his stereotypes challenged: Robert travels alone on trains, he has a beard, he eats his food neatly (though he uses his fingers), he smokes, and he sits up at night watching a TV program on cathedrals to keep the narrator company. Robert is even willing to try some of the narrator's marijuana. <u>In Carver's story, we have an interesting example of the blind leading the blind, as Robert leads the narrator to conceive of a world beyond his immediate needs and fears.</u>

DEFINE SOMETHING

To understand R. W. Connell's concept of "hegemonic masculinity," it is useful to know what we mean by *hegemonic*; as an adjective, it means "supreme" or "ruling." Hegemonic masculinity, then, is a society's ideal of powerful masculinity. It is sometimes modelled by leaders, military men, movie stars, or superheroes. At the same time, however, it is highly unstable, and no single individual achieves hegemonic masculinity, or at least not for very long. Keifer Sutherland's Agent Jack Bauer and Bruce Willis's John McClane are contemporary examples of hegemonic masculinity. But their performances of this role are aided by Hollywood plots, special effects, and stunt men; it's not a role any man could ever play for very long. <u>So these models of hegemonic masculinity, in the long run, leave many men feeling they'll never be manly enough.</u>

USE AN INTERESTING OR PERTINENT QUOTATION

Last week at his press conference, the premier said, "It is with regret that I announce a 20 percent cut in subsidies for higher education. I believe, however, that this cut is the least painful way to balance the provincial budget." <u>The premier is wrong: these cuts will have a catastrophic effect on the people of this province.</u>

Note: Avoid quotations such as "The early bird gets the worm" or "Better late than never." These are clichés more likely to bore than interest a reader.

Do not limit yourself to the approaches explained above, as they are just some common strategies. Additional approaches are given in Chapters 4 through 11, and you will likely come up with your own methods that seem natural and effective given the task at hand. Furthermore, when you are writing in different disciplines or in the workplace, specific conventions may apply for introductions. For example, a report for your boss presenting a solution to a personnel problem would likely open with a description of the problem and then move on to your explanation of the solution. In papers for science classes, you may be expected to open with a review of the relevant research on your topic. In papers for business classes, you may be expected to open with your thesis. Always investigate the conventions for the field in which you are writing.

Body Paragraphs

The **body paragraphs,** which form the middle of an essay, prove or explain your thesis. For that reason, you cannot overestimate the importance of body paragraphs because they are the heart of your essay.

Each body paragraph has two parts. One part expresses the paragraph's main idea, the point the paragraph will develop to help support or explain the thesis. That part is the **topic sentence**, which can be specifically stated or strongly implied. The second part includes all the points you make to support, explain, or clarify the topic sentence. Those are the **supporting details.**

The following body paragraph, taken from the final version of Jeff's essay, illustrates these two parts.

Another source of deception is the advertising industry.
Advertisers bombard us every day with powerful male athletes endorsing products. Men are enticed to buy the products
because they are led to believe they will be similarly powerful if
they do. At one time, Michael Jordan, in all his athletic, superhero grandeur, seduced us into buying Nikes. Now that torch
has been passed to the latest basketball phenomenon, LeBron
James. Superstars from many sports, including Lance Armstrong,
Tiger Woods, and Derek Jeter, make us want the shoes with the
swoosh, but even more, they make males long for their ability, acclaim, and lifestyles. We buy the shoes hoping to be more
like the athletes we envy and then feel inferior because we don't
achieve athletic superstardom or any of its trappings. Jason
Giambi and Jeff Gordon may have sold a lot of Pepsi, but they
also sold the notion that the ideal male has the strength and
physique to hit a baseball out of the park or drive a race car at
160 k.p.h. Most males can't do that, so we feel inferior, less than
the ideal. Advertising sends two messages: You should buy this
product because this man should be your idol, and if you want to
be a "real man," you should have the athletic prowess, physique,
and other characteristics of a sports star.

Topic sentence (gives main idea of paragraph)

Supporting details (back up the topic sentence by showing it is true)

In a successful essay, body paragraphs have *adequate supporting detail,* and they have *relevant supporting detail.* These points are discussed next.

Adequate Supporting Detail

You cannot expect your reader to believe what you say just because you say it. You must explain and prove your points convincingly. To do so, think of your thesis and each of your topic sentences as a **generalization,** a broad statement that asserts that something is true in most cases or in every case. To have *adequate supporting detail,* you must back up every generalization, including your thesis and every topic sentence, with enough detail to prove or explain it to your reader's satisfaction.

If, for instance, you write that your roommate is a practical joker, you have made a generalization. You then must prove that generalization with examples of your roommate's practical jokes. If you say that Chez Paris is the most beautiful restaurant in town, you are making a generalization and must support it with descriptive details, showing why you find it beautiful. If you say that schoolchildren should not be grouped by ability because such grouping discourages achievement, you must explain that generalization by showing how grouping by ability discourages achievement. A good way to remember the need to provide adequate detail is to remind yourself that a writer must "show and not just tell." You can show and not just tell if you first state a generalization, and then go on to give specific points to prove or support that generalization.

Be aware that in an assignment for a college or university class, the most interesting and relevant supporting details are not going to come simply from your own experience. In this context, the phrase "learning to write" has two meanings. One is reflected in this text: Writing is a complicated undertaking, and we need to master many tools that will allow us to write well. The other is that we often need to learn—to learn independently by reading and doing research—in order to make our writing fully effective. If you were working on an essay on "hegemonic masculinity" (see the example above), it's true that your knowledge of popular culture and your observations of the men around you might provide some of the necessary details. But you would need to go to the source of the concept—R. W. Connell—and to see what sociologists have thought about this concept in the two decades since Connell proposed it. You might also want to know what other models of masculinity are available to young men and how young men are encouraged to choose a masculine style for themselves. Your sociology textbook probably says something about this; at the least it will provide you with a bibliography that you can use to begin your own quest to learn on your own.

To appreciate the need to show and not just tell, and to see how a writer can move from the general to the specific, contrast the following two drafts. Draft A does not support generalizations, but draft B does—by moving from the general to the specific. The specific points are underscored.

DRAFT A

Dr. Garcia is a dedicated teacher. She is concerned about students and always willing to give a struggling young scholar extra attention. In addition, she takes pains to include everyone in class discussions, even the shy students who ordinarily do not participate. Particularly impressive is the personal interest she takes in each of her students. No wonder her class is always one of the first to fill up every semester.

DRAFT B

Dr. Garcia is a dedicated teacher. She is concerned about students and always willing to give a struggling young scholar extra attention. Last week, for example, two students were having trouble finding topics for their research papers, so Dr. Garcia met them at the library and helped them explore the possibilities. In addition, she takes pains to include everyone in class discussions, even the shy students who ordinarily do not participate. One way she does this is to ask people their opinions on subjects under discussion. That way, they do not have to worry about giving a wrong answer. Another way she brings students into discussions is to plan group work so students can talk to each other in more comfortable, smaller groups.

Particularly impressive is the personal interest Dr. Garcia takes in each of her students. Everyone writes a journal, and from the journals Dr. Garcia learns about her students' interests, successes, problems, and family life. Because she comes to know her students so well, she can talk to them about things important to them, which creates a bond between student and teacher. As a result, all her students come to understand that Dr. Garcia cares about them. No wonder her class is always one of the first to fill up every semester.

Relevant Supporting Detail

Supporting details must be *relevant,* which means they must be clearly related to the thesis. Most readers will grow annoyed when details are not related to the matter at hand. If you want to argue for the elimination of the physical education requirement at your school, you would not mention that it would also be a good idea to eliminate the foreign language requirement. When you read the following draft, you will notice the distraction created by one sentence that presents irrelevant detail.

Many universities are altering their teacher education curricula to require prospective teachers to get into the classroom as soon as possible, even in the first year. These future teachers observe, tutor, and in general get the feel of a teacher's responsibilities. The plan is a good one because students can decide early on if they are suited to teaching and change their majors if necessary. In the more traditional curriculum, an education major waits until the third or fourth year to get into the classroom, when it can be too late to change majors without serious inconvenience and expense. Many students in all programs change majors and problems are to be expected. Certainly it makes sense to move prospective teachers into the classroom as early as possible, so the plan should catch on.

You probably found the next to last sentence annoying and distracting because it is not related closely enough to the matter at hand. To avoid such irrelevant detail in your own writing, outline carefully to be sure everything you write is related to the thesis.

Using the Patterns of Development to Convey Supporting Details

Your supporting details can come from your own experience and observation, as well as from what you learn in the classroom and as a result of reading, watching television, listening to the radio, or surfing the Internet. If necessary and appropriate, you can use facts, statistics, and opinions of experts, some of which you may find in this book and some of which you can research in the library and on the Internet. If you do use such material, be sure to check Chapter 14 for information on paraphrasing, quoting, and documenting source material. In addition, Chapter 1 offers advice for summarizing and synthesizing ideas from sources.

Most of the rest of this book explains various forms your supporting details can take. These forms, called *patterns of development,* are description, narration, exemplification, definition, process analysis, comparison-contrast, cause-and-effect analysis, and classification-division. You can use these patterns—alone or in combination—to organize and present your supporting details.

Each pattern of development is treated in its own chapter; however, the inside front cover of this book also gives a brief explanation of each pattern. Take a look now at that information and refer to it whenever a particular pattern is mentioned and you are unsure of its nature.

So you can see how the patterns of development can help you prove your thesis and achieve your purpose, here are examples of how each pattern could support the thesis used earlier in the chapter, that Dr. Garcia is a dedicated teacher.

DESCRIPTION   Give details that show how Dr. Garcia looks and acts

NARRATION	Tell a story about a time Dr. Garcia helped a student
EXEMPLIFICATION	Give examples of ways Dr. Garcia shows interest in students
DEFINITION	Define a "good teacher" and show how Dr. Garcia conforms to that definition
PROCESS ANALYSIS	Explain Dr. Garcia's process for using groups to help students learn
COMPARISON-CONTRAST	Compare and/or contrast Dr. Garcia with other teachers to show how good she is
CAUSE-AND-EFFECT ANALYSIS	Explain the effects of one or more of Dr. Garcia's teaching methods
CLASSIFICATION-DIVISION	Classify all the ways Dr. Garcia helps students

You would not use all these patterns in a single essay, but they do provide options to consider as you develop your supporting details. These patterns of development can also be very useful when you are generating ideas.

Combining the Patterns of Development

To achieve their purpose and meet their readers' needs, writers sometimes use a single pattern of development. Frequently, though, they combine two or more patterns. Essays with multiple patterns often are developed by a dominant pattern with a few paragraphs organized by one or more other patterns. Sometimes, multiple patterns are combined in roughly equal amounts. In the next chapters, you will read both essays that rely primarily on a single pattern and ones that combine multiple patterns to achieve their purpose. In addition, Chapter 13 focuses solely on essays that combine patterns. In your own writing, your purpose and audience will determine whether you use one or more patterns. To see how patterns can be combined in a single paragraph, read again this excerpt from the final version of Jeff's essay and notice the use of both exemplification and cause-and-effect analysis.

Another source of deception is the advertising industry. Advertisers bombard us every day with powerful male athletes endorsing products. Men are enticed to buy the products because they are led to believe they will be similarly powerful if they do. At one time, Michael Jordan, in all his athletic, superhero grandeur, seduced us into buying Nikes. Now that torch has been passed to

Cause-and-effect analysis: Advertisers cause males to envy sports superstars, a feeling that leads males to buy the products athletes endorse and ultimately, to feel inferior.

Exemplification: James, Jeter, Woods, are examples of athletes who endorse products and make males feel inferior. Nike shoes and Pepsi are examples of products advertised.

the latest basketball phenomenon, LeBron James. Superstars from many sports, including Lance Armstrong, Tiger Woods, and Derek Jeter, make us want the shoes with the swoosh, but even more, they make males long for their ability, acclaim, and lifestyles. We buy the shoes hoping to be more like the athletes we envy and then feel inferior because we don't achieve athletic superstardom or any of its trappings. Jason Giambi and Jeff Gordon may have sold a lot of Pepsi, but they also sold the notion that the ideal male has the strength and physique to hit a baseball out of the park or drive a race car at 160 k.p.h. Most males can't do that, so we feel inferior, less than the ideal. Advertising sends two messages: You should buy this product because this man should be your idol, and if you want to be a "real man," you should have the athletic prowess, physique, and other characteristics of a sports star.

Organizing Body Paragraphs

Each body paragraph typically focuses on one main idea, to support or explain the thesis. (A main idea that requires considerable explanation can be the focus of more than one body paragraph.) When the main idea of a body paragraph is written rather than implied, it is expressed in a topic sentence. The **topic sentence** is a generalization that must be developed with adequate, relevant supporting details.

You may find it easiest to compose body paragraphs that begin with a topic sentence followed by the supporting details meant to explain or prove the idea in that topic sentence. If you were writing an essay with the thesis "Dr. Garcia is a dedicated teacher," for example, your essay might have three body paragraphs, each beginning with a version of one of these topic sentences:

Dr. Garcia makes sure every student is relaxed in class.
Dr. Garcia is always willing to give students extra help.
Dr. Garcia takes a personal interest in each of her students.

Notice that each of these topic sentences is relevant to the thesis. Similarly, the supporting details in each body paragraph should be relevant to the topic sentence of that paragraph. Thus, the first body paragraph would include only details about helping students relax, the second only details about providing students with extra help, and the third only details about taking a personal interest in students.

Coherence

To have **coherence,** the supporting details in your body paragraphs, and the body paragraphs themselves, must connect to each other in ways your reader can easily understand and follow. Four strategies can help you achieve coherence.

Use Transitional Words and Phrases

Transitional words and phrases signal the relationship between ideas. The chart that follows lists and illustrates transitions.

Transition Chart

RELATIONSHIP	TRANSITIONS	EXAMPLE
addition	also, and, too, in addition, furthermore, first, further	The apartment has all the features I want. In addition, the rent is low.
time	now, then, before, after, earlier, later, soon, finally, first, next	First, measure the flour. Then add it to the butter and eggs.
space	near, next to, away from, beside, inside, on the left, on the right, along-side, behind	Go two blocks west to the light. On the right is the park.
comparison	similarly, likewise, in the same way, in like manner	The mayor will recommend some layoffs. Similarly, she will not approve any new hirings.
contrast	however, in contrast, but, still, on the contrary, nevertheless, yet	The House of Commons will pass the jobs bill. However, the Senate will vote it down.
cause and effect	since, because, so, as a result, consequently, thus, therefore, hence	Because half the students are sick with the flu, school will be closed.
emphasis	indeed, in fact, surely, certainly, without a doubt	Everyone enjoys Dr. Hill's class. In fact, it is always the first to close.
illustration	for example, for instance, specifically, in particular	Counting fat grams is a good way to diet. Dana, for example, lost a pound a week that way.
summary or clarification	in summary, in conclusion, in brief, in short, in other words, all in all	In other words, ideas of masculinity subject men to unreasonable expectations.

Repeat Words or Ideas

Repeating key words or ideas can help a writer achieve coherence and improve the flow of writing. Here are two examples:

REPEATING
A WORD

Chronic fatigue <u>syndrome</u> is becoming more widely recognized in the medical community and therefore more frequently diagnosed. This <u>syndrome</u> is so debilitating that its sufferers often cannot work.

REPEATING
AN IDEA

<u>A group of volunteer parents is now working cooperatively with school authorities</u> to introduce more extracurricular activities into the schools and to begin a drug awareness program. <u>These worthy efforts</u> will no doubt improve the quality of education in our township.

Use Synonyms

Another way to achieve coherence is to use a synonym for a word or idea mentioned earlier, as in these two sentences:

The workers expressed their <u>dissatisfaction</u> with management's latest wage offer. Their <u>discontent</u> may well lead to a strike.

Although your computer may have its own thesaurus, it's more appropriate for business use than for writing college and university essays. Check out online thesauruses at www.merriam-webster.com or thesaurus.reference. com. Use a thesaurus to find synonyms that haven't come to mind, not to discover new words; you're likely to use new words without knowing their connotations. The time for learning new vocabulary is when you read: try to look up most of the words you're not familiar with.

Use Sentences That Look Backward and Forward

You can make an effective transition from one paragraph to another—and thereby achieve coherence—by beginning with a sentence that looks back to something in the previous paragraph and forward to an idea in the one coming up. Assume, for example, that you have just written a paragraph about the fact that Dr. Garcia gives students extra help, and you are about to write a paragraph about how she makes students feel comfortable in class. You could write one of these sentences to connect the two paragraphs.

looking back   looking forward
[In addition to giving students extra help,] [Dr. Garcia always makes them feel comfortable in class.]

looking back   looking forward

[Dr. Garcia does more than provide extra help to those in need;] [she also makes sure that everyone feels comfortable in class.]

When to Paragraph

Typically, writers begin a new body paragraph each time they move to a new main idea to support the thesis. However, if you have a great deal to say about one point, you can break up the discussion into two or more paragraphs. If you have a point that deserves special emphasis, you can place it in its own paragraph, or if you have an extended example or narration (a story), you can set it off by placing it in its own paragraph.

It is helpful to remember that effective paragraphs are usually between four and ten sentences long. Paragraphs shorter than four sentences are probably undeveloped or deal with relatively unimportant points. When your draft has short paragraphs, you will need to decide whether these paragraphs need more detail or should be eliminated or combined with other material. Paragraphs longer than ten sentences don't give the reader a much-needed mental breath. As well, students who write very long paragraphs often miss opportunities to emphasize important ideas. Readers know, almost intuitively, that when you start a new paragraph you are changing the subject, however slightly, and they will pay attention, thus giving you a natural opportunity to emphasize a point.

Tone

Speakers can use tone of voice to help convey feelings and meaning. Similarly, writers can establish a *tone* for their writing. **Tone** is the writer's attitude or feelings toward the reader or the subject. The tone can be angry, sarcastic, serious, preachy, argumentative, conciliatory, hurtful, playful, earnest, scornful, hostile, enthusiastic, neutral, and so forth.

Most often, tone is established by the words you choose to convey supporting details. Notice, for example, how word choice creates the different tones in the following sentences on the same subject.

ANGRY AND JUDGMENTAL TONE	Many so-called citizens who are too tight-fisted to invest in the future of our children refuse to vote for the school levy.
NEUTRAL TONE	A significant number of citizens hesitate to pass the school levy and thereby increase their taxes.

Using Visual Material for Support

You are accustomed to encountering visual material in your reading. Newspapers and magazines, textbooks, Web pages, journal articles, reports at work—much of what you read is accompanied by photos, charts, graphs, illustrations, and other images. In Chapter 1, you learned that this visual material needs to be "read" critically, in the same way you read written text.

Technological advances make it so much easier for you to include visual material in your writing. With the Internet, you can locate and import images; with digital photography, you can insert photos into documents; and with computer programs, you can create graphs from data you supply. Before you include visual materials, however, ask your instructor whether you may use them in your submissions. If yes, follow your instructor's guidelines. In addition, keep these points in mind:

- **Use images *only* when they help explain, illustrate, or prove a point.** Visual material should support the text, not be a substitute for it. Never use visual material to pad a piece of writing that is too short. But do select visuals if they can amplify or complement what you have written.
- **Consider your audience and purpose.** Make sure the visuals you select suit your audience and help fulfill your purpose. A complicated diagram explaining how plants turn carbon dioxide into oxygen might confuse a ten-year-old, but a simple flow chart might work perfectly. If you import visual material from another source, remember that it was developed for a different writer's purpose and audience, so evaluate it carefully. Its tone must be in keeping with your tone. A humorous cartoon may not be appropriate for a research paper examining spousal abuse, but a bar graph showing the frequency of spousal abuse by age group may be informative.
- **Consider the quality of the visual.** An image of poor quality or a graph that is difficult to decipher will detract from your writing. Select or prepare visual material that is attractive, easy to read, and easy to understand. Make sure the colour, font, spacing, and other features are appropriate for your paper.
- **Write the caption carefully.** Most images require captions. Take this opportunity to guide your reader's interpretation. Provide the reader background information about the creator of the image or the purpose for which it was created. Establish the authority or reliability of the image by indicating its source and/or date. See the caption for the Veronica Geminder photograph in Chapter 1 (p. 25) for an example of the way caption information can guide interpretation.

Troubleshooting Guide

Using Images in Classroom Writing

If you have trouble selecting or integrating images into your writing, consider this advice:

- Select or create your visual material only after writing your first draft. That way, you can be certain this material supplements the written text, fulfills your writing purpose, and meets the needs of your audience.

- Place the visual as close as possible to the material it supports. If design and layout considerations prevent that, add a cross-reference for the reader, such as, "The chart on page 3 shows how different people will benefit from the tax cut."

- If you use an image from another source, provide proper credit. Refer to Chapter 14 for information on evaluating and documenting source materials.

The Conclusion

The **conclusion,** the last sentences or paragraph that provides closure, is an important part of a successful essay because it influences the reader's final, lasting impression. No matter how strong your introduction and body paragraphs are, if your ending is weak, your reader will come away from the essay feeling let down.

Many approaches for concluding an essay are possible. If your essay is long, with many ideas, you can summarize your main points as a helpful reminder to your reader. However, if your essay is brief and the ideas are easily remembered, summarizing is not a good idea because it will bore rather than help a reader.

Repeating the thesis or another important idea is an effective way to conclude an essay when the repetition provides emphasis or dramatic effect. Be careful, though. The repetition will bore a reader if it fails to provide drama or emphasis. Sometimes, writers delay the thesis until the conclusion because they want to build up to it.

Another common technique is to introduce a new but related idea in the conclusion. The idea must be clearly related to the rest of the essay to avoid dismaying the reader with new material that seems unconnected to the topic. Finally, writers often craft effective conclusions by combining approaches.

If you are having difficult writing a conclusion, reread your introduction. Have you given away too much? Does your reader already know how your essay is going to end? Often, when a writer is having trouble writing a conclusion, it's because he or she has already written it. It's simply in the wrong place!

Other approaches to the conclusion are illustrated below. In addition, the introductory sections in Chapters 4 through 11 suggest ways to handle conclusions.

DRAW A CONCLUSION FROM THE INFORMATION IN THE ESSAY (THIS ILLUSTRATION IS FROM AN ESSAY ABOUT THE EFFECTS OF DIVORCE.)

Recent evidence suggests that the children of divorced parents suffer a number of difficulties, regardless of their age at the time of the divorce. For this reason, parents who stay together "for the sake of the children" may be doing the right thing.

PRESENT THE FINAL, MOST IMPORTANT POINT (THIS ILLUSTRATION IS FROM AN ESSAY ARGUING AGAINST CENSORSHIP.)

The most compelling reason to oppose censorship is the threat it poses to Canadian democracy. Once we feel comfortable about taking away the freedom of speech for individuals who engage in hate speech, we're on our way to taking away the freedom of speech for individuals whose political opinions differ from the governing majority. A healthy democracy thrives on contentious debate. Once we limit free speech, we establish a climate that permits the chipping away at our freedoms until our rights are severely curtailed.

OFFER A SOLUTION TO A PROBLEM MENTIONED IN THE ESSAY (THIS ILLUSTRATION IS FROM AN ESSAY THAT EXPLAINS PROBLEMS ASSOCIATED WITH UNIVERSITY ATHLETICS.)

University athletics will remain controversial until we reform the system dramatically. Perhaps the most honest thing to do is to hire the athletes to play and pay them salaries. If they want to use their paycheques to pay for tuition, fine. If not, they can just be university employees. The fans will still turn out to see the teams, regardless of whether the players are student athletes or professional athletes.

CALL YOUR READERS TO ACTION (THIS ILLUSTRATION IS FROM AN ESSAY ARGUING FOR INCREASING THE SALARY OF TEACHERS.)

To improve the quality of education, we must increase teachers' salaries to make them compatible with those in business and industry. Only then will we attract the best people to the profession. Thus, we must support school levies that fund pay increases and lobby boards of education to do whatever it takes to increase teachers' salaries.

> ## Troubleshooting Guide
>
> ### Drafting Introductions and Conclusions
> If you have trouble drafting your introduction, keep it short. Begin with your prelimi- nary thesis and move on. During revising, you can add details to stimulate interest. Similarly, an effective conclusion can be brief, even one or two sentences. If you are stuck for a closing, end with your final point and improve the conclusion during revi- sion, if necessary.

LOOK TO THE FUTURE (THIS ILLUSTRATION IS FROM AN ESSAY EXPLAINING THE EFFECTS OF THE ROUTE 8 BYPASS.)

Once the Route 8 bypass is built, our area will become a major crossroads. In ten years, our economy will be flourishing from the business and commerce that will result from our strategic location, and our tax base will broaden to the benefit of our schools and infrastructure.

LEAVE YOUR READER WITH A FINAL IMPRESSION (THIS ILLUSTRATION IS FROM AN ESSAY ON DISCRIMINATION AGAINST OVERWEIGHT PEOPLE.)

Our society discriminates against overweight people, and it's a shame. Many capable people never get a chance to show what they can do because of our narrow-mindedness.

The Title

Although the title is the first thing a reader sees, many people compose it last because a good title often suggests itself after the essay is written. There are many ways to approach the title. Sometimes a clever or funny title is a good way to pique your reader's interest. However, not everyone can be clever or funny, so it is fine to write a title that suggests the content of the essay, like "What Is the Good Life?" which is in this book. Sometimes an intriguing title like "The Watcher at the Gates" (which also appears in this book) can stimu- late a reader's interest. Avoid a title that presents your thesis. If your title is "Capital Punishment Is Inhumane," you will tip your hand too soon. Also, avoid very broad titles that do not suggest your content. "Television" is too broad, but "The Effects of Television Violence" is fine.

VISUALIZING AN ESSAY

The essay structure explained in this chapter is not the only one—or even the best one in all circumstances—and many of the essays in this text will illustrate departures from this structure. Nonetheless, this structure is a very serviceable one, so you can use it in many writing situations. To review the structure and help you visualize it, examine this graphic representation.

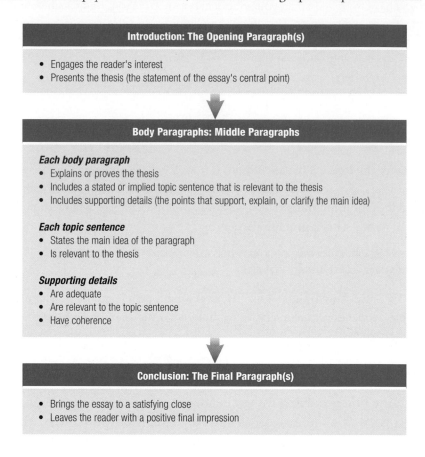

An Essay in Progress: Drafting

Using his informal outline as a guide (see page 55), Jeff wrote the first draft that appears below. You will notice that Jeff departed from his outline at times, which is fine. Writers should always be open to new ideas and ways of organizing their material. Knowing that he would polish the draft during revision, Jeff concentrated on writing his ideas down as best he could without labouring over anything. Notice that Jeff realized some problems while drafting and wrote reminders to himself in brackets about revisions to make.

The Not-So-Ideal Ideal Male

1   Canadians are being bullied, tricked, and led astray by products of our own North American culture. We are being fed falsehoods, and we digest them happily, but we are being poisoned.

Our own culture—our own heritage and popular society—is feeding us misinformation; we are being led to believe in an absurd concept of the ideal male. [fix intro.]

2   The root of the inappropriateness of this idealization lies in the nature of its main perpet-uators—the movie and advertising industries, and folktales and childhood stories. The most obvious of these sources is the movie industry, which produces totally unrealistic plots typically having (perhaps subtly, but still) superhuman males as heroes. We watch these movies and feel that this is what our men are supposed to be like. [give examples] The cartoonish action movies are generally the most extreme, and these are targeted at the most vulnerable audience—teen-age boys who are ready to become men. They see these heroes on the screen and see visions of themselves in ten years. This is tragic. An equally prevalent but less glaring source of deception is the advertising industry. They bombard us everyday with quick scenes of powerful, intimidating male atheletes endorsing their products. [give examples] The message is this: you should buy this product because this man should be your idol. Physical dominance is put in the spotlight as much as the product. A third projector of this concept comes from our heritage, and that is its problem. Folktales and childhood stories are usually legends that have been passed down through generations of people. Nobody even remembers how long ago they were created. That is precisely the trouble. Triumphant men like Robin Hood originated in an entirely different society; they are heroes of the distant past, and they do not befit the present.

3   The problem these unsuitable sources of the ideal male present is that their admired and discouraged qualities are out of place. In action movies and folk tales, the hero wins the battle because his instincts are flawless. He knows just where every attacker will be in a battle, and he knows by sight which fair maiden will be faithful to him. But in the real world today, how often does a man fend off a small mob in hand-to-hand combat or choose his wife from a lineup of beautiful princesses? To apply the power of understatement—rarely. In our highly complex, and civilized, society, the considered decision is more important then the instinctive or rash one. Also, the men of advertising, movies, and legends are loners. Their great strength stems from the fact that they need no one else to help them accomplish their goals. Again, this clashes with modern society. Our world is becoming increasingly cooperative on all levels—from inter-personal to international. A realistic man knows that the help of others is esential in achieving his dream.

4   Finally, the men these sources give us often are deplorable in their relations to women. Many times the entire purpose of the movie, advertisement, or tale is for the hero to "get" the woman. He is almost invariably her protector, saviour, or unrepellable lover. In a world in which possibly the characteristic of modern history is the rise of women nearer and nearer to equality, how can the ideal man have this type of relationship with women? The answer is simple: he is not the ideal man.

| EXERCISE 3.1 |

Drafting

1. Refer to the thesis statements and supporting details you used for numbers 2 and 3 of Exercise 2.4 on page 59. For each thesis and set of supporting details, do the following:

   a. Decide on a possible approach to the introduction and explain why the approach is a good one.
   b. Write two topic sentences that could open two body paragraphs.
   c. Decide on a possible approach to the conclusion and explain why the approach is a good one.

2. Using the material you have from number 4 of Exercise 2.4 (and adding and deleting ideas as you wish), write a first draft.

REVISING YOUR DRAFT

Revising is shaping and refining your draft until it is ready for your reader. Most experienced writers will tell you that revising is the heart of their writing processes and that it is time-consuming. Unfortunately, many inexperienced writers believe that revision simply involves changing a few words, adding a comma here and there, and checking spellings. In truth, when you revise you should completely rethink your essay to be sure everything in it suits your purpose, audience, and role. To that end, revision requires you to consider the aspects of your draft covered in the following checklist and make changes as necessary. As you look over the checklist, you can tell that revision is a complex process. Thus, you will often write multiple drafts until you are satisfied that your essay is reader-ready. And because you have so much to consider, the first rule of revision is *be sure to allow plenty of time.*

At least since the ancient Greeks, we have valued clarity, wholeness, and unity in writing. That is, we don't want writing to raise questions it doesn't answer or to veer into topics it doesn't develop. In an age of text messaging and sound bytes, such qualities don't come easily. Good ideas don't occur to us with all the detail we need to reach the reader, or with our ideas in the most effective and convincing order. This means that writing is recursive: It doesn't proceed in a straight line from idea to finished essay. Often, when we find our essay has a logical gap or raises questions, we have to go back to earlier stages, like brainstorming, generating ideas, and finding examples, in order to achieve the wholeness we ourselves appreciate in a piece of writing. Simply put, that takes time.

✔ Revision Checklist

FOR YOUR THESIS (see page 49), be sure:

1. _____ Your essay has a clearly stated or strongly implied thesis.

2. _____ Your thesis is not a statement of fact.

3. _____ Your thesis can be treated in a manageable length.

4. _____ Your thesis is not a formal announcement and is expressed in specific language.

5. _____ Your thesis allows you to achieve your purpose and is geared toward your reader's traits and needs.

6. _____ Your thesis is compatible with your role.

FOR YOUR INTRODUCTION (see page 66), be sure:

1. _____ Your introduction makes a good first impression.

2. _____ Your introduction is suited to your purpose, audience, and role.

FOR YOUR SUPPORTING DETAILS (see page 69), be sure:

1. _____ All your details are suited to your purpose, audience, and role.

2. _____ Your details are in a logical order and arranged in body paragraphs.

3. _____ Each body paragraph has a clearly stated or strongly implied topic sentence.

4. _____ All your details are relevant to the thesis and appropriate topic sentence.

5. _____ You have enough details to support the thesis and each topic sentence.

6. _____ Transitions move the reader smoothly from idea to idea and from paragraph to paragraph.

7. _____ You avoid errors in logic (p. 9).

FOR YOUR CONCLUSION (see page 79):

1. _____ Your essay comes to a satisfying finish.

2. _____ Your conclusion is appropriate to your purpose, audience, and role.

FOR EFFECTIVE EXPRESSION, be sure:

1. _____ Unnecessary words are eliminated.

2. _____ All your ideas are clearly expressed.

3. _____ Specific words are substituted for vague ones.

4. _____ Words are compatible with your audience, role, and tone.

5. _____ Tired expressions (clichés) such as "cold as ice" are rewritten.

6. _____ Choppy, repetitive, or singsong prose is eliminated.

FOR YOUR TITLE (see page 81), be sure:

1. _____ Your title suggests the content of the essay without being too broad.

2. _____ Your thesis is not given in the title.

Tips for Revising

- **Remember that revising is not editing.** To revise means literally to "re-see" what you have written. You need enough time away from your draft to be able to see all its flaws in argument, construction, use (or lack) of evidence, and expression. In fact, it's a good idea to avoid editing during the revision process, for two reasons. First, the material you laboriously edit may in the end be cut from your essay. Second, focusing on spelling, grammar, and punctuation will distract you and make it hard to focus on the task at hand: seeing your draft the way an intelligent reader will see it..

- **Allow plenty of time** because revising is time-consuming. Pace your work so you will have a period of several days to revise.

- **Remember your writing context.** Every evaluation of your draft and every change you make should be done with your audience, purpose, and role in mind. However, because idea generation is ongoing, you may decide to change some aspect of the context as you revise.

- **Revise in stages** by considering one or two of the revision concerns at a time. (Use the revision checklist to be sure you consider everything.) As an alternative, revise one or two paragraphs at a time. Be sure to take a break whenever you get tired.

- **Return to idea generation or adjust your thesis, if necessary.** If you have trouble coming up with adequate detail, try one of the idea generation techniques covered on pages 38–47 to develop more material. If that does not work, reconsider your thesis. Should you broaden it or refocus it to have enough to say?

- **Revise typed copy** because you are less likely to overlook problems in type than in your own handwriting or on the computer screen.

- **In Microsoft Word®, use Track Changes.** Located on the dropdown "Tools" menu on your toolbar, Track Changes allows you to revise while preserving the original draft. Your changes will not become permanent until and unless you want them to, so you can easily return to and restore all or part of your earlier work.

Revising with Peer Review

Because feedback can be so helpful to writers, you should always consider asking other people to read your drafts, react, and suggest changes. In fact, your instructor may arrange for you and your classmates to exchange drafts. When you find readers on your own, be sure to use *reliable readers*, people who know the qualities of effective writing and who will not hesitate to offer constructive criticism. It makes no sense to ask a friend for help if that friend has not yet taken a writing course, nor is it useful to ask people who always hesitate to tell you what they really think. Also, use more than one reader, so you have the advantage of multiple perspectives and so you can look for consensus. Remember, though, that you have the final say. Rather than accepting everything your readers offer, consider their reactions critically and revise accordingly.

If you have particular concerns about your draft, you can ask your readers to read and react just to those concerns. Ask them to tell you what they think of your introduction, to help you think of another example to support a point in paragraph 4, to help you clarify an idea, and so forth. Otherwise, ask your readers to use the revision checklist on page 85 as a guide to reacting to your draft.

When readers help you, always return the favour by offering to react to *their* drafts. When it is your turn to respond, follow these guidelines.

- **Comment on strengths and weaknesses.** Offering praise alone makes a writer feel good but does little to help that writer improve a draft. Offering criticism alone is demoralizing.
- **Put your responses in writing.** That way, the writer has a record to refer to. (If you are given an electronic copy of a draft and you use Microsoft Word®, you can insert comments using the Comment feature of the program, located in the drop down "Insert" menu on the toolbar.)
- **Be specific.** Rather than say, "Paragraph 2 is unclear," write "In paragraph 2, I do not understand why you say that men experience discrimination in the workplace."
- **Offer suggestions.** When you comment on a weakness, suggest a revision strategy, like this: "If you could give an example of discrimination against males in the workplace, I would be able to accept your point more readily."

An Essay in Progress: Writing a Second Draft

Jeff knew some of the changes needed in his first draft and indicated them on the draft in brackets. (See page 82.) Before revising to compose a second draft, Jeff reread his first draft and considered his bracketed comments. In addition, he sought responses from two classmates and his teacher. He was reassured to discover that his readers' reactions to the draft were very similar to his own. As a result, he felt confident in his ability to judge his writing accurately. The teacher's response, which helped guide Jeff's revision, appears here.

Jeff,

Your draft held my interest every step of the way. I was particularly taken by the energy in your writing. You feel very strongly about your topic. You even seem passionate about it. Your energy and your honest emotions really propelled me forward, and I am hoping you can retain that spirit in your revision. I'd take a careful look at the introduction, though. It's a place where your emotion creates a problem. The introduction makes you seem very angry, even a bit out of control, so it is a little off-putting, especially in the opening. Remember, you want your reader to see you as a reasonable, thoughtful person. Anger is fine, but you don't want to appear more emotional than thoughtful. You indicate that you want to work on your intro; I think softening the angry tone will help considerably.

Your thesis is very clear, so I have no trouble determining your focus, and you make excellent points in paragraph 2. These points can go a long way to support your thesis, but right now you have too many main ideas in one paragraph (movies, advertising, and folktales and stories). You noted yourself that you need specific examples, and I agree. Perhaps if you give each of your main points its own body paragraph, you could more easily incorporate your examples.

You state important ideas in your last body paragraph. I was particularly intrigued by your contrast of the loner not being well adapted to today's cooperative environment—very astute. In fact, all of your points are interesting and significant.

I look forward to your revision. One last thing, though: Your last paragraph brings up your final points and is rather like a body paragraph. Do you feel the need for a separate conclusion? Frankly, I'm not sure because your final sentence provides some closure. Think about it and maybe get some other opinions.

Jeff's Second Draft

The introduction is less angry. The thesis now indicates three of the main points to be discussed.

1   On the movie screen, characters played by actors like Bruce Willis, Arnold Schwarzenegger, Tom Cruise, and Pierce Brosnan are men of action and resolve. They depict the ideal male that men strive to be but can never achieve. However, the truth is that men are being tricked and led astray by these characterizations. We are being led to believe in an absurd image of the ideal male, not just in movies, but in advertising and childhood stories.

The first body paragraph now discusses only one main idea. Two examples have been added for support.

2   An obvious perpetrator of this idealization is the movie industry, which produces totally unrealistic plots typically having (perhaps subtly but still) super-human males as heroes. We watch these movies and feel that this is what our men are supposed to be like. Arnold slams through walls and saves the beautiful woman from the jaws of death and The Rock does away with bad guys by

single handedly fighting an entire compound and throwing himself through a pillar. Granted, the cartoonish action movies are generally the most extreme, but these are targeted at the most vulnerable audience—teenage boys who are ready to become men. They see these heroes on the screen and see visions of themselves in ten years. This is tragic because the boys can never be what movie action heroes are.

3   An equally prevalent but less glaring source of deception is the advertising industry. They bombard us every day with quick scenes of powerful, intimidating male athletes endorsing their products. Michael Jordan who everybody worshipped in his superathlete glory made us want Nikes and now LeBron James does the same. But at the same time the image makes males want to be an athlete like them but that can never be. Sports superstars like Derek Jeter and Jason Giambi sell products, but they sell more. Physical dominance is in the spotlight as much as the product, but how likely is it that the average viewer can attain such physical dominance? Advertising sends two messages. One is to buy the product, but the more harmful one is that to be a "real man" you must look and perform like a star athelete. Once again, the male is left feeling inadequate.

The second body paragraph now focuses on only one main idea. Examples have been added for support.

4   A third projector of this concept comes from our heritage, and that is the source of the problem. Folktales and childhood stories are usually legends that have been passed down through generations. Triumphant men like Robin Hood, Sir Lancelot, and Davy Crockett originated in an entirely different society; they are heroes of the distant past, and they do not befit the present. As legends, they risked their lives for the underdog, but their feats are impossible to emulate, so males exposed to these stories are made to feel inadequate.

This body paragraph now has just one main idea. Examples and explanation have been added for support.

5   The ideal men depicted in advertising, movies, and legends are loners. Their great strength stems from the fact that they need no one else to help them accomplish their goals. For example, the Marlboro man always rides out alone; the action hero single handedly saves the day. Again, this clashes with modern society because it leads men to wall themselves off from others. Also, our world is becoming more cooperative on all levels. The loner will not succeed in the workplace where collaboration is increasingly valued.

This body paragraph now focuses on the idea of loners and omits the discussion of the hero in battle and with women. The Marlboro man example has been added.

6   Finally, the men these sources give us are often deplorable to women. Many times the entire purpose of the movie, advertisement, or tale is for the hero to "get" the woman. He is almost invariably her protector, saviour, or

Jeff chose to retain his approach to the last paragraph, although he revised to create more closure in the final sentence.

unrepellable lover. In a world in which possibly the main characteristic of modern history is the rise of women to equality, how can the ideal man have this type of relationship with women? The answer is simple: he cannot because except in advertising, movies, and folktales, he is not the ideal male.

EXERCISE 3.2

Revising the Draft

1. Read the first draft that follows and then make four suggestions you think the author should consider during revising.

IS TODAY'S ATHLETE A GOOD SPORT?

I have been playing soccer for a long time and I can see that players are playing much more violently now than they used to. Players will do anything to win, even stuff they would never consider doing off the field. I think that today's athlete is one person on the field and another person off the field.

Players think that hurting someone is okay because it's just part of the game. My roommate, for example, is a real gentle guy until he gets on the basketball court, then he's rough and ready and violent. If he didn't play that way, the coach would keep him on the bench.

Many players say they have to be violent to beat the other players. They don't feel they've done anything wrong as long as they win. In one of my soccer games, for example, an opposing player intentionally spiked the sweeper and cheated to get the goal.

A lot of times, players justify violence by saying "it's only a game" and not reality. Yes, it's a game but the injuries are real and can cause a lot of problems and pain. For example, a player on my soccer team missed a month of school as a result of an opposing player who knocked him into the goal. I'm sure the player didn't think twice about the consequences of his actions.

Unfortunately, fans love the violence. The more violence, the more cheering. They're violent in the stands, too.

The violence must stop and players should be penalized for it. Otherwise, people will get hurt more and more.

2. Revise the draft you wrote in response to number 2 of Exercise 3.1 on page 84.

EDITING YOUR DRAFT

Editing is finding and correcting mistakes in grammar, spelling, punctuation, capitalization, and usage. Finding and eliminating such errors is important because a reader can lose confidence in a writer if the essay has many errors, and if you undermine your reader's confidence, you may fail to achieve your purpose for writing. To be efficient, do most or all of your editing after you revise. Why look for errors in sentences that you ultimately strike during revision?

Tips for Editing

- **Know the kinds of mistakes you typically make and be on the lookout for them.** For example, if spelling is a problem for you, pay particular attention to this aspect of your draft.
- **Learn the rules.** You cannot edit effectively if you do not know the rules. Buy a good handbook of grammar and usage at your bookstore, consult it as needed, and learn the rules for matters that cause you problems.
- **Use computer grammar and spell-checks with caution.** These tools are not foolproof. For example, they will not tell you whether you have substituted *here* for *hear* or *then* for *than*.
- **Trust your instincts.** If you have a feeling that something is wrong, the odds are good that a problem exists—even if you cannot give the problem a name or figure out a solution at the moment.
- **Think like your reader.** Identify the characteristics of your reader and then read your draft the way someone with those characteristics would. Think about where such a reader might need more information and where he or she might lose interest. Then revise accordingly.
- **Edit print copy.** You are less likely to overlook errors in print copy than on the computer screen. At the same time, be aware that computer-generated print material often looks so professional that you can be fooled into overlooking problems and mistakes.

Troubleshooting Guide

Making Revising and Editing Decisions

If you have trouble knowing what changes to make, try the following:

- **Leave your work for at least a day** to gain some objectivity about your draft. After a break, you will be better able to identify material to revise and edit.

- **Read your work aloud** to listen for problems you have overlooked visually. Be careful, though, to read exactly what is on the page, not what you intended to write.

- **Point to each word with a pen or pencil** and linger over it for a second or two. This procedure will prevent you from building the kind of speed that can lead you to overlook errors.

- **Place a ruler under each line as you edit** to block out other material and prevent it from distracting you.

PROOFREADING THE FINAL COPY

After editing, use your computer to type your essay into the proper form for your reader. Then, check carefully for typing errors. Read very slowly, lingering over each word and punctuation mark, so you do not build up too much speed and miss something. If your instructor permits, neatly ink in corrections; otherwise, type in the correction and print a new copy.

An Essay in Progress: The Final Copy

Below is the final version of the essay that Jeff wrote in response to "The Men from the Boys: Bull Riding Is Dangerous, Irrelevant and a Rare Expression of Old-Style Masculinity" (page 12). (The notes in the margin point out some key features of the essay.) You have already viewed the idea generation (pages 43 and 47), outlining (page 58), and two of the drafts (pages 82 and 88) that preceded this final copy. Between the second draft and the final version, Jeff wrote two additional drafts in the course of revising and editing. In those drafts, he added more detail and improved his word choice.

The Not-So-Ideal Male

The introduction engages the reader's interest by providing background information and specific examples.

The thesis presents the subject as the image of the ideal male and the writer's assertion that the image is absurd. The thesis also notes main points to be covered (movies, advertising, and childhood stories).

1   First there was Errol Flynn; then there was John Wayne; after him came Bruce Willis, Sylvester Stallone, Jean-Claude Van Damme, and Arnold Schwarzenegger. Now we have Pierce Brosnan, Tom Cruise, Russell Crowe, Denzel Washington—and the most recent entry, The Rock. These men of action and resolve are the celluloid depictions of the ideal male. They are the model that men strive for, but the goal they can never achieve. They are the men that women want but never find (off the big screen, that is). They are the reason men feel inferior. The image of these movie action heroes is one reason men feel inferior, but it is not the only reason. The truth is that we are being led to believe in an absurd image of the ideal male, and the source of this image is not just movies; it is also advertising and childhood stories.

The topic sentence presents a generalization about the movie industry. The examples in the paragraph provide support.

From the beginning, the tone (one of strong feeling and concern) is clear.

2   An obvious contributor to the falsehood is the movie industry, which produces unrealistic plots with superhuman male heroes. Arnold (pre-governor days) slammed through brick walls and snatched the beautiful woman from the jaws of death. The Rock does away with the bad guys by single-handedly fighting an entire compound of evil-doers and throwing himself through a support pillar. Dangling on a wire, Tom Cruise breaks into an impenetrable government agency, scales mountains of heart-stopping heights, and clings to the top of a

speeding train without ever losing his cool or mussing his hair. As 007, Pierce Brosnan stays similarly unruffled as he saves the world, gets the beautiful, aloof woman, and escapes from no fewer than ten near-death experiences—and that's just ten minutes after the opening credits roll. Even aging Harrison Ford performs superhuman heroics worthy of a much younger action hero, including hanging from the back of a 747 jetliner flying at top speed. We watch these movies and feel that this is what men are supposed to be like. Granted, cartoonish action movies are generally the most extreme, but they appeal to the most vulnerable audience— teenage boys. Adolescent males see in these screen heroes visions of what they should be like when they become men. The goal is, of course, unattainable, so males feel inadequate because they do not perform remarkable deeds or look like this image of The Rock in *The Scorpion King*.

The author's informative and persuasive purposes are clear. His role (a concerned male) and his audience (the average, general reader, both males and females) are also becoming clear. The purpose seems to be to inform the reader about how the image of the ideal male is manipulated. The paragraph includes cause-and-effect analysis.

The image illustrates the unattainable goal depicted in movies.

The Rock in *The Scorpion King* (2002; dir. Check Russell)

3   Another source of deception is the advertising industry. Advertisers bombard us every day with powerful male athletes endorsing products. Men are enticed to buy the products because they are led to believe they will be similarly powerful if they do. At one time, Michael Jordan, in all his athletic, superhero grandeur, seduced us into buying Nikes. Now that torch has been passed to the latest basketball phenomenon, LeBron James. Superstars from many sports, including Lance Armstrong, Tiger Woods, and Derek Jeter, make us want the shoes with the swoosh, but even more, they make males long for their ability, acclaim, and lifestyles. We buy the shoes hoping to be more like the athletes we envy and then feel inferior because we don't achieve athletic superstardom or any of its trappings. Jason Giambi and Jeff Gordon may have sold a lot of Pepsi, but they also sold the notion that the ideal male has the strength and physique to hit a baseball out of the park or drive a race car at 160 k.p.h. Most males can't do that, so we feel inferior, less than the ideal. Advertising sends two messages: You should buy this product because this man should be your idol, and if you want to be a "real man," you should have the athletic prowess, physique, and other characteristics of a sports star.

4   A third perpetrator of the misconception is folktales and childhood stories, legends that have been passed down through generations. Triumphant men who confront danger and risk their lives for the underdog are everywhere in our myths, and they cause males to feel inadequate. The likes of Robin Hood, Sir Lancelot, and Davy Crockett originated in an entirely different time and society; they are heroes of the past who do not befit the present, yet their legendary (and impossible to emulate) feats shape the psyches of males. The tradition continues into more recent times, as Superman, Batman, and Spiderman fight injustice, rescue the weak, and generally contribute to the notion that real men are action figures.

5   The ideal men depicted in advertising, movies, and legends are loners. Their strength stems from the fact that they need no one to help them accomplish their goals. The Marlboro man always rides out alone; the action hero single-handedly saves the day. This fact causes problems for males who try to live up to the perceived ideal. It leads them to wall themselves off from others, depriving themselves of enjoyable, satisfying relationships. Further, our world is becoming increasingly cooperative on all levels—from interpersonal to international. A successful male knows that the help of others is essential to achieving

his dream and that collaboration is increasingly valued in the workplace. The loner may not perform as well on the job.

6   Finally, the unfortunate image of the ideal male perpetrated by advertising, movies, and myth damages relations with women. Many times the point of the movie, advertisement, or tale is that the male hero "gets" the woman. He is almost invariably her protector, saviour, or unrepellable lover. In a world whose defining characteristic is the advancement of women nearer and nearer to equality, how can the ideal man have such a relationship with women? The answer is simple: he cannot. Indeed, once outside the worlds of advertising, movies, and folktales, he is not the ideal male.

The conclusion provides closure by presenting a final point and leaving the reader with a final impression. Coherence is achieved with the transition "finally."

Works Cited

The Rock as The Scorpion King. 2002. Photograph. Photofest, New York.

Photograph is documented as explained in Chapter 14.

READING SELECTION

Background

Paul Roberts (1917–1967) was a teacher, linguist, and textbook author. His writing books include *English Syntax* (1954) and *Patterns of English* (1956). "How to Say Nothing in 500 Words" comes from Roberts's best-known book, *Understanding English* (1958).

Reading with a Purpose

Although written almost 50 years ago, "How to Say Nothing in 500 Words" is one of the most frequently anthologized essays in first-year composition readers because it says so much about writing that remains true to this day. (You will notice the author's use of the masculine "he" to refer to the instructor and student, who could be either male or female. At the time the essay was written, using "he" was the conventional way to refer to groups that included both genders.) The essay's lively style makes this a most entertaining piece, but do not be fooled—Roberts is very serious about his advice to writers. As you read, think about whether you know many student writers who behave the way Roberts describes.

Assignment

After your read this essay, stop and think a little about your own writing practice. You might write about what happens to your own writing style when you use more words than necessary. Or you might consider the colourless expressions of your own time. What are these expressions? How do they work in casual conversation? How do they fail to work when we are writing?

Alternatively, you might make a list of topics your instructor should never use and explain why they encourage poor writing.

How to Say Nothing in 500 Words
Paul Roberts

NOTHING ABOUT SOMETHING

1   It's Friday afternoon, and you have almost survived another week of classes. You are just looking forward dreamily to the weekend when the English instructor says: "For Monday you will turn in a five-hundred-word composition on college football."

2   Well, that puts a good big hole in the weekend. You don't have any strong views on college football one way or the other. You get rather excited during the season and go to all the home games and find it rather more fun than not. On the other hand, the class has been reading Robert Hutchins in the anthology and perhaps Shaw's "Eighty-Yard Run," and from the class discussion you have got the idea that the instructor thinks college football is for the birds. You are no fool, you. You can figure out what side to take.

3   After dinner you get out the portable typewriter that you got for high school graduation. You might as well get it over with and enjoy Saturday and Sunday. Five

hundred words is about two double-spaced pages with normal margins. You put in a sheet of paper, think up a title, and you're off:

Why College Football Should Be Abolished

4   College football should be abolished because it's bad for the school and also bad for the players. The players are so busy practicing that they don't have any time for their studies.

5   This, you feel, is a mighty good start. The only trouble is that it's only thirty-two words. You still have four hundred and sixty-eight to go, and you've pretty well exhausted the subject. It comes to you that you do your best thinking in the morning, so you put away the typewriter and go to the movies. But the next morning you have to do your washing and some math problems, and in the afternoon you go to the game. The English instructor turns up too, and you wonder if you've taken the right side after all. Saturday night you have a date, and Sunday morning you have to go to church. (You shouldn't let English assignments interfere with your religion.) What with one thing and another, it's ten o'clock Sunday night before you get out the typewriter again. You make a pot of coffee and start to fill out your views on college football. Put a little meat on the bones.

Why College Football Should Be Abolished

6   In my opinion, it seems to me that college football should be abolished. The reason why I think this to be true is because I feel that football is bad for the colleges in nearly every respect. As Robert Hutchins says in his article in our anthology in which he discusses college football, it would be better if the colleges had race horses and had races with one another, because then the horses would not have to attend classes. I firmly agree with Mr. Hutchins on this point, and I am sure that many other students would agree too.

7   One reason why it seems to me that college football is bad is that it has become too commercial. In the olden times when people played football just for the fun of it, maybe college football was all right, but they do not play football just for the fun of it now as they used to in the old days. Nowadays college football is what you might call a big business. Maybe this is not true at all schools, and I don't think it is especially true here at State, but certainly this is the case at most colleges and universities in America nowadays, as Mr. Hutchins points out in his very interesting article. Actually the coaches and alumni go around to the high schools and offer the high school stars large salaries to come to their colleges and play football for them. There was one case where a high school star was offered a convertible if he would play football for a certain college.

8   Another reason for abolishing college football is that it is bad for the players. They do not have time to get a college education, because they are so busy playing football. A football player has to practice every afternoon

from three to six, and then he is so tired that he can't concentrate on his studies. He just feels like dropping off to sleep after dinner, and then the next day he goes to his classes without having studied and maybe he fails the test.

(Good ripe stuff so far, but you're still a hundred and fifty-one words from home. One more push.)

9   Also I think college football is bad for the colleges and the universities because not very many students get to participate in it. Out of a college of ten thousand students only seventy-five or a hundred play football, if that many. Football is what you might call a spectator sport. That means that most people go to watch it but do not play it themselves.

(Four hundred and fifteen. Well, you still have the conclusion, and when you retype it, you can make the margins a little wider.)

10   These are the reasons why I agree with Mr. Hutchins that college football should be abolished in American colleges and universities.

11   On Monday you turn it in, moderately hopeful, and on Friday it comes back marked "weak in content" and sporting a big "D."

12   This essay is exaggerated a little, not much. The English instructor will recognize it as reasonably typical of what an assignment on college football will bring in. He knows that nearly half of the class will contrive in five hundred words to say that college football is too commercial and bad for the players. Most of the other half will inform him that college football builds character and prepares one for life and brings prestige to the school. As he reads paper after paper all saying the same thing in almost the same words, all bloodless, five hundred words dripping out of nothing, he wonders how he allowed himself to get trapped into teaching English when he might have had a happy and interesting life as an electrician or a confidence man.

13   Well, you may ask, what can you do about it? The subject is one on which you have few convictions and little information. Can you be expected to make a dull subject interesting? As a matter of fact, this is precisely what you are expected to do. This is the writer's essential task. All subjects, except sex, are dull until somebody makes them interesting. The writer's job is to find the argument, the approach, the angle, the wording that will take the reader with him. This is seldom easy, and it is particularly hard in subjects that have been much discussed: College Football, Fraternities, Popular Music, Is Chivalry Dead?, and the like. You will feel that there is nothing you can do with such subjects except repeat the old bromides. But there are some things you can do which will make your papers, if not throbbingly alive, at least less insufferably tedious than they might otherwise be.

AVOID THE OBVIOUS CONTENT

14   Say the assignment is college football. Say that you've decided to be against it. Begin by putting down the arguments that come to your mind: it is too commercial, it

takes the students' minds off their studies, it is hard on the players, it makes the university a kind of circus instead of an intellectual center, for most schools it is financially ruinous. Can you think of any more arguments just off hand? All right. Now when you write your paper, *make sure that you don't use any of the material on this list.* If these are the points that leap to your mind, they will leap to everyone else's too, and whether you get a "C" or a "D" may depend on whether the instructor reads your paper early when he is fresh and tolerant or late, when the sentence "In my opinion, college football has become too commercial," inexorably repeated, has brought him to the brink of lunacy.

15   Be against college football for some reason or reasons of your own. If they are keen and perceptive ones, that's splendid. But even if they are trivial or foolish or indefensible, you are still ahead so long as they are not everybody else's reasons too. Be against it because the colleges don't spend enough money on it to make it worth while, because it is bad for the characters of the spectators, because the players are forced to attend classes, because the football stars hog all the beautiful women, because it competes with baseball and is therefore un-American and possibly Communist inspired. There are lots of more or less unused reasons for being against college football.

16   Sometimes it is a good idea to sum up and dispose of the trite and conventional points before going on to your own. This has the advantage of indicating to the reader that you are going to be neither trite nor conventional. Something like this:

17   We are often told that college football should be abolished because
        it has become too commercial or because it is bad for the players. These
        arguments are no doubt very cogent, but they don't really go to the heart of
        the matter.

Then you go to the heart of the matter.

TAKE THE LESS USUAL SIDE

18   One rather simple way of getting interest into your paper is to take the side of the argument that most of the citizens will want to avoid. If the assignment is an essay on dogs, you can, if you choose, explain that dogs are faithful and lovable companions, intelligent, useful as guardians of the house and protectors of children, indispensable in police work—in short, when all is said and done, man's best friends. Or you can suggest that those big brown eyes conceal, more often than not, a vacuity of mind and an inconstancy of purpose; that the dogs you have known most intimately have been mangy, ill-tempered brutes, incapable of instruction; and that only your nobility of mind and fear of arrest prevent you from kicking the flea-ridden animals when you pass them on the street.

19   Naturally, personal convictions will sometimes dictate your approach. If the assigned subject is "Is Methodism Rewarding to the Individual?" and you are a pious Methodist, you have really no choice. But few assigned subjects, if any, will fall in this category. Most of them will lie in broad areas of discussion with much to be said on

both sides. They are intellectual exercises and it is legitimate to argue now one way and now another, as debaters do in similar circumstances. Always take the side that looks to you hardest, least defensible. It will almost always turn out to be easier to write interestingly on that side.

20   This general advice applies where you have a choice of subjects. If you are to choose among "The Value of Fraternities" and "My Favorite High School Teacher" and "What I Think About Beetles," by all means plump for the beetles. By the time the instructor gets to your paper, he will be up to his ears in tedious tales about the French teacher at Bloombury High and assertions about how fraternities build character and prepare one for life. Your views on beetles, whatever they are, are bound to be a refreshing change.

21   Don't worry too much about figuring out what the instructor thinks about the subject so that you can cuddle up with him. Chances are his views are no stronger than yours. If he does have convictions and you oppose them, his problem is to keep from grading you higher than you deserve in order to show he is not biased. This doesn't mean that you should always cantankerously dissent from what the instructor says; that gets tiresome too. And if the subject assigned is "My Pet Peeve," do not begin, "My pet peeve is the English instructor who assigns papers on 'my pet peeve.'" This was still funny during the War of 1812, but it has sort of lost its edge since then. It is in general good manners to avoid personalities.

SLIP OUT OF ABSTRACTION

22   If you will study the essay on college football . . . you will perceive that one reason for its appalling dullness is that it never gets down to particulars. It is just a series of not very glittering generalities: "football is bad for the colleges," "it has become too commercial," "football is a big business," "it is bad for the players," and so on. Such round phrases thudding against the reader's brain are unlikely to convince him, though they may well render him unconscious.

23   If you want the reader to believe that college football is bad for the players, you have to do more than say so. You have to display the evil. Take your roommate, Alfred Simkins, the second-string center. Picture poor old Alfy coming home from football practice every evening, bruised and aching, agonizingly tired, scarcely able to shovel the mashed potatoes into his mouth. Let us see him staggering up to the room, getting out his econ textbook, peering desperately at it with his good eye, falling asleep and failing the test in the morning. Let us share his unbearable tension as Saturday draws near. Will he fail, be demoted, lose his monthly allowance, be forced to return to the coal mines? And if he succeeds, what will be his reward? Perhaps a slight ripple of applause when the third-string center replaces him, a moment of elation in the locker room if the team wins, of despair if it loses. What will he look back on when he graduates from college? Toil and torn ligaments. And what will be his future? He is not good enough for pro football, and he is too obscure and weak in econ to succeed in stocks

and bonds. College football is tearing the heart from Alfy Simkins and, when it finishes with him, will callously toss aside the shattered hulk.

24   This is no doubt a weak enough argument for the abolition of college football, but it is a sight better than saying, in three or four variations, that college football (in your opinion) is bad for the players.

25   Look at the work of any professional writer and notice how constantly he is moving from the generality, the abstract statement, to the concrete example, the facts and figures, the illustration. If he is writing on juvenile delinquency, he does not just tell you that juveniles are (it seems to him) delinquent and that (in his opinion) something should be done about it. He shows you juveniles being delinquent, tearing up movie theatres in Buffalo, stabbing high school principals in Dallas, smoking marijuana in Palo Alto. And more than likely he is moving toward some specific remedy, not just a general wringing of the hands.

26   It is no doubt possible to be *too* concrete, too illustrative or anecdotal, but few inexperienced writers err this way. For most the soundest advice is to be seeking always for the picture, to be always turning general remarks into seeable examples. Don't say, "Sororities teach girls the social graces." Say "Sorority life teaches a girl how to carry on a conversation while pouring tea, without sloshing the tea into the saucer." Don't say, "I like certain kinds of popular music very much." Say, "Whenever I hear Gerber Spinklittle play 'Mississippi Man' on the trombone, my socks creep up my ankles."

GET RID OF OBVIOUS PADDING

27   The student toiling away at his weekly English theme is too often tormented by a figure: five hundred words. How, he asks himself, is he to achieve this staggering total? Obviously by never using one word when he can somehow work in ten.

28   He is therefore seldom content with a plain statement like "Fast driving is dangerous." This has only four words in it. He takes thought, and the sentence becomes:

In my opinion, fast driving is dangerous.

Better, but he can do better still:

In my opinion, fast driving would seem to be rather dangerous.

If he is really adept, it may come out:

In my humble opinion, though I do not claim to be an expert on this complicated subject, fast driving, in most circumstances, would seem to be rather dangerous in many respects, or at least so it would seem to me.

Thus four words have been turned into forty, and not an iota of content has been added.

29   Now this is a way to go about reaching five hundred words, and if you are content with a "D" grade, it is as good a way as any. But if you aim higher, you must work

differently. Instead of stuffing your sentences with straw, you must try steadily to get rid of the padding, to make your sentences lean and tough. If you are really working at it, your first draft will greatly exceed the required total, and then you will work it down, thus:

> It is thought in some quarters that fraternities do not contribute as much as might be expected to campus life.
> Some people think that fraternities contribute little to campus life.

> The average doctor who practices in small towns or in the country must toil night and day to heal the sick.
> Most country doctors work long hours.

> When I was a little girl, I suffered from shyness and embarrassment in the presence of others.
> I was a shy little girl.

> It is absolutely necessary for the person employed as a marine fireman to give the matter of steam pressure his undivided attention at all times.
> The fireman has to keep his eye on the steam gauge.

30   You may ask how you can arrive at five hundred words at this rate. Simply. You dig up more real content. Instead of taking a couple of obvious points off the surface of the topic and then circling warily around them for six paragraphs, you work in and explore, figure out the details. You illustrate. You say that fast driving is dangerous, and then you prove it. How long does it take to stop a car at forty and at eighty? How far can you see at night? What happens when a tire blows? What happens in a head-on collision at fifty miles an hour? Pretty soon your paper will be full of broken glass and blood and headless torsos, and reaching five hundred words will not really be a problem.

CALL A FOOL A FOOL

31   Some of the padding in freshman themes is to be blamed not on anxiety about the word minimum but on excessive timidity. The student writes, "In my opinion, the principal of my high school acted in ways that I believe every unbiased person would have to call foolish." This isn't exactly what he means. What he means is, "My high school principal was a fool." If he was a fool, call him a fool. Hedging the thing about with "in-my-opinion's" and "it-seems-to-me's" and "as-I-see-it's" and "at-least-from-my-point-of-view's" gains you nothing. Delete these phrases whenever they creep into your paper.

32   The student's tendency to hedge stems from a modesty that in other circumstances would be commendable. He is, he realizes, young and inexperienced, and he half suspects that he is dopey and fuzzy-minded beyond the average. Probably only too true. But it doesn't help to announce your incompetence six times in every

paragraph. Decide what you want to say and say it as vigorously as possible, without apology and in plain words.

33   Linguistic diffidence can take various forms. One is what we call *euphemism*. This is the tendency to call a spade "a certain garden implement" or women's underwear "unmentionables." It is stronger in some eras than others and in some people than others but it always operates more or less in subjects that are touchy or taboo: death, sex, madness, and so on. Thus we shrink from saying "He died last night" but say instead "passed away," "left us," "joined his Maker," "went to his reward." Or we try to take off the tension with a lighter cliché: "kicked the bucket," "cashed in his chips," "handed in his dinner pail." We have found all sorts of ways to avoid saying *mad*: "mentally ill," "touched," "not quite right upstairs," "feeble-minded," "innocent," "simple," "off his trolley," "not in his right mind." Even such a now plain word as *insane* began as a euphemism with the meaning "not healthy."

34   Modern science, particularly psychology, contributes many polysyllables in which we can wrap our thoughts and blunt their force. To many writers there is no such thing as a bad schoolboy. Schoolboys are maladjusted or unoriented or misunderstood or in need of guidance or lacking in continued success toward satisfactory integration of the personality as a social unit, but they are never bad. Psychology no doubt makes us better men or women, more sympathetic and tolerant, but it doesn't make writing any easier. Had Shakespeare been confronted with psychology, "To be or not to be" might have come out, "To continue as a social unit or not to do so. That is the personality problem Whether 'tis a better sign of integration at the conscious level to display a psychic tolerance toward the maladjustments and repressions induced by one's lack of orientation in one's environment or—" But Hamlet would never have finished the soliloquy.

35   Writing in the modern world, you cannot altogether avoid modern jargon. Nor, in an effort to get away from euphemism, should you salt your paper with four-letter words. But you can do much if you will mount guard against those roundabout phrases, those echoing polysyllables that tend to slip into your writing to rob it of its crispness and force.

BEWARE OF THE PAT EXPRESSION

36   Other things being equal, avoid phrases like "other things being equal." Those sentences that come to you whole, or in two or three doughy lumps, are sure to be bad sentences. They are no creation of yours but pieces of common thought floating in the community soup.

37   Pat expressions are hard, often impossible, to avoid, because they come too easily to be noticed and seem too necessary to be dispensed with. No writer avoids them altogether, but good writers avoid them more often than poor writers.

38   By "pat expressions" we mean such tags as "to all practical intents and purposes," "the pure and simple truth," "from where I sit," "the time of his life," "to the ends

of the earth," "in the twinkling of an eye," "as sure as you're born," "over my dead body," "under cover of darkness," "took the easy way out," "when all is said and done," "told him time and time again," "parted the best of friends," "stand up and be counted," "gave him the best years of her life," "worked her fingers to the bone." Like other clichés, these expressions were once forceful. Now we should use them only when we can't possibly think of anything else.

39   Some pat expressions stand like a wall between the writer and thought. Such a one is "the American way of life." Many student writers feel that when they have said that something accords with the American way of life or does not they have exhausted the subject. Actually, they have stopped at the highest level of abstraction. The American way of life is the complicated set of bonds between a hundred and eighty million ways. All of us know this when we think about it, but the tag phrase too often keeps us from thinking about it.

40   So with many another phrase dear to the politician: "this great land of ours," "the man in the street," "our national heritage." These may prove our patriotism or give a clue to our political beliefs, but otherwise they add nothing to the paper except words.

COLORFUL WORDS

41   The writer builds with words, and no builder uses a raw material more slippery and elusive and treacherous. A writer's work is a constant struggle to get the right word in the right place, to find that particular word that will convey his meaning exactly, that will persuade the reader or soothe him or startle or amuse him. He never succeeds altogether—sometimes he feels that he scarcely succeeds at all—but such successes as he has are what make the thing worth doing.

42   There is no book of rules for this game. One progresses through everlasting experiment on the basis of ever-widening experience. There are few useful general-izations that one can make about words as words, but there are perhaps a few.

43   Some words are what we call "colorful." By this we mean that they are calculated to produce a picture or induce an emotion. They are dressy instead of plain, specific instead of general, loud instead of soft. Thus, in place of "Her heart beat," we may write "Her heart *pounded, throbbed, fluttered, danced.*" Instead of "He sat in his chair," we may say, "He *lounged, sprawled, coiled.*" Instead of "It was hot," we may say, "It was *blistering, sultry, muggy, suffocating, steamy, wilting.*"

44   However, it should not be supposed that the fancy word is always better. Often it is as well to write "Her heart beat" or "It was hot" if that is all it did or all it was. Ages differ in how they like their prose. The nineteenth century liked it rich and smoky. The twentieth has usually preferred it lean and cool. The twentieth-century writer, like all writers, is forever seeking the exact word, but he is wary of sounding feverish. He tends to pitch it low, to understate it, to throw it away. He knows that if he gets too colorful, the audience is likely to giggle.

45   See how this strikes you: "As the rich, golden glow of the sunset died away along the eternal western hills, Angela's limpid blue eyes looked softly and trustingly into Montague's flashing brown ones, and her heart pounded like a drum in time with the joyous song surging in her soul." Some people like that sort of thing, but most modern readers would say, "Good grief," and turn on the television.

COLORED WORDS

46   Some words we would call not so much colorful as colored—that is, loaded with associations, good or bad. All words—except perhaps structure words—have associations of some sort. We have said that the meaning of a word is the sum of the contexts in which it occurs. When we hear a word, we hear with it an echo of all the situations in which we have heard it before.

47   In some words, these echoes are obvious and discussable. The word *mother*, for example, has, for most people, agreeable associations. When you hear *mother* you probably think of home, safety, love, food, and various other pleasant things. If one writes, "She was like a mother to me," he gets an effect which he would not get in "She was like an aunt to me." The advertiser makes use of the associations of *mother* by working it in when he talks about his product. The politician works it in when he talks about himself.

48   So also with such words as *home, liberty, fireside, contentment, patriot, tenderness, sacrifice, childlike, manly, bluff, limpid.* All of these words are loaded with favorable associations that would be rather hard to indicate in a straightforward definition. There is more than a literal difference between "They sat around the fireside" and "They sat around the stove." They might have been equally warm and happy around the stove, but *fireside* suggests leisure, grace, quiet tradition, congenial company, and *stove* does not.

49   Conversely, some words have bad associations. *Mother* suggests pleasant things, but *mother-in-law* does not. Many mothers-in-law are heroically lovable and some mothers drink gin all day and beat their children insensible, but these facts of life are beside the point. The thing is that *mother* sounds good and *mother-in-law* does not.

50   Or consider the word *intellectual*. This would seem to be a complimentary term, but in point of fact it is not, for it has picked up associations of impracticality and ineffectuality and general dopiness. So also with such words as *liberal, reactionary, Communist, socialist, capitalist, radical, schoolteacher, truck driver, undertaker, operator, salesman, huckster, speculator.* These convey meanings on the literal level, but beyond that—sometimes, in some places—they convey contempt on the part of the speaker.

51   The question of whether to use loaded words or not depends on what is being written. The scientist, the scholar, try to avoid them; for the poet, the advertising writer, the public speaker, they are standard equipment. But every writer should take care that they do not substitute for thought. If you write, "Anyone who thinks that is

nothing but a Socialist (or Communist or capitalist)," you have said nothing except that you don't like people who think that, and such remarks are effective only with the most naive readers. It is always a bad mistake to think your readers more naive than they really are.

COLORLESS WORDS

52   But probably most student writers come to grief not with words that are colorful or those that are colored but with those that have no color at all. A pet example is *nice,* a word we would find it hard to dispense with in casual conversation but which is no longer capable of adding much to a description. Colorless words are those of such general meaning that in a particular sentence they mean nothing. Slang adjectives, like *cool* ("That's real cool") tend to explode all over the language. They are applied to everything, lose their original force, and quickly die.

53   Beware also of nouns of very general meaning, like *circumstances, cases, instances, aspects, factors, relationships, attitudes, eventualities,* etc. In most circumstances you will find that those cases of writing which contain too many instances of words like these will in this and other aspects have factors leading to unsatisfactory relationships with the reader resulting in unfavorable attitudes on his part and perhaps other eventualities, like a grade of "D." Notice also what "etc." means. It means "I'd like to make this list longer, but I can't think of any more examples."

Chapter 4

Description

Among branches
a bird lands fluttering,
a soft gray glove
with a heart.

The land at twilight.
Swamp of black mist.
A first planet. A swordtip.
The bird chanting
in a jail of darkness.

This is the last unclassified bird,
the one one never sees,
but hears when alone, walking.

You can see how far I've gone
not to speak of you.
Birds have made a simple bargain
with the land.

The only song I know
is the one I see with my eyes,
the one I'd give up my eyes
in order for you to hear.

— Roo Borson, *Gray Glove*, 1981

THE PATTERN

What happens when you encounter a striking landscape, hear a moving song on the radio, smell a peculiar scent in your apartment, taste a delightful dessert in a restaurant, or touch a velvety sweater in a store? Like most people, you probably want to share the experience with others, so you find yourself saying things like

"Quick, come see this!"
"You've got to listen to this song."

"Do you smell that?"

"Here, you have to have a bite of this cake."

"Oh, feel how soft this sweater is."

Writers have the same impulse. They want to share their sensory impressions, so they use words to create mental pictures that will help their readers experience a bit of what they did.

When writers use words to create mental pictures, they are writing **description.** To appreciate how description can allow writers to convey sensory impressions, consider this sentence, from Trevor Herriot's *River in a Dry Land*:

> Beside tables that seem endless, women stand hip to hip, and between their gingham and paisley-printed backsides come glimpses of cut flowers, jams and jellies, pies, loaves of bread, bunches of carrots, squashes, tomatoes.

Can you picture that scene? You can probably picture it more clearly than you would with this less descriptive sentence:

> Women stand hip to hip at long tables heaped with produce and baking.

The first sentence shows the power of words to create mental pictures, which is a primary purpose of description: using words to move your reader to mentally see, hear, smell, taste, and touch in a particular manner. In a similar way, writers can use words to convey how it feels to experience a situation or emotion, as is the case in this example from "A Sleuth of Bears" by Brian Payton:

> We wandered the rainforest in heavy downpours and soft, persistent mist. More than nine feet of precipitation soaks this part of the coast each year and the resulting jungle is dark and primeval. Grizzly bears play an integral role in this environment, consuming huge quantities of salmon and conveying valuable nitrogen fertilizer deep into the forest. They are the unwitting gardeners of some of the world's oldest, biggest trees.

USING DESCRIPTION FOR A PURPOSE

Description can entertain, convey feelings, relate experience, inform, and persuade. When people on vacation want to share their good times, for example, they often write description on postcards to relate their experience and express to friends and relatives back home how they see and react to the beautiful vistas, local cuisine, and interesting people they encounter. Newspaper and magazine columnists often use description to entertain their readers, as Brian Payton does when he describes the antics of a young grizzly bear on page 128. On the job, people can use description to inform a reader. For example, the public relations director of your university might include description of your campus in the catalogue to inform prospective students about what the campus is like. Description can also be an important component of writing meant to persuade. Because well-written description can move a reader's emotions, it is often used to convince a reader to think or act a particular way. A travel agent trying to persuade people to take a Caribbean cruise might write a letter to clients describing the luxurious ship and breathtaking ports of call to get them excited about the trip and convince them to send a deposit.

Although it can serve a variety of purposes, description is most often expressive, so it most often helps writers share their perceptions. As human beings, we have a compelling desire to connect with other people by sharing our experiences with them. Description helps us do that. In addition, because well-written description can be beautiful and therefore pleasurable to read, a secondary purpose of description is often to entertain.

Since description helps the reader form mental pictures, writers often rely on it to add interest and vividness. That is, description helps writers do more than just *tell* that something is true; it allows them to *show* that something is true. For this reason, writers often combine description with other patterns of development. For example, suppose you are writing an explanation of how to make the perfect spaghetti sauce (this would be *process analysis,* an explanation of how something is made) If you tell your reader to pick only the best tomatoes, you might go on to describe how those tomatoes look, feel, and smell, so your reader knows how to select them. Now suppose you are telling a story about the time you wrecked your uncle's classic car (this would be *narration*). You might include a vivid description of what the car looked like after the wreck to help your reader appreciate how badly the car was damaged.

Description at School, at Work, and in the Community

One mark of an educated person is the ability to observe closely and assess the significance of what is observed. Thus, in your college and university classes, you will frequently be asked to observe, describe, and evaluate. For example, in an art history course, you might be asked to describe two paintings by Van Gogh to show their similarities and differences. In a music appreciation course, you might be asked to describe a Chopin nocturne to explain the technique the performer used. In an advertising course, you might be required to describe an ad for a particular product to learn about persuasive strategies. In your history courses, you might be asked to describe conditions after events such as wars, coups, economic reversals, and social reforms to assess their effects. In an English class, you will probably need to describe a character. In a biology lab, you might need to describe organs after dissection in order to understand their characteristics, and in a psychology lab, you might need to describe the behaviour of a mouse following a particular experiment to learn about the effects of certain stimuli. In a fashion design class, you might need to describe classic Gucci designs, and in a dental hygiene class, you might need to describe the appearance of a healthy bicuspid.

You will also find description in most of your textbooks, whatever discipline you are studying. Here, for example, is description taken from *The People of New France,* by Allan Greer:

> Four days out of Montreal in August 1749, Peter Kalm's bateau rounded a curve in the St Lawrence, and the Swedish naturalist caught his first sight of the fortifications of Quebec, looming over the rocky heights. Unlike other travellers who would have arrived from the sea by way of the mammoth funnel of the St Lawrence, Kalm was approaching the city through its back door. Even so, Quebec did not fail to impress Kalm with its spectacular setting against a backdrop of mountains. After landing at the docks, he made his way up the narrow, winding road to the upper town—so steep, he marvelled at the drivers of carriages and wagons attempting the descent—and, at the top, he stopped to admire the "amazing" view from the galleries of the governor's château. Earlier visitors had called this "the noblest and most extensive Prospect in the World," with the Île d'Orléans in the distance and the broad St Lawrence, where "snow white" belugas frolicked over the waves. Right below Kalm were the wharves and the busy streets of Lower Town. "Most of the merchants live in the lower city, where the houses are built very close together. The streets in it are narrow, very rough, and almost always set. There is likewise a church and a small marketplace. The upper city is inhabited by people of quality, by several persons belonging to the different offices, by tradesmen and others. In this part are the chief buildings of the town."

Notice how Allan Greer gives you a clear picture of New France by including a wide range of details—from the organization of neighbourhoods to the cavorting belugas in the harbour.

Beyond the classroom, you will likely use description. For example, description is common in workplace writing. Real estate agents describe properties in classified advertisements, and police officers describe crime scenes in crime reports. Psychologists describe their patients' demeanours in therapy notes, and scientists describe specimens before and after experiments. Nurses describe patients' appearances in medical charts, and insurance adjusters describe the condition of cars after accidents.

Description is also helpful in community-based writing. For instance, assume you are writing a letter to the editor of your campus newspaper to persuade students to recycle pop cans. You might describe the appearance of the campus quad littered with used aluminium cans. Or assume you are emailing friends asking them to volunteer their time at a homeless shelter. You could create sympathy by describing the conditions of those forced to live on the street.

The Patterns and Their Purposes

In academic writing, description is more likely to *contribute* to the effectiveness of your writing; simply describing an historical figure, a heritage building, the anatomy of a salamander, or the plants found in a bog is unlikely to be the sole focus of an essay. Similarly, you aren't likely to write essays that only tell a story (narration) or define a concept (definition). Rather, you will be writing what is broadly termed expository essays—essays that explain something to your reader. If, for example, your assignment is to write an expository essay explaining the changes that affect the narrator in Raymond Carver's story "Cathedral," you will probably portray the character (description), tell what happens to him in the story (narration), and analyze why he changes toward the end of the story (cause and effect).

In doing so, you will have discovered what are called the rhetorical patterns of development. Early rhetoricians noticed that our minds manipulate information in a limited number of ways when we try to understand something: we describe, tell stories, define, collect examples, consider differences and similarities to what we already know, and reflect on causes and their effects. In short, we use the patterns that structure this book. But we seldom use a single approach.

At the same time, though, each of these rhetorical patterns involves a particular way of thinking and writing. To make exposition manageable, then, most composition textbooks treat one pattern at a time. While the chapters in this book focus on a single pattern, the essays are often more broadly expository. The first reading you encounter in a chapter will use the pattern we're focusing on; other readings may show you how these patterns can be combined.

DECIDING ON A DOMINANT IMPRESSION

If you describe something small and uncomplicated, such as a chair, you can probably describe all its features. However, if you are describing something larger or more complex, including all of its characteristics would be difficult for you and overwhelming to your reader. To keep complex descriptions manageable, settle on a **dominant impression** (one notable quality) and write only those details that express that impression.

The quality is not "dominant" because it is the most significant or noticeable feature of what you are describing. The quality is dominant because it is the characteristic your description will focus on—it is "dominant" in your essay. For example, suppose you decide to describe the house you grew up in. Do you *really* want the task of describing all aspects of that house? Probably not. For most purposes, you can cut the job of describing your house down to a manageable size by choosing only those details that convey some opinion you have of the house. Once you decide on that opinion, you have the dominant impression, and you can safely ignore details that do not convey that impression.

Let's say the house you grew up in was an architectural nightmare, cluttered, but nonetheless cheerful. You can settle on one of those characteristics for your dominant impression. If you decided to convey the impression that the house was an architectural nightmare, you would describe the sagging porch and leaky roof rather than the beauty of the stained glass windows in the dining room. If you decided to convey how cluttered the house was, you would describe the collection of glass bottles that covered every tabletop, but not the crisply starched and pressed curtains. If you decided to convey the cheerfulness of the house, you would describe the sun flooding the front room, but not the tattered sofa. You can also form a dominant impression from more than one quality, if doing so still gives you a manageable writing task. You could, for example, describe your house as rundown but cheerful. In that case, you would describe the sagging porch and the leaky roof as well as the beautiful stained glass windows and starched, pressed curtains.

SUPPORTING DETAILS

Supporting details in a description essay should give your reader a clear mental image of your subject. In addition, they should convey your dominant impression of your subject and establish why you have formed that impression. The strategies explained next will help you choose supporting details that accomplish these goals.

Objective and Expressive Details

Objective details give a factual, impartial, unemotional account of your subject. You don't choose these details to tell us about your reaction to the subject, but to describe the subject as carefully as you can. **Expressive details**

present a more subjective, personal, or emotional view; you choose expressive details to convey something about your reaction to or feelings about the subject. A bank appraiser describing a piece of property would use objective details because his or her personal opinion about the property is not relevant. However, an advertising executive writing a description of a new car would use expressive detail to create an emotional appeal that will persuade the consumer to buy the car. Notice the difference between objective and expressive details in these examples, taken from readings in this chapter.

OBJECTIVE DETAILS   Convinced he'd established who was in charge, the cub scrambled up a large rock for a better view. He yawned, licked his paws, and even dozed off for a while. He resembled a young royal, aware of the flashing cameras but intent on maintaining the pretense of normalcy. A few minutes later, the pair slowly ambled away from the water's edge and disappeared into the forest. (From "A Sleuth of Bears," page 128)

EXPRESSIVE DETAILS   It's a strange thing to witness the dismantling of a community and the concurrent construction of something new, particularly in a city undergoing change at a rate nobody can absorb. Every few blocks there is another newly bulldozed lot. Deep holes gape like enormous, empty mouths from which boulders protrude like broken teeth. Each empty lot signifies something lost and something being born. (From "Inner City," page 124)

Whether expressive or objective, descriptive details are **sensory details** (details that pertain to the senses: sight, sound, taste, smell, and touch). Sometimes a writer will use only one sense—typically sight—and other times a writer will appeal to several senses.

To see how writers can appeal to the five senses, consider the following sentences taken from essays in this book.

SIGHT   On one of our forest walks, we found a bear trail below an old hemlock tree. Unlike other animal or human paths, where an unbroken line is traced on the earth, here each bear carefully placed its paws in exactly the same spot as the bears that passed before it. The result was a series of round, measured paw pads in the bright green moss. Some speculate that these trails are ancient pathways trod by untold generations. ("A Sleuth of Bears," page 129)

SOUND   There, among jewelled headpieces, gleaming costumes, and prop curtains, [my mother] played mah-jong with members of the troop, while I was being spoiled by sweetmeats or left alone to play with costumed opera dolls with fierce warrior faces. Alone, I became a prince and a warrior, my parents the Emperor and Empress. All the adventures of the world were possible, and I the hero of them all. Finally, I remember the laughter and sing-song voices, the *clack-click* of the bamboo and ivory game tiles, lulling me to sleep. ("The Ten Thousand Things," page 162)

TASTE

With our fingers we pulled soft fragments of [the cooked fish] from its sides to our plates, and ate; it was delicate fish-flesh, fresh and mild. Someone found the roe, and I ate of that too—it was fat and stronger, like egg yolk, naturally enough, and warm. ("The Deer at Providencia," page 136)

SMELL

[My mother] lay gasping for breath: the result of decades of smoking. I stroked her forehead, and with my other hand I clasped her thin motionless fingers. Around two in the morning, half asleep and weary, I closed my eyes to catnap. Suddenly, the last striving for breath shook her thin body. I snapped awake, conscious again of the smell of acetone, of death burning away her body. The silence deepened; the room chilled. The mother I had known all my life was gone. ("The Ten Thousand Things," page 158. Note how the sound of the mother's breathing and the chill in the room also contribute to the effect of this passage.)

TOUCH

Autumn has slipped into the room. It is cold everywhere. It crept in through the cracks in the window, enveloping everything. It holds me where I am. I am safe as long as I don't leave the warmth of her bed. The comforter and pillows are goose down and the sheets are soft and they cradle me as I doze. My bed doesn't do this. It is cold and firm, too big for one person. ("Cold Hangs," page 123)

Descriptive Words

Whether you are writing objective or expressive description, choose your words carefully. This does *not* mean that you should dash for the dictionary or thesaurus to find as many big words as possible. While these sources can be helpful, relying on them too heavily can lead you to write an overbearing sentence like this one:

The pulchritudinous rose imparted delightful olfactory sensations upon me.

This sentence illustrates two problems that can occur when writers abandon their own natural styles and pile on words taken from the thesaurus and dictionary: The writing becomes stiff, pretentious, and unnatural, and the reader has a hard time understanding.

You can always turn to a dictionary or thesaurus when you are stuck, but usually you can write effective description with words you already know. The key is to use *specific* nouns, verbs, and modifiers rather than general ones because specific words are more descriptive. *General words* give readers a broad sense of what you are referring to, while *specific words* offer them a narrower, more focused meaning. The following list will help you see the difference between general and specific words.

GENERAL NOUNS	SPECIFIC NOUNS
car	Ford Taurus
sweater	cardigan
shoe	Nike Shox
class	Physics 103
meat	filet mignon
magazine	*Maclean's*

GENERAL VERBS	SPECIFIC VERBS
walk	stroll
spoke	shouted
look	glance
went	raced

GENERAL MODIFIERS	SPECIFIC MODIFIERS
nice	elegant
awesome	overwhelming
terrible	frightening
bad	gaudy

To develop effective descriptive language, expect to work through a series of refinements as you revise your drafts.

FIRST DRAFT	The house stood in the shadow of the huge tree.
REVISION 1	The huge tree cast a shadow over the house.
REVISION 2	The enormous poplar cast a shadow over the house.
REVISION 3	The enormous poplar cast an eerie shadow over the house.

As you refine your descriptions in stages, look for opportunities to substitute specific nouns, verbs, and modifiers for more general words. Consider the following sentence for example.

The tree moved in the wind.

The nouns are *tree* and *wind*. As a first refinement, you might make *tree* more specific:

The <u>poplar</u> moved in the wind.

Now you might make the verb *moved* more specific:

The poplar <u>swayed</u> in the wind.

Next, you might add specific modifiers:

The <u>newly planted</u> poplar swayed in the <u>gusting</u> wind.

Eventually, striving for specific nouns, verbs, and modifiers might lead you to rewrite the entire sentence to make it more active and vivid.

The gale-force wind whipped the branches of the young poplar. Mother's favourite poplar was whipped by the powerful gusts.

How you describe the tree and the wind will depend upon the mental picture you want to create. However, a little description can go a long way. Do not overwhelm your reader by stringing together too many modifiers, or you will create an overburdened sentence like this one:

The emaciated, spindly, waxen old man stared vacantly into the barren, colourless hallway as his bony, arthritic, pale fingers played absently with the beige fringes of the faded blue bedspread.

When you do have highly descriptive sentences, balance them with less descriptive ones so your reader is not overwhelmed. For example, consider this passage from "Inner City," where a highly descriptive sentence is followed by a less descriptive one:

The pictures are brightly coloured, and the buildings are tall and glassy and the trees are mature and the sidewalks are bustling with smiling people carrying grocery bags and briefcases; the streetscape shimmers and there are no broken windows and no sleeping bags on sidewalks and no empty, outstretched hands. The sky is blue.

Similes and Metaphors

Writers often use similes and metaphors in description because they help create mental images. A **simile** uses the words *like* or *as* to compare two things

> ### Troubleshooting Guide
>
> ### Avoiding Clichés
>
> Poet Robert Hall has written that "Clichés are little cinder blocks of crushed and reprocessed experience. When we use them in writing, we violate our agreement to construct sentences in order to reach someone else" (*Writing Well*, 4). Clichés come in and out of style; they float in the social air around us and are often the expressions we turn to in conversation, when we need words quickly. But in conversation, we can add some nuance to clichés with our tone of voice, facial expression, or body language. When we write, we do not have that option.
>
> When we choose a cliché, we haven't thought about what we really want to say but have chosen the first words that come to mind. Maybe we also don't believe it's important enough to find fresh, vivid language to "reach someone else," as Hall puts it. But then we can't blame our reader for being bored or for not getting the point.
>
> If you have trouble finding and eliminating clichés (overused expressions like "sadder but wiser" and "the last straw," or over-used text-messaging shorthand like "lol" or "roflmao"), the following suggestions may be helpful.
>
> 1. To identify clichés in your own writing, look for similes (see above) that are not original—ones you have heard before, like these:
>
>   **cold as ice   free as a bird   crazy like a fox   dark as night**
>
> 2. To eliminate a cliché that is a simile, rewrite the simile in a new way:
>
>   FIRST DRAFT: **Some sit on the railing like ducks in a row . . .**
>   REVISION: **Some perch like chickens on the railing . . .**
>
>   If you cannot rewrite the simile in a new way, rewrite without the simile:
>
>   FIRST DRAFT: **Some sit on the railing like ducks in a row . . .**
>   REVISION: **Some sit on the railing shoulder to shoulder.**
>
> 3. Not all clichés are similes, and not all similes are clichés. To become more familiar with clichés, visit these Web sites and browse the cliché lists:
>
>   **www.clichesite.com**
>   **www.lssu.edu/banished/current.php**
>   **www.westegg.com/cliche/random.cgi**

that are not usually seen as similar. Here is an example of a simile from "A Sleuth of Bears":

The light and weather were changing, casting the mountains in shadow and bathing the shore in amber hues. At the far end of the estuary, shafts of light beamed down from the heavens as in a Renaissance painting.

A **metaphor** compares two items not usually seen as similar, but without *like* or *as*. In this metaphor from "Gray Glove," the poem printed at the beginning of this chapter, Borson compares a gray bird to a glove:

> Among branches
> a bird lands fluttering,
> a soft gray glove
> with a heart.

ORGANIZING DETAILS

An essay developed with description will often include a thesis that mentions both what is being described and the dominant impression. Here are two examples:

> I was always embarrassed by the rundown house I grew up in. (*The house will be described; the dominant impression is "rundown."*)

> At noon, the park comes alive with businesspeople taking a midday break from the pressures of work. (*The park at noon will be described; the dominant impression is that it is alive with the activity of businesspeople.*)

The thesis of a descriptive essay can be implied rather than stated. (See page 51 on the implied thesis.) If your thesis is implied, be sure the cumulative effect of your descriptive details gives your reader a clear sense of your dominant impression.

To order your descriptive details, ask yourself what arrangement will best help you convey your dominant impression and achieve your purpose for writing the description. Often, you will opt for a **spatial order,** especially when you are describing a room or other contained space where it is logical to move from front to back, left to right, top to bottom, and so on. If you describe the rundown house you grew up in, for example, you can begin at the front door and move clockwise through the rooms on the first floor. Other times, a **progressive order** will serve your purpose, particularly when your description is meant to persuade your reader to think or act a particular way. A real estate agent trying to convince people to buy the house you grew up in would probably describe the best features last to leave the reader with the strongest possible final impression of the place. **Chronological order** is another option in which you describe a place as if you were moving through it. Say you want to describe the house you grew up in as it was when you returned there last Thanksgiving. You could arrange the details according to what you noticed first, second, and so on as you entered and moved through the house.

VISUALIZING A DESCRIPTIVE ESSAY

The following chart can help you visualize the structure for a descriptive essay. Like all good models, however, this one can be altered as needed.

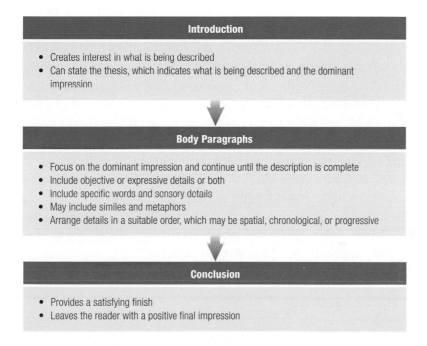

Introduction
- Creates interest in what is being described
- Can state the thesis, which indicates what is being described and the dominant impression

Body Paragraphs
- Focus on the dominant impression and continue until the description is complete
- Include objective or expressive details or both
- Include specific words and sensory details
- May include similes and metaphors
- Arrange details in a suitable order, which may be spatial, chronological, or progressive

Conclusion
- Provides a satisfying finish
- Leaves the reader with a positive final impression

PROCESS GUIDELINES: STRATEGIES FOR WRITING DESCRIPTION

1. **Selecting a topic.** You need not worry about finding a magnificent, dramatic, or unusual subject to describe. Concentrate on finding a topic and settling on a dominant impression that will allow you to write vivid descriptions that convey the significance of your subject and help you achieve a particular purpose. Also, try to describe something you can visit and observe, such as a doctor's waiting room, a bus station, a popular campus gathering place, or a restaurant with a theme decor. When you visit the spot, take notes about sensory details to make drafting easier. If

you describe a subject from memory, such as a childhood haunt, your high school cafeteria, or a tree house you used to have, be sure the memory is fresh enough to allow you to come up with vivid, specific details.

2. **Establishing a dominant impression.** If you have trouble settling on a dominant impression, list all the emotions your subject arouses in you and all the reactions you have to your subject. Then choose one of those feelings or reactions as your dominant impression. You need not choose your strongest reaction. You can select the one you find most interesting or surprising, or the one you think you can write about the best.

3. **Drafting.** When you write your first draft, be as descriptive as you can comfortably be, but do not labour too long over individual sentences or particular words. Descriptive language often does not come easily; choosing specific nouns, verbs, and modifiers takes time and often involves a series of revisions, so do not expect too much too soon. When you revise, you can shape your descriptive language to get it just right.

4. **Revising.** Remember to use specific words to show rather than tell. Instead of writing "The child looked tired," be specific about how the child acted: "Little Alfie rubbed his fists into his eyes and stretched his mouth into a wide yawn." Also, revise vague words like *good, nice, awful, terrible, cool, bad,* and *great.* Aim for more specific alternatives. Instead of "bad food," revise to get "over-seasoned, stringy steak"; instead of "awful headache," revise to get "throbbing headache."

Troubleshooting Guide

Using the Dictionary, Thesaurus, and OneLook Reverse Dictionary

If you have trouble finding the right descriptive word, a dictionary or thesaurus can help. But be aware of the connotations—the implied or secondary meanings—of words you take from these sources because synonyms are not always interchangeable. While *stern* is a synonym for *fierce*, you would not write that you encountered a stern bear in the woods.

If you have a concept in mind, but can't think of the word or phrase you want, use OneLook Reverse Dictionary at www.onelook.com/reverse-dictionary.shtml. You can use this site to find a word if you already know the definition, get a list of related concepts and words, and answer identification questions.

✔ Checklist for Revising Description

Be sure:

_____ Details work together to convey a single dominant impression.

_____ Nouns, verbs, and modifiers are specific and appeal to the appropriate senses.

_____ Less descriptive sentences follow highly descriptive sentences.

_____ Details work to fulfill your purpose or combination of purposes.

_____ Details are arranged in a suitable order, indicated by topic sentences and transitions, as needed.

ANNOTATED STUDENT ESSAY

In this descriptive essay, student writer Adrien Sala calls on many of the reader's senses to create a portrait of "the morning after the night before." We hear the sounds of the apartment, we taste the bitterness of the water in the kettle, we feel the softness of the sheets, and we see the chaos of the young woman's bedroom. All of these details create an impression of the narrator's sense that he has done something that damages himself—again.

Cold Hangs

Paragraph 1
The first and last sentences function as a thesis: the writer is uneasy about being here. It's not yet clear where "here" is, nor who "she" is, echoing the narrator's sense of puzzlement.

1   I've woken up here before, though I don't know why I let it happen again. It must be mid-morning—the sun is strong and the sounds from the neighbouring apartments have shifted from groggy bathroom noise to television and crying kids. I am alone and my head aches. Down the hall I can hear her turning the taps for the shower. She will spend the next few minutes adjusting the hot and cold until the water is perfect, and almost finished being hot. Part of my punishment for coming here is to always be left with cold showers.

Paragraph 2
The focus of this paragraph is the tea kettle. Just as the narrator's life has changed because of his involvement with "her," so the tea kettle has moved from his place to hers. The bitterness of the coffee echoes the bitterness he feels. This is largely subjective description.

2   I don't have to leave the comfort of her bed to know what is going on inside the apartment. There is an old, half-copper kettle warming on the stove. It creaks and moans, long haunting breaths as it gets hotter. The kettle used to be mine. I had it before I met her, when I spent all of my time alone and drank too much coffee. It leaves water with a bitter metallic taste that lingers long after you've finished any drink made from it. After we started spending more time together, and I wasn't alone as much, I wanted to throw it out. She wouldn't let me and it wound up here. These days I hate the kettle more than I did when it just gave my coffee a metal flavour. I know now that I'm not the only one who drinks from it; I'm not the only stranger who wakes up here.

Paragraph 3
The description of the room is slightly chaotic: there is no unifying spatial principle guiding his choice of things to describe; this echoes, once again, the narrator's feelings. The closing comparison of "her" to Hugh Hefner is rather unsympathetic.

3   Looking around I see the room in its usual state. Clothes are tossed, forgotten and wilted on the back of her grandmother's antique chair. More are piled behind the door. Old 45s are stacked beside the bed, with the frayed album covers creating a soft table that holds her earrings, watch, and money. There is also a glass, a quarter full of water, left for me to drink. The only thing missing from the room is her worn, burgundy dressing gown. I close my eyes and imagine her right then, walking bare-foot back and forth between the kitchen and bathroom, with her gown carelessly tied around her, falling from her shoulders. I think to myself that if Hugh Hefner were a 5'3'' woman, he would look like her in the morning: replace the pipe for a coffee mug, keep the desperate need for attention and marry it with a relentless desire to be single, and you would have her, pacing around the apartment, wondering what urge made her call me last night, and how she was going to get me out of her bed and her apartment.

4   Autumn has slipped into the room. It is cold everywhere. It crept in through the cracks in the window, enveloping everything. It holds me where I am. I am safe as long as I don't leave the warmth of her bed. The comforter and pillows are goose down and the sheets are soft and they cradle me as I doze. My bed doesn't do this. It is cold and firm, too big for one person. Directly over her bed is a skylight and, directly over that, nothing—it is a window to infinity I have stared out of many times. This morning I gaze out of it as I have all the other mornings here since last December, and regret coming. It isn't good for me. I told her so last night after I had driven over. I was opening a bottle of wine I brought and said with a mixture of clarity and courage, "This isn't right you know."

Paragraph 4
This description is spatially organized: the narrator turns from the bed to the skylight and from the present to the past.

5   "Shut up," she replied.

Paragraph 5
The one-sentence paragraph is emphatic.

6   So here I am, hiding from the cold that hangs everywhere in the room, keeping my eyes closed. I can feel the frigid air coming up from the floor and in through the windows. I think that if I opened my eyes I could see it, but I don't have to—I can hear the coldest part of the apartment pacing, letting the water run, leaving nothing to keep me warm.

Paragraph 6
The topic sentence (sentence 1) describes both the apartment and the writer's frame of mind. There's nothing in this relationship or the room to keep him warm.

PEER REVIEW

Responding to "Cold Hangs"

Evaluate "Cold Hangs" by responding to these questions:

1. What is the narrator's frame of mind in the few moments it takes him to describe his situation? How does his description give you access to his mood?
2. Insofar as there is a thesis for this essay, it is split in two. Is this an effective strategy, or should the author write a clearer thesis or do without one altogether? Explain your reaction.
3. Does the author use objective details well? Does he use expressive details well? Explain and cite examples to support your view.
4. What do you think of the author's word choice? Why? Cite an example to support your view.
5. Are the details arranged in a suitable order? Explain.
6. What are the chief strengths of the essay? Why do you find these features strong?
7. Mention one revision you would like to see. How will that revision improve the essay and help the author achieve his purpose?

READING SELECTIONS

Background

Jill Boettger is a poet and a prose writer from southern Alberta, where she teaches writing at Mount Royal College and is on the editorial board of *Geist*.

Reading with a Purpose

Jill Boettger finds herself faced with enormous changes to the social and architectural fabric of Calgary. Unsure of her reactions to the demolition and building she finds around her, she juxtaposes descriptions of the dismantled inner city community with billboards promising tall glass buildings and blue sky, trying to decide whether the grieving over the loss of community or the dream of a new city "has the greater purchase on [her] heart."

Inner City

Jill Boettger

As you read
Consider the changes you've seen in your neighbourhood. How have you felt about them?

1   Last fall a newspaper headline read that vacant schools would be used as temporary shelters for homeless people in the coming winter. In my neighbourhood in downtown southeast Calgary, the number of people working construction on the streets is almost equal to the number of people living on the streets, and everywhere there are billboards of glossy pictures that show us what's to come. The pictures are brightly coloured, and the buildings are tall and glassy and the trees are mature and the sidewalks are bustling with smiling people carrying grocery bags and briefcases; the streetscape shimmers and there are no broken windows and no sleeping bags on sidewalks and no empty, outstretched hands. The sky is blue.

2   In Calgary's inner city it seems another rooming house comes down every week. Or a hospital, or a school. A small white church is still standing—the only structure left on an entire city block that's been flattened to make way for the new Stampede Casino. This community, newly named the East Village, was once called Victoria Park but now Victoria Park is barely breathing. All that is left is a row of ill-kept, dilapidated character houses and a small grocery store. The pizza joint has been replaced by a real estate office. The community centre has been levelled and the lot used as parking for the Stampede grounds; Victoria Park Community School has been demolished to make way for Arriva, the tallest residential tower in Alberta.

3   It's a strange thing to witness the dismantling of a community and the concurrent construction of something new, particularly in a city undergoing change at a rate nobody can absorb. Every few blocks there is another newly bulldozed lot. Deep holes gape like enormous, empty mouths from which boulders protrude like broken teeth. Each empty lot signifies something lost and something being born. Here grieving and dreaming happen side by side, and I don't know which has greater purchase on my heart. The new condo high-rises will increase urban density and perhaps contain

the growing urban sprawl, and the Stampede Park expansion is being marketed as "a gathering place for Calgary and the world." Meanwhile, the signs and structures that once told me I was home don't exist any more; they're rubble. They've been replaced with comic book images of the future, and I feel as though I'm occupying a storyboard or a movie set I somehow wandered onto without a role or a script.

4   For those whose houses have become the rubble, the question of home is not a theoretical one. One of Calgary's only low-income, inner-city residential neighbour-hoods has been cleared to make way for "inner city revitalization" and the Stampede ground expansion, and while some residents have been relocated, no equivalent community has been created to replace it. Ironically, this meant that the Stampede Grandstand was opened as a temporary shelter for homeless people during a cold snap because all of the regular shelters were full.

5   For a week in late February, snow fell every day, and then, a Chinook. The tem-perature rose sixteen degrees over the course of six hours, and the next day the city was melting: the impressive, hulking snowbanks sagged into the streets. I wonder if the weather is taking its cues from the city's frenzied pace, or if the city is mimicking the havoc of our new climate. Either way, everything is changing at the same freakish rate.

6   Today, in all the melting, I go for a walk: leave my house in Ramsay, cross the Elbow River into Victoria Park and pass through the abandoned and semi-abandoned lots and the crashing construction zones. Somehow, in the middle of this prairie city rushing its way to big, on a street corner on the brink of a dying and blooming downtown community, there's the Haymarket Café, a worker-owned co-operative bookstore and coffee shop run by a small pod of self-identified anarchists. I leave the noisy street for the living-room comfort of the café with its curiously gathered furniture and cozy, colourful walls and bookshelves and chalkboards and its menu of homemade organic foods. A small stack of handbills on the counter show a picture of a scheming girl in black and the words *Come plot something at Haymarket.* The room has a small stage and large speakers and an amp, and the entrance is papered in posters advertising underground film festivals and public forums and local music and fair-trade clothing. The anarchists move around behind the counter brewing coffee and spreading vegan margarine on whole-wheat bagels, and they perch on stools at the lunch bar discussing shipments of veggies and coffee beans. When I walk in they welcome me with their smiles but don't say anything.

7   I order chai and browse the bookshelves stocked with radical ideas, looking for clues on how to handle what I'm in the middle of, an explanation—perfect and clear—to tell me how the heart is supposed to manage the dizzying flux of home. Instead, I find instructions on the multiple uses of baking soda, notes on the pitfalls and triumphs of launching a revolution, a vagina owner's manual and a short intro-duction to Marxism.

8   While I'm hunting through books and sipping tea, outside the lineup for the Mustard Seed Street Ministry's evening meal is already curling around the block.

> Sirens blare and fade. Gradually the dump trucks and cement mixers slow to a halt, and the sidewalks busy with people leaving downtown, carrying leather satchels and shopping bags and briefcases and lunch boxes and hardhats, moving through the city with a steady, distracted grace. It's the people who catch my attention, and from my warm window in the Haymarket Café I wonder where everyone's going.

Reading Closely and Thinking Critically

1. How does place play a role in our sense of who we are as individuals?
2. Given your answer to the previous question, consider how place plays a role in our sense of communal identity. Is it possible to simply demolish one community hockey rink or a group of small neighbourhood stores and replace it with a newer, more modern building? Why or why not?
3. What should city councillors and city planning authorities consider when they are deliberating on changes to the fabric of a town or city?
4. Should the fate of the homeless be the concern of urban developers? Why or why not?

Examining Structure and Strategy

1. Juxtaposition involves simply setting two things side by side and allowing the viewers or readers to draw their own conclusions. Boettger repeatedly tells us that she's not sure how to react to the change she sees. She acknowledges, standing at construction sites, that "Here grieving and dreaming happen side by side, and I don't know which has the greater purchase on my heart." Her basic strategy here is simply to juxtapose description of demolition, along with its consequences, to the billboards depicting new buildings, or to juxtapose soup lines to visions of construction and departing office workers. How does her use of juxtaposition reflect her uncertainty?
2. Why does Boettger end her essay with her visit to the Haymarket Café? Why does she seek answers from self-described "anarchists"? Does the mission or the reading at the café offer her any answers to her dilemma? Why or why not?
3. What does Boettger's description of the Haymarket Café contribute to her portrait of the area of Calgary that is undergoing so much demolition and construction? Does this description give you some uneasy sense of why city planners have decided to raze this area?

Considering Language and Style

1. Boettger uses a freight train sentence (a sentence that, like a freight train, seems to build up steam and just keep going) at the end of her first paragraph. The long sentence is followed by a very brief "The sky is blue." How is Boettger using the rhythm of her sentence to convey something of her reaction to the changes she's seeing in Calgary?
2. In paragraph 3, Boettger uses a simile to describe the construction sites: "Deep holes gape like enormous, empty mouths from which boulders protrude like broken teeth." How does the simile reflect her reaction to the construction taking place in Calgary?
3. At the end of paragraph 3, Boettger uses a simile to compare her experience of walking through the construction zone to "occupying a storyboard of a movie set I somehow wandered onto without a role or a script." What does this simile convey about this experience?

4. Boettger's use of juxtaposition is echoed at the sentence level. In paragraph 3 she writes that "Each empty lot signifies something lost and something being born. Here grieving and dreaming happen side by side, and I don't know which has greater purchase on my heart." How do these sentences reflect her reactions to the construction? Is the reader encouraged to share her ambivalence?

For Discussion in Class or Online

What values are reflected in the changes being made to your own town, city, or neighbourhood? How do you feel about these changes? If your instructor so directs, post your responses on your class Web site.

Writing Assignments

1. **In your journal.** Consider how a place now gone has contributed to your existential sense of who you are or where you come from. Describe that place with an eye to making its particular contribution to your life a key component of the description.

2. **Using description for a purpose.** The purposes given in the assignments are possibilities. You may establish whatever purposes you like, within your instructor's guidelines.
   - To entertain your reader or express feelings, describe two places, one of which was torn down and the other that replaced it.
   - To inform your reader, describe a new building that has contributed something new to a neighbourhood or community.
   - To persuade your reader, describe a building or a neighbourhood that has been torn down and consider what was lost or gained in the process.

3. **Combining patterns.**
   - To inform your reader, describe a building that has been torn down. Use narrative to trace the changes that this destruction has had on the people who used that building,
   - To inform your audience, describe a neighbourhood (which might include a suburb or a portion of the inner city) and consider the effect that its character has on how we use that space. You might consider, for example, whether the neighbourhood you are describing invites you to walk places or necessitates the use of your car.

4. **Connecting the readings.**
   - In Mark Kingwell's essay "What Is the Good Life?" he argues that one of the things we value most is a sense of community. How would Kingwell weigh in on the destruction of community that Boettger depicts in paragraphs 2 and 3?
   - In Tim Falconer's essay "Toronto Cars. Can't Live with 'Em, Can't Live without 'Em," (Chapter 12), Falconer discusses Jane Jacobs's work and credits her with saving Toronto neighbourhoods by protesting against the Spadina Expressway. Compare what Falconer says about the Toronto neighbourhoods she saved with the destruction that Boettger is seeing in Calgary. Which model of "urban renewal" would you prefer, and why?

5. **Drawing on sources.** Douglas Martin wrote in *The New York Times* that "At a time when both common and inspired wisdom called for bulldozing slums and opening up city space, Ms. Jacobs's prescription was ever more diversity, density and dynamism—in effect, to crowd people and activities together in a jumping, joyous urban jumble." Jacobs believed that it was partaking of the joyous jumble, meeting people on the street and being part of the street life, that allowed us to negotiate, sometimes even without talking about it, what it is we want from cities. Read *Death and Life of Great American Cities* or other books or articles by or about Jane Jacobs and her ideas, and with her ideas in mind, describe an area of the city (or your campus) where such exchanges go on.

Background

Brian Payton has written about adventure, wildlife, and the environment for *The New York Times, Los Angeles Times, Chicago Tribune, Boston Globe, The Globe and Mail,* and *Canadian Geographic.* In 2001 and 2002 his work earned a Lowell Thomas Silver Award for best North American travel essay from the Society of American Travel Writers. The selection below comes from *Shadow of the Bear: Travels in Vanishing Wilderness.* Here, he explores both our ancient interest in bears and the fact that they are a reliable indicator of the health of the ecosystem where they live. Payton lives in Vancouver with his wife.

Combined Patterns and Their Purposes

In this introduction to his book *Shadow of the Bear: Travels in Vanishing Wilderness*, Payton intertwines descriptions of encounters with bears, discussions of the place bears have held in our collective imaginations, and considerations of the effects of our encroachment on their habitats. The result is a powerful argument for recognizing that we are not the only, much less the most important, creatures on this planet.

A Sleuth of Bears

Brian Payton

As you read
Think about your own relation to nature. What forces have shaped your view of the natural world?

1   There are moments of clarity in life, instances that so completely focus the senses, there is no yesterday or tomorrow—only the absolute here and now. Such a moment came for me in the spring of 2000, on the coast of British Columbia, when my guide reached for the oar in the bottom of our boat and accidentally spooked a grizzly cub on shore.

2   The overgrown three-year-old bawled and temporarily lost his footing. His mother, grazing sedge nearby, spun around and stopped mid-chew. We were so close, I could see the foamy, green saliva at the corners of her mouth—so close I could see her eyes focus on me. Several heart-pounding seconds passed as we stared at one another, reading body language, plotting possible outcomes. Then all at once she turned and sat down. Seemingly unconcerned with our presence, she kept her back to us and her cub as she continued munching on stems and blades.

3   From what I'd gathered about meeting bears in the wilderness, coming upon a mother and cub seemed like the worst-case scenario. And yet somehow these bears put me at ease. Convinced he'd established who was in charge, the cub scrambled up a large rock for a better view. He yawned, licked his paws, and even dozed off for a while. He resembled a young royal, aware of the flashing cameras but intent on maintaining the pretense of normalcy. A few minutes later, the pair slowly ambled away from the water's edge and disappeared into the forest.

4   We've been meeting them in the wilderness, and in our dreams, since the dawn of human history. Bears have been celebrated in art and myth since we began drawing on the walls of caves. No beast casts a longer shadow over our collective subconscious. Perhaps more than any other animal, the bear remains at the very heart of our concept of wilderness.

> Perhaps more than any other animal, the bear remains
> at the very heart of our concept of wilderness.

5   The hope of seeing grizzlies in their natural habitat brought me and six companions to the mouth of the Khutzeymateen (KOOT-suh-mah-teen) River in Canada's only grizzly bear sanctuary. The inlet reaches twelve miles in from Chatham Sound, forming an arm of the Pacific Ocean that ends in fingers full of rich green sedge. After emerging from hibernation, grizzlies make their way down to the marsh to feast on the bounty of new shoots that offer up to 28 percent protein. A place of plenty, the marsh attracts dozens of bears each spring. After establishing a pecking order, these ordinarily solitary creatures graze in close proximity. This gathering, known as a sleuth of bears, is something that rarely happens in the wild.

6   I was determined to get up close and experience being in a place where humans are not the masters of all we see—a place where we are at least one link down the food chain. For four days, guide Tom Ellison's seventy-two-foot ketch served as our mother ship for exploration. Anchored in a sheltered cove, we were surrounded by slopes of old-growth cedar and snowy peaks soaring nearly seven thousand feet above the tide. Himself an imposing figure, Ellison's weathered features betrayed a long association with the wilderness and the sea. He knew these bears better than anyone.

7   We wandered the rainforest in heavy downpours and soft, persistent mist. More than nine feet of precipitation soaks this part of the coast each year and the resulting jungle is dark and primeval. Grizzly bears play an integral role in this environment, consuming huge quantities of salmon and conveying valuable nitrogen fertilizer deep into the forest. They are the unwitting gardeners of some of the world's oldest, biggest trees. In North America, before the advent of industrial logging, temperate rainforests once stretched along the West Coast from California's giant sequoias to Alaska's majestic Sitka spruce. Among the world's rarest ecosystems, temperate rainforests never covered more than one-fifth of percent of the planet's land surface. Today, less than one-half of that small amount remains.

8   On one of our forest walks, we found a bear trail below an old hemlock tree. Unlike other animal or human paths, where an unbroken line is traced on the earth, here each bear carefully placed its paws in exactly the same spot as the bears that passed before it. The result was a series of round, measured paw pads in the bright green moss. Some speculate that these trails are ancient pathways, trod by untold generations. Passing bears have also left their marks on nearby scratch trees, which provide temporary relief from an itchy back and serve as a kind of social register with scent, bits of fur, and claw marks that let other bears know who's in the neighborhood.

9   I was fully aware that these bears could tear me apart. Although the vast majority of encounters between people and bears are peaceful in this part of the world, every couple of years someone gets killed. However, within this protected, pristine environment, bears have not learned to fear humans or associate us with handouts or garbage. Here, it is possible to meet them on unencumbered terms.

10   I discovered that the same government that protects the sixty grizzlies in this estuary sanctions the killing of approximately three hundred others in British Columbia's annual grizzly bear hunt. It is estimated that another three hundred are victims of poaching. A considerable number of these are killed only for their gallbladders, which end up as medicine in Asian apothecaries, or for their paws, which are served as exotic delicacies in restaurants around the world. Despite the numbers directly killed by humans, it is believed that habitat destruction remains the most serious threat to the survival of these and most other bears.

11   "We're losing this coast," Ellison said one night over dinner. "If people can't be bothered to save the salmon or trees, maybe they'll be motivated to save these magnificent creatures. And the only way they're going to want to save the bears is if they get to know them."

12   Ellison spent a long time becoming acquainted with the female bear we met a few days before. Her story began in the early 1990s, when a dominant male encountered her family when she was just a yearling. Male grizzlies are known to attack and kill cubs. This tactic is used to bring females into estrus so they will be receptive to mating, according to some researchers; others are not so sure. Whatever the motivation, the family was attacked. The mother was killed along with one of her cubs. The surviving cub wasn't expected to make it through the season.

13   "When winter came, we were sure we'd never see her again," Ellison said. "But in the spring, there she was—alive and kicking. She had survived the winter alone in the den. Sometimes she'd see us coming and swim to the boat: I'd have to gently push her paw away with the oar so she wouldn't climb aboard.

14   "As she matured, she would lure the big males out of the forest to dance with them and tease them on shore. When she was in estrus, she would chase them if they wandered off. She wanted to be mated. One time, we saw her lure a big male into a secluded spot in the bush and make quite a lot of noise. She re-emerged with fur rubbed off her shoulders. Then we realized who she was mating with—the same bear who killed her mother and sibling. The result was the cub you've been watching the past two days.

15   "When the fight was really heating up to save this place, we were able to bring influential people to see the bears," Ellison explained. "She gave many of them an opportunity to get up close and have a personal experience. That bear let us into her life and helped save this valley. This is a special place where these kinds of meetings can happen."

16   Over a stretch of four unforgettable days, I saw grizzlies crash through the brush, dig up clams, and paddle along the shore. I saw male and female grizzlies, cubs, and numerous shy black bears. On the final day, we set a course for a waist-high field of sedge.

17   The light and weather were changing, casting the mountains in shadow and bathing the shore in amber hues. At the far end of the estuary, shafts of light beamed down

from the heavens as in a Renaissance painting. We landed near a patch of purple lupine and proceeded unarmed (save for a large can of bear spray) in the general direction of an adult male grizzly. Ellison didn't recognize this bear but guessed it was a fifteen-year-old male, perhaps 550 pounds. Once we were within a hundred yards, we quietly sat down.

18   Despite his powerful build, this bear was the picture of laziness. He ate the sedge within easy reach, then sprawled on his stomach to reach some more. When those blades were finally clipped, he got up, took a deep breath, and moved in our direction. He sauntered for thirty yards or so, stopped, and stuck his nose in the air. He took a long, ponderous whiff. Satisfied with our nonthreatening odor, he resumed his grazing.

19   Then the bear moved closer still. All was silent, save the click and whirr of our cameras. I stopped staring through the viewfinder and slowly rested the camera in my lap. As we sat frozen, mouths agape, it dawned on me that we were in a rare place in our modern world—at the mercy of a large, wild animal.

20   As it closed the gap between us, I had another of those moments of clarity. My heart was not racing, I felt no panic welling up inside. But I did feel as if the tables had turned, as if I had become the object of curiosity. Ellison spoke in a soothing voice, informing the bear of our intentions, then quietly suggested that we take a few steps back—which I was happy to do. Choosing to leave us unchallenged and undisturbed, the bear continued past and up an embankment. I inhaled deeply through my nose in a vain attempt to pick up his scent. At the top of the rise, he stopped, took a final look over his shoulder, then lumbered into the woods.

21   My journey began with a dream. Before I left for the Khutzeymateen, I dreamt that I was walking in the woods and saw something, or someone, sitting on a log in the distance. It had its back to me, but I knew it was a bear. It was wearing tattered overalls and mumbling unintelligible words. It turned and acknowledged me with a grunt. As I approached, I saw that it held something in its paws. A book? It was trying to sound out words as it squinted through old, broken spectacles. I sat down next to the bear and began to teach it how to read.

22   A product of North American culture, I've had two distinct and competing images of the bear imprinted in my subconscious: the clown of enchanted forests and the relentless killing machine that stalks the night. As infants, teddy bears are among the first items placed inside our cribs. As we grow, we are fed a steady diet of children's stories and cartoons about lovable, huggable bears. Eventually, we are exposed to society's enduring and macabre fascination with bear attacks. The result is that many of us tend to either anthropomorphize or demonize bears out of ignorance or expediency. I was determined to move beyond all that and hopefully get a glimpse of what these creatures really are.

23   The connection between bears and humans is primal—it reaches back into the shadows beyond both myth and memory. We have always recognized bears as

extraordinary, intelligent, and powerful beasts that share our preferred environments. More than that; they can stand on their hind legs like us. This ability inspires awe in modern viewers, just as it did our ancestors. Archeologists report that bears have been feared, revered, and even worshiped since the earliest times.

> We have always recognized bears as extraordinary, intelligent, and powerful beasts that share our preferred environments.

24   Now they fill a new and emerging role. Where bears still roam, biologists say they act as an indicator of the general health of the ecosystem that supports them. Bears are considered an "umbrella" species. If they are protected and thriving, so the theory goes, then so too will a whole range of animals and plants on the food chain below them. Inspired by this idea, conservationists launched an international campaign to rechristen a five-million-acre chunk of Canada's West Coast "the Great Bear Rainforest." The area is home to thousands of bears: grizzlies, black bear, and even a rare, all-white subspecies of black bear known as the Kermode, or Spirit Bear. If people wouldn't save the wilderness for its own sake, perhaps they would save it for the bears. Following a ten-year struggle, a historic agreement was reached among Native groups, government, and industry to protect the world's largest remaining intact coastal rainforest. Proof of the power of metaphor.

25   When I returned from the Khutzeymateen, I continued my research. Aside from North America's three bear species—grizzly/brown bear, black bear, and polar bear—I was aware only of China's giant panda and Russia's brown bear. To my surprise, I discovered there are bears in Southeast Asia, Western Europe, India, and South America—eight surviving species in all. Termite-eating bears, feisty little jungle bears, and even bears with pale rings around their eyes that make them appear as if they're wearing spectacles. I found numerous books about bears, including many natural histories of bears living in or near U.S. national parks. Information about bears beyond North America was scarce in the extreme.

26   It seemed to me that one could probably tell a lot about a society by the way it treats its bears. Outside rare environments like the Khutzeymateen Grizzly Bear Sanctuary, people and bears compete for shrinking space and resources. From the beginning, bears and other large predators have shaped our development by forcing us to cooperate for the protection of each other's lives and, eventually, livestock. Now we shape their destiny.

27   Scientists tell us that we are in the midst of the Sixth Extinction, a time when species are disappearing at a rate one hundred times faster than normal. All bear species have declined in number and range due to human activities. The IUCN, the World Conservation Union, publishes a Red List of Threatened Species to call attention to those animals facing a high risk of global extinction. Six out of the eight bear species are on that list: the Asiatic black bear, the spectacled bear, the sun bear, the sloth bear, the giant panda, and the polar bear. Saving them will require an enormous test of our

ability to cooperate; failing—at the very least—will mean the irretrievable loss of a way to understand ourselves.

All bear species have declined in number
and range due to human activities.

28   Too many fundamental questions about bears remain unanswered, questions only disciplined scientific study can address. But beyond biology and ecology, what kind of political, economic, and cultural environments do bears inhabit? I felt compelled to go and find out. As I embarked on this series of journeys, I was unsure what I hoped to gain, other than some understanding of our relationship to these remarkable beasts and why they continue to inspire fear, fascination, and reverence.

29   It has been said that there are two concentric circles of knowledge. The inner circle holds everything you know, while the outer circle contains those things you know you don't know (like how to speak Phoenician). Beyond is that universe of things of which you are completely unaware. In my limited experience, I had already moved one small but unassailable fact into my inner circle—spend time in bear country and something interesting is bound to happen. Armed with little more knowledge than this, I set out to wander beyond the outer ring.

Reading Closely and Thinking Critically

1. What are the many ways that human lives been tied to those of the bear? Why do bears appear in our cribs, fairy tales, myths, news stories, and nightmares?
2. How does Payton want to exploit this tie between people and bears to make an argument for preserving the habitats of endangered species?
3. What does the fact that six out of the eight species of bear are on the endangered list kept by the World Conservation Union tell us?
4. Why, at the close of Payton's encounter with the fifteen-year-old male, does he inhale deeply through his nose, attempting to catch the bear's scent? What does that have to do with being at the bear's mercy?
5. Discuss the concentric circles of knowledge Payton describes in his final paragraph. How does your time at college or university change what is contained by those concentric circles? Are you, like Payton, wandering "beyond the outer ring"?

Examining Structure and Strategy

1. What is Payton's purpose in this essay? Is his description of his encounters with bears a means to an end or an end in itself—or both?
2. Payton describes two startling moments of clarity in his essay. How are these related? How do they create a structure for the essay?
3. Why does Payton close the essay with a description of the concentric rings of our knowledge? Is this an effective conclusion?

Noting Combined Patterns

1. From paragraph 12 to paragraph 15, Payton tells the story of an orphaned cub that isn't frightened of people. Why does he interrupt his descriptive essay with a narrative? Why this narrative?

2. Similarly, from paragraphs 17 to 20, Payton tells the story of his encounter with a fifteen-year old male. What does that narrative contribute?
3. In paragraphs 23 and 24, Payton uses exposition and analysis to tell us about the bear's place in our ecosystem, indicating that the well-being of bears speaks to the well-being of the entire ecosystem. What is the relationship between this "discussion" on saving habitats and his description of encounters with bears?

Considering Language and Style

1. The collective noun for a group of bears is "a sleuth of bears." What does this expression suggest to you? How does it suit Brian Payton's purpose? Visit one of the Web sites that explore the odd collective nouns available in English—expressions like "a murder of crows," or "an ascension of larks"—to discover what the expression actually means (http://www.rinkworks.com/words/collective. shtml or http://www.hintsandthings.co.uk/kennel/collectives.htm). Does this lend a different note to Payton's story?
2. In paragraph 9, Payton says that in the Khutzeymateen you can meet bears on "unencumbered terms"? What does he mean by that expression? How is it connected to the purpose of his essay?
3. In paragraph 22, Payton observes that we demonize or anthropomorphize bears. What does "anthropomorphize" mean? Are either of these ways of understanding bears appropriate?

For Discussion in Class or Online

Describe the last time you found yourself awed and perhaps even frightened by the natural world? What does such experience—or the lack of it—tell us about our contemporary relationship with the natural world?

Writing Assignments

1. **In your journal.** Write about your own encounter with an animal, even a pet, that gave you a glimpse into an entirely different way of viewing the world.
2. **Using description for a purpose.** The purposes given in the assignments are possibilities. You may establish whatever purposes you like, within your instructor's guidelines.
   - To entertain your reader, describe an animal you have known well—or as well as we know any animal. What does your knowledge of that animal, or your lack of knowledge, tell us about our relationships to the natural world?
   - To inform and persuade your reader, describe a species of animal that is endangered. Explain why protecting the species is important.
   - To persuade your reader, use both objective and subjective details to describe a species or a habit with such precision and intensity that readers will be willing to change their behaviour to protect it. You might also describe the changes that are necessary.
3. **Combining patterns.** Describe a species that is near distinction and use cause and effect to explain what imbalances will result if the species becomes extinct.
4. **Connecting the readings.** In Chapter 12, Wayne Grady's essay "On Walking" implicitly argues that only when we walk in our world do we have the kind of awareness of it that is required if we're going to value the planet that we're living on. Describe a walk that you frequently take or a walk that you've taken (perhaps even a hike through wilderness) to show what we gain when we get out of our cars, take out our ear buds, and experience the natural world around us.
5. **Drawing on sources.** Begin with an Internet search using the terms "endangered species" and "Canada" to discover what species of animals are endangered near where you live. What is being done to ensure the animals' survival? What else should be done?

Background

Both a writer and a teacher of writing (at Wesleyan University in Connecticut), Annie Dillard has been a columnist for *The Living Wilderness* and a contributing editor for *Harper's* magazine. Born in 1945, Dillard won a Pulitzer Prize in 1975 for her first book of prose, *The Pilgrim at Tinker Creek,* a collection of observations about the beauty and violence of the natural world near her Virginia home. Dillard's other works include poetry; *For the Time Being* (1999), a personal narrative; *Encounters with Chinese Writers* (1984), a work about her visit to China as part of a United States cultural delegation; *The Writing Life* (1989), a narrative about the writing process; and a book of essays, *Teaching a Stone to Talk* (1982). "The Deer at Providencia," is from *Teaching a Stone to Talk*.

Combined Patterns and Their Purposes

"The Deer at Providencia" is a description of the torment of a deer. This description is a powerful component of Dillard's narration (story) about the suffering of humans and animals. The weaving of the descriptive and narrative elements allows Dillard to relate her experience in the Ecuadorian jungle and express her feelings of uncertainty.

The Deer at Providencia
Annie Dillard

1   There were four of us North Americans in the jungle, in the Ecuadorian jungle on the banks of the Napo River in the Amazon watershed. The other three North Americans were metropolitan men. We stayed in tents in one riverside village, and visited others. At the village called Providencia we saw a sight which moved us, and which shocked the men.

As you read
Think about the suffering people and animals experience. How much of that suffering is avoidable?

2   The first thing we saw when we climbed the riverbank to the village of Providencia was the deer. It was roped to a tree on the grass clearing near the thatch shelter where we would eat lunch.

3   The deer was small, about the size of a whitetail fawn, but apparently full-grown. It had a rope around its neck and three feet caught in the rope. Someone said that the dogs had caught it that morning and the villagers were going to cook and eat it that night.

4   This clearing lay at the edge of the little thatched-hut village. We could see the villagers going about their business, scattering feed corn for hens about their houses, and wandering down paths to the river to bathe. The village headman was our host; he stood beside us as we watched the deer struggle. Several village boys were interested in the deer; they formed part of the circle we made around it in the clearing. So also did four businessmen from Quito who were attempting to guide us around the jungle. Few of the very different people standing in this circle had a common language. We watched the deer, and no one said much.

5   The deer lay on its side at the rope's very end, so the rope lacked slack to let it rest its head in the dust. It was "pretty," delicate of bone like all deer, and thin-skinned

for the tropics. Its skin looked virtually hairless, in fact, and almost translucent, like a membrane. Its neck was no thicker than my wrist; it was rubbed open on the rope, and gashed. Trying to paw itself free of the rope, the deer had scratched its own neck with its hooves. The raw underside of its neck showed red stripes and some bruises bleeding inside the muscles. Now three of its feet were hooked in the rope under its jaw. It could not stand, of course, on one leg, so it could not move to slacken the rope and ease the pull on its throat and enable it to rest its head.

6   Repeatedly the deer paused, motionless, its eyes veiled, with only its rib cage in motion, and its breaths the only sound. Then, after I would think, "It has given up; now it will die," it would heave. The rope twanged; the tree leaves clattered; the deer's free foot beat the ground. We stepped back and held our breaths. It thrashed, kicking, but only one leg moved; the other three legs tightened inside the rope's loop. Its hip jerked; its spine shook. Its eyes rolled; its tongue, thick with spittle, pushed in and out. Then it would rest again. We watched this for fifteen minutes.

7   Once three young native boys charged in, released its trapped legs, and jumped back to the circle of people. But instantly the deer scratched up its neck with its hooves and snared its forelegs in the rope again. It was easy to imagine a third and then a fourth leg soon stuck, like Brer Rabbit and the Tar Baby.

8   We watched the deer from the circle, and then we drifted on to lunch. Our palm-roofed shelter stood on a grassy promontory from which we would see the deer tied to the tree, pigs and hens walking under village houses, and black-and-white cattle standing in the river. There was even a breeze.

9   Lunch, which was the second and better lunch we had that day, was hot and fried. There was a big fish called *doncella,* a kind of catfish, dipped whole in corn flour and beaten egg, then deep fried. With our fingers we pulled soft fragments of it from its sides to our plates, and ate; it was delicate fish-flesh, fresh and mild. Someone found the roe, and I ate of that too—it was fat and stronger, like egg yolk, naturally enough, and warm.

10   There was also a stew of meat in shreds with rice and pale brown gravy. I had asked what kind of deer it was tied to the tree; Pepe had answered in Spanish, "*Gama.*" Now they told us this was *gama* too, stewed. I suspect the word means merely game or venison. At any rate, I heard that the village dogs had cornered another deer just yesterday, and it was this deer which we were now eating in full sight of the whole article. It was good. I was surprised at its tenderness. But it is a fact that high levels of lactic acid, which builds up in muscle tissues during exertion, tenderizes.

11   After the fish and meat we ate bananas fried in chunks and served on a tray; they were sweet and full of flavor. I felt terrific. My shirt was wet and cool from swimming; I had had a night's sleep, two decent walks, three meals, and a swim— everything tasted good. From time to time each one of us, separately, would look beyond our

shaded roof to the sunny spot where the deer was still convulsing in the dust. Our meal completed, we walked around the deer and back to the boats.

12   That night I learned that while we were watching the deer, the others were watching me.

13   We four North Americans grew close in the jungle in a way that was not the usual artificial intimacy of travelers. We liked each other. We stayed up all that night talking, murmuring, as though we rocked on hammocks slung above time. The others were from big cities: New York, Washington, Boston. They all said that I had no expression on my face when I was watching the deer—or at any rate, not the expression they expected.

14   They had looked to see how I, the only woman, and the youngest, was taking the sight of the deer's struggles. I looked detached, apparently, or hard, or calm, or focused, still. I don't know. I was thinking. I remember feeling very old and energetic. I could say like Thoreau that I have traveled widely in Roanoke, Virginia. I have thought a great deal about carnivorousness; I eat meat. These things are not issues; they are mysteries.

15   Gentlemen of the city, what surprises you? That there is suffering here, or that I know it?

16   We lay in the tent and talked. "If it had been my wife," one man said with special vigor, amazed, "she wouldn't have cared *what* was going on; she would have dropped *everything* right at that moment and gone in the village from here to there to there, she would not have *stopped* until that animal was out of its suffering one way or another. She couldn't *bear* to see a creature in agony like that."

17   I nodded.

18   Now I am home. When I wake I comb my hair before the mirror above my dresser. Every morning for the past two years I have seen in that mirror, beside my sleep-softened face, the blacked face of a burnt man. It is a wire-service photo-graph clipped from a newspaper and taped to my mirror. The caption reads: "Alan McDonald in Miami hospital bed." All you can see in the photograph is a smudged triangle of face from his eyelids to his lower lip; the rest is bandages. You cannot see the expression in his eyes; the bandages shade them.

19   The story, headed MAN BURNED FOR SECOND TIME, begins:

> "Why does God hate me?" Alan McDonald asked from his hospital bed.
> "When the gunpowder went off, I couldn't believe it," he said. "I just
> couldn't believe it. I said, 'No, God couldn't do this to me again.'"

He was in a burn ward in Miami, in serious condition. I do not even know if he lived. I wrote him a letter at the time, cringing.

20   He had been burned before, thirteen years previously, by flaming gasoline. For years he had been having his body restored and his face remade in dozens of

operations. He had been a boy, and then a burnt boy. He had already been stunned by what could happen, by how life could veer.

21   Once I read that people who survive bad burns tend to go crazy; they have a very high suicide rate. Medicine cannot ease their pain; drugs just leak away, soaking the sheets, because there is no skin to hold them in. The people just lie there and weep. Later they kill themselves. They had not known, before they were burned, that the world included such suffering, that life could permit them personally such pain.

22   This time a bowl of gunpowder had exploded on McDonald.

> "I didn't realize what had happened at first," he recounted. "And then I heard that sound from 13 years ago. I was burning. I rolled to put the fire out and I thought, 'Oh God, not again.'
> "If my friend hadn't been there, I would have jumped into a canal with a rock around my neck." His wife concludes the piece, "Man, it just isn't fair."

23   I read the whole clipping again every morning. This is the Big Time here, every minute of it. Will someone please explain to Alan McDonald in his dignity, to the deer at Providencia in his dignity, what is going on? And mail me the carbon.

24   When we walked by the deer at Providencia for the last time, I said to Pepe, with a pitying glance at the deer, *"Pobrecito"*—"poor little thing." But I was trying out Spanish. I knew at the time it was a ridiculous thing to say.

Reading Closely and Thinking Critically

1. In your own words, write a sentence or two that expresses the thesis of "The Deer of Providencia."
2. Describe the way the men react to the deer. How is their reaction different from Dillard's? Why are the men surprised by Dillard's reaction to the deer?
3. Why does Dillard note (in paragraph 10) that high levels of lactic acid tenderize meat?
4. What view of women is referred to in paragraphs 15 and 16?
5. Do you agree with Dillard that *"Pobrecito"* ("poor little thing") was a ridiculous thing for her to say as she walked by the deer? Explain.
6. Why do you think that Dillard kept the picture and article about Alan McDonald?

Examining Structure and Strategy

1. What approach does Dillard take to her introduction (see page 66)?
2. Dillard writes of the deer at Providencia and of Alan McDonald. What do these two have in common? That is, how is it possible to discuss both in the same essay? How does each discussion relate to Dillard's purpose?
3. Which of the descriptive paragraphs are developed primarily with objective detail and which with expressive detail?
4. What attitude toward the deer is Dillard's audience likely to have? How is the reader likely to react to the deer's plight? How does Dillard respond to her audience's probable reaction? How does her response further her purpose?

Noting Combined Patterns

1. Which paragraphs are developed primarily with description?
2. Which paragraphs are developed primarily with narration (storytelling)?

Considering Language and Style

1. Dillard uses descriptive language to portray the deer as fragile. Cite two examples of such language.
2. What is significant about the name of the village (Providencia)?
3. Consult a dictionary if you are unsure of the meaning of any of these words: *watershed* (paragraph 1), *thatch* (paragraph 2), *translucent* (paragraph 5), *spittle* (paragraph 6), *promontory* (paragraph 8), *carnivorousness* (paragraph 14).

For Discussion in Class or Online

With your classmates, consider this question: Do you see a difference between the suffering of the deer and the suffering of Alan McDonald? If so, explain what that difference is. If not, explain why. If your instructor so directs, post your response to your class Web site.

Writing Assignments

1. **In your journal.** At one time, killing animals for food was a necessity, but many people claim that we no longer need to do so, that vegetarianism eliminates the need for animals to suffer and die for us. Attack or defend the killing of animals for food.
2. **Using description for a purpose.** The purposes given in the assignments are possibilities. You may establish whatever purposes you like, within your instructor's guidelines.
   - Like Dillard, describe an animal engaged in some activity. For example, you could describe a kitten at play, a cat washing itself, a dog chasing a ball, or fish swimming in a tank. Use expressive detail to entertain your reader (if the activity is a pleasant one), to relate the animal's experience, and to inform your reader about the animal's level of comfort.
   - If you have experienced considerable pain, describe what you went through. For example, you can describe having a broken leg, a migraine headache, or a sports injury. Your purpose can be to relate your experience, to express your feelings about it, and/or to inform your reader of what the experience was like.
   - To entertain and perhaps inform your reader, describe an animal in its natural habitat or its common surroundings. For example, you can describe a squirrel on the campus commons, a monkey in the zoo, a dog in your yard, or a cat in a pet store.
3. **Combining patterns.** Like Dillard, narrate a story that teaches something about life. Include a considerable amount of description.
4. **Connecting the readings.** Do you think we do enough to reduce suffering in the world? Explain your view. The information in "The Keys of Paradise" (page 193) and "Imagining an Enlightened Social Policy on Drugs" (page 422) might give you some ideas.
5. **Drawing on sources.** Part of "The Deer at Providencia" focuses on the tremendous suffering endured by Alan McDonald. Many people believe that those who are suffering and who have little or no chance to recover should be allowed to request euthanasia, sometimes called "mercy killing." Many others believe that euthanasia is wrong. To examine this controversial issue, summarize the chief arguments on both sides of the euthanasia debate. Use description to provide examples that support either or both sides. If you need a starting point, look up *euthanasia* in the *Social Sciences Index* and the *Humanities Index*. These volumes, located in your library's reference room, will direct you to articles on the subject. If you prefer to use the Internet, type in the keyword *euthanasia* into your favourite search engine. Your search results will lead you to a number of helpful sites.

Additional Essay Assignments
See pages 119 and 121 for strategies for writing description and for a revising checklist.

1. Describe a place you go to relax: a park, a spot on campus, the gym, or the zoo, for example. Try to convey why the place helps you unwind.
2. Describe a character in a story or film. While you may use expressive detail to capture the character's personality, use some objective analysis to consider what that character contributes to the theme or intent of the story, novel, or movie.
3. Describe a view from a window, using expressive detail to convey a dominant impression.
4. Describe a landscape. Use objective details to capture the dominant features of the landscape; then consider how this has influenced the way we have come to use this land.
5. Describe an urban space, using objective details to capture its dominant features. Consider how the appearance of this space influences how people use it.
6. Describe the room you liked best in the house you grew up in. Your dominant impression will be how the room made you feel.
7. Describe a place during a ceremony or holiday celebration. For example, you could describe a pow-wow, picnics and fireworks on July 1, or a mall during the Christmas season.
8. Describe your favourite vacation spot, using expressive detail to convey why you enjoy this place.
9. Describe a winter scene, a fall scene, a spring scene, or a summer scene.
10. Describe one of your classrooms. Try to convey whether or not the room is conducive to learning.
11. Describe your bedroom. Use expressive detail to reveal what the bedroom says about you.
12. Describe a room after a party has been held there.
13. Using objective detail, describe the place where you work to show whether or not your work environment is pleasant.
14. Describe part of an amusement park.
15. Describe your favourite restaurant to persuade other people to try it.
16. Describe the neighbourhood you grew up in to share a portion of your past with your reader.
17. Describe a scene at a sporting event.
18. Describe a rock concert for someone who has never been to one.
19. Describe a painting or sculpture you enjoy.
20. **Description in context:** Assume that you are a student employee in your campus admissions office. As part of its recruiting efforts, the director of admissions is putting together a large, glossy brochure that presents information about the school. You have been asked to contribute to the brochure by photographing a favourite campus spot and writing a description of it. Visit a suitable spot, decide on a dominant impression, and develop your description. Keep in mind that your purpose is to present the campus attractively so that potential students will want to attend your school.

Chapter 5

Narration

Why, you might ask, should we care about how other people think and feel about stories? Why do we talk about them in this language of value? One answer is just that it is part of being human. People tell stories and discuss them in every culture, and we know they have done so back as far as the record goes. The *Iliad* and the *Odyssey*, the *Epic of Gilgamesh*, the *Tale of the Genji*, the Ananse stories I grew up with in Asante, weren't just read or recited: they were discussed, evaluated, referred to in everyday life. We wouldn't recognize a community as human if it had no stories, if its people had no narrative imagination. So one answer to the question why we do it is: it's just one of the things that humans do.

But a deeper answer is that evaluating stories together is one of the central human ways of learning to align our responses to the world. And that alignment of responses is, in turn, one of the ways we maintain the social fabric, the texture of our relationships.

— Kwame Anthony Appiah, *Cosmopolitanism: Ethics in a World of Strangers*

THE PATTERN

Everyone likes a good story. We go to movies for good stories, we read books for good stories, and we gravitate toward people at parties who tell good stories. We tell them to our children before they go to sleep and to our friends when we happen to meet them in a store or on a street corner. Another name for a story is a **narration,** and this chapter will discuss writing effective narration.

USING NARRATION FOR A PURPOSE

Obviously, a narration can *entertain* because a good story can amuse readers and help them forget about themselves for a time. Romance novels and detective fiction are two popular types of stories that provide escapist entertainment. Narration can do more than entertain, however. Say, for example, that for many years you visited your grandfather at a retirement home every week, and as a result you learned much about such facilities. To express your feelings about retirement homes and relate your experience with them, you could narrate an account of your final visit with your grandfather. For this purpose, you would tell what happened during the visit and how the events made you feel. To inform your reader about the benefits of retirement homes, you could narrate an account of a typical day for your grandfather, pointing out the advantages he enjoyed because he lived at the retirement home. To persuade your reader to volunteer at a retirement home, you could narrate an account of one or more of your own experiences as a volunteer and the benefits you and the residents enjoyed as a result.

A brief narration, called an **anecdote,** is often useful as a secondary pattern in other essays. For example, in an exemplification essay, an anecdote can be an example. If you want to illustrate your mother's courage, you can include a moving anecdote about the time she fended off an attack by a mugger. A comparison-contrast that notes the differences between two mayoral candidates can include a telling anecdote about the time you met both candidates at a meeting. A cause-and-effect analysis that explains the effects of the treatment of juveniles in the courts can include a powerful anecdote from the newspaper about a young offender who was jailed with adults for a long period because he could not afford a good lawyer. A process analysis that explains how to surf can tell the story of the time you broke your leg because you failed to follow a procedure you mention in the essay.

Narration at School, at Work, and in the Community

Narration is important in many kinds of university and college writing. For instance, a history paper on the events leading up to the Holocaust can tell the story of "The Night of the Broken Glass," when Jewish homes and businesses were looted and destroyed. A political science paper can narrate an account of the events leading up to Gomery investigation of the Federal Sponsorship scandal in 2004. A women's studies or history paper on women's roles in public office can begin with the story of Nellie McClung and the 1929 Privy Council decision that women were indeed persons under the British North America Act and could be appointed to the Senate. In journalism classes, students write newspaper-style accounts of current events or campus happenings.

Brief narrations, or anecdotes, are particularly useful for illustrating a point. If you write a paper for an education class and argue that people with learning disabilities do not get appropriate support in the classroom, you might tell the story of the time a learning-disabled friend was ignored in a high school algebra class. In a paper for a criminal justice class, you could support your point that judges should give out harsher penalties by telling the story of an offender who was repeatedly released, only to commit more crimes.

Narration is a frequent component of textbooks in most disciplines. Here, for example, is an excerpt from a section of an introduction to psychology text that focuses on sleep and dreams:

> The crowd roared as running back Donald Dorff, age 67, took the pitch from his quarterback and accelerated smoothly across the artificial turf. As Dorff braked and pivoted to cut back over a tackle, a huge defensive lineman loomed in his path. One hundred twenty pounds of pluck, Dorff did not hesitate. But let the retired grocery merchandiser from Golden Valley, Minnesota, tell it:
>
> "There was a 280-pound tackle waiting for me, so I decided to give him my shoulder. When I came to, I was on the floor in my bedroom. I had smashed into the dresser and knocked everything off it and broke the mirror and just made one heck of a mess. It was 1:30 A.M." (Long, 1987, p. 787).
>
> Dorff, it turned out, was suffering from a rare condition afflicting some older men. The problem occurs when the mechanism that usually shuts down bodily movement during dreams does not function properly. People suffering from the malady have been known to hit others, smash windows, punch holes in walls— all while fast asleep. (Feldman, *Understanding Psychology*)

In this example, the textbook author uses narration to illustrate a particular kind of sleep disturbance and how serious its consequences can be. Because the narration comes at the beginning of the section on sleep and dreams and because it is a very interesting story, the narration also creates interest in the discussion to come. Notice how dialogue and description help create that interest.

Narration is also a component of workplace writing. Police officers write crime reports, and insurance investigators write accident reports, both of which narrate sequences of events. Physical therapists and nurses write narrative accounts of their patients' progress, and teachers narrate events for disciplinary reports. Supervisors write narrative accounts of employees' actions for individual personnel files, and company officials use narration to report on the company's performance during the fiscal year for its stockholders.

Outside school and work, you already use narration often and will continue to do so. You may narrate events in your life in letters and email you write to friends and in your diary or journal entries. If you are a recording secretary for an organization, you will write narrative minutes of meetings. In fact, anecdotes appear in all kinds of writing. For example, if you write to a company to complain about a pair of shoes that wore out prematurely, you could narrate an account of what happened when you wore the shoes to work. If you are speaking at a dinner honouring a friend, you could illustrate that friend's kindness with an anecdote about the time she helped a stranger search for his lost dog.

SUPPORTING DETAILS

Your narration should make a point, and your point is tied to your purpose. Without focusing on your point and purpose, you can go off on a narrative tangent, which will cause your readers to scratch their heads and wonder why they are reading your essay. Thus, you should choose supporting details that help your readers see the point of your narration. Say, for example, that you are narrating an account of being accused of shoplifting at the mall. If your point is that sales personnel accused you because you appeared to be poor, and your purpose is to inform your reader that salespeople are biased against the poor, you would emphasize your appearance—your dirty hair and face, torn jeans, oversized T-shirt, and so forth. However, if your point is that you suffered public humiliation and your purpose is to relate an experience and express your feelings, then you may want to emphasize your appearance less than the people who stared at you when you were stopped and accused.

If you are using narrative in an academic essay, it's particularly important to keep your point in mind as you choose your details. Writing an essay about a novel or an historical event, it is easy to get caught up in following one episode with another (and satisfying to see the word count mount up) without considering what this sequence of events *means*. Remember that when you write a thesis statement you must focus on saying something arguable and significant. So when you are writing academic essays with narrative illustrations, you need to decide how you understand the importance of the events *before* you choose which details to include. These details will support your thesis.

A narration usually includes the answers to the **journalist's questions** *who? what? when? where? why?* and *how?* The narrative explains *who* was involved, *what* happened, *when* it happened, *where* it happened, *why* it happened, and *how* it happened. Of course, you may not need to include the answers to each of these questions in every narrative you write, but they are a good starting point for generating ideas. Also, you might emphasize different answers in different narrations. Thus, in some stories you might pay more attention to *who* was involved, but in other stories, you might consider *when* the event happened more significant and treat the time element in more detail. To decide which journalist's questions to emphasize, carefully consider the point of your narration and your purpose.

In addition to the answers to the journalist's questions, narration often includes descriptive detail. When a person's appearance is important to the story, that person will be described; when locale, or scene, is important, a place will be described. For example, in her essay, "Encounter," Carol Shields describes the exhaustion of travelling to explain the importance of the events that follow:

> I had hoped for more; what traveller doesn't? Travelling is expensive, exhausting, and often lonely—the cultural confusion, the acres of concrete, the bitter coffee, the unreadable maps, and the rates of exchange that are almost always unfavourable. And then, like a punishment at the end of the traveller's day, there wait a solitary room, and a bed that, however comfortable, is not your bed. What makes all this worth the effort is the shock of otherness that arrives from time to time, rattling loose your bearings and making you suddenly alert to an altered world.

Note how Shields balances between using language that makes clear how alienated we can feel when we travel in phrases like "acres of concrete" and "unreadable maps," and language that is general enough to apply to anyone's circumstances.

If your reader needs additional information to appreciate the story, you can provide background information or an explanation. For example, in "'You'll Never Believe What Happened' Is Always a Great Way to Start" (p. 465), Thomas King tells us about his father to explain why his stories so often revolve around him:

> My father is a different story. I didn't know him. He left when I was three or four. I have one memory of a man who took me to a small café that had wooden booths with high backs and a green parrot that pulled at my hair. I don't think this was my father, but it might have been.

Dialogue

Dialogue has many uses. You can use someone's words to create a verbal portrait. Dialogue conveys a person's age (through slang), their world-view (through the attitudes expressed), or their idiosyncrasies (through the metaphors used or the colours of speech). Think about how quickly you know characters in movies simply from what they say and how they say it. Dialogue can also be used in narratives to advance the story and make it more vivid. To appreciate what dialogue can add, consider the difference between these examples; the first one is taken from "The Ten Thousand Things"; the second one paraphrases the dialogue:

1. "But I have one [a birth certificate]," I insisted.

    "That was because *my* mother was a midwife," Hazel said. "My mother told the government clerk you born at home." She sipped from her teacup and laughed. "What do they know? What do they care?" Her eyes sparkled with memory. "Those old days! Here was a China baby, just a few weeks old! They maybe think, things done differently in Chinatown! Anyway, nobody care about one more China baby! Everybody worry about the war."

2. Hazel explained that I have a birth certificate because her mother was a midwife who told the authorities he was born at home and because they were more concerned with the war than with one extra Chinese baby.

While the second version contains most of the relevant facts, the dialogue makes the first version more lively, vivid, and interesting. We get a sense of Hazel's character from the way she speaks—Choy has left some of her grammatical irregularities in place—and from the gestures that punctuate her words.

When you write dialogue, follow the conventions for capitalizing and punctuating **quotations,** a speaker's or writer's exact words. The conventions for punctuating quotations are illustrated here, and you can use these examples as models. (Pay particular attention to the location of quotation marks, commas, periods, question marks, and capital letters.) For other situations, consult a writing handbook.

Dialogue and Paragraphing

If you have trouble paragraphing to identify speakers when you write dialogue, use the convention of beginning a new paragraph each time a different person speaks. The paragraph indentation signals the change in speaker, as illustrated by this passage from "The Keys of Paradise" (page 198). In this passage, Dr. Gabor Maté is talking to one of the drug addicts he treats in his clinic:

"Man, I can't face the day without the rock," says Greg, a multi-drug addict in his early forties. "I'm dying for one right now."

"You're not dying *for* it, I venture. "You're dying *because* of it."

Greg is tickled. "Nah, not me. I'm Irish and half Indian."

"Right. There are no dead Irish or dead Indians around."

From Greg, more jollity. "Everybody has to go sometime. When your number comes up, that's it."

If one person speaks for more than a paragraph, begin that speaker's new paragraphs with quotation marks, but use closing quotation marks at the end of the quotation only, not at the end of each paragraph.

When the Quotation Comes Before the Speaker or Writer Is Mentioned

Note that between the quotation and the identification of the speaker, we typically place a comma. It goes within the punctuation marks.

> "Most people overestimate their ability to handle threatening situations," the police officer explained.

> "How will price controls affect foreign trade?" the MP asked. (*Here, we've placed a question mark inside the quotation marks because the speaker is asking a question.*)

When the Quotation Comes After the Speaker or Writer Is Mentioned

Note that a comma goes between the introduction of the speaker and the quotation. It goes outside the quotation marks because it isn't part of the quotation.

> The police officer explained, "Most people overestimate their ability to handle threatening situations."

> The senator asked, "How will price controls affect foreign trade?"

> Do you believe the senator asked, "How will price controls affect foreign trade"? (*The entire sentence, not just the quoted words, forms a question.*)

ORGANIZING DETAILS

If you've ever listened to someone tell a story and drone on and on, you know how important it is to select narrative details carefully to avoid boring your reader with unnecessary information. Choose carefully which *who? what? when? where? why?* and *how?* questions to answer, and be careful not to include insignificant details or over-emphasize minor points. In other words, there are two keys to a successful narrative. One is pacing; you need create an appropriate balance between including important and telling details and moving the story forward at a pace that intrigues your reader. The other is knowing the meaning of your story. The *Oxford English Dictionary* reminds us that the Latin root of "narrate" is both *narrare*, which means "to relate or recount," and *gnarus*, which means "knowing, skilled." Skilled narrators know the meaning of their stories.

One way to communicate the point of your narration is to express it in a thesis, such as the following:

> After my recent experience with a credit card company, I realize that university students should be cautious about accepting those bank cards they get in the mail. *(The narration is about the writer's experience with a credit card company, and the point is that students should be careful about accepting the credit cards that are mailed to them.)*

If a stated thesis will disturb the flow of your story, you can imply rather than state your thesis, but be sure your reader can infer your point from the details you have included. (For more on an implied thesis, see page 51.) Another alternative is to state the point at the end of the narration, so it forms the conclusion of your essay. For example, in "'You'll Never Believe What Happened' Is Always a Great Way to Start," King explains in his final paragraph why he has told us this story:

> I tell the stories not to play on your sympathies but to suggest how stories can control our lives, for there is a part of me that has never been able to move past these stories, a part of me that will be chained to these stories as long as I live.

Arranging narrative details usually involves placing the events in **chronological order.** Most often this means beginning with the first event, moving to the second, on to the third, and so on. Variations of this pattern are possible, however. For some stories, you may want to begin at the end or in the middle, then shift back to the beginning, using **flashback.**

Say, for example, you want to narrate an account of a car accident you were involved in. You could begin with the first event and move forward to the last event, like this:

> A year ago, I was on my way to pick up my girlfriend, looking forward to a pleasant dinner. As I approached the intersection at Fifth and Grove, the light turned yellow, but I figured I had plenty of time to slide through.

After this opening, you would narrate an account of the accident and then go on to tell about its aftermath.

You could also begin at the end and flash back to the beginning, like this:

> As I walked out of my last physical therapy session, I thought about how remarkable it is that I can walk at all. An accident nine months earlier had left me in critical condition with a smashed pelvis.

From here, you would flash back to the beginning and narrate an account of the accident and all the events leading up to the time you walked out of your last physical therapy session.

You could also begin in the middle of the chronology, like this:

I remember waking up in the hospital with my parents and sister at my side. Mom was crying and Dad looked worried. In an instant the pain overwhelmed me and I could not remember what happened. Then all at once I remembered the accident.

From this point in the middle, you would flash back to the beginning and narrate an account of the accident. You would then move chronologically through the events until you reached the last event, walking out of your final physical therapy session.

To signal chronological order, move smoothly through your time sequence, and help your reader follow the events in your narrative, you can use *transitions* such as the following:

at first	later	second
at the same time	meanwhile	soon
in the meantime	next	the next day

When a story is told in chronological order, the time sequence provides a clear structure, so the reader often does not need the organizational signposts provided by topic sentences.

VISUALIZING A NARRATIVE ESSAY

The chart on page 150 can help you visualize the structure for a narrative essay. Like all good models, however, this one can be altered as needed.

PROCESS GUIDELINES: STRATEGIES FOR WRITING NARRATION

1. **Selecting a Topic.** Pick a story that you want to tell for a reason. Rather than tell a story for the sake of telling a story, have a specific purpose in mind: While you'll want to entertain, express feelings, relate experience, inform, or persuade, you should also be aware of the significance of this *particular* story.
2. **Establishing the Point.** Write out a statement of the point of your narration. You can use a version of this statement as your thesis or imply your point through your choice of details.
3. **Generating Ideas.** List the answers to the *who? what? when? where? why?* and *how?* questions. Decide which of these answers should be emphasized, based on your audience and purpose. Also, identify important

Introduction
• Creates interest in the story • States the thesis, which may indicate the point of the story

Body Paragraphs
• Begin the story and continue until the story is complete • Answer the appropriate journalist's questions • May include description • May include background information or explanation • May include dialogue • Arrange details in chronological order, which may include flashback

Conclusion
• Provides a satisfying finish • May state the point of the narration if not done elsewhere

features about the people and scenes of your story. Look for points in the narration where you may want to add these descriptive details.

4. **Drafting.** As you write your first draft, concentrate on getting all the events down on paper or on your computer screen and answering all the appropriate journalist's questions. During revision you can consider using flashback and adding description, transitions, and other elements of an effective essay.

5. **Revising.** Consider adding dialogue to make your narrative more vivid, and decide whether to describe people or scenes. Does the narration make a readily identifiable point? Read your draft aloud; if you hear any abrupt shifts, consider whether transitions are needed.

Troubleshooting Guide

Avoiding Tense Shifts

If you have trouble maintaining tense in narration, edit carefully. A distorted time sequence can confuse your reader. The most common tense shifts in narration occur when the writer moves between the past and present tense inappropriately, like this:

INAPPROPRIATE TENSE SHIFT FROM PAST TO PRESENT	I <u>walked</u> into the classroom and <u>found</u> a seat in the back. As soon as I <u>sit</u> down, Luis <u>cracks</u> a joke.
CORRECTION	I <u>walked</u> into the classroom and <u>found</u> a seat in the back. As soon as I <u>sat</u> down, Luis <u>cracked</u> a joke.

When you write dialogue, moving between the past tense and present tense can be appropriate.

APPROPRIATE TENSE SHIFT	Katrina announced, "I am quitting my job and joining the Peace Corps."

✔ Checklist for Revising Narration

Be sure:

_____ The journalist's questions are answered and appropriately emphasized.

_____ Descriptions of people and scenes are included when they are important.

_____ Dialogue is included where it can advance the narrative and make it more vivid.

_____ Background information required by your reader is included.

_____ Your narration's point is easily determined.

_____ Extraneous details are deleted.

_____ Details are arranged in a chronological or other suitable order.

_____ Transitions help your reader follow the chronology or other order.

ANNOTATED STUDENT ESSAY

In the following essay, student Cari Siebrits shares an account of watching sharks. After you read, you will have an opportunity to evaluate this essay.

Shark Alley

Paragraph 1
This paragraphs sets the scene quite vividly. How effective is the simile, which compares the tossing of the small boat to the tossing of a baseball? What does this simile contribute to the overall mood of the paragraph?

1   A crew member kills the engine. This leaves us passengers uneasy, missing the familiarity of its constant murmur of comfort. Our little boat rocks to and fro, keeping pace with the rolling water. We are idly tossed back and forth between waves, much like a baseball team might toss a ball during an all-too-early morning warm-up. A gleaming sun beats down on our bodies, scalding our fragile skin in spite of the many meticulously distributed layers of sunscreen. Gusts of wind cause the surf to break against the sides of the vessel, while strands of slimy green kelp drift lazily around us. The glint of sunlight on the rough waves creates the illusion of moving through a shimmering sea of crystals.

Paragraph 2
Siebrits doesn't tell us what's happening until the second paragraph. What's the effect of this delay? Again, consider the simile comparing Shark Week to Christmas.

2   The salty breath of the ocean has left my throat dry. Or likely, a combination of the salt air and my anxiety. Don't get me wrong, I was thrilled to be here! I'd pictured this moment for as long as I could remember; for years I had faithfully watched the brave zoologists on *Animal Planet* take the plunge. For me, the Discovery Channel's annual "Shark Week" was better than Christmas. I dreamt of the day it would finally be my turn to get into the cage.

Paragraph 3
What's the purpose of this paragraph? How effective is the closing metaphor?

3   I spot our good-natured skipper, Steve. He seems dressed for the part, sporting a white polo and tan shorts. He jokes with passengers while absentmindedly tossing the chum, the bait, overboard. On today's menu, the blocky, thawing head of an unlucky tuna fish. While passengers mirror each others' identical looks of disgust, hopeful gulls circle hungrily overhead. We are informed that it will only be a matter of time now. The crew leaps into action, helping us squeeze into stiff, skin-tight wetsuits. My breaths grow short and quick, while the butterflies in my stomach busy themselves with what I assume to be either full-fledged aerial combat or a gymnastics routine, consisting of various flips and somersaults.

Paragraph 4
What's the purpose of this brief paragraph? Should Siebrits have expanded any of her ideas here?

4   The spot was appropriately, if unoriginally, named "Shark Alley." Renowned for its enormous population of cape fur seals, it was a location equally popular among tourists and ocean's most lethal predator. Waves continue to lap eagerly at the boat's side, while passengers peer nervously over the edge.

5   Both seagulls and passengers fall silent when the first fin breaks the surface, commanding the attention of land, sky and ocean dwellers alike. More soon follow, and within minutes we find ourselves surrounded by half a dozen ominously circling great white sharks. We watch with a

mixture of fear and awe. The spell is broken when the exuberant skipper asks who wants to go in first.

6   No feeling can compare to lowering yourself into that shark cage. Every part of your body screams for you to get back into the boat, while unpleasant images of *Jaws* flood your mind. The stinging cold of the Atlantic penetrates your wetsuit instantly, leaving you unable to breathe, move, or think clearly. With furiously trembling fingers, you grip the metal bars and lower yourself beneath the swell of the waves. The top of the cage descends, sealing your only pathway to the safety of the surface. Disorientated, you stare intently out into the murky water, past the bits of chum that have broken off and are now floating freely around you. Struck with terror, you await the arrival of the nefarious creatures.

> **Paragraph 6**
> As Siebrits describes getting into the cage, she addresses the reader as "you." What effect does this have on our reaction?

7   Then, always catching you completely off guard, you glimpse the first perilous shadow as it glides towards you. Surprisingly, the fear soon vanishes. Awe quickly overpowers panic; you press your body against the bars and will the figure to come closer. It seems strange, to call a shark graceful or beautiful, but these are the words that seem most fitting. Light rays that have penetrated the ocean surface reflect from their bodies, causing them to glow a pale bluish-white. They aren't aggressive, they don't attack the cage. Instead, they approach cautiously. As they circle the confines of cage, they eye you with notable curiosity. They are exquisite. Ghost-like, they move effortlessly, converging from all directions; left, right, or vertically from the depths below. You feel as though you are part of an extraordinary dream and become completely entranced by the beautiful creatures.

> **Paragraph 7**
> How has her description of the shark challenged the view of sharks we have as a result of watching *Jaws*?

8   When I am finally forced back into the boat, my skin is wrinkled and I'm shaking so uncontrollably that I need to be lifted out of the cage. But I am beaming.

PEER REVIEW

Responding to "Shark Alley"

Evaluate "Shark Alley" by responding to these questions:

1. Does the narration hold your interest? Why or why not?
2. How does Siebrits balance narration and description here?
3. What do you think of the writer's use of similes and metaphors?
4. Is the word choice effective? Should the writer revise for more effective word choice?
5. Does the writer use description effectively? Explain.
6. Is anything unclear?

READING SELECTIONS

Background

Born Carol Warner in Oak Park, Illinois, Carol Shields met her husband Donald while on a college exchange in Scotland. After their marriage they moved to Canada, where she became one of the country's most beloved and most critically acclaimed authors. Her novel *The Stone Diaries* won both a Governor General's Award in 1993 and a Pulitzer Prize in 1995, the only book to have won both those awards. In addition, it was nominated for a Critics' Circle Award and the Orange Prize. Often considered a novelist who understood and celebrated the lives of women and who uncovered what *The Guardian* called "the dramatic in the domestic," Shields turned to the lives of men with equal compassion and insight in *Larry's Party,* which won the Orange Prize and the National Book Critics Circle Award in 1997. Her last novel before her death from breast cancer in 2003 was *Unless.*

The Pattern and Its Purpose

In this selection from a collection of travel writing, Shields attempts to uncover what kind of experience we seek when we travel and perhaps suggests why, in a global economy, such experience is becoming more and more rare. Still, her narrative reveals how people—even when they don't speak the same language or have the same cultural assumptions—manage to touch one another's lives.

Encounter

Carol Shields

> **As you read**
> Consider how someone who seems strange or different can understand what you need or feel.

1   I was in Tokyo to attend a conference, one of a thousand or so delegates—and that probably was my problem: the plasticized name card and the logo of my organization marked me as someone who desired only to be cheerfully accommodated.

2   The allotted two weeks had passed. A single day in Japan remained, and at last I admitted to myself that I was disappointed. The terrible banality of tourist desire invaded me like a kind of flu. Walking the broad, busy boulevards, I caught myself looking too eagerly, too preciously, for minor cultural manifestations—the charming way the bank teller bowed when presenting me with my bundle of cash, the colourful plastic food in the windows of restaurants; these were items I was able to record in my travel journal, touching them up in the way of desperate travellers, shaping them into humorous or appreciative annotation on the Japanese people and the exotic city they inhabited.

3   But Tokyo with its hotels and subways and department stores was a modern industrial complex. Its citizens went to work in the morning, earned money, and travelled home again at night. These homes, to be sure, were impenetrable to me, but the busy working days bore the same rhythms as those found in any large North American city. The traffic noises, the scent of pollution, and the civility of people in the street made me think of—home.

4   I had hoped for more; what traveller doesn't? Travelling is expensive, exhausting, and often lonely—the cultural confusion, the acres of concrete, the bitter coffee, the

unreadable maps, and the rates of exchange that are almost always unfavourable. And then, like a punishment at the end of the traveller's day, there waits a solitary room, and a bed that, however comfortable, is not your bed. What makes all this worth the effort is the shock of otherness that arrives from time to time, rattling loose your bearings and making you suddenly alert to an altered world. But Tokyo was determinedly polite, fulsomely western, a city with a bland, smiling face, ready to welcome me not on its terms but on my own.

5   I already know that the banquet that was to conclude the conference would be a model of French cuisine. Seven courses, seven different wines. No rice, no noodles, no sushi, no hot radish. It was to be held at the famous Imperial Hotel, which was fifteen or twenty minutes' walk from the somewhat less expensive hotel where I was staying.

6   I started out in good time. It was a soft spring evening, and the thought of a leisurely stroll was appealing. I would be able to look around one last time, breathe in a final impression that I could perhaps test against my accumulated disappointment, acquiring some fresh point of perception with which to colour and preserve my Japanese sojourn.

7   At that moment it began to rain. A few drops at first, then it came down in earnest, spotting the silk dinner suit I was wearing and threatening to flatten my carefully arranged hair. I looked about for a taxi or a roof to shelter under, but neither presented itself. The only thing to do, I decided, was to run as quickly as I could the rest of the way.

8   But a tall man was standing directly in front of me, a man with an umbrella. He was smiling tentatively, and gesturing, and his mouth was moving. But what was he saying? I wasn't sure, since the accent was unfamiliar, but it sounded like "Imperial Hotel?" With a question mark behind it. "Yes," I said, nodding and speaking with great deliberation, "Imperial Hotel," and at that he lifted his umbrella slightly, and invited me under.

9   The umbrella was large and black, resolutely standard, the sort of umbrella found in every city or backwater of the world. "Thank you," I said in Japanese—the only phrase I had mastered—but he only repeated what he had said earlier: "Imperial Hotel?" And tipped his head quizzically in an eastward direction. "Yes," I said again. And we began walking.

10   It seemed only polite to make an effort at conversation. Where was he from? Was he with the conference? Was he a stranger in Japan like myself? He shook his head, uncomprehending, and released a shower of words in an unidentifiable language. Now it was my turn to shake my head. After that, smiling, we continued our walk in a contained silence, as though we had each admitted to the other that language was absurd, that rhetoric was a laughable formality that could be set aside for this brief interval.

11   Suddenly careless of social taboos, and because it's difficult for a short woman to walk with a tall man under an umbrella, I took the stranger's arm. (Thinking about this later, I theorized that he must have gestured minutely with his elbow, inviting my intimacy.) Now, arms linked, we were able to walk together smoothly, stepping over and around the puddles without losing our stride, pausing at traffic lights, stepping down from curbs.

12   We had arrived quickly at our congenial gliding pace, left foot, right foot, left foot again, a forward rhythm with a very slight sideways roll like a kind of swimming. Our mutually constrained tongues, the sound of the pelting rain, and our random possession of a random moment in time, seemed to seal us in a temporary vacuum that had nothing to do with Japan, nor with gender or age or with Hollywood notions about men and women walking in the rain. This was good walking, though, I knew that much—walking that transcended mere movement. Hypnotic walking. Walking toward the unimaginable. And I found myself wanting it to go on and on.

13   But there we suddenly were, at the brilliantly lit entrance of the Imperial Hotel, caught in a throng of people arriving and departing, people who had come from every corner of the globe, and trailing after them their separate languages, their lives, their ribbons of chance connection. The stranger with the umbrella abruptly disappeared. I looked around for him but was unable to recall his face, how he had been dressed. One minute he was there and the next minute he'd vanished, leaving me alone with that primary shiver of mystery that travellers, if they're lucky, hope to hang on to: the shock of the known and the unknown colliding in space.

Reading Closely and Thinking Critically

1. What does Shields mean by "the terrible banality of tourist desire" in paragraph 1? Why has Tokyo not assuaged that desire?
2. Travel, as Shields points out, is often difficult, tiring, disorienting, and lonely. Why do we do it?
3. What's the significance of the fact that Shields doesn't know or identify the nationality of the gentleman who shares his umbrella with her?
4. How do we communicate with people when we don't share a language? Describe the way Shields and the strange gentleman manage to establish a common goal.
5. What's the significance of the final sentence? How does it "answer" what Shields has been looking for during her time in Tokyo?

Examining Structure and Strategy

1. Shields begins her essay clearly unsatisfied with her experience of Japan. She has been sheltered by her two-week conference and by the fact that Tokyo seems too typically Western to give her the experience of congenial unfamiliarity she's looking for in her interactions with people and in shop windows. Why is her almost wordless walk to the hotel an antidote for her dissatisfaction?
2. Shields has been in Tokyo for two weeks. Why does she limit her essay to an event that took, perhaps, ten minutes?
3. Why does she devote a whole paragraph to a description of her walk with her partner?

Considering Language and Style

1. In her first paragraph, Shields uses the world "preciously." What does she mean by this?
2. In paragraph 9, Shields describes the gentleman's umbrella as "resolutely standard." What does she mean by this? How does that description belie his surprising gesture?
3. Why does walking with this tall stranger in paragraph 12 transcend mere movement? Why does Shields describe it as "Walking toward the unimaginable"?

For Discussion in Class or Online

North American culture is becoming more culturally heterogeneous. Consider how travel helps us to embrace—rather than to be frightened of—that heterogeneity. If your instructor so directs, post your responses to your class Web site.

Writing Assignments

1. **In your journal.** Write about a trip you made, focussing on the way early disappointment, loneliness, or dissatisfaction was transformed into an occasion to grasp something important about the world outside your everyday experience. If this change never occurred, try to explain why.
2. **Using narration for a purpose.** The purposes given in the assignments are possibilities. You may establish whatever purposes you like, within your instructor's guidelines.
   - To entertain your reader, use narration to tell the story of a surprising encounter with a stranger.
   - Use a narrative to persuade your reader that travel is an important way of encountering an unfamiliar world and finding ways of including it within the circle of your own knowledge.
   - Write an expressive essay that records your frustration or loneliness on a trip. How did you overcome these feelings?
3. **Combining patterns.** Contrast or compare travelling within Canada to travelling abroad. Use narrative to illustrate the differences or similarities.
4. **Connecting the readings.** In Chapter 12, Tim Falconer's essay on "Toronto Cars" suggests how profoundly the car has changed our lives and Wayne Grady suggests how car travel changes our perception of the world in "On Walking." Ask yourself if Shields would have had this experience if she had driven to the hotel; then write a narrative about an experience you could have missed if you have travelled in a car instead of walking or taking public transit.
5. **Drawing on sources.** Travel writing is a genre unto itself. Canada's magazine *The Walrus* opens each issue with a section called "Field Notes," which usually contains two or three travel narratives. Read several of these in two or three issues of *The Walrus* and write your own travel narrative that would be appropriate for "Field Notes."

Background

Wayson Choy was born in Vancouver's Chinatown in 1939. After studying creative writing at UBC and publishing some early stories, he moved to Toronto to teach English and creative writing at Humber College. But he didn't begin his own creative work again until 1977, when he began to expand his short story "The Jade Peony" into his first novel. *The Jade Peony*, published in 1995, was a bestseller and won the prestigious Trillium Award, as did the sequel novel *All That Matters* in 2004. Between these novels he wrote his memoir *Paper Shadows: A Chinatown Childhood*, which was nominated for a Governor General's Award and was a *Globe and Mail* notable book for 1999. Given that his writing is dominated by memories of Vancouver's Chinatown, it comes as no surprise that Choy values storytelling as a way of making human connections. In Sandra Martin's profile of Choy for *Quill and Quire,* she quotes his observation that when he writes he is "wrapped in a world where words matter, because they are allowing me to understand what I am writing, what I have lived, what I have perceived. That is the flashpoint in my head that makes me realize I may be a writer."

The Pattern and Its Purpose

In this excerpt from *Paper Shadows: A Chinatown Childhood,* Choy tells the story of discovering, just before his fifty-seventh birthday, that he was adopted by the people he thought to be his parents. Just as our own complicated lives are composed of multiple strands of narrative, so this discovery reveals that the narratives of his life are more complicated than he had imagined. Choy doesn't try to sort these strands out for us, reducing his life to a handful of simple narratives, but allows the narratives to mix and mingle.

The Ten Thousand Things

Wayson Choy

As you read
Think about the secrets and mysteries every family has.

1   "I saw your mother last week."

2   The stranger's voice on the phone surprised me. She spoke firmly, clearly, with the accents of Vancouver's Old Chinatown: "I saw your *mah-ma* on the streetcar."

3   Not possible. Mother died nineteen years ago.

4   Nineteen years ago I had sat on a St. Paul's hospital bed beside her skeletal frame, while the last cells of her lungs clogged up. She lay gasping for breath: the result of decades of smoking. I stroked her forehead, and with my other hand I clasped her thin motionless fingers. Around two in the morning, half asleep and weary, I closed my eyes to catnap. Suddenly, the last striving for breath shook her thin body. I snapped awake, conscious again of the smell of acetone, of death burning away her body. The silence deepened; the room chilled. The mother I had known all my life was gone.

5   Nineteen years later, in response to a lively radio interview about my first novel, a woman left a mysterious message, URGENT WAYSON CHOY CALL THIS NUMBER.

6   Back at my hotel room, message in hand, I dialled the number and heard an older woman's voice tell me she has seen my mother on the streetcar. She insisted.

7   "You must be mistaken," I said, confident that this woman, her voice charged with nervous energy, would recognize her error and sign off.

8   "No, no, not your mother," the voice persisted. "I mean your *real* mother."

9   "My first crazy," I remember thinking. *The Jade Peony* had been launched just two days before at the Vancouver Writers' Festival, and already I had a crazy. "Watch out for crazies!" my agent had, half-whimsically, warned me. The crazies had declared open season upon another of her clients, a young woman who had written frankly of sexual matters. I was flattered, hardly believing that my novel about Vancouver's Old Chinatown could provoke such perverse attention. Surely, my caller was simply mistaken.

10   "I saw your *real* mother," the voice insisted, repeating the word "real" as if it were an incantation.

11   My *real* mother? I looked down at the polished desk, absently studied the Hotel Vancouver room-service menu. My real mother was dead; I had been there to witness her going. I had come home that same morning nineteen years ago and seen her flowered apron carefully draped over the kitchen chair, folded precisely, as it had been every day of my life. I remember taking the apron, quickly hiding it from my father's eyes as he, in his pyjamas, shuffled on his cane into the kitchen. Seeing the apron missing from the chair, he asked, "She's—?" but could not finish the question. He stood staring at the back of the chair. He leaned his frail eighty-plus years against me. Speechless, I led him back to his bed.

12   The voice on the hotel phone chattered on, spilling out details and relationships, talking of Pender *Gai*[1] and noting how my brand-new book talked of the "secrets of Chinatown." I suddenly caught my family name pronounced distinctively and correctly, *Tuey*. Then my grandfather's, my mother's, and my father's formal Chinese names, rarely heard, sang into my consciousness over the earpiece.

13   "Yes, yes," the voice went on, "those are your family names?"

14   "Yes, they are," I answered, "but who are you?"

15   "Call me Hazel," she said.

16   Months later, Hazel turned up to be interviewed; we had tea, some dumplings, and bowls of *jook*.[2] In 1939, when she herself was in her teens, Hazel had taken care of a baby named *Way Sun*. Her family home had been a kind of short-term foster home for in-transit Chinatown children. It was 1939, the year of the Royal Visit, and Hazel's own mother had desperately wanted to see the King and Queen parade down Hastings and Granville streets.

17   "That's why I remember your name," Hazel said. She proved to be a friendly, talkative woman in her late sixties, wisps of grey hair floating about her. "Unusual name, *Way Sun*. Your new mother worried that you wouldn't have a birth certificate.

---

[1]Street (pron. "guy").
[2]Rice gruel.

18   "But I have one," I insisted.

19   "That was because *my* mother was a midwife," Hazel said. "My mother told the government clerk you born at home." She sipped from her teacup and laughed. "What do they know? What do they care?" Her eyes sparkled with memory. "Those old days! Here was a China baby, just a few weeks old! They maybe think, things done differently in Chinatown! Anyway, nobody care about one more China baby! Everybody worry about the war."

20   A few months before Hazel and I met, I had cornered my two aunts, to whom I had dedicated my book. Was I adopted, I wanted to know, as Hazel had told me? My two aunts looked at each other. In an interview with me, the reporter from *Maclean's* magazine had noted that "a caller" had left me perplexed about my birth. Surely Aunt Freda and Aunt Mary knew the truth.

21   I had written a novel about the secrets of Chinatown, and in the kaleidoscope of my life, one single phone call had altered the picture significantly, shifted all the pieces: my life held secrets, too. This real-life drama beginning to unfold, this eerie echo of the life of one of my fictional characters, seemed absurd. Suddenly, nothing of my family, of home, seemed solid and specific. Nothing in my past seemed to be what it had always been.

22   During the Depression and the War years, the trading and selling of children, especially the giving and taking of male children, were not uncommon practices either of Old China or of the Old Chinatowns of North America. Canada's 1923 Exclusion Act and similar racist laws passed earlier in the United States all forbade the immigration of Chinese women and children. Thus, there were only limited numbers of Chinese families in North America. Chinatowns became social and sexual pressure cookers; bachelor-men dominated the population. Children were being born, wanted and unwanted. Scandals and suicides multiplied. Family joys were balanced by family suffering.

23   In the hothouse climate of Vancouver's Chinatown in the 1920s, '30s, and mid-'40s, children were born and kept mainly within their own families, or family tongs;[3] however, a secret few were sold, traded, or given away to fill a childless couple's empty nest, or to balance a family that lacked a first-born son to carry on their kinship name; family pride and Confucian tradition[4] demanded a son to inherit the family artefacts. And so, I must have been sold, traded, or given away to balance my adoptive parents' empty nest. I was to be the only child, a son, heir to the family name and worldly goods.

_____

[3]Associations, often secret.
[4]Philosophical system named for Confucius (551–479 B.C.E.)

24   My adopted parents had both died, believing that I would never discover that they were not my birth parents, that my memory of home had been fraudulent in a sense, lovingly fraudulent. Now the truth was trickling out. The ground shifted under me. Was it true? Was I adopted?

25   As the airport restaurant where we spoke, my two aunts looked sheepishly at each other, and then, eyes full of loving concern, they turned to look at me. I said nothing. At last, Freda confessed, "Yes, yes, you are adopted." Mary quickly added, "So what? To me, you're just as much a part of our family."

26   "You're even better than that!" Freda laughed. "You were chosen. We just got born into the damn family!"

27   I didn't laugh. Hearing them confirm Hazel's claim made me pause: all those years that I had taken "home" for granted. . . . A long drawn-out sigh escaped from me: I had become an orphan three weeks before my fifty-seventh birthday. I glanced at the date registered on my watch.

28   "Tomorrow is April Fool's Day," I finally said, voice maudlin. Then, barely able to contain ourselves, we all three burst out laughing.

29   "Life has no beginning . . . nor ending." The man whom I thought was my father had said this to me three days before he died. "Good things go on being good," he said, sighing that long sigh that I had learned from him. "Bad things go on being bad."

30   Unlike the woman whom I had thought was my mother, the man whom I'd taken for my father was not afraid to talk of other mysteries and losses, of life past, and even of his own eventual dying that summer's end at St. Paul's Hospital.

31   In this hospital, throughout the '30s, the nuns had lobbied the city fathers and the health authorities to admit the people of Chinatown into its ill-lit, mildewed basement. In this hospital, the Chinese and other undesirables—"Resident Aliens"—were to be nursed back to health or to die there, at least in the care of God's holy servants. *His* father died there, in the basement; and in September of 1982, the man I had known as *my* father ended his life, at eighty-five, of a stomach cancer he accepted as the last indignity.

32   He stayed, not in the basement, but in a sixth-floor bed that looked over the West End, in a newly built wing of St. Paul's, in a room that was flooded with morning light, free of dampness and mildew. His eyes had grown too cloudy to see anything but light. I rubbed his back with mineral oil, his skin like a baby's. He barely smiled. He had been happy to greet my friend Marie, who had flown in from Toronto to be with both of us. That last evening, with Marie's gentle encouragement, he accepted from me a spoonful of fruit salad. He took into his dry mouth a seedless grape, but would not swallow.

33   The next morning at eight o'clock, when he died, a torrential rainstorm lashed the city. Marie, so beloved of my father, touched my father's stiff hands and brought

them together. As his only son, I kissed his still-warm forehead and marvelled at life and death.

34   I did not know then that he was not my *real* father; I only knew that this old man—whose outward frailty betrayed the tough spirit within—was the man I had loved as my father all my life. There was no other.

35   Since hearing from Hazel, I have thought often of the Chinese phrase "the ten thousand things," whose number symbolically suggests how countless are the ways of living and dying, how much of love and life cannot be fathomed. And I have thought of the Cantonese opera.

36   "My Aunt Helena says that your father was a member of one of the opera companies," Hazel told me, much later, in her young-again, excited voice.

37   On my behalf, Hazel had been earnestly digging up as much information from the Elders as she could. She had already learned that the person she thought was my *real* mother, the old woman she saw on the streetcar, was not my real mother after all. She, it turns out, had died decades ago. And, yes, the man who fathered me was a member of one of the opera companies. Alas, there was no more information; at least, no more was revealed by the Elders. Not even Mrs. Lee, a best friend of my adoptive parents, would admit she knew anything. So much you can know, and no more.

38   For the past two years, long before Hazel's first telephone call sent her seismic quake through my world, I had been, ironically, researching the Cantonese Opera, especially the touring Chinese opera companies that had thrived all through the '30s and '40s from Canton to Hong Kong, from San Francisco to Seattle to Vancouver, the semi-professional companies that formed "the Bamboo Circuit." My second novel, the one I'm writing now, is centred around the Vancouver opera companies of Old Chinatown.

39   Since childhood, I had been enthralled with the high drama and acrobatics of Chinese opera. The woman who was known to me as my mother had taken me to see the operas and then, afterwards, to visit Shanghai Alley and the smoky backstage of the opera company. There, among jewelled headpieces, gleaming costumes, and prop curtains, she played mah-jong[5] with members of the troop, while I was being spoiled by sweetmeats or left alone to play with costumed opera dolls with fierce warrior faces. Alone, I became a prince and a warrior, my parents the Emperor and Empress. All the adventures of the world were possible, and I the hero of them all. Finally, I remember the laughter and sing-song voices, the *clack-click* of the bamboo and ivory game tiles, lulling me to sleep.

---

[5]A game for four, played with 144 tiles.

40　Even today I recall, as a child, dreaming of the fabled opera costumes, how they swirled to glittering life, how I flew acrobatically through the air between spinning red banners and clouds of yellow silk and heard the roar and clanging of drums and cymbals. And how I fought off demons and ghosts to great applause. Were those dreams in my blood?

41　"The way things were in those old days," Hazel said, pushing back a strand of her salt-and-pepper hair, "best to let the old stories rest. Your father belonged to the opera company, that's what my Aunt Helena says."

42　For the past two summers, I had pored over the tinted cast and production photos of the opera companies in Vancouver. For intense seconds, without realizing it, I must have caught a smile, a glimpse of a hairline as familiar as my own; I must have seen eyes looking back through the photographer's plates, eyes like my own: I might have seen, staring back at me, the man who surely was my father. I cannot help myself: I imagine the man who fathered me, dressed in imperial splendour, sword in hand; he is flying above me, majestic and detached, If I were seventeen, and not fifty-seven, would I weep to know that this man abandoned me?

43　"Best to let the stories rest," Hazel repeated.

44　And so I do, I let the stories rest, though not quite. My writer's mind races on, unstoppable. I had always thought of my family, my home, in such a solid, no-nonsense, no-mystery manner, how could I possibly think that the untold stories would never be told?

45　I think of myself as the child I was, playing with the fierce-faced dolls among the backstage wooden swords and stretched drums of the opera company. I see myself, five years old, being watched and wondered at by a tall figure behind me, a figure who slips away if I turn my head towards him. Was that the man who fathered me? And perhaps a woman—the birth mother—raises her hand at the mah-jong table and smiles at me, briefly noting how blessed my life now seems. How lucky I am, to share the fate of the man and woman I came to know as Mother and Father, decent and good people, who, all my life, loved me as their own.

46　I marvel that the ten thousand things should raise questions I never thought to ask, should weave abiding mystery into my life. How did most of us come to think of parents and family and home, as if there were no mysteries, really? How did most of us contrive for decades to speak neither of the unknown nor of the knowable? And how, with the blessing of a community that knew when to keep silent and when—at last—to speak up, I am come home again, like a child, opened up again to dreams and possibility.

47　At home, I turn on my computer to begin tapping out the second novel; in the middle of a sentence—like this one, in fact—I laugh aloud. I had been writing fiction about life in Chinatown; Chinatown, all these years, had been writing me.

Reading Closely and Thinking Critically

1. Most of us assume that the stories of our childhood are intimate family stories barely connected to larger historical forces or circumstances. In what ways does Choy discover that his childhood has been profoundly shaped by historical circumstances, cultural forces, and government policies? How does this discovery relate to the final sentence of the essay?

2. What is Choy trying to articulate when he queries of his writerly interest in the Chinese opera, "Were those dreams in my blood?" When we think about our characters or curiosities or abilities, how do we distinguish between "nature," and some inherited predisposition or gift, and "culture," the way our upbringings have shaped us? Do we favour one over the other? Why? What does this tell us about the way we conceive our "selves"?

3. In paragraph 43, Hazel suggests it is "best to let the stories rest." If that's the case, why has she started Choy on this quest for his origins?

4. In paragraph 44 Choy remarks, "I had always thought of my family, my home, in such a solid, no-nonsense, no-mystery manner, how could I possibly think that the untold stories would never be told?" Two paragraphs later he asks, "How did most of us come to think of parents and family and home, as if there were no mysteries, really?" Why are we all torn between believing there are no mysteries in our lives and searching to uncover mysteries of whose existence we are certain?

Examining Structure and Strategy

Several narratives are intertwined in this essay: the story of Choy's meeting with Hazel and his uncovering some of the secrets of his past, the stories of both his parents' deaths, and the meeting with his aunts, who admit that he was adopted. This interweaving leads us to ask a number of questions.

1. Why doesn't Choy present a single narrative in chronological order, beginning with his mother's death, going on to his father's death, his phone conversation with Hazel, his query of his aunts, and then his meeting with Hazel and the fact she subsequently uncovered at his request? Why are the facts of his life woven in and out of his conversation with Hazel?

2. How has Hazel's assertion that Choy was adopted put these various stories into a different perspective?

Considering Language and Style

1. Consider carefully Choy's descriptions of his mother's death in paragraph 4, of his father's response to her death in paragraph 11, and of his father's death in paragraphs 29 through 34. Remembering that writers create a dominant impression through details, point out the details that capture most clearly Choy's love for these two people and his reaction to their deaths.

2. Choy uses numerous metaphors to suggest how he feels about the way Hazel's information affects his frame of mind. In paragraph 21, he writes that "in the kaleidoscope of my life, one single phone call has altered the picture significantly, shifted all the pieces." In paragraph 38, he observes that Hazel's first telephone call had sent a "seismic quake through my world." What purposes do these metaphors serve?

3. In paragraphs 27 and 28, Choy observes first that he'd become "an orphan three weeks before his fifty-seventh birthday" and that the next day was "April Fool's Day." What does his expression here tell you about his frame of mind?

4. In paragraph 29, Choy quotes his father's saying, "Life has no beginning . . . nor ending." He later refers to the expression that gives this essay its title, "the ten thousand things," which encapsulates the complexity of life. How do these two expressions represent Choy's purpose in this essay?

For Discussion in Class or Online

Are the childhoods of some groups of people (such as immigrants or women) more likely to be profoundly influenced by historical or cultural events, or are we all equally vulnerable to having our childhood taken over and shaped by its historical context? If your instructor so directs, post your responses on your class Web site.

Writing Assignments

1. **In your journal.** If you could tell a friend only one story that explained the complexity of your childhood, what would it be? Tell the story without explaining its significance to see if that can be conveyed by the story itself.

2. **Using narration for a purpose.** The purposes given in the assignments are possibilities. You may establish whatever purposes you like, within your instructor's guidelines.

   • To express feelings and relate experience, tell the story of a discovery that shifted your sense of who you are.

   • To express feelings and relate experience, tell a story that illustrates your ties to previous generations of your family.

   • To inform your reader, tell the story about yourself, a close friend, or a family member that illustrates the way our seemingly innocent youths are coloured by larger historical or cultural forces.

3. **Combining patterns.** Using narration and contrast-comparison, tell two stories of people from two generations, arguing either that little about childhood changes over time or that over the years childhood changes profoundly.

4. **Connecting the readings.** Both Wayson Choy in "The Ten Thousand Things" and Thomas King in "'You'll Never Believe What Happened' Is a Great Way to Begin a Story" find themselves drawn to the gaps and the mysteries in the narratives about their early lives with their parents. Realistically, we know we can never retrieve all the facts about our early years, yet we keep trying to know more. In your introductory paragraphs, discuss what drives Choy and King to recreate stories; in the remainder of your essay, use a narrative recovered by you, a family member, or an acquaintance to explain what illumination we are all looking for.

5. **Drawing on sources.** Read several memoirs from *The Vintage Book of Canadian Memoirs*. Using these and "The Ten Thousand Things" as examples, discuss how memoirs accomplish what Kwame Anthony Appiah, the writer quoted at the beginning of this chapter, argues is one of the most important tasks of stories: to maintain the social fabric and connect us to the people around us.

Background

Natalie Kusz is the author of the memoir *Road Song* (1990) and of essays published in *Harper's, Threepenny Review, McCall's, Allure* (where "Ring Leader" was first published in 1990), and other periodicals. Her work has earned, among others, a Whiting Writer's Award, a Pushcart Prize, and fellowships from the NEA, the Bush Foundation, and the Bunting Institute of Radcliffe College. A former faculty member of Bethel College and Harvard University, she now teaches in the MFA (master of fine arts) program at Eastern Washington University.

Combined Patterns and Their Purposes

In "Ring Leader," Natalie Kusz relates her experience as an unconventional adolescent and adult and expresses her feelings about her physical appearance. Using narration, she tells something about herself, first as a high school student and then as a college teacher. Using cause-and-effect analysis, she explains what led her to get her nose pierced and the results of that action.

Ring Leader

Natalie Kusz

1   I was thirty years old when I had my right nostril pierced, and back-home friends fell speechless at the news, lapsing into long telephone pauses of the sort that June Cleaver would employ if the Beave had ever called to report, "Mom, I'm married. His name's Eddie." Not that I resemble a Cleaver or have friends who wear pearls in the shower, but people who have known me the longest would say that for me to *draw* attention to my body rather than to work all out to *repel* it is at least as out of character as the Beave's abrupt urge for his-and-his golf ensembles. A nose ring, they might tell you, would be my last choice for a fashion accessory, way down on the list with a sag-enhancing specialty bra or a sign on my butt reading "Wide Load."

As you read
Notice the humour in the essay. Try to determine what purpose that humour serves.

2   The fact is, I grew up ugly—no, worse than that, I grew up unusual, that unforgivable sin among youth. We lived in Alaska, where, despite what you might have heard about the Rugged Individualist, teenagers still adhere to the universal rules of conformity: If Popular Patty wears contact lenses, then you will by gum get contacts too, or else pocket those glasses and pray you can distinguish the girls' bathroom door from the boys'. The bad news was that I had only one eye, having lost the other in a dog attack at age seven; so although contacts, at half the two-eyed price, were easy to talk my parents into, I was still left with an eye patch and many facial scars, signs as gaudy as neon, telling everyone, "Here is a girl who is Not Like You." And Not Like Them, remember, was equivalent to Not from This Dimension, only half (maybe one third) as interesting.

> "The fact is, I grew up ugly— no, worse than that,
> I grew up unusual, that unforgivable sin. . . ."

3   The rest of my anatomy did nothing to help matters. I come from a long line of famine-surviving ancestors—on my father's side, Polish and Russian, on my mother's, everything from Irish to French Canadian—and thus I have an excellent, thrifty, Ebenezer Scrooge of a metabolism. I can ingest but a single calorie, and before quitting time at the Scrooge office, my system will have spent that calorie to replace an old blood cell, to secrete a vital hormone, to send a few chemicals around the old nervous system, and still have enough left over to deposit ten fat cells in my inner thigh—a nifty little investment for the future, in case the Irish potato famine ever recurs. These metabolic wonders are delightful if you are planning a move to central Africa, but for an American kid wiggling to Jane Fonda* as if her life depended on it (which, in high school, it did), the luckiest people on earth seemed to be anorexics, those wispy and hollow-cheeked beings whose primary part in the locker room drama was to stand at the mirror and announce, "My God, I disgust myself, I am *so fat*." While the other girls recited their lines ("No, Samantha, don't talk like that, you're beautiful, you really *are!*"), I tried to pull on a gym shirt without removing any other shirt first, writhing inside the cloth like a cat trapped among the bedsheets.

4   Thus, if you add the oversized body to the disfigured face, and add again my family's low income and my second-hand wardrobe, you have a formula for pure, excruciating teenage angst. Hiding from public scrutiny became for me, as for many people like me, a way of life. I developed a bouncy sense of humor, the kind that makes people say, "That Natalie, she is always so *up*," and keeps them from probing for deep emotion. After teaching myself to sew, I made myself cheap versions of those Popular Patty clothes or at least the items (*never* halter tops, although this was the seventies) that a large girl could wear with any aplomb. And above all, I studied the other kids, their physical posture, their music, their methods of blow-dryer artistry, hoping one day to emerge from my body, invisible. I suppose I came as close to invisibility as my appearance would allow, for if you look at the year-book photos from that time, you will find on my face the same "too cool to say 'cheese'" expression as on Popular Patty's eleven-man entourage.

"Hiding from public scrutiny became . . . a way of life."

5   But at age thirty, I found myself living in the (to me) incomprehensible politeness of America's Midwest, teaching at a small private college that I found suffocating, and anticipating the arrival of that all-affirming desire of college professors everywhere, that professional certification indicating you are now "one of the family": academic tenure. A first-time visitor to any college campus can easily differentiate between tenured and nontenured faculty by keeping in mind a learning institution's two main expectations: (1) that a young professor will spend her first several years on the job proving herself indispensable (sucking up), working to advance the interests of the

---

*Jane Fonda's exercise videos were very popular in the 1980s and early 1990s.

college (sucking up), and making a name for herself in her field of study (sucking up); and (2) that a senior, tenured professor, having achieved indispensability, institutional usefulness, and fame will thereafter lend her widely recognized name to the school's public relations office, which will use that name to attract prospective new students and faculty, who will in turn be encouraged to call on senior professors for the purpose of asking deep, scholarly questions (sucking up). Thus, a visitor touring any random campus can quickly distinguish tenured faculty persons from nontenured ones simply by noting the habitual shape and amount of chapping of their lips.

6   I anticipated a future of senior-faculty meetings with academia's own version of Popular Patty—not a nubile, cheerleading fashion plate, but a somber and scholarly denture wearer who, under the legal terms of tenure, cannot be fired except for the most grievous unprofessional behavior, such as igniting plastique under the dean's new Lexus. When that official notice landed in my In box, my sucking-up days would be over. I would have arrived. I would be family.

7   I couldn't bear it. In addition to the fact that I possessed all my own teeth, I was unsuited to Become As One with the other tenured beings because I was by nature boisterous, a collector of Elvis memorabilia, and given to not washing my car—in short, I was and always would be from Alaska.

8   Even in my leisure hours, my roots made my life of that period disorienting. Having moved to the immaculate Midwest from the far-from-immaculate wilderness, I found myself incapable of understanding, say, the nature of cul-de-sacs, those little circles of pristine homes where all the children were named Chris, and where all the parents got to vote on whether the Johnsons (they were all Johnsons) could paint their house beige. I would go to potluck suppers where the dishes were foreign to me, and twelve people at my table would take a bite, savor it with closed eyes, and say, "Ah, Tater Tot casserole. Now *that* takes me back." It got to the point where I felt defensive all the time, professing my out-of-townness whenever I was mistaken for a local, someone who understood the conversational subtexts and genteel body language of a Minnesotan. Moreover, I could never be sure what I myself said to these people with my subtextual language or my body. For all I knew, my posture during one of those impossible kaffeeklatsches proclaimed to everyone, "I am about to steal the silverware," or "I subscribe to the beliefs of Reverend Sun Myung Moon."

9   I grew depressed. Before long, I was feeling nostalgic for Alaskan eccentricities I had avoided even when I had lived there—unshaven legs and armpits, for example, and automobiles held together entirely by duct tape. I began decorating my office with absurd and nonprofessional items: velvet paintings, Mr. Potato Head, and a growing collection of snow globes from each of the fifty states. Students took to coming by to play with Legos, or to blow bubbles from those little circular wands, and a wish started to grow in my brain, a yearning for some way to transport the paraphernalia around with me, to carry it along as an indication that I was truly unconventional at heart.

"Before long, I was feeling nostalgic for Alaskan eccentricities . . ."

10   So the week that I received tenure, when they could no longer fire me and when a sore nose would not get bumped during the course of any future sucking-up maneuver, I entered a little shop in the black-leather part of town and emerged within minutes with my right nostril duly pierced. The gesture was, for me, a celebration, a visible statement that said, "Assume nothing. I might be a punk from Hennepin Avenue, or a belly dancer with brass knuckles in my purse." Polite as was the society of that region, my colleagues never referred to my nose, but I could see them looking and wondering a bit, which was exactly the thing I had wanted—a lingering question in the minds of the natives, the possibility of forces they had never fathomed.

11   After this, my comfort level changed some, and almost entirely for the better. I had warned my father, who lived with me those years, that I was thinking of piercing my nose. When I arrived home that day and the hole was through the side instead of the center—he had expected, I found out, a Maori-style bone beneath the nostrils—he looked at me, his color improved, and he asked if I wanted chicken for dinner. So that was all fine. At school, students got over their initial shock relatively quickly, having already seen the trailer-park ambience of my office, and they became less apt to question my judgment on their papers; I could hear them thinking, She looks like she must understand *something* about where I'm coming from. And my daughter—this is the best part of all—declared I was the hippest parent she knew, and decided it was O.K. to introduce me to her junior high friends; even Cool Chris—the Midwestern variety of Popular Patty—couldn't boast a body-pierced mom.

12   I have since moved away from Minnesota, and old friends (those of the aforementioned June Cleaver–type stunned silence) have begun to ask if I have decided to stop wearing a nose stud now that my initial reason for acquiring it has passed. And here, to me, is the interesting part: the answer, categorically, is no. Nonconformity, or something like it, may have been the initial reason behind shooting a new hole through my proboscis, but a whole set of side effects, a broad and unexpected brand of liberation, has provided me a reason for keeping it. Because the one-eyed fat girl who couldn't wear Popular Patty's clothes, much less aspire to steal her boyfriends, who was long accustomed to the grocery-store stares of adults and small children ("Mommy, what happened to that fat lady's face?"), who had learned over the years to hide whenever possible, slathering her facial scars with cover stick, is now—am I dreaming?—in charge. I have now, after all, deliberately chosen a "facial flaw," a remarkable aspect of appearance. Somehow now, the glances of strangers seem less invasive, nothing to incite me to nunhood; a long look is just that—a look—and what of it? I've invited it, I've made room for it, it is no longer inflicted upon me against my will.

Reading Closely and Thinking Critically

1. Why does Kusz get her nose pierced?
2. What were the various reactions to the author's pierced nose? Why did people react the way they did?
3. In paragraph 2, Kusz says that among youth, looking unusual is worse than being ugly. What does she mean?
4. Did Kusz fit in as a faculty member? Explain.
5. Kusz felt self-conscious about her appearance, and that self-consciousness influenced her behaviour. How did it influence her behaviour as an adolescent? As an adult?

Examining Structure and Strategy

1. How does Kusz use flashback? How does the flashback help the author achieve her purpose?
2. What words describe the tone of the essay? (See page 77 on tone.)
3. What purpose does the humour in the essay serve? How does that purpose compare to the purpose humour served in the author's life?

Noting Combined Patterns

1. Where does Kusz use cause-and-effect analysis? (Cause-and-effect analysis is explained in Chapter 10.)
2. Do you consider "Ring Leader" a cause-and-effect analysis with elements of narration, or a narration with elements of cause-and-effect analysis? Explain.

Considering Language and Style

1. In paragraph 1, Kusz refers to characters from *Leave It to Beaver,* a popular television program of the late '50s and early '60s that depicted middle-class whites in an overly wholesome way. June Cleaver was the ideal wife and mother. Her son Beaver was an all-American child. Friend Eddie was a troublemaker. How does Kusz use these references?
2. Explain the metaphor and simile that appear in paragraph 3. How does Kusz use these figures of speech?
3. Consult a dictionary if you are unsure of the meaning of any of these words: *angst* (paragraph 4), *aplomb* (paragraph 4), *entourage* (paragraph 4), *nubile* (paragraph 6), *plastique* (paragraph 6), *cul-de-sacs* (paragraph 8), *kaffeeklatsches* (paragraph 8), *ambience* (paragraph 11), *proboscis* (paragraph 12).

For Discussion in Class or Online

Body piercing and tattooing have become popular in recent years, particularly among young people. With your classmates, discuss why you think these practices are so popular. If your instructor so directs, post your responses to your class Web site.

Writing Assignments

1. **In your journal.** When you were in high school, how did you feel about your appearance? To what extent did that feeling affect your behaviour then, and how does it affect you now? Answer in a page or two.
2. **Using narration for a purpose.** The purposes given in the assignments are possibilities. You may establish whatever purposes you like, within your instructor's guidelines.
    *   To relate your experience and perhaps express your feelings, narrate a story that reveals something about what high school was like for you.
    *   In paragraph 4, Kusz refers to teenage angst. What is angst? Do some searching of the Internet to understand this word. Then narrate an account of a time when you or a friend suffered from teenage angst. Your purpose is to inform your reader, and relate your experience.

- Narrate a story that reveals you or someone you know as unconventional to inform your reader about the nature of the person who is your subject. Be sure to consider the context that created the need or desire to rebel against convention. Attempt to explain why the context created that need.
- Tell a story about a time you did not fit in to relate your experience and perhaps express your feelings.

3. **Combining patterns.** Kusz notes that in addition to being affected by her physical appearance, she was shaped by living in Alaska. Use narration and cause-and-effect analysis to tell a story that illustrates how you were affected by the town or neighbourhood where you grew up. If you like, you can also explain why the town affected you the way it did. (Cause-and-effect analysis is explained in Chapter 9.)

4. **Connecting the readings.** Discuss the connection between our self-concepts and how the world judges us. To what extent does society's view of us as an outsider or as someone who is not "normal" influence how we feel about ourselves? In addition to the ideas in "Ring Leader," the ideas in "The Keys of Paradise" (page 193) may be helpful.

5. **Drawing on sources.** Many people have body image problems because they look in the mirror and do not like what they see, even though they look perfectly fine. Some people speculate that the impossible standard of beauty presented in magazine and television advertisements contributes to body image problems. Study a sampling of advertisements in magazines and on television and then agree or disagree with this speculation. You can also look in the *Social Sciences Index* under the heading "body image."

Additional Essay Assignments
See pages 149–151 for strategies for writing narration and for a revision checklist.

1. Narrate an account of an event that caused you to change your view of someone or something. It might be useful to the academic writing you do in other classes to relate the story of a class reading or lecture that changed your views.

2. Examine an element of our culture that we take for granted—the Internet or cell phones, for example. Write a narrative that explains the changes—positive and negative—that occurred in an individual's life when he or she acquired Internet access at home or finally bought a cellphone.

3. Narrate an account of the discovery or development of a common part of our current culture. You might consider the use of computer-generated graphics in film or computer games, or animation techniques. Ensure that your thesis statement outlines the significance of this development.

4. Tell the story of a time when things did not go as you expected them to.

5. Narrate the events of a movie, graphic novel, or conventional novel as a way of explaining the surprising transformation of a character. Make sure your thesis makes reference to this change and that you keep the character's change in mind as you write your essay. Avoid simple plot summary.

6. Tell the story of an event that marked a turning point in your life. Be sure to indicate how you were affected by this event.

7. Tell the story of a time when you displayed or witnessed courage.

8. Tell the story of an athletic event in which you were involved.

9. Tell the story of a disappointment someone you know experienced.

10. Tell a story that shows that people can be cruel (or kind).

11. Tell a story that shows that we rely heavily on technology.

12. Tell the story of a time that you or someone you know overcame an obstacle.

13. Tell the story of a time when hard work did (or did not) pay off.

14. Tell a story about a school experience you have had.

15. Tell a story that reveals a personality trait of someone. For example, if you have a friend who is reckless, tell a story that illustrates that recklessness. Try to use description and dialogue.

16. Tell a story that shows that things are not always what they seem.

17. Tell a story that shows that some modern device (the car, the DVD player, the computer, the microwave, for example) is more trouble than it is worth. If you like, you can make the narration humorous.

18. Tell a story that shows we should be careful of what we wish for because we may get it.

19. Narrate an account of a difficult decision that you had to make. Be sure to indicate the effect the decision had on you.

20. **Narration in context.** Assume that you are contributing a piece for a "My Life" column in your campus newspaper. The piece will be a narration about a first-time experience: the first time you drove a car, a first kiss, your first day of college or university, your first job, your first time away from home, and so on. If you want, you can make the narration humorous. To come up with ideas, list all the "firsts" you can think of.

Chapter 6

Exemplification

Example is the school of mankind, and they will learn at no other.

— Edmund Burke, 1796

THE PATTERN

"Can you give me an example?" How many times have you asked that question? Like most people, you probably ask for examples often—and for good reason, because nothing clarifies a point better. Usually, examples clarify by making the general more specific or by showing that something is true. To understand how examples work to clarify, consider this statement:

> Living in a high-tech society has its drawbacks.

To clarify that general statement, specific examples can be added, like this:

> Living in a high-tech society has its drawbacks. For example, our devices have become so complicated that many people can no longer operate them. I don't know anyone who can program a DVD recorder or figure out how to get the message light to stop blinking on an answering machine after a power outage.

In addition to clarifying points, specific examples can keep your writing interesting. In "What I've Learned from Men" (page 205), Barbara Ehrenreich uses examples for that purpose in this passage, which comments on the belief she once held that men could teach her little:

> What else would we possibly want to learn from them [men]? How to interrupt someone in midsentence as if you were performing an act of conversational euthanasia? How to drop a pair of socks three feet from an open hamper and keep right on walking? How to make those weird guttural gargling sounds in the bathroom?

To make the point that for years she mistakenly believed she had little to learn from men, she does not just ask, "What else would we possibly want to learn from them?" She creates interest and humour by adding questions as examples of how little she once thought men could teach her.

Examples can also help you persuade your reader. In "Forgiveness," June Callwood uses an example to illustrate how forgiveness empowers the person who forgives:

> Some people are marvellously unbroken by great injustices. Nelson Mandela smiled gently at his adversaries after twenty-seven years of brutal imprisonment. A worldwide figure of wonder, he even invited his white jailer to his inauguration as South Africa's president.

When you use specific examples (specific instances) to clarify a point, add interest, or persuade, you are using **exemplification.**

USING EXEMPLIFICATION FOR A PURPOSE

Because examples are so important for clarification, adding interest, and persuasion, writers rely on them all the time, even when they use other patterns of development. Thus, you will see examples in essays developed largely with cause-and-effect analysis, process analysis, comparison-contrast, and other patterns or combination of patterns. Say, for instance, that you are using cause-and-effect analysis to explain why sexually active teenagers often do not use birth control. Once you note that teenagers may not always understand when and how pregnancy can occur, you can illustrate with an example you read of a 15-year-old who became pregnant because she thought she was "safe" since it was her first sexual experience. Although examples are often a part of essays developed with any pattern or combination of patterns, exemplification also can form the primary pattern of development to help you entertain, relate experience and express feelings, inform, and persuade.

Chapter 1 on critical reading identified overgeneralization as a common logical fallacy. Exemplification can provide a useful strategy for ensuring that you're not oversimplifying your ideas or making claims you cannot support. When you go in search of examples to illustrate your thoughts or observations, you have an opportunity to ensure that you haven't overgeneralized, particularly if you search for examples that do not fully support your claim. Such examples give us the opportunity to revise our assertions to make them more reflective of the complex world we write about.

Using examples solves a number of other problems college and university writers find themselves encountering, even when they're not writing essays designed to be models of exemplification. When you are faced with an essay on feminist antiwar movements for your women's studies class, or one on silent films for your film class, you'll want to think about examples at several stages of the writing process. During your initial brainstorming, thinking about examples can help you in two ways. Examples that immediately come to mind can help you formulate a direction for your essay. Examples that come to mind but that you know little about give you a place to begin your research. Knowing you have to provide examples to support your theories helps motivate and direct your curiosity. Once you've formulated a thesis—one that is both significant and arguable—the recognition that you will need examples further directs your thinking and any research you still need to do.

Examples are also crucial to well-developed paragraphs. If you have ever tried to build a paragraph out of general statements, you'll know how difficult and frustrating it is. Remember "How to Say Nothing in 500 Words"? One of the reasons that young writer had such difficulty getting started was that he had no experiences or knowledge—examples, in short—that would allow him to say something that wasn't hopelessly general. On the other hand, paragraphs that contain evidence are much easier to write, and much easier to shape to follow the contours of your argument. One good strategy is to begin a paragraph with a generalization (how bold you want to be is determined by your audience), followed by some well-considered examples. At the end of the paragraph, once you've carefully analyzed and elucidated the significance of your evidence, you'll find you can return to that original generalized idea and now say something much more nuanced and responsible—not to mention interesting.

If you've really crafted a thesis that is arguable, you need evidence—which is exactly what examples are. In fact, your post-secondary career revolves around the issue of evidence: what your instructors teach you, the research and reading you do for all your courses, is all about having your own body of evidence from which you can draw conclusions. Similarly, the different styles of thinking provided by science classes or art history classes are an attempt to give you different tools for understanding and using evidence.

Regardless of your purpose for using exemplification, your examples will support, clarify, or explain a **generalization,** which is a statement of something you consider to be true in your own life or in a broader context. For example, if you want to write about your post-secondary experience in a way that would entertain your reader, you could give examples of your humorous mishaps on campus to support the generalization that your first week was a comedy of errors. You can also use examples to express feelings and relate experience. For example, in "The Keys of Paradise," Gabor Maté's many examples of drug addicts who feel they cannot live without their addictions give the reader the sense that drug addictions meet real needs of the addict. Examples can help you inform a reader as well. In the same essay, Maté provides examples of addicts who were abused as children to help the reader understand that pain always lies behind addiction. Finally, examples can persuade your reader. To persuade your reader to support tax incentives for businesses relocating to your area, you can provide examples to support the generalization that other communities benefited when they offered similar incentives.

Exemplification at School, at Work, and in the Community

You will use exemplification in most of your academic writing, including essay examinations and required papers. Assignments that direct you to "explain and illustrate . . . ," "define and provide examples of . . . ," and "cite illustrations to show that . . . ," are requiring you to use examples. In a world history class, you may be asked to explain and illustrate the role of women in ancient Egypt. In a political science class, you may argue for or against gun control legislation, and to do so you may cite examples of murder rates in countries that either have or lack such legislation. In an education class, you might be called upon to argue against proficiency exams by citing examples of problems such tests cause or fail to address. In a marketing class, you might be asked to define and illustrate target marketing, and in a biology class, you might be asked to define and illustrate natural selection.

Because examples clarify points so well, they help students understand important concepts. For that reason, you will encounter examples frequently in all your textbooks, as in this excerpt from an introduction to business textbook:

> Business is perhaps the most crucial institution of civil society. For its own well-being, business depends on its employees being active in politics, law, churches, arts, charities, and so on. For example, some folks at the General Electric plastics division helped their community while developing their own team-building skills. Rather than heading to a resort hotel to participate in some isolated team-building activities, the group went into the neighborhood surrounding their offices and helped rebuild the community, barn-raising style. The result back on the job was a sense of team camaraderie that proved as lasting as the buildings that were rebuilt. (Nickels, McHugh, and McHugh, *Understanding Business*)

Notice that the textbook authors use examples twice. The first time, they give examples of the kinds of civic institutions a business needs its employees to be involved in: "politics, law, churches, arts, charities, and so on." The second time, they give a more extended example to illustrate civic involvement more specifically and to illustrate how the involvement helps a business: rebuilding a neighbourhood around the business improved both the neighbourhood and the employees' camaraderie. For students trying to learn material, such clear examples aid understanding by making general concepts very specific.

Workplace writing also requires examples. Job application letters highlight examples of accomplishments: "As an intern in a local advertising agency, I learned a great deal about copywriting, including how to target an audience, how to assess that audience, and how to write colourfully yet succinctly." Written job descriptions state and illustrate responsibilities: "The regional sales manager supports the sales staff in any way needed. The support can include providing budget funds for travel, visiting important clients, and brainstorming for marketing ideas." Performance evaluations give examples of workplace behaviour: "Lee is unreliable. He consistently arrives late, leaves early, and reports off sick."

Examples are also an important part of writing outside the classroom and workplace. If you are writing to persuade a friend to vote for a particular candidate, you might provide examples of that person's accomplishments: "Grace Wang is a sound fiscal manager. She has been financial vice president for First Asset Mortgage Company for 12 years, and she has successfully managed the investments of Park Street Church for 10 years." When you write a condolence note to a person who lost a loved one, you can share an example of your memories of the deceased: "Whenever I talked to Juan, he always made me laugh." If you place a classified ad for a garage sale, you might give examples of your wares to attract certain kinds of customers: "Children's toys, including Star Wars figures, Hot Wheels cars, and numerous board games."

SUPPORTING DETAILS

The examples you use to support a generalization can come from a variety of sources: personal experience, observation, general knowledge, class lectures, reading research, and so forth. In "The Keys of Paradise," Maté's personal experience has led him to believe that society doesn't provide us with much guidance for a meaningful life; consequently, he includes examples of addicts who report that drugs alleviate their sense of boredom and meaninglessness. In "What I've Learned from Men" (page 205), Barbara Ehrenreich gives an example of an encounter she had with a professor, an encounter from her own experience, to illustrate that at one time she was too "ladylike." If you wanted to illustrate that people lie about unimportant things, you could do so with examples taken from a recent psychology class lecture you attended about why people lie.

Examples can take many forms. Sometimes an example is an explanation. In "The Keys of Paradise," Maté uses the example of a young man who was tied to a chair as a child in an effort to control his hyperactivity to explain that some addicts are individuals with attention deficit hyperactivity disorder who use drugs to ameliorate this condition.

An example can also take the form of a narration. In order to argue that travel enlarges our perspective, you could tell the story of your trip to China to explain how it led you to question your belief that helpful, friendly people are found only in small Canadian towns.

Sometimes examples take the form of description. For example, if you wanted to illustrate that people do not care about cleaning up the planet, you could describe the litter in a public park and the pollution of a local river.

You may be wondering how many examples you should use; there is no one number that applies in all instances. The appropriate number of examples to use is a decision you should make based upon audience and purpose. How much does your audience know about your topic? How difficult is the material? The less your readers know and the more challenging the material, the more examples your readers may require. Are you attempting to persuade your readers to think or act a particular way? If so, you may need more examples than if you want to entertain.

Examples can be brief or extended, and sometimes the length of your examples factors into your decision about how many to use. If your examples are extended, you may be able to use fewer than you would if your examples were brief. For example, as Maté tries to explain the many causes of addiction, he uses numerous examples to illustrate how complex these causes are. Your essay on how travel broadens our perspectives might consist of two examples, one dealing with your trip, another—in order to show that your experience wasn't exceptional—to tell how a friend had a similar experience. Your goal is to provide enough examples in enough detail to achieve your purpose.

Hypothetical Examples

Sometimes writers use **hypothetical examples.** These are not drawn from any single observation or experience of the writer but are created from what the writer knows *could* happen, based on common knowledge, past experience, past observation, and logic. To be effective, hypothetical examples must be plausible, and they must not be overused. For example, say that you wanted to illustrate that advertisements make drinking beer look cool. Rather than point to specific advertisements, you could say something like this:

Beer advertisements make it seem that beer drinkers have more fun. The ads show beautiful people frolicking on the beach, playing volleyball, sitting by a campfire, and laughing away the hours. Other ads show beautiful people bundled in ski clothes, nestled by the fire, listening to jazz.

The examples in the above passage are not from specific beer ads. They are hypothetical. However, they are sufficiently like real advertisements to be effective. In other words, to be effective, a hypothetical example must be representative enough of reality that it *could* happen.

ORGANIZING DETAILS

In an essay developed primarily with exemplification, the thesis can embody the generalization that your examples will prove or clarify. For example, consider the thesis of "What I've Learned from Men":

After more than a decade of consciousness-raising, assertiveness training, and hand-to-hand combat in the battle of the sexes, we're [women] still too ladylike.

The rest of the essay provides examples of ways women are too ladylike; that is, it provides examples of ladylike behaviours that cause problems. Many times, the clarifying examples can be introduced with topic sentences, like this one from "What I've Learned from Men":

The essence of ladylikeness is a persistent servility masked as "niceness."

Following this topic sentence, Ehrenreich notes several instances of women's ladylike niceness casting them in servile roles.

The order in which you present your examples should be carefully considered. For a **progressive order,** arrange your examples from the least to the most compelling. As an effective alternative, place your two strongest examples first and last, with the others in between. Progressive order is particularly effective for a persuasive purpose because it provides a strong final impression with its convincing example at the end.

Sometimes **chronological** (time) **order** is effective. For example, if you want to illustrate that a particular politician's record is problematic, you could do so with examples arranged in chronological order from the time the politician took office up to the present.

On occasion, **a spatial order** is desirable. If, for example, you want to demonstrate that your campus presents obstacles for the physically disabled, you could move across campus space (maybe north to south) giving examples of physical barriers.

VISUALIZING AN EXEMPLIFICATION ESSAY

The following chart can help you visualize the structure for an exemplification essay. Like all good models, however, this one can be altered as needed.

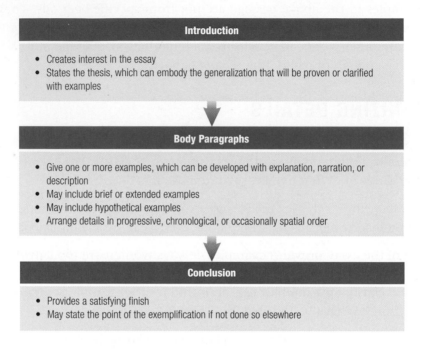

Introduction

- Creates interest in the essay
- States the thesis, which can embody the generalization that will be proven or clarified with examples

Body Paragraphs

- Give one or more examples, which can be developed with explanation, narration, or description
- May include brief or extended examples
- May include hypothetical examples
- Arrange details in progressive, chronological, or occasionally spatial order

Conclusion

- Provides a satisfying finish
- May state the point of the exemplification if not done so elsewhere

PROCESS GUIDELINES: STRATEGIES FOR WRITING EXEMPLIFICATION

1. **Selecting a Topic.** For a generalization to clarify with examples, fill in the blanks in one of these sentences:

   _____ is the best (worst) _____ I know.
   _____ is the most (least) _____ I know.

   You may end up with generalizations like these:

   Television advertising is the most manipulative form of communication I know.
   Nurses are the least appreciated professionals I know.

2. **Shaping a Thesis.** The sentences you formed by filling in the blanks above, however, are overgeneralizations. Your next task is to consider what examples have prompted you to draw this conclusion and then to

> ### Troubleshooting Guide
>
> #### Introducing Examples in a Series
> If you have trouble introducing examples in a series using *such as* or *including*, follow these guidelines:
>
> 1. Use a colon if the words before that colon are an independent clause (a word group that can stand alone as a sentence).
>
>   YES   **The union had many grievances: mandatory overtime, lack of layoff procedures based on seniority, and suspension of pay raises.**
>
>   YES   **The union had many grievances, such as mandatory overtime, lack of layoff procedures based on seniority, and suspension of pay raises.**
>
>   NO   **The union had many grievances, such as: mandatory overtime, lack of layoff procedures based on seniority, and suspension of pay raises.**
>
> 2. Use a comma before—but not after—these words. Do not use a colon.
>
>   YES   **The teacher had many innovative ideas, including collaborative test-taking, morning yoga instruction, and self-grading.**
>
>   NO   **The teacher had many innovative ideas including, collaborative test-taking, morning yoga instruction, and self-grading.**
>
>   NO   **The teacher had many innovative ideas, including: collaborative test-taking, morning yoga instruction, and self-grading.**

think how you can restate the idea in an arguable and convincing thesis. For example, you can shape the generalization "Television advertising is the most manipulative form of communication I know" into the thesis "Television advertisements use manipulative techniques to persuade people to buy products they do not need." You can then support that thesis by giving examples of manipulative advertisements for unnecessary products.

3. **Generating Ideas.** To generate examples for supporting details, you can ask yourself these questions:

   a. What have I experienced that illustrates my generalization?

   b. What have I observed that illustrates my generalization?

  c. What have I read that illustrates my generalization?

  d. What have I learned in school that illustrates my generalization?

  e. What stories can I tell to illustrate my generalization?

  f. What can I describe to illustrate my generalization?

4. **Organizing Details.** List all the examples you will use and number them in the order you will present them.

5. **Drafting.** Write your draft using your numbered list as a scratch outline. Do not worry about polished prose now. Just write your ideas any way you can; you can refine later.

6. **Revising.** Ask a classmate or friend who has good judgment about writing to read your draft and evaluate whether you have enough examples and have included the right amount of detail for each.

✔ Checklist for Revising Exemplification

Be sure:

_____   The generalization is clearly stated in a thesis or is strongly implied.

_____   Examples clarify the generalization and/or show that it is true.

_____   Examples are suited to your audience and purpose.

_____   You have enough examples developed in enough detail.

_____   Hypothetical examples, if you use them, are plausible.

_____   Examples are arranged in a progressive or other suitable order.

ANNOTATED STUDENT ESSAY

In the following essay, student author Shane Arbuthnott uses examples to describe how unromantic and frustrating independent filmmaking can be. Once the independent filmmaker has struggled with weather, people, and holding a day job, there is little time for the everyday activities that make our lives pleasant. After reading, you will have an opportunity to evaluate the essay.

The Trials of Glamour: A Journey into and out of Filmmaking

1   In 2001 I packed my bags, hopped on a bus in Regina, Saskatchewan, and travelled 2670 kilometers to Toronto, Ontario. There are several sane reasons that one might want to move from Regina to Toronto. One might move for the sake of a job; I did not do this, however, as I already had a satisfactory (if menial) job in Regina, and the one I had awaiting me in Toronto was no better. One might be lured by the big-city mystique of Toronto, with the uber-chic Yonge Street shopping and the brilliantly bohemian cafes on every corner; but I had never liked big cities, and have never been described as chic or bohemian in my life. One might want to move to Toronto for the varied, vibrant culture of its inhabitants; this I did enjoy, but I must admit that when I climbed onto that bus, I had no notion of Greektown with its street fairs and endless kebabs, or of the Asian mall on the outskirts of the city which seems more like a misplaced fragment of Tokyo than part of Canada. I did not move to Toronto for any of these perfectly reasonable motives. Instead, I was uprooting myself to take part in an independent film project. If this seems sane, glamorous or cool to you, then you have likely not worked in the independent film industry. Once the work is done and the images hit the screen, as long as the filmmakers have done their jobs properly then it should seem effortless; but the effort is there, in the invisible spaces behind the camera and between takes. The images left on the film are an accrual of struggle, often against weather, people and time, and represent more sacrifice than can be easily seen.

2   First, a little background information may be helpful. In the film world, "independent" is generally synonymous with "dirt cheap," and this was certainly true in our project. We were not financed, save by our own pockets, and so our equipment was an interesting hodge-podge of professional-grade, amateur-grade, and constructed-with-duct-tape. We had a lovely camera, but in order to move it around we were using a wheeled wooden platform instead of the smooth camera tracks found on high-budget film sets. Our lighting equipment was bought in Canadian Tire, and intended for use in unlit garages. Our editing equipment consisted of one computer running several excellent editing programs, none

Paragraph 1
The introduction engages interest with examples of reasons a young person might move to Toronto, reasons that are not the case here. The purpose of these examples is to provide contrast to the unglamorous work on an independent film. The final sentence of the paragraph is Shane's thesis.

Paragraph 2
The examples here provide background on independent filmmaking and give the reader a precise sense of the challenges independent filmmakers with small budgets face. Both the first and last sentences are topic sentences.

of which were designed to work with each other; generally, when we combined sound and picture, we all had our fingers crossed in hopes that nothing would explode. In fact, most of the year and a half spent on the project was spent with crossed fingers.

3   The Canadian climate offers some unique challenges for the independent filmmaker. Even high-end film equipment will struggle when the harshness of a Canadian winter hits, and as discussed, our equipment was anything but high-end. In our case, we discovered that our ancient-but-reliable microphone was only reliable above minus thirty degrees Celsius; after that, it went on strike. One particular night, we were filming a short scene at a public phone. We hooked up all our gear, got everything running, and began shooting. Five seconds into the scene, our sound recorder stopped us to tell us that all he could hear was wind. We hastily constructed a windbreak out of cardboard and broomsticks, and started again. We made it ten seconds into the scene this time, and then the microphone simply stopped working. No amount of cajoling or bullying could revive the expensive piece of equipment, and so we had to switch to a secondary microphone, this one being a small wireless model, to be clipped to a tie or shirt collar. This microphone, of course, is designed with a controlled studio in mind. When you try to connect it to the kind of clothing that a northern winter requires, all you can hear is the rustling of layered jackets. After half an hour of repositioning with this microphone, we gave up, filmed the scene, and recorded the sound later—a process of several hours, instead of the ten minutes it should have taken.

4   However, despite all of this, the weather is less of a challenge than the people. I should point out that no one who worked on this film was being paid; any money or time contributed to the project was entirely on a volunteer basis. As much as I appreciate the generosity of these people, however, it was not always easy to work with them. Take, for example, the group of sketch comedians who regularly appeared in the series. We were making a comedy, and as such we wanted funny people working with us; however, the comedic temperament is often accompanied by a high level of distractability. In my experience, herding cats is challenging but possible; if you want a true challenge, try herding sketch comedians. One short scene, meant to comprise a third of our day's shooting schedule, stretched to a ten-hour marathon, as attention wandered and a scripted scene became an improvisational exercise with the other filmmakers and me trying desperately to regain a hold on the reins. If I may use a cliché in the film industry, hilarity ensued. After ten hours, however, hilarity is not as funny as it usually is.

Paragraph 3
The first sentence is the topic sentence. The paragraph consists of an extended example that illustrates both the kinds of difficulties Canadian weather creates for a filmmaker and the way such difficulties eat up the filmmaker's time.

Paragraph 4
The topic sentence is the first sentence. The first three sentences link back to the thesis statement about the challenges of independent filmmaking. Shane has used two clichés here—the image of herding cats and the expression "hilarity ensued." Do these work? Why or why not?

5 But these were only periodic problems—there were periods in which neither weather nor people posed a problem; time, on the other hand, was a problem which never abated. Creating any type of film or video project is a very large time commitment. On average, roughly eight pages of a script can be filmed in one day. This pace slows if there are many changes of location within those pages—which there always were in our scripts. It should also be remembered that filming is only a small part of creating a film. The scripts must first be created. Then the filming itself must be planned extensively; locations must be found; permission to film in these places must be acquired; props and costumes must be collected or constructed (in a subsequent project, eight hours were spent hand-crafting Alpha-Bit cereal pieces—luckily, I was absent); the schedules of actors, crew and general hangers-on must be coordinated (around jobs, since we could not pay our cast and crew); and once everything is filmed, it must all be edited into a form recognizable as "film." Through this all, of course, was the special imposition Toronto makes on time: commuting. I cannot count the hours I spent shuddering along the subway tracks below the city, watching tunnel walls pass by the windows. Last, but certainly not least, we were required to feed ourselves and provide our own shelter, which meant that every one of the filmmakers also held a full-time job while filming. We kept ourselves busy, to say the least.

6 A life only contains so many hours. As time grows short, certain ingredients of a happy life tend to be left by the wayside. Whether one likes to read, watch television, go to concerts, play sports or simply sit quietly, time is required for such leisure activities, and it is hard to understand how much such trivialities are needed until one has gone entirely without them for a long period. As well, aside from on-set banter, social life is abandoned. The only time one could hold a conversation was when something—the location, the schedule, the camera—fell apart and work was, by necessity, stopped. I began to look forward to catastrophe for this very reason. Sleep is another time-consuming activity which, unfortunately, the life of an independent filmmaker does not generally allow. Over the course of the year and a half I devoted to this particular project, I generally slept no more than four or five hours a night—a workable feat for a few weeks, but after a few months health and happiness quickly deteriorate. In those years, I learned that the adage "Time is money" is false; time is infinitely more precious, and for myself, happiness cannot be had without it.

7 The truth of filmmaking, particularly independent filmmaking, is much less appealing than the fiction. While cinema in general is

Paragraph 5
The topic sentence is the first sentence. Once again, the first three sentences support the essay's thesis. Shane then provides examples of what must be done to organize and complete a day's filming. Two more examples provide a sense of how full the days of independent filmmakers can be.

Paragraph 6
The topic sentence is the second sentence. This idea is reinforced by the final sentence, which challenges a cliché.

Paragraph 7
The topic sentence is the first sentence, though once again the topic is reiterated in the final sentence.

considered cool or glamorous, the life of a filmmaker is arduous, frenetic, and in my own experience, unhappy. While working in this creative, interesting medium can certainly be rewarding, that work comes at a cost to every other part of one's life. When the choice is between filmmaking and the rest of life, given my experience I would most certainly choose the latter.

PEER REVIEW

Responding to "The Trials of Glamour: A Journey into and out of Filmmaking"

Evaluate "The Trials of Glamour" by responding to these questions:

1. Does the essay hold your interest? Why or why not?
2. What does the thesis tell us about independent filmmaking?
3. Are the examples good ones? Does the essay include enough examples? Explain.
4. The writer frequently opens and closes his paragraphs with something similar to a topic sentence. Why might this be an effective strategy for an exemplification essay?
5. Are the examples arranged in a suitable order? Explain.
6. What do you think of the author's word choice? Cite examples to support your opinion.
7. What are the chief strengths of the essay? Why do you find these features strong?
8. Mention one revision you would like to see. How will that revision improve the essay and help the author achieve his purpose?

READING SELECTIONS

Background

June Callwood (1924–2007) was born in Chatham, Ontario, and grew up in the village of Belle River, Ontario. Her first job as a journalist for the *Brantford Expositor* led to a career in journalism, with her first serious job at *The Globe and Mail*. There she met Trent Frayne, whom she later married; she kept her maiden name, however, as *The Globe and Mail* didn't hire married women in the 1940s. When she became a mother, she started freelancing and ghostwriting. Callwood's work has always had a social justice focus that is particularly concerned with the needs of women and children. Her biography on the Library and Archives Canada Web site lists just some of the many social action organizations she founded or co-founded: "These include Digger House, a youth hostel; Nellie's hostel for women; Jessie's, a centre for teenage parents; Casey House Hospice for those with AIDS; PEN Canada; the Canadian Civil Liberties Foundation and Feminists Against Censorship." A professorship in social justice has been established in her honour at Victoria College, University of Toronto. Callwood is the author of more than two dozen books. "Each person is like a stone in a pond," she observed near the end of her life. "Individual actions, good or bad, send out tiny ripples that change the surface of the public pond. People, by choice, can spread warm understanding or cold indifference."

The Pattern and Its Purposes

June Callwood reflects on the reasons that twenty-first-century society is mired in anger: there are conflicts in every corner of the planet; religious beliefs, when held, too often embrace an extremist concept of purity rather than of inclusiveness; life is too short and is moving too quickly so our human spirits are frayed. Into this turmoil comes the quiet possibility for forgiveness, a generosity often not deserved, but good for the giver as well as the receiver. Callwood uses examples to explore the complex issues of this difficult act.

Forgiveness

June Callwood

1   A small boy in an industrial city in Ontario was beaten severely many times by his father, to the extent that the boy not infrequently required a doctor to stitch up the wounds. His father, a policeman, sincerely believed that if he beat his son with chains, belts, sticks, and his fists, the boy would not grow up to be gay. That boy, now in his thirties and indelibly a gay man, says he will never forgive his father.

> **As you read**
> Think about the examples you find most compelling and consider why they are effective.

2   "What he did is not forgivable," the man says with composure. "How can it ever be all right to abuse a child? But I have let it go."

3   And a woman, raised on the Prairies in a Finnish home, married a black man and had a son. She showed the infant proudly to her mother, whose reaction was a look of naked disgust. Her mother and that son, now a charming and successful adult, have since developed an affectionate relationship, but the daughter has not forgotten or forgiven the expression on her mother's face.

4   "The best I can do," she says, "is that I have stopped hating her."

5   The ability to forgive is a central tenet of every major religion in the world—Christian, Judaic, Hindu, Buddhist, and Islamic. Those faiths urge followers to forgive their enemies and, indeed, even to find a way to love those who wrong them. As the twenty-first century dawns, however, the world is making a spectacular mess of such pious admonitions. Instead of goodwill, this is the age of anger, the polar opposite of forgiveness. Merciless ethnic, tribal, and religious conflicts dominate every corner of the planet, and in North America individuals live with high levels of wrath that explode as domestic brutality, road rage, vile epithets, and acts of random slaughter.

> "Conflicts dominate every corner of the planet, and in North America individuals live with high levels of wrath that explode as domestic brutality, road rage, vile epithets, and acts of random slaughter."

6   Many people, like the gay man or the woman in a biracial marriage, find forgiveness an unreasonable dictate. Some assaults on the body or soul are unconscionable, they feel, and forgiveness is simply out of the question. It satisfies the requirements of their humanity that they gradually ease away from the primitive thoughts of revenge that once obsessed them.

7   When Simon Wiesenthal, the famed Nazi hunter, was in a German concentration camp, he found himself in a strange situation. He was taken to the bedside of a dying SS officer, a youth who had killed many Jews, and the young man asked him, a Jew, for forgiveness. Wiesenthal was silent and left the room, but was haunted ever after. Thirty years later, he contacted some of the world's great thinkers and asked, what should I have done? Theologians such as Bishop Desmond Tutu and the Dalai Lama gently hinted that he should have been forgiving, for his own sake, but others, notably philosopher Herbert Marcuse, said that great evil should never be forgiven. In *The Sunflower*, a collection of fifty-three responses to Wiesenthal's question, Marcuse wrote sternly that forgiveness condones the crime.

8   The moral vacuum left by the pervasive disuse and misuse of religious tenets has allowed a secular forgiveness industry to spring into being. People who yearn desperately to rid themselves of an obsession for vengeance will seek help in curious places. Since 1985, the University of Wisconsin–Madison has offered forgiveness studies, and an International Forgiveness Institute was founded there. Four years ago, the world's first international conference on forgiveness drew hundreds of delegates to Madison. Stanford University has a forgiveness research project and people in California, a state on the cutting edge of self-absorption, are taking part in studies on the art and science of forgiveness. Self-help shelves in bookstores abound in titles such as *Forgive Your Parents: Heal Yourself*.

9   An odious US daytime television show, *Forgive or Forget*, features guests who say they owe someone an apology. They describe their offence, and then, *ta-dah*, the injured party appears on the appropriately tacky set and either grants or withholds forgiveness. Will the former foes embrace one another? The titillated audience can't wait.

10   Apologies are iffy because often they are contrived or coerced. Apologies extracted by judges, mediators, and parents are thin gruel for the wronged person. One familiar genre of apology, the one which commences, "I am sorry you are feeling badly," is particularly counterproductive because there is no admission of any responsibility; it is the other person's problem for being thin-skinned. A sincere and remorseful acceptance of blame, however, can close a wound.

11   Psychologists are engrossed by the topic and so are theologians, philosophers, psychiatrists, and—surprise—cardiologists. Unforgiving people, some studies show, are three times more likely to have heart disease as people who don't carry grudges. These findings raise the suspicion that the researchers may have the cart before the horse. Heart attacks occur more often in blow-top people who have unfortified egos, the very ones most apt to be relentlessly unforgiving. On the other hand, people who hold tolerant views of human nature and don't seem to nurse grievances unduly tend to have blood pressures in the normal range.

12   Clergy, counsellors, and people who lecture and write books about forgiveness all preach reductionism as a strategy for overcoming hot resentment of someone's nasty behaviour. They say that people who have been harmed should see the hurtful as deeply flawed human beings working out nameless aggressions. Pitiable and inferior, they are examples of failure to thrive. Adults still distressed by abuse, neglect, or rejection in childhood are urged to consider what happened in their parents' childhoods—often, bad parenting comes from being badly parented. The theory is that understanding the reasons for their parents' limitations will enable the offspring to acquire a measure of compassion.

13   Maybe it works. Hillary Clinton apparently forgave her sleazy husband because she knows he had an unhappy childhood.

14   This technique can be applied to almost any injustice and falls within the rapists-were-beaten-as-children, *poor them* school of thought, which for some skeptics veers perilously close to nonaccountability. The law and commonsense hold that adults are responsible for what they do. While empathy may help people appreciate why others behave badly, the exercise is somewhat patronizing. The offender is reduced to a contemptible hive of neuroses and ungovernable aberrations, which accordingly elevates the injured party to a morally superior person.

15   Demonizing the enemy is a common coping mechanism in times of adversity. In military terms, it captures the high ground.

16   Catastrophes such as divorce, job loss, rape, robbery, infidelity, and slander are all assaults on personal dignity and self-respect. A sense of being intact—*safe*—has been violated, and people are dismayed to find themselves for some time emotionally crippled by anger and grief. Betrayal and loss take big chunks out of people's confidence and leave them feeling excruciatingly vulnerable to random harm.

17   The starting place, some therapists say, is to accept that something appalling has happened, and it hurts. Denial, a recourse more favoured by men than by women, won't help. The next step, they say, is to develop an off switch. When fury threatens to make the brain reel, people should grasp for distractions. Brooding about revenge only serves to unhinge reason. If people don't rid themselves of wrath, personal growth stops cold. The hard part comes at the end of the process. The choices are to enter a state of forgiveness, which is a triumph of generosity, or just to put the matter in a box, cover it with a lid, place a brick on the lid, and move on. In healthy people, a perverse state of mind eventually wears itself out.

> "The starting place, some therapists say, is to accept that
> something appalling has happened, and it hurts."

18   In yoga, they say that it takes six years of regularly practising meditation to gain spiritual insight. Forgiveness of a great wrong may take longer. The process can't even begin until the injured person stops crying.

19   Some people are marvellously unbroken by great injustices. Nelson Mandela smiled gently at his adversaries after twenty-seven years of brutal imprisonment. A worldwide figure of wonder, he even invited his white jailers to his inauguration as South Africa's president. In Cambodia, a pastor whose family had been wiped out by the Khmer Rouge baptized and forgave a notorious Khmer Rouge leader known as Duch. A university professor in Virginia had an urge to kill the intruder who beat his mother to death, but stopped himself with the thought, "Whose heart is darker?" And the father of a young girl casually murdered in a street encounter with a teenager she didn't know attended the trial and sat quietly throughout the appalling testimony. He said he would visit the youth in prison. "I do not think I can forgive him," he explained, "but perhaps if I know him I will not hate him."

20   Forgiveness is hard work. A woman, a devout Roman Catholic who forgave the man who tortured and killed her seven-year-old daughter, said, "Anyone who says forgiveness is for wimps hasn't tried it." The reward for giving up scalding thoughts of reprisal is peace of mind. It is worth the candle.

Reading Closely and Thinking Critically

1. Why is there so much anger and so little forgiveness in contemporary society?
2. What does Callwood think of the strategy of forgiving people who have hurt you because they themselves were hurt? How does this practice create a moral quandary for the person trying to forgive?
3. What process can be useful for people who have been hurt and want to forgive? Why is it so hard?
4. Callwood gives us a number of reasons that it's a good idea to forgive. The great faith traditions urge us to do so. Holding a grudge is hard work. Forgiving liberates us. It's good for our health and our hearts—literally. Which of her arguments do you find most compelling? Why?
5. What's the distinction between putting the matter in a box and putting a lid on it and forgiveness? Might one lead to the other?

Examining Structure and Strategy

1. Callwood begins her essay with two examples before she poses the question about forgiveness in "the age of anger." Are these an effective opening? Do you relate to the stories? How do you feel, by the end of the essay, about the absence of forgiveness in these lives? Does your reaction change over the course of the essay?
2. Two of Callwood's major examples are men famous for their thoughtfulness and reflectiveness: Simon Wiesenthal and Nelson Mandela. Wiesenthal refused to forgive and is supported in that decision by the philosopher Herbert Marcuse, who says some things are so morally reprehensible that to forgive them condones evil. Nelson Mandela, in contrast, invited those who imprisoned him to his inauguration. Find out who these men are if need be. Why has Callwood used examples of well-known men that conflict with respect to their ability to forgive? Which carries the most weight with the reader? Why?
3. Do Callwood's examples include enough detail? Too much? Does she have enough examples, too many, or too few? Would a couple of longer examples have given us more insight into the process or do Callwood's numerous examples highlight the common difficulties of forgiving?

Considering Language and Style

1. What does it mean to be "worth the candle"? Search online references such as Bartleby.com or the online *Oxford English Dictionary* to find out what it means. Does this expression provide an effective conclusion to Callwood's essay?
2. Callwood doesn't comment on many of her examples; in effect, she doesn't suggest whether the people's decisions to forgive or not were appropriate or effective. Why? Is such reticence effective?

For Discussion in Class or Online

Consider moments in your own life or in history when forgiveness seemed inappropriate. Why do we think of some acts as unforgivable? If your instructor so directs, post your response on your class Web site.

Writing Assignments

1. **In your journal.** In a page or two, relate how your capacity for forgiveness has been challenged. Explain why you could or could not find forgiveness.
2. **Using exemplification for a purpose.** The purposes given in the assignments are possibilities. You may establish whatever purposes you like, within your instructor's guidelines.
    *   To inform your reader, use examples from a range of historical time periods or literary or popular texts to explain how a concept or a behaviour has changed over time. You could look at women's magazines over the last 50 years and use examples to discuss how concepts of male and female beauty have changed. If you have a background in economics, you could use examples to consider how government has reacted in times of financial crisis.
    *   To persuade your reader, write an essay using examples where the person who forgives receives the most good from the process.
    *   To inform your reader, use examples of frustrated and angry behaviour to explore why people in the twenty-first century have such short fuses.
    *   To entertain your reader, use examples of misunderstanding that are suddenly resolved by understanding another person's motives. What do these examples say about one of the first things we need to do when we are frustrated or angry?
3. **Combining patterns.**
    *   Use definition to explain a concept such as forgiveness or empathy. Then use cause-and-effect analysis to explain the effects, on others as well as on yourself, of practising it.

- Use examples to discuss the conventions of a particular kind of genre fiction, such as romance or science fiction, and contrast or compare examples that look similar but aren't. Or you could contrast or compare imaginative with conventional writing in the genre.

4. **Connecting the readings.** In Thomas King's essay "'You'll Never Believe What Happened' Is Always a Good Way to Start," King talks about his fantasy meeting with his absent father in a barroom: just as it dawns on his father who King is, King leaves. Contrast or compare King's response to one of the individuals whose life is referred to in "Forgiveness." How do the similarities or differences help us understand how hard it is to forgive?

5. **Drawing on sources.** Find Wiesenthal's book *The Sunflower,* and read the individual responses to his question about forgiveness that suggest it's important to forgive atrocities as well as those that demur. Choose two of the opposing viewpoints and write about them, attempting to understand the writers' perspectives on forgiveness.

Background

Gabor Maté is the author or co-author of numerous books, including *Scattered Minds*, on attention deficit disorder, and *When the Body Says No*, on the effects of stress. He frequently writes for the *Vancouver Sun* and *The Globe and Mail*. Born in Hungary, he emigrated to Canada when he was 13. He spent several years as a high school English teacher, then returned to university to train as a doctor. Currently he is the staff physician at the Portland Hotel, a residence and resource centre for the people of Vancouver's Downtown Eastside. Many of his patients suffer from mental illness, drug addiction, HIV, or all three.

Combined Patterns and Their Purposes

In "The Keys of Paradise," Maté explores the causes of addiction. Blending his scientific knowledge with the voices of addicts who explain their own needs in very human terms, Maté helps us understand that addicts are not weak-willed people with destructive habits, but are people searching for the same things we are: emotional security, the sense of safety that allows them to engage in the world, a community, an identity. While Maté provides social and scientific explanations, he relies on the voices of the addicts he treats to provide examples that question our tendency to view the drug addict as "other."

The Keys of Paradise: Addiction as a Flight from Distress
Gabor Maté

1   It is impossible to understand addiction without asking what relief the addict finds, or hopes to find, in the drug or the addictive behaviour.

> **As you read**
> Consider the kinds of stress or distress in your life that prompt you to seek your drug of choice—whether it's chocolate or a new CD.

2   The early-nineteenth-century literary figure Thomas De Quincey was an opium user. "The subtle powers lodged in this mighty drug," he rhapsodized, "tranquilize all irritations of the nervous system . . . sustain through twenty-four hours the else drooping animal energies . . . O just, subtle and all-conquering opium . . . Thou only givest these gifts to man; and thou hast the keys of Paradise." De Quincey's words encapsulate the blessings of all drugs as the addict experiences them—indeed, as we shall see later, the appeal of all addictive obsessions, with or without drugs.

3   Far more than a quest for pleasure, chronic substance use is the addict's attempt to escape distress. From a medical point of view, addicts are self-medicating conditions like depression, anxiety, post-traumatic stress or even ADHD (attention-deficit hyperactivity disorder).

4   Addictions always originate in pain, whether felt openly or hidden in the unconscious. They are emotional anaesthetics. Heroin and cocaine, both powerful physical painkillers, also ease psychological discomfort. Infant animals separated from their mothers can be soothed readily by low doses of narcotics, just as if it was actual physical pain they were enduring.[1]

---

[1] In popular usage "narcotic" may refer loosely to any illicit drug. In this book, as in medical language, narcotics is a term only for opioid drugs either derived from the Asian poppy, like heroin and morphine, or synthetic, like oxycodone. J. Panksepp, "Social Support and Pain: How Does the Brain Feel the Ache of a Broken Heart?" *Journal of Cancer Pain and Symptom Palliation* 1(1) (2005): 29–65.

5   The pain pathways in humans are no different. The very same brain centres that interpret and "feel" physical pain also become activated during the experience of emotional rejection: on brain scans they "light up" in response to social ostracism just as they would when triggered by physically harmful stimuli.[2] When people speak of feeling "hurt" or of having emotional "pain," they are not being abstract or poetic but scientifically quite precise.

6   The hard-drug addict's life has been marked by a surfeit of pain. No wonder she desperately craves relief. "In moments I go from complete misery and vulnerability to total invulnerability," says Judy, a thirty-six-year-old heroin and cocaine addict who is now trying to kick her two-decade habit. "I have a lot of issues. A lot of the reason why I use is to get rid of those thoughts and emotions and cover them up."

7   The question is never "Why the addiction?" but "Why the pain?"

8   The research literature is unequivocal: most hard-core substance abusers come from abusive homes.[3] The majority of my Skid Row patients suffered severe neglect and maltreatment early in life. Almost all the addicted women inhabiting the Downtown Eastside were sexually assaulted in childhood, as were many of the men. The autobiographical accounts and case files of Portland residents tell stories of pain upon pain: rape, beatings, humiliation, rejection, abandonment, relentless character assassination. As children they were obliged to witness the violent relationships, self-harming life patterns or suicidal addictions of their parents—and often had to take care of them. Or they had to look after younger siblings and defend them from being abused even as they themselves endured the daily violation of their own bodies and souls. One man grew up in a hotel room where his prostitute mother hosted a nightly procession of men as her child slept, or tried to, on his cot on the floor.

9   Carl, a thirty-six-year-old Native man, was banished from one foster home after another, had dishwashing liquid poured down his throat at age five for using foul language and was tied to a chair in a dark room in attempts to control his hyperactivity. When he's angry at himself—as he was one day for having used cocaine—he gouges his foot with a knife as punishment. He confessed his "sin" to me with the look of a terrorized urchin who'd just smashed some family heirloom and dreaded the harshest retribution.

10   Another man described the way his mother used a mechanical babysitter when he was three years old. "She went to the bar to drink and pick up men. Her idea of keeping me safe and from getting into trouble was to stick me in the dryer. She put a heavy box on top so I couldn't get out." The air vent ensured that the boy wouldn't suffocate.

11   My prose is unequal to the task of depicting such nearly inconceivable trauma. "Our difficulty or inability to perceive the experience of others . . . is all the more

---

[2]N. I. Eisenberger, "Does Rejection Hurt? An FMRI Study of Social Exclusion," *Science,* 10 October 2003, 290–92.

[3]R. Shanta et al., "Childhood Abuse, Neglect and Household Dysfunction and the Risk of Illicit Drug Use: The Adverse Childhood Experiences Study," *Pediatrics* 111 (2003): 565–72.

pronounced the more distant these experiences are from ours in time, space, or qual-ity," wrote the Auschwitz survivor Primo Levi.[4] We can be moved by the tragedy of mass starvation on a far continent; after all, we have all known physical hunger, if only temporarily. But it takes a greater effort of emotional imagination to empathize with the addict. We readily feel for a suffering child, but cannot see the child in the adult who, his soul fragmented and isolated, hustles for survival a few blocks away from where we shop or work.

> "We readily feel for a suffering child, but cannot see the child
> in the adult who, his soul fragmented and isolated, hustles for
> survival a few blocks away from where we shop or work."

12   Levi quotes Jean Améry, a Jewish-Austrian philosopher and resistance fighter who fell into the grasp of the Gestapo. "Anyone who was tortured remains tortured . . . Anyone who has suffered torture never again will be able to be at ease in the world . . . Faith in humanity, already cracked by the first slap in the face, then demolished by torture, is never acquired again."[5] Améry was a full-grown adult when he was trau-matized, an accomplished intellectual captured by the foe in the course of a war of liberation. We may then imagine the shock, loss of faith and unfathomable despair of the child who is traumatized not by hated enemies but by loved ones.

13   Not all addictions are rooted in abuse or trauma, but I do believe they can be traced to painful experience. A hurt is at the centre of *all* addictive behaviours. It is present in the gambler, the Internet addict, the compulsive shopper and the worka-holic. The wound may not be as deep and the ache not as excruciating, and it may even be entirely hidden—but it's there. As we'll see, the effects of early stress or adverse experiences directly shape both the psychology and the neurobiology of addiction in the brain.

14   I asked fifty-seven-year-old Richard, an addict since his teens, why he kept using. "I don't know, I'm just trying to fill a void," he replied. "Emptiness in my life. Boredom. Lack of direction." I knew all too well what he meant. "Here I am, in my late fifties," he said. "I have no wife, no children. I appear to be a failure, Society says you should be married and have children, a job, that kind of stuff. This way, with the cocaine, I can sit there and do some little thing like rewire the toaster that wasn't working, and not feel like I've lost out on life." He died a few months after our interview, succumb-ing to a combination of lung disease, kidney cancer and overdose.

15   "I didn't use for six years," says Cathy, forty-two-year-old heroin and cocaine user, back in a grubby Downtown Eastside hotel after a long absence. She's contracted HIV

---

[4]Primo Levi, *The Drowned and the Saved,* trans. Raymond Rosenthal (New York: Vintage International, 1989), 158.
[5]Levi, *The Drowned and the Saved,* 25.

since her return. "The whole six years I craved. It was the lifestyle. I thought I was missing something. And now I look around myself and I think, What the hell was I missing?" Cathy reveals that when she wasn't using, she missed not only the effect of the drugs but also the excitement of drug seeking and the rituals the drug habit entails. "I just didn't know what to do with myself. It felt empty."

16   A sense of deficient emptiness pervades our entire culture. The drug addict is more painfully conscious of this void than most people and has limited means of escaping it. The rest of us find other ways of suppressing our fear of emptiness or of distracting ourselves from it. When we have nothing to occupy our minds, bad memories, troubling anxieties, unease or the nagging mental stupor we call boredom can arise. At all costs, drug addicts want to escape spending "alone time" with their minds. To a lesser degree, behavioural addictions are also responses to this terror of the void.

17   Opium, wrote Thomas De Quincey, is a powerful "counter agent . . to the formidable curse of *taedium vitae*"—the tedium of life.

18   Human beings want not only to survive, but also to live. We long to experience life in all its vividness, with full, untrammelled emotion. Adults envy the open-hearted and open-minded explorations of children; seeing their joy and curiosity, we pine for our own lost capacity for wide-eyed wonder. Boredom, rooted in a fundamental discomfort with the self, is one of the least tolerable mental states.

19   For the addict the drug provides a route to feeling alive again, if only temporarily. "I am in profound awe of the ordinary," recalls author and bank robber Stephen Reid of his first hit of morphine. Thomas De Quincey extols opium's power "to stimulate the capacities of enjoyment."

> "For the addict the drug provides a route to feeling
> alive again, if only temporarily."

20   Carol is a twenty-three-year-old resident of the Portland Hotel Society's Stanley Hotel. Her nose and lips are pierced with rings. Around her neck she wears a chain with a black metal cross. Her hairdo is a pink-dyed Mohawk that tapers to blond locks cascading at the back to her shoulders. A bright, mentally agile young woman, Carol has been an injection crystal meth user and heroin addict since she ran away from home at age fifteen. The Stanley is her first stable domicile after five years on the streets. These days she is active in promoting harm reduction and in supporting fellow addicts. She has attended international conferences, and her writings have been quoted by addiction experts.

21   During a methadone appointment, she explains what she cherishes about the crystal meth experience. She speaks nervously and rapidly and fidgets incessantly, effects that result from her long-standing stimulant habit and likely from the early-onset hyperactivity disorder she had before she ever used drugs. As befits a street-educated child of her generation, Carol's every second word seems to be "like" or "whatever."

22   "When you do, like, a good hit or whatever you get like a cough or whatever, like a warm feeling, you really feel a hit, start breathing hard or whatever," she says. "Kind of like a good orgasm if you are a more sexual person—I never really thought of it that way, but my body still experiences the same physical sensations. I just don't associate it with sex.

23   "I get all excited, whatever you're into . . . I like playing with clothes, or I like going out at night in the West End when there's not a whole lot of people, walking down back alleys, singing to myself. People leave stuff out, I look for what I can find, scavenging, and it's all so interesting."

24   The addict's reliance on the drug to reawaken her dulled feelings is no adolescent caprice. The dullness is itself a consequence of an emotional malfunction not of her making: the internal shutdown of vulnerability.

25   From the Latin word *vulnerare*, "to wound," vulnerability is our susceptibility to be wounded. This fragility is part of our nature and cannot be escaped. The best the brain can do is to shut down conscious awareness of it when pain becomes so vast or unbearable that it threatens to overwhelm our capacity to function. The automatic repression of painful emotion is a helpless child's prime defence mechanism and can enable the child to endure trauma that would otherwise be catastrophic. The unfortunate consequence is a wholesale dulling of emotional awareness. "Everybody knows there is no fineness or accuracy of suppression," wrote the American novelist Saul Bellow in *The Adventures of Augie March*; "if you hold down one thing you hold down the adjoining."[6]

26   Intuitively, we all know that it's better to feel than not to feel. Beyond their energizing subjective charge, emotions have crucial survival value. They orient us, interpret the world for us and offer us vital information. They tell us what is dangerous and what is benign, what threatens our existence and what will nurture our growth. Imagine how disabled we would be if we could not see or hear or taste or sense heat or cold or physical pain. Emotional shutdown is similar. Our emotions are an indispensable part of our sensory apparatus and an essential part of who we are. They make life worthwhile, exciting, challenging, beautiful and meaningful.

27   When we flee our vulnerability, we lose our full capacity for feeling emotion. We may even become emotional amnesiacs, not remembering ever having felt truly elated or truly sad. A nagging void opens, and we experience it as alienation, as profound *ennui*, as the sense of deficient emptiness described above.

28   The wondrous power of a drug is to offer the addict protection from pain while at the same time enabling her to engage the world with excitement and meaning. "It's not that my senses are dulled—no, they open, expanded," explained a young woman whose substances of choice are cocaine and marijuana. "But the anxiety is removed,

---

[6]Saul Bellow, *The Adventures of Augie March* (New York: Penguin Books, 1996), 1.

and the nagging guilt and—yeah!" The drug restores to the addict the childhood vivacity she suppressed long ago.

29   Emotionally drained people often lack physical energy, as anyone who has experienced depression knows, and this is a prime cause of the bodily weariness that beleaguers many addicts. There are many more: dismal nutrition; a debilitating lifestyle; diseases like HIV, hepatitis C and their complications; disturbed sleep patterns that date back, in many cases, to childhood—another consequence of abuse or neglect. "I just couldn't go to sleep, ever," says Maureen, a sex-trade worker and heroin addict. "I never even knew there was such a thing as a good sleep until I was twenty-nine years old." Like Thomas De Quincey, who used opium to "sustain through twenty-four hours the else drooping animal energies," present-day addicts turn to drugs for a reliable energy boost.

30   "I can't give up cocaine," a pregnant patient named Celia once told me. "With my HIV, I have no energy. The rock gives me strength." Her phrasing sounded like a morbid reconfiguration of the psalmist's words: *"He only is my rock and my salvation; he is my defence. I shall not be moved."*

31   "I enjoy the rush, the smell and the taste," says Charlotte, long-time cocaine and heroin user, pot smoker and self-confessed speed freak. "I guess I've been smoking or doing some form of drugs for so long, I don't know . . . I think, What if I stopped? Then what? That's where I get my energy from."

32   "Man, I can't face the day without the rock," says Greg, a multi-drug addict in his early forties. "I'm dying for one right now."

33   "You're not dying *for* it," I venture. "You're dying *because* of it." Greg is tickled. "Nah, not me. I'm Irish and half Indian."

34   "Right. There are no dead Irish or dead Indians around."

35   From Greg, more jollity. "Everybody has to go sometime. When your number comes up, that's it."

36   These four don't know it, but beyond illness or the inertia of emotional and physical exhaustion, they are also up against the brain physiology of addiction.

37   Cocaine, as we shall see, exerts its euphoric effect by increasing the availability of the reward chemical dopamine in key brain circuits, and this is necessary for motivation and for mental and physical energy. Flooded with artificially high levels of dopamine triggered by external substances, the brain's own mechanisms of dopamine secretion become lazy. They stop functioning at anywhere near full capacity, relying on the artificial boosters instead. Only long months of abstinence allow the intrinsic machinery of dopamine production to regenerate, and in the meantime, the addict will experience extremes of physical and emotional exhaustion.

"Flooded with artificially high levels of dopamine . . . the brain's own mechanisms of dopamine secretion become lazy."

38   Aubrey, a tall, rangy, solitary man now approaching middle age, is also hooked on cocaine. His face is permanently lined by sadness, and his customary tone is one of resignation and regret. He feels incomplete and incompetent as a person without the drug, a self-concept that has nothing to do with his real abilities and everything to do with his formative experiences as a child. By his own assessment, inadequacy and the sense that he was a failed human being were part and parcel of his personality before he ever touched drugs.

39   "After Grade Eight I grew up on drugs," Aubrey says. "When I turned to drugs, I found that I fit in with other kids . . . Yeah, it was a big important thing, to fit in. See, as a kid when you picked somebody for a soccer game, I was always the last guy to be picked.

40   "See," he continues, "I've been in institutions a lot, I've spent a long time in a four-by-eight cell. So I've been by myself a lot. And before then, too. See, I had a rough childhood, going from foster home to foster home. I was shipped off quite a bit, eh."

41   "At what age were you sent to foster homes?" I ask.

42   "About eleven. My father was killed, hit by a truck. My mother couldn't take care of all of us kids, and so Children's Aid stepped in. Me being the oldest, they took me out. I got two brothers. They were younger. They stayed home."

43   Aubrey believes he was chosen for foster care because he was "so hyper as a kid" that his mother couldn't handle him.

44   "I was there for five years. Well, not in one place. No. I got shipped around. They'd keep me for maybe a year and then they couldn't . . . and I had to go to another one."

45   "How did it feel to be shunted about like that?"

46   "It hurt me. I was feeling like I wasn't wanted. I was just a kid . . . It's like, I'm a kid and nobody wants me. Even in school. The nuns taught me, but I never learned to read or write or nothing. They just pushed me from one class to another . . . I was always disciplined for something, and they'd take me out of that class and put me in a class for four- or five-year-old kids . . . so I felt so uncomfortable. It was hard for me. I felt stupid. I'm sitting there with all these little kids around me, looking at me. The teacher is teaching spelling . . . And they're doing it and I can't do it . . . I kept it all to myself. I didn't want to talk for the longest time . . . I couldn't even talk to people. I stuttered; I had a hard time explaining myself. I kept it all inside me for so long. When I get hyper I can't talk proper . . .

47   "Strange, the cocaine calms me down.[7] And the pot. I smoke five or six joints a day. That relaxes me, too. It takes the edge off. At the end of the day I just lay back with it. That's just what happens, that's my life. I smoke a joint and I go to sleep."

48   Shirley, in her forties, addicted to both opiates and stimulants and stricken with the usual roster of diseases, also confesses to a sense of inadequacy without her drugs and sees cocaine as a life necessity. "I was thirteen when I first used. It took most of my inhibitions away, and my uneasiness, my inadequacies—how we feel about our- selves I guess is a better way to put it."

49   "When you say inhibitions, what do you mean?" I ask.

50   "Inhibitions . . . it's like the awkwardness a man and a woman feel when you first meet, and you don't know whether to kiss each other, except I always felt that way. It makes everything go easier . . . your movements are more relaxed, so you're not awk- ward anymore."

51   No less a figure than the young Dr. Sigmund Freud was enthralled with cocaine for a while, relying on it "to control his intermittent depressed moods, improve his general sense of well-being, help him relax in tense social encounters, and *just make him feel more like a man*."[8] Freud was slow to accept that cocaine could create a dependence problem.

52   Enhancing the personality, the drug also eases social interactions, as Aubrey and Shirley both testify. "Usually, I'm feeling down," says Aubrey. "I do coke, I'm totally a different person. I could talk to you a lot better now if I was high on cocaine. I don't slur my words. It wakes me. It makes it easier to see people. I'll want to start a conver- sation with somebody. I'm usually not very interesting to talk to . . . That's why most of the time I don't want to be with other people. I don't have that drive. I stay in my room by myself."

53   Many addicts report similar improvements in their social abilities under the influ- ence, in contrast to the intolerable aloneness they experience when sober. "It makes me talk, it opens me up; I can be friendly," says one young man wired on crystal meth. "I'm never like this normally." We shouldn't underestimate how desperate a chronically lonely person is to escape the prison of solitude. It's not a matter here of common shyness but of a deep psychological sense of isolation experienced from early childhood by people who felt rejected by everyone, beginning with their caregivers.

> "We shouldn't underestimate how desperate a chronically
> lonely person is to escape the prison of solitude."

---

[7]A patient's report that a stimulant drug like cocaine or crystal meth has a calming effect is virtual confirmation that he or she has ADHD (Attention Deficit Hyperactivity Disorder). . . .

[8]Italics mine throughout unless otherwise noted. Peter Gay, *Freud: A Life for Our Time* (New York: W.W. Norton, 1998), 44.

54   Nicole is in her early fifties. After five years as my patient she revealed that, as a teenager, she'd been repeatedly raped by her father. She, too, has HIV, and the ravages of an old hip infection have left her hobbling around with a cane. "I'm more social with the drug," she says. "I get talkative and confident. Usually I'm shy and withdrawn and not very impressive. I let people walk all over me."

55   Another powerful dynamic perpetuates addiction despite the abundance of disastrous consequences: the addict sees no other possible existence for himself. His outlook on the future is restricted by his entrenched self-image as addict. No matter how much he may acknowledge the costs of his addiction, he fears a loss of self if it were absent from his life. In his own mind, he would cease to exist as he knows himself.

56   Carol says she was able to experience herself in a completely new and positive way under the influence of crystal meth. "I felt like I was smarter, like a floodgate of information or whatever just opened in my head . . . It opened my creativity. . . ." Asked if she has any regrets about her eight years of amphetamine addiction, she is quick to respond: "Not really, 'cause it helped bring me to who I am today." That may sound bizarre, but Carol's perspective is that drug use helped her escape an abusive family home, survive years of street living and connect her with a community of people with shared experiences. As many crystal meth users see it, this drug offers benefits to young street dwellers. Strange to say, it makes their lives more livable in the short term. It's hard to get a good night's sleep on the street: crystal meth keeps you awake and alert. No money for food? No need for hunger: crystal meth is an appetite suppressant. Tired, lacking energy? Crystal meth gives a user boundless energy.

57   Chris, a personable man with a mischievous sense of humour, whose well-muscled arms sport a kaleidoscope of tattoos, completed a year-long prison term a few months ago and is now back on the methadone program. In the Downtown Eastside he's known by the strange sobriquet "Toecutter," which he earned, legend has it, when he dropped a sharp, heavy industrial blade on someone's foot. He continues to inject crystal meth with dogged determination. "Helps me concentrate," he says. There's no doubt he's had Attention Deficit Disorder all his life and he accepts the diagnosis, but he declines treatment. "This smart doctor once told me I'm self-medicating," he smirks, recalling a conversation we had years ago.

58   Chris recently came into the clinic with a fracture of his facial bones, sustained in a street brawl over a "paper" of heroin. Had the blow struck an inch higher, his left eye would have been destroyed. "I don't want to give up being an addict," he says when I ask him if it's all worth it. "I know this sounds pretty fucked up, but I like who I am."

59   "You're sitting here with your face smashed in by a metal pipe, and you're telling me you like who you are?"

60   "Yes, but I like who *I* am. I'm Toecutter, I'm an addict and I'm a nice guy."

61   Jake, methadone-treated opiate addict and heavy cocaine user, is in his mid-thirties. With his wispy blond facial stubble and lively body movements and a black baseball cap pulled rakishly low over his eyes, he could pass for ten years younger. "You've been injecting a lot of cocaine recently," I remark to him one day.

62   "It's hard to get away from it," he replies with his gap-toothed grin.

63   "You make coke sound like it's some wild animal, stalking you. Yet you're the one who's chasing it. What does it do for you?"

64   "It cuts the edge off everyday life down here, of dealing with everything."

65   "What is everything?"

66   "Responsibilities. I guess you could call it that—responsibilities. So long as I'm using, I don't care about responsibilities . . . When I'm older, I'll worry about pension plans and stuff like that. But right now, I don't care about nothin' except my old lady."

67   "Your old lady . . ."

68   "Yeah, I look upon the coke as my old lady, my family. It's my partner. I don't see my own family for a year, and I don't care, 'cause I've got my partner."

69   "So the coke is your life."

70   "Yeah, the coke's my life . . . I care more about the dope than my loved ones or anything else. For the past fifteen years . . . it's part of me now. It's part of my every day . . . I don't know how to be without it. I don't know how to live everyday life without it. You take it away, I don't know what I'm going to do . . . If you were to change me and put me in a regular-style life, I wouldn't know how to retain it. I was there once in my life, but it feels like I don't know how to go back. I don't have the . . . It's not the will I don't have; I just don't know how."

71   "What about the desire? Do you even want that regular life?"

72   "No, not really," Jake says quietly and sadly.

73   I don't believe that's true. I think deep in his heart there must live a desire for a life of wholeness and integrity that may be too painful to acknowledge—painful because, in his eyes, it's unattainable. Jake is so identified with his addiction that he doesn't dare imagine himself sober. "It feels like everyday life for me," he says. "It doesn't seem any different from anyone else's life. It's normal for me."

74   That reminds me of the frog, I tell Jake. "They say that if you take a frog and drop him in hot water, he'll jump out. But if you take the same frog, put him in water at room temperature and then slowly heat up the water, he'll boil to death because gradually, degree by degree, he becomes used to it. He perceives it as normal.

75   "If you had a regular life and somebody said to you, `Hey, you could be in the Downtown Eastside hustling all day and blowing three or four hundred dollars a day on rock,' you'd say, `What? Are you crazy? That's not for me!' But you've been doing it for so long it's become normal for you."

76   Jake then shows me his hands and arms, covered with patches of silvery scales on a red, inflamed field of skin. On top of everything else, his psoriasis is acting up. "Do you think you could send me to a skin specialist?" he asks.

77   "I could," I reply, "but the last time I did, you didn't show for the appointment. If you miss this one, I won't refer you again."

78   "I'll go, Doc. Don't worry, I'll go."

79   I write out the prescriptions for methadone and for the dermatological creams Jake needs. We chat a little more, and then he leaves. He's my last patient of the day.

80   A few minutes later, as I'm about to check my voicemail messages, there's a knock. I pull the door ajar. It's Jake, who made it to the front gate of the Portland but has returned to tell me something. "You were right, you know," he says, grinning again.

81   "Right about what?"

82   "That frog you're talking about. That's me."

Reading Closely and Thinking Critically

1. What preconceptions about addiction and addicts is Maté attempting to challenge?
2. What needs are met by addictions?
3. What are the various causes of addiction? How do these many causes bring into question the common model of the addict as an individual who lacks self-control?
4. "A sense of deficient emptiness pervades our entire culture," Maté writes in paragraph 16. Use examples to agree or disagree with Maté's observation.
5. "Boredom, rooted in a fundamental discomfort with the self, is one of the least tolerable mental states," Maté asserts, without explanation or defence, at the end of paragraph 18. Is this something he should explain? Do you see this phenomenon at work in the society around you?
6. While our vulnerability is "our susceptibility to be wounded," it also plays positive roles in our lives, as if it were two sides of the same coin. Explain the positive role that vulnerability has in human life as well as how the desire to be invulnerable sabotages the addict.

Examining Structure and Strategy

1. Maté explains the causes of addiction in this essay. What role do his examples play in this explanation? Do the examples suggest that he has a second, equally important purpose?
2. In paragraphs 4 and 5, Maté explains that the brain responds to mental and physical pain in much the same way. Why does he draw attention to this similarity?
3. Generally speaking, we consider paragraphs of one or two sentences undeveloped. Paragraph 7 is a single sentence: "The question is never 'Why the addiction?' but 'Why the pain?'" Is this an effective strategy? Why or why not?
4. In paragraph 11, after he has allowed us to hear the stories and voices of three addicts, Maté writes, "My prose is unequal to the task of depicting such nearly inconceivable trauma." Does this lessen or increase your trust in him as a writer?
5. Consider the parable of the boiled frog that closes the essay. Is this an effective way to conclude?

Considering Language and Style

1. Why does Maté tell the stories of addicts using their own words?
2. Many of Maté's examples come from the lives of the patients he sees in his role as physician at the Portland Hotel. But in other cases, he gives us the words of people like Thomas De Quincey, Primo Levi, Jean Améry, and Sigmund Freud. What does this variety of examples accomplish?
3. On of the street names for cocaine is "the rock." In paragraph 30, Maté draws an implicit comparison between cocaine and religious belief by quoting the Bible. Why does he do this?

For Discussion in Class or Online

What preconceptions do you have about addiction and addicts? Has Maté prompted you to question any of your beliefs? If your instructor so directs, post your response to your class Web site.

Writing Assignments

1. **In your journal.** In his book on addiction, *In the Realm of Hungry Ghosts,* Maté talks about his own addiction to buying classical CDs—not something you think of as an addiction. He also thinks of addiction as a continuum that includes behaviours as well as drug use. Do you have any addictions? Must you watch cartoons when you are avoiding writing an essay? Do you need chocolate or Red Bull to get through an all-nighter? Write about your own addictions, however minor they are, and attempt to understand what needs they meet in your life.
2. **Using exemplification for a purpose.** The purposes given in the assignments are possibilities. You may establish whatever purposes you like, within your instructor's guidelines.
    - To inform your reader, use exemplification to explain different ways in which people learn.
    - To inform your reader, use exemplification to explain a concept like repression or projection that you have learned about in psychology class.
    - To inform your reader, use examples to explain how students balance school and work.
    - To explore your feelings, use examples to people whose lives you admire that might illustrate how you want to live your life.
    - To persuade your reader, use examples to suggest how North Americans are addicted to cars or fast food or cruising the malls.
3. **Combining patterns.** Use both exemplification and contrast and comparison to consider the effects of two different addictions (not necessarily to illicit drugs).
4. **Connecting the readings.** "A sense of deficient emptiness pervades our entire culture," Maté writes in "The Keys of Paradise." Mark Kingwell similarly argues that although our culture promises happiness with the acquisition of material goods, they do not really make us happier. Contrast or compare the ability of money and drugs to give us the illusion of happiness.
5. **Drawing on sources.** Consult the *Canadian Periodical Index* for magazine articles in the popular press that address the causes of drug addiction. Do more extensive research on the cause that seems most convincing to you.

Background

Born in Butte, Montana, in 1941, award-winning political essayist and social activist Barbara Ehrenreich has lent her support to many progressive causes, including the women's movement. She comes from a science background, having earned her PhD in biology from Rockefeller University. After teaching college for a time, she turned to writing. She is a social critic whose sometimes scathing commentaries have appeared in *The Nation, Harper's, Z Magazine, Atlantic Monthly, New York Times Magazine, TV Guide,* and *Mother Jones.* Ehrenreich also writes regularly for *The Progressive* and *Time.* A popular guest on television programs, Ehrenreich has appeared on both *Good Morning America* and *Today.* She is the author of many books, including *Nickel and Dimed: On (Not) Getting by in America* (2001) and *Dancing in the Streets: A History of Collective Joy (2007).* "What I've Learned from Men" first appeared in *Ms.* in 1985.

Combined Patterns and Their Purposes

In "What I've Learned from Men," Barbara Ehrenreich combines exemplification with cause-and-effect analysis, definition, contrast, and narration to inform her audience about a problem she thinks women have: they are too "ladylike." She goes on to persuade her readers that women should become more like men— that is, tougher and more assertive. Although the essay originally appeared in 1985 in a magazine aimed at women, it has relevance today for both male and female readers.

What I've Learned from Men: Lessons for a Full-Grown Feminist

Barbara Ehrenreich

1   For many years I believed that women had only one thing to learn from men: how to get the attention of a waiter by some means short of kicking over the table and shrieking. Never in my life have I gotten the attention of a waiter, unless it was an off-duty waiter whose car I'd accidentally scraped in a parking lot somewhere. Men, however, can summon a maître d' just by thinking the word "coffee," and this is a power women would be well-advised to study. What else would we possibly want to learn from them? How to interrupt someone in midsentence as if you were performing an act of conversational euthanasia? How to drop a pair of socks three feet from an open hamper and keep right on walking? How to make those weird guttural gargling sounds in the bathroom?

> **As you read**
> Think about what it means to be "ladylike."

2   But now, at mid-life, I am willing to admit that there are some real and useful things to learn from men. Not from all men—in fact, we may have the most to learn from some of the men we like the least. This realization does not mean that my feminist principles have gone soft with age: what I think women could learn from men is how to get *tough.* After more than a decade of consciousness-raising, assertiveness training, and hand-to-hand combat in the battle of the sexes, we're still too ladylike. Let me try that again—we're just too *damn* ladylike.

3   Here is an example from my own experience, a story that I blush to recount. A few years ago, at an international conference held in an exotic and luxurious setting, a prestigious professor invited me to his room for what he said would be an intellectual

discussion on matters of theoretical importance. So far, so good. I showed up promptly. But only minutes into the conversation—held in all-too-adjacent chairs—it emerged that he was interested in something more substantial than a meeting of minds. I was disgusted, but not enough to overcome 30-odd years of programming in ladylikeness. Every time his comments took a lecherous turn, I chattered distractingly; every time his hand found its way to my knee, I returned it as if it were something he had misplaced. This went on for an unconscionable period (as much as 20 minutes); then there was a minor scuffle, a dash for the door, and I was out—with nothing violated but my self-esteem. I, a full-grown feminist, conversant with such matters as rape crisis counseling and sexual harassment at the workplace, had behaved like a ninny—or, as I now understand it, like a lady.

4   The essence of ladylikeness is a persistent servility masked as "niceness." For example, we (women) tend to assume that it is our responsibility to keep everything "nice" even when the person we are with is rude, aggressive, or emotionally AWOL. (In the above example, I was so busy taking responsibility for preserving the veneer of "niceness" that I almost forgot to take responsibility for myself.) In conversations with men, we do almost all the work: sociologists have observed that in male-female social interactions it's the woman who throws out leading questions and verbal encouragements ("So how did you *feel* about that?" and so on) while the man, typically, says "Hmmmm." Wherever we go, we're perpetually smiling—the on-cue smile, like the now-outmoded curtsy, being one of our culture's little rituals of submission. We're trained to feel embarrassed if we're praised, but if we see a criticism coming at us from miles down the road, we rush to acknowledge it. And when we're feeling aggressive or angry or resentful, we just tighten up our smiles or turn them into rueful little moues. In short, we spend a great deal of time acting like wimps.

5   For contrast, think of the macho stars we love to watch. Think, for example, of Mel Gibson facing down punk marauders in "The Road Warrior" . . . John Travolta swaggering his way through the early scenes of "Saturday Night Fever" . . . or Marlon Brando shrugging off the local law in "The Wild One." Would they simper their way through tight spots? Chatter aimlessly to keep the conversation going? Get all clutched up whenever they think they might—just might—have hurt someone's feelings? No, of course not, and therein, I think, lies their fascination for us.

> "Think, for example, of Mel Gibson facing down
> punk marauders in 'The Road Warrior.'"

6   The attraction of the "tough guy" is that he has—or at least seems to have—what most of us lack, and that is an aura of power and control. In an article, feminist psychiatrist Jean Baker Miller writes that "a woman's using self-determined power for herself is equivalent to selfishness [and] destructiveness—an equation that makes us want to avoid even the appearance of power." Miller cites cases of women who get depressed just when they're on the verge of success—and of women who do succeed and then bury their achievement in self-deprecation. As an example, she

describes one company's periodic meetings to recognize outstanding salespeople: when a woman is asked to say a few words about her achievement, she tends to say something like, "Well, I really don't know how it happened. I guess I was just lucky this time." In contrast, the men will cheerfully own up to the hard work, intelligence, and so on, to which they owe their success. By putting herself down, a woman avoids feeling brazenly powerful and potentially "selfish"; she also does the traditional lady's work of trying to make everyone else feel better ("She's not really so smart, after all, just lucky").

7   So we might as well get a little tougher. And a good place to start is by cutting back on the small acts of deference that we've been programmed to perform since girlhood. Like unnecessary smiling. For many women—waitresses, flight attendants, receptionists—smiling is an occupational requirement, but there's no reason for anyone to go around grinning when she's not being paid for it. I'd suggest that we save our off-duty smiles for when we truly feel like sharing them, and if you're not sure what to do with your face in the meantime, study Clint Eastwood's expressions—both of them.

8   Along the same lines, I think women should stop taking responsibility for every human interaction we engage in. In a social encounter with a woman, the average man can go 25 minutes saying nothing more than "You don't say?" "Izzat so?" and, of course, "Hmmmm." Why should we do all the work? By taking so much responsibility for making conversations go well, we act as if we had much more at stake in the encounter than the other party—and that gives him (or her) the power advantage. Every now and then, we deserve to get more out of a conversation than we put into it: I'd suggest not offering information you'd rather not share ("I'm really terrified that my sales plan won't work") and not, out of sheer politeness, soliciting information you don't really want ("Wherever did you get that lovely tie?"). There will be pauses, but they don't have to be awkward for *you.*

9   It is true that some, perhaps most, men will interpret any decrease in female deference as a deliberate act of hostility. Omit the free smiles and perky conversation-boosters and someone is bound to ask, "Well, what's come over *you* today?" For most of us, the first impulse is to stare at our feet and make vague references to a terminally ill aunt in Atlanta, but we should have as much right to be taciturn as the average (male) taxi driver. If you're taking a vacation from smiles and small talk and some fellow is moved to inquire about what's "bothering" you, just stare back levelly and say, the international debt crisis, the arms race, or the death of God.

10   There are all kinds of ways to toughen up—and potentially move up—at work, and I leave the details to the purveyors of assertiveness training. But Jean Baker Miller's study underscores a fundamental principle that anyone can master on her own. We can stop acting less capable than we actually are. For example, in the matter of taking credit when credit is due, there's a key difference between saying "I was just lucky" and saying "I had a plan and it worked." If you take the credit you deserve, you're

letting people know that you were confident you'd succeed all along, and that you fully intend to do so again.

"We can stop acting less capable than we actually are."

11   Finally, we may be able to learn something from men about what to do with anger. As a general rule, women get irritated; men get *mad*. We make tight little smiles of ladylike exasperation; they pound on desks and roar. I wouldn't recommend emulating the full basso profundo male tantrum, but women do need ways of expressing justified anger clearly, colorfully, and when necessary, crudely. If you're not just irritated, but *pissed off,* it might help to say so.

12   I, for example, have rerun the scene with the prestigious professor many times in my mind. And in my mind, I play it like Bogart. I start by moving my chair over to where I can look the professor full in the face. I let him do the chattering, and when it becomes evident that he has nothing serious to say, I lean back and cross my arms, just to let him know that he's wasting my time. I do not smile, neither do I nod encouragement. Nor, of course, do I respond to his blandishments with apologetic shrugs and blushes. Then, at the first flicker of lechery, I stand up and announce coolly, "All right, I've had enough of this crap." Then I walk out—slowly, deliberately, confidently. Just like a man.

13   Or—now that I think of it—just like a woman.

Reading Closely and Thinking Critically
1. What three things has Barbara Ehrenreich *really* learned from men?
2. Why do you think that Ehrenreich "blush[es] to recount" the story of her encounter at the conference? Do you think she has good reason to blush? Explain.
3. Why wasn't Ehrenreich more assertive with the lecherous professor?
4. Why do you think some women get depressed when "they're on the verge of success," and why do others "bury their achievement in self-deprecation" (see paragraph 6)?
5. Using the evidence in the essay, write a one- or two-sentence definition of *lady* or *ladylike* that reflects Ehrenreich's meaning of one of these terms.

Examining Structure and Strategy
1. Ehrenreich delays her thesis until paragraph 2. Which sentence presents that thesis? The material before the thesis is humorous. How does the humour help her achieve her purpose? Do you think that beginning a discussion of a serious topic in an amusing way is an effective strategy?
2. What paragraph marks Ehrenreich's move from an informative to a persuasive purpose?
3. How would you describe Ehrenreich's original audience (see the headnote on page 205)? Was this audience likely to be receptive to her message? Explain.

Noting Combined Patterns
1. What is the function of the narrative example in paragraph 3? Does this example clarify by showing that something is true, by making the general specific, or both? What contrast does the example set up? (Contrast, discussed in Chapter 9, points out differences.) What other paragraphs include contrast?

2. Brief examples appear in paragraphs 4, 5, 6, 7, 8, and 10. How do these examples help the author achieve her purpose? Which paragraph provides a definition of *ladylikeness* and *lady?* What is the purpose of that definition? (Definition, which explains the meaning of something, is discussed in Chapter 7.)

3. Paragraphs 6, 9, and 10 include cause-and-effect analysis. (Cause-and-effect analysis, which explains the causes and/or effects of something, is explained in Chapter 10.) How does this analysis help the author achieve her purpose?

Considering Language and Style

1. What connotations does the word *lady* have for most people? What connotations does it have in "What I've Learned from Men"?

2. How does the language in the last two sentences echo Ehrenreich's thesis and create closure?

3. Consult a dictionary if you are unsure of the meaning of any of these words: *maître d'* (paragraph 1), *euthanasia* (paragraph 1), *guttural* (paragraph 1), *lecherous* (paragraph 3), *unconscionable* (paragraph 3), *veneer* (paragraph 4), *rueful* (paragraph 4), *taciturn* (paragraph 9), *purveyors* (paragraph 10).

For Discussion in Class or Online

What do you think "What I've Learned from Men" has to offer to male readers? Do you think the essay is relevant today? Explain why you think as you do. If your instructor so directs, post your response to your class Web site.

Writing Assignments

1. **In your journal.** Compose a one- or two-paragraph narration to illustrate what Ehrenreich should have done when she was in the company of the lecherous professor.

2. **Using exemplification for a purpose.** The purposes given in the assignments are possibilities. You may establish whatever purposes you like, within your instructor's guidelines.
   - Write an essay with the title, "What I've Learned from _____." Fill in the blank with the name of a teacher, a boss, a coach, a member of the clergy, a relative, and so on. To relate your experience and to inform, give examples to illustrate the lessons you learned from the person's behaviour.
   - Ehrenreich writes about what women can learn from men. To inform, turn the tables and write about what men can learn from women. Use examples to illustrate your points. If you want to make your essay humorous, your purpose can be to entertain.
   - Do you agree with Ehrenreich? Using illustrations to support your stand, persuade your reader that Ehrenreich is right (or wrong).

3. **Combining patterns.** Select something about yourself you would like to change. Perhaps you are impulsive, a procrastinator, short-tempered, easily intimidated, or afraid to take risks. Give examples of times you exhibited the behaviour and explain a process for changing the behaviour. (Process analysis is explained in Chapter 8.)

4. **Connecting the readings.** In "The Mirror of the Internet" (page 362), Serge Tisseron notes that students in a wired world communicate differently. Consider Tisseron's points along with those of Ehrenreich and then discuss the ways less assertive students might respond to distance learning, paperless classrooms, and email communication.

5. **Drawing on sources.** For two or three days, observe the way male and female students behave in the classroom. Pay attention to such things as how they speak, what they say, how many questions they ask, how often they are called upon, where they sit, how they interact with the instructor, and how they interact with classmates. Then write an essay that notes and gives examples of similarities in and differences between the way male and female students behave in the classroom.

Additional Essay Assignments

See pages 180 and 182 for strategies for writing exemplification and for a revising checklist.

1. Use examples of a particular kind of music to help explain the characteristics of the genre.
2. Use examples of fantasy or science fiction to explain the characteristics of the genre.
3. Use examples to distinguish between well-written and poorly written genre fiction such as mysteries or horror.
4. Use examples to prove that advertisements cause people to want things that they do not really need.
5. Use examples to explain a concept you are learning in one of your other classes..
6. Use examples to illustrate the benefits or drawbacks of computers or some other form of technology.
7. Form a generalization about the way some group is depicted on television (women, police officers, the elderly, teenagers, or fathers, for instance) and provide examples to illustrate that generalization. Evaluate the accuracy of the depiction.
8. Use examples to show that advertisements can mislead the consumer.
9. Use illustrations to persuade your reader that sometimes a lie is better than the truth.
10. Provide humorous examples to illustrate Murphy's First Law ("What *can* go wrong, *will* go wrong").
11. Provide examples to show that people are at their worst when they are behind the wheel of their cars.
12. Use examples to persuade your reader that athletics have (or have not) assumed excessive importance in this country.
13. Use examples to persuade your reader that the Canadian family is (or is not) changing for the better.
14. Use examples to persuade your reader that the Canadian education system is in need of a major overhaul.
16. Use examples to illustrate the fact that sometimes people can surprise you.
17. Use examples to illustrate some aspect of the relationship you had with your best friend when you were growing up.
18. Provide examples to illustrate the fact that jealousy can be a destructive emotion.
19. Provide examples to illustrate the fact that people make their own luck.
20. **Exemplification in context:** Assume that your local Home and School Association has asked families and schools to consider a month-long ban on television viewing for school-age children. The organization's goal is to get children away from their television sets and engaged in "more worthwhile" activities, such as reading, interacting with family members, studying, playing sports, enjoying hobbies, and so forth. A public forum is being held to look at the advantages and disadvantages of the proposal. Write a position paper to be distributed at the forum, a paper in which you support or attack the moratorium by offering illustrations to convince people that television has negative (or positive) effects on children.

Chapter 7

Definition

Absurdity, *n.*: A statement or belief manifestly inconsistent with one's own opinion.

Acquaintance, *n.*: A person whom we know well enough to borrow from but not well enough to lend to.

Admiration, *n.*: A polite recognition of another's resemblance to ourselves.

Bore, *n.*: A person who talks when you wish him to listen.

Politics, *n.*: A strife of interests masquerading as a contest of principles.

— Ambrose Bierce, *The Devil's Dictionary*

Common sense and a sense of humor are the same thing, moving at different speeds. A sense of humor is just common sense, dancing.

— William James

THE PATTERN

Except for the phone book, the dictionary may be the most frequently consulted reference book. Since grade school, we have gone to the dictionary to check the meaning of a word we don't know, and now when we work on the computer, we can strike a key or two and consult an online dictionary even faster. When we consult a dictionary, we get a **formal definition,** which often explains a term by giving the class it belongs to and how it differs from other members of that class.

TERM	CLASS	DIFFERENTIATION
A formula is	a set of words	that indicates a procedure to be followed.
An embryo is	an organism	in its early stages of development, particularly before it has achieved recognizable form.
Repression is	the unconscious exclusion from one's conscious mind	of painful or taboo memories, thoughts, or desires.

Definitions play a significant role in post-secondary education, partly because it is in the very nature of the academy to explore new and unfamiliar concepts. When scholars formulate a new idea, make a new observation, or suggest a new procedure, one of the first things they have to do is create an expression that seems to capture the phenomenon and define it. For example, trying to figure out how to encourage industries to produce less CO_2, economists and environmentalists came up with two solutions. One, which they came to call a cap-and-trade system, proposes that industrial producers of carbon be given limits with respect to how much carbon they can produce. If they put energy-saving measures into place and produce less, they can trade their potential but unused CO_2 credits with another company. If they produce more, they have to buy those credits from another company. The second solution is a carbon tax. Such a tax simply charges a company for every tonne of CO_2 it produces. (Please see Jane Hoffman and Michael Hoffman's book, *Green*, for a further discussion of these concepts.) In order to convince citizens to support one idea or the other, however, environmentalists need clear definitions. Let's see how we can use the paradigm for definitions to create one.

TERM	CLASS	DIFFERENTIATION
The cap-and-trade system	is a means of encouraging companies to produce less greenhouse gas	by first setting limits (measured by credits) on how much carbon a company can produce, and then allowing it to sell credits if it produces less carbon than expected, or forcing it to buy credits if it produces more.
Carbon tax	is a means of encouraging companies to produce less greenhouse gas	by charging a company for every tonne of CO_2 it produces.

You can see from these definitions that a carbon tax and a cap-and-trade system are trying to accomplish the same thing, so you can focus your attention now on the effectiveness of the ways companies are being encouraged to produce fewer greenhouse gases.

Similarly, scholars in the sciences and humanities have been trying since the 1960s to understand how gender plays out in our private and social lives.

Observing that in many cultures masculinity is associated with being power-ful, R. W. Connell coined the term "hegemonic masculinity" in his 1995 book *Masculinities*:

> The concept of "hegemony," deriving from Antonio Gramsci's analysis of class relations, refers to the cultural dynamic by which a group claims and sustains a leading position in social life. At any given time, one form of masculinity rather than others is culturally exalted. Hegemonic masculinity can be defined as the configuration of gender practice which embodies the currently accepted answer to the problem of the legitimacy of patriarchy, which guarantees (or is taken to guarantee) the dominant position of men and the subordinate position of women.
>
> This is not to say that the most visible bearers of hegemonic masculinity are always the most powerful people. They may be exemplars, such as film actors, or even fantasy figures, such as film characters. Individual holders of institu-tional power or great wealth may be far from the hegemonic pattern in their personal lives. (Thus a male member of a prominent business dynasty was a key figure in the gay/transvestite social scene in Sydney in the 1950s, because of his wealth and the protection this gave in the cold-war climate of political and police harassment.) (77)

Note how Connell needs to define "hegemony" before he can define hege-monic masculinity. Also note the role that examples play in his discussion of the concept. Again, let's try to apply the elements of a formal definition to this discussion.

TERM	CLASS	DIFFERENTIATION
Hegemony	is a cultural dynamic, or the way people interact with one another,	that allows a particular group of people to claim and play a leading position in social life.
Hegemonic masculinity	is a particular way of acting and being manly	that is used to account for why men are dominant and women are subordinate.

Sometimes, however, simply saying what something *is* isn't enough. In that case you use a **negative definition:** You say what something isn't. This strategy is often welcome when you are having difficulty defining some-thing. (Gender, of course, comes to mind here as one of the hardest things to define.) You could say, for example, "It isn't manly to beat your wife or to abuse people who are powerless, even if you have the power to do so." Or we could write, "Being a woman does not necessarily mean wanting to be a mother."

Another kind of definition is the **stipulative definition,** which states a particular, special way a term is being used. Writers who want to use a term in a way a reader might not expect can include a stipulative definition. For example, if you were writing an essay to convince the dean of student services to offer more night classes for adult learners, you might write something like this:

> By adult learner, I mean any student over 25 who has been out of school for at least 5 years. The adult learner typically works full-time and helps support a family.

You can use a stipulative definition to ensure that your reader understands precisely how you are using a term.

Sometimes you want to go beyond a word's literal dictionary meaning to explain the significance, associations, private meanings, and personal experiences associated with the word. This information can only come from an **extended definition,** the kind of essay this chapter treats. For example, consider the word *sled*. A dictionary will tell a reader that it is a vehicle on runners used for coasting on snow. However, an extended definition can tell the reader that a sled contributed to the happiest times you shared with your brother and father. Now consider the word *prejudice*, which can mean different things to different people. An extended definition allows you to explain the meaning and significance *you* ascribe to the word. Thus, an extended definition affords a writer the opportunity to go beyond the formal or stipulative meaning to express feelings, opinions, knowledge, unusual views, and personal experiences associated with a word.

USING DEFINITION FOR A PURPOSE

More often than not, an extended definition informs. Sometimes you inform by clarifying something that is complex. For example, an essay that defines *freedom* can help the reader understand this very difficult concept. A definition can also inform by bringing the reader to a fresh appreciation of something familiar or taken for granted. For example, if you think that Canadians do not sufficiently appreciate free speech, you could define *free speech* to help readers renew their appreciation for this important liberty. A definition can also bring a reader to an understanding of something new or unfamiliar—or something the reader simply hasn't thought much about. In "What Is the Good Life," Mark Kingwell defines reflection as "the always incomplete attempt to make sense of who we are and what we are up to, trying all the while to do that most difficult of things, to live better" (page 225). An extended definition of the cap-and-trade system and of carbon taxes would go beyond the basic definition above to consider how these different systems might do more or less to encourage companies to reduce their emissions. It would also discuss how their administrations differ. Extended definitions go beyond simple meanings of words to consider the implications of a concept.

In addition to informing, an extended definition can allow you to express feelings and relate experiences. For example, you could define *teenager* by explaining what your own teenage years were like and in this way relate part of your experience with adolescence.

A definition can also entertain, as when you write a humorous definition of *first-year university student*, to amuse your reader. Finally, an extended definition can serve a persuasive purpose, particularly when it points to a conclusion about a controversial issue. For example, Mark Kingwell's definition of the good life, his sense that it involves not "more stuff" but "more meaning," and that we seek this meaning in commitments to community, common goals, and more time to reflect, seeks to persuade readers that a competitive quest for more material goods will not give meaning to their lives (page 224). Similarly, Judy Brady defines *wife* in "I Want a Wife" (page 232) to convince the reader that the traditional wifely role is unfair to women.

In addition to using definition to develop entire essays, you will often use this pattern with other methods of development. For example, if you classify kinds of folk art, you might first define what folk art is; if you provide examples of courage, you might begin with your personal definition of courage; and if you explain the causes and effects of anorexia nervosa, you will probably define anorexia nervosa early on.

Definition at School, at Work, and in the Community

Post-secondary work requires you to learn the meaning of terms and concepts, and a good way to demonstrate your understanding of these terms and concepts is to write definitions. Sometimes these definitions will be extended, as when you define *existentialism* in a paper for a philosophy class or when you define *naturalism* for an essay for an American literature class. You might also write an extended definition of *natural selection* for a biology class, of *the enclosure movement* for an economics class, or of *cultural relativity* for an anthropology class.

Many times, you will incorporate formal definition with other patterns of development. For example, a history paper might require you to define the *chivalric code* and then go on to explain its effects. Similarly, a paper for an introductory psychology course might require you to define and classify *defence mechanisms* and then go on to give examples of each kind.

Definition is an important part of college and university textbooks. Here is one example, taken from the introductory textbook *Sociology*.

> It is tempting to evaluate the practices of other cultures on the basis of our own perspectives. Sociologist William Graham Sumner (1906) coined the term *ethnocentrism* to refer to the tendency to assume that one's culture and way of life constitute the norm or are superior to all others. The ethnocentric person sees his or her own group as the center or defining point of culture and views all other cultures as deviations from what is "normal."
>
> Those westerners who are contemptuous of India's Hindu religion and culture because of its view of cattle as sacred are engaged in ethnocentrism. As another manifestation of ethnocentrism, people in one culture may dismiss as unthinkable the mate selection or child rearing practices of another culture . . . (Schaefer, *Sociology*).

To clarify unfamiliar terms and concepts, textbooks often follow definitions with examples. In the above excerpt, notice that the definition of ethnocentrism comes in the first paragraph and examples of ethnocentrism come in the second paragraph to help students grasp the concept and remember the definition.

On the job, definition is also important. A teacher might write a stipulative definition of "competency testing" in a memo to parents in order to help them understand how the tests are used in their children's classrooms. A dietitian might write formal definitions of "good cholesterol" and "bad cholesterol" to help clients make better food choices. A human resources manager might combine formal, stipulative, and extended definitions of "mutual gains bargaining" to persuade a labour union to adopt this negotiating practice.

Outside the classroom, writers have many occasions to use definition. As editor of your religious congregation's newsletter, you might write an editorial that is an extended definition of *charity* to encourage congregants to give more generously. In a letter to the editor of your local newspaper, you might define *good citizen* to encourage readers to vote.

SUPPORTING DETAILS

In general, an extended definition presents the characteristics of what is being defined. Thus, to define *courage*, you might note that its characteristics include doing what needs to be done without regard to personal cost and even when afraid.

Often when you present the characteristics, you rely on other patterns. For example, if you define *sinus headache* to relate your own experiences with this misery, you could describe the pain. To define *math anxiety* to inform the reader of what this condition is like, part of your essay could narrate an account of a time you experienced this anxiety. To define a *good teacher* to inform your reader of what a teacher should be like, you could include examples of good teachers from your past. To define *maturity,* you could include a contrast of maturity with immaturity. To define *sexual harassment* to convince people to take action against this practice, part of your piece could analyze the causes and effects of sexual harassment to show why it is such a problem.

Sometimes you should explain what your subject is *not,* especially if you need to correct a misconception. For example, if you were defining *poverty,* you could note that poverty is not necessarily something that people can escape if they just try hard enough.

When you write your definition, avoid stating the obvious, and avoid using a dictionary style unless you are writing a formal definition. If you state the obvious, you will bore your reader. Thus, if you are defining *mother,* you need not state that a mother is a female parent. Similarly, a dictionary style in an extended definition is likely to bore a reader because it is stiff and unlike your own natural style. Thus, avoid defining *teenager* as "a person in that developmental period of hormonal and social change marking the transition from childhood to adulthood."

Troubleshooting Guide

Avoiding Circular Definitions

If you have trouble avoiding circular definitions, remember to avoid repeating the words you are defining or merely using synonyms for those words.

CIRCULAR	**Male liberation is the liberation of men.**
CIRCULAR	**Male liberation involves freeing men.**
BETTER	**Male liberation allows men to relinquish their historical roles to assume roles formerly held only by women.**

As you can see, circular definitions communicate very little, so they are not helpful.

ORGANIZING DETAILS

The thesis for an extended definition can state what will be defined and your assertion about what will be defined, like this:

Adolescence is not the happy time many people remember it to be.

This thesis indicates you will define *adolescence* and show that it can be a difficult period.

You can also shape a thesis by noting what will be defined and why it is important to understand the term, like this:

If we do not understand the meaning of free speech, we will be in danger of losing it.

To create interest in your essay, your introduction can explain the significance of the definition. Thus, if you are defining *homelessness,* you can note the extent of homelessness in this country to show why readers need to understand it. You can also tell a story related to what you are defining. In addition, if the meaning of your term has changed over the years, you can explain what your term used to mean before going on to give a current definition. For example, if you are defining *dating,* you could open by noting that dating used to mean sitting in the parlour with a girl's parents or attending a church social together.

Since definition often includes other patterns, the order of details will be influenced by these patterns. Thus, narrations will use chronological order, cause-and-effect analysis will reproduce causal chains, and so on. Purpose, too, can influence order. Thus, if your purpose is persuasive, you may want to place the characteristics of what you are defining in a progressive order to save the most important points for last.

VISUALIZING A DEFINITION ESSAY

The following chart can help you visualize the structure for a definition essay. Like all good models, however, this one can be altered as needed.

PROCESS GUIDELINES: STRATEGIES FOR WRITING DEFINITION

1. **Selecting a Topic.** Consider the roles you play in your life and the aspects of those roles. For example, if you are an athlete, you can define

Introduction
• Creates interest in the essay, perhaps by explaining the significance of the definition, explaining how its meaning has changed over the years, or telling a story related to the term • States the thesis, which can state what will be defined and your assertion about what will be defined or why it is important to understand the term

Body Paragraphs
• Give and explain all characteristics of the term • May include any patterns of development • May explain what the term is not • Avoid stating the obvious, circular definitions, and dictionary style • Arrange details according to the patterns used

Conclusion
• Provides a satisfying finish • Leaves the reader with a positive final impression

student athlete or *competition.* Or consider the emotions and moods you have experienced lately and define one of them: *love, anger, anxiety, anticipation, jealousy,* and so forth.

2. **Generating Ideas.** List all the characteristics of what you are defining. Then circle the ones you want to treat.

   a. For each circled characteristic, ask these questions:
   - Can I tell a story to reveal or illustrate the characteristic?
   - What examples illustrate the characteristic?
   - Can I describe the characteristic?
   - Can I compare or contrast the characteristic with something?
   - Can I explain how the characteristic works?
   - What are the causes and effects of the characteristic?

   b. Decide whether you need to clear up any reader misconceptions by explaining what your subject is not.

   c. Write a statement of the significance of your term and why it is important to define it. You can use a version of this statement in your introduction, as your thesis, or in your conclusion.

✔ Checklist for Revising Definition

Be sure:

_____   Your thesis notes what you are defining.

_____   You have avoided stating the obvious.

_____   You have avoided an inappropriate dictionary style.

_____   You have developed all the relevant characteristics of your term.

_____   You have used appropriate patterns of development and organized accordingly.

_____   You have explained what your term is *not,* as needed.

_____   You have stated or strongly implied the significance of your definition.

_____   You have avoided "is when" constructions and circular definitions.

ANNOTATED STUDENT ESSAY

Student writer Nick Hickman defines a technical term for a non-technical reader in order to inform and—surprisingly—entertain. To address the needs of his audience, Nick uses process analysis, exemplification, and an image. After you read, you will have an opportunity to evaluate the essay.

Why Did the Chicken Cross the Möbius Strip?
(Or Babysitting for Dummies)

1   Ask anyone over the age of three why the chicken crossed the road, and you will immediately get the response: "to get to the other side." Ask the question in the title (Why did the chicken cross the Möbius strip?), and you will get a far different response: "What is a Möbius strip?" The answer is that the *Möbius strip* is an example of a nonorientable surface. It is a seemingly impossible object of great interest to mathematicians, yet a person can hold it in the palm of one hand.

2   To understand the Möbius strip, a person must know what a nonorientable surface is, which means first knowing the definition of a surface. Think of a *surface* as anything that can be created by taping together sheets of paper. The only restriction is that the sheets must be taped flat-side-to-flat side or edge-to-edge. In other words, long strips of paper are surfaces, and an L-shape made by two sheets taped at their edges is a surface. A cylinder can be thought of as a surface in two different ways—by putting two pieces of paper together or by connecting the opposite edges of one sheet. A person who gets really creative can even build a pair of pants or a shirt this way but not a set of bookshelves. Bookshelves cannot be a surface because the edges and back of each shelf make a T-shape with the outer casing.

3   In addition to all of them being surfaces, a cylinder, a pair of pants, and a shirt have something else in common. They all have a clearly distinguishable inside and outside. That is, a person who touches a pair of pants with a finger can readily tell whether the outside or the inside of the object is being touched. The same is true for a tabletop, a drinking glass, or a funhouse mirror because all of these are surfaces with a well-defined front and back, inside and outside, or top and bottom. This is what it means to be an *orientable surface*.

4   Obviously, that means that a *nonorientable surface* must be a surface with only one side! Orientable surfaces are boring everyday objects—certainly no fun at parties—but a one-sided object could really be something to show off to a crowd!

Paragraph 1
The introduction creates interest with a twist on a children's riddle. The thesis is the last two sentences. It combines a formal technical definition with the intriguing notion (that also creates interest) that the Möbius strip is "seemingly impossible."

Paragraph 2
The paragraph opens with a topic sentence noting that a necessary background definition will be given (of *surface*). The supporting details give a characteristic of the term being defined and explain the characteristic with examples.

Paragraph 3
The topic sentence is the last sentence. It notes that another background definition (*orientable surface*) is given. The supporting details give a characteristic of the term, which is explained with examples.

Paragraph 4
This is a transitional paragraph, linking the definitions of orientable and nonorientable surfaces. Notice the touch of humour. How is it likely to appeal to the author's intended audience?

Paragraph 5

The paragraph opens with a topic sentence that notes the paragraph will be about how to make a Möbius strip. Knowing how to make the strip helps the reader understand its nature. The detail is process analysis.

5   The best way to demonstrate that a Möbius strip is a nonorientable surface is to construct one. Take a standard pants belt, unbuckled. Bring the tip around toward the buckle, just as if you were putting the belt around your waist, but do not buckle it. Notice that if you buckled the belt normally it would clearly have two sides, an inside and an outside. Now take the tip and give it half a twist so the "inside" is facing out, and buckle it in this position. This is a Möbius strip, a one-sided surface right in your own home that looks like this:

The drawing helps the reader visualize the strip. How important is the drawing?

Paragraph 6

The process analysis further clarifies the nature of the term.

6   To test for nonorientability, take your finger and place it by the buckle. Now trace the belt around until it gets back to the buckle again. Your finger should be on the "other side" of the belt. Without lifting your finger, keep tracing. When you get back to the buckle a second time, your finger will have returned to the "correct side" of the belt. You have now touched every part of the surface, but you changed sides without lifting your finger!

7   To mathematicians, a nonorientable surface is a two-dimensional manifold with no consistent choice of fundamental class in its second homology group. The Möbius strip, which was discovered by German mathematician August Ferdinand Möbius in 1868, can be thought of as one of two canonical vector bundles over the circle or as a topological quotient space of the closed unit square. At heart, though, a Möbius strip is just a twisted belt. Advanced abstract mathematics is actually that close to our boring everyday lives, and if you don't think a twisted belt is really all that exciting, give one to a child and explain how the finger-tracing works. Imagine a house cat trying to come to terms with a hologram of a mouse, and you will understand how the Möbius strip can be an amazing babysitting tool.

Paragraph 7

This paragraph contrasts a technical definition with a non-technical one and brings the technical down to the everyday level for the average reader. Notice the energetic, non-scientific tone.

8   So, why did the chicken cross the Möbius strip? You should have figured that out by now: to get to the same side.

Paragraph 8

The conclusion provides closure by connecting to the introduction and cleverly playing on the opening riddle.

PEER REVIEW

Responding to "Why Did the Chicken Cross the Möbius Strip? (Or Babysitting for Dummies)"

Evaluate "Why Did the Chicken Cross the Möbius Strip? (Or Babysitting for Dummies)" by responding to these questions:

1. How does the essay effectively combine humour with a definition of complex mathematical concepts?
2. Is the thesis effective? Why or why not?
3. Is there enough of the right kind of detail to define the term adequately? Explain.
4. Is the organization effective? Why or why not?
5. Is the drawing effective and helpful? Explain.
6. What do you like best about the essay?
7. What single change do you think would make the essay better?

READING SELECTIONS

Background

Mark Kingwell took his philosophy degrees at Edinburgh University and at Yale. He currently teaches philosophy at the University of Toronto, though he has also taught at Cambridge and the University of California at Berkeley. A list of a few of his dozen books gives some sense of the breadth of his interests. Three recent publications include "*A Civil Tongue: Justice, Dialogue, and the Politics of Pluralism* (1997), *In Pursuit of Happiness: Plato to Prozac* (2000), and *The World We Want* (2001). He has written for *Harper's Magazine*, *Saturday Night, The National Post,* and *The Globe and Mail*. He has also written a book on mixing drinks, published by McClelland and Stewart, illustrating that even philosophers know how to live the good life.

Patterns and Their Purposes

Mark Kingwell asks one of the basic questions that fascinate philosophers: What is the good life, the life worth living? In order to answer that question for a general and contemporary audience (the essay was first published in *The World We Want: Virtue, Vice, and the Good Citizen*) he asks sociologists what makes us happy—and it's not money or material goods!—before he defines the good life as one that has meaning for us. Not surprisingly, he finds that we want more creative leisure time, a community of friends, and more time to reflect.

What Is the Good Life?

Mark Kingwell

As you read
Think about the definitions of "the good life" represented in popular culture. What are these images telling you?

1   When my first-year philosophy students write their final examination each year they are asked, among other things, to comment on this statement taken from the philosopher Alasdair MacIntyre: "The good life is the life spent seeking the good life." *Discuss. True or false. Agree or disagree.*

2   Don't worry. I always tell them this beforehand. There isn't much point, after all, in springing something like that on a nineteen-year-old who's sitting in a chilly gym at 9 a.m., probably wondering what she's going to do for a summer job or, maybe more to the point, why he signed up for philosophy in the first place. I try to give them all the breaks I can. On the other hand, I also want to unsettle them as much as possible. What is the good life? MacIntyre's deliberately puzzling formulation is an attempt to rise above the shifting sands of time and fashion. It neatly captures the paradoxical nature of critical reflection on the possibilities of life, because its logic undermines the blithe assurance of those whose knowingness gives them all the answers to our problems, usually doled out during dinner-party debates or in 750-word chunks on the op-ed pages of newspapers. This odd-sounding answer to the basic ethical question constantly reminds us of the disruptive elements in our attempts to make sense of ourselves and our place in the world.

3   That is an important reminder, even if we are rightly suspicious of philosophers (or anyone else, for that matter) who seem to think that the answer to all our problems

lies in further theorizing and more explanation. *Reflection* . . . is conceptually distinct from *theory*. It is much more modest in its aims and aware of the intellect's shortcomings—but also much more searching and powerful in its potential effects. Reflection involves the always incomplete attempt to make sense of who we are and what we are up to, trying all the while to do that most difficult of things, to live better. Theory believes it provides answers. Reflection knows that it merely pursues questions, and does that often enough only tentatively or in the midst of perplexity and sadness.

4   Even reflection has limits when it must cut so much against the spirit of the age. What constitutes success in living seems always to be changing, and that variation can lead to a judgment of relativism: the ultimately self-defeating notion that there is no fact of the matter about the good life—so knock yourself out in your chosen quest, for power or money or sexual pleasure. You might as well live like a depraved moral lunatic! Why not? What is there to stop you? These days, such judgments even draw a measure of social sanction and become the nihilistic common sense of the age. In the process they send ethical debate to the bleakly humorous margins so effectively rendered in contemporary films, usually about Los Angeles. The bickering armed robbers of *Reservoir Dogs,* the morally decentred group of bachelor-party buddies in *Very Bad Things,* the nuance-disputing drug dealers of *Go:* they all enact a kind of twisted Platonic dialogue about how to go on. "Sure we'll kill him, but not *that* way. Of *course* I'm going to commit a hit-and-run, but not without leaving the body where it can be discovered." Nobody sane would draw their notions of the good life from such material, of course, but these visions do serve to mark the decline of our reasoning about what Socrates considered the foundational philosophical question, What is the life worth living?

> "The phrase 'living well' has almost entirely
> shed its ethical connotations."

5   That question has lately become more about things than wisdom, more about brand names than the common good. These days, indeed, it is difficult to keep any discussion of "the good life" from sliding, sometimes immediately and sometimes by imperceptible stages, into a seminar on material comforts and lifestyle aids. The phrase "living well" has almost entirely shed its ethical connotations. That is why looking at certain lifestyle magazines can make you feel faintly sick: their lack of shame about materialism is, at one remove, shaming. This is certainly not to say that material goods are irrelevant to happiness, or that the good life involves nothing of what those tasty, coated-paper magazines deliver to us in their backlit visions. Try telling someone without the means to buy a television, or to make a phone call, that they shouldn't long for these double-edged toys of modern life. And anyone who has had the luck to enjoy some luxury now and then must agree with Aristotle that a truly blessed life involves a measure of wealth and the chance to enjoy its fruits. But we seem to have

lost our ability to think clearly about these matters, and for fairly precise historical and economic reasons.

6   Today we are not really materialists. We are, rather, fetishists of the material. If we were truly materialist, as the critic Raymond Williams once pointed out, we would be *satisfied* with the acquisition of material goods; they would make us happy in themselves. We are precisely the opposite of this, ever-conflicted victims of the vice the ancient Greek philosophers called *pleonexia:* wanting more, the more we have. We do not really desire the goods most of the time, only the complicated feelings of pleasure that acquiring the goods makes possible. Strummed by advertisers and marketers, like plummy mandolins, surrendering to our own internalized desires, we are forever in search of the next consumer hit. Well, so what? This is hardly news. Lots of people will tell you that it was ever thus, or that we can't expect anything else. Actually, both claims are false—it was not, and we can. But it is worth wondering why such argument-ending claims have the cachet they do, given how weak they are.

7   Part of the motivation for thinking in that reductive way, maybe a large part, is defensive. Consider an example. There is nothing more common in disputes about the state of the world today than what we might agree to call the Evasive Elision. I mean the way important distinctions, say between art and advertising, or between argument and self-promotion, are these days eagerly rubbed out in a face-saving attempt to suggest that everything is for sale and therefore nothing is untainted. Ironically, the arguments about a lack of purity are most often made by those who would otherwise shrink from the idea that purity matters, and from the idea that engagement with the market signifies impurity. This is a clear sign of the cynicism of the position, which proceeds not from conviction but from self-protection. Levelling charges of hypocrisy is always the fastest, and cheapest, route to the moral high ground. . . . The trouble is, that move doesn't help anybody except the leveller, who now gets to dodge criticism but only at the cost of shutting down debate altogether.

8   Indeed, such erasures recall Oscar Wilde's definition of the cynic as the person who knows the price of everything but the value of nothing. And that kind of apparently sophisticated attitude, perversely, makes us more comfortable with our weaknesses, not less. If the nihilism of the fastidious professional killer or mildly scrupulous drug dealer is not for all of us, this more general piece of cynical self-protection certainly is. The good life? Nowadays it is the life spent fending off all those naive challenges to one's acquisitiveness, throwing out facile charges of bad faith at those who dare to suggest things might be better, and claiming to find it baffling that anyone really thinks the adventitious privilege of birth might entail positive duties to the less fortunate. In this weirdly protracted battle for the modern soul, the glossy consumer objects, so ubiquitous and fetching, are themselves an unanswerable challenge to political awareness, a carapace of brand-name armour. [German Marxist literary critic Walter] Benjamin . . . circa 1928: "The luxury goods swaggering before us now parade such brazen solidity that all the mind's shafts break harmlessly on their surface."

9   The real trouble, of course, is that all this acquisition does not seem to make us any happier. In this sense, the Evasive Elision and its cousins are mere window-dressing, the distracting appearance of argument that does not touch the core problem. The renegade economist Robert Frank notes that there is no logical stopping point to acquisition, and yet beyond a certain level there is no correlation between wealth and happiness. "Behavioral scientists," he says, "have found persuasive evidence that once a threshold level of affluence is achieved, the average life-satisfaction level in any country is essentially independent of its per capita income." Which is one reason why the 39 percent rise in U.S. per capita income between 1972 and 1991, say, left a legacy of lower average happiness levels. At the heart of this apparently bizarre result is the confused nature of our conceptions of happiness. We are competitive and envious creatures, whether by nature or by some complex of natural and social factors, and so our sense of well-being is dangerously dependent on what is going on with others.

10   Thus studies consistently indicate results surprising only in their honesty about human desire. Beyond the levels of basic subsistence, we want to have things and wealth relative to what other people have, not for themselves. Most people, for example, would prefer earning $50,000 while others made $25,000 to earning $100,000 while others made $250,000. This kind of result holds even when it is true that a flatter income-distribution level would be advantageous to everyone. As long as individuals measure themselves against other individuals, we are caught in what Frank calls the "smart for one, dumb for all" trap. Instead of channelling money into cheap and reliable public transit, for example, we all strive to buy sporty convertibles or massive trucks—though they clog the highways, pollute the air, cut us off from one another, and regularly crash. Instead of reflecting on the possibility that need and want may be distinct concepts, we immerse ourselves in the nearly overwhelming pleasures of the unstable material world.

> "Beyond the levels of basic subsistence, we want
> to have things and wealth relative to what other
> people have, not for themselves."

11   These are real pleasures, of course, and there is real joy to be found in the marketplace. That is why merely denunciatory critics of consumerism are doing nobody but themselves any good. If we want to engage this world of ours with real results, we have to accept and understand the fact that watching a thirty-second television ad can sometimes be an exhilarating experience, that shopping is indeed a form of release and pleasure for many people, that putting on an expensive suit can occasion a liberating and wonderful feeling of well-being. Only then should we even attempt to separate that kind of exhilaration or pleasure from the consumer impulse that seems to accompany it. Why attempt that separation at all, ever? Well, because, once we take a first step on the road to luxury, there is little to prevent a kind of consumerist arms race, with small gaps or advantages in material goods closing as fast as they open.

Ever in search of a competitive advantage or pocket of enviable happiness, we are now driven to newer and more inventive forms of acquisition. Standard luxury items like Rolexes and ChrisCraft speedboats sell on the basis of their exclusivity, a combination of outrageous cost and artificially limited supply, in order to make them markers of success in the envy stakes. *I have it—and you don't!*

12   By the same token, the contemporary branding and narrativizing of consumer products, which compresses desire and expectation into the slick miniature plot of a television commercial, makes all of us into de facto experts on names and logos and spokespeople. Our overwhelming exposure to these micro-tales of success and beauty transforms acquisition into a kind of hypercompetitive graduate school, with Phil Knight or Bill Gates or Michael Jordan our presumptive professors. All the buying and selling of cool naturally comes down to this: I know more than you do about the available brands, I am more *au courant* with the latest narrative, I discovered this logo sooner, and therefore I have an advantage over you. You may catch up, finally buying your Kangol golf cap or FUBU shirt—or whatever it now is, for time overtakes a writer's examples as relentlessly as a person's expectations—but I will already be gone. We all know this is true, because marketers and their critics (who are sometimes, in another elision, the very same people) have been telling us this for years. And yet we seem unwilling to act on that knowledge.

13   It is hard to know whether the sharply unequal distribution of wealth we now observe in the world is a direct result of these aspects of our current notions of the good life, or whether we construct visions to match our situation. I think the relationship is symbiotic, complex, and hard to analyze with anything like a clarity that would issue in a course of action. The competitive impulse of all this envy drives a system away from horizontal distributions, even as it sharpens the unhappiness felt by the majority that, of necessity, finds itself unable to scale the pinnacles of the resulting x-y curve. It is certainly the case, for example, as the economist Robert Samuelson has argued persuasively, that most North Americans are far better off in absolute material terms now than during the 1950s. Rare today is the home without running water, a television or two, even a car. North Americans eat out more than twice as often now as they did during the 1950s, and spend vastly more on toys, travel, and entertainment.

14   There are fewer servants in North America today, it's true, because local wage expectations make them too expensive. Appliances and home shopping alleviate the need for most people, while cheaper foreign labour is once more making the domestic servant a familiar sight, at least in the homes of the very wealthy. Some people still live in abject poverty, but a larger proportion of the population is provably more comfortable than their parents' generation—and yet they think of themselves as poor because, compared with what they see and expect, they are. Visions of luxurious living clearly contribute strongly to this impression, since in the contemporary media-scape it becomes nearly impossible to avoid images of a life more desirable than your own. From Martha Stewart's mad domestic perfectionism to the cool-to-rule kids of

the fashion glossies, there's always somebody somewhere who has it better than you. This leads in turn to a sense that life is letting you down, that there is no good reason for relative differences in comfort, and therefore no good reason for the social structures that permit them.

15   Envy may be the basis of democracy, as [the English philosopher] Bertrand Russell once said, but it is also the most common source of unhappiness. By 1995, household debt in the United States had grown to 81 percent of disposable income, not least because going into debt is the only way most people can acquire the things they crave. Those of us in the most prosperous parts of the world now work longer hours, commute farther, and sleep less—all in the service of the good life. People will do anything, apparently even to their own detriment, to find some manner of what they think constitutes "better living." On the surface, then, we observe more luxury goods, more seductive visions of individual achievement and self-creation, and more subtle comparisons. But we also see more unhappiness, more resentment, and more imminent social unrest. Programs of voluntary simplicity or renewed spirituality, the countertenor of the era's loud chorus, keen and warble their dissent but don't really affect the dominant melody of getting and spending.

16   Is there a solution to this crazy merry-go-round? Some economists propose a luxury tax to counter our upward spiral of acquisition, a bold attempt to turn individual self-interest away from itself by sharply raising the opportunity costs of indulgence. Individuals would have to decide on and declare a single luxury pursuit, preserving a measure of choice thereby, but would then be bound in their spending by the redistributive constraints of steep marginal tax rates. (The argument is that such a directed tax is fairer than across-the-board progressive income tax, which is indiscriminate its application of redistributive burdens.)

17   Others would have us return, as if that were possible, to a less rapacious, fifties-style version of North America. For those who would not actually endorse the social and tax policies of any allegedly simpler era, there is always the costless option of nostalgia. Wander through the high-end home stores of Chelsea or Yorkville or SoHo and you will be struck by the ubiquity of a watered-down modernist style, a generalized and somehow bleakly appealing version of the good life as distributed, in the main, by cinematic imagery: skyscrapers in cool black and white, silver frames, bullet-headed cocktail shakers. We all want to live on this film set, to inhabit this fantasy. But like all fantasies, it is structurally unstable, important for what it hides more than what it reveals. The more of these literally fantastic goods there are to purchase, the more they, and the well-being they promise, seem to slip through our fingers. Nostalgia cannot aid us here, because its wispy attractions are meretricious; it leaves everything as it is.

18   I have a different suggestion. Denunciations of materialism and consumerism so often fall on deaf ears because at a deep level they miss the point. Appearances sometimes to the contrary, we are all struggling, in our different ways, to bestow meaning

on the world of our everyday experience. We are trying to forge identities from the play of cultural materials. And the basics of the good life have not really changed, though this became harder and harder to see as we reached the end of the expiring decadent century and sifted through our trunks of mechanically reproduced images, faux memories, and siren calls to comfort. The relentless acquisition of goods is just a symptom of a deeper ailment, a lack of secure placement in a world of shared under-standing, a failure to be at home. Denouncing the symptom instead of the illness, we would miss the point—and fail in our duty as social critics.

> "We are, finally, happier not with more
> stuff but with more meaning."

19   The important thing to see here is the currents of desire beneath the pretty surfaces, the wishes and fantasies there facilitated. What do they point to? The socio-logical studies bear out something that philosophical inquiry can see without taking a survey. We are, finally, happier not with more stuff but with more meaning: more creative leisure time, stronger connections to groups of friends, deeper commitment to common social projects, and a greater opportunity to reflect. In short, the life of the well-rounded person, including crucially the orienting aspect of life associated with virtuous citizenship. Nor is this basic social commitment something we should pursue for ourselves alone, a project simply to promote our personal happiness. At its best, it is an expression of commonality that creates something greater than the sum of its—let us be honest—often self-interested and distracted members. It creates a community.

Reading Closely and Thinking Critically

1. Answers to the question "What is the life worth living," Kingwell tells us, often reflect the spirit of the age. The current answer, he fears, "is more about things than wisdom, more about brand names than the common good." Considering the people around you, particularly those who have influenced your view of life, consider whether Kingwell's hypothesis is accurate and attempt to explain why.

2. In paragraph 5, Kingwell notes that "the phrase 'living well' has almost entirely shed its ethical connotations," using the glossy lifestyle magazines as examples of "the good life" that very few people can live. Why, then, does he suggest that material things are important? What balance do you think he wants his readers to find?

3. What is the difference between a materialist and a fetishist of the material?

4. What role does envy play in pursuing the good life? How does it make that life impossible?

5. What is the relationship between media depictions of the pursuit of "the good life" and a rise in unhappiness, resentment, and social unrest?

Examining Structure and Strategy

1. After examining some of the philosophical challenges of the search for the good life, Kingwell turns to economists and social scientists for theories about the nuts and bolts of what makes us happy. Is this a sound strategy in an essay that considers a philosophical problem?

2. Time and again, Kingwell tells us that things don't make us happy even while illustrating that sometimes things are an important part of our happiness (see paragraphs 5, 11, and 18.) How is he appealing to his reader? Is he attempting to find a non-existent balance?

3. In paragraph 18, Kingwell notes that "denunciations of materialism and consumerism so often fall on deaf ears because at a deep level they miss the point." Hasn't he been denouncing consumerism? What has he been doing?

Considering Language and Style

1. Kingwell opens his essay by describing a question on his Philosophy 100 final exam, and exhorting his reader, "Don't worry," while explaining that he gives his students warning. What kind of relationship is he trying to create with his reader?

2. What, according to Kingwell, is *reflection*? How does it differ from theory?

3. What is *pleonexia*? Please give some examples that will illustrate your definition.

4. Kingwell's definition of the good life is included mainly in the last two paragraphs. Why does he spend so much time talking about what the good life is not?

For Discussion in Class or Online

What do you think your peers believe is a good life? Does that correspond with your own desires or beliefs? Why or why not? If your instructor directs you to do so, post your thoughts on your class Web site.

Writing Assignments

1. **In your journal.** Describe your idea of the good life and try to identify where that vision came from.

2. **Using definition for a purpose.** The purposes given in the assignments are possibilities. You may establish whatever purposes you like, within your instructor's guidelines.
   - To entertain your reader, use Ambrose Bierce's example in *The Devil's Dictionary* and define a principle you think is widely held in Canada. Go beyond Bierce's aphoristic style, using examples to illustrate those principles.
   - To inform your reader, define "a good university class," "a good learning experience," or "a good professor." You can use Judy Brady's strategy of defining something with a careful catalogue of its characteristics.
   - To persuade your reader, define "success." Is it consonant with "the good life"?

3. **Combining patterns.** Describe a person you've known who has lived what you believe to be a good life. Contrast that person's ideas about the good life with your own or with those you think society holds.

4. **Connecting the readings.** Contrast or compare Mark Kingwell's idea of "the good life" with those of the drug addicts described in "The Keys of Paradise." What surprising similarities do you find?

5. **Drawing on sources.** Many pop songs, movies, even novels have been titled "The Good Life." Choose a popular culture description of "the good life" and contrast or compare it to Kingwell's definition.

Background

Born in San Francisco in 1937, Judy Brady earned a degree in painting from the University of Iowa in 1962. She is a political activist, feminist, and freelance writer who has written on abortion, education, the labour movement, and the women's movement. In 1973, she travelled to Cuba to learn about the relationship between social class and change. Brady writes a column for the Women's Cancer Research Center and has also edited *Women and Cancer* (1990) and *One in Three: Women with Cancer Confront an Epidemic* (1991), a collection of writings by women. Involved in women's issues since 1969, Brady published "I Want a Wife" in 1972 for the first issue of *Ms.* magazine, and it quickly became a classic piece of satire.

The Pattern and Its Purposes

In "I Want a Wife," Judy Brady defines the traditional wifely role to inform the reader of its servile nature. While the typical reader of *Ms.* does not need to be persuaded of the fundamental injustice of that role, the essay also works to persuade other readers of that injustice.

I Want a Wife

Judy Brady

1   I belong to that classification of people known as wives. I am A Wife. And, not altogether incidentally, I am a mother.

> **As you read**
> Decide whether much of what the author says is still true today.

2   Not too long ago a male friend appeared on the scene from the Midwest fresh from a recent divorce. He had one child, who is, of course, with his ex-wife. He is obviously looking for another wife. As I thought about him while I was ironing one evening, it suddenly occurred to me that I, too, would like to have a wife. Why do I want a wife?

3   I would like to go back to school so that I can become economically independent, support myself, and, if need be, support those dependent upon me. I want a wife who will work and send me to school. And while I am going to school I want a wife to take care of my children. I want a wife to keep track of the children's doctor and dentist appointments. And to keep track of mine, too. I want a wife to make sure my children eat properly and are kept clean. I want a wife who will wash the children's clothes and keep them mended. I want a wife who is a good nurturant attendant to my children, arranges for their schooling, makes sure that they have an adequate social life with their peers, takes them to the park, the zoo, etc. I want a wife who takes care of the children when they are sick, a wife who arranges to be around when the children need special care, because, of course, I cannot miss classes at school. My wife must arrange to lose time at work and not lose the job. It may mean a small cut in my wife's income from time to time, but I guess I can tolerate that. Needless to say, my wife will arrange and pay for the care of the children while my wife is working.

"I want a wife who will work and send me to school."

4   I want a wife who will take care of *my* physical needs. I want a wife who will keep my house clean. A wife who will pick up after my children, a wife who will pick

up after me. I want a wife who will keep my clothes clean, ironed, mended, replaced when need be, and who will see to it that my personal things are kept in their proper place so that I can find what I need the minute I need it. I want a wife who cooks the meals, a wife who is a *good* cook. I want a wife who will plan the menus, do the necessary grocery shopping, prepare the meals, serve them pleasantly, and then do the cleaning up while I do my studying. I want a wife who will care for me when I am sick and sympathize with my pain and loss of time from school. I want a wife to go along when our family takes a vacation so that someone can continue to care for me and my children when I need a rest and a change of scene.

> "I want a wife who will not bother me with
> rambling complaints about a wife's duties."

5   I want a wife who will not bother me with rambling complaints about a wife's duties. But I want a wife who will listen to me when I feel the need to explain a rather difficult point I have come across in my course of studies. And I want a wife who will type my papers for me when I have written them.

6   I want a wife who will take care of the details of my social life. When my wife and I are invited out by my friends, I want a wife who will take care of the babysitting arrangements. When I meet people at school that I like and want to entertain, I want a wife who will have the house clean, will prepare a special meal, serve it to me and my friends, and not interrupt when I talk about the things that interest me and my friends. I want a wife who will have arranged that the children are fed and ready for bed before my guests arrive so that the children do not bother us. I want a wife who takes care of the needs of my guests so that they feel comfortable, who makes sure that they have an ashtray, that they are passed the hors d'oeuvres, that they are offered a second helping of the food, that their wine glasses are replenished when necessary, that their coffee is served to them as they like it. And I want a wife who knows that sometimes I need a night out by myself.

7   I want a wife who is sensitive to my sexual needs, a wife who makes love passionately and eagerly when I feel like it, a wife who makes sure that I am satisfied. And, of course, I want a wife who will not demand sexual attention when I am not in the mood for it. I want a wife who assumes the complete responsibility for birth control, because I do not want more children. I want a wife who will remain sexually faithful to me so that I do not have to clutter up my intellectual life with jealousies. And I want a wife who understands that *my* sexual needs may entail more than strict adherence to monogamy. I must, after all, be able to relate to people as fully as possible.

8   If, by chance, I find another person more suitable as a wife than the wife I already have, I want the liberty to replace my present wife with another one. Naturally, I will expect a fresh, new life; my wife will take the children and be solely responsible for them so that I am left free.

> 9   When I am through with school and have acquired a job, I want my wife to quit working and remain at home so that my wife can more fully and completely take care of a wife's duties.
>
> 10   My God, who *wouldn't* want a wife?

Reading Closely and Thinking Critically
1. What is Brady's attitude toward the wifely role she depicts in the essay?
2. What view of men does Brady present in her essay? Do you think she is being fair to men? Explain.
3. Why does Brady say she wants a wife? Does she imply more reasons than she gives? Explain.
4. Can Brady be taken literally? That is, does she mean *exactly* what she says? Explain.

Examining Structure and Strategy
1. Paragraphs 1 and 2 form the introduction of "I Want a Wife." What strategy does Brady use in that introduction?
2. In your own words, state the thesis of "I Want a Wife."
3. Brady uses classification and division to help develop her definition. (Classification and division, discussed in Chapter 11, sort items into categories and divide them into parts.) What categories does Brady establish for the wife's duties?
4. Why does Brady open with a statement that she is a wife and mother?

Considering Language and Style
1. Brady frequently repeats the words "I want." What is the effect of this repetition?
2. A speaker or writer who asks a *rhetorical question* does not expect an answer. Brady closes "I Want a Wife" with a rhetorical question. Do you think it creates an effective conclusion? Explain.
3. Consult a dictionary if you are unsure of the meaning of any of these words: *nurturant* (paragraph 3), *hors d'oeuvres* (paragraph 6), *entail* (paragraph 7), *monogamy* (paragraph 7).

For Discussion in Class or Online
Is "I Want a Wife" as relevant today as it was when it was first published in 1972? Explain. If your instructor directs you to do so, post your response to your class Web site.

Writing Assignments
1. **In your journal.** Write a description of the ideal spouse.
2. **Using definition for a purpose.** The purposes given in the assignments are possibilities. You may establish whatever purposes you like, within your instructor's guidelines.
   - Write an essay entitled "I Want a _____." Fill in the blank with some family role (husband, child, older brother, younger sister, mother, father, grandparent, and so on). To inform and persuade your reader that the role can be difficult, define that role and point out its difficulty and/or unfairness. If you like, you can borrow Brady's technique and repeat the words "I want a _____ who. . . ."
   - To inform and perhaps persuade, define what you think the role of a *wife* should be. As an alternative, define what the role of *husband* should be.
   - To inform and convince your reader that the role is unjust, define the role of someone who has traditionally been exploited, such as a table server, a babysitter, or a cleaning person.

- Write a definition of one of the roles you currently play or have played in the past: wife, husband, mother, father, child, friend, soldier, student, track star, musician, younger brother, older sister, student athlete, non-traditional student, international student, coach, and so on. Like Brady, let your definition convey how you feel about the role.

3. **Combining patterns.** Brady's definition of the ideal wife depicts a stereotype as it existed in 1972. Write your own definition of the ideal wife or husband to depict today's stereotype. Use cause-and-effect analysis (discussed in Chapter 9) to explain what factors are responsible for that stereotype (such as television, movies, the women's movement, or advertisements).

4. **Connecting the readings.** Compare and contrast the wife that Judy Brady depicts with the image of his mother Wayson Choy provides in "The Ten Thousand Things" (page 158). Is either woman typical of women today?

5. **Drawing on sources.** In your library, examine the advertisements and articles in magazines from a specific decade of the twentieth century. Based on what you see, define the image of women in that decade.

Background

Former contributing editor and economic policy correspondent to the *National Journal,* an American non-partisan journal on government and public policy, political writer and journalist Jonathan Rauch is currently the publication's opinion columnist. He is also a correspondent for *The Atlantic Monthly,* a liberal American magazine. A 1982 graduate of Yale, Rauch writes on a range of topics, including American politics, economic issues, and animal rights. He has written for many periodicals, including London's *The Economist,* the *Winston-Salem* (North Carolina) *Journal,* and *The New Republic.* Rauch's books include *Kindly Inquisitors: The New Attacks on Free Thought* (1993), *Government's End: Why Washington Stopped Working* (1999), and *Gay Marriage: Why It Is Good for Gays, Good for Straights, and Good for America* (2004). "Caring for Your Introvert" first appeared in *The Atlantic Monthly* (2003).

Combined Patterns and Their Purposes

In "Caring for Your Introvert," Jonathan Rauch combines a definition of introvert with contrast to inform readers of the characteristics of a little-understood personality type. In addition, Rauch works to persuade readers that although introverts are an oppressed group, they are superior to extroverts. You will, no doubt, notice elements of humour in the essay that entertain readers.

Caring for Your Introvert
Jonathan Rauch

As you read
Consider why Rauch organizes part of his essay with a question-and-answer format.

1   Do you know someone who needs hours alone every day? Who loves quiet conversations about feelings or ideas, and can give a dynamite presentation to a big audience, but seems awkward in groups and maladroit at small talk? Who has to be dragged to parties and then needs the rest of the day to recuperate? Who growls or scowls or grunts or winces when accosted with pleasantries by people who are just trying to be nice?

2   If so, do you tell this person he is "too serious," or ask if he is okay? Regard him as aloof, arrogant, rude? Redouble your efforts to draw him out?

3   If you answered yes to these questions, chances are that you have an introvert on your hands—and that you aren't caring for him properly. Science has learned a good deal in recent years about the habits and requirements of introverts. It has even learned, by means of brain scans, that introverts process information differently from other people (I am not making this up). If you are behind the curve on this important matter, be reassured that you are not alone. Introverts may be common, but they are also among the most misunderstood and aggrieved groups in America, possibly the world.

"My name is Jonathan, and I am an introvert."

4   I know. My name is Jonathan, and I am an introvert.

5   Oh, for years I denied it. After all, I have good social skills. I am not morose or misanthropic. Usually. I am far from shy. I love long conversations that explore intimate thoughts or passionate interests. But at last I have self-identified and come out to

my friends and colleagues. In doing so, I have found myself liberated from any number of damaging misconceptions and stereotypes. Now I am here to tell you what you need to know in order to respond sensitively and supportively to your own introverted family members, friends, and colleagues. Remember, someone you know, respect, and interact with every day is an introvert, and you are probably driving this person nuts. It pays to learn the warning signs.

WHAT IS INTROVERSION?

6   In its modern sense, the concept goes back to the 1920s and the psychologist Carl Jung. Today it is a mainstay of personality tests, including the widely used Myers-Briggs Type Indicator. Introverts are not necessarily shy. Shy people are anxious or frightened or self-excoriating in social settings; introverts generally are not. Introverts are also not misanthropic, though some of us do go along with Sartre[1] as far as to say "Hell is other people at breakfast." Rather, introverts are people who find other people tiring.

7   Extroverts are energized by people, and wilt or fade when alone. They often seem bored by themselves, in both senses of the expression. Leave an extrovert alone for two minutes and he will reach for his cell phone. In contrast, after an hour or two of being socially "on," we introverts need to turn off and recharge. My own formula is roughly two hours alone for every hour of socializing. This isn't antisocial. It isn't a sign of depression. It does not call for medication. For introverts, to be alone with our thoughts is as restorative as sleeping, as nourishing as eating. Our motto: "I'm okay, you're okay—in small doses."[2]

HOW MANY PEOPLE ARE INTROVERTS?

8   I performed exhaustive research on this question, in the form of a quick Google search. The answer: About 25 percent. Or: Just under half. Or—my favorite—"a minority in the regular population but a majority in the gifted population."

ARE INTROVERTS MISUNDERSTOOD?

9   Wildly. That, it appears, is our lot in life. "It is very difficult for an extrovert to understand an introvert," write the education experts Jill D. Burruss and Lisa Kaenzig. (They are also the source of the quotation in the previous paragraph.) Extroverts are easy for introverts to understand, because extroverts spend so much of their time working out who they are in voluble, and frequently inescapable, interaction with other people. They are as inscrutable as puppy dogs. But the street does not run both ways. Extroverts have little or no grasp of introversion. They assume that company, especially their own, is always welcome. They cannot imagine why someone

---

[1]Jean-Paul Sartre (1905–1980), a French philosopher; "hell is other people" is a quotation from his 1947 play *No Exit*.

[2]*I'm OK—You're OK* (1967), a self-help book by Thomas Harris, M.D.

would need to be alone; indeed, they often take umbrage at the suggestion. As often as I have tried to explain the matter to extroverts, I have never sensed that any of them really understood. They listen for a moment and then go back to barking and yipping.

ARE INTROVERTS OPPRESSED?

10   I would have to say so. For one thing, extroverts are overrepresented in politics, a profession in which only the garrulous are really comfortable. Look at George W. Bush. Look at Bill Clinton. They seem to come fully to life only around other people. To think of the few introverts who did rise to the top in politics—Calvin Coolidge, Richard Nixon—is merely to drive home the point. With the possible exception of Ronald Reagan, whose fabled aloofness and privateness were probably signs of a deep introverted streak (many actors, I've read, are introverts, and many introverts, when socializing, feel like actors), introverts are not considered "naturals" in politics.

11   Extroverts therefore dominate public life. This is a pity. If we introverts ran the world, it would no doubt be a calmer, saner, more peaceful sort of place. As Coolidge is supposed to have said, "Don't you know that four fifths of all our troubles in this life would disappear if we would just sit down and keep still?" (He is also supposed to have said, "If you don't say anything, you won't be called on to repeat it." The only thing a true introvert dislikes more than talking about himself is repeating himself.)

12   With their endless appetite for talk and attention, extroverts also dominate social life, so they tend to set expectations. In our extrovertist society, being outgoing is considered normal and therefore desirable, a mark of happiness, confidence, leadership. Extroverts are seen as big-hearted, vibrant, warm, empathic. "People person" is a compliment. Introverts are described with words like "guarded," "loner," "reserved," "taciturn," "self-contained," "private"—narrow, ungenerous words, words that suggest emotional parsimony and smallness of personality. Female introverts, I suspect, must suffer especially. In certain circles, particularly in the Midwest, a man can still sometimes get away with being what they used to call a strong and silent type; introverted women, lacking that alternative, are even more likely than men to be perceived as timid, withdrawn, haughty.

ARE INTROVERTS ARROGANT?

13   Hardly. I suppose this common misconception has to do with our being more intelligent, more reflective, more independent, more level-headed, more refined, and more sensitive than extroverts. Also, it is probably due to our lack of small talk, a lack that extroverts often mistake for disdain. We tend to think before talking, whereas extroverts tend to think by talking, which is why their meetings never last less than six hours. "Introverts," writes a perceptive fellow named Thomas P. Crouser, in an online review of a recent book called Why Should Extroverts Make All the Money? (I'm not making that up, either), "are driven to distraction by the semi-internal dialogue

extroverts tend to conduct. Introverts don't outwardly complain, instead roll their eyes and silently curse the darkness." Just so.

14   The worst of it is that extroverts have no idea of the torment they put us through. Sometimes, as we gasp for air amid the fog of their 98-percent-content-free talk, we wonder if extroverts even bother to listen to themselves. Still, we endure stoically, because the etiquette books—written, no doubt, by extroverts— regard declining to banter as rude and gaps in conversation as awkward. We can only dream that some-day, when our condition is more widely understood, when perhaps an Introverts' Rights movement has blossomed and borne fruit, it will not be impolite to say "I'm an introvert. You are a wonderful person and I like you. But now please shush."

HOW CAN I LET THE INTROVERT IN MY LIFE KNOW THAT I SUPPORT HIM AND RESPECT HIS CHOICE?

15   First, recognize that it's not a choice. It's not a lifestyle. It's an *orientation.*

16   Second, when you see an introvert lost in thought, don't say "What's the matter?" or "Are you all right?"

17   Third, don't say any thing else, either.

Reading Closely and Thinking Critically

1. Which sentence is the thesis of the essay?
2. Why does Rauch want readers to understand what introverts are like? That is, what is the significance of the definition?
3. Some of the essay is humorous, and some of the points are exaggerated. Cite one humorous detail and one exaggerated detail. Given the humour and exaggeration, how serious is Rauch?
4. According to Rauch, what misconceptions do people have about introverts?
5. Rauch says the fact that Calvin Coolidge and Richard Nixon were introverts helps make the point that introverts are not natural politicians. Explain what Rauch means.

Examining Structure and Strategy

1. Why does Rauch open his essay with questions that include the characteristics of an introvert rather than state the introvert's characteristics in declarative sentences?
2. Rauch cites scientific and other sources throughout the essay. (See, for example, paragraphs 3 and 6). How does this material help the author achieve his purpose?
3. Why does Rauch use the question-and-answer format in paragraphs 6–15? Do you think this format provides an effective organizational structure? Explain.
4. What techniques does Rauch use to create humour and entertain his reader?

Noting Combined Patterns

1. What is the purpose of the contrast in paragraphs 6 and 7?
2. What is the purpose of the contrast in paragraphs 10–12?
3. What is the purpose of the contrast in paragraph 13?

Considering Language and Style

1. At times, Rauch uses exaggeration and mock seriousness. For example, in paragraph 3, he exaggerates by saying that introverts are one of the "most misunderstood and aggrieved groups in America, possibly the world." Cite three other examples of exaggeration or mock seriousness.
2. Consult a dictionary if you are unsure of the meaning of these words: *maladroit* (paragraph 1), *misanthropic* (paragraph 5, 6), *self-excoriating* (paragraph 6), *garrulous* (paragraph 10), *parsimony* (paragraph 12).

For Discussion in Class or Online

Rauch says that extroverts "dominate public life" (paragraph 11). Is it possible for introverts to dominate public life? Why or why not? If your instructor directs you to do so, post your response to your class Web site.

Writing Assignments

1. **In your journal.** In a page or so, explain whether you are an introvert or an extrovert. Cite examples to illustrate your characterization.
2. **Using definition for a purpose.** The purposes given in the assignments are possibilities. You may establish whatever purposes you like, within your instructor's guidelines.
   - To inform and perhaps entertain, write your own definition of *introvert.*
   - To inform and perhaps entertain, define *extrovert.* You can also try to convince readers that extroverts are superior to introverts.
   - Psychologists tell us that introversion and extroversion are fairly stable qualities of personality. Undertake some research to find out why and incorporate that into a definition of either and introvert or an extrovert.
   - Rauch says that introverts are oppressed. To entertain your reader, define another such oppressed group, perhaps impulsive people, procrastinators, the fashion-challenged, or clumsy people.
   - In paragraph 12, Rauch says that "being outgoing is considered normal." To inform, and perhaps persuade or entertain, define *normal.*
3. **Combining patterns.** Define some characteristic or condition that you have, such as shyness, self-consciousness, attention deficit disorder, dyslexia, or hearing impairment. Using narration (explained in Chapter 5), tell one or more brief stories to illustrate how you are affected by the characteristic or condition.
4. **Connecting the readings.** In "Neat People vs. Sloppy People" (page 298), Suzanne Britt contrasts those who are neat and sloppy, and she argues that sloppy people are better than neat ones. Using the ideas in that essay along with those in "Caring for Your Introvert," explain the advantages of being either a sloppy extrovert or neat introvert.
5. **Drawing on sources.** Observe people in gatherings you are regularly a part of, such as those that occur in the classroom, at social functions with your friends, at the gym, in houses of worship, and in grocery stores. What differences do you notice between introverts and extroverts? Do you agree with Rauch's characterizations of introverts and extroverts? Do you agree with his conclusion that extroverts "dominate public life" (paragraph 11)? Support your responses with examples of the people you observe.

Additional Essay Assignments
See pages 218 and 220 for strategies for writing definition and for a revising checklist.

1. Define *stereotype* to help your readers recognize stereotypes and their dangers.
2. Define and illustrate *politically correct* to help your readers better understand this concept and its effect on society.
3. Define something that can be positive but that has the potential to tyrannize a person: aerobics, running, weight training, video games, getting As, vegetarianism, and so forth.
4. To convince your reader that it is either good or bad, define *censorship.*
5. Define *science fiction movie* to help your reader appreciate the appeal of this genre.
6. Define *one* of any of the following genres of fiction: the realistic novel, the science fiction novel, detective fiction, the police procedural, the coming-of-age novel.
7. Use examples to define an expression from the specialized terminology found in one of your other classes. If you are taking psychology, you might define *repression* or *projection.* If you are taking a math class, define a concept you are learning there. Be particularly aware of who your audience is.
8. Define *power* in a way that expresses an opinion.
9. If you have a hobby or special interest, define it to help your reader appreciate its appeal.
10. To give your readers a fresh appreciation of the familiar, define *friend* or *family.*
11. If you have a job, define your role to help your reader appreciate what you do. For example, you could define *nurse, lifeguard, camp counsellor,* or *security guard.*
12. Define something that helps you simplify your life: an answering machine, a microwave oven, a computer, inline skates, and so forth.
13. Define *bureaucracy* to show the frustrations that can be associated with it. If you like, you can make this a humorous definition.
14. Write a definition of a news source: your local paper, your campus paper, the national news on TV, a Web site. Your goal is to convince your reader that the source is or is not a useful one.
15. Define *peer pressure* to help your reader understand what a potent force it is.
16. To clarify something not well understood, define *creativity.*
17. To entertain and/or to inform, define *style.*
18. To entertain and/or to inform, define *tacky.*
19. Define *frustration.* If you want to make the piece amusing, your purpose can be to entertain.
20. Define a custom or concept unique to your ethnic heritage so someone who does not share your heritage will understand it.
21. **Definition In context:** Assume you are a tutor in your campus writing centre and the director has asked you to develop a pamphlet on writer's block to be given to students who come to the centre. Write a definition of *writer's block* and its effects, suitable for inclusion in the pamphlet. You may also include narrations about experiencing writer's block if those narrations help illustrate its characteristics.

Chapter 8

Process Analysis

A kiss is one of the most intimate and sensuous things you can experience with another person. Fortunately, while there's no "right" way to kiss, many people experience anxiety about kissing or don't know how to ask for a kiss. Fear not! Whether you're getting ready for your first kiss, or you're an experienced kisser and just want to improve your game for your first kiss with a new partner, you've come to the right place.

- Be kissable. Use lip balm, especially if your lips tend to get dry and chapped. Soft lips are simply more inviting. Most importantly, nobody wants to kiss someone with a stinky mouth, so carry some breath mints or gum with you, especially if you're going out on a date. Breath mints are preferable, because you can use them in a pinch and not have to worry about getting rid of them. Be sure to stay hydrated, because a dry mouth is more likely to have bad breath. Drink water; other drinks (especially sweet ones) can leave an aftertaste that'll affect your breath, and some drinks (like milk) will linger in a bad way. Also, don't drink anything colored that might leave a ring around your mouth.

- Test the waters. Pay attention to signals that the other person is into you and is ready for a kiss. Do they brush up against you or frequently enter your personal space with playful, innocent touches? Has the subject of kissing come up in conversation? If you haven't noticed any of these signals, but the person does seem "into you," try discreetly and innocently breaking the touch barrier (guys will generally be very receptive to this, many girls might not). The key is to be subtle and to watch the other person's reaction.

— WikiHow, "How to Kiss" (http://www.wikihow.com/Kiss)

THE PATTERN

A **process analysis** explains how something works, how something is made, or how something is done. There are two kinds of process analyses:

- The directional process analysis
- The explanatory process analysis

A **directional process analysis** gives the steps in a procedure the reader may want to perform. For example, when you buy a watch, the accompanying instruction booklet explains how to set the time, how to change the battery, and how to work the alarm. Each of these explanations is a directional process analysis. When you consult a recipe to prepare a new dish, you are reading and following a directional process analysis. Similarly, if you apply for a scholarship, the instructions for completing the application are a directional process analysis.

An **explanatory process analysis** is a bit different. Like a directional process analysis, it tells how something works, how something is made, or how something is done, but the procedure explained will *not* be performed by the reader. Explanatory process analyses are also common. Your biology textbook explains how plants convert carbon dioxide to oxygen with the process of photosynthesis. Since no reader will engage in photosynthesis, the process analysis is purely explanatory, meant to increase understanding. Similar explanations of how an internal combustion engine works, how natural selection occurs, and how rivers become polluted are examples of explanatory process analyses.

USING PROCESS ANALYSIS FOR A PURPOSE

A directional process analysis can inform a reader how to perform a particular procedure or process. For example, a process analysis that explains how to install a computer program serves this informational purpose. A directional process analysis can also inform a reader who wants to discover a better or different way to do something. For example, you already know how to study, but you still might be interested in a process analysis essay with the title "Six Steps to More Efficient Studying" because the essay may help you save time and improve your grades by showing you an even better way. An explanatory process analysis can inform a reader who desires a better understanding of how a procedure works. This is the case with "How Men Choose Women" (page 256), which explains how men "pick out which women they are going to *try* for." Kearns clearly addresses a heterosexual female audience that is probably curious about how this process is performed because it clearly affects their lives.

Finally, an explanatory process analysis can inform a reader about the beauty, difficulty, or complexity of a process so the reader can better appreciate it. For example, say that you are a distance runner. If you want your reader to appreciate the rigour and discipline that go into running a cross-country race, you can describe the process of running that race to impress the reader with its difficulty.

In addition to informing a reader, a process analysis can entertain. In "How Men Choose Women" (page 256), for example, the author entertains

Troubleshooting Guide

Using Imperative and Declarative Sentences

If you have trouble keeping your approach consistent in a process analysis, remember the difference between imperative and declarative sentences. An imperative sentence gives a directive. Its subject is *you*, which can be stated or unstated. A declarative sentence makes a statement. Its subject, which is stated, can be any noun or pronoun. Use imperative sentences with directional process analyses and declarative sentences with explanatory process analyses. The following examples for process analyses about bread baking illustrate the difference:

IMPERATIVE SENTENCES (FOR DIRECTIONAL PROCESS ANALYSIS):	**Dissolve the yeast in the water and let it sit for 10 minutes. In a large bowl, combine the water and yeast mixture, milk, sugar, salt, and oil.**
DECLARATIVE SENTENCES (FOR EXPLANATORY PROCESS ANALYSIS):	**Yeast eats sugar, and from the sugar it creates alcohol and carbon dioxide gas. The carbon dioxide gas gives bread its texture, and the alcohol flavours the bread.**

with a humorous account of a man's inability to send the right signals to a woman he was interested in dating.

A process analysis can also express feelings and relate experience. For example, assume one of your happiest childhood memories is of your annual fishing trips with your grandfather. You could relate part of that experience by explaining how you and your grandfather prepared for the trip and by noting the special ways you interacted during the process.

Finally, a process analysis can persuade a reader. For example, if you want to convince your reader that current gun registration procedures are inadequate, you can explain the registration process and point out its flaws. If you want to persuade your reader to use a particular computer security system, you can explain how the system works and point out its superior features.

Process Analysis at School, at Work, and in the Community

You are likely to use both directional and explanatory process analyses in much of your university and college writing. An obvious use of directional process analysis is for biology, chemistry, and physics lab reports, where you must explain the process you followed to complete various experiments. In a marketing class, an examination question might require you to write a directional process analysis to explain how to conduct a consumer survey. A report you write for a computer science class would use directional process analysis to explain how to develop a certain kind of computer program. In an art class, you would write a directional process analysis if you were to explain how to mix paints to achieve a desired effect.

Similarly, you will often write explanatory process analyses. For example, for a geology mid-term exam you may need to explain how erosion occurs; for a political science exam you may need to explain how the Senate works; for a psychology class, you may need to write a research paper that explains how children acquire language.

Process analysis—particularly explanatory process analysis—is a common component in textbooks of all kinds. Here, for example, is an excerpt from an introductory psychology textbook. It explains the classic experiments that Russian psychologist Ivan Pavlov performed to learn about a form of learning called *classical conditioning*, which occurs when an organism is trained or "conditioned" to produce a response not ordinarily associated with a particular stimulus.

> To demonstrate and analyze classical conditioning, Pavlov conducted a series of experiments (Pavlov, 1927). In one, he attached a tube to the salivary gland of a dog, allowing him to measure precisely the amount of salivation that occurred. He then sounded a tuning fork and, just a few seconds later, presented the dog with meat powder. This pairing, carefully planned so that exactly the same amount of time elapsed between the presentation of the sound and the meat powder, occurred repeatedly. At first the dog would salivate only when the meat powder itself was presented, but soon it began to salivate at the sound of the tuning fork. In fact, even when Pavlov stopped presenting the meat powder, the dog still salivated after hearing the sound. The dog had been classically conditioned to salivate to the tone. (Feldman, *Understanding Psychology*)

In the textbook, the process analysis helps students understand that an animal (in this case, a dog) can be conditioned to produce a response (salivating) that is normally unrelated to the stimulus (the sound of the tuning fork). The process analysis helps students better remember the concept of classical conditioning by helping them visualize the concept in action.

Beyond the classroom, process analysis can be an important component of workplace communications. A restaurant manager might send a memo to employees with an explanatory process analysis that describes how food poisoning occurs. Human resource managers send memos explaining procedures for using vacation days, physical therapists write out instructions for performing exercises, and safety officers write out procedures for emergency evacuations of buildings. To help a colleague with online research, you might write an explanation of how to use a specific kind of search engine.

Process analysis is also important to writing you do in the community. When you write out directions to your home or another location, you are writing a directional process analysis. If you email a friend about how to install a computer firewall to protect against viruses, you are writing a directional process analysis, as you are if you send a letter to the editor urging people to donate blood by explaining how simple the procedure is.

SUPPORTING DETAILS

Because a process analysis explains how something is made, how something works, or how something is done, the primary detail will be the steps in the process. Sometimes, you will find it necessary to go on to explain *how* a particular step is performed. For example, in "Don't Just Stand There" (page 266), Diane Cole describes how to deal with racial, ethnic, and sexist remarks. At one point she tells what to do when the remark occurs at a large meeting or public talk, and then she goes on to explain *how* to perform the step:

> At a large meeting or public talk, you might consider passing the speaker a note . . . You could write, "You may not realize it, but your remarks were offensive because . . ."

At times, you may want to explain *why* a step is performed so your reader appreciates the importance of the step. For example, assume you are explaining the best job application procedure, and you mention that you should follow every interview with a letter of thanks that also reaffirms your interest in the position. To help your reader appreciate the importance of this step, you can explain that the letter marks you as someone who is courteous and as someone who follows through—two qualities that can help you land the job.

If you need to clarify a step to be sure your reader understands, an example may help. In this excerpt from "Don't Just Stand There," notice that the author uses an example to clarify how the host of a gathering can control the behaviour of guests:

> If you, yourself, are the host, you can exercise more control; you are, after all, the one who sets the rules and the tone of behavior in your home. Once, when Professor Kahn's party guests began singing offensive, racist songs, for instance, he kicked them all out, saying "You don't sing songs like that in my house!" And, he adds, "they never did again."

If you think your reader might perform a step incorrectly or might perform an unnecessary step, you can explain what *not* to do and why. For example, in "Don't Just Stand There," the author cautions the reader not to deal with offensive remarks by embarrassing a person publicly:

> But in general, psychologists say, shaming a person in public may have the opposite effect of the one you want: The speaker may deny his offence all the more strongly in order to save face.

If a particular part of the process can be crucial, you can point that out to the reader, as J. M. Kearns does in "How Men Choose Women":

> So the first rule is, *let men see you*. This may seem too obvious to even mention, but in fact it is the key to the whole thing. If you make it difficult to be seen—for instance, if you sit in the back booth with shades on—you stop Step One from happening. So none of the other steps can happen. (Note that being seen is particularly crucial—and achievable—if you are trying to meet Mr. Right online.)

Description can be an important element of a process analysis when you want your reader to visualize some aspect of the process in order to better appreciate it. (See Chapter 4 for more information on writing description.) In "In the Kitchen," (page 273), for example, Henry Louis Gates, Jr., explains how his mother used to straighten the hair of her African-American clients and includes this description:

> Mama would stroke that red-hot iron—which by this time had been in the gas fire for half an hour or more—slowly but firmly through their hair, from scalp to strand's end. It made a scorching, crinkly sound, the hot iron did, as it burned its way through kink, leaving in its wake straight strands of hair, standing long and tall but drooping over at the ends, their shape like the top of a heavy willow tree.

If your reader is unlikely to understand specialized vocabulary, your process analysis may include definition, as in this excerpt from "In the Kitchen," which defines a potentially unfamiliar use of *kitchen*:

> But the word has another meaning, and the kitchen that I'm speaking of is the very kinky bit of hair at the back of your head, where your neck meets your shirt collar.

Deciding whether or not to define specific terms requires an understanding of who your audience is and what your reader knows. For that reason, careful audience assessment is important.

ORGANIZING DETAILS

The thesis for a process analysis can mention the process to be explained:

> A person should take great care when choosing a personal physician. (*Thesis indicates that the essay will explain how to choose a personal physician.*)

In addition to mentioning the process, the thesis can also explain why it is important to understand the process:

> To avoid making a costly mistake, follow this procedure when you shop for a car. (*Thesis indicates that the process is important because it can save the reader money.*)

If you do not mention the importance of the process in the thesis, you can do so elsewhere in the essay. In "Don't Just Stand There," Diane Cole uses her fourth paragraph to explain why it is important to know a process for dealing with racial and ethnic insults:

> But left unchecked, racial slurs and offensive ethnic jokes "can poison the atmosphere," says Michael McQuillan, adviser for racial/ethnic affairs for the Brooklyn borough president's office. "Hearing these remarks conditions us to accept them; and if we accept these, we can become accepting of other acts."

If you want your reader to know why you are qualified to describe the process, you can give your credentials in your introduction. For example, if you are explaining an efficient note-taking system you have devised, you can explain that you have made the dean's list every term since you started using the system.

If completing the process requires particular materials, make note of that fact early, perhaps even in the first paragraph. If, for example, you are explaining how to build a bookcase, note the lumber sizes, tools, and other materials needed.

When the steps in the process must be performed in a particular order, details are arranged in a **chronological** (or time) order. To help your reader follow the chronological order, transitions like these can help:

> *First,* you must . . .
> *Next,* be careful to . . .
> *Now,* you can . . .
> *After that,* try . . .
> *Finally,* you should . . .

Similarly, in an explanatory process analysis, the steps may follow in a chronological order that is based on cause and effect. In addition to some of the transitions above, you might make use of phrases like these:

This behaviour causes . . .
In turn . . .
The effect of this outcome is . . .

If you need to mention what *not* to do so your reader does not make a mistake or misunderstand a step, include this information at the point in the process when the confusion can occur. If you need to define a term, do so the first time the term is used. Finally, if you need to explain why a step is performed, do so when the step is given.

Process Guidelines: Strategies for Writing a Process Analysis

1. **Selecting a Topic.** Select a process you know well so you are not struggling for detail or presenting the process incompletely.
2. **Establishing a Purpose.** To establish your purpose, ask yourself these questions:
   - Am I writing a directional process analysis to inform my audience so my reader can perform the process?
   - Am I writing an explanatory process analysis to inform a reader who will not perform the process?
   - Do I want my reader to appreciate the beauty, difficulty, or complexity of the process?
   - Do I want to entertain my reader? Do I want to relate part of my experience or express my feelings about something associated with the process?
   - Do I want to convince my reader that the process is a better way to do something?
   - Do I want to show my reader the flaws in a specific process and suggest ways in which that process might be improved?
3. **Assessing Your Audience.** To assess your audience, ask yourself whether your reader appreciates the importance of the process, understands any part of the process, or would find any of the steps difficult to perform or understand. In addition, consider why your reader might be interested in the process.
4. **Generating Ideas.** List every step in the process in the order it is performed. Then write a statement that explains the importance of the process.

5. **Drafting.** With your list of steps as a guide, write out the process. Try to visualize the process as you are describing it. Are you providing enough information? Do the steps follow a logical order? Try to include a statement that indicates the importance of understanding the process. If you wish, this statement can be your thesis.

Troubleshooting Guide

Avoiding Person and Pronoun Shifts

If you have trouble knowing when to use *you* and *your*, remember that these words refer to the reader. If you use one of these pronouns to refer to a noun or to yourself—that is, if you are *not* referring to the reader—you create a problem called *person shift*.

PERSON SHIFT: **Women often overestimate their ability to handle dangerous situations. For example, women think they can talk themselves out of a confrontation, but you should always remember that your first step should be to walk—or run—away.**

CORRECTION: **Women often overestimate their ability to handle dangerous situations. For example, women think they can talk themselves out of a confrontation, but they should always remember that their first step should be to walk—or run—away.**

When you try to be gender neutral and avoid using gendered pronouns like *he* or *she*, preferring the safety of *they*, you can create pronoun shifts. You can avoid these shifts by making generalizations about groups, such as *students* or *workers*, rather than about *a student* or *a worker*. Note also that when you change your entire passage to plural you must also change the verb forms.

PRONOUN SHIFT: **When a woman finds herself in a conflict at work, they might be inclined to capitulate, believing that it's woman's role to keep the peace. Such a response, however, may naturally lead to further conflict if they overreact to the assumption they will always back down. It's a much better policy, then, to be calmly assertive about one's needs and principles.**

CORRECTION: **When women find [*note the change to a plural verb*] themselves in a conflict at work, they might be inclined to capitulate, believing that it's women's role to keep the peace. Such a response, however, may naturally lead to further conflict if they overreact to the assumption they will always back down. It's a much better policy, then, for women to be calmly assertive about their needs and principles.**

6. **Revising.** Be sure you are not stating the obvious or explaining how to do something the reader already knows how to do. For example, if you are explaining how to use a particular search engine, you do not need to tell your reader to turn on the computer. Be sure to define any specialized terms.

VISUALIZING A PROCESS ANALYSIS ESSAY

The following chart can help you visualize the structure for a process analysis. Like all good models, however, this one can be altered as needed.

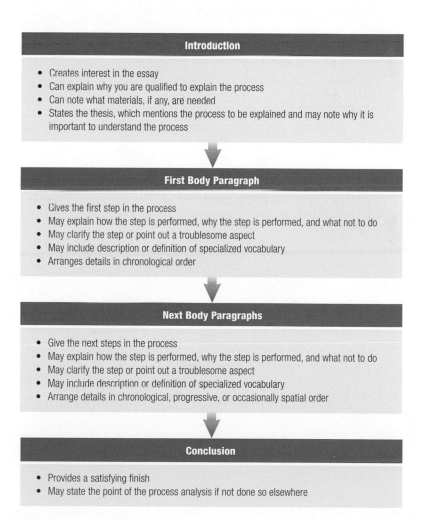

Introduction

- Creates interest in the essay
- Can explain why you are qualified to explain the process
- Can note what materials, if any, are needed
- States the thesis, which mentions the process to be explained and may note why it is important to understand the process

First Body Paragraph

- Gives the first step in the process
- May explain how the step is performed, why the step is performed, and what not to do
- May clarify the step or point out a troublesome aspect
- May include description or definition of specialized vocabulary
- Arranges details in chronological order

Next Body Paragraphs

- Give the next steps in the process
- May explain how the step is performed, why the step is performed, and what not to do
- May clarify the step or point out a troublesome aspect
- May include description or definition of specialized vocabulary
- Arrange details in chronological, progressive, or occasionally spatial order

Conclusion

- Provides a satisfying finish
- May state the point of the process analysis if not done so elsewhere

✔ Checklist for Revising a Process Analysis

Be sure to:

_____ Explain how steps are performed, if necessary.

_____ Mention what not to do, if necessary.

_____ Explain why steps are performed, if necessary.

_____ Provide clarifying examples, if needed.

_____ Describe, as necessary.

_____ Define terms your reader may not understand.

_____ Point out troublesome aspects of the process.

_____ Indicate the importance of understanding the process.

_____ Avoid stating the obvious.

_____ Use transitions to indicate sequence.

ANNOTATED STUDENT ESSAY

The following student essay is an informational process analysis that says as much about the joy of performing the process as it does about how to perform the process. After you read, you will have an opportunity to evaluate this essay.

A Visit to Candyland

1   You may have been to the supermarket around Christmastime and seen a gingerbread house kit. It probably involved graham-cracker slabs meant to be stuck together with thick white frosting and decorated with gumdrops. In my family, making gingerbread houses is a long-standing tradition, and one that involves far more than simply slapping some cookies and frosting together. Each year, in early December, we decide on a theme and go on to create an elaborate gingerbread structure that reflects the season and our interests. Our cardinal rule in gingerbread house making often comes as a surprise to the friends who visit to marvel at our creations: absolutely everything in the gingerbread house must be edible, and not only edible, but tasty.

2   We begin by coming up with a concept. One year, it was a crèche scene with Mary, Joseph, the baby Jesus, and various animals, shepherds, and angels. Another year, it was a covered bridge under snow, with a horse-drawn carriage. Once we've decided on a theme, we might visit the library or go on the Internet to find visual ideas we can incorporate in to our design. Then, after we've done some preliminary sketches, we make a pattern, measuring carefully with a ruler to make sure each piece will fit with the others. These pattern pieces are drawn onto thin paper and then precisely cut out with sharp scissors. We've found it helps to note on each pattern piece how many need to be made—a roof, for example, is usually made of two equal rectangles, and only one pattern piece is needed.

3   The next step is to make the gingerbread. We use an old family recipe that produces a sturdy but extremely tasty gingerbread cookie, flavoured with molasses, cinnamon, ground cloves, and lots of ginger. In order to make a really tough cookie, many cups of flour have to be incorporated into the batter. Once all the flour has been added, the dough is so dense it's almost impossible to stir, so we hand it off to my father, whose arms are the strongest. After the dough is finished it has to sit in the refrigerator for a time period ranging from several hours to a week. This cooling period makes the dough easier to handle and the finished cookie even tougher.

Paragraph 1
The introduction gives background information. The thesis is not stated but the paragraph suggests a focus on making gingerbread houses.

Paragraph 2
The paragraph gives the first two steps in the process. The details include examples of the first step and information on how the second step is performed.

Paragraph 3
The topic sentence (the first sentence) gives the next step in the process. Detail is included on why part of the step is performed.

Paragraph 4
The topic sentence (the first sentence) gives the next step in the process. Notice the transition, "once that's done."

4   Once the dough is ready to bake, it's time to make the pieces of the house. We do this by rolling out the dough onto sheets of tinfoil. We try to avoid handling the dough too much—if it gets warm before it goes into the oven, it loses some of its resilience. The dough is rolled until it's a little less than a quarter of an inch thick. Then we place the pattern pieces onto the rolled dough. Using a small knife, we cut around the pattern piece, discarding the excess dough. After we've cut out the windows on the wall pieces, we fill the holes with broken bits of hard candy. In the oven, these candy pieces melt and harden, forming what looks like stained glass. Once that's done, we slide the tinfoil with the cookie pieces on it onto a cookie sheet and put them into the oven.

Paragraph 5
The paragraph opens with the transition "seven to ten minutes later." The paragraph also notes a troublesome aspect of the process.

5   Seven to ten minutes later, the cookies are done, and we slide them onto wire racks to cool. After they've cooled, we peel off the tinfoil backing and admire the coloured light through the little stained-glass windows. Now we're ready for the hardest part of the whole process: putting the house together. Frosting is simply not tough enough for the elaborate structures we make, so instead we use melted sugar. We sprinkle regular granulated sugar into a wide, flat pan and heat it over a medium-high flame. In a few minutes it forms a glossy, dark-brown liquid. The ends of the gingerbread pieces that are to be stuck together have to be dipped very quickly into the melted sugar and then speedily and precisely joined to their intended mates. If this process is done too quickly, there may not be enough sugar to make the pieces stick, or we may stick them on at the wrong angle. If it's done too slowly, the sugar can harden, its sticking powers completely lost. When my brothers and I were little, we were not allowed to participate in the melted-sugar operation, but now we've developed the necessary manual dexterity and nerves of steel.

Paragraph 6
The topic sentence (the first sentence) gives the next step and includes a transition.

6   Now the house is assembled and ready for everyone's favourite stage: decoration. We make frosting out of butter, confectioner's sugar, and food coloring, and add a base coat to the parts of the house that seem to need it, like the roof. We generally leave the sides bare, because the dark brown gingerbread is such a pretty color, but we add details with frosting piped out of a wax-paper tube. Then we add decorations. In the past we've used raisins, cinnamon sticks, star anise, nuts, and, of course, many different kinds of candy. Necco wafers, broken in half, make particularly good shingles.

Paragraph 7
The conclusion provides closure by explaining what is done with the gingerbread house. It also highlights a family tradition.

7   When we're finished, we've usually consumed a substantial quantity of decorations, spoonfuls of frosting, and cookie scraps. Naturally we make gingerbread men to live in the house, but their lifespans tend to be extremely short—sometimes they don't even get frosted. We're too full to do anything but sit and admire our handiwork. A few days later,

however, we host our annual holiday party, where the final part of the tradition comes into play. The youngest child at the event (apart from babies, of course) is handed an orange suspended from a red satin ribbon. This is the gingerbread wrecking ball, and it's swung at the house until total destruction has been achieved. We're always sorry to see the house ruined, but then we have the pleasure, along with our guests, of eating our annual masterpiece.

PEER REVIEW

Responding to "A Visit to Candyland"

Evaluate "A Visit to Candyland" by responding to these questions:

1. Does the essay hold your interest? Why or why not?
2. Are the introduction and conclusion effective? Explain.
3. Is the essay a directional or an explanatory process analysis? If it is the former, could you perform the process after reading the essay? If it is the latter, do you understand and appreciate the process after reading the essay?
4. What do you think of the author's word choice? Why? Cite an example to support your view.
5. What are the chief strengths of the essay? Why do you find these features strong?
6. Mention one revision you would like to see. How will that revision improve the essay or help the author achieve his purpose?

READING SELECTIONS

Background

J. M. Kearns grew up in Ontario. After making his living as a bureaucrat in L.A., he returned to his Canadian roots for a while before moving back to the States. He now lives in Nashville, Tennessee, where he writes and indulges in the other love of his life: producing recordings for some of Nashville's most talented indie artists. In 2007, he published his bestselling *Why Mr. Right Can't Find You.* In 2008, he published his first novel, *ex-Cottagers in Love.* Holding a PhD in the philosophy of perception, he brings the philosopher's analytic approach and the novelist/songwriter's curiosity about human relationships to understanding the challenges people face when they seek Mr. or Ms. Right. The essay was first published in *What I Meant to Say: The Private Lives of Men*.

The Combined Patterns and Their Purposes

Kearns's essay is an example of an explanatory process analysis: obviously written for women, it details the mysterious process through which men with romance on their minds connect with women. The essay's generous and sometimes funny use of examples helps the reader to understand the kinds of choices men unconsciously make and the role of chance in successful "sightings." Yet despite addressing a female audience, the essay might help couples figure out how they got so lucky or how men might improve their odds. There may be a little directional process analysis lurking here.

How Men Choose Women

J. M. Kearns

1   Let me say at the start, I don't mean to imply that men get to do the choosing. It isn't like a vegetable stand, where a man can say, "I'll take this onion here, not these others," and the onion has nothing to say about it. What we're talking about is, how do men pick out which women they are going to *try* for. Nor am I condoning, excusing or endorsing men's methods. Interesting essays could be written on how men *should* choose women, or how men *wish* they chose women. But we will focus on a topic of more practical interest: in the real world, how do men actually choose women? We will take a clear-eyed look at that question, and maybe we will find that the truth has some redeeming qualities.

> **As you read**
> Is Kearns's tone appropriate to the topic? Does it mock men and women or does it acknowledge the complexities of attractions?

2   The first thing we need to face about men is this: they are animals. More accurately, they are loons. They have their own ways of doing things. They don't proceed in a politically correct, enlightened way to select a woman. They may end up valuing her for the "right" things, the things she wants to be valued for. But that is not how they start.

3   Men are hard-wired to look for certain features. Evolution wants the mating process to succeed, and so it makes sure that men home in on that which will be conducive to success, regardless of how unrefined this strategy may be.

4   But no matter how strange men are, if you're a woman who wants to meet the right man, you have to clue in to how men think. (Okay, "think" is a bit of a stretch.) If you try to change men or just don't get them, you'll be stymied—but if you accept how they are and forgive them and work with them, you will have enormous power and effectiveness.

5   Men want to look. First, foremost and always, men are visual. Men's eyes are always wandering, seeking out that which they could and would impregnate. Why is this so, Mr. Darwin? "Well, it's because the genes that triggered that kind of behaviour had the best chance of survival down through the ages, until all the men who were left had those genes." In other words, an obsession with reproduction leads to a better reproductive score . . . or something—let's not get too technical. The fact is men can't help looking, even happily married men, even codgers who think Viagra is better than money.

6   So the first rule is, *let men see you.* This may seem too obvious to even mention, but in fact it is the key to the whole thing. If you make it difficult to be seen—for instance, if you sit in the back booth with shades on—you stop Step One from happening. So none of the other steps can happen. (Note that being seen is particularly crucial—and achievable—if you are trying to meet Mr. Right online.)

7   Now let us ask, what are men looking *for*? What are they hoping to see? If you're feeling cynical, your answer may be, "Cameron Diaz." Or if you happen to look like Cameron Diaz, your equally discouraged answer may be "Kiera Knightly." But this is so wrong it is laughable.

8   Men are, in the first place, looking for "attractive." Now what on earth does that mean? Well, the good news is, it means completely different things to different men—but it almost always involves a combination of face, and body shape and size.

9   Different men like completely different bodies. Many men in our culture like slender, athletic female figures—some men really do, and some *say they do*, because they are ashamed of admitting anything else to their male peer group. Some men want the rail-thin model type. But many men in our culture do not want a slender woman: they want someone with riper curves, someone who is larger, more "Rubenesque." Some men like pear-shaped women; some men like inverted pears. Some men want very large women. And some men don't really care that much about body size or shape.

"There are no objective standards concerning faces."

10   Then we have faces. Here there is even less consensus. No one agrees on faces. A face that strikes one man as masculine may seem feminine to another. A face that strikes Tom as sexy may look shallow to Harry. Ralph may hate a lot of makeup on a woman, while Shawn considers it a turn-on. There are no objective standards concerning faces. Even in the realm of extremely good-looking celebrities, you will find a whole gamut of opinions. I know men who think Britney Spears is homely. I know men who think Pamela Anderson is grotesque.

11   I know men who hate all blondes. Men who hate brunettes. Men who appreciate a good tan. Men who adore very pale skin. Boob men. Leg men. I knew a guy who got very turned on by a woman's handshake, if it was "as strong as a man's." His friends told him he was in the closet, but he stuck to his guns.

12   All this may strike the sensitive, intelligent woman as superficial, even offensive. "How shallow can guys get?" you may ask. Surely the cultured, educated, spiritual (yet masculine) man of *your* dreams doesn't look only at the outside of a woman. "*True beauty is on the inside*," women cry out from the salons of the world. "Besides," I hear them say, "we women are forgiving of men's looks—why can't men return the favour?"

13   Scientists say men and women are both designed to be ruthlessly pragmatic in their criteria for a mate. Women are programmed by evolution to choose men based on their father potential, which is closely associated with status in the group—what we now call money and power. Men—regardless of their conscious attitude to having kids—are designed to look for good reproducers; a low waist-to-hip ratio of around .70 signifies "likely to be a success at bearing children." (Larger waists relative to the hips have been linked to lower estrogen levels, less body fat available to sustain pregnancy and lower fertility.) And in both sexes, facial beauty is associated with grace, intelligence, popularity and, in general, fitness for survival.

14   So forget about how superficial men may be and realize that they, like you, are hard-wired in mysterious ways, which may or may not be as shallow as you think. (Fortunately, many of them don't toe the evolutionary line anyway—apparently their wiring has come loose.)

15   Take faces, for example. It's clear that we read far more in a face than looks. We think we are reading souls. We look into the eyes of the person we are talking to, and we feel as if we can tell who they are, deep down—what they value, what they love. With certain people, something about the face feels familiar, even familial. Many people strike us as somehow alien; but some faces arouse in us a strange empathy from the first time we set eyes on them.

> "It's clear that we read far more in a face than looks.
> We think we are reading souls."

16   What is a man doing when he looks you over? On some level, quite possibly unconscious, he (or his genes) are trying to decide, could this person be a lover or is she just a potential friend? If the answer comes up "lover," his charm will probably kick in, and there will be a lot of twinkling eyes and banter and smiling (read: spreading of plumage) that might not take place if his circuits decided on "friend." And how is the decision made? Let's assume he finds you to be above some basic threshold of attractiveness—what other factors come into play?

17   Well, as odd as it may sound, you are being checked out in a number of ways to determine whether you are *too intimidating*. You are being studied to see whether

you are likely to defeat him as a lover. I mean this in the most literal way: he wants to know whether in your presence he might be *unable to perform*.

18   The average male who is old enough and mature enough to want to marry has realized that sex is not always a triumph. I'm not saying he is sexually insecure: indeed, with the right woman he may be easygoing, studly and confident. But therein lies the rub: how does he know which women are "right"?

19   Our evolving male has tried, with those few cells in his brain devoted to self-knowledge, to wrestle with this question. This has made him attentive to factors that influence his chemistry with women. Many of these factors are hard to pin down: who knows what creates that magical heat for some couples? And how many men have bravely catalogued the qualities of particular women that threaten their ego, and thereby their arousal? But one area, at least, seems to be a no-brainer: a man's own physical likes and dislikes. So he tries to screen out anything that might lessen his prowess if a woman invites him to perform.

20   This isn't all selfish. When a man spies a woman who is really "his type"—whatever this may be—he thinks he has found someone whose sexual needs he could enthusiastically fulfill. Shall we blame him for thinking this is good news for her too?

INTIMIDATION AND ATTRACTION: A SHORT VIGNETTE

21   It's lunch time. Randy and Tom find themselves sitting next to a rather elegant woman in a yuppie bar in the business district. They strike up a conversation with her while they wait for their respective tables. The woman, Rachel, is friendly, glad to have someone to talk to while she waits for a friend to show up. The men are responding in kind, but meanwhile they are both, as discreetly as they can, checking Rachel out.

22   Now it happens that Rachel, though strikingly attractive, has a slightly hawk-like cast to her features, a slight fierceness built into her face, that reads to Randy as intimidating and as slightly masculine. He senses in her an unswerving confidence in herself and in the cosmos, and a capacity for aggression, that make him feel he may be out of his league. So Randy is leaning toward a no on the "lover" issue, except for one thing: he has noticed that Rachel (who is wearing an attractive taupe business suit) has long, very good legs, and Randy is a confirmed leg man. (He is having trouble getting good views of her legs, because he is right next to her, and has to lean back and tilt his head to inspect them.) To make matters worse, Rachel has said she is a criminal lawyer. Randy is a tax lawyer, and they are bantering about the legal scene. But he opted out of court work because it was too scary, and he is very conscious of a threat to his ego in this woman. Those legs make him wish that she didn't intimidate him, but he can't fight the verdict of his genes.

23   Meanwhile Tom, who is one barstool over, is caught in a different struggle. Tom does not perceive Rachel as hawk-like or aggressive; he came from a family of women who had features somewhat like Rachel's, and to him her face represents not only beauty, but comfort, femininity and warmth. Tom is half in love already. He is not

a lawyer and is not directly threatened by any status Rachel may have in that area. Tom's problem is that he can't seem to get into the conversation (because Randy is the one sitting next to Rachel and they're talking shop), and is therefore unable to tell how he and Rachel might get along, or even how she might react to him. Tom is divorced, has been lonely and horny for ages, and he has checked Rachel's hand and found no ring.

24   Tom has one other problem. Don't laugh at him, girls, or think he's a lout: he didn't choose this problem. Tom is a breast man. This does not mean that Tom thinks he deserves more goodies than the next guy—that he wants a luxury that he could do without. Rather, Tom's problem is that his sexual confidence is tied to the large female bosom: he becomes just a little insecure without it because a large bust is the catalyst that sparks his sexual chemistry.

25   I said he didn't choose to be this way. Tom didn't sit down with a notepad at age thirteen and write, "I now decide that I will find the following features of the female anatomy unbearably exciting." He just discovered what moved him. Like a man who hears western swing music for the first time and knows he has found his Holy Grail. So what *did* determine the matter? It could be cultural: the TV did it to him, men's magazines did it. The problem with that theory is we have too many different men liking too many different body types: they seem to extract different images from the media. It could be genetic: his grandfather liked the same type. Or perhaps it was early childhood experience, or lack thereof. Maybe he imprinted on the first woman he fell in love with—and maybe that was his art teacher in Grade Four.

26   At any rate, ever since he noticed how lovely Rachel is, Tom has been trying to lean around his stocky friend Randy and get a gander at Rachel's chest. But Randy is always in the way, and unfortunately Rachel is wearing a business suit and the jacket pretty much hides her shape.

27   Just as the men's table is announced, two things happen. Rachel says to Randy, "The only place that really matters to me is our family cottage on the lake," and Rachel twists toward them on her stool, her jacket falls open, and Tom has his first unobstructed view of the generous curve of her chest in a cream blouse. Tom is now completely smitten, because his own sacred place happens to be a cottage on a lake, and he is absolutely clear that Rachel, as a physical specimen, is his wet dream.

28   Tom now has achieved what we will call a "sighting." Tom is beside himself, if you must know the truth. He knows right now, with the same certainty that he knows his own address, that he could be happy with this woman. Behind his exterior calm he is hyperventilating, because *this never happens.* He sees women whom he finds attractive, sometimes, but they are not alone. And they are usually married. Mostly he sees them across a room or across the street. And he never gets to hear them talk about their lives, never gets even a hint as to whether he might be compatible with them in a personal sense. On this occasion in the restaurant, all these sad rules have found an exception.

29   This woman is classy, she is smart and she cares about lakes. And in Tom's eyes, she is a goddess.

30   Randy gets up to go to their table. He says goodbye to Rachel, who gives him a warm smile. Tom suspects that Rachel is attracted to Randy. Tom has no sense at all of Rachel even noticing him. He smiles at her but his smile comes out anxious and stiff, because for him there is too much at stake and he has no cards to play. Randy says, "Let's go, bud," a little sarcastically—and Tom realizes he is just standing there in a haze, gazing at Rachel. Randy tugs him away and says to Rachel, "This guy needs to eat."

31   Tom flushes and follows Randy into the restaurant area, and they order. Randy says dismissively, "She was nice, but kind of butch-looking. A little hefty, too." Tom, who knows his own taste for fuller-figured women is atypical of his male peer group, keeps quiet, doesn't mention that he just lost the love of his life. A few minutes later, they see Rachel sit down in a nearby booth with a very good-looking, well-dressed man, who seems to be locked in constant hilarity with her. Tom abandons a half-formed plan of somehow talking to her before heading back to work.

32   This is how it happens to us men.

33   A typical session in the endless male search: what can we learn from it? Let's inventory a few useful points:

34   1.   Facial looks are totally subjective: the same woman can look feminine and pretty to one man and just the opposite to another. Same for body shapes and sizes.

35   2.   Total accidents of seating and attitude can stop major connections from being made.

36   3.   Men very rarely have positive "sightings," and usually are not in a position to act even on those.

37   4.   Men's relentless scrutiny of women, the thing that drives feminists crazy, is just as much *a screening out of that which is intimidating* as it is a judging of whether someone is up to par. If truth be known, Randy's dismissal of Rachel had little to do with her being not pretty or too heavy. These were excuses. The truth was, he found her intimidating as a lawyer and as a woman.

38   5.   The most confident, forward man in the group is not always the most interested one. He may be confident because he isn't interested, and therefore has nothing to lose. The one who can't get a word out may be the one who is stricken with attraction. *Above all, remember this.*

39   6.   Qualities of character are often in play from the beginning. Men may seem to be judging solely on appearance—but in fact *they see in appearance many other levels of humanity.* In Rachel's face, Tom saw warmth, familial comfort, kindness, intelligence. In her words he heard a love for a type of

sacred place that he too values. Even her body's sexual appeal to him holds other levels of connection—in her full figure he sees a reassuring quality, and a sensual opulence, that speaks to his emotional needs. (Randy saw qualities of mind that scared him off.) Both men were reacting to a whole person, through her appearance.

40   And what did Rachel think?

41   Here we encounter an amazing disparity—a gap like the Grand Canyon. Her experience was so unlike that of the men as to seem like a cruel cosmic joke. Rachel did not have "finding a man" on her agenda. She wanted to meet her friend Pete and have lunch, and she was preoccupied with a trial she is in the middle of. Pete works at the same firm she does, and they hang out together a lot, but there is no chemistry between them and that is why they have the relaxed, hilarious rapport that Tom noticed later.

> "And what did Rachel think? Here we encounter an amazing disparity—a gap like the Grand Canyon."

42   Rachel broke up with a long-term lover six months ago when she discovered he was cheating on her. Although she is lonely and occasionally makes a slight effort to meet new people, she is skeptical of all men. And anyway, *she does not think of a bar as a place where she could ever meet a man.* She was perfectly happy to talk to Randy, but did not even ask herself whether he was relationship material—he was just a fellow lawyer. Tom she hardly noticed. She did observe that he had a nice face, but it never occurred to her for a moment that he was interested in her, and he seemed sort of uptight and sad compared to his friend.

43   Rachel's attitude to her body is even more tragically counterproductive. Rachel has regretted since about age sixteen that she is not skinnier. She thinks of herself as full-figured, because although she has a model's legs, she has rounded hips and a full bosom. Actually, she thinks she's fat. If she could only lose thirty pounds, she might be acceptable in her own eyes. She has an older sister who still weighs 115 pounds and this torments her daily. Somewhere inside her, a voice still says, "You're beautiful," but lately she has trouble hearing it.

44   Oh Rachel! The truth is, you have a classic hourglass figure, and plenty of men would find you almost overwhelmingly sexy if you would let them—and if they could escape the caustic stereotypes of their peer group. So Rachel wears her business jackets in such a way as to conceal her generous chest—she is ambivalent at best about it. It certainly never occurred to her that Tom is a man who absolutely cherishes the very body type that she represents, at the weight where she is. Or that her jacket was preventing such an admirer from even verifying that she is what he admires!

45   Tom, a man who is normally cheerful and entertaining, managed only to seem a bit sad to her. And if he seemed sad, maybe he had a right to be. Because something sad did just happen. Rachel just walked away from Mr. Right. Tom was it.

46   Don't get me wrong here: I am not saying that Rachel did anything wrong, though she could be accused of being somewhat unaware.

47   What I *am* saying is that near-misses like this happen all the time. People who would be perfect together pass like the proverbial ships in the night. Then they trudge on down life's path, forever lonely. Women cruise through situations, blissfully unaware of the life-and-death struggle going on in the man who is right next to them.

48   For it *is* a life-and-death struggle. Biologically, nothing is more important than successful mating. And for an average male who is old enough and mature enough to want to marry, that challenge is an awesome test, a labour of Hercules, fraught with perils and obstacles. The main peril is rejection (intensified by the competition of other males, many of whom have him beaten in one way or another—looks, money, physique, smarts, style, confidence . . .*). The main obstacle is rarity: too seldom does our eligible male encounter an unattached and approachable female whom he senses could really be the one.

49   No wonder a man goes a little crazy when a true sighting happens—success and happiness and an end to loneliness are beckoning to him, if he can only make the right moves. In our example, Tom froze up completely, even managed to make himself less attractive! Became stiff and sad-looking, tongue-tied.

50   Must we leave our little story of the yuppie lovers with a bad ending? Could Rachel have done anything to change the outcome?

51   Well, suppose we replay the scene with just a few tiny changes. This time, Rachel keeps in mind that any place is a good place to meet Mr. Right.

52   Let's say that again. *Any place is a good place to meet Mr. Right.*

53   So she has her antennae switched on. Then she may well notice that lawyer Randy is not really interested in her. And that he is a bit of a bore—too needy in the ego department. And she may well pick up on the fact that Tom is eyeing her in an almost stressed way. Why is he doing that? Maybe he fancies her. Maybe she should make a point to speak to him, instead of letting this insecure tax lawyer hog all her time. Tom does have a very nice face, after all. So she leans across Randy, smiles at Tom, realizes that her jacket has fallen open, which is fine, and says to Tom, "Why do you hang out with this lawyer boy, anyway? Can't you do any better?"

---

*Or if he is the rare bird with looks, money, physique, smarts, style and confidence, then he meets some woman who wants him to be more sensitive, more creative, more humble.

   In recent years the "Am I as good-looking as the other guys?" issue has intensified, as the media have done to men what they always did to women: assaulted them with a barrage of images of "perfect" male specimens with perfect faces, hair, clothing, pecs and abs, as they conspire to sell exercise machines, diets, erectile dysfunction pills and plastic surgery to men.

54   Tom lights up at this suggestion that she has noticed him, at her sense of humour, and at the curves that he has just detected. Tom starts to talk to her; Randy decides to go to the rest room; Tom cannot resist moving over next to her. They discover their mutual love of lakes and cottages. He asks her if she is meeting someone for lunch. She says yes, but he's just a friend. Finally Tom cannot restrain himself. He asks for her card. She gives it to him. They smile at each other. Love is born.

55   (Somewhere, Cupid frowns: because two people who will be *happy together* have found each other.)

Reading Closely and Thinking Critically

1. There are two basic, antithetical ways of thinking about gender roles (with all kinds of positions in between them). One extreme suggests that men and women are hard-wired for certain characteristics or behaviours: that men are "naturally" aggressive, while women are "naturally" nurturing. The other extreme suggests that we are entirely the products of our cultures and that hormones and the structures of our brains play no roles at all. Where does Kearns fall on the continuum between these two positions?
2. What evidence do you have that Kearns believes, at least to some extent, in the role of biology in shaping gender?
3. What evidence do you have that Kearns thinks society shapes our desires and expectations?
4. How does Kearns try to reconcile men's focus on the visual with some deeper motives for finding a particular woman attractive?
5. In a footnote, Kearns observes that "the media have done to men what they always did to women: assaulted them with a barrage of images of 'perfect' male specimens with perfect faces, hair, clothing, pecs and abs, as they conspire to sell exercise machines, diets, erectile dysfunction pills and plastic surgery to men." How might this observation help to reveal that Kearns is also writing for men?

Examining Structure and Strategy

1. Kearns entitles his essay "How Men Choose Women," and then spends the first paragraph saying that this is not exactly what he's talking about. Why does he do this? Is it an effective strategy?
2. One of Kearns' basic strategies is to use examples. Attempting to describe what women assume men are looking for, he offers the examples of Cameron Diaz or "Kiera Knightly" (paragraph 7). Questioning objective standards of beauty, he notes that "I know men who think Britney Spears is homely. I know men who think Pamela Anderson is grotesque" (paragraph 10). Are these brief examples helpful? Why has he chosen examples from popular culture rather than mentioning, for example, the Mona Lisa?
3. Consider the extended example Kearns ends the essay with that has two different endings. Has he made effective decisions about when to use brief examples and when to use longer ones? Are the two endings of the essay effective?
4. In such a short essay, does Kearns need a list of the points he's made? What's the effect of this list?
5. Why does the essay end with Cupid frowning "because two people who will be *happy together* have found each other"? Doesn't Cupid try to get people to fall in love?

Considering Language and Style

1. Kearns regularly uses language that is implicitly, if not explicitly, critical of the way men conduct themselves in order to achieve a "sighting." He calls men "animals" and "loons"; he says that "'think' is a bit of a stretch" when we're trying to describe what motivates men to be attracted to one woman and not another. He suggests that the male brain only has a "few cells . . . devoted to self-knowledge."

What are his motives for such put-downs? What effect do they have on you? Are those effects different for men and women?

2. What kinds of observations suggest, contrary to some of the language he uses, that Kearns is sympathetic to men?

3. How can you tell he's sympathetic about women's experience?

4. Kearns regularly uses metaphors and similes. The "dating scene" is not a "vegetable stand" and women are not onions (paragraph 1). A man's attraction to long legs or full figures is "Like a man who hears western swing music for the first time and knows he has found his Holy Grail" (paragraph 25; be sure to pay attention to both metaphors here.) The disparity between Rachel's experience of the brief moment at the bar and Tom's is "a gap like the Grand Canyon" (paragraph 41). Why does he need to use metaphors at these particular moments? Are there other strategies that would similarly make the unfamiliar familiar?

5. Tone is the sum of *all* the decisions a writer makes, from word choice to sentence structure to the shape and argument of the overall essay. Tone reveals writers' attitudes toward their subjects and their readers. How would you summarize Kearns' tone? Does it shift from time to time? Why or why not? Do you find it appropriate?

For Discussion in Class or Online

What assumptions do you have about whether being a man or woman is a matter of nature or nurture? What evidence do you have for your assumptions? Are they shared with your generation? Do you share them with your parents' generation? Why or why not? If your instructor so directs, post your responses on your class Web site.

Writing Assignments

1. **In your journal.** What does popular culture say about the process of two people finding one another? Consider what your favourite singer or your favourite romantic comedy has to say about this process. Why do you think popular culture is so preoccupied with this process?

2. **Using process analysis for a purpose.** The purposes given in the assignments are possibilities. You may establish whatever purposes you like, within your instructor's guidelines.
    *   To entertain your reader, describe the process involved in setting up the perfect blind date.
    *   To entertain and inform your reader, write an explanatory process analysis that analyzes the steps to perfect happiness suggested by Hollywood's formula for the romantic comedy. (You will probably need to consider a sub-genre of the romantic comedy in order to find films that are similar enough to draw conclusions from.)
    *   To persuade your reader, describe the perfect (even if unrealistic) process by which men and women interested in romance might meet their ideal partners.
    *   To persuade your reader, consider the way the Internet has changed some of the dynamics of dating for the better—or, if you like, for the worse.

3. **Combining patterns.** Using process analysis and contrast and comparison, write about the similarities or differences in two generations of romantic comedies to see how the process by which the characters achieve lasting happiness changes over time—say from your parents' generation to your own.

4. **Connecting the readings.** Barbara Ehrenrich's essay "What I've Learned from Men" was written in 1985; J. M. Kearns published "How Men Choose Women" in 2007. Both essays give you snapshots of gender roles in their time. Compare the "full-grown feminist" of 1985 with the young woman seeking a partner in the twenty-first century. Or contrast the men of Ehrenrich's generation with those depicted in Kearns' essay.

5. **Drawing on sources.** Consult Google Scholar to learn how being involved parents is changing men's ideas and experiences of masculinity.

Background

Born in Baltimore, Maryland, in 1952, Diane Cole attended Radcliffe College and Johns Hopkins University. In addition to serving as a contributing editor to *Psychology Today*, she has written for *The Wall Street Journal*, the *Washington Post*, the *New York Times, Parents, Newsweek, Ms.*, and *Glamour*. Her writing topics frequently include psychology and women's careers. Cole's books include *Hunting the Headhunters: A Woman's Guide* (1988), *After Great Pain: A New Life Emerges* (1992), and, with Scott Wetzler, *Is It You or Is It Me? How We Turn Our Emotions Inside Out and Blame Each Other* (1998). "Don't Just Stand There" was first published in 1989 in a *New York Times* supplement called *A World of Difference*, which was part of a campaign against bigotry sponsored by the Anti-Defamation League of B'nai B'rith, a Jewish fraternal order.

The Pattern and Its Purposes

Have you ever been unsure how to respond to a bigoted remark? If so, "Don't Just Stand There" can help, because Diane Cole uses process analysis to inform her audience about how to react to bigoted comments and jokes. At the same time, she makes her readers more sensitive to the hurtful nature of such slurs and persuades them to take action when they hear them.

Don't Just Stand There
Diane Cole

As you read
Cole uses a great many quotations in the essay. Consider how they help achieve her purpose for writing.

1   It was my office farewell party, and colleagues at the job I was about to leave were wishing me well. My mood was one of ebullience tinged with regret, and it was in this spirit that I spoke to the office neighbor to whom I had waved hello every morning for the past two years. He smiled broadly as he launched into a long, rambling story, pausing only after he delivered the punch line. It was a very long pause because, although he laughed, I did not: This joke was unmistakably anti-Semitic.

2   I froze. Everyone in the office knew I was Jewish; what could he have possibly meant? Shaken and hurt, not knowing what else to do, I turned in stunned silence to the next well-wisher. Later, still angry, I wondered, what else should I—could I—have done?

3   Prejudice can make its presence felt in any setting, but hearing its nasty voice in this way can be particularly unnerving. We do not know what to do and often we feel another form of paralysis as well: We think, "Nothing I say or do will change this person's attitude, so why bother?"

4   But left unchecked, racial slurs and offensive ethnic jokes "can poison the atmosphere," says Michael McQuillan, adviser for racial/ethnic affairs for the Brooklyn borough president's office. "Hearing these remarks conditions us to accept them; and if we accept these, we can become accepting of other acts."

5   Speaking up may not magically change a biased attitude, but it can change a person's behavior by putting a strong message across. And the more messages there are, the more likely a person is to change that behavior, says Arnold Kahn, professor

of psychology at James Madison University, Harrisonburg, Va., who makes this analogy: "You can't keep people from smoking in *their* house, but you can ask them not to smoke in *your* house."

6   At the same time, "Even if the other party ignores or discounts what you say, people always reflect on how others perceive them. Speaking up always counts," says LeNorman Strong, director of campus life at George Washington University, Washington, D.C.

"Speaking up always counts."

7   Finally, learning to respond effectively also helps people feel better about themselves, asserts Cherie Brown, executive director of the National Coalition Building Institute, a Boston-based training organization. "We've found that, when people felt they could at least in this small way make a difference, that made them more eager to take on other activities on a larger scale," she says. Although there is no "cook-book approach" to confronting such remarks—every situation is different, experts stress—there are some effective strategies.

8   *When the "joke" turns on who you are— as a member of an ethnic or religious group, a person of color, a woman, a gay or lesbian, an elderly person, or someone with a physical handicap—shocked paralysis is often the first response. Then, wounded and vulnerable, on some level you want to strike back.*

9   Lashing out or responding in kind is seldom the most effective response, however. "That can give you momentary satisfaction, but you also feel as if you've lowered yourself to that other person's level," Mr. McQuillan explains. Such a response may further label you in the speaker's mind as thin-skinned, someone not to be taken seriously. Or it may up the ante, making the speaker, and then you, reach for new insults—or physical blows.

10   "If you don't laugh at the joke, or fight, or respond in kind to the slur," says Mr. McQuillan, "that will take the person by surprise, and that can give you more control over the situation." Therefore, in situations like the one in which I found myself—a private conversation in which I knew the person making the remark—he suggests voicing your anger calmly but pointedly: "I don't know if you realize what that sounded like to me. If that's what you meant, it really hurt me."

11   State how *you* feel, rather than making an abstract statement like, "Not everyone who hears that joke might find it funny." Counsels Mr. Strong: "Personalize the sense of 'this is how I feel when you say this.' That makes it very concrete"—and harder to dismiss.

12   Make sure you heard the words and their intent correctly by repeating or rephrasing the statement: "This is what I heard you say. Is that what you meant?" It's important to give the other person the benefit of the doubt because, in fact, he may *not* have realized that the comment was offensive and, if you had not spoken up, would have had no idea of its impact on you.

13   For instance, Professor Kahn relates that he used to include in his exams multiple-choice questions that occasionally contained "incorrect funny answers." After one exam, a student came up to him in private and said, "I don't think you intended this, but I found a number of those jokes offensive to me as a woman." She explained why. "What she said made immediate sense to me," he says. "I apologized at the next class, and I never did it again."

14   But what if the speaker dismisses your objection, saying, "Oh, you're just being sensitive. Can't you take a joke?" In that case, you might say, "I'm not so sure about that, let's talk about that a little more." The key, Mr. Strong says, is to continue the dialogue, hear the other person's concerns, and point out your own. "There are times when you're just going to have to admit defeat and end it," he adds, "but I have to feel that I did the best I could."

15   When the offending remark is made in the presence of others—at a staff meeting, for example—it can be even more distressing than an insult made privately.

16   "You have two options," says William Newlin, director of field services for the Community Relations division of the New York City Commission on Human Rights. "You can respond immediately at the meeting, or you can delay your response until afterward in private. But a response has to come."

17   Some remarks or actions may be so outrageous that they cannot go unnoted at the moment, regardless of the speaker or the setting. But in general, psychologists say, shaming a person in public may have the opposite effect of the one you want: The speaker will deny his offense all the more strongly in order to save face. Further, few people enjoy being put on the spot, and if the remark really was not intended to be offensive, publicly embarrassing the person who made it may cause an unnecessary rift or further misunderstanding. Finally, most people just don't react as well or thoughtfully under a public spotlight as they would in private.

18   Keeping that in mind, an excellent alternative is to take the offender aside afterward: "Could we talk for a minute in private?" Then use the strategies suggested above for calmly stating how you feel, giving the speaker the benefit of the doubt, and proceeding from there.

19   At a large meeting or public talk, you might consider passing the speaker a note, says David Wertheimer, executive director of the New York City Gay and Lesbian Anti-Violence Project: You could write, "You may not realize it, but your remarks were offensive because . . ."

20   "Think of your role as that of an educator," suggests James M. Jones, Ph.D., executive director for public interest at the American Psychological Association. "You have to be controlled."

21   Regardless of the setting or situation, speaking up always raises the risk of rocking the boat. If the person who made the offending remark is your boss, there may be

an even bigger risk to consider: How will this affect my job? Several things can help minimize the risk, however. First, know what other resources you may have at work, suggests Caryl Stern, director of the A World of Difference—New York City campaign: Does your personnel office handle discrimination complaints? Are other grievance procedures in place?

22   You won't necessarily need to use any of these procedures, Ms. Stern stresses. In fact, she advises, "It's usually better to try a one-on-one approach first." But simply knowing a formal system exists can make you feel secure enough to set up that meeting.

23   You can also raise the issue with other colleagues who heard the remark: Did they feel the same way you did? The more support you have, the less alone you will feel. Your point will also carry more validity and be more difficult to shrug off. Finally, give your boss credit—and the benefit of the doubt: "I know you've worked hard for the company's affirmative action programs, so I'm sure you didn't realize what those remarks sounded like to me as well as the others at the meeting last week . . ."

24   If, even after this discussion, the problem persists, go back for another meeting, Ms. Stern advises. And if that, too, fails, you'll know what other options are available to you.

25   *It's a spirited dinner party, and everyone's having a good time, until one guest starts reciting a racist joke. Everyone at the table is white, including you. The others are still laughing, as you wonder what to say or do.*

"The others are still laughing, as you wonder what to say or do."

26   No one likes being seen as a party-pooper, but before deciding that you'd prefer not to take on this role, you might remember that the person who told the offensive joke has already ruined your good time.

27   If it's a group that you feel comfortable in—a family gathering, for instance—you will feel freer to speak up. Still, shaming the person by shouting, "You're wrong" or "That's not funny!" probably won't get your point across as effectively as other strategies. "If you interrupt people to condemn them, it just makes it harder," says Cherie Brown. She suggests trying instead to get at the resentments that lie beneath the joke by asking open-ended questions: "Grandpa, I know you always treat everyone with such respect. Why do people in our family talk that way about black people?" The key, Ms. Brown says, "is to listen to them first, so they will be more likely to listen to you."

28   If you don't know your fellow guests well, before speaking up you could turn discreetly to your neighbors (or excuse yourself to help the host or hostess in the kitchen) to get a reading on how they felt, and whether or not you'll find support for speaking up: "I know you probably didn't mean anything by that joke, Jim, but it really offended me . . ." It's important to say that *you* were offended—not state how

the group that is the butt of the joke would feel. "Otherwise," Le Norman Strong says, "you risk coming off as a goody-two-shoes."

29   If you yourself are the host, you can exercise more control; you are, after all, the one who sets the rules and the tone of behavior in your home. Once, when Professor Kahn's party guests began singing offensive, racist songs, for instance, he kicked them all out, saying, "You don't sing songs like that in my house!" And, he adds, "they never did again."

30   *At school one day, a friend comes over and says, "Who do you think you are, hanging out with Joe? If you can be friends with those people, I'm through with you!"*

31   Peer pressure can weigh heavily on kids. They feel vulnerable and, because they are kids, they aren't as able to control the urge to fight. "But if you learn to handle these situations as kids, you'll be better able to handle them as an adult," William Newlin points out.

32   Begin by redefining to yourself what a friend is and examining what friendship means, advises Amy Lee, a human relations specialist at Panel of Americans, an intergroup-relations training and educational organization. If that person from a different group fits your requirement for a friend, ask, "Why shouldn't I be friends with Joe? We have a lot in common." Try to get more information about whatever stereotypes or resentments lie beneath your friend's statement. Ms. Lee suggests: "What makes you think they're so different from us? Where did you get that information?" She explains: "People are learning these stereotypes from somewhere, and they cannot be blamed for that. So examine where these ideas come from." Then talk about how your own experience rebuts them.

33   Kids, like adults, should also be aware of other resources to back them up: Does the school offer special programs for fighting prejudice? How supportive will the principal, the teachers, or other students be? If the school atmosphere is volatile, experts warn, make sure that taking a stand at that moment won't put you in physical danger. If that is the case, it's better to look for other alternatives.

34   These can include programs or organizations that bring kids from different backgrounds together. "When kids work together across race lines, that is how you break down the barriers and see that the stereotypes are not true," says Laurie Meadoff, president of CityKids Foundation, a nonprofit group whose programs attempt to do just that. Such programs can also provide what Cherie Brown calls a "safe place" to express the anger and pain that slurs and other offenses cause, whether the bigotry is directed against you or others.

35   In learning to speak up, everyone will develop a different style and a slightly different message to get across, experts agree. But it would be hard to do better than these two messages suggested by teenagers at CityKids: "Everyone on the face of the earth has the same intestines," said one. Another added, "Cross over the bridge. There's a lot of love on the streets."

Reading Closely and Thinking Critically

1. According to Cole, why is it important to respond to racial, ethnic, and sexist slurs?
2. Why does Cole say it is best not to laugh at racial slurs and offensive ethnic jokes?
3. When a person makes an offensive remark, why is it best not to shame that person publicly?
4. Cole offers procedures to help children deal with bigotry. Why do you think she includes information for children?
5. Did you learn anything as a result of reading "Don't Just Stand There"? If so, explain what you learned.

Examining Structure and Strategy

1. Which sentence is Cole's thesis because it presents the process under consideration?
2. Cite three paragraphs that explain what not to do and why. Which paragraph presents a troublesome aspect of the process?
3. Cole includes a considerable number of quotations. What do you think these quotations contribute? Do they help the author achieve her purpose? Explain.

Noting Combined Patterns

1. How does the narration in paragraphs 1 and 2 help Cole achieve her purpose?
2. Cole frequently uses exemplification. Cite at least three examples and explain how they help Cole achieve her purpose.

Considering Language and Style

1. Cole uses first- and second-person pronouns (I, we, you, me, us). Why does she use these pronouns rather than third-person pronouns (he, she, they)?
2. Paragraphs 8, 25, and 30 are set off with extra spacing and italics. Why?
3. Consult a dictionary if you are unsure of the meaning of any of these words: *ebullience* (paragraph 1), *tinged* (paragraph 1), *anti-Semitic* (paragraph 1), *rift* (paragraph 17), *volatile* (paragraph 33).

For Discussion in Class or Online

Is any of the advice in the essay "easier said than done"? Explain why or why not. If your instructor so directs, post your response to your class Web site.

Writing Assignments

1. **In your journal.** Write about a time when you overheard a racial, sexist, or ethnic slur. How did you respond and why did you respond that way? After reading Cole's essay, do you think you could have handled yourself differently? Explain.
2. **Using process analysis for a purpose.** The purposes given in the assignments are possibilities. You may establish whatever purposes you like, within your instructor's guidelines.
   - Select a hurtful behaviour (for example, classroom cheating, lying, or teenage drinking) and, to inform your reader, describe a process for dealing with it.
   - Select a bothersome behaviour that is not harmful (for example, talking in theatres, rudeness by salespeople, channel-switching by the person with the remote control, or inattentive table servers). To inform your reader, explain a process for dealing with the behaviour.
   - Inform your reader and relate your experience by explaining your own procedure for dealing with ethnic, sexist, and/or racial slurs.
3. **Combining patterns.** Racial, ethnic, gender, and other forms of bias are current facts of life. Using cause-and-effect analysis (explained in Chapter 10), explain how you think bias originates in people or

why people and society allow the bias to persist. Then use process analysis to explain what you think can be done to address the bias.

4. **Connecting the readings.** Stereotypes of people who are different from us depend on lack of knowledge. At the end of her essay, Cole suggests ways of counteracting prejudiced stereotypes. At the beginning of Chapter 5 (p. 141), you'll find a quotation from *Cosmopolitanism* that suggests stories are one way of getting to know individuals and cultures that seem different. Beginning with Cole's suggestions about countering prejudice, make some suggestions of your own and consider the power of stories. Choose an essay in this book that introduces you to new viewpoints and questions stereotypes. You might consider "In the Kitchen," (the next essay in this chapter), "The Ten Thousand Things" from Chapter 5, or "You'll Never Believe What Happened" in Chapter 13. Alternatively, you may find that the viewpoint of "You'll Never Believe What Happened" is second nature, and that essays like "Once More to the Lake" introduce you to people who are unfamiliar. If you're a vegetarian or vegan, you might consider using "The Deer at Providencia" to help you understand the viewpoints of meat eaters.

5. **Drawing on sources.** Research the policy and procedure for handling discrimination and harassment at either your college or university or your workplace. Explain whether or not the policy and procedure are satisfactory and why.

Background

Born in 1950 in West Virginia, Henry Louis Gates, Jr., taught at Yale, Cornell (where he was the first African-American male to hold an endowed chair), and Duke before joining the faculty of Harvard as the director of the W.E.B. DuBois Institute for Afro-American Research. He is also the chair of Harvard's Afro-American Studies Department. His many honours and grants include a MacArthur Foundation "genius grant" (1981), and a mention as one of *Time* magazine's "25 Most Influential Americans" (1997). Gates's book of critical theory, *The Signifying Monkey: A Theory of African-American Literary Criticism* (1989) earned him the American Book Award and brought him great public attention. A prolific author, Gates has written many volumes of literary criticism. He has also written *Colored People: A Memoir* (1994); *The Future of the Race* (1996); and with Cornel West, *Thirteen Ways of Looking at a Black Man* (1997). His most recent work is *Lincoln on Race and Slavery* (2009), which he edited with Donald Yacovone. "In the Kitchen" first appeared in 1994 in *The New Yorker,* a weekly magazine of literature, commentary, and in-depth reporting as well as entertainment reviews and listings for New York City.

Combined Patterns and Their Purposes

"In the Kitchen" is part memoir, part political statement. In the essay, Henry Louis Gates Jr., uses process analysis, definition, and description to inform the reader of several processes African Americans used to straighten their hair, including the one he remembers his mother performing on her clients. At the same time, Gates asks readers to consider the political significance of why African Americans altered their appearance. As Gates explains the processes, he also relates his own experience observing his mother, and he expresses his feelings about what people went through to straighten their hair.

In the Kitchen
Henry Louis Gates, Jr.

1   We always had a gas stove in the kitchen, in our house in Piedmont, West Virginia, where I grew up. Never electric, though using electric became fashionable in Piedmont in the sixties, like using Crest toothpaste rather than Colgate, or watching Huntley and Brinkley rather than Walter Cronkite.[1] But not us: gas, Colgate, and good ole Walter Cronkite, come what may. We used gas partly out of loyalty to Big Mom, Mama's Mama, because she was mostly blind and still loved to cook, and could feel her way more easily with gas than with electric. But the most important thing about our gas-equipped kitchen was that Mama used to do hair there. The "hot comb" was a fine-toothed iron instrument with a long wooden handle and a pair of iron curlers that opened and closed like scissors. Mama would put it in the gas fire until it glowed. You could smell those prongs heating up.

As you read
Think about the ways things have changed—and the ways they have not— since the time of the essay.

---

[1]Chet Huntley and David Brinkley were the anchors of the *Huntley-Brinkley Report,* a nightly news program on NBC that ran from 1956 to 1970. Walter Cronkite anchored *The CBS Evening News* from 1962 to 1981.

2   I liked that smell. Not the smell so much, I guess, as what the smell meant for the shape of my day. There was an intimate warmth in the women's tones as they talked with my Mama, doing their hair. I knew what the women had been through to get their hair ready to be "done," because I would watch Mama do it to herself. How that kink could be transformed through grease and fire into that magnificent head of wavy hair was a miracle to me, and still is.

3   Mama would wash her hair over the sink, a towel wrapped around her shoulders, wearing just her slip and her white bra. (We had no shower—just a galvanized tub that we stored in the kitchen—until we moved down Rat Tail Road into Doc Wolverton's house, in 1954.) After she dried it, she would grease her scalp thoroughly with blue Bergamot hair grease, which came in a short, fat jar with a picture of a beautiful colored lady on it. It's important to grease your scalp real good, my Mama would explain, to keep from burning yourself. Of course, her hair would return to its natural kink almost as soon as the hot water and shampoo hit it. To me, it was another miracle how hair so "straight" would so quickly become kinky again the second it even approached some water.

> "It's important to grease your scalp . . . to keep from burning yourself."

4   My Mama had only a few "clients" whose heads she "did"—did, I think, because she enjoyed it, rather than for the few pennies it brought in. They would sit on one of our red plastic kitchen chairs, the kind with the shiny metal legs, and brace themselves for the process. Mama would stroke that red-hot iron—which by this time had been in the gas fire for half an hour or more—slowly but firmly through their hair, from scalp to strand's end. It made a scorching, crinkly sound, the hot iron did, as it burned its way through kink, leaving in its wake straight strands of hair, standing long and tall but drooping over at the ends, their shape like the top of a heavy willow tree. Slowly, steadily, Mama's hands would transform a round mound of Odetta kink into a darkened swamp of everglades. The Bergamot made the hair shiny; the heat of the hot iron gave it a brownish-red cast. Once all the hair was as straight as God allows kink to get, Mama would take the well-heated curling iron and twirl the straightened strands into more or less loosely wrapped curls. She claimed that she owed her skill as a hairdresser to the strength in her wrists, and as she worked her little finger would poke out, the way it did when she sipped tea. Mama was a southpaw, and wrote upside down and backward to produce the cleanest, roundest letters you've ever seen.

5   The "kitchen" she would all but remove from sight with a handheld pair of shears, bought just for this purpose. Now, the kitchen was the room in which we were sitting—the room where Mama did hair and washed clothes, and where we all took a bath in that galvanized tub. But the word has another meaning, and the kitchen that I'm speaking of is the very kinky bit of hair at the back of your head, where your neck meets your shirt collar. If there was ever a part of your African past that resisted assimilation, it was the kitchen. No matter how hot the iron, no matter how powerful the chemical, no matter how stringent the mashed-potatoes-and-lye formula of a man's

"process," neither God nor woman nor Sammy Davis, Jr., could straighten the kitchen. The kitchen was permanent, irredeemable, irresistible kink. Unassimilably African. No matter what you did, no matter how hard you tried, you couldn't de-kink a person's kitchen. So you trimmed it off as best you could.

6   When hair had begun to "turn," as they'd say—to return to its natural kinky glory—it was the kitchen that turned first (the kitchen around the back, and nappy edges at the temples). When the kitchen started creeping up the back of the neck, it was time to get your hair done again.

7   Sometimes, after dark, a man would come to have his hair done. It was Mr. Charlie Carroll. He was very light-complected and had a ruddy nose—it made me think of Edmund Gwenn, who played Kris Kringle in "Miracle on 34th Street." At first, Mama did him after my brother, Rocky, and I had gone to sleep. It was only later that we found out that he had come to our house so Mama could iron his hair—not with a hot comb or a curling iron but with our very own Proctor-Silex steam iron. For some reason I never understood, Mr. Charlie would conceal his Frederick Douglass-like[2] mane under a big white Stetson hat. I never saw him take it off except when he came to our house, at night, to have his hair pressed. (Later, Daddy would tell us about Mr. Charlie's most prized piece of knowledge, something that the man would only confide after his hair had been pressed, as a token of intimacy. "Not many people know this," he'd say, in a tone of circumspection, "but George Washington was Abraham Lincoln's daddy." Nodding solemnly, he'd add the clincher: "A white man told me." Though he was in dead earnest, this became a humorous refrain around our house—"a white man told me"—which we used to punctuate especially preposterous assertions.)

8   My mother examined my daughters' kitchens whenever we went home to visit, in the early eighties. It became a game between us. I had told her not to do it, because I didn't like the politics it suggested—the notion of "good" and "bad" hair. "Good" hair was "straight," "bad" hair kinky. Even in the late sixties, at the height of Black Power, almost nobody could bring themselves to say "bad" for good and "good" for bad. People still said that hair like white people's hair was "good," even if they encapsulated it in a disclaimer, like "what we used to call 'good.'"

9   Maggie would be seated in her high chair, throwing food this way and that, and Mama would be cooing about how cute it all was, how I used to do just like Maggie was doing, and wondering whether her flinging her food with her left hand meant that she was going to be left-handed like Mama. When my daughter was just about covered with Chef Boyardee Spaghetti-O's, Mama would seize the opportunity: wiping her clean, she would tilt Maggie's head to one side and reach down the back of her neck. Sometimes Mama would even rub a curl between her fingers, just to make sure that her bifocals had not deceived her. Then she'd sigh with satisfaction and relief: No

[2]Frederick Douglass (1818–1895), prominent abolitionist and writer.

kink . . . yet. Mama! I'd shout, pretending to be angry. Every once in a while, if no one was looking, I'd peek, too.

10   I say "yet" because most black babies are born with soft, silken hair. But after a few months it begins to turn, as inevitably as do the seasons or the leaves on a tree. People once thought baby oil would stop it. They were wrong.

11   Everybody I knew as a child wanted to have good hair. You could be as ugly as homemade sin dipped in misery and still be thought attractive if you had good hair. "Jesus moss," the girls at Camp Lee, Virginia, had called Daddy's naturally "good" hair during the war. I know that he played that thick head of hair for all it was worth, too.

12   My own hair was "not a bad grade," as barbers would tell me when they cut it for the first time. It was like a doctor reporting the results of the first full physical he has given you. Like "You're in good shape" or "Blood pressure's kind of high—better cut down on salt."

13   I spent most of my childhood and adolescence messing with my hair. I definitely wanted straight hair. Like Pop's. When I was about three, I tried to stick a wad of Bazooka bubblegum to that straight hair of his. I suppose what fixed that memory for me is the spanking I got for doing so: he turned me upside down, holding me by my feet, the better to paddle my behind. Little *nigger,* he had shouted, walloping away. I started to laugh about it two days later, when my behind stopped hurting.

"I definitely wanted straight hair. Like Pop's."

14   When black people say "straight," of course, they don't usually mean literally straight—they're not describing hair like, say, Peggy Lipton's (she was the white girl on "The Mod Squad"), or like Mary's of Peter, Paul & Mary fame; black people call that "stringy" hair. No, "straight" just means not kinky, no matter what contours the curl may take. I would have done *anything* to have straight hair—and I used to try everything, short of getting a process.

15   Of the wide variety of techniques and methods I came to master in the challenging prestidigitation of the follicle, almost all had two things in common: a heavy grease and the application of pressure. It's not an accident that some of the biggest black-owned companies in the fifties and sixties made hair products. And I tried them all, in search of that certain silken touch, the one that would leave neither the hand nor the pillow sullied by grease.

16   I always wondered what Frederick Douglass put on *his* hair, or what Phillis Wheatley[3] put on hers. Or why Wheatley has that rag on her head in the little engraving in the frontispiece of her book. One thing is for sure: you can bet that when Phillis

---

[3]Phillis Wheatley (1753–1784), poet who wrote the first book published by an African American.

Wheatley went to England and saw the Countess of Huntingdon she did not stop by the Queen's coiffeur on her way there. So many black people still get their hair straightened that it's a wonder we don't have a national holiday for Madame C. J. Walker, the woman who invented the process of straightening kinky hair. Call it Jheri-Kurled or call it "relaxed," it's still fried hair.

17   I used all the greases, from sea-blue Bergamot and creamy vanilla Duke (in its clear jar with the orange-white-and-green label) to the godfather of grease, the formidable Murray's. Now, Murray's was some *serious* grease. Whereas Bergamot was like oily jello, and Duke was viscous and sickly sweet, Murray's was light brown and *hard*. Hard as lard and twice as greasy, Daddy used to say. Murray's came in an orange can with a press-on top. It was so hard that some people would put a match to the can, just to soften the stuff and make it more manageable. Then, in the late sixties, when Afros came into style, I used Afro Sheen. From Murray's to Duke to Afro Sheen: that was my progression in black consciousness.

18   We used to put hot towels or washrags over our Murray-coated heads, in order to melt the wax into the scalp and the follicles. Unfortunately, the wax also had the habit of running down your neck, ears, and forehead. Not to mention your pillowcase. Another problem was that if you put two palmfuls of Murray's on your head your hair turned white. (Duke did the same thing.) The challenge was to get rid of that white color. Because if you got rid of the white stuff you had a magnificent head of wavy hair. That was the beauty of it: Murray's was so hard that it froze your hair into the wavy style you brushed it into. It looked really good if you wore a part. A lot of guys had parts *cut* into their hair by a barber, either with the clippers or with a straight-edge razor. Especially if you had kinky hair—then you'd generally wear a short razor cut, or what we called a Quo Vadis.

19   We tried to be as innovative as possible. Everyone knew about using a stocking cap, because your father or your uncle wore one whenever something really big was about to happen, whether sacred or secular: a funeral or a dance, a wedding or a trip in which you confronted official white people. Any time you were trying to look really sharp, you wore a stocking cap in preparation. And if the event was really a big one, you made a new cap. You asked your mother for a pair of her hose, and cut it with scissors about six inches or so from the open end—the end with the elastic that goes up to the top of the thigh. Then you knotted the cut end, and it became a beehive-shaped hat, with an elastic band that you pulled down low on your forehead and down around your neck in the back. To work well, the cap had to fit tightly and snugly, like a press. And it had to fit that tightly because it *was* a press: it pressed your hair with the force of the hose's elastic. If you greased your hair down real good, and left the stocking cap on long enough, voilà: you got a head of pressed-against-the-scalp waves. (You also got a ring around your forehead when you woke up, but it went away.) And then you could enjoy your concrete do. Swore we were bad, too, with all that grease and those flat heads. My brother and I would brush it out a bit in

the mornings, so that it looked—well, "natural." Grown men still wear stocking caps—especially older men, who generally keep their stocking caps in their top drawers, along with their cufflinks and their see-through silk socks, their "Maverick" ties, their silk handkerchiefs, and whatever else they prize the most.

20   A Murrayed-down stocking cap was the respectable version of the process, which, by contrast, was most definitely not a cool thing to have unless you were an entertainer by trade. Zeke and Keith and Poochie and a few other stars of the high-school basketball team all used to get a process once or twice a year. It was expensive, and you had to go somewhere like Pittsburgh or D.C. or Uniontown—somewhere where there were enough colored people to support a trade. The guys would disappear, then reappear a day or two later, strutting like peacocks, their hair burned slightly red from the lye base. They'd also wear "rags"—cloths or handkerchiefs—around their heads when they slept or played basketball. Do-rags, they were called. But the result was straight hair, with just a hint of wave. No curl. Do-it-yourselfers took their chances at home with a concoction of mashed potatoes and lye.

21   The most famous process of all, however, outside of the process Malcolm X describes in his "Autobiography," and maybe the process of Sammy Davis, Jr.,[4] was Nat King Cole's process. Nat King Cole[5] had patent-leather hair. That man's got the finest process money can buy, or so Daddy said the night we saw Cole's TV show on NBC. It was November 5, 1956. I remember the date because everyone came to our house to watch it and to celebrate one of Daddy's buddies' birthdays. Yeah, Uncle Joe chimed in, they can do shit to his hair that the average Negro can't even *think* about—secret shit.

22   Nat King Cole was *clean*. I've had an ongoing argument with a Nigerian friend about Nat King Cole for twenty years now. Not about whether he could sing—any fool knows that he could—but about whether or not he was a handkerchief head for wearing that patent-leather process.

23   Sammy Davis, Jr.'s process was the one I detested. It didn't look good on him. Worse still, he liked to have a fried strand dangling down the middle of his forehead, so he could shake it out from the crown when he sang. But Nat King Cole's hair was a thing unto itself, a beautifully sculpted work of art that he and he alone had the right to wear. The only difference between a process and a stocking cap, really, was taste; but Nat King Cole, unlike, say, Michael Jackson, looked *good* in his. His head looked like Valentino's head in the twenties, and some say it was Valentino the process was imitating. But Nat King Cole wore a process because it suited his face, his demeanor, his name, his style. He was as clean as he wanted to be.

---

[4]Sammy Davis, Jr. (1925–1990), African-American singer, actor, and dancer.
[5]Nat King Cole (1919–1965), African-American singer and musician.

24   I had forgotten all about that patent-leather look until one day in 1971, when I was sitting in an Arab restaurant on the island of Zanzibar surrounded by men in fezzes and white caftans, trying to learn how to eat curried goat and rice with the fingers of my right hand and feeling two million miles from home. All of a sudden, an old transistor radio sitting on top of a china cupboard stopped blaring out its Swahili music and started playing "Fly Me to the Moon," by Nat King Cole. The restaurant's din was not affected at all, but in my mind's eye I saw it: the King's magnificent sleek black tiara. I managed, barely, to blink back the tears.

Reading Closely and Thinking Critically
1. Why is Gates so interested in the process his mother used to straighten hair? Why does he find that process and other hair-straightening processes important enough to write an essay about them?
2. Why did African Americans endure the difficult process of straightening their hair? Why have many people discontinued the practice in more recent years?
3. Why does Gates check his daughter's hair for kink? Why does he do so only when no one is looking?
4. What is the "patent-leather" look? Why did it suit Nat King Cole?
5. Why did Gates have to "blink back the tears" when he heard a Nat King Cole recording in Zanzibar?

Examining Structure and Strategy
1. Paragraph 18 includes information about why a step was performed and problems associated with a step. Why does Gates include this information?
2. Why do you think Gates titled his essay "In the Kitchen" rather than "Straightening Hair"?

Noting Combined Patterns
1. Gates includes quite a bit of description in the essay. For example, paragraph 1 describes the hot comb; paragraph 4 includes description in the explanation of the hair-straightening process; paragraph 17 describes hair grease. What does the extensive use of description suggest about Gates's intended audience? How does it help the author achieve his purpose with that audience?
2. Which paragraphs include definition? How does the definition help Gates achieve his purpose?
3. Gates describes the processed hair of entertainers Nat King Cole and Sammy Davis, Jr., but he does not explain the process they used to achieve their hairstyles. Why not?

Considering Language and Style
1. Gates often uses specific product names. For example, he uses *Bergamot* (paragraph 3), *Murray's* (paragraph 17), and *Afro Sheen* (paragraph 17), rather than "hair grease" or "hair product." Why do you think he uses specific product names?
2. Gates describes Nat King Cole as "clean," but he does not explain his use of the term. Using evidence in the essay for clues, what do you think he means by "clean"?
3. Consult a dictionary if you are unsure of the meaning of any of these words: *galvanized* (paragraphs 3, 5), *southpaw* (paragraph 4), *assimilation* (paragraph 5), *circumspection* (paragraph 7), *refrain* (paragraph 7), *prestidigitation* (paragraph 15), *sullied* (paragraph 15), *viscous* (paragraph 17), *voilà* (paragraph 19).

For Discussion in Class or Online

Some employers require their employees to conform to specific standards of appearance. They may specify no facial hair, no dreadlocks, no long hair on males, no tattoos, or no body piercing. Consider whether such requirements are fair and appropriate. If your instructor so directs, post your response on your class Web site.

Writing Assignments

1. **In your journal.** To what extent have the times since Gates's childhood changed and to what extent have they stayed the same? Answer in a page or two.

2. **Using process analysis for a purpose.** The purposes given in the assignments are possibilities. You may establish whatever purposes you like, within your instructor's guidelines.

   - To relate your experience, express your feelings, and perhaps entertain, explain a process you endure in order to meet society's standard of beauty: shaving, dying your hair, applying makeup, dieting, exercising, getting a permanent, using a hair-piece or wig, and so on.

   - To inform and perhaps persuade, explain the process whereby people decide what looks "good" and what looks "bad." If you like, consider one or more of the following: advertising, parental influence, peer influence, sports figures, the music industry, movies, or television.

   - To inform, write a directional process analysis that will help people avoid being manipulated by society's standards of beauty.

   - To relate your experience, express your feelings, and perhaps entertain, explain a process for purchasing something that affects your appearance, such as clothes, makeup, hair care products, or skin care products.

3. **Combining patterns.** Tell about a time you tried to look a particular way in order to be more like another person or group. Explain the process you followed. For example, in high school, you may have tried to look more like the cheerleaders or more like the football players, or even like a favourite rock star. At work, you may have tried to look more like your supervisor. Use cause-and-effect analysis (explained in Chapter 9) to explain what motivated you and how you were affected by your attempt.

4. **Connecting the readings.** Discuss one way people are affected by their childhood contexts. For ideas, you can draw on your own experience, along with "In the Kitchen" and "'You'll Never Believe What Happened' is Always A Great Way to Start," (Chapter 13, page 463).

5. **Drawing on sources.** Hairstyles have always changed with the times, but one thing has remained constant: For much of history, people have cut, coloured, curled, straightened, and otherwise forced their hair into unnatural styles and colours. Why are people so obsessed with hair? How far will we go to alter our hair's natural looks? For ideas, you can go to www.google.com and type in the keywords, "history of hairstyles," or in your library's reference room check the *Reader's Guide to Periodical Literature* or the *Encyclopedia of Popular Culture* under the heading "hairstyles."

Additional Essay Assignments

See pages 249 and 252 for strategies for writing a process analysis and for a revising checklist.

1. Explain a process you know that other people should know so they can cope with an emergency: for instance, how to administer CPR, how to administer first aid to someone badly cut, what to do if a tornado strikes, what to do if fire breaks out in the home, or how to rescue a drowning person. Your purpose is to inform your reader.

2. Write a process analysis that describes how to perform and write up a laboratory experiment. You might want to limit your instructions in a meaningful way, describing, for example, how to perform and write up a chemistry experiment.

3. Write a process analysis that describes how an individual might respond to a racist, sexist, ageist, or "fat-ist" remark.

4. Write a process analysis that explains how your readers can make changes to their routines to be more environmentally responsible. You might describe how they can organize and recycle their trash or how to organize their day to make use of public transit, or how to install weather stripping on doors.

5. To inform your reader, explain how something common—such as paper, decaffeinated coffee, or a baseball—is made. If necessary, do some research to learn about the process. (Consult Chapter 14 on how to handle material taken from sources.)

6. Explain a process associated with computers—how to create a web page, how to program a computer, how to use shortcuts in your word-processing program. Before you begin, however, consider whether you want to write a directional or explanatory process analysis. Perhaps you want your reader to simply understand how complex computer programming is.

7. To entertain your reader, write a humorous explanation of a process: how to flunk a test, how to make a bad impression on a date, how to irritate a teacher, how to make a bad impression on a job interview, or how to be a slob. Use verbal irony, if appropriate.

8. To convince your reader that people suffer unfairly to conform to society's concept of beauty, explain a process they go through.

9. Explain the wedding ritual for the religious, ethnic, or cultural group you belong to. Your purpose is to relate your experience and inform your reader. Try to use description to make aspects of the process as vivid as possible.

10. Explain some process for improving relationships between people: how to fight fairly, how to communicate better, how to respect differences, how to offer constructive criticism, and so on.

11. To inform college or university students, explain a process for coping with stress.

12. To entertain your reader, explain how to survive adolescence. You may write from a parent's or child's point of view.

13. Explain how to relax.

14. **Process Analysis in Context:** Assume that your college or university is putting together a handbook for first-year students to help them adjust to school and be successful. As an experienced student, you have been asked to contribute to the handbook by describing an important academic survival skill: taking notes, taking an examination, getting along with a difficult roommate, reading a textbook, studying for finals, and so on. Be sure your process analysis is written in such a way that it is genuinely useful to a new student.

Chapter 9

Comparison and Contrast

Reason respects the differences, and imagination the similitudes of things

— Percy Bysshe Shelley, *A Defence of Poetry*

Our Similarities bring us to a common ground; Our Differences allow us to be fascinated by each other

— Tom Robbins

THE PATTERN

Comparison points out similarities; **contrast** points out differences; **comparison-contrast** points out both similarities and differences. Because comparison-contrast allows us to examine the features of two or more subjects, it is an important component of decision making. Should you buy a notebook computer or upgrade your current desktop? Is this political candidate better for the country or is that one? Will the job in Montreal make me happier than the one in Saskatoon? Will the anthropology course be more interesting than the psychology course? To decide, you compare and contrast the merits of the two computers, the two candidates, the two jobs, and the two courses. Comparison-contrast is so integral to decision making that you engage in it many times each day.

USING COMPARISON AND CONTRAST FOR A PURPOSE

In addition to helping you make decisions, comparison and contrast can help a writer inform a reader about the nature of something that is not well understood. For example, to explain rugby to a reader who knows little about the sport, you could compare and contrast it with the better-known game of football. Comparison-contrast can also help you inform by clarifying the nature of *both* subjects under consideration. For example, to help the reader understand how different people react to a cancer diagnosis in "Two Faces of Hope" (page 302), Stefan Riches compares the approach of his mother, which was to be hopeful until the very end, to that of his brother-in-law, who accepted a death that seemed inevitable. In Riches' essay, both responses make sense.

Another way comparison-contrast can inform is by providing new insight into something already familiar. In this case, the purpose of the comparison-contrast is to sharpen the reader's awareness or appreciation. For example, in "It's Not Easy Being Green" (page 308), Michael Adams and Keith Neuman compare Canadians' desire to be environmentally responsible to religion. Making this comparison allows them to suggest, playfully, that our environmental choices have an ethical dimension.

In addition to informing, comparison-contrast can allow the writer to express feelings and relate experience. To relate the effects of your parents' divorce and express your feelings about it, for example, you could contrast your life before and after the divorce to reveal the impact the event had on you.

By showing that one subject is superior to the other, comparison-contrast also can work to persuade a reader to think or act a particular way. For instance, to convince a reader to vote for a particular candidate, you could contrast that candidate with the opposition to show that your choice is better.

An amusing comparison-contrast will entertain a reader—often at the same time it informs, relates experience, expresses feelings, or persuades. Suzanne Britt's "Neat People vs. Sloppy People" (page 298) is such a piece. Its humorous contrast of neat and sloppy people entertains at the same time it expresses some of Britt's feelings about these distinct types and argues for the superiority of sloppiness.

Comparison-Contrast at School, at Work, and in the Community

Comparison-contrast has many uses in the classroom. Often you will use it to clarify and evaluate the nature of two subjects. In a political science class, you could be asked to compare and contrast two political ideologies such as socialism and communism. In a music appreciation class, you could be asked to compare and contrast the techniques of two composers; in a literature class, you could be asked to compare and contrast the symbolism in two poems; and in a cultural anthropology class, you could be asked to compare and contrast the marriage rituals in two cultures.

You are also likely to use comparison-contrast to show the superiority of one of the subjects. For example, in a clinical psychology class, you might compare and contrast two treatments for depression to show which one is better; in an advertising class, you might compare and contrast two advertising campaigns to determine which one is more effective; and in a history class, you might compare and contrast two World War II generals to determine who was the better strategist.

Because comparison-contrast clarifies ideas and concepts by showing how they are similar to and different from other ideas and concepts, textbook authors use it often. For example, the authors of *History of the Canadian Peoples* explain the ways historians have come to change the language they use to describe groups of people marginalized by histories that focused largely on the actions of the powerful and the rich:

> Contemporary political movements have forced historians to think about the words they use to describe Canadians. Thirty years ago most textbooks used the term "negroes" to refer to people with black skin. In the 1960s "black" became the politically conscious way to refer to people of African descent. More recently "African Canadian" has become the more popular term. Similarly, the words used to describe aboriginal peoples have changed in recent years. "Savages" was quickly dropped from textbooks in the 1960s, and although the misnomer "Indian" is still widely used today—and has particular applications that as yet seem unavoidable—the preferred terms seem to be "Native peoples" and "First Nations." "Amerindian" is a scholarly term to encompass the wide range of Native peoples and cultures.
>
> Women, too, have insisted on being described in more respectful terms. Feminists objected strongly to the use of the word "girl" when adult women were being discussed, and they dismissed "lady" as being too condescending or elitist. Because "man" was adequate for the male of the species, "women" seemed the most appropriate term, although some radical feminists have used the spelling "wymyn." Only the most hidebound of scholars still insist that the word "man" can be used to describe the entire human species.
>
> Many scholars complained loudly about being asked to abandon words long established in their vocabularies. A few even argued that "political correctness" restricted freedom of speech. We do not hold such views. Because English is a living language and changes over time, we see no reason why it should not continue to change to reflect the new consciousness of groups in Canadian society. Indeed the importance of language is obvious in the sometimes derisive phrase "politically correct." In our view, the words "politically conscious" more accurately describe the attempts by groups to name their own experience. Language, of course, is not only about naming things but about power. Attempts by oppressed groups to find their own language to fit their experiences should be seen in the context of their struggles for empowerment. (Finkel and Conrad, *History of the Canadian Peoples* xv–xvi)

Here, Finkel and Conrad discuss the similarities between the way language about African Canadians, Native Peoples, and women has changed. Besides drawing attention to the way the language we use determines what we see and how we make judgments, this discussion points out that these three changes occurred in tandem, during the 1960s, as our attention was drawn to issues of human rights and potentials. While these paragraphs employ exemplification, providing examples of the relationship between the language we use and the opinions we hold, together, as comparisons, they illustrate a wider trend.

Comparison and contrast are also frequent components of writing on the job. For example, professionals often write reports that compare such things as computer systems and phone systems in order to recommend a particular purchase. A construction manager may compare two bid proposals from general contractors to determine which company to award a building project to, and a caterer might compare several menus, themes, and decorations for a reception to help a client make a selection.

Outside the classroom and workplace, you will have many opportunities to use comparison or contrast as part of your decision-making process. For a particularly difficult choice such as choosing which job to take, try writing out a comparison of the items. Not only does writing stimulate your thinking and lead you to ideas that might not otherwise occur to you, but it also gives you something concrete to study as you mull over the choice. If you are a member of an organization, you might use comparison or contrast in a committee report evaluating different fund-raising projects or membership campaigns. If you are trying to decide how to respond to someone at work who is bullying you, you can contrast the different approaches to bullying, trying to decide whether, in your situation, it's going to be more effective for you to ignore the bully, take him or her aside and discuss the effects of his or her behaviour, or call the bully to task publicly.

CHOOSING SUBJECTS

The subjects you choose for comparison-contrast should allow you to cite comparisons and contrasts that go beyond trivial points. Do not compare and contrast the bicycle and automobile, for example, if you can note only the number of wheels and speed of travel. However, you can use these subjects if you have a fresh approach, perhaps comparing and contrasting the lifestyles associated with using each vehicle as a principal mode of transportation.

In general, the subjects you choose to compare and contrast should be from the same category, or general type of thing or idea. Thus, you can compare and contrast two kinds of computers, two Elizabethan sonnets that describe the beauty of the speaker's beloved, two politicians' approaches to leadership, and so forth. If your purpose is to entertain, however, you may be able to compare and contrast subjects from different categories. A political satirist, for example, might compare a former prime minister of Canada to Ronald McDonald, and a campus humour columnist might compare studying for exams and preparing for war.

The comparison of subjects from different categories is an **analogy.** With an analogy, you can compare subjects from different categories if they have surprising and compelling similarities or ones that shed light on one or both subjects. For example, author Robert Jastrow once compared the human brain with a computer because the two subjects, although from different categories, function similarly in a number of ways. The analogy helped the reader better understand how both subjects work. Other analogies might be comparing the human eye to a camera or comparing an ant colony to New York City. Writers often use brief analogies to add surprising insight or interest to their writing. For example, Christopher, the young autistic narrator of Mark Haddon's novel *The Curious Incident of the Dog in the Night-Time*, uses an analogy to help the reader understand how the brain of an autistic child experiences the world:

> And when I am in a new place, because I see everything, it is like when a computer is doing too many things at the same time and the central processor unit is blocked up and there isn't any space left to think about other things. And when I am in a new place and there are lots of people there it is even harder because people are not like cows and flowers and grass and they can talk to you and do things that you don't expect, so you have to notice everything that is in the place, and also you have to notice things that might happen as well. And sometimes when I am in a new place and there are lots of people there it is like a computer crashing and I have to close my eyes and put my hands over my ears and groan, which is like pressing **CTRL + ALT + DEL**, and shutting down programs and turning the computer off and rebooting so that I can remember what I am doing and where I am meant to be going.

We often make sense of the chaotic world by noting similarities and differences as well as by questioning our first impressions of similarities and differences. If there's a young woman in your class with a foreign accent, you might initially lump her in a category you've labelled "foreigner," while hearing her contributions to class discussion helps you see that in spite of the fact that four years ago she was in a refugee camp in Darfur, many of her thoughts, anxieties, and hopes are much like your own. Or you might make the assumption that people living on the street are profoundly different from those of us that buy houses and live in stable communities. But when your social work professor encourages you to volunteer at a homeless shelter, you begin to hear snippets of people's stories that make clear how much like you they are. On the other hand, the young man sitting next to you with his baseball cap on backwards looks just like you but is a math genius and a computer geek, and consequently finds writing about his personal life quite difficult. Because there are interesting differences between things that appear similar and unexpected similarities between things that appear different, the most surprising and useful rule for choosing subjects is this: If you want to go beyond the obvious and write an essay that truly probes the way we see our world—which is often in terms of differences and similarities—you need to choose subjects for contrast essays that on the surface appear similar, while good subjects for comparison essays should seem to the casual observer to be different. Two subjects you *contrast* should be similar enough for the contrast to be both meaningful and unanticipated. You might contrast graphic novels and comic books because to many people they appear similar, while you challenge this view by focusing on their differences. Similarly, two subjects you *compare* should be different enough to warrant the treatment of illustrating their similarities. In effect, you want to be able to say, "You think graphic novels and literary fiction are entirely different, but I want you to see that both are examples of art that seeks to probe and question the society we live in."

SUPPORTING DETAILS

Because mentioning every possible point of comparison and contrast is undesirable—if not impossible—you must select your details with regard to your purpose for writing. Say, for instance, that you are comparing and contrasting public and private schools. If your purpose is to convince your reader that public schools are better, then you might mention that the ethnic diversity often found in these schools can teach students more about people and their cultural heritage. If your purpose is to relate your experiences in these schools, you can tell which school you were happier in and why. If your purpose is to inform, you might discuss the academic programs in each kind of school so parents can make up their own minds about which is better for their children. If your purpose is to entertain, you can give humorous portraits of the students and teachers in each kind of school.

Your audience will also influence the points you choose to compare and contrast. Say you are contrasting public and private schools to persuade your reader to increase support of public schools. If your audience includes politicians, and you do not want them to support legislation increasing funding to private schools, you can contrast enrolments in the two kinds of schools to show that more voters send children to public schools than to private ones. However, if your audience includes parents, and you want them to send their children to public rather than private schools, you can compare and contrast extracurricular activities to show that students have more options in public schools.

In addition to purpose and audience, a sense of balance will influence your selection of details. Most times, any point you make about one of your subjects should also be made about the other subject. Thus, if you are comparing and contrasting public and private schools and you discuss the teachers in public school, you should also discuss the teachers in private school; if you discuss course offerings in public school, you should also discuss course offerings in private school, and so on. You may notice that the authors in this chapter do not always adhere strictly to this principle of balance. An author can depart from this principle only if the essay does not become a random collection of points about the subjects. That is, if you do not maintain enough balance, your essay will not be a comparison-contrast.

Although you are likely to discuss the same points about each of your subjects, you need not do so in equal detail. A point can be discussed in more detail for one subject than for the other. For example, if you are contrasting online classrooms and traditional classrooms, you could make the point that in traditional classrooms, teachers can read facial expressions and body language to determine whether students understand a point. Then you could give examples of expressions and posture that signal understanding and those that signal confusion. When you discuss the same point for online classrooms, you can simply write that online instructors do not have the opportunity to read expressions and body language; further explanation may not be required.

Sometimes writers fall into the trap of stating the obvious. Avoid making self-evident statements that could bore and alienate your reader. If, for example, you are contrasting online and traditional classrooms, you need not mention that students in online classrooms require computer access, but students in traditional classrooms do not.

Comparison-contrast may include other patterns of development. For example, to compare and contrast the techniques of two artists, you would probably describe the styles of each person. Examples are also a frequent component of comparison-contrast, particularly when a point of comparison or contrast requires clarification. For instance, if you were comparing two political candidates, and you stated that they both favoured progressive legislation, you could clarify and support that point of comparison with an example. You could note that both candidates voted for a bill that would provide tax credits for working parents with children in daycare centres.

Because a story can serve as an example, narration can be a part of comparison-contrast. Say that you want to compare and contrast your relationship with two friends. To show the differences in the way you interact with each person, you can tell the story of the time the three of you went away for the weekend.

Process analysis, too, can form part of comparison-contrast. For example, to contrast the styles of two baseball coaches, you could explain the process each one follows to motivate players.

ORGANIZING DETAILS

The thesis for a comparison-contrast essay can present the subjects under consideration and indicate whether these subjects will be compared, contrasted, or both compared and contrasted. Consider, for example, this thesis from "Neat People vs. Sloppy People":

> Neat people are lazier and meaner than sloppy people.

This thesis notes that the subjects under consideration are neat people and sloppy people, and it also indicates that the subjects will be contrasted, particularly with respect to laziness and meanness. Now consider these two thesis statements:

> Islam and Christianity are both monotheistic, are based on texts their followers believe have been revealed by their god to their prophets, and anticipate a final day of judgment.
> Smith and Jones have different political philosophies, but they implement those philosophies with similar styles, so the differences between the men are not readily apparent.

The first thesis indicates that the essay will compare Islam and Christianity to make an important point about both religions. Notice that the specific points to be compared are a component of the thesis—the informational purpose is made clear. The second thesis indicates that politicians Smith and Jones will be both compared and contrasted. Again, the informational purpose is apparent—the thesis will make the point that the similarities between the two politicians mask their differences.

Ordering detail in a comparison-contrast essay requires some thought. One possible arrangement is the **block pattern** whereby all the points about one subject are made (in a block), then all the points about the other subject are made (in a second block.) To appreciate how the block arrangement works, look at the following outline for an essay contrasting political candidates Smith and Jones. Notice that balance is achieved by discussing the same points for both subjects. Also notice that the points are discussed in the same order for both subjects.

I.   Smith
     A.   Believes in provinces funding their own health care plans
     B.   Believes in supporting education with a provincial income tax
     C.   Wants to form a task force to study lake pollution
II. Jones
     A.   Believes the federal government should fund health care
     B.   Believes in supporting education with a property tax
     C.   Believes lake pollution is not a priority

A second possible arrangement for the details of comparison-contrast is the **alternating pattern,** whereby a point is made for one subject, then for the other. A second point is made for the first subject, then for the other. This alternating pattern continues until all the points are made for both subjects. An outline for an essay contrasting Smith and Jones could look like this if the alternating pattern were used:

I.   View on financing health care
     A.   Smith believes provinces should fund their own plans
     B.   Jones believes the federal government should fund the plan
II. View on financing education
     A.   Smith believes in a provincial income tax
     B.   Jones believes in a property tax
III. View on lake pollution
     A.   Smith wants to form a task force to study pollution
     B.   Jones believes pollution is not a priority

Although comparison-contrast can be arranged using a block or an alternating pattern, the two strategies are not interchangeable. In general, the block method works better for essays with fewer points of comparison or contrast that are not extensively developed because the reader is not forced to remember many ideas about the first subject while reading about the second. When you have many points to discuss, or points that are very detailed, you can easily lose track of them with the block method, and your reader can easily get lost.

An alternating pattern is usually a better choice for an essay with many points of comparison and contrast or an essay with extensively developed ideas because readers can keep track of the ideas more easily. However, the points must be well developed, or you risk creating a "ping-pong" effect as you switch back and forth between subjects.

If you are both comparing and contrasting, you can organize by treating similarities first and differences next. Or you can reverse this order, leaving for last the points you think are most significant.

In Chapter 2, we discussed writing thesis statements that are arguable and significant and suggested that writers need to do a considerable amount of brainstorming before crafting a thesis statement. Some of the patterns up to this point—like narration and description—can be successful without a lot of brainstorming and without thesis statements. But because contrast and comparison essays require careful attention to the essay's structure, because decisions about structure are best made *before* you start drafting, and because

---

Troubleshooting Guide

Using Transitions in Comparison-Contrast

If you have trouble moving smoothly from point to point or subject to subject, use transitions:

TO SHOW SIMILARITY   similarly, likewise, in similar fashion, in like manner, in the same way

Smith believes in tax reform. Similarly, Jones wants to close tax loopholes.

TO SHOW CONTRAST   however, on the other hand, conversely, in contrast

Smith favours tax reform. However, Jones believes current tax laws are adequate.

Repetition of key words, particularly when combined with transitions, can also help you move smoothly between points and maintain coherence.

Smith believes in tax reform. However, tax reform is equally important to Jones, who wants to close tax loopholes.

Smith favours tax reform. Such reform is not a priority for Jones, though, because he believes current tax laws are adequate.

For more on transitional phrases, see p. 75 in Chapter 3.

good contrast and comparison essays are built on an element of surprise, you need to work even harder on careful, considered brainstorming and drafting and redrafting a thesis statement in order to write an essay that is effectively structured and not a predictable exercise.

VISUALIZING A COMPARISON-CONTRAST ESSAY

The following chart can help you visualize either the block or alternating structure for a comparison-contrast essay. Like all good models, however, this one can be altered as needed.

Introduction

- Creates interest in the essay
- States the thesis, which mentions the subjects being considered and may indicate whether the subjects will be compared, contrasted, or both

First Body Paragraph(s)

- In a block pattern, make and explain all the points about the first subject
- In an alternating pattern, make and explain a point about the first subject, and then make and explain the same point for the second subject
- Discuss the same points for both subjects, but not necessarily in the same amount of detail
- May include any other patterns of development

Next Body Paragraph(s)

- In a block pattern, make and explain all the points about the second subject
- In an alternating pattern, make and explain the next point about the first subject and then make and explain the same point for the second subject, continuing this way until all points are made
- Discuss the same points for both subjects, but not necessarily in the same amount of detail
- May include any other patterns of development

Conclusion

- Provides a satisfying finish
- May state the point of the comparison-contrast if not done so elsewhere

---

Troubleshooting Guide

Using Modifiers in Comparison-Contrast

If you have trouble using modifiers (adjectives and adverbs) correctly to compare and contrast, this explanation may be helpful.

Modifiers have *comparative forms* and *superlative forms*. Use the comparative form to compare or contrast two items and the superlative form to compare and contrast more than two items.

BASE FORM	COMPARATIVE FORM	SUPERLATIVE FORM
fast	faster	fastest
unusual	more unusual	most unusual
good	better	best
bad	worse	worst

NO   Both cities have low unemployment rates, but Calgary has the *best* average income.

YES   Both cities have low unemployment rates, but Calgary has a *better* average income. [only two cities]

NO   Of all the tutors observed, the writing centre tutors were *friendlier*.

YES   Of all the tutors observed, the writing centre tutors were *friendliest*. [more than two tutors]

PROCESS GUIDELINES: STRATEGIES FOR WRITING COMPARISON-CONTRAST

1. **Selecting a Topic.** Try explaining the similarities between two things usually considered different or the differences between two things thought of as alike. For example, you could discuss the similarities between madness and genius or the differences between getting a degree and getting an education. Be sure to select subjects from the same category.

2. **Establishing a Purpose.** To establish your purpose, answer these questions:
   - Do I want to inform readers about the nature of something not well understood?
   - Do I want to clarify the nature of one or both subjects?
   - Do I want to offer a new insight into something familiar?
   - Do I want to convince my reader that one subject is better than the other?
   - Do I want to express feelings or relate experience?
   - Do I want to entertain my reader?

3. **Assessing Your Audience.** To assess your audience, determine how much your reader knows about your subjects and how interested your reader is likely to be in your subjects.
4. **Writing a Thesis.** Write out an early version of your thesis in a sentence that names your subjects, indicates whether you will compare, contrast, or both, and suggests your purpose.
5. **Generating ideas.** Try these techniques if you need help thinking of ideas:
   a. List every similarity you can think of or every difference (whichever is appropriate for your topic). Study the list and eliminate ideas not suited to your audience and purpose.
   b. Ask yourself these questions about the points on your list: Should I describe anything? Should I tell a story? Should I explain a process? Should I provide examples?
6. **Organizing.** Organizing comparison-contrast requires careful planning, so even if you do not ordinarily write detailed outlines, consider doing so for this essay. Try outlining your ideas, using a block or alternating pattern to see which will be most effective.
7. **Revising.** Ask a friend whose judgment about writing you trust to read your draft and note anything that is unclear and any places where you are not moving smoothly from point to point or from subject to subject.

✔ Checklist for Revising Comparison-Contrast

Be sure:

_____   You have a sound basis for considering your subjects side by side and that your subjects are from the same category.

_____   Your thesis presents your subjects and notes whether they will be compared, contrasted, or both.

_____   Your details suit your audience and purpose.

_____   You have discussed the same points for both subjects—or if you haven't, that the lack of balance does not create a problem.

_____   You have avoided stating obvious comparisons and contrasts.

_____   You have used a block or alternating pattern to best advantage.

_____   You have used transitions and repetition to move from point to point and subject to subject.

ANNOTATED STUDENT ESSAY

The student author of "Teaching a New Dog Old Tricks" contrasts her dog Rufus with an electronic dog. You will have no trouble recognizing the writer's opinion about electronic pets. After you read, you will have an opportunity to evaluate this essay.

Teaching a New Dog Old Tricks

1   When I was eight, I got the perfect interactive toy: a new puppy. Rufus was a scrawny mutt with big floppy ears and unsteady legs, but I couldn't have loved him more if he'd been a champion show dog. I considered myself very lucky; some of my friends begged for a pet and were told it would be too messy, too expensive, or too high-maintenance. It seems that many of today's children have found a way to counter these objections. Poo-Chi, an interactive puppy robot made by the Japanese toy manufacturer Sega Toys, took second place on a list of the bestselling toys of 2000 ("Old Favorites" A57). Although its creators claim the robot mimics some of the engaging qualities of a real puppy, I don't think Poo-Chi would have made an adequate substitute for Rufus.

2   Poo-Chi, priced at between $20 and $30, is one of several robot dogs on the market, including the $1,500 Sony Aibo, which "can recognize about 50 words, bark, dance, move [its] ears and take pictures with a camera mounted on [its] nose" (Barnes C1). Rufus, born in the local pound, came free to a good home (ours). Of course, there are highly bred puppies that cost as much as or more than the Aibo, but there will always be good-natured mutts and strays that, for no money at all, can learn a range of tricks, skills, and behaviors that would put the Aibo, let alone the simpler Poo-Chi, to shame. Like Poo-Chi, Rufus could interact with others of his kind, but unlike Poo-Chi, Rufus had special friends among the dogs he knew, and knew by smell when one of his friends had been somewhere.

3   For all Rufus' scruffiness, he did have a coat of warm, glossy light-brown fur; big, wet brown eyes; and a lolling pink tongue. Poo-Chi is made out of two-tone plastic; one of its colors is silver and the other is purple, blue, or another un-doglike hue. The Poo-Chi I examined in a recent visit to a toy store was designed to resemble a bulldog, but in general the toy's appearance is extremely stylized. It looks like what it is: a dog-shaped robot. When my father brought him home from the pound, Rufus was about a foot tall, and he soon grew much bigger. Poo-Chi is around five inches tall, and, naturally, will never grow. One of my favorite things to do with Rufus was roughhouse with him and pet him;

Paragraph 1
The introduction creates interest with background information and some description. The thesis, the last sentence, gives the subjects and notes that differences will be discussed.

Paragraph 2
Details, which include information from sources, are given in an alternating pattern.

Paragraph 3
Details include description. The alternating pattern continues.

I don't think rolling on the floor with a little plastic robot would be nearly as fun.

Paragraph 4
The paragraph opens with a transitional sentence. Notice the humour in the paragraph.

4   Rufus was certainly cuddly and playful, but he was also extremely messy. It took us several months to get him housetrained, and even after he learned to wait for his walk he would still knock over his food bowl, trample mud on the kitchen floor, and leave hair on the couch. Despite its name, Poo-Chi will never need to be taken for a walk or fed, and no one will ever need to clean up after it. Its plastic surface can be wiped clean with a damp cloth—no sloppy tub or hose baths needed. Rufus ate like a horse, and my parents sometimes complained about all the dog food they had to buy for him. Poo-Chi runs on batteries, which can last for several weeks before they need to be changed. The silver plastic "bone" packaged with Poo-Chi might get lost, but it won't be because Poo-Chi buried it in the back yard.

Paragraph 5
The point of contrast is emotions. Notice the specific word choice.

5   Poo-Chi, claims Tiger Electronics, which introduced the toy to the United States, "is so lifelike, he needs love." The manufacturers used biorhythm technology to "create realistic emotional responses that adapt and change as you play with [Poo-Chi]" (Willman E-2). These responses are somewhat limited; Poo-Chi's eyes flash red or green stars when it is happy, half-circles when it is asleep, and so on. It can sing, stand, or sit, but it can't walk. Rufus, by contrast, leaped and wagged his tail when he was happy, flopped on the floor and snored when sleeping, and displayed dozens of other emotions and states of being in complex ways. When I left each morning for school, Rufus would stand by the door and howl, and when I returned he was dizzy with excitement. Poo-Chi may need love, but it probably won't scratch grooves into the front door if you leave it alone for too long.

Paragraph 6
The essay concludes with the final point of contrast: emotional attachment to a living creature vs. a replaceable toy. Source material is included.

6   Ten-year-old Kurt Roeder, one of the first Chicagoans to play with a Poo-Chi, reported, "They're really fun. They sing songs, and they're usually happy" (Fitch). Rufus yodeled and barked, but he didn't sing songs, and he wasn't always happy. It's understandable that some children, not to mention their parents, would opt for a pet that is entertaining, inexpensive, and easy to take care of, but I hope that those with enough space, time, and money will consider paying a visit to the pound. Still, in doing so, they'd be taking a big risk: getting attached to a unique and irreplaceable pet with a finite lifespan. Fortunately, Rufus lived a long and happy life, but I was miserable when he finally passed away last year. If my pet had been Poo-Chi, I could simply have gone to the store and picked up another one.

Works Cited

Barnes, Julian E. "As Visions of E-Toys Danced in Their Heads." *New York Times* 11 Nov. 2000: C1. Print.

Fitch, Jessica Madore. "Hoping to Be Top Dog." *Chicago Sun-Times.* Chicago Sun-Times, 3 May 2000. Web. 31 March 2001.

"Old Favorites Led Holiday Toy Sales." *Newsday* 8 Feb. 2001: A57. Print.

Willman, Martha L. "Bark Versus Byte." *Los Angeles Times* 3 Feb. 2000: E2.

PEER REVIEW

Responding to "Teaching a New Dog Old Tricks"

Evaluate "Teaching a New Dog Old Tricks" by responding to these questions:

1. Does the essay hold your interest? Why or why not?
2. Does the introduction effectively establish whether similarities and/or differences will be focused on? Is the topic significant and surprising? If not, what could the author have done to improve her treatment of the topic?
3. Is there material in the conclusion that warrants further development?
4. Do the supporting details adequately develop the thesis? Explain.
5. Is the source material effective? Explain.
6. Is the alternating pattern a suitable organization? Why or why not? Try outlining the essay in block pattern and consider whether this would provide a more suitable structure.
7. Is the word choice effective? Explain.
8. What do you like best about the essay?
9. What change or changes would you advise the writer to make? Would you suggest that the writer change the essay's structure? Do you think that either similarities between Rufus and Poo-Chi or the differences should be further emphasized?

READING SELECTIONS

Background

Born in North Carolina, Suzanne Britt is a poet, essayist, teacher, and textbook author. She graduated from Salem Academy and College with majors in English and Latin and earned her master's degree in English from Washington University in St. Louis. She has taught at North Carolina State University, Pace College, and Duke Divinity School and is now teaching at Meredith College. Her poems have appeared in the literary magazines *Denver Quarterly, Lake Superior Review, Greensboro Review,* and *Southern Poetry Review.* Her essays and articles have appeared in many newspapers and magazines, including *Newsweek, Books and Religion,* the *Boston Globe,* the *Cleveland Plain Dealer,* the *Charlotte Observer,* and *Newsday.* If you enjoy Britt's humour, you might want to read some of her other essays, which have been collected in *Skinny People Are Dull and Crunchy Like Carrots* (1982) and *Show and Tell* (1982). "Neat People vs. Sloppy People" is from her collection *Show and Tell.*

Combined Patterns and Their Purpose

In "Neat People vs. Sloppy People," an entertaining essay, Britt contrasts neat and sloppy people using examples and description to help make her points.

Neat People vs. Sloppy People
Suzanne Britt

As you read
Determine whether Britt means everything she says, or whether she is just going for laughs.

1   I've finally figured out the difference between neat people and sloppy people. The distinction is, as always, moral. Neat people are lazier and meaner than sloppy people.

2   Sloppy people, you see, are not really sloppy. Their sloppiness is merely the unfortunate consequence of their extreme moral rectitude. Sloppy people carry in their mind's eye a heavenly vision, a precise plan, that is so stupendous, so perfect, it can't be achieved in this world or the next.

3   Sloppy people live in Never-Never Land. Someday is their métier. Someday they are planning to alphabetize all their books and set up home catalogs. Someday they will go through their wardrobes and mark certain items for tentative mending and certain items for passing on to relatives of similar shape and size. Someday sloppy people will make family scrapbooks into which they will put newspaper clippings, postcards, locks of hair, and the dried corsage from their senior prom. Someday they will file everything on the surface of their desks, including the cash receipts from coffee purchases at the snack shop. Someday they will sit down and read all the back issues of *The New Yorker.*

4   For all these noble reasons and more, sloppy people never get neat. They aim too high and wide. They save everything, planning someday to file, order, and straighten out the world. But while these ambitious plans take clearer and clearer shape in their

heads, the books spill from the shelves onto the floor, the clothes pile up in the hamper and closet, the family mementos accumulate in every drawer, the surface of the desk is buried under mounds of paper and the unread magazines threaten to reach the ceiling.

5   Sloppy people can't bear to part with anything. They give loving attention to every detail. When sloppy people say they're going to tackle the surface of the desk, they really mean it. Not a paper will go unturned; not a rubber band will go unboxed. Four hours or two weeks into the excavation, the desk looks exactly the same, primarily because the sloppy person is meticulously creating new piles of papers with new headings and scrupulously stopping to read all the old book catalogs before he throws them away. A neat person would just bulldoze the desk.

6   Neat people are bums and clods at heart. They have cavalier attitudes toward possessions, including family heirlooms. Everything is just another dustcatcher to them. If anything collects dust, it's got to go and that's that. Neat people will toy with the idea of throwing the children out of the house just to cut down on the clutter.

7   Neat people don't care about process. They like results. What they want to do is get the whole thing over with so they can sit down and watch the rasslin' on TV. Neat people operate on two unvarying principles: Never handle any item twice, and throw everything away.

8   The only thing messy in a neat person's house is the trash can. The minute something comes to a neat person's hand, he will look at it, try to decide if it has immediate use and, finding none, throw it in the trash.

9   Neat people are especially vicious with mail. They never go through their mail unless they are standing directly over a trash can. If the trash can is beside the mailbox, even better. All ads, catalogs, pleas for charitable contributions, church bulletins and money-saving coupons go straight into the trash can without being opened. All letters from home, postcards from Europe, bills and paychecks are opened, immediately responded to, then dropped in the trash can. Neat people keep their receipts only for tax purposes. That's it. No sentimental salvaging of birthday cards or the last letter a dying relative ever wrote. Into the trash it goes.

10   Neat people place neatness above everything, even economics. They are incredibly wasteful. Neat people throw away several toys every time they walk through the den. I knew a neat person once who threw away a perfectly good dish drainer because it had mold on it. The drainer was too much trouble to wash. And neat people sell their furniture when they move. They will sell a La-Z-Boy recliner while you are reclining in it.

11   Neat people are no good to borrow from. Neat people buy everything in expensive little single portions. They get their flour and sugar in two-pound bags. They wouldn't consider clipping a coupon, saving a leftover, reusing plastic nondairy whipped cream containers or rinsing off tin foil and draping it over the unmoldy dish

drainer. You can never borrow a neat person's newspaper to see what's playing at the movies. Neat people have the paper all wadded up and in the trash by 7:05 A.M.

12   Neat people cut a clean swath through the organic as well as the inorganic world. People, animals, and things are all one to them. They are so insensitive. After they've finished with the pantry, the medicine cabinet, and the attic, they will throw out the red geranium (too many leaves), sell the dog (too many fleas), and send the children off to boarding school (too many scuffmarks on the hardwood floors).

Reading Closely and Thinking Critically

1. Is Britt serious when she claims, in paragraph 1, that the distinction between neat and sloppy people is a moral one? Explain.
2. Britt says that neat people are insensitive, that they are bums and clods. How serious is she in this assessment? If she cannot be taken literally, then how would you describe her attitude toward neat people?
3. Do you think that Britt is being fair to neat people? To sloppy people? Explain.
4. What kind of audience do you think Britt had in mind? Does it include neat people or sloppy people?

Examining Structure and Strategy

1. Does Britt use an alternating or block pattern to organize her details?
2. Does Britt achieve balance by treating the same points about both of her subjects? If not, is the lack of balance a problem? Explain.
3. Why does Britt wait until the end of her essay to discuss how neat people treat living things?

Noting Combined Patterns

1. In which paragraphs does Britt use examples to clarify a point of contrast?
2. Three paragraphs describe sloppy people and seven paragraphs describe neat people. How does the description help Britt achieve her purpose for writing? Why does she have more description about neat people than sloppy people?

Considering Language and Style

1. How does Britt's tone contribute to the humour of the essay? (Tone is discussed on page 77). Cite at least two examples to illustrate your view.
2. Almost all of Britt's paragraphs begin with the words "Neat people" or the words "Sloppy people." Why?
3. Consult a dictionary if you are unsure of the meaning of any of these words: *rectitude* (paragraph 2), *métier* (paragraph 3), *meticulously* (paragraph 5), *scrupulously* (paragraph 5), *cavalier* (paragraph 6), *swath* (paragraph 12).

For Discussion in Class or Online

Consider Britt's word choice, examples, detail selection, and tone, and then explain how Britt achieves humour. If your instructor directs you to do so, post your response to your class Web site.

Writing Assignments

1. **In your journal.** Are you a neat person or a sloppy person? Identify yourself as one or the other and go on to explain whether any of Britt's characterizations are true of you. Also, note to what extent you are happy to be either neat or sloppy.

2. **Using comparison-contrast for a purpose.** The purposes in the assignments are possibilities. You may establish whatever purposes you like, within your instructor's guidelines.
   - To entertain, turn the tables on Britt and write a contrast that proclaims the superiority of neat people.
   - To entertain, contrast those who plan ahead and those who are impulsive. As an alternative contrast those who procrastinate and those who do not put things off.
   - To entertain and perhaps inform, contrast those who are technologically savvy and those who know little about technology.

3. **Combining patterns.** Contrast any of these campus types, drawing on description (explained in Chapter 4) and examples (explained in Chapter 6) to help make your points: professors and deans; commuter students and residential students; adult learners and younger students.

4. **Connecting the readings.** Humorous essays entertain, but humour can also make serious points as well. Barbara Ehrenrich uses humour to suggest that women can learn toughness from men. In "'You'll Never Believe What Happened' Is Always a Great Way to Start" (Chapter 13, page 463), Thomas King uses humour to suggest that the Christian belief system encourages a belief in autocratic power and competition. Explain how the authors use humour both to entertain and to make serious points. How does humour help the authors achieve persuasive and informative purposes?

5. **Drawing on sources.** Interview one student, one teacher, one business or professional person, and one other person of your choice. Ask each of these people the following questions:
   - Are there times when neatness is important in your life or work? If so, explain when and why.
   - Are there times when neatness is not important in your life or work? If so, explain when and why
   - Are there times when sloppiness is acceptable? If so explain when.

   Using the information from the interviews along with your own experience and observation, write an essay that proves either that neatness counts or that neatness does not count.

Background

Born in Hong Kong and raised in Saskatchewan, Stefan Riches graduated with a BA (Distinction) in English from the University of Regina in 1997. After stints in New York and Taipei, he moved to Toronto where he is working and completing the University of British Columbia's online Optional-Residency Creative Writing MFA program. *Tales from the Gap*, written by Joel Fafard with Stefan Riches, was produced by the Regina Globe Theatre in 2008, and he is the author *of Moving Forward, Looking Back: Saskatchewan Rowing in the 20th Century*. A shorter version of his essay "The Two Faces of Hope" originally appeared in *The Globe and Mail*

Combined Patterns and Their Purposes

Riches' essay uses narrative to describe the ways his brother-in-law and his mother reacted to their diagnoses of terminal cancer, and to explore his own reactions to death. At the same time, he contrasts their very different responses to the diagnosis—one accepting it, the other hoping for a cure until her final days. Riches asks, as many of us will, what constitutes hope.

Two Faces of Hope

Stefan Riches

I

1   My sister called in August, crying and scared. I have bad news, she said. I braced myself. Then the words Ken, cancer, oesophagus, spread, inoperable all came crashing down, her sobs rendering further speech impossible. A doctor had just delivered her 47-year-old husband a death sentence.

As you read
What does this essay convey about our sense that there is a type of person who gets cancer? Why do we think in these terms?

2   Although a smoker, Ken was not the type of person you would associate with disease. A successful oil and gas land agent, he ran his demanding business with the energy and passion you would expect from someone who truly loved his work. He rode a Harley, coached his oldest son's hockey team, and fixed everything around the house. He did the laundry and cooking. He treasured playtime with his 2-year-old son, Mason. It never crossed my mind to imagine him ill, let alone terminally.

3   When I arrived in Regina from Toronto two days after my sister's call, like everyone else I looked for signs of hope, only to find none. The doctor's report stated that his cancer was in stage four—there is no stage five—and the oncology tests proved it to be an extremely aggressive form. But it didn't take a medical professional to know how sick Ken was. He'd lost 25 pounds. Every movement caused him pain even morphine couldn't soothe. He had thrown up blood.

4   There was brief talk of flying to the Mayo Clinic for chemo, but Ken knew it was too late to fight. I can't imagine the courage it took when he decided to forgo treatment and live the rest of his days doing the things he loved: late night talks around the fire at the cabin, taking the boat out on the lake, watching his family grow. Chemo might buy him a few more weeks, but it would erode the quality of the little time he had left.

5   People, feeling helpless, offered what they could. A friend brought over a bottle of concentrated blueberry and pomegranate juice, the label proudly boasting its antioxidant power. The gesture, of course, came from a place of love, even though it seemed like handing someone on the Titanic a champagne flute and saying: "Here. Bail."

6   Someone else suggested to me that Ken drink his own urine. Mid-flow with lots of water, she instructed, assuring me (she'd tried it) it tastes better if you haven't been consuming alcohol, meat, or greasy foods. "Do you think Ken would be receptive?" the friend asked. Later that day, I watched Ken eat a dinner of steak and potatoes washed back with rye and coke. His was a diet many associate with disease, but also one many others had consumed until well into old age. Even though he could barely eat two bites without it hurting, I didn't mention the urine.

7   Although my visit was difficult, it was not without laughter. Perhaps it was the morphine, but Ken quickly developed a dark sense of humour about his fate. When someone mentioned a timeshare in Hawaii, he quipped that he didn't have any time to share. When a friend was cold, he offered her a pair of his sweats. "Lucky you," he said. "You don't have to bring them back." When a piece of melon fell on the cabin deck, landing on loose flecks of paint, Ken picked it up and ate it, flecks and all. "What's it going to do, kill me?"

8   Other moments were not so light. "He's not going to remember me," Ken said of Mason one afternoon. As Mason, oblivious to the tragic weight of Ken's remark, laughed and played, the rest of us cried, not just because Mason's best buddy was dying, but because it was true, making Mason the second person in my immediate family to have no memory of his father. His grandfather, my dad, lost his own father at the age of one, not to a battle with cancer, but with Nazis. But although I'd accepted that there was no hope for Ken, I do have hope that Mason will remember his father's boundless love. Not in conscious detail, but in his future capacity to love others, and himself. Ken's immortality, and my hope for Mason, is tied to this.

II

9   Death has a smell. I don't want to describe it, not sure that I can, but it has a smell. I remembered this when I walked into my sister's home for my last visit with Ken, four months after his diagnosis. I say remembered because Ken's wasn't the first death in my family. My mother, a poet and teacher, passed away of cancer at 52. First breast, then colon, then everywhere. Her death sentence had come several years before she died, the word "terminal" written on a report similar to the one Ken had received. Chemo, radiation, surgery—nothing halted her cancer's march. A few months before her death, no longer able to teach and having given up on conventional therapies, she left Regina for Vancouver to immerse herself in its alt-healing environment. She would be back, she assured us. She would beat cancer.

10   Mom and Ken, who never met, were very different people, as their gravestones attest. "We are such stuff" hers reads; a Harley Davidson is etched on his.

But what took them from this earth will forever connect them. Ken chose to die at home; my mother stayed in her Vancouver apartment until a coma forced her into the hospital for the last two days of her life. My final visit with Ken began a week before he died on December 1, 2007, the same length of time I spent with my mom before she passed away on July 12, 1994. Vancouver was sunny and warm while I was there, Regina frigidly cold, proof, perhaps, that death is oblivious to simple metaphors.

11   I was different, too. At 24, a competitive rower at the height of my physical conditioning, my body was a stark contrast to Mom's decaying flesh. I could power a scull down a course faster than most, but there was nothing I could do to prevent the demise of the woman who gave me life. When she died I was still young enough to believe that I was going to live, if not forever, then at least to a point in the future I could not yet conceive. Thirteen years later, I feel the fragility of time, live daily with the weight of my mortality. Ken, after all, was only ten years my senior. I can't see that point—who can?—but I can conceive it now.

12   When it comes, will I need homecare, like Mom and Ken? In the "second child-ishness" of my "strange eventful history," will someone relieve my brittle and flecking lips with water-soaked and colourful sponge swabs that look like lollipops? Will I need diapers to collect shit from bowels I can no longer control? Will nurses be on constant watch, bringing what comfort they can to my bedsores and the pain caused by movements as simple as breathing? Will I take the morphine, like Ken, or rely only on codeine for the pain, like Mom? (How did she bear the agony?) And when oblivion comes, will someone remove a ring from my finger when I am gone, and if so, what will become of it?

13   On her last conscious day on Earth, Mom wanted to go to the Hotel Vancouver for Sunday brunch. It was absurd paying the thirty odd dollars for food she could barely eat, and people kept looking over at the dying woman in the wheelchair being fed chocolate pudding, the last thing she ate, by her scared son. But looking back, I understand that Mom, like Ken, wanted to indulge her senses as often as she could, while she could. I suppose that's why, a few days prior, we took a taxi up Mount Seymour, so she could feel the breeze on her face one last time, look out over the city that couldn't provide the miracle she'd come to find, to "smell the flowers while you can," she might have said, reading the slogan off a U2 concert t-shirt I frequently wore.

14   As I wheeled her back from brunch to the Somerset Apartments (a building she chose, I am sure, because she grew up in Somerset in the UK), we stopped at a sidewalk merchant selling jewellery. Mom bought two silver rings, one with yin and yang symbols, the other a dolphin, a symbol of spiritual wisdom and insight. Days later, this merchant brought me to tears on crowded Robson street when she told me she had experienced Mom's peaceful and loving spirit in the few brief minutes she had spent with her.

15 When Mom was gone, a nurse removed the rings from her fingers. I kept the dolphin ring, my sister the yin/yang. My sister also kept the wedding ring she removed from Ken's hand shortly after he died. Although they were a couple for a dozen years, ran a business together, had a son, they didn't marry until after Ken was diagnosed. They flew to Vegas, got hitched in a chapel without any guests, returned with a DVD of the ceremony that no one who knows them can watch without crying. He died, not happy, but at least happily married.

16 Death is harder on the living than on the dead, my sister told me after Mom died. I think I know what she was talking about. Death is a release from suffering for the dead, an accumulation for the living. I was relieved when Ken died, relieved that he no longer had to moan in agony, but his death retriggered the almost diabolical fear of being alive that had attacked me after Mom died. It left me feeling defenceless against the random power of killer cancer cells; it drained me emotionally and spiritually. It made me angry.

17 Yet both their deaths also connected me to something deeper, to an intimacy with life, filling me at times with a sense of calm and purpose. In seeing how strong Mom and Ken were in handling their hellish fates, I got a sense that our existence goes beyond the corporeal. Their strength was not a question of mind over matter; it was spirit over death, putting a twist on Nietzsche's axiom that "What does not destroy us makes us stronger." What destroys us can make us stronger, too.

18 In short, their deaths put me in touch with a central paradox: that both for the dying and the living who bear witness, death, especially death as cruel and harrowing as death by cancer, can be demonic, unfathomably painful, and life denying, yet at the same time divine, life affirming, and capable of summoning courage and love you never thought existed. I have never felt more present, more alive than when surrounded by death; have never been more afraid.

III

19 My mother died long before the pomegranate craze hit, and I don't know if she ever drank her own urine. But I do know she would have been receptive to such suggestions. Her hope had opened her up to endless possibilities. "Dear God," she wrote in her journal as she watched game three of the 1994 Canucks-Rangers Stanley Cup Finals on TV, "Let me resist the temptation to say: if the Canucks win, I shall be healed."

20 Ken died a week after his hometown Saskatchewan Roughriders captured the Grey Cup. I'm sure, as he lay in his deathbed, aware that the game was on but unable to watch, he didn't pin any hope on the Rider squad saving him from his fate. In his mind, his death sentence was a death sentence.

21 Hope is "exceedingly deceitful," French author François de La Rochefoucauld wrote, something I'm sure Ken would have agreed with. But in the same quote, La

Rochefoucauld also observed that hope is "of good use to us, that . . . it conducts us in an easier and more pleasant way to our journey's end," words to which my mother would have no doubt attested.

22   Did Ken's lack of hope render him, in the eyes of whoever doles them out, ineligible for a miracle cure? Is that how it works? In light of my mother's experience, surely not. "I'm not dying," she told a friend only weeks before she died. "I'm just sick." By that time, she was in a wheelchair, her legs swollen with edema, her emaciated face and bloated stomach reminiscent of a famine victim. Yet still she talked of coming home, of returning to teaching, of finishing her latest book. Hope may have made her journey more bearable, but it didn't spur any miracles.

23   I wanted to be angry with my mother for not being honest with us, or herself, about how sick she really was. Did her hope cost us time? I also wanted to be angry because Ken gave up hope when he perhaps could have fought for his life. Did his lack of hope cost us time? But I can't be angry with either. My love for them doesn't work that way, and besides, who am I to know what would have happened if they had chosen different paths?

24   Mom and Ken's experiences have left me facing a terrifying question: Who was right, my mother for denying her fate or Ken for accepting his? If one day I am faced with the same death sentence, should I take my mother's approach and bravely battle my disease with the blind hope that a cure is imminent? Or should I, as Ken equally bravely did, plan my funeral and wake and suck the marrow out of my final days?

25   It's an impossible question, of course; I won't know unless it happens. My only hope is that I will have the courage, as Mom and Ken did, to take control of the time I have left, in whatever way I need.

Reading Closely and Thinking Critically

1. Many obituaries refer to an individual's "battle with cancer." In light of Riches' essay, how useful is that phrase? Is it reflective of the complex ways human beings approach their deaths?

2. Why does Riches spend so much time considering his own reaction to these deaths? What is he saying about our relationship with mortality?

3. Riches also examines moments of physical and emotional pleasure for the dying—his brother's sense of humour, his mother's lunch at the Hotel Vancouver eating chocolate pudding. How do these moments cause us to question our own sense of what it means to face death?

4. Riches' mother was a poet and teacher whose effect on a street merchant brought the author near tears; his brother-in-law's legacy to his son will be "boundless love." What do the effects of the dead upon the living suggest about mortality and immortality?

Examining Structure and Strategy

1. Riches divides his essay into three distinct sections. How do these help to orient the reader? Are they unnecessary, or are they integral to the process of considering one's reaction to two different approaches to death?

2. Riches doesn't politely ignore the ugly difficulties of death—its smell, the appearance of his mother, the pain morphine can't soothe. What does he accomplish by doing this?
3. Riches quotes La Rouchefoucauld, Nietzsche, and a U2 t-shirt. Do these quotations undermine or strengthen his ideas? Why has he combined references to philosophers with those to popular culture?

Considering Language and Style
1. Riches compares giving a person with a diagnosis of terminal cancer a bottle of juice to giving "someone on the Titanic a champagne flute and saying 'Here. Bail.'" Is this an appropriate simile? How does it work on multiple levels?
2. Why does Riches observe, in paragraph 10, that "death is oblivious to simple metaphors"?
3. Following the paragraph in which Riches discusses the smell of death, he enumerates some of the obvious differences between his mother and his brother-in-law. Yet he has told us in the previous paragraph that the smell of death is the same for both of them. Are their differences or their similarities more profound? How are their differences and similarities articulated through the essay's structure?
4. Think for a moment what you know about Riches. He's not a distant authorial voice, but a real presence in the essay. How does the immediacy of his voice affect your reaction to the essay? Do you trust him more or less than you'd trust a more distanced presence?

For Discussion in Class or Online
How does our culture view death? Consider its representation on TV or in the movies. What kinds of representations make us feel immune to death? What kinds of representations make us feel vulnerable? Do you think popular culture can represent death "realistically"? Alternatively, you could read the obituary columns of your newspapers for a couple of days to infer how people dealing with the death of a family member experience that death. If your instructor so directs, post your responses on your class Web site.

Writing Assignments
1. **In your journal.** Consider a moment when you faced your own mortality. Perhaps it was a car accident you narrowly avoided, or a fairly serious accident you had while playing sports. What were your first thoughts? What were your more considered reflections?
2. **Using contrast or comparison for a purpose.** The purposes in the assignments are possibilities. You may establish whatever purposes you like, within your instructor's guidelines.
   - To entertain your reader, contrast or compare the way young animals and young children play. What do the differences and similarities say about joie de vivre?
   - To entertain and inform your reader, contrast the way you approach your studies in college or university with the way you approached them in high school. How do you account for the difference?
3. **Combining patterns.** Use narration or description to contrast or compare how two of your contemporaries approach activities that might be dangerous, whether it's rock climbing, downhill skiing, or writing an essay the night before it's due.
4. **Connecting the readings.** Riches, in "Two Faces of Hope," and Dillard, in "The Deer at Providencia," both write of how individuals face circumstances that are painful and seemingly hopeless. Explore their different attitudes toward the challenges of the human condition.
5. **Drawing on sources.** In the last chapter of his book *How We Die*, Sherwin Nuland considers how terminal illness forces people to redefine the concept of hope. Read this chapter in Nuland's book and interview someone with a terminal illness. Write a comparison-contrast essay on the way the individual's understanding of hope has changed or has remained unchanged.

Background

Michael Adams is the president of the Environics Institute for Survey Research and writes books (four of them bestsellers) and articles to explain the changing patterns in opinions, attitudes, and values that his research reveals. In 2007 he published *Unlikely Utopia: The Surprising Triumph of Canadian Pluralism*. Keith Neuman has more than 20 years at senior levels in public opinion research organizations and is a frequent media commentator on social trends and public opinion. He is a vice president at Environics. This essay was originally written for the Forest Stewardship Council of Canada Business Forum, and was then reprinted in *The Globe and Mail* (2006).

The Pattern and Its Purpose

In their essay, Adams and Neuman use an analogy, which explores the similarities between two otherwise seemingly different concepts (see page 286). By likening environmentalism to religion, Adams and Neuman encourage readers to think about their commitment to protecting the environment in a different way, persuading us of the ethical importance of our decisions and actions, while helping us to understand why we sometimes fall short of perfection.

It's Not Easy Being Green
Michael Adams and Keith Neuman

As you read
Consider which environmental principles—like not buying bottled water—you're willing to live by; also consider which sacrifices you are not willing to make.

1   In June of 1989, a remarkable thing happened. When Environics asked Canadians what they saw as the top problem facing the country, the most common answer was the environment. We've asked this question quarterly since 1983, and answers have varied. Health care and national unity are common as top issues; unemployment and inflation appear depending on the economic weather. But 1989 was the first time the environment emerged as Canadians' most pressing concern.

2   It was an important signal. Certainly, Canadians were alarmed by the environmental disasters in the news then. The Exxon Valdez oil spill occurred in March, 1989, dousing that iconic oil-soaked seabird in Prince William Sound. Talk of acid rain and the depleted ozone layer were causing unease, and the summer of 1988 was the hottest on record, with droughts throughout North America.

3   But in addition to alarm about these events, Canadians were developing a new orientation to the environment, and a new understanding of where they fit into the ecosystem. In a sense, as Canadians moved away from traditional religion and the rules and relationships it entailed, environmentalism became a kind of secular religion; we moved from deference to a patriarchal God to harmony with a matriarchal Gaia. Like religion, environmentalism involves a commitment to something larger than oneself—the earth and its systems. Environmentalism asks people to suppress their egotism and say, "I will make this sacrifice—be it walking when I would rather drive, or kicking hard-earned dollars into the collection plate—because my own desires are not the only things that count."

"Like religion, environmentalism involves a commitment to something larger than oneself—the earth and its systems."

4   Today, amid mounting evidence of global climate change, we see the environment once again moving to the top of the public agenda. At our last measure, Canadians saw the environment as second only to health care as a pressing issue facing the country. It remains to be seen now whether Canadians will view the Conservatives' "made-in-Canada" environmental policy as a sufficiently serious offering to the green gods.

5   Like religion, environmentalism offers opportunities to individuals and their governments for both guilt and redemption. And like religion, the imperatives of environmentalism can be sufficiently demanding that we sometimes believe in them more than we actually adhere to them. If Canadian environmentalism was baptized in the sludge of the Exxon Valdez and underwent its confirmation in Kyoto, it still manages on occasion to lapse into sin.

6   When we have polled Canadians about their views on the environment over the past decade, they have consistently told us that they:

7   • View environmental threats to be significant, and more serious than nuclear war or worldwide pandemics.

8   • Believe that individual citizens can make a difference in helping to protect the environment.

9   • Are willing to do their part, in terms of environmental purchases, recycling, and supporting regulations and taxes to further environmental protection.

10   • Report taking some green steps, cutting back on home energy use and reducing unnecessary driving.

11   Despite these eco-pieties, we see behaviour among Canadians that is not entirely green. We see rising levels of per capita energy and resource consumption, as well as the growing popularity of SUVs, whose share of the Canadian new car market has almost quadrupled since 1990. Household waste is a perennial issue across Canada.

12   Are Canadians hypocrites who talk a good game but in the end do not really care about the Earth? We think not. Like righteous souls in a fallen world, Canadians are doing their best but encounter obstacles in their efforts to act green.

13   First, there is the matter of where we live. An increasing proportion of us live in low-density suburban housing tracts with limited public transit options, where a car is the only way to get by.

14   Second, like the rewards and punishments of the afterlife, fallout from the environmental damage we cause is difficult to predict and sometimes does not show itself until it's too late. Most people take it on faith that they should conserve energy and reduce waste, but don't feel immediate negative effects of environmental damage.

15   Third, Canadians receive mixed signals about the environment. On one channel, Rick Mercer tells us to reduce our consumption; on the next, we find an ad for a Hummer. Often, glossy ads from marketers make a stronger impression than devout messages about restraint and conservation.

16   This brings us to perhaps the greatest factor in the inconsistency between Canadians' claims about the environment and their actual behaviour: the tension between our roles as citizens and consumers. As citizens, we have a collective interest in a sustainable future. As individuals, we have daily needs—and desires that our consumer society encourages us to see as needs.

> "As citizens, we have a collective interest in a sustainable future. As individuals, we have daily needs—and desires that our consumer society encourages us to see as needs."

17   This dual identity is every bit as true of governments that must balance the long-term necessity of maintaining an environment in which its citizens can live and work healthfully, and the short-term need to foster industry. Often the economic demands of today edge out ecological concerns about tomorrow—whether for the individual getting to work or the government making a policy trade-off.

18   Government, of course, cannot fix everything on its own; we are all consumers and all guilty in some way. To a great extent, Canadians' behaviour vis-à-vis the environment will come from peer pressure. The country's many successful blue-box programs offer a perfect example of social norms evolving around green behaviour: Everyone sees who puts out their box in the morning. It's like going to confession in the public square.

19   Our research suggests that Canadians genuinely want to lighten their footprints on the Earth; their expressions of concern about the environment are neither superficial nor hypocritical. But they cannot walk the narrow path of ecological righteousness alone. Canadians will look to government, institutions, and the private sector for active and visible leadership. It will be fascinating to see whether the current government, with its emphasis on traditional values including religiosity, will be able to integrate Canadians' secular religion into their policy agenda.

Reading Closely and Thinking Critically

1. Writers use analogies when they want us to give us a fresh view of an issue or a concept. How does "It's Not Easy Being Green" encourage readers to see their environmental choices and actions differently?

2. Writers also use analogies to persuade readers by giving them a new perspective on an issue or a concept. Do you find the comparison between religion and environmentalism persuasive? What does it persuade you to do or think?

3. The writers also discuss, with a degree of tolerance, our lack of perfection. Does this make their essay more or less persuasive?

4. How do we decide what sacrifices we are or are not willing to make in the face of our lack of perfection? If we recycle, buy a fuel-efficient car, and use energy-efficient light bulbs, is that enough? What is enough? Why don't we all give up our cars? Why do we tolerate box-store land and suburbs, both configurations of urban space that depend on the use of a car?
5. Do Adams and Neuman suggest any way that we might examine our behaviour from time to time to see whether it needs to be reconsidered?

Examining Structure and Strategy

1. The first three paragraphs take us from the present back to June 1989, when an Environics poll noted a change in respondents' attitudes toward the environment. Why do Adams and Neuman go back to that event?
2. How does the fact that we've thought the environment was an important issue for over 20 years accord with their observation that our actions don't necessarily reflect our beliefs?
3. In paragraphs 9, 10, and 11, Adams and Neuman identify four reasons for the gap between our beliefs and our behaviour. What principles govern the order in which they present these reasons?

Considering Language and Style

1. Analogies have their limitations: one thing is not like another in *all* respects; otherwise, they'd be the same thing. In order to highlight the discussion of our environmental responsibilities, the authors cannot make the comparison between environmentalism and religion the focus of attention at all times. In that light, what is the effect of sprinkling expressions that have religious overtones throughout the essay?
2. The task of comparing environmentalism to religion might encourage writers to use a very formal style to reflect the seriousness of the discussion. Is this what Adams and Neuman do? Is their tone appropriate?

For Discussion in Class or Online

Adams and Neuman suggest that the greatest factor contributing to our inconsistency vis-à-vis the environment is "the tension between our roles as citizens and consumers" (paragraph 16). How does that tension play itself out in your life? In the lives of your family or peers? What other aspects of your life are shaped by this tension? If your instructor so directs, post your responses on your class Web site.

Writing Assignments

1. **In your journal.** Consider your own behaviour with respect to the environment. How much of a sacrifice are you willing to make? What would make you a perfect environmental citizen? Is being perfect possible? What do your commitments tell you about yourself as an environmental citizen?
2. **Using contrast or comparison for a purpose.** The purposes in the assignments are possibilities. You may establish whatever purposes you like, within your instructor's guidelines.
    *   To entertain your reader, use an analogy to explain a facet of your life that other people aren't likely to understand. Is being a student like taking religious vows? Is working at a minimum wage job like being a beast of burden? Is looking for a meaningful summer job like running a marathon?
    *   To inform your reader, contrast or compare two environmentally friendly changes an individual could make with respect to their ease or effectiveness.
    *   To persuade your reader, contrast or compare environmentally responsible changes individuals can make with respect to how much they cost (in dollars or in damage) or how much they save (also in dollars or damage).

3. **Combining patterns.** After contrasting your current environmental habits to ones you held earlier, use narrative to relate how and why you made those changes.

4. **Connecting the readings.** In "Toronto Cars" (page 411), Tim Falconer writes of how he loves the freedom and speed of cars but feels guilty about depending on his. Using "It's Not Easy Being Green," and "Toronto Cars," as examples, write your own essay on the seductions of an environmental bad habit, like drinking bottled water or driving around the city looking at gardens or Christmas lights. Use the contrast or comparison form to consider how we resolve this particular contradiction in our lives.

5. **Drawing on sources.** Polls show that most Canadians think the environment is one of the most important challenges we face. But at the same time, most of us probably don't know what to do to personally address that challenge. Do energy-saving light bulbs help? Do we all have to give up our cars or would driving differently make a difference? After researching the effects of the various changes individuals can make, write an essay contrasting the two most effective changes individuals can make with the two that are easiest to incorporate into one's life.

Additional Essay Assignments

See pages 293 and 294 for strategies for writing comparison-contrast and for a revising checklist.

1. Compare and/or contrast a place on campus at two different times of the day. For example, you can compare and/or contrast a campus eating spot at the noon rush hour and again at the 3:00 lull, the football stadium during and after a game, or the library before and after finals week. Use description for vividness.

2. Compare and/or contrast the way two disciplines might view the same problem. For example, consider how history and English classes might treat the historical background of Canadian novels like Ondaatje's *The English Patient* or Sinclair Ross's *As for Me and My House.* Or write about how classes in psychology and justice studies consider the problem of juvenile crime.

3. Compare and/or contrast a movie to the novel that it's based on. Which medium is more successful? Why?

4. Contrast the way a group of people (for example, mothers, police officers, fathers, or teens) is portrayed on television with the way the group is in real life.

5. Consider your circumstances before and after some change in your life: getting married, having children, going to college or university, getting a job, or joining an athletic team, for example. If you wish, make your details humorous and entertain your reader.

6. In your campus library, look up advertisements in *Life* and *Look* magazines from the 1950s and compare and contrast one or two of these ads with ads for similar products in contemporary magazines to inform your reader of the changes. Use cause-and-effect analysis to explain the cause and/or the effects of the changes. (See Chapter 10.)

7. Compare and contrast the styles of two comedians, actors, or musicians to inform your reader about the characteristics of each one.

8. Compare and contrast the chief arguments on both sides of a controversial issue (for example, abortion, capital punishment, euthanasia, animal rights, distributing condoms in schools, or bilingual education) to inform your reader of the thinking on both sides. If necessary, research the issue in your campus library or on the Internet.

9. If you have lived in more than one place, compare and contrast life in two of those places.

10. If you or someone close to you has lived with chronic illness, contrast life as a healthy and a sick person to heighten your reader's awareness of what it is like to be ill.

11. Using vivid description, compare and/or contrast your current view of a particular place and the view you held as a child. For example, you could compare and/or contrast your views of your elementary school, a family vacation spot, your old bedroom, or your old neighbourhood.

12. Compare and/or contrast the ways men are portrayed on television with the ways women are portrayed. Use specific examples from shows and commercials to clarify and support your points. If possible, explain the effects these portrayals have on the viewer.

13. Contrast your view of a parent now with your view at some point in the past.

14. Compare and/or contrast your life today with what you once thought your life would be like. If there are striking contrasts, try to explain what accounts for those contrasts.

15. **Comparison/contrast in context.** For a humour column for your student newspaper, compare and/or contrasts the food in your campus cafeteria and the food you grew up on.

Chapter 10

Cause-and-Effect Analysis

Why do writers write? Because it isn't there.

— Thomas Berger

Patience and perseverance have a magical effect before which difficulties disappear and obstacles vanish.

— John Quincy Adams

THE PATTERN

Human beings need to make sense of the world by understanding why events occur and how they affect us. Thus, we examine the causes of earthquakes, try to determine how a political party's victory will change the economy, work to figure out why the car does not get the gas mileage it should, struggle to understand why our best friend suddenly seems distant, and so on. An understanding of causes and effects is important to our sense of security and our need to deal with forces in our environment. Thus, we often use **cause-and-effect analysis** to examine causes, effects, or both. When you explore causes, you identify the reasons for an event; when you explore effects, you identify the results of an event; when you look at both causes and effects, you examine reasons *and* results.

USING CAUSE-AND-EFFECT ANALYSIS FOR A PURPOSE

Cause-and-effect analysis can entertain, inform, persuade, or express feelings and relate experience. For example, you could entertain with a funny account of the causes and effects of your attempt to throw a surprise party—which was ultimately a disaster. If you were to explain the causes of inflation, you would inform a reader about an economic force, or if you explained the effects of computers on reading instruction, you would inform your reader about a trend in education. Similarly, if you explained the causes of math anxiety, you could do so to persuade your reader that women are often conditioned by our culture to avoid math, and if you explained the possible effects of the failure to pass a private member's bill on lowering the voting age to 16, you might be able to persuade your readers to contact their MPs to argue that young people would be more likely to become regular voters if they started voting at the same time they were studying Canadian history and culture in secondary schools. Cause-and-effect analysis can also allow you to express feelings and relate experience, as when you explain the causes and effects of your decision to leave home and move to another province.

An essay is often developed solely with cause-and-effect analysis, but the pattern can also form part of an essay developed primarily with another pattern. For example, if you wrote a process analysis to explain how heat lightning works, part of the essay might include a discussion of the effects of heat lightning. Similarly, if you told the story of the time you were involved in a serious car accident, the narration could also include a discussion of what caused the accident.

Cause-and-Effect Analysis at School, at Work, and in the Community

Cause-and-effect analysis is a frequent component of writing in many university and college classes. For instance, in a mathematics class, you might be asked to write a journal entry explaining how math affects your life. In history and political science classes, you will often be asked to explain the causes and effects of important events. For example, you could be asked on an essay exam to explain the causes of rejection of the Charlottetown Accord, or you could be asked to write a report evaluating the causes and effects of residential schools. In a sociology class, you could be asked to explain the effects of the AIDS crisis on dating practices, and in a physics, chemistry, or biology class you will likely be asked to write lab reports explaining the effects of experiments. In an education class, you could detail the causes of teacher burnout or the effects of whole language instruction, and in a marketing class, you could write a paper on the effects of telemarketing.

Cause-and-effect analysis is one of the most frequently occurring patterns in college and university textbooks. Here, for example, is a paragraph from a business textbook that explains causes—in this case, the complex reasons people are unemployed.

> People are unemployed in Canada for various reasons. Perhaps their employer goes out of business or their company cuts staff. Young persons enter

the job market looking for their first job and other employees quit their jobs but have trouble finding new ones. Companies merge and jobs are consolidated or trimmed. Companies transfer their operations to another country, or a branch of a foreign company is closed down. Of course, in a period of economic recession, such as the early 1990s and 2000 and 2001, unemployment increases. (Nickels, McHugh, McHugh, and Cossa, *Understanding Canadian Busines*)

It is sometimes easy to assume that the causes of unemployment are relatively simple: the economy is in a slump and some people are lazy. These examples give a sense of how complex and impersonal the causes of unemployment can be.

Here is another paragraph from the same textbook. This paragraph explains effects—specifically the effect of managers who do not understand their local cultures:

> Understanding sociocultural differences can also be important when managing employees. In Latin American countries, workers believe that managers are placed in positions of authority to make decisions and be responsible for the well-being of their workers. Consider what happened to one North American manager in Peru who was unaware of this characteristic and believed that workers should participate in managerial functions. This manager was convinced that he could motivate his workers to higher levels of productivity by instituting a more democratic decision-making style than the one already in place. Soon workers began quitting their jobs in droves. When asked why, the workers said the new manager did not know his job and was asking the workers what to do. All stated that they wanted to find new jobs, since obviously this company was doomed due to incompetent managers. (Nickels, McHugh, McHugh, and Cossa, *Understanding Canadian Business*)

The textbook authors could have simply said that businesses benefit from being sensitive to local cultures, but the example illustrates why cultural sensitivity benefits everyone.

On the job, people frequently use cause-and-effect analysis. Teachers write explanations of the causes of declining test scores, and social workers write reports for social service agencies explaining the positive effects of services on a family or community. Marketing managers write reports noting the reasons for a decline in sales, and dieticians give their clients a written explanation of the effects of sugar on insulin production. A police officer will fill out a report explaining the causes of an accident, and an official with Environment Canada may write a study of the effects of a dam on river ecology.

Outside the classroom and workplace, cause-and-effect analysis is likely to be an important component of your writing. For example, when you write a letter of complaint to a company about a faulty product, you will describe what went wrong with the product and the damaging effects of that fault. If you ever deliver a eulogy, you will explain the positive ways the deceased affected you and others.

SUPPORTING DETAILS

A number of patterns can help you achieve your purpose. In particular, narration, exemplification, description, and process analysis can be very useful. For an essay explaining reasons people graduate from high school without being able to read, you might cite one cause as social promotions. You can help establish this point by narrating the story of Stella, a non-reader you know who was frequently passed on from grade to grade because she was a troublemaker, and teachers did not want to have her in their classrooms another year. You could also give several examples of other people who have been promoted without knowing how to read. Description can also contribute to cause-and-effect analysis. For example, if you want to explain the effects of littering, you can clarify the problem by describing a section of roadside that has been heavily littered. Sometimes, process analysis helps make a point. For example, if you want to explain the effects of tax reduction, you can note the process whereby lowering taxes creates more disposable income, which leads to increased spending, which spurs manufacturing, which ultimately creates jobs.

Note that the example on page 316 about the importance of cultural sensitivity is in the form of a narrative. In some ways, cause-and-effect analysis always involves a narrative, given that causes come first and bring about effects. But don't let this fact handcuff you to a narrative form. In reasoning out causes and their effects, we always proceed from what we know (the effect: people were quitting in droves) to what we don't know (the cause: Peruvians prefer authoritative managers). Similarly, we write from what we know, regardless of whether it's a cause or an effect, toward what we've tried to reason out. Better yet, write from what your audience knows (the effects of being unemployed) to what they don't know (the complex causes—which helps your parents understand why you haven't moved out yet).

Events typically have more than one cause and more than one effect. Say, for example, that you are looking at the causes and effects of an enrolment decline at your college or university. The causes are likely to be many and might include these: a weak economy that means fewer people have the money to go to college or university, the creation of two new post-secondary institutions in a 200-kilometre radius, lack of a recruitment drive, and less financial aid available for prospective students. Similarly, the effects of the enrolment decline are likely to be many, including loss of revenue, loss of prestige, low employee morale, and fewer course offerings. When an event has multiple causes and effects, you do not want to omit any significant ones, or you will give your reader an incomplete picture. At the same time, the multiple causes and effects may not be of equal significance, so you need not develop them all in the same detail. If the primary reasons for the enrolment decline are the weak economy and the two new schools, you should discuss those causes in considerably more detail than the reduced financial aid and lack of recruitment. When you organize an essay that considers multiple causes or multiple effects, it's effective to put them in the order of their importance, from least important to most important.

When an event has more than one cause, you may need to distinguish between causes that are *immediate* and those that are *remote*. Say, for example, that you are explaining why AIDS has reached epidemic proportions. Obviously, there are many reasons, but you may cite as one *immediate* cause the U.S. laws prohibiting notification of those exposed to the disease through their HIV-positive partners without the consent of those partners. To explain the lack of laws in the U.S., you can cite a more *remote* cause: Gay and HIV activists successfully lobbied against such legislation because they feared discrimination against those publicly identified as gay and/or infected.

Sometimes cause-and-effect details include an explanation of causal chains. In a **causal chain,** a cause leads to an effect; that effect becomes a cause that leads to another effect; then that effect becomes a cause, and so on. For example, if you wanted to explain the effects of being very tall, you might reproduce a causal chain like this one: being tall made you feel awkward (effect); feeling awkward (cause) reduced your self-confidence (effect); your reduced self-confidence (cause) made it hard for you to date (effect); not dating (cause) made you depressed (effect).

In addition to reproducing causal chains, you may want to point out something that is *not,* despite popular belief, a cause or an effect. This strategy is especially effective if you need to correct your reader's understanding. For example, assume that you are explaining the effects of sex education in the schools, and you think your reader mistakenly believes that sex education leads to increased sexual activity. You can note that increased sexual activity has not been proven to be an effect of sex education.

To identify causes and effects, ask yourself the questions "Why?" and "Then what?" as you develop your details. For example, say you are explaining the causes of your shyness, and you give as one reason the fact that you do not feel comfortable around people. If you ask why you do not feel comfortable, you may remember that your family moved so frequently that you never got to know anyone very well. A new cause for your discussion, then, is those frequent moves. In a different essay, you might explain the effects of your parents' divorce on you, indicating that the divorce meant you saw less of your father. Ask "Then what?" and you might answer that you and your father drifted apart, so you never got to know him well—that is another effect you can write about.

Avoiding Errors in Logic

In Chapter 1 you will find a section entitled "Detecting Errors in Logic" (page 9), which you should revisit. There, the focus was on finding the errors in other people's writing; reread it now from the point of view of preventing errors in your own writing.

The most common logical error in cause-and-effect writing is *post hoc, ergo propter hoc* ("after this, therefore because of this"), which is automatically assuming that an earlier event caused a later one. For example, you cannot assume that an increase in traffic accidents at a street corner after a traffic light was installed is necessarily a result of that traffic light. Other factors must be considered, such as a change in the speed limit and an increase in the number of cars along the route as a result of a new shopping plaza. Taken to its extreme, *post hoc, ergo propter hoc* can lead to superstitious thinking. For example, it can cause a person who sprains an ankle after breaking a mirror to assume that breaking a mirror causes bad luck. The most effective way of avoiding this causal fallacy is to explain, to yourself if not to your reader, *how* the cause produced the effect.

The other common errors you should watch for as you write cause-and-effect essays all involve seeing the world as a simpler place than it actually is. The first of these errors is *oversimplifying*. Most cause-and-effect relationships are complex; they often involve multiple causes and effects. If you fail to consider important causes or effects, you are oversimplifying. Thus, to state that violence against women is solely the result of pornography is to ignore an array of other factors that contribute to the problem. A related error is *overgeneralizing*. If you are writing about the causes of the spread of AIDS and cited a newspaper story about a trial of a gay man who did not inform his partners that he was infected, you would be overgeneralizing to conclude that gay men do not care about the health of their partners. When we draw conclusions based on insufficient evidence, we overgeneralize. To avoid hasty

Troubleshooting Guide

Using *Affect* and *Effect* Correctly

If you have trouble understanding the difference between *affect* and *effect*, remember the following:

- *Affect* is a verb meaning "to influence," as in "Explain how hockey affects Canadian culture."

- *Effect* is most often a noun meaning "result," as in "Explain the effects of hockey on Canadian culture."

generalizations, we need to ensure that our assertion is based on a representative sampling of a group.

Two other fallacies can creep into our cause-and-effect writing. One is the *either/or fallacy.* If you were writing about the misunderstandings that arise when people instant message one another and aren't careful about their language or their tone, you would be committing the either/or fallacy if you wrote, "Either we return to face-to-fact contact, or we're going to forget how to relate to people in a considerate and caring way." Surely there are other options, which include being more careful about our language, thinking before we press "send," or considering whether instant messaging is the best way to deal with the circumstances at hand. Instant messaging may provide a great way to make a date, but it's probably a poor way to break up. The second fallacy, the *appeal to tradition,* involves the assertion that the old ways are the best ways. Once again, writing on the problems created by instant messaging, you would be appealing to tradition if you wrote, "Talking to one another face to face has served humanity well for centuries. We should stick to what has worked, regardless of the options technology has made available to us." This appeal to tradition ignores the way communication is always changing. Where once we had to write letters to communicate with people far away, in the twentieth century long distance phone calls made it possible to speak directly to them. Now we have email, and web cameras are built right into our computers.

ORGANIZING DETAILS

The thesis for your cause-and-effect analysis can indicate your topic and whether you will explain causes, effects, or both. In addition, your thesis can suggest your purpose by noting the point your cause-and-effect analysis is making. Here is an example:

THESIS When athletes use performance-enhancing drugs to give themselves a competitive edge, they not only give themselves an unfair advantage, but they put their own health at risk.

This thesis indicates that the essay will explain the causes of drug use among athletes and that the purpose is to inform the reader that the short-term seemingly positive effects (in the form of a competitive edge) are accompanied by long-term health risks.

For clear organization, use topic sentences to introduce your discussion of each cause or effect. Here are the sample thesis and some topic sentences that could appear in an essay about the causes of drug abuse among athletes.

THESIS While athletes may be told that performance-enhancing drugs are unhealthy and unsportsmanlike, the reasons they take them anyway are understandable.

TOPIC SENTENCE The pressure for professional athletes to justify their huge salaries is so great that they often see performance-enhancing drugs as the answer. (*Topic sentence presents the first cause: pressure on professional athletes.*)

TOPIC SENTENCE Furthermore, athletes may feel that they must take the drugs in order to be competitive, since so many other athletes are taking them. (*Topic sentence presents second cause: others take drugs.*)

TOPIC SENTENCE Finally, some athletes get hooked on drugs because their coaches and trainers administer them. (*Topic sentence presents third reason: coaches and trainers give out the drugs.*)

If you are explaining both causes and effects, you may want to discuss causes first and then move on to effects. Otherwise, a particular order may be called for. If your purpose is persuasive, you may want a progressive order so you can save your most dramatic, compelling, or significant cause or effect for the end. If you are reproducing causal chains, you need a chronological order, so you can cite the causes and effects in the order they occur. Chronological order is also called for when you are discussing causes and effects as they occurred across time. For example, a discussion of the effects of your musical talent could begin with your first music lessons, then go into your increasing commitment to practising as you grew up, and conclude with your decision to become a music teacher. At times, you may want to arrange your details in categories. If, for example, you are explaining the effects of raising property taxes to provide more school funding, you can discuss together all the effects on teachers, then the effects on students, and finally the effects on curriculum.

Two kinds of transitions can help you signal cause-and-effect relationships to your reader. First, the following transitions signal that one thing is the effect of another: *as a result, consequently, thus, hence, therefore,* and *for this reason.* Here are two examples:

> The midterm grades were very low. *For this reason,* Professor Werner reviewed the material with the class.
> The storm damage was extensive. *As a result,* the tourist trade in the coastal town declined.

Transitions of addition (*also, in addition, additionally, furthermore,* and *another*) can also signal cause-and-effect analysis, as in the following examples:

> *Another* effect of MTV is . . .
> *In addition,* stress fractures can be caused by . . .

VISUALIZING A CAUSE-AND-EFFECT ANALYSIS

The chart on page 323 can help you visualize the structure for a cause-and-effect analysis. Like all good models, however, this one can be altered as needed.

PROCESS GUIDELINES: STRATEGIES FOR WRITING CAUSE-AND-EFFECT ANALYSIS

1. **Selecting a Topic.** Consider writing about the causes and/or effects of some aspect of your life or personality. Possible topics include shyness, math anxiety, birth order, fear of heights, your parents' divorce, or living on a farm.
2. **Generating Ideas.** To generate ideas,
    - List every cause and/or effect of your topic that you can think of, without pausing to evaluate whether your ideas are good or not.
    - Ask "why?" and/or "then what?" of every item on your list to explore additional causes and effects.
    - Consider whether you can tell a story, provide an example, describe, or explain a process to clarify any of the points on your list.
    - Consider whether your audience needs to be told whether something is not a cause or effect, even though some people mistakenly believe it to be.
    - Review your list of ideas. Based on your audience and purpose, is there anything you should cross off?
3. **Organizing.** Number the remaining ideas on your list in the order you will treat them in your first draft. Consider causal chains and remote and immediate causes.

Introduction

- Creates interest in the essay
- States the thesis, which can indicate your topic, whether you will explain causes, effects, or both, and the point the cause-and-effect analysis will make

First Body Paragraph

- Gives the first cause or effect, which can be stated in a topic sentence
- Can be developed with any patterns of development
- May reproduce causal chains
- May indicate something that is not a cause or effect
- May arrange causes before effects
- May arrange details in a progressive order or in order events in causal chain occur

Next Body Paragraphs

- Give the next causes or effects, which can be stated in a topic sentence
- Can be developed with any patterns of development
- May reproduce causal chains
- May indicate something that is not a cause or effect
- May arrange causes before effects
- May arrange details in a progressive order or in order events in causal chain occur

Conclusion

- Provides a satisfying finish
- Leaves the reader with a positive final impression

Troubleshooting Guide

Avoiding "the Reason Is Because"

If you have trouble avoiding "the reason is because," remember that this expression is redundant because "the reason" means "because." Two alternatives are *the reason is that* and *because*.

NO   **Economic development on the west side has lagged behind other areas of the city. The reason is because the Route 7 connector bridge has not been completed.**

YES   **Economic development on the west side has lagged behind other areas of the city. The reason is that the Route 7 connector bridge has not been completed.**

YES   **Economic development on the west side has lagged behind other areas of the city because the Route 7 connector bridge has not been completed.**

✔ Checklist for Revising Cause-and-Effect Analysis

Be sure:

_____ The thesis indicates whether you are explaining causes, effects, or both—and, perhaps, the point your analysis will make.

_____ Topic sentences introduce the discussion of each cause and effect.

_____ You have noted all significant causes and effects.

_____ You have clarified all causes and effects, as needed, with explanation, description, narration, examples, or process analysis.

_____ You have reproduced causal chains, where appropriate.

_____ You have accounted for both immediate and remote causes, without going further back than necessary.

_____ You have avoided oversimplifying, overgeneralizing, and *post hoc, ergo propter hoc* errors in logic.

_____ You have used transitions, as needed, to introduce causes and effects.

ANNOTATED STUDENT ESSAY

Student writer Carl Benedict informs his reader by explaining the causes of steroid use among athletes. As you read, notice how carefully each cause is presented and explained. After you read, you will have an opportunity to evaluate this essay.

Why Athletes Use Steroids

1   One of the most heated controversies in athletics centres is the use of anabolic steroids. Behind the dispute is the evidence that steroids pose a health hazard. They are linked to cardiovascular disease, liver disorders, and cancerous tumours. In addition, there is evidence that they cause personality aberrations. Still, an alarming number of athletes are willing to risk their health for the enhanced performance steroids provide—and it is not hard to understand why.

2   First of all, many athletes are so blinded by the obvious benefits of steroid use that they fail to note their adverse effects. They are so focused on the increased strength, stamina, and size that result from steroid use, they may overlook the abuse their bodies are sustaining—often until it is too late. That is, athletes who are delighting in turning in the best performance of their lives are not likely to think about future deleterious effects. This is the same psychology that keeps the nicotine addict smoking three packs a day, until the x-ray shows the lung cancer is so advanced that nothing can be done.

3   Some athletes rationalize steroid use another way. They claim that anabolic steroids pose no greater health hazard than participation in such contact sports as football, boxing, and wrestling. However, these athletes fail to understand that in addition to harming the body, steroids also heighten the danger of contact sports by making the participants larger and stronger, thereby increasing their momentum and impact.

4   Some people think steroid use continues despite the life-threatening effects because athletes are just "dumb jocks" who are not smart enough to appreciate the risks. I don't accept that explanation. Instead, I suspect that steroid use continues partly because most athletes are young, and young people never feel threatened. Part of being young is feeling invulnerable. That is why young people drive too fast, drink too much, and bungee jump. They just do not believe that anything can happen to them. The same psychology is at work with athletes. They are young people who feel they will live forever.

5   In addition, athletes assume that because their bodies are so physically conditioned they can withstand more punishment than the average person, so they feel even less at risk by steroid use. They think, "The

Paragraph 1
The introduction gives background information. The thesis (the last sentence) indicates that the subject is steroid use and the essay will present causes.

Paragraph 2
Sentence 1 is the topic sentence. It begins with a transition of addition and presents the first cause under consideration.

Paragraph 3
The second cause is presented in the first two sentences. The paragraph also presents an effect: Contact sports become more dangerous.

Paragraph 4
This paragraph explains something that is not a cause, then goes on to give a real cause. Note the transition *instead.*

Paragraph 5
The first sentence is the topic sentence. It begins with a transition and presents the next cause. Does this paragraph need more detail?

average person should not do this, but I can because my body is finely tuned."

6   Perhaps the biggest reason athletes use steroids can be explained by the spirit that lies at the heart of all athletes: competition. Once a handful of athletes enhance their performance artificially, then others follow in order to stay competitive. Eventually, steroid users dominate a sport, and anyone who wants to compete at the highest levels is forced to use steroids or lose out. This fact explains why unscrupulous coaches and trainers who want to win at any cost have contributed to the problem by offering steroids to their players and urging them to use them. Sadly, this practice has even filtered down to the high school level in some cases.

7   Competition for the thrill of winning is only part of the explanation, however. Big-time athletics means big-time money. As the financial rewards rise in a given sport, so does the pressure to win at any cost. Huge salaries, enormous purses, big bonuses, and incredibly lucrative commercial endorsements all tempt athletes to enhance their performances any way they can.

8   Despite drug testing before competition and dissemination of information about the dangers of anabolic steroids, athletes still use steroids because the pressures to do so are so compelling. The truth is, too many athletes think steroids only hurt the other person, or else they think using steroids is worth the risk.

Paragraph 6
The first sentence is the topic sentence. "The biggest reason" notes that detail is in a progressive order. The paragraph presents a causal chain.

Paragraph 7
This paragraph presents a cause that is an extension of the one given in the previous paragraph.

Paragraph 8
The conclusion summarizes the main causes.

PEER REVIEW

Responding to "Why Athletes Use Steroids"

Evaluate "Why Athletes Use Steroids" by responding to these questions:

1. Does the writer treat the causes and effects of steroid use in a significant and logical order?
2. Are the introduction and conclusion effective? Why or why not?
3. Are causes and effects explained in sufficient detail? Explain.
4. Has the author accounted for both immediate and remote causes? If not, is that a problem? Explain.
5. Are there any errors in logic?
6. What do you like best about the essay?
7. Name one revision that would make the essay better.

READING SELECTIONS

Background

Nora Underwood spent a decade writing for a variety of Canadian publications such as *Maclean's*, *The Globe and Mail*, the *National Post,* and *Canadian Living* before becoming a senior editor at *The Walrus.* She specializes in health, behaviour, and social issues. This essay on the teenage brain appeared in a slightly different form in *The Walrus* in November 2006, for which it won a National Magazine Award.

The Pattern and Its Purposes

Because causes precede effects in time, we often assume that we need to write from causes to effects. In this essay, Nora Underwood often writes from effect to cause. She examines the effects many parents observe—teenage behaviours like being emotionally over-sensitive, not considering the long-term consequences of actions, or wanting to sleep until noon—and considers what science has to say about the development of the teenage brain—the causes—that produce those effects.

The Teenage Brain
Nora Underwood

You don't have to suffer to be a poet. Adolescence is enough suffering for anyone.

— American poet John Ciardi, 1962

1   In his speech at the launch of the 1997 I Am Your Child campaign, director and actor Rob Reiner stated that "by the age of ten, your brain is cooked." And until recently, most child experts, including Dr. Spock, would have agreed. They considered the first few years of a child's life to be the most important—and the experiences a child had during those years to play a crucial role in defining the kind of person he or she would ultimately become. That understanding also helped create a whole generation of obsessively child-focused parents, who, with the best of intentions, have tried to cram a lifetime of "educating" into a few short years, subjecting their unwitting fetuses to a diet of *Eine kleine Nachtmusik* and their pre-verbal toddlers to basic arithmetic and multiple viewings of *Baby Einstein* DVDs. (A wise elementary-school principal once noted, "I very much doubt Einstein was doing any of this when *he* was young.")

As you read
How does Underwood account for the difference between parents' expectations of grownup behaviour and the experience of continuing to grow?

2   Somewhere along the line, or so many parents believed, the window of opportunity would close. The foundations of the adult-to-be would be laid, and the worst damage would be done. The majority of brain development does, in fact, take place in the early years, when billions of synaptic circuits that will last the child's lifetime are forming. But growth and change don't end there. Important developmental changes, scientists are discovering, are still taking place in a big way through the adolescent years—and into the mid-twenties. Perhaps this helps to explain the growing

phenomenon of adult children who linger on under the parental roof; their growing may not be over, despite their arrival at "adulthood."

3   In recent years, researchers have finally been able to get real insight into the workings of the brain thanks to magnetic resonance imaging (MRI), using the technology to map blood flow to the areas of the brain that are activated by exposure to various stimuli. By scanning the same group of adolescents over a period of years or by comparing the brain responses of teenagers to those of adults, researchers are putting together a portrait of adolescence that confirms what many parents have always suspected: adolescents might as well be a whole different species. They are, as one neuroscientist puts it, a "work-in-progress."

"Adolescents might as well be a whole different species."

4   Over the past decade, scientists have started to grasp exactly how distinctive the adolescent brain is and how crucial the years between ten and twenty-five are in terms of its development. And their discoveries have wide-ranging implications—for parents, educators, and the medical community but also for policymakers. "I wouldn't disagree with Rob Reiner that the first three years are important," says Jay Giedd, chief of brain imaging in the child-psychiatry branch of the National Institute of Mental Health in Bethesda, Maryland. "I would just say that so are the next three and the next three and the next three, up to twenty-five and perhaps even beyond."

5   This news may not come as a surprise to the mother who still lies awake at 3 a.m., waiting for her basement-dwelling, twenty-two-year-old post-grad son to come home. What science suggests is that "adulthood" as we have defined it doesn't necessarily signal the end of childhood development—or of parental worries. If the media is to be believed, the stereotypical teen is a selfish, volatile, rude, rebellious hormone-head, capable of little more than taking outrageous risks, ingesting too many harmful substances (legal and otherwise), committing crimes, crashing parties, trashing houses, and generally being a layabout. Of course, this is a gross misrepresentation: many teenagers pass through adolescence smoothly and happily, without becoming parents themselves, dropping out of school, or acquiring a criminal record instead of a degree. Still, there's a stubborn tendency in the culture to ascribe every negative teen moment to "hormones." Recent brain research, however, relieves hormones of much of the blame for this period of "storm and stress," as psychologist G. Stanley Hall, father of adolescent research, called it.

6   The full extent to which hormones actually influence adolescent behaviour remains unknown. So is what role they play in brain development. Hormones are certainly responsible for the most obvious hallmarks of puberty; at some mysterious point in a child's life, a protein called kisspeptin causes the hypothalamus—an area in the brain that orchestrates certain autonomic nervous-system functions—to secrete the gonadotropin-releasing hormone, which sets the pubertal changes in motion.

Ultimately, estrogen and testosterone are responsible for the physical transforma-
tions—breast and genital development, body-hair growth, deepening of the voice,
and so on—but by no means all the behavioural changes of adolescence. Hormones
may have nothing to do with the fact that your daughter can't bear your singing voice,
for instance; it's a safe bet, however, that a teenager's fixation on sex and social standing is pretty much hormone-related.

7   But puberty does have an impact on how they think. For instance, as Giedd points
out, boys fairly predictably base their decisions on the question "Will this lead to sex?"
Giedd adds: "They may not say it in that way or it may not be that blatant, but if you
just sort of go with that model it works pretty well." When girls make decisions, he
adds, they are more likely to keep the social group, and their place in it, in mind. But
Giedd feels that puberty's influence doesn't extend much outside that realm. "Your
ability to do a logic problem or to do geometry or to do other things seems to be more
[related to] age itself." Researchers have also found that the onslaught of testosterone
in both male and female adolescents at puberty literally swells the amygdala—the
brain centre associated with the emotions. Perhaps the amygdala is to blame for the
slammed doors and sudden tears that overcome previously sunny children when they
hit adolescence.

8   So hormones are not the only players in the changes that characterize adolescence. And while it is difficult to tease out the varying roles played by chromosomes,
hormones, and other factors in teen behaviour, the insights that MRI reveals are nothing short of astounding.

9   A father compliments his thirteen-year-old daughter on her new dress, only to
have her swivel around, glare at him, and hiss, "What's *that* supposed to mean?"
Nervous parents can rarely tell when an adolescent is going to fly off the handle. Why
do they often have such hair-trigger responses? Two different MRI studies indicate
that teenagers do not process emotion the same way adults do. In fact, one study
shows that the adolescent brain actually reads emotion through a different area of
the brain. Dr. Deborah Yurgelun-Todd, director of neuropsychology and cognitive
neuroimaging at McLean Hospital in Belmont, Massachusetts, has scanned both adults
and teenagers as they were shown images of faces that are clearly expressing fear.
All the adults correctly identified the emotion; many of the teens got it wrong (about
half labeled the expression one of "shock," "sadness," or "confusion"). Yurgelun-
Todd found that during the scan of the adults, both the limbic area of the brain—the
area especially connected to emotions—and the prefrontal cortex, the home of the
so-called "executive functions" such as planning, organization, judgment, impulse
control, and reasoning, lit up. When teens were seeing the same pictures, the limbic
area was bright but there was almost no activity in the prefrontal cortex—the last area
of the brain to mature. They were having an emotional response essentially unmedi-
ated by judgment and reasoning.

10   In another brain-imaging study, Daniel Pine, a researcher at the National Institute of Mental Health, tried to determine how the brain was able to stay focused on a task while the subject was being exposed to faces that were registering strong emotion. The result: activity in the frontal cortex of the adults was steadier, indicating they were better able to stay on task than teenagers. The emotional faces seemed to activate key areas in the brains of both age groups but only the adults were able to mute that activity so they could stay focused. Teenagers are more at the mercy of their feelings. As if having to walk on eggshells weren't enough, there is another fascinating phenomenon that plays havoc with the family of a teen: the adolescent sleep pattern. Suddenly, the kid who always woke the parents up at sunrise, when they were desperate to sleep, turns thirteen or fourteen and can neither be dragged from bed in the morning nor forced into it at night. Making matters worse, this change invariably occurs as the sleep needs of the middle-aged parents are flipping around the other way. It may seem like just another case of teenage passive aggression, but it's actually biology; the circadian rhythm of the brain has changed and teenagers simply don't want to—or can't—go to bed before 12 or 1 a.m.

11   Why this happens has been the focus of some interest. Researchers at Brown University and Bradley Hospital in Providence, Rhode Island, measured the amount of melatonin, the hormone that helps regulate the sleep-wake cycle, in teenagers' saliva over the course of the day. They discovered that the levels of the hormone increased later in the day and decreased later in the morning in teenagers than in adults and children. A separate study indicated that the biological trigger for sleep—called the sleep pressure rate—slowed down during adolescence.

> "Teenagers are chronically sleep-deprived, which can
> have consequences ranging from superficial to severe."

12   So if teenagers appear to be cycling through the day at a different pace from the rest of the world, it's because they are. In fact, because they are waking up when the world dictates—rather than when their bodies tell them to—teenagers are chronically sleep-deprived, which can have consequences ranging from superficial to severe. For starters, as Carlyle Smith, a psychology professor at Trent University in Peterborough, Ontario, who has studied how the adolescent brain processes information during sleep, notes, "They're just sleepy." They go to school tired, unfocused, and—because nobody likes to eat breakfast when they'd rather be sleeping—typically unfed. And as many teachers can attest, teenagers are also generally less able to absorb information in the morning. But by later in the afternoon, as the rest of the world is struggling not to nod off at their desks, teenagers begin to fire on all cylinders. "[As an adult], your temperature is at its high point shortly after lunch," explains Smith, "and then it starts its way down and drops all night until 3 or 4 a.m., when it starts to go up again. Theirs doesn't reach its height until later in the day." As a result, teenagers are just starting to focus and become more verbally adept as the rest of the world is crashing. By

midnight, while the rest of the family is doing its best to fall asleep, teenagers are wide awake and instant messaging away.

13   What is the fallout from a world that runs against the adolescent clock? There are four non-REM stages of sleep, and stages three and four, the deepest, which occur during the first third to first half of the night, are particularly useful to adolescents, who still have those frontal lobes to myelinate—during myelination, neurons, or nerve fibres, are insulated to enhance their performance—and lots of overall growing left to do (growth hormone is released during deep sleep). But because teenagers are so often deprived of REM sleep, which occurs during the last part of the night, their memories can suffer; they lose out on the stage of sleep that sees the information they've absorbed throughout the day replayed and consolidated. "Kids should be getting over nine hours of sleep," says Smith. "Most are getting one to two hours less than they should. They're missing quite a chunk of REM sleep and that's important for understanding new things. If you don't get much REM sleep, you're not going to learn as fast as people who do."

14   In one study, Smith set his subjects, who ranged in age from eighteen to twenty-two, to learning a logic task and then deprived them of the last half of the night of sleep. A week later, after the participants had recovered, the researchers tested them again. All had forgotten between 20 and 30 percent of what they'd learned. Once in a while, this kind of sleep loss is no problem. People can catch up. But when sleep deprivation becomes chronic, the consequences are compounded. "You're forgetting 20 percent, but 20 percent every day," says Smith. "And that goes on for months and months and months. That's an inefficient system."

15   Chronic sleep deprivation also increases the risk of developing depression (though, paradoxically, if someone is already depressed, sleep deprivation tends to help them feel better). This is a particularly serious issue for adolescents, as certain mental-health disorders tend to manifest themselves during these years. "There's so much confusion over this," Smith admits, "but one of the worries is if you just keep on with the sleep deprivation, eventually [that person] will become depressed. And we're seeing a lot more depressed kids around now."

> "Chronic sleep deprivation also increases the risk of developing depression."

16   But it's not easy to fight nature; probably the best thing to do when your own rhythm doesn't fit with the world at large is slow down at a reasonable time in the evening, keep technology out of the bedroom and caffeine to a minimum, and use the weekends for catching up.

17   Most adults remember their own night-owl days. While they might not confess it to their kids, they may have dabbled in a little rule-breaking, underage drinking, and

general wildness as teenagers and now they shudder at the thought of their own children doing the same or worse. They were lucky, but will their kids inherit their luck? (The bad news for former hell raisers: some research suggests a person's tendency to take risks is partly genetic.)

18   In fact, there's some indication that cultivating unhealthy habits through this whole tumultuous period of development can have serious long-term effects. Those who start smoking during adolescence, for example, will likely have a much harder time quitting later in life than those who take up smoking in their twenties; the addiction, according to researchers at Duke University in Durham, North Carolina, appears to get hard-wired during the teen years. Evidence from some studies also suggests that alcohol is more likely to damage memory and learning ability in the hippocampus of the evolving adolescent brain. At the same time, adolescent rats—whose brains are relatively similar to those of adolescent humans—suffer less from some of alcohol's other effects, including sedation. That sounds like a good thing, but if it is indeed true for adolescents (and for obvious ethical reasons researchers don't put adolescents through alcohol-related trials), it means they can drink more, and for longer periods—and therefore run a greater risk of long-term damage. Repeated alcohol use during these years may also lead to lasting memory and learning impairment—not to mention the fact that young binge drinkers are more likely to set themselves up with a lifetime alcohol-abuse problem.

19   This is one area where brain-research findings have affected how Giedd, the father of four, behaves as a parent. "In terms of substance abuse and alcohol, I'm a lot less hip now," he says. "I wouldn't have the mentality of, 'Oh it's better to have them do it at home.' [Adolescence is] a very vulnerable time in brain development to be exposed to these other substances." Giedd is surprised by how many parents say that their kids are going to drink and take drugs anyway, so they might as well do it at home, in a safe environment. "Biologically, it's a time when the cement is setting. If people cannot do these things until the age of nineteen, the odds of them not having trouble as adults go up enormously."

20   But experimenting, taking risks, and searching for good times are, it would seem, all part of the adolescent picture. As difficult as it is for parents to grasp, adolescents don't always make poor choices just to get their goats or because they're suddenly gripped by temporary insanity. This sort of behaviour appears to be a predictable part of the identity-formation process, which begins in the early years but dramatically accelerates during adolescence. That's when children begin playing different roles, trying on different hats, figuring out if they're gay, straight, or bisexual, whether they're a geek, a jock, or cool. At the same time, their frontal lobes aren't fully developed, which means that the appetite for experimentation doesn't necessarily go hand in hand with the capacity to make sound judgments or to see into the not-so-distant future. In other words, by their very nature, teenagers are not especially focused on, or equipped to assess, the consequences of their actions.

21   A 2004 MRI study suggested that adolescent brains are less active than those of adults in regions that motivate reward-based behaviour. James Bjork, a neuroscientist at the National Institute on Alcohol Abuse and Alcoholism, and his colleagues conducted a brain scan on twelve adolescents between the ages of twelve and seventeen and a dozen adults aged twenty-two to twenty-eight. During the scan, the participants responded to targets on a screen by pressing a button; the object was to win (or avoid losing) varying amounts of money. The researchers found that areas of the brain associated with seeking gain lit up in both age groups. But in the adolescents, there was less activity. Adults, says Bjork, may have developed circuitry that enables them to motivate themselves to earn relatively modest rewards—the satisfaction felt after volunteering at church, say, or walking through a ravine. Adolescents, on the other hand, "may need activities that either have a very high thrill payoff or reduced effort requirement or a combination of the two." Examples, he adds, would be "sitting on the couch playing violent video games or sitting on the couch and pounding alcohol."

22   Even if, in quiet conversation, teenagers understand the risks of certain actions—drinking and driving, sex without protection, jumping off cliffs—when the moment of truth actually arrives, reason can be shot to hell. In the heat of the moment, the limbic area of the brain lights up like a pinball machine while the prefrontal cortex, the good angel that tamps down intense feeling and helps us navigate through emotional situations, is essentially asleep. In addition, experts have found that teenagers have a higher level of dopamine, a neurotransmitter connected to pleasure, movement, and sexual desire, which may increase the need for extra stimulation through risk-taking.

23   Some teenagers slide through adolescence unscathed. But there's no doubt that adolescents in the throes of hormone surges and brain development are extremely vulnerable—to making poor choices, to mental-health problems, to death and injury. A quick look at the statistics paints a troubling picture. According to Statistics Canada, adolescents between fourteen and nineteen are more likely to commit property crimes and violent offences than any other age group; 25 percent of teenagers reported binge drinking at least once a month in 2000–2001, a rate second only to the twenty- to thirty-four-year-olds. During that same period, the pregnancy rate for girls between fifteen and nineteen was thirty-six out of 1,000. Most discouraging is the suicide rate for teenagers: currently about eighteen for every 100,000, with the highest rate occurring among teenaged boys (although girls are hospitalized for attempted suicide at a far greater rate than boys). In fact, the three leading causes of death for teenagers in North America are accidents, suicide, and homicide.

24   Unsurprisingly, the majority of accidents involve motor vehicles; in 2004, in the United States, about 20 percent of accidents that resulted in fatalities were due to a driver who had a high blood-alcohol level. According to the Insurance Institute for Highway Safety, injuries suffered by teenagers in car crashes have become a pressing public-health problem. Sixty-two percent of teenage passenger deaths in 2004

occurred when another teenager was driving. And teenage drivers are more likely to be at fault in crashes.

"Teenage drivers are more likely to be at fault in crashes."

25   All of which is not going to make parents sleep any better—if indeed they can get to sleep in the first place. Teenage speeding, irresponsibility, and status-seeking are not the only explanations for the statistics (though teenagers have been shown to take greater risks behind the wheel when their friends are with them). In fact, they also appear to be at a disadvantage because they have not refined the ability to multi-task—driving while drinking a beverage, listening to music, talking on a cellphone, or even chatting with a passenger. One sensible response to this, according to many scientists and policy-makers, is graduated licensing, which is already in place everywhere in Canada except Nunavut. In 1996, many American states started to introduce some aspects of graduated licensing, and according to a 2003 report in the *Journal of Safety Research*, they have seen a decrease in crash rates.

26   So if adolescents are a work-in-progress in terms of judgment, should they be held accountable for their crimes in the same way adults are? Recent adolescent brain-development research was used in arguments against the juvenile death penalty in the United States. If adolescents aren't yet fully capable of controlling their emotional responses or understanding the consequences of their actions, groups like the International Justice Project said, then they should not be punishable by death. In March 2005, when the US Supreme Court finally abolished the juvenile death penalty, there were seventy-three people on death rows across the United States for crimes they had committed before the age of eighteen. Many brain researchers believe that science should be part of the debate. But, Giedd adds, "it becomes a very slippery slope: the same data that might support abolishing the juvenile death penalty could be used to take away teenagers' ability to make their own reproductive-rights decisions."

27   Despite these new findings, has brain science told us anything we don't already know? Bjork's answer: "As Jay Giedd says, a lot of what we're finding out in brain research is the neuroanatomical, neurometabolic correlate of what grandma always told you." Indeed, brain mapping has provided proof of a neurological and biological basis for what sometimes ails the still-forming adult (and the adults who love and live with them).

28   One task for scientists is to determine which things in a teenager's environment and experience will, for better or worse, influence brain development. "So many things have already been put forward—music, education in general, learning a second language, bacteria, viruses, video games, diet, sleep, exercise," says Giedd, "and all of them are probably true to some extent."

29   But what the general culture has to offer to teenagers is only one part of the equation. The brain has always been built for learning by example and experience—which experiences lead to pain, which lead to good outcomes. And for Giedd, that

facility is what will give adolescents the best chance to grow up well—the ability to learn from the people around them. "It's the little things, the day-to-day things that we say in the car or when we're solving problems, how we handle relationships, emotions, our work ethic," he says. "They will believe much more what we *do* than what we tell them."

30   In fact, if there is anything parents can take away from all the scientific research into adolescent brain development, it's that their influence, patience, understanding, and guidance are very necessary—even when the teenager or young adult shrinks away from affection, grunts, slams doors, blasts music, rolls eyes, breaks house rules, and seems incapable of following simple instructions. Developing brains often can't handle organizational problems; they have more trouble making social, political, and moral judgments; they have to be reminded of potential consequences and carefully directed toward risks that aren't quite so, well, risky. Developing adults need appropriate amounts of independence, freedom, and responsibility.

31   "I would say with a clear conscience that the teen brain is different than the adult brain," says Giedd. "Just as I would feel comfortable saying men are taller than women." We ignore those differences at our peril, he adds. Teenagers may drive the family car, move away from home, go to college, and spend their early twenties wrestling with life decisions, all of which are a normal part of growing up. But as Giedd says, just because adolescents have left childhood behind, "parents shouldn't say, 'My work is done.'"

Reading Closely and Thinking Critically

1. Should the fact that their brains don't give teenagers all the information they need about feelings and consequences absolve them of emotional thunderstorms and risk-taking behaviour? If so, how far should that absolution go?
2. Find an example where Underwood reasons from a known effect to a cause and one where she reasons from a cause to an effect.
3. In paragraph 19, Underwood discusses the fact that smoking and drinking can have long-term effects; teenagers who smoke find it harder to quit and those who binge drink are more likely to have lifelong alcohol-abuse problems. Knowing this, what advice would you give parents? What advice would you give younger siblings?
4. How would you suggest adolescents resolve the conflict between trying to understand who they are and their place in the world and the tendency to experiment and rebel that goes along with this quest?
5. Does Underwood's essay motivate you to change any of your own behaviours? Why or why not?

Examining Structure and Strategy

1. Underwood is dealing with the unfamiliar. What are the pre-frontal cortex and the amygdala? How does she structure her essay to help you manage all the unfamiliar material? Do you sometimes wish for more information?
2. Could you add headings to this essay, the way Bruce Mau has done in the next reading? Would they be helpful?

3. In paragraph 5, Underwood paints a picture of the media's representation of a stereotypical teen. To what extent is her depiction accurate? What's her purpose in creating such a composite of risky and annoying teen behaviours? Did it alienate you as a reader? Why or why not?

Considering Language and Style

1. Underwood's style is pretty matter-of-fact; she doesn't use language in a way that alerts the reader to her attitudes about teenagers or magnetic resonance imaging. (See Kearns, "How Men Choose Women," page 256, for an essay that uses a more personal tone.) Try to find several reasons Underwood's style is appropriate in this context.
2. If Underwood is writing for a young audience—like you—should she try to sound more hip? Why or why not?
3. Find the original version of this essay, which was written for parents, and consider some of the changes Underwood has made. What changes would have made it even more appropriate for a young audience?
4. Underwood's writing is more colourful in paragraph 22, when she describes how even sensible teenagers can behave unpredictably "in the heat of the moment." She writes that "the limbic area of the brain lights up like a pinball machine while the prefrontal cortex, the good angel that tamps down intense feeling and helps us navigate through emotional situations, is essentially asleep." Is this moment of colour appropriate? Would you have wished for more colourful writing or would such strategies undermine her authority? How do you resolve the conflict between the temptation to entertain a bored professor who is marking 50 essays and the desire to have a voice that's credible?

For Discussion in Class or Online

What kinds of things did you do as a teenager (or what kinds of things are you *still* doing) that might have their source in an undeveloped teenage brain? Did you feel as if you weren't on the same planet as your parents or older siblings? If your instructor so directs, post your responses on your class Web site.

Writing Assignments

1. **In your journal.** Using Underwood's epigraph as a point of departure, consider the "suffering" of adolescence. What are the main causes of this suffering? The most significant effects? Is there anything parents can do to help?
2. **Using cause-and-effect analysis for a purpose.** The purposes in the assignments are possibilities. You may establish whatever purposes you like, within your instructor's guidelines.
   - To entertain your reader, explain the reasonable causes of some of your more "out there" behaviour.
   - To express feelings, consider those moments in your earlier years when you didn't understand the powerful feelings that seemed to take control of you. What caused them? What effects did they have on others?
   - To inform your reader, use a narrative to explain the complex causes of a social problem, like homelessness, pathological gambling, or alcoholism,
   - To persuade your reader, begin with what you now know about one facet of the teenage brain and the resulting behaviour. Then argue for a change that might ameliorate it. Should high schools start their day at 10 a.m.? Should people not be eligible for a driver's licence until they are 20? Should your campus pub be better at checking ID and making sure its patrons are old enough to drink legally?
3. **Combining patterns.** Write a narrative that describes some typically teenage behaviour you engaged in, one that gives your reader some sympathy with the feelings that led to your actions. Then use Underwood's explanations of the structure of the teenage brain to explain your actions.

4. **Connecting the readings.** How does Underwood's discussion of the teenage brain help to explain the experience of Brad Whetstine in "Augustinian Influences" (page 482)? Although Whetstine credits watching the movie *Lonesome Dove* with his decision to enter university, how might the maturity of his brain also explain this change in his life?

5. **Drawing on sources.** We know shockingly little about the brain. We are, however, learning about some of the chemicals that shape our moods and behaviour. Choose an affective or behavioural problem like drug addiction or depression, and learn about its roots in the brain and its biochemical stew. Alternatively, you can choose to research the reasons that some individuals excel at what others struggle to understand—like higher mathematics or poetry. How is the structure of the brain implicated in these profound differences in ability?

Background

Canadian designer Bruce Mau was born in Sudbury, Ontario. He began his studies at the Ontario College of Art and Design, but left them unfinished to pursue opportunities in Britain before returning to Toronto. While he has one foot in the world of the university and the art gallery, acting as a professor at Rice University and a visiting scholar at the Getty Institute of Research in Los Angeles, his other foot is firmly planted in organizations that use the potential of design to address global problems. His Toronto-based Bruce Mau Design is an interdisciplinary design studio whose mandate is to help people "design the change they want to see in the world." He won the Chrysler Award for Design Innovation in 1998, and the Toronto Arts Award for Architecture and Design in 1999. His project Massive Change is a collaboration between Bruce Mau Design and the Institute without Borders, an interdisciplinary design program at Brown College. The mandate of Massive Change is to explore "the legacy and potential, the promise and power of design in improving the welfare of humanity" by researching "the capacities and limitations of human efforts to change the world for the better" (Massive Change Web site).

Combined Patterns and Their Purposes

In "Imagining the Future," Mau follows two causal threads. One considers the way "design," broadly conceived, has improved the lives of nearly everyone on the planet. The other concerns the way in which continuing improvement is threatened by the media's representation of global conditions; when people are pessimistic, "they circle their wagons, hunker down, and close the border. They move to gated communities in their cities and in their hearts. They take what they can get while they can still get it." Optimism, unlike cynicism, creates hope and possibilities. Mau uses the contrast pattern to consider these two options. Part of being optimistic involves redefining progress to include our commitments to a better world, redefining design as an "art that is charged with looking forward," and redefining wealth to include "freedom, education, literacy, mobility, human rights."

Imagining the Future
Bruce Mau

As you read
Think about what makes you feel optimistic or pessimistic about the age we're living through.

1   Let me begin with an admission. I am a designer, which means I cannot afford the luxury of cynicism. Designers are called upon to come up with solutions to problems of every imaginable description, from designing a machine to provide kidney dialysis at home to creating an interface for complex critical systems like air-traffic control. No matter what the specific nature of a project—whether it's a park or a product, a book or a business—optimism is always central to my work. It's as important to what I do as research tools, computer systems, or a sense of colour.

2   Three years ago, the Vancouver Art Gallery invited me to produce a major exhibition on the future of design. They had no fixed ideas as to what that might mean, except for the scale; they wanted something that would mark a significant commitment by their museum to the design field.

3   My first impulse was to say no. To discover what is happening in design around the world and to explore its potential across all the disciplines seemed too daunting.

Besides, I was happily working on a full slate of projects that were already very demanding and personally rewarding.

4   But something was irritating me. There was something floating around in our culture that I found deeply troubling. It got under my skin until it became an itch I had to scratch. There seemed to be a growing split between reality and mood, a conflict between what is actually happening in the world—what we are capable of, what we are committed to, what we are achieving—and our perception of how we're doing. The prevailing mood feels dark, negative, harrowingly pessimistic, and tending to the cynical. Bizarrely, this kind of negativity has become the vogue even in creative fields, which are traditionally committed to vision, beauty, and pleasure, to notions of utopia—to possibility, in other words. This is especially true in design. How, I wondered, had the virus of pessimism crept into the one area of art that is charged with looking forward?

> "There was something floating around in our
> culture that I found deeply troubling."

5   First and foremost, design is committed to a better, smarter future. It's the art form pragmatically focused on finding solutions for how we live in the world. But it seems we have mistakenly conflated the word "critical" with the word "negative" and embraced a cynical perspective. Art speaks mostly in dystopian terms, while business is charged with envisioning our future. Today the talent to make beautiful paintings is a bus pass to the suburbs of art discourse; cranky architects scowl from magazine covers and moan, absurdly, about their powerlessness. Gloom and doom are everywhere.

6   These days, to express optimism in educated company suggests that you are either wilfully ignorant of the facts or simply a fool. To be serious, to be critical, to have a voice, we have to be cynical. To strive for something—something better—is a Pollyanna project for the naive.

7   In stark contrast to this prevailing wind of negativity, the experience of the team that worked with me on Massive Change (as the Vancouver project came to be called) was quite the opposite. In the face of global challenges—and there are many of unprecedented seriousness, from the AIDS disaster in Africa to the environmental impact of our growing population—we nevertheless witnessed action coming to bear on almost every significant problem. We saw new possibilities in collaboration and connectedness, which, along with the Internet, would allow designers around the world to draw on knowledge and expertise that had never before been accessible.

8   My experience with this project has been delightful, with one startling exception: I discovered how controversial optimism can be.

THE CASE FOR OPTIMISM

9   Despite our collective despondency, we live in a time when more people are richer, healthier, better educated, more literate, and more productive. We live longer, travel more, and enjoy greater access to knowledge and freedom than at any other

time in human history. Worldwide, we now number more than six billion people—partly because we are able, with varying degrees of success, to sustain that number. We have beaten back the Malthusians.

10   And there are other victories worth noting.

WE HAVE BEATEN BACK HUNGER

11   Through ongoing innovations in agriculture and the development of crops that produce a higher yield—India has become a net exporter of rice, for instance—we are feeding more people. Not the whole world, it must be said, but we have come a long way. According to a 2004 report from the United Nations, more than thirty countries reduced the number of hungry people by at least 25 percent during the 1990s.

WE HAVE BEATEN BACK DISEASE

12   I don't want to sound overly optimistic here. AIDS continues to ravage Africa, and until we find ways to deal with that tragedy, a deep shadow will haunt our future. However, there is a genuine commitment to finding a cure for big killers like malaria and dysentery. In the past, a disease like SARS in China, Hong Kong, and Toronto would have wiped out tens or even hundreds of thousands of people. It didn't. Because we collaborated globally to fight SARS, we lost only hundreds.

WE HAVE BEATEN BACK CHILD MORTALITY

13   Since the sixties, we have halved the rates of child mortality for most of the developing world, including China, India, and Brazil, and at the same time we have increased global life expectancy by seventeen years. The average number of children per woman in most of the developing world has gone from more than five to fewer than four, while child mortality in some countries has gone from between 10 and 40 percent of the population under five to less than 10 percent. According to *Gapminder. org*, "Today most countries in Asia, Latin America, and the Arab world have small families and infant mortality is low. We now have a completely different world!"

> "If you want to do something for the
> environment, educate and liberate women."

14   Related to this shift is the changing role of women. In a conversation I had with E.O. Wilson, the author of *The Future of Life*, he said, "If you want to do something for the environment, educate and liberate women," because "when women are educated and liberated, the birth rate declines." The statistics suggest that this is exactly what is happening.

WE HAVE BEATEN BACK DEATH

15   Not literally, of course. I am not that optimistic! But for most of recorded history, life expectancy hovered around thirty years. Many died in infancy. If we survived,

we married young, and died young. Even by the end of the nineteenth century, life expectancy was just over thirty-two years. Today, average life expectancy worldwide is now sixty-five years.

16   One way to measure global progress is through the United Nations Human Development Index. The HDI measures a basket of factors including life expectancy, school enrolment, adult literacy, and gross domestic product per capita. Taken together, these offer a useful portrait of the development of a society and its ability to meet the needs of its citizens.

17   Looking at human development around the world since 1975, it is striking to see that with few exceptions the trends are all positive. Not only do the United States, Canada, and other Western nations show steady improvement, but more recently countries like India, China, and Brazil are moving in the same direction. With the glaring exception of Africa, we are moving to a more developed world. Of the thirty-two countries still classified as low development, with an HDI of less than 0.5, thirty are in Africa. But public awareness of Africa's situation is at least on an upward swing, a dramatic change in its long and tortured history with the West.

18   Another way to consider progress is to look at our commitment to reach certain objectives. At the Millennium Summit in September 2000, 189 countries adopted a global to-do list. The eight goals are to eradicate extreme poverty and hunger; achieve universal primary education; promote gender equality and the empowerment of women; reduce child mortality by two-thirds; improve maternal health; combat HIV/ AIDS, malaria, and other diseases; ensure environmental sustainability; and cultivate a global partnership for development. The fact that we have come together to articulate these goals, and committed ourselves to meeting them, gives a sense of the true nature of our human project.

19   Are we on target to get through the list by the deadline of 2015? No. Are some places getting worse, not better? Certainly, but very few. Are some developed countries negligent in meeting their obligations? Yes. But are we making progress? Absolutely. We may be behind schedule but we are mostly moving forward. For instance, based on current trends, child mortality rates will be 15 percent lower in 2015 than they were in 1990. If the trend continues, we won't meet the Millennium goal until 2045. Thirty years late—but still a staggering human accomplishment, made possible by collective global collaboration.

20   Another way of measuring progress is to look at not only what we have defeated but what we have embraced. We have embraced wealth in all of its dimensions. In fact, one accomplishment of Massive Change was to reconfigure notions of wealth to include freedom, education, literacy, mobility, human rights, health, sanitation, communication, collaboration, science, technology, knowledge, and now, increasingly, sustainability.

21   To a large degree, the greatest challenge we face as a global culture—sustainability—is a consequence of our great success. We are six billion people today, not

because we have failed in designing solutions to the problems we have faced, but because we have overcome many of the worst problems afflicting people around the world.

CIRCLING THE WAGONS

22   In the course of our work on Massive Change, we met an extraordinary man named Stewart Brand. An innovator and entrepreneur, he was the founder of *Whole Earth Catalog*, a countercultural landmark in the late sixties and early seventies. He led a campaign to convince NASA to make a photograph of the Earth from space, an image that has become a defining icon of our age.

23   Brand is also a founder of The Long Now Foundation, an effort to expand our cultural time horizon from the next fiscal quarter to the long term. He believes that when people think things are bad and getting worse, they do the usual things people do to protect themselves: They circle their wagons, hunker down, and close the border. They move to gated communities in their cities and in their hearts. They take what they can get while they can still get it.

24   However, if they come to understand that things are improving—that we are working together to make things better—they will invest in their communities and their businesses, in their children and their family, in their culture and education. They will do so because once they discover that things are actually getting better, enlightened self-interest will make them want to be part of the improvement.

25   I think we have been missing something quite important in assessing where we really stand, and this gap limits our forward momentum. We have been missing it because the old politics of Left versus Right are no longer relevant or helpful. A more collaborative approach is emerging. Rather than seeing things in terms of Left or Right, this approach seeks indicators of social and economic progress along a continuum running from retrograde to advanced.

26   To grasp the approach, think of an image whose pixels have been distributed to a million citizens worldwide. It is an image of collaboration, shared problem-solving, accessibility, and collective enterprise. It is a complex and beautiful image, perhaps the most beautiful image of all time. In contrast, our understanding of the world is driven by a media culture obsessed with violence and conflict. The tenor is one of negativity and crisis, which translates into pessimism and cynicism, and from there to apathy and paralysis. This negative world view can erode human agency—and without that, we're basically sunk.

27   As a global culture we are beginning to outgrow polarized and binary divisions but we still confuse the media with reality. If we were to publish a newspaper called *Reality*, it would be a mile thick. The first quarter-inch would arrive on your doorstep, scare the hell out of you, push the worst of human possibility into your world, make you want to lock your doors, inhibit your impulse toward community, and drive you to xenophobia, resentful and fearful of all the violent others determined to ruin your

life. The rest of the mile of newspaper—the reality of our world, the part that never gets published—would be Massive Change, the story of how millions of people from every part of the world are working together to confront the dilemmas we face as a global society.

28   The media is our siren and our lullaby. In a neverending cycle, it shakes us up, alerts us to danger, then puts us back to sleep, reassured that someone else is taking care of things.

> "We have the power to make change on a global scale, to solve the problems we are facing today."

29   But what we need to be reminded of is our own potential. We have the power to make change on a global scale, to solve the problems we are facing today. We have the means to make the things we love more intelligent and more delightful. We have the imagination and the ability to invent new ways of sustainable living in advanced, courageous, and open societies.

30   All we need is the optimism to realize it.

Reading Closely and Thinking Critically

1. Mau suggests in paragraph 4 that there is a "split between reality and mood, a conflict between what is actually happening in the world . . . and our perception of how we're doing." How does he explain that split? Do you think there are other explanations?
2. Mau has facts to back his argument. In paragraphs 11 through 15, he provides a brief sketch of the ways the world has improved. How do you explain the headlines in your newspaper?
3. In paragraph 18, Mau suggests that "another way to consider progress is to look at our commitment to reach certain objectives." Are intentions enough? Do you believe they will lead to actions? Is he being too optimistic here?
4. What are the benefits of redefining progress and wealth?
5. Does the world need a Long Now Foundation? What evidence do you see around you of people's inability to consider the consequences of actions and choices beyond the next day—or even the next few minutes?
6. Mau more or less sums up his argument in paragraph 26, where he describes the following causal chain: a media culture obsessed with violence and conflict leads to pessimism and cynicism, which in turn erodes a sense of human agency, producing apathy and paralysis. How compelling do you find this argument?

Examining Structure and Strategy

1. While Mau is largely optimistic, he is occasionally quite blunt about what remains to be done. In paragraph 12, he admits that AIDS is a "deep shadow," particularly in Africa. In paragraph 17, he admits that Africa is a "glaring exception" to the world's tendency to move forward. Consider how he manages to acknowledge the challenges while keeping our attention on human potential.
2. A classic persuasive strategy is to use what is termed a "concession statement," which concedes the opposing argument in a subordinate clause while presenting your own position in a main clause. How

does this rhetorical strategy keep control of the writer's emphasis while still being honest about the complexities of the argument?

Considering Language and Style

1. Why does Mau begin his essay by admitting that, as a designer, he's by definition an optimist? How do his examples of what designers do place that assertion in a particular context?
2. Google the phrase "enlightened self-interest." How is Mau tapping into the long history of this phrase? Do you think people really act with enlightened self-interest in mind?
3. In paragraph 26, Mau uses an analogy to explain how he sees retrograde and advanced thinking. He compares advanced thinking to a distribution of pixels of an image worldwide. What do you think he means by this? What *practical* actions does this suggest?

For Discussion in Class or Online

In paragraph 4, Mau tells the reader that he decided to undertake the major exhibition on the future of design because "something was irritating me." Consider times when you have solved an important problem—whether it's the interpretation of a poem or the resolution of a conflict—because something was irritating you. If your instructor so directs, post your responses on your class Web site.

Writing Assignments

1. **In your journal.** What's the hardest thing you ever tried to change about yourself or the people around you? What was the cause of the difficulty?
2. **Using cause-and-effect analysis for a purpose.** The purposes in the assignments are possibilities. You may establish whatever purposes you like, within your instructor's guidelines.
   - To entertain and to persuade your reader, describe the effects of instant messaging on your writing skills.
   - Google the Long Now Foundation, which is dedicated to counteracting our tendency to live for the next five minutes. To inform your reader, consider the causes of this mindset. What are its effects?
   - To persuade and inform your reader, describe how making a few changes in their lifestyles or attitudes could have a lasting effect on the planet or on the human condition.
3. **Combining patterns.** To illustrate how improvements in women's rights and economic status affect their community, write a narrative about a woman whose accomplishments improved the conditions of her entire family or community.
4. **Connecting the readings.** Since the 1960s, teens have been an economic force in Western society. They both drive market niches and critique the culture adults have handed down to them. Consider the teen brain as described in "The Teenage Brain" (page 327) and what it might bring to a critique of culture that's distinctive to addressing the problems Mau identifies.
5. **Drawing on sources.** There has been a recent controversy about the value of happiness. While self-help books like *The How of Happiness* continue to be published, others think that some dissatisfaction with our lives or our world is necessary to motivate us to undertake and accept change. Using Mau's essay and a current book on happiness, consider how both critical and positive attitudes are important forces for change. It would be helpful to focus on a particular change, like the status of women in developing countries or environmental change here in Canada.

Background

James Surowiecki is the financial columnist for *The New Yorker* and a regular contributor to other publications, including *Salon* and *New York* magazine. He has written on a variety of financial and business topics, including bank mergers, the stock market, and the music industry. He has also edited *Best Crime Writing of the Year* (2002) and written *The Wisdom of Crowds: Why the Many Are Smarter Than the Few and How Collective Wisdom Shapes Business, Economies, Societies, and Nations* (2004). "Paying to Play" first appeared in *The New Yorker* (2004).

Combined Patterns and Their Purposes

Hundreds of CDs come out each week, and radio stations cannot possibly play them all. Using cause-and-effect analysis and exemplification, James Surowiecki informs the reader about one way stations decide what to play: Music publishers buy air time for their recordings. Surowiecki also has a persuasive purpose, as he aims to convince the reader (in part, with comparison-contrast) that pay-for-play is a flawed system.

Paying to Play
James Surowiecki

1   Pop music thrives on repetition. You know a song's a hit when you've heard it so often that you'll be happy never to hear it again. Even by Top 40 standards, though, the play list adopted a few weeks ago by the Nashville radio station WQZQ was extreme. On May 23rd, *Billboard*[1] reported, the station played "Don't Tell Me," the new single by Avril Lavigne, three times an hour, every hour, between midnight and 6 A.M. This didn't have much to do with the tastes of WQZQ's d.j.s or listeners. Instead, an independent promoter working for Lavigne's record label had effectively paid the station to play the song. "Don't Tell Me" had been hovering just outside *Billboard's* list of the country's ten most frequently played songs, which radio programmers use to decide what singles get airtime. The extra spins the promoter bought—sometimes called "spot buys," because what's really being bought are blocks of ad time, as with an infomercial—were meant to bump "Don't Tell Me" up the list. By early June, Lavigne had a Top 10 hit.

> *As you read*
> Pay attention to how the author achieves coherence in the essay.

> "By early June, Lavigne had a Top 10 hit. She also
> had a lot of angry music fans to contend with."

2   She also had a lot of angry music fans to contend with. Spot buys may be legal, but to most people they're the "new payola," a modern-day equivalent of Alan Freed's[2]

---

[1] *Billboard* is an international news weekly about the music industry. Among its features are charts of music sales and airplay.

[2] Alan Freed (1922–1965) was a disc jockey and rock-and-roll promoter. In 1962, he plead guilty to accepting money to play records. Some say he was a scapegoat, punished because he played records by black artists for white audiences.

taking money under the table to play rock-and-roll records. (Freed called the pay-ments "consulting fees.") It's an obvious comparison, but a misplaced one. Spot buys aren't the same as old-fashioned payola. They're worse.

3   "Payola" became a household word in the fifties, when a host of d.j.s were found to be playing songs in exchange for favors and money, but the practice is as old as pop music itself. A century ago, songwriters routinely paid vaudeville singers to perform their tunes, hoping to goose demand for sheet music. In the thirties, music publishers paid off radio bandleaders. And although some forms of payola were outlawed after the mid-century scandals, various loopholes allowed other incarnations to thrive, under the guise of independent promotion. With money from the record companies, promoters used oblique tactics—subsidies, gifts, "research funds"—to encourage radio stations to add new singles to their playlists. By 2000, tens of millions of dollars a year were being spent on what you might call legal payola, and although bad publicity has severely cur-tailed the promotion business, paying to play is still integral to the way radio works.

4   Despite its sleazy reputation, payola has a certain rationale. In a typical year, upward of seven or eight hundred CDs are issued each week. Not even the most dedicated program director can hope to sift through all the new songs. So stations need a way to filter the possible hits from the certain bombs. Pay-for-play schemes provide one rough-and-ready way to do this, because they involve what economists call signalling. By putting money behind a record, a label signals its belief that the record has a chance to be a hit; no company will spend a lot of money trying to sell something it doesn't have high hopes for. And hits, of course, are the only thing that radio cares about.

"And hits, of course, are the only thing that radio cares about."

5   You can see the same process at work in many other businesses, too. Supermarkets and drugstores accept billions of dollars a year in "slotting fees" to position products at the end of an aisle or at eye level. Book chains sell space on the tables at the front of their stores. And record stores accept advertising dollars from labels to push certain albums. Here, too, being willing to shell out for a good space on the shelf is a state-ment about how much you think people will want your product.

6   This is, at best, a flawed way to find hits. Unless a record label has a good sense of what people want to hear, it could be buying airtime for flops. And labels that don't have the cash to promote their records are out of luck. But the surprising truth is that, historically speaking, payola has often fostered musical diversity, rather than squelch-ing it. In the fifties, the music industry was dominated by a few giant labels, much as it is today; because of payola (and payola-takers, like Alan Freed), the smaller labels that revolutionized the industry—including Atlantic, Chess, and King Records—were able to get their music on the air. In retail, too, paying for space hasn't necessarily hindered innovation. Even as slotting fees have become more common in supermarkets, for instance, the number of new products that reach the shelves each year has exploded.

And the same is true with books. We tend to assume that payola favors the big play-ers because they are the ones with the big money. But the big players also have big sales forces, big brand names, and big connections. They'd win without having to ante up to get in on the action. Paying to play, then, creates a rough marketplace democ-racy: if you can come up with the cash, you get a shot. But that's all. Labels can buy themselves exposure; they can't buy themselves a hit. If people don't want to hear a record, radio stations won't keep playing it of their own accord.

7   And that's where spot buys come in. Unlike conventional pay-for-play deals, spot buys like the one that propelled Avril Lavigne into the Top 10 aren't meant to introduce listeners to songs; they're meant to game the playlist system. It's a salient feature of modern media that being thought to be popular can make you more popu-lar. Best-selling books and records are discounted more than slow-selling ones and are positioned more prominently. Songs in *Billboard's* Top 10 automatically end up being spun more. And if you invest lots of money in creating an illusion of popularity—by, say, buying hours of airplay on the radio— you may end up making yourself more pop-ular. In the process, what real listeners want matters less than it ever did. In "Payola Blues," Neil Young sang to Alan Freed, "The things they're doing today / Will make a saint out of you." He didn't know the half of it.

Reading Closely and Thinking Critically
1. What is the thesis of the essay?
2. Why does Surowiecki believe that spot buys are worse than payola? Do you agree? Why or why not?
3. What are the negative effects of pay-for-play?
4. Do you think record sales would decline if more people knew about pay-for-play? Why or why not?

Examining Structure and Strategy
1. What approach does Surowiecki use for his introduction? Why does he use this approach?
2. In paragraph 3, Surowiecki gives the history of pay-for-play. Why does he include this information? How does it help him achieve his purpose for writing?
3. Which paragraphs have topic sentences that introduce a discussion of a cause or effect of pay-for-play?
4. How does Surowiecki achieve coherence between paragraphs 1 and 2? Between paragraphs 2 and 3? Between paragraphs 3 and 4? Between paragraphs 4 and 5? (See page 75 on coherence.)
5. How does the repetition of *Avril Lavigne* in the conclusion help achieve coherence?

Noting Combined Patterns
1. How does Surowiecki use comparison-contrast to help achieve his writing purpose?
2. Why does Surowiecki compare spot buying of radio time to paying slotting fees in retail stores?
3. The opening paragraph includes an extended example, and examples appear in paragraphs 3, 5, and 6. How does this exemplification help the author achieve his writing purpose?

Considering Language and Style
1. In paragraph 6, Surowiecki says that paying to play creates a "marketplace democracy." In your opinion, is this phrase accurate? Why or why not?

2. Surowiecki uses informal language, including "goose" (paragraph 3), "shell out" (paragraph 5), and "game the playlist" (paragraph 7). What effect does this informal usage create? Is the informal usage appropriate? Explain.
3. Consult a dictionary if you do not know the meaning of any of these words and phrases: *under-the-table* (paragraph 2), *incarnations* (paragraph 3), *guise* (paragraph 3), *salient* (paragraph 7).

For Discussion in Class or Online

Is signalling (paragraph 4) a valid way to filter "possible hits from the certain bombs"? Why or why not? Can you think of a better alternative to signalling and pay-for-play? If your instructor so directs, post your response on your class Web site.

Writing Assignments

1. **In your journal.** What do you think of the manipulation of the marketplace revealed in the essay? In what other ways are consumers' choices and preferences manipulated? Who benefits, and how does that make you feel? Answer one or more of these questions in a page or so.
2. **Using cause-and-effect analysis for a purpose.** The purposes in the assignments are possibilities. You may establish whatever purposes you like, within your instructor's guidelines.
   - To express your feelings and inform, explain what causes you to like one of the following: a song, a movie, a television show, a video game, a music video, or a book. How much of the title's appeal is the result of how often you see or hear it?
   - Explain why you buy particular items in the grocery store, pharmacy, book store, or from a Web site. Are you influenced by the location of the product in the store or on the Web site? Your purpose can be to inform and perhaps persuade that positioning does or does not influence buyers.
   - To inform and perhaps relate experience, explain the causes and effects of the illusions we create. You can consider such illusions as those we create in chat rooms, on resumés, and in the classroom with such artifices as posturing, lying, makeup, hair dye, wigs, and plastic surgery.
3. **Combining patterns.** In paragraph 7, Surowiecki says that "if you invest lots of money in creating an illusion of popularity . . . you may end up making yourself more popular." Use definition (explained in Chapter 7) to explain what popularity is in a particular context, such as high school, politics, the media, or athletics. In addition, use cause-and-effect analysis to explain how money can create the "illusion of popularity" in that context. You can also use process analysis (explained in Chapter 8) to track the process whereby popularity is achieved.
4. **Connecting the readings.** Surowiecki says that "being thought to be popular can make you more popular" (paragraph 7). Explain what he means and whether or not you agree with him. For ideas, you can draw on your own experience and observation as well as on "Ring Leader" (page 166).
5. **Drawing on sources.** Research the payola scandal of the 1950s and Alan Freed's alleged role in it. Then write a brief summary of what happened. For information, you can type "Alan Freed payola" into your favourite search engine or look up "Alan Freed" and "payola" in *Infotrac* or *Social Sciences Index*.

Additional Essay Assignments

See pages 322 and 324 for strategies for writing cause-and-effect analysis and for a revising checklist.

1. Analyze the effects of the teenage brain on a particular risk-taking behaviour. Are there other contributory causes for the behaviour?
2. Analyze the effects of gender on risk-taking behaviour. What expectations about masculine or feminine qualities or behaviours shape risk-taking behaviour? You might find it productive to focus on a particular behaviour like drinking and driving or participating in extreme sports.
3. Visit the Canadian government's Web site on literacy at www.hrsdc.gc.ca/eng/hip/lld/nls/About/new.shtml. Consider the effects of a program like "Canada Reads" or of workplace training on individuals' literacy. This topic may require you to define literacy before you can discuss it.
4. If you have difficulty with a particular subject (English, math, science, etc.), explain why the subject causes you problems and/or the effect of having difficulty with that subject.
5. Explain the effects on people or society of some aspect of the Internet, such as chat rooms, online shopping, access to information, online gambling, or online games.
6. Explain the techniques television commercials (or magazine ads) use to influence consumers. As an alternative, explain the effects of commercials (or magazine ads) on us.
7. Select a bad habit you have (for example, procrastinating, smoking, overeating, or nail biting) and explain its causes and effects.
8. Select a problem on your campus (for example, inadequate student housing, high tuition, or limited course offerings) and analyze the effects on students to persuade those in authority to remedy the problem.
9. Analyze how the neighbourhood in which you grew up affected you.
10. Explain why students cheat and the effects cheating has on students.
11. If you have a particular fear (of heights, of math, of failure, and so on), explain the causes and/or effects of that fear.
12. Pick a harmless human characteristic or behaviour (for example, checking the alarm even though we know it is set, habitually choosing the wrong bank or supermarket line, losing car keys, and so on). Then write a humorous essay that explains the causes and/or effects of this behaviour or characteristic.
13. Select something inconsequential that Canadians can no longer do, such as cook without a microwave, walk places, or change channels without a remote control. Then write a humorous account of the causes and effects of the "problem."
14. If you ever moved to a new town, explain how the move affected you.
15. If you have children, explain the effects of becoming a parent. If you want, you can make this essay humorous.
16. If you are an international student, explain how you have been affected by living and attending school in this country.
17. Explain why hockey (or football or baseball) is so popular in this country and how the sport affects Canadian culture.
18. Select a person who has had a significant impact on you (for example, a coach, a clergyperson, a teacher, or a friend) and explain the effects this individual has had on you.
19. **Cause-and-effect analysis in context:** Assume you are a member of a consumer affairs panel that has secured a grant to study violence in the media. Write a report that explains why some people enjoy violent movies. Your audience is other members of the panel, and your purpose is to provide them with information.

Chapter 11

Classification and Division

Science is the systematic classification of experience.

— George H. Lewes

Instead of this absurd *division* into sexes they ought to class people as static and dynamic.

— Evelyn Waugh

THE PATTERN

Both classification and division are methods of grouping and ordering. Although both patterns are instances of analysis—dividing something into its components to understand it better—classification and division work quite differently. **Classification** takes a number of items and groups them into categories; **division** takes one entity and breaks it down into its parts. Take people, for example. We are constantly grouping the class we call "people" by gender, age, or race; this is classification. But when we take a single individual, we can only divide that person into his or her constituent parts. We might divide a person according to a number of paradigms. Such schemes for division might include head and heart; body and soul; skeletal system, digestive system, cardiovascular system, muscular system, and nervous system.

You do not have to look very far to find examples of classification. The Yellow Pages of your phone book groups telephone numbers according to the kinds of businesses; your biology textbook classifies animals according to whether they are mammals, reptiles, and so on; your local grocery store arranges items in aisles by classifying them according to whether they are canned goods, cleaning products, pet products, meats, produce, or frozen foods.

Division is also common. The laboratory technician examines your blood by breaking it down into its components and studying each of them (the red cells, the white cells, the plasma, and so on), a movie reviewer evaluates different parts of a film (the actors, the director, the script, the cinematography, and so on); and a real estate appraiser analyzes the separate components of your property (the location, the size, the condition, and so on). When you analyze a story, you divide it into its parts so you can see how the whole works together. Since it's not possible to talk meaningfully about a whole story, you consider character, plot, theme, language, and style. Similarly, you've been analyzing the essays in this book, examining the content and the steps in the argument, the writer's style and how the writer relates to the reader, and the writer's use of words. (As you can see, the pedagogy at the end of each essay reflects these categories of analysis.)

Classification and division are common because they help us order items or pieces of information to study them or to retrieve them more efficiently. Imagine a world without categories or divisions. How hard would it be to locate a book in the library or to study plant and animal life? How would we characterize the neighbourhoods we live in or describe our friends?

Sometimes classification and division are each performed alone, but often they are companion operations performed together for a specific purpose. For example, the manager of a video store can use both classification and division to organize all the tapes and DVDs so customers can locate titles easily. First the manager would use *division* to establish a breakdown into categories or parts, such as westerns, musicals, science fiction, romance, horror films, and adventure movies. Then he or she would use *classification* to sort the videos into the appropriate categories—*Star Wars* into the science fiction area, *Friday the 13th* into the horror movie area, and so on.

USING CLASSIFICATION AND DIVISION FOR A PURPOSE

Writers often classify or divide in order to inform. Sometimes a writer wants to inform a reader of the relative merits of the items classified so the reader can choose one wisely. For example, you can classify various health clubs according to expense and variety of equipment and classes to help exercisers decide which club to join. Sometimes a writer wants to inform a reader of the characteristics of the parts that have been divided. For example, to inform people about how to write grant proposals more successfully, a writer could divide the effective grant proposal into its parts and explain how to write each of those parts. Sometimes a writer classifies or divides to give the reader a fresh appreciation of the familiar. In "White Lies" (page 367), Sissela Bok classifies the variety of white lies in order to help readers more carefully consider them and their moral significance. Sometimes a writer wants to help a reader see the familiar in a new light.

Classification and division can also allow you to express feelings and relate experience. This would be the case if you classified various ways to celebrate Halloween in order to relate your own childhood experiences with the holiday or if you divided your best Halloween celebration into its components.

Very often, classification and division can have a persuasive purpose, as is the case with "The Ways of Meeting Oppression" (page 371). In this essay, Dr. Martin Luther King, Jr., classifies the ways to deal with oppression in order to convince the average reader that one of those ways is more effective than the rest and should be employed.

Finally, classification and division can entertain a reader. For example, to amuse your audience, you could classify all your eccentric relatives according to their funny traits and behaviours, or you could examine your most eccentric relative by dividing that person's behaviour and personality into their most amusing parts.

Classification and division can function alone or with other patterns as well. For example, in an essay explaining the causes and effects of age discrimination in the workplace, you could include a classification of the most common kinds of age discrimination.

Classification and Division at School, at Work, and in the Community

You will have many occasions to use classification and division in your postsecondary classes. For example, in an education class, you may need to divide a lesson plan into its components and explain the characteristics of effective components to demonstrate that you can write a useful plan. Similarly, a business class might require you to note the components of a sound business plan to demonstrate that you could develop such a plan, and a marketing class may require you to give the components of an effective survey to show that you know how to construct one.

At times, you will write classification and division to show that you understand the relative merits and uses of various categories of something. For example, in an advertising class, you could write a paper that classifies the kinds of direct mail campaigns, noting what kind of audience each approach appeals to and what kind of product each approach is best suited for. Such a paper would demonstrate that you knew when to use each kind of campaign.

Perhaps most frequently, you will write classification and division to demonstrate your comprehension of information. This would be the case in a biology class that required you to classify the mating behaviour of birds or in a communications class that required you to divide political rhetoric into its components.

Classification and division are found in many textbooks; these two strategies allow writers to find a systematic way of approaching a large body of material. In the following excerpt from *Canadian Folklore,* Edith Fowke classifies the large body of texts we think of as folklore in order to make its study comprehensible:

> The tales that came to Canada from the Old World fall into the categories that Antii Aarne and Stith Thompson classify in *The Types of the Folktale.* The first group, "Animal Tales," are mainly fables— animal stories used to teach lessons— and stories in which animals take on human characteristics. Apart from Indian legends, few of these have been told in Canada, although Fauset found some among the blacks in Nova Scotia, and a few have come here more recently with immigrants from the West Indies.
>
> In the second and largest group, labelled simply "Ordinary Folktales," most of the plots have supernatural elements. These are what most people think of when folktales are mentioned—the kind of stories that the Germans call *Märchen,* the French *contes populaires,* and the English fairy-tales—although they are better termed wonder tales, for few are about fairies. Some have their roots in a pre-Christian era; most date back hundreds of years; many came originally from the Orient or Egypt; and nearly all have international plots.
>
> Much more common than the wonder tales are "Jokes and Anecdotes," the third of the four Aarne and Thompson types. Where comparatively few tell the old supernatural stories today, practically everyone occasionally tells a joke or anecdotes. The two most common groups are tales of lying and numbskull jokes.
>
> Particularly popular are tales of lying—termed tall tales—that depend on exaggeration for their humour. They are often linked to legendary or semi-legendary characters like Paul Bunyan or Joe Mufferaw, or occasionally to less well-known local characters. Common themes are extraordinary weather, enormous insects, or the fantastic exploits of hunters or fisherman. (Fowke, *Canadian Folklore* 26–27)

Outlining that you do for any writing, no matter where it occurs, involves classification and division because you divide your topic into ideas and group those ideas together according to the point they develop. In addition, when you write to-do lists, whether at home, at school, or at work, you engage in classification and division if you divide your tasks into their parts and then group the parts according to their deadlines and importance so you can decide how to proceed.

On the job, classification and division are essential. For example, to develop a solid business plan, you must group elements of the plan according to categories such as marketing, acquisition of capital, management structure, and growth potential. You may need to classify kinds of customer-incentive programs or group insurance plans to decide which one to use. Even before you get your job, you use classification and division to write a resumé, where you must divide and group your skills, education, and experience.

In your life outside school and work, you may also draw on classification and division. For example, if you were planning a large party, such as a wedding reception or retirement dinner, and needed place cards, you might classify the people on your guest list according to friendships or compatibility in order to draw up a seating chart. If you were apartment hunting, you could divide your ideal place into its components (location, size, rent, whether it has air-conditioning, furnishings, and so on). When you look at places, you could check off whether each apartment has the features.

THE ORDERING PRINCIPLE FOR CLASSIFICATION AND DIVISION

Most things can be classified or divided more than one way, depending on the ordering principle used. For example, you could classify post-secondary institutions according to their cost, their location, the degrees or programs they offer, their faculty, or prestige. Cost, location, programs, degrees offered, faculty, prestige—each of these is an *ordering principle*. Your ordering principle should be significant, consistent, and complete. A significant ordering principle allows you to reveal something important or generally unnoticed about your topic. If you decided to analyze the narrators of short stories and your classification system referred to omniscient and first-person narrators, you would be hard pressed to say something new. If, however, you considered narrators who invited the reader into the story and those who pretended to be authoritative and cast the reader as a mere observer, you would be able to say something more significant about how writers use narrators.

Your ordering principle also ought to be complete. Say, for example, that you are classifying the forms of financial aid to inform students of ways to get help paying for their educations. You could include these categories: loans, grants, and scholarships. However, by omitting work-study programs, your system is incomplete and your essay is less helpful than it could—and should—be. Or say that you were analyzing the components of an effective political campaign. You could break the campaign down into these parts: grassroots support, publicity, and the focus on issues. However, you would be omitting an important component—financing.

On the other hand, you should avoid including groups and parts that are not compatible with your ordering principle. For example, if you are classifying coaches according to how important winning is to them, you might have these categories: coaches who think winning is everything; coaches who think winning is less important than learning and having fun; coaches who think winning is completely unimportant. In such a classification, you could not include coaches who are inexperienced, because that group is not consistent with the ordering principle.

SUPPORTING DETAILS

Your supporting details can include a wide range of patterns of development to explain the characteristics of each category or part. Examples provide the backbone of a classification or division essay, but these two rhetorical modes should not be confused. Classification and division require that examples are used as evidence of the ordering system. If you are classifying Halloween celebrations into three types, the sedate, the jolly, and the scary, you could use examples to illustrate the kinds of harmless pranks people play for a jolly celebration. You could also describe the frightening costumes people wear for a scary celebration; you could narrate the story of your last Halloween celebration, which was sedate. In addition, you could use process analysis to tell how to prepare for a scary Halloween celebration; you could use cause-and-effect analysis to explain the effects of the pranks played during the jolly celebration; you could use definition to explain the meaning of a sedate celebration; you could use comparison-contrast to show the similarities and differences among the three kinds of celebrations. Of course, you will not use all these patterns in a single essay, but they are all available for your consideration as ways to achieve your writing purpose.

ORGANIZING DETAILS

The thesis for classification or division can be handled a variety of ways. First, you can indicate what you are classifying or dividing and the ordering principle you will use:

> The current crop of television talk shows can be classified according to the kinds of guests that appear. (*Television talk shows will be classified; the ordering principle is the guests that appear.*)

A second way to handle the thesis is to indicate what will be classified or divided, along with the specific groupings that will be discussed:

> Television talk shows can be distinguished according to whether the guests are primarily entertainers, politicians, or oddballs. (*The thesis indicates that television talk shows will be classified and the categories will be those with guests who are entertainers, those with guests who are politicians, and those with guests who are oddballs.*)

Remember that one of the purposes of a thesis statement is to give you a chance to consider your thinking before you've written the whole essay. Once you've written your thesis statement, stop to consider whether your ordering principle is significant, complete, and consistent.

Organizing a classification or division essay can be easier when topic sentences introduce the discussion of each grouping. For example, if you were classifying talk shows, you might have topic sentences like these:

> In the most common variety of talk show the guests are entertainers. (*A discussion of talk shows with entertainers as guests would follow.*)

> Somewhat more intellectual than the first type, another common variety of show has politicians for guests. (*A discussion of talk shows with politicians as guests would follow.*)

> Increasingly popular is the talk show that showcases oddballs. (*A discussion of talk shows with oddballs as guests would follow.*)

To move smoothly from one grouping to another, you can include transitional phrases in your topic sentences:

> Another category . . .
> A more significant group . . .
> A more common kind . . .
> A second division of . . .

When you order your details, consider your thesis. If it includes categories or divisions, then you should present them in the same order they appear in the thesis. Otherwise, order is not much of an issue, unless your purpose is persuasive. Then you are likely to present the recommended category or the most important division last. In "The Ways of Meeting Oppression," for example, Dr. Martin Luther King, Jr., presents the method he wants people to adopt last.

When you are discussing the same characteristics for each category or division, you should present those characteristics in the same order each time. Thus, if you group Halloween celebrations and discuss decorations, costumes,

> **Troubleshooting Guide**
>
> **Maintaining Parallelism**
>
> If you have trouble expressing categories or divisions smoothly in your thesis, state them in the same grammatical form to maintain parallel structure. Here is a thesis that lacks parallelism:
>
> > Television talk shows can be divided into three types: <u>shows with entertainers for guests</u>, <u>those with guests who are politicians</u>, and <u>shows with oddballs for guests</u>.
>
> Notice that the following revision is much more pleasing because of the parallel structure:
>
> > Television talk shows can be divided into three types: <u>shows with entertainers for guests</u>, <u>shows with politicians for guests</u>, and <u>shows with oddballs for guests</u>.

and degree of scariness for each kind of celebration, then you should discuss these features in the same order for each one.

VISUALIZING A CLASSIFICATION AND DIVISION ESSAY

The chart on page 358 can help you visualize the structure for a classification and division essay. Like all good models, however, this one can be altered as needed.

PROCESS GUIDELINES: STRATEGIES FOR WRITING CLASSIFICATION AND DIVISION

1. **Planning.** Write your ordering principle at the top of a sheet of paper or your computer screen. Below that, write each of your categories or divisions at the top of a column. Three categories or divisions will give you three columns, four will give you four columns, and so on. Under each column list the elements in the category or the characteristics of the division.

2. **Generating Supporting Details.** Ask yourself these questions of every element or characteristic in your columns. Make notes of the answers on your planning sheet.
   - Can I narrate a story to develop this element or characteristic?
   - Can I describe something to develop this element or characteristic?

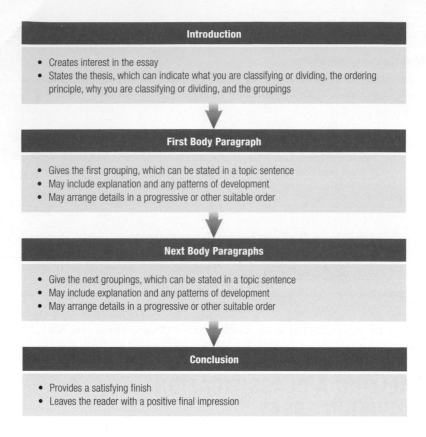

Introduction

- Creates interest in the essay
- States the thesis, which can indicate what you are classifying or dividing, the ordering principle, why you are classifying or dividing, and the groupings

First Body Paragraph

- Gives the first grouping, which can be stated in a topic sentence
- May include explanation and any patterns of development
- May arrange details in a progressive or other suitable order

Next Body Paragraphs

- Give the next groupings, which can be stated in a topic sentence
- May include explanation and any patterns of development
- May arrange details in a progressive or other suitable order

Conclusion

- Provides a satisfying finish
- Leaves the reader with a positive final impression

– Can I analyze causes or effects to develop this element or characteristic?
– Can I give an example to develop this element or characteristic?
– Can I define something to develop this element or characteristic?
– Can I compare or contrast to develop this element or characteristic?
– Can I use process analysis to develop this element or characteristic?

3. **Organizing.** Number the columns on your sheet in the order you want to treat them. You now have an outline to guide your draft.

4. **Revising.** As you evaluate your draft, consider everything in light of your audience and purpose. Be sure you have included all relevant categories and divisions and that they are compatible with your ordering principle.

✔ Checklist for Revising Classification and Division

Be sure:

_____ To include all relevant categories or divisions.

_____ To omit categories or division unrelated to your ordering principle.

_____ Your thesis indicates whether you are classifying or dividing and, if appropriate, your ordering principle.

_____ Transitions help you move smoothly from one category or division to the next.

_____ If you have discussed the same characteristics for each category or division, they appear in the same order.

ANNOTATED STUDENT ESSAY

Student-author David Wolfe uses classification to inform his reader about the origins of some common expressions. Be sure to notice how the author uses examples to help make his point. After you read, you will have an opportunity to evaluate this essay.

Strictly Speaking

Paragraph 1
This is the introduction. The thesis (the last sentence) indicates that Wolfe will use classification. It also indicates that expressions derived from outdoor life will be classified according to their sporting origins.

1   Expressions derived from outdoor life are so ingrained in everyday English that we fail to notice them or consider their origins. However, it is interesting to pause and think about these terms, and one way to do that is to look at three basic categories of expressions: those derived from the use of firearms, those derived from hunting, and those derived from the characteristics of wildlife or game.

Paragraph 2
The first sentence is the topic sentence. It presents the first category given in the thesis. The supporting details are examples of expressions in the category.

2   Some common sayings come directly from the use of firearms. For example, if we buy something "lock, stock, and barrel," we have purchased the whole object or believed the whole story. This expression originally meant to buy the whole gun by purchasing its three parts: the "lock" as in the flintlock, the wooden "stock," and the metal "barrel." We also talk about "going off half-cocked," which means taking action or setting out without being fully prepared. This expression goes back to having a gun on "half-cock." In the half-cocked position, the hammer is between the relaxed position and the fully cocked position, which means the gun is halfway between unready and fully ready for firing. Often we say we had our "sights set on" something or had a goal "in our sights." Both of these expressions refer to aiming a gun at something. Also, we can be "primed and ready," or fully prepared, as when a flintlock rifle is fully primed or prepared and ready to fire.

Paragraph 3
The topic sentence is the first sentence. It presents the second category. The supporting details are examples. Note the transition provided by *a second group, for example, another example,* and *similarly.*

3   A second group of expressions is derived from hunting. For example, the word "hello" has its origins there. It comes from hunters calling out "hulloa" or "haloo" when they saw other hunters in the woods in order to attract attention and avoid being accidentally hurt. "Stop beating around the bush" is another example of a hunting expression. It comes from the European practice of using "beaters" or people to drive game out of the brush for the hunter to shoot at. To do the job properly, beaters had to get into the middle of the bush where the game was. Otherwise, they were not getting the job done because they were beating around the bush. If we "make tracks," we hurry. Originally, this expression referred to an animal going in a hurry and thus leaving behind a set of tracks that were easy to follow. Being on "the right trail" refers to doing something properly or going in the right direction, but its original meaning referred to a hunter being on the right trail while tracking game. Similarly, if we

are "barking up the wrong tree," we are as mistaken as the hunting dogs that are howling up one tree when the raccoon is out on the limb of a different tree.

4   Sayings related to wildlife or game are also interesting. We brag about saving money when we are "feathering our nests" or "building up our nest eggs," the way a bird does in the spring. We may be called "owl-eyed" for wearing glasses or be "wise as an owl" for knowing the right answers. If we are "blind as a bat," we can't see very well, just as a bat has poor vision. If we have a bad disposition, we are "grouchy as a bear" or told "don't be such a bear," since bears have angry temperaments. In addition, there are two ways we can get "skunked." We can actually get sprayed by a skunk, or we can lose a game of some kind very badly—in either case, we lose.

Paragraph 4
The first sentence is the topic sentence. It includes the transition also and presents the final category. The supporting details are examples.

5   Expressions from the outdoors are so common that even those of us who never hunt, shoot, or get close to animals will find ourselves drawing on vocabulary derived from these sources, a fact you may be more aware of from now on.

Paragraph 5
The conclusion repeats the idea in the introduction that these expressions are ingrained in English.

PEER REVIEW

Responding to "Strictly Speaking"

Evaluate "Strictly Speaking" by responding to these questions:

1. Is the writer's classification system significant, complete, and consistent?
2. Is the thesis effective? Why or why not?
3. Are the supporting details adequate? Explain.
4. Is the organization effective? Why or why not?
5. What do you like best about the essay?
6. What single change do you think would make the essay better?

READING SELECTIONS

Background

Serge Tisseron is a psychoanalyst who teaches at the University of Paris X. He has published studies on many subjects, including the effects of violence in the media on young teenagers. As well as a writer, Tisseron is a cartoonist, and has written widely on the image and its effect on our cultural and private lives. His latest work, *Intimacy Overexposed* (2002), received a France-television Award.

Combined Patterns and Their Purposes

Often students confess that they can draft their essays or their poems only by hand; others insist that they can draft only with a computer screen in front of them. In this essay, Tisseron classifies the methods we use to express ourselves—whether in speech, in writing for school, or in writing online for our peers—by the emotional associations we have with those means of expression. This essay was originally published in the Canadian journal *Queen's Quarterly* in 2002.

The Mirror of the Internet

Serge Tisseron

As you read
Consider how social networks made possible by new technology influence your relationships.

1   The history of writing is the history of transcription onto paper of language, something that has become more and more complex through the millennia. But for almost all of its history, writing has been essentially the technique of using a marking liquid which seeps from the sharp edge of the hand-held writing instrument.

2   The development of the typewriter and then the computer has introduced a way of writing that is radically new. Now the writer types at a keyboard and sees what he has written appearing before his eyes on a monitor screen. But this is more than just a technological improvement. This fundamental change in the writing process carries very important consequences for *what is being written*. Every writing technique carries within it a sort of psychological posture induced by the very act of writing. And these postures cannot help but influence the content of the message. Consider that before you place yourself before your blank sheet of paper, your blank computer screen, or even before a lectern and microphone, you generally have only a very approximate idea of the concrete shape of your thought. Indeed the thinking process is constructed through the constraints imposed by the device one uses to communicate, the freedom that the device allows, and the project of the text, which becomes modified and transformed at every instant.

3   Let us compare the three different psychological postures that manifest themselves when we use these three different modes of communication: speaking, writing with a pen on paper, and using a computer.

4   Spoken language is first learned in the warm atmosphere of the family. Parents, brothers, sisters, grandparents, aunts, and uncles are the first to share language with

us, and this is generally done with the great interest and empathy adults reserve for the very young. And for the rest of our lives, to speak is always to create a link with the warm sounds in which one first learned to communicate. Every family possesses its own style of speaking, with its own unique intonations and accents, its own expressions and favourite locutions. Spoken language has even deeper warm memories at its core, since this language is created in the mouth and in some sense takes the speaker back to the time when his mother nursed him, providing both physical nourishment and delighted encouragement for every infantile sound. And this very human connection helps spoken language spin the illusion that whomever one speaks to must have at least some sympathy and understanding of our views. If we didn't believe that, it would be hard to take the risk of opening one's mouth.

5   Writing, on the other hand, is developed against a background of reminiscences that are starkly different. Many people admit to being terribly inhibited when they have to write, and they often find it impossible to express the same things they can formulate easily through spoken language. This is because learning to write has generally taken place in a school environment where the constant red ink corrections of the teacher are so intimidating and distressing for the child. The act of writing has become for most of us inseparable from the fear that an authorized and scholarly glance can, at any second, condemn us. This psychological posture is awakened every time we take up a pen. Where spoken language is more closely tied to our warm maternal feelings, writing feels more sternly paternal, marked by the constraints and rigour of grammar and accepted form.

6   In contrast to this speaking/writing opposition of maternal indulgence and paternal discipline, writing with a computer involves a third possibility, and this is the one brought forth by being so aware of the act of communication within a very specific community of one's peers. Writing on a computer is an act of declaring, without shame, the facets of our own peculiar personalities in the hope of finding a listener who will receive, accept and validate these traits of personality.

7   Another interesting trait is inherent in writing on a keyboard, especially during "chat room" conversations. Here writing is not constrained by the same injunctions of perfection that writing on paper demands, because such Internet conversations are totally free from the requirement of perfection that has marked our learning to write. Hence we should not be astonished that most young people in such a forum write with great freedom and with a certain joyous abandon—they freely create their own phonetic transcriptions, evolve myriad shared and individual forms of slang, and take great liberties with grammar and style.

8   The final characteristic of the psychological posture that characterizes keyboard writing is the illusion of a privileged rapport with a chosen community of peers. This is quite distinct from our sense of spoken language, which is inseparable from the family in which we happened to be raised, and our sense of written language, which owes its posture to the school environment that drilled its rules into our heads. In either case,

we had little choice about the group with which we were expected to communicate. In contrast, today's keyboard communication is very much influenced by the idea of a community of individuals who choose to participate in the same project, ideally with the same enthusiasm and the same aspirations as their cyberspace peers.

9   Once the Internet writer has selected the site where he hopes to find the maximum number of people sharing his interest, the writer can soon feel that his Internet circle knows him well enough to be sensitive to his moods, and feels that sharing these subtle emotions is welcomed within the community. Writing symbols—such as "☺" and "!!!!!"—can replace parts of text and sometimes whole sentences. In other words, writing on a computer keyboard is focused on one's *extimacy*, and that is why this type of communication does not fret about its future. A number of old sayings have contrasted spoken words, which are often fleeting and forgotten, to writing, which by nature is meant to endure. But consigning one's writing to the Internet's opinion polls, chat rooms, and bulletin boards should remind us that writing may soon disappear even faster than spoken words.

10   The practice of chat rooms, like the practice of e-mail, has presupposed that writing, like language, contains a truth, valid during the moment of its formulation. This sort of truth is not connected to what has been said but to the emotional validity that spawns what is said. Writing on the Internet is, first of all, creating an image of one's emotion and intuition and presenting this image to the Other in the expectation that he or she will recognize and validate these feelings. The desire driving us to write in this way is not only a longing for encouragement but also a need to encounter "out there" a receptive partner, as interested as we are in an instantaneous exchange in order to know *ourselves* better.

11   So this new exchange, we must understand, is a form of communication with oneself as much as with another person or a group. At its core, it is a search and evaluation of one's own emotions and ideas as much as it is a reciprocal conversation.

Reading Closely and Thinking Critically

1. Tisseron's classification of writing focuses mainly on the writer's relationship to the medium and on the way our past relationship with that medium influences what we might say. What other variables in the writing situation might influence our expression? Give examples to support your ideas.
2. Do you agree with Tisseron's observation that self-reflection goes into expressing ourselves on the Web? What other motives or desires constitute part of our self-presentation?
3. When describing the context in which we learn to speak, Tisseron observes that "this very human connection helps spoken language spin the illusion that whomever one speaks to must have at least some sympathy and understanding of our views." His use of the phrase "spin the illusion" suggests that there are contexts where saying what we think isn't welcome. Gives examples of such contexts. In what other ways can speech be risky?
4. Tisseron appeals to the old maxim that speech disappears more quickly than writing. Does this principle need re-examining? In the days of Twitter and Facebook, could you formulate a different

principle that predicts how quickly an act of communication will disappear—such as the amount of embarrassment involved?

Examining Structure and Strategy

1. In a classic example of classification, the writer gives equal space and time to each class and examines them with the same lens, as far as possible. In contrast, Tisseron spends one paragraph each on speaking and writing, while his discussion of expressing oneself on a computer takes five paragraphs. His examinations of speaking and writing consider the context in which these skills were learned, whereas his consideration of our use of the computer considers our search for an audience. What rhetorical effect do these inconsistencies have? Are these deviations from the "classical" pattern warranted? Do they make the essay more interesting? Do they ever frustrate you?

2. As a French psychiatrist, Tisseron describes kinds of communication in terms of gender. For example, he asserts that spoken language "in some sense takes the speaker back to the time when his mother nursed him, providing both physical nourishment and delighted encouragement for every infantile sound" (paragraph 4). Similarly he claims that speech is associated with maternal indulgence and that writing reminds one of paternal discipline (paragraph 6). Is his appeal to gender roles convincing? Why or why not?

Considering Language and Style

1. Tisseron observes that "every writing technique carries within it a sort of psychological posture induced by the very act of writing." What does he mean, in this context, by "posture"?

2. In paragraph 9, Tisseron coins the expression "extimacy," perhaps by conflating the words "external" and "intimacy." What do you think he means by this expression? Is this indeed what you find in a chat room or on Facebook?

3. In paragraph 10, Tisseron observes that "Writing on the Internet is, first of all, creating an image of one's emotion and intuition and presenting this image to the Other in the expectation that he or she will recognize and validate these feelings." Who is this "Other" and why is he or she capitalized?

For Discussion in Class or Online

Consider how the various ways and contexts in which you communicate—through instant messaging, Facebook, emails, essays for professors—colour your sense of what it means to communicate with someone else. Does the variety of contexts available to you make it easier or harder to communicate? Why? If your instructor so directs, post your responses on your class Web site.

Writing Assignments

1. **In your journal.** Tisseron's essay doesn't consider the writing people might do in journals. Consider what you are learning or accomplishing by writing in your journal and add a hypothetical paragraph to Tisseron's essay that discusses the journal as a medium and a context.

2. **Using classification or division for a purpose.** The purposes in the assignments are possibilities. You may establish whatever purposes you like, within your instructor's guidelines.

   - To entertain your reader, classify your friends on Facebook according to either how they present themselves or what they seek to gain with their Facebook profiles.

   - To inform your reader, classify the writing situations faced by your generation. Think carefully about what the principles of your classification would be. How grammatically correct one's expression must be? How honest (or fanciful) you are expected to be? How long the communication will hang around?

   - To persuade your reader, classify types of writing by whether they support or interfere with one another. Should serious college or university students give up instant messaging?

3. **Combining patterns.** Classify instructors or professors by the kinds of writing they expect from you. What effects on your writing did these expectations have?

4. **Connecting the readings.** In his essay, "Imagining the Future" (page 338), Bruce Mau talks about how design can contribute to a better world. Using Tisseron's observations about the way the Internet influences how we communicate, consider how the design of sites like Facebook or YouTube might contribute to a world where we know more about other people's lives. Classify the knowledge we might gain from well-designed sites.

5. **Drawing on sources.** Interview half a dozen fellow students to find out how they feel about writing for their classes, and construct a system of classification that illuminates their different attitudes and experiences.

Background

Born in 1934 in Sweden, writer and philosopher Sissela Bok was educated in Switzerland and France before going to the United States. She earned her PhD in philosophy from Harvard University. Bok is currently a senior fellow at the Harvard Center for Population and Development Studies. She is a frequent writer on ethics in medicine and government and has lectured on medical ethics at Harvard and the Massachusetts Institute of Technology. Bok won the Orwell Award for her book *Lying: Moral Choice in Private and Public Life* (1978, reissued in 1999), from which "White Lies" is taken. Her other books include *Secrets: On the Ethics of Concealment and Revelation* (1982); *A Strategy for Peace: Human Values and the Threat of War* (1989); *Alva Myrdal: A Daughter's Memoir* (1991), for which Bok received the Melcher Book Award; *Common Values* (1996); and *Mayhem: Violence as Public Entertainment* (1998). Bok is also a former member of the Pulitzer Prize Board and a member of the Academic Advisory Council of the National Campaign Against Youth Violence.

Combined Patterns and Their Purposes

In "White Lies," Sissela Bok classifies and defines white lies to inform her reader of the various kinds. She also makes a persuasive point about the harm these lies cause, drawing on examples and cause-and-effect analysis.

White Lies
Sissela Bok

1   White lies are at the other end of the spectrum of deception from lies in a serious crisis. They are the most common and the most trivial forms that duplicity can take. The fact that they are so common provides their protective coloring. And their very triviality, when compared to more threatening lies, makes it seem unnecessary or even absurd to condemn them. Some consider *all* well-intentioned lies, however momentous, to be white; in this book, I shall adhere to the narrower usage: a white lie, in this sense, is a falsehood not meant to injure anyone, and of little moral import. I want to ask whether there *are* such lies; and if there are, whether their cumulative consequences are still without harm; and, finally whether many lies are defended as "white" which are in fact harmful in their own right.

> **As you read**
> What's Bok's system of classification here? Is it significant, complete, and consistent?

2   Many small subterfuges may not even be intended to mislead. They are only "white lies" in the most marginal sense. Take, for example, the many social exchanges: "How nice to see you!" or "Cordially Yours." These and a thousand other polite expressions are so much taken for granted that if someone decided, in the name of total honesty, not to employ them, he might well give the impression of an indifference he did not possess. The justification for continuing to use such accepted formulations is that they deceive no one, except possibly those unfamiliar with the language.

3   A social practice more clearly deceptive is that of giving a false excuse so as not to hurt the feelings of someone making an invitation or request: to say one "can't" do what in reality one may not *want* to do. Once again, the false excuse may prevent

unwarranted inferences of greater hostility to the undertaking than one may well feel. Merely to say that one can't do something, moreover, is not deceptive in the sense that an elaborately concocted story can be.

4   Still other white lies are told in an effort to flatter, to throw a cheerful interpretation on depressing circumstances, or to show gratitude for unwanted gifts. In the eyes of many, such white lies do not harm, provide needed support and cheer, and help dispel gloom and boredom. They preserve the equilibrium and often the humaneness of social relationships, and are usually accepted as excusable so long as they do not become excessive. Many argue, moreover, that such deception is so helpful and at times so necessary that it must be tolerated as an exception to a general policy against lying. Thus Bacon[1] observed:

> Doth any man doubt, that if there were taken out of men's minds vain opinions, flattering hopes, false valuations, imaginations as one would, and the like, but it would leave the minds of a number of men poor shrunken things, full of melancholy and indisposition, and unpleasing to themselves?

5   Another kind of lie may actually be advocated as bringing a more substantial benefit, or avoiding a real harm, while seeming quite innocuous to those who tell the lies. Such are the placebos given for innumerable common ailments, and the pervasive use of inflated grades and recommendations for employment and promotion.

6   A large number of lies without such redeeming features are nevertheless often regarded as so trivial that they should be grouped with white lies. They are the lies told on the spur of the moment, for want of reflection, or to get out of a scrape, or even simply to pass the time. Such are the lies told to boast or exaggerate, or on the contrary to deprecate and understate; the many lies told or repeated in gossip; Rousseau's[2] lies told simply "in order to say something"; the embroidering on facts that seem too tedious in their own right; and the substitution of a quick lie for the lengthy explanations one might otherwise have to provide for something not worth spending time on.

7   Utilitarians often cite white lies as the *kind* of deception where their theory shows the benefits of common sense and clear thinking. A white lie, they hold, is trivial; it is either completely harmless, or so marginally harmful that the cost of detecting and evaluating the harm is much greater than the minute harm itself. In addition, the white lie can often actually be beneficial, thus further tipping the scales of utility. In a world with so many difficult problems, utilitarians might ask: Why take the time to weigh the minute pros and cons in telling someone that his tie is attractive when it is an abomination, or of saying to a guest that a broken vase was worthless? Why bother even to

---

[1]Francis Bacon (1561–1626), British philosopher and statesman.
[2]Jean-Jacques Rousseau (1712–1778), a French philosopher and author.

define such insignificant distortions or make mountains out of molehills by seeking to justify them?

8   Triviality surely does set limits to when moral inquiry is reasonable. But when we look more closely at practices such as placebo-giving, it becomes clear that all lies defended as "white" cannot be so easily dismissed. In the first place, the harmlessness of lies is notoriously disputable. What the liar perceives as harmless or even beneficial may not be so in the eyes of the deceived. Second, the failure to look at an entire practice rather than at their own isolated case often blinds liars to cumulative harm and expanding deceptive activities. Those who begin with white lies can come to resort to more frequent and more serious ones. Where some tell a few white lies, others may tell more. Because lines are so hard to draw, the indiscriminate use of such lies can lead to other deceptive practices. The aggregate harm from a large number of marginally harmful instances may, therefore, be highly undesirable in the end—for liars, those deceived, and honesty and trust more generally.

Reading Closely and Thinking Critically
1. What does Bok mean when she says in paragraph 1, "The fact that [white lies] are so common provides their protective coloring"?
2. What kinds of white lies does Bok classify? What are the justifications for each of these kinds of white lies?
3. Who are the utilitarians that Bok refers to in paragraph 7? What is their view of white lies?
4. What is Bok's view of the white lie?
5. Is there any kind of white lie that Bok might find acceptable? Cite evidence from the selection to support your view.

Examining Structure and Strategy
1. What is Bok's ordering principle?
2. In what kind of order does Bok arrange her categories?
3. Bok introduces her categories with topic sentences. What are those topic sentences? What transitions appear in the topic sentences in paragraphs 4 and 5? What purpose do these transitions serve?

Noting Combined Patterns
1. In paragraph 2, Bok gives examples of items in one of her categories. How do these examples help Bok achieve her purpose? Would any other paragraphs benefit from the addition of examples? Explain.
2. How does Bok use cause-and-effect analysis?
3. Is it possible to think of "White Lies" as a definition? Explain.

Considering Language and Style
1. What is a *placebo* (paragraphs 5 and 8) and how is it a form of lie?
2. Consult a dictionary if you are unsure of the meaning of any of these words: *spectrum* (paragraph 1), *duplicity* (paragraph 1), *innocuous* (paragraph 5), *utilitarians* (paragraph 7), *aggregate* (paragraph 8).

For Discussion in Class or Online

Discuss what day-to-day living would be like if people never told white lies. Would some kinds of lies be missed more than others? If your instructor directs you to do so, post your responses to your class Web site.

Writing Assignments

1. **In your journal.** In a page or two, respond to these questions: How often do you tell white lies? What kinds of white lies do you usually tell? Have you ever told a white lie that has hurt someone? Have you ever been hurt by a white lie?

2. **Using classification or division for a purpose.** The purposes in the assignments are possibilities. You may establish whatever purposes you like, within your instructor's guidelines.

   - Rather than focus on white lies as Bok does, inform your reader with a classification of all lies. If you want, you can also persuade your reader that one kind of lie is more or less serious than the others. As an alternative, use division to break down one kind of lie into its components.
   - To inform and perhaps persuade your reader of the seriousness of the lies, classify the lies told in some specific context, such as in school, on a date, at family gatherings, or in the workplace.
   - To inform and perhaps persuade, classify the types of one kind of undesirable behaviour, such as cheating, disloyalty, or procrastination. As an alternative, use division to break down one type of undesirable behaviour into its components and evaluate its degree of harm.

3. **Combining patterns.** Classify the lies parents tell their children or the lies that teenagers tell their parents. Use exemplification to illustrate the lies and cause-and-effect analysis to explain the causes and effects of the lies. (Exemplification is explained in Chapter 6, and cause-and-effect analysis is explained in Chapter 10.)

4. **Connecting the readings.** White lies are a common—and even accepted—form of deception. Do you think that deception is so common that it is woven into the fabric of our society? Or do you think people are honest for the most part? Be sure to cite examples to support your assertion. You can draw on "White Lies" and "How Men Choose Women" (page 256) for ideas.

5. **Drawing on sources.** Select a kind of product frequently advertised, such as toothpaste, soft drinks, or cleaning products. Examine advertisements for the product type on television and/or in print and write a classification of the ways the product is advertised. Draw a conclusion about how deceptive or truthful the advertising is.

Background

Dr. Martin Luther King, Jr., (1929–1968) was a Baptist minister and the most prominent U.S. civil rights leader of the 1950s and 1960s. He founded the Southern Christian Leadership Conference in 1957 and worked tirelessly to achieve racial integration through non-violent means, especially peaceful demonstrations. Named *Time* magazine's Man of the Year in 1963, King became the youngest winner ever of the Nobel Peace Prize in 1964. King graduated from Morehouse College, an all-black university in Atlanta, and went on to Crozer Theological Seminary to continue preparing for the ministry. In 1955, he received his doctorate from Boston University. While at Crozer, King attended a lecture on Indian pacifist Mahatma Gandhi. The lecture charted the course of King's philosophy of non-violent resistance: "His message was so profound and electrifying," King later said, "that I left the meeting and bought a half dozen books on Gandhi's life and works." On April 4, 1968, King was assassinated in Memphis, Tennessee. King's writings include *Letter from Birmingham City Jail* (1963) and *Where Do We Go from Here: Chaos or Community* (1967). "The Ways of Meeting Oppression" is taken from *Stride toward Freedom* (1958).

Combined Patterns and Their Purposes

Using classification combined with cause-and-effect analysis and definition, Martin Luther King, Jr., informs his reader of the options oppressed people have and works to persuade them that non-violent resistance is the best way to oppose oppression.

The Ways of Meeting Oppression
Martin Luther King, Jr.

1   Oppressed people deal with their oppression in three characteristic ways. One way is acquiescence: the oppressed resign themselves to their doom. They tacitly adjust themselves to oppression, and thereby become conditioned to it. In every movement toward freedom some of the oppressed prefer to remain oppressed. Almost 2800 years ago Moses set out to lead the children of Israel from the slavery of Egypt to the freedom of the promised land. He soon discovered that slaves do not always welcome their deliverers. They become accustomed to being slaves. They would rather bear those ills they have, as Shakespeare pointed out, than flee to others that they know not of. They prefer the "fleshpots of Egypt" to the ordeals of emancipation.

As you read
Notice the biblical references and imagery.

2   There is such a thing as the freedom of exhaustion. Some people are so worn down by the yoke of oppression that they give up. A few years ago in the slum areas of Atlanta, a Negro guitarist used to sing almost daily: "Been down so long that down don't bother me." This is the type of negative freedom and resignation that often engulfs the life of the oppressed.

3   But this is not the way out. To accept passively an unjust system is to cooperate with that system; thereby the oppressed become as evil as the oppressor. Noncooperation with evil is as much a moral obligation as is cooperation with good. The oppressed must never allow the conscience of the oppressor to slumber. Religion reminds every man that he is his brother's keeper. To accept injustice or segregation

passively is to say to the oppressor that his actions are morally right. It is a way of allowing his conscience to fall asleep. At this moment the oppressed fails to be his brother's keeper. So acquiescence—while often the easier way—is not the moral way. It is the way of the coward. The Negro cannot win the respect of his oppressor by acquiescing; he merely increases the oppressor's arrogance and contempt. Acquiescence is interpreted as proof of the Negro's inferiority. The Negro cannot win the respect of the white people of the South or the peoples of the world if he is willing to sell the future of his children for his personal and immediate comfort and safety.

> "Noncooperation with evil is as much a moral
> obligation as is cooperation with good."

4   A second way that oppressed people sometimes deal with oppression is to resort to physical violence and corroding hatred. Violence often brings about momentary results. Nations have frequently won their independence in battle. But in spite of temporary victories, violence never brings permanent peace. It solves no social problem; it merely creates new and more complicated ones.

5   Violence as a way of achieving racial justice is both impractical and immoral. It is impractical because it is a descending spiral ending in destruction for all. The old law of an eye for an eye leaves everybody blind. It is immoral because it seeks to humiliate the opponent rather than win his understanding; it seeks to annihilate rather than to convert. Violence is immoral because it thrives on hatred rather than love. It destroys community and makes brotherhood impossible. It leaves society in monologue rather than dialogue. Violence ends by defeating itself. It creates bitterness in the survivors and brutality in the destroyers. A voice echoes through time saying to every potential Peter, "Put up your sword."[1] History is cluttered with the wreckage of nations that failed to follow this command.

6   If the American Negro and other victims of oppression succumb to the temptation of using violence in the struggle for freedom, future generations will be the recipients of a desolate night of bitterness, and our chief legacy to them will be an endless reign of meaningless chaos. Violence is not the way.

7   The third way open to oppressed people in their quest for freedom is the way of nonviolent resistance. Like the synthesis in Hegelian philosophy,[2] the principle of nonviolent resistance seeks to reconcile the truths of two opposites—the acquiescence and violence—while avoiding the extremes and immoralities of both. The nonviolent resister agrees with the person who acquiesces that one should not be physically

---

[1]The apostle Peter had drawn his sword to defend Christ from arrest. The voice was Christ's, who surrendered himself for trial and crucifixion (John 18:11).
[2]Georg Wilhelm Hegel (1770–1831) was a German philosopher who said that contradictions could be synthesized to achieve truth.

aggressive toward his opponent; but he balances the equation by agreeing with the person of violence that evil must be resisted. He avoids the nonresistance of the former and the violent resistance of the latter. With nonviolent resistance, no individual or group need submit to any wrong, nor need anyone resort to violence in order to right a wrong.

8   It seems to me that this is the method that must guide the actions of the Negro in the present crisis in race relations. Through nonviolent resistance the Negro will be able to rise to the noble height of opposing the unjust system while loving the perpetrators of the system. The Negro must work passionately and unrelentingly for full stature as a citizen, but he must not use inferior methods to gain it. He must never come to terms with falsehood, malice, hate, or destruction.

9   Nonviolent resistance makes it possible for the Negro to remain in the South and struggle for his rights. The Negro's problem will not be solved by running away. He cannot listen to the glib suggestion of those who would urge him to migrate en masse to other sections of the country. By grasping his great opportunity in the South he can make a lasting contribution to the moral strength of the nation and set a sublime example of courage for generations yet unborn.

> "Nonviolent resistance is not aimed against
> oppressors but against oppression."

10   By nonviolent resistance, the Negro can also enlist all men of good will in his struggle for equality. The problem is not a purely racial one, with Negroes set against whites. In the end, it is not a struggle between people at all, but a tension between justice and injustice. Nonviolent resistance is not aimed against oppressors but against oppression. Under its banner consciences, not racial groups, are enlisted.

Reading Closely and Thinking Critically

1. According to King, what are the problems with acquiescence? With physical violence?
2. In paragraph 2, King refers to the "freedom of exhaustion." What does this phrase mean?
3. In paragraph 1, King says that some "would rather bear those ills they have . . . than flee to others they know not of." What does King mean? Why do you think that he makes this point?
4. According to King, how does non-violent resistance balance the approaches of those who acquiesce and those who engage in physical violence?
5. Why does King advocate non-violent resistance?

Examining Structure and Strategy

1. What ordering principle does King use? What are his categories?
2. Which sentence is the thesis of "The Ways of Meeting Oppression"?
3. King presents his categories in topic sentences. What are those topic sentences?
4. Where in the essay does King make his persuasive purpose clear? Why do you think he establishes his persuasive point at this stage of his essay?

Noting Combined Patterns

1. Cause-and-effect analysis appears in paragraphs 5 and 6, and 8 through 10. (Cause-and-effect analysis, the explanation of the causes or the effects of something, is discussed in Chapter 10.) How does the analysis help advance the classification?
2. Which paragraph includes definition? (Definition, an explanation of what something means, is discussed in Chapter 7.) What purpose does that definition serve? What paragraphs include examples? What purpose do those examples serve?

Considering Language and Style

1. Paragraph 5 includes two biblical references: the mention of "an eye for an eye" and the mention of Peter. Explain these references and evaluate their appropriateness. Why is it natural for King to use biblical references?
2. "The Ways of Meeting Oppression" comes from King's 1958 book *Stride toward Freedom*. What elements of King's language are clues to the era in which King was writing? How does this language contribute to our understanding of the circumstances King was addressing?
3. Consult a dictionary if you are unsure of the meaning of any of these words: *tacitly* (paragraph 1), *fleshpots* (paragraph 1), *desolate* (paragraph 6), *legacy* (paragraph 6), *perpetrators* (paragraph 8), *glib* (paragraph 9), *en masse* (paragraph 9).

For Discussion in Class or Online

When King writes, "The old law of an eye for an eye leaves everybody blind," he is paraphrasing Mahatma Gandhi, who said, "An eye for an eye only ends up making the whole world blind." Consider the extent to which revenge is all too common in our lives and in our culture. What kinds of blindness do you see as a result?

Writing Assignments

1. **In your journal.** Write about a time when you witnessed, experienced, or heard about some form of oppression or discrimination. Describe the incident and how it made you feel.
2. **Using classification or division for a purpose.** The purposes in the assignments are possibilities. You may establish whatever purposes you like, within your instructor's guidelines.
   - To inform readers and persuade them that one way is better than the others, classify the ways of dealing with a bully. Give the chief advantages and/or disadvantages of each technique.
   - To inform readers and persuade them that one way is better than the others, classify the ways of dealing with either stress or depression. Give the chief advantages and disadvantages of each way.
   - To inform readers and persuade them that one way is better than the others, classify the ways of dealing with gender discrimination, age discrimination, or sexual harassment. Give the advantages and disadvantages of each way.
3. **Combining patterns.** Using definition (explained in Chapter 7), explain what a *bully* is and classify ways of dealing with one, being sure to indicate the methods that are most effective. As an alternative, classify kinds of bullying behaviour, indicating which are the most harmful.
4. **Connecting the readings.** Read "The Keys of Paradise" (page 193) and "Imagining an Enlightened Social Policy on Drugs" (page 422). Then write an essay that explains to what extent addicts are victims of oppression. Indicate whether or not you think King's policy of non-violent resistance would help addicts and explain why you believe as you do.
5. **Drawing on sources.** Interview three people who have found themselves embroiled in conflict in recent times. Ask them to tell you about the conflict and their response to it. Then ask them whether the non-violent approach that eschews revenge would have been helpful to them. It might be helpful to quote Gandhi or King and see whether they think revenge blinds us in our everyday lives.

Additional Essay Assignments
See pages 357 and 359 for strategies for writing classification and division and for a revising checklist.

1. Classify popular music to inform people who do not know much about this music.
2. Classify either television talk shows or situation comedies to explain the nature of these forms of entertainment. As an alternative, use division to break down one of these shows into its various parts.
3. Classify "genre fiction"—mysteries, fantasy, science fiction, true crime. Or classify a single kind of genre fiction. You might classify mysteries according to the kind of detective authors use, contrasting the police procedural with the mystery involving amateur detectives like Sherlock Holmes or Peter Wimsey. Or you might classify fantasy novels with respect to their settings: do they happen on our world, between our world and another world, or in an entirely different world altogether? Remember that your classification system needs to be significant: what categories can you create that inform a reader who knows little about genre fiction?
4. Divide a genre of fiction or film into its component parts. What elements must every horror movie have? What common characteristics are shared by every novel written by Terry Pratchett?
5. Classify hockey goalies, baseball pitchers, football quarterbacks, basketball forwards, or others who play a particular position on an athletic team.
6. Classify kinds of dishonesty.
7. Classify kinds of shoppers.
8. Classify radio disc jockeys or television newscasters or talk show hosts.
9. Classify sources of frustration.
10. Classify kinds of superheroes, limiting yourself to a particular medium, such as comic books, movies, graphic novels.
11. Classify types of inner strength or types of courage.
12. Classify parenting styles. If you wish, your purpose can be to persuade your reader that a particular style is the best.
13. Classify types of drivers. If you like, your purpose can be to entertain.
14. Classify soft drink advertisements on television or makeup advertisements in magazines to inform your reader of the persuasive strategies that are employed. As an alternative, analyze the components of a typical advertisement for one of these products.
15. Classify the kinds of parties college students attend. As an alternative, use division to present the various aspects of a college party.
16. Classify hockey, football, baseball, or basketball fans.
17. Classify the kinds of neighbours people can have.
18. Write a classification of the kinds of good luck or bad luck.
19. Classify the different kinds of theme parks or roller coasters.
20. **Classification and division in context:** Assume you are the entertainment editor for your campus newspaper. For the first issue of the fall term, write an article that classifies the kinds of entertainment available to students at your school. Your purpose is to inform first-year students of the options available to them and the chief features of each kind of entertainment in order to help them adjust to your campus.

Chapter 12

A Casebook for Argumentation and Persuasion

To convert somebody, go and take them by the hand and guide them.

— Thomas Aquinas (1224–1274)

Let one who wants to move and convince others, first be convinced and moved themselves. If a person speaks with genuine earnestness the thoughts, the emotion and the actual condition of their own heart, others will listen because we all are knit together by the tie of sympathy.

— Thomas Carlyle, British historian and essayist (1795–1881)

THE DIFFERENCE BETWEEN ARGUMENTATION AND PERSUASION

Both **argumentation** and **persuasion** aim to convince a reader to adopt a particular view or to take a particular action. In the purest sense, argumentation relies on sound reasoning and logic to move the reader, while persuasion employs appeals to emotion, values, and beliefs. Say, for example, that you want to convince a female friend to vote for a particular candidate for leadership of a political party. You would employ argumentation if you noted the candidate's prior experience in the provincial legislature and strong political ties to Ottawa; you would employ persuasion if you noted the need for more women in high political office. Although argumentation and persuasion are technically different, in practice, the distinction is blurred because reason and logic are usually combined with appeals to emotions, values, and beliefs. Thus, to convince your friend to vote for your candidate, you might mention her political credentials *and* her gender.

Already in this book, you have dealt with a number of essays with a persuasive purpose because each chapter of readings has included one or more selections meant to move the reader to think or act a particular way. In this chapter, however, you will study argumentative-persuasive technique in greater detail.

PURPOSE AND AUDIENCE

As explained, argumentation and persuasion work to convince the reader to think or act a particular way. For example, a newspaper editorial argues that the city's layoff of municipal employees is unnecessary in order to convince readers that the layoffs are a mistake. An advertisement extols the virtues of a car to persuade people to buy it.

Sometimes you have no hope of convincing your reader, so you must establish a less ambitious goal, such as softening your reader's objection or convincing your reader that your view has some merit. Say, for example, that you are arguing that your province's premier should increase the sales tax to support public education. If your reader has children in school, you can reasonably aim to convince your audience to agree with you. However, if your reader is a retired person on a fixed income, expecting agreement may be unreasonable. In this case, a more suitable goal is to convince your reader that there are some good reasons to raise the sales tax—even if he or she does not fully support the idea. Perhaps you are wondering what good it is to soften a reader's objection or convince that person that your view has some merit. The answer is that if you can lessen a reader's resistance to your view, he or she may come around to your thinking eventually or work less hard to oppose you. Thus, if you convince a retired person that there are some valid reasons for the sales tax, he or she still might not vote for it but also might not campaign actively against it.

If you don't adopt these more modest goals, you may attempt to win your audience over, no matter what you have to do. The strategies you use when you feel this way are usually neither sound arguments nor reasonable emotional appeals. Rather, you might resort to bullying, ridiculing the other person's position, and claiming more for your arguments than they will bear under close scrutiny. People who say to themselves, "I'm right and I'm going to show them," have, in all likelihood, already lost the argument.

Audience assessment is particularly important in argumentation and persuasion. You must assess your reader's interest in order to establish a reasonable purpose for your writing, and you must understand the characteristics of your audience so you know which points need to be stated and proven, what kind of evidence will be the most effective, how hard you must work to convince your reader, and how your audience will respond to emotional appeals.

Argumentation and Persuasion at School, at Work, and in the Community

Argumentation will be a considerable part of your post-secondary writing. While you often will be tested on your ability to recall information, at other times you will need to do more than restate what you have read in a text or heard in a lecture. To show that you have thoughtfully considered that information, you will be asked to analyze it, consider different points of view, and then draw your own conclusions, which your instructors will ask you to present and defend with argumentation that relies on reason.

For example, in a political science or Canadian studies class, you may be asked to do more that just explain employment equity and its history; you may also have to argue whether or not such initiatives have hurt or helped minority populations. In an ethics class, you may need to do more than explain what is possible with genetic engineering; you may have to develop guidelines governing genetic screening and argue for their acceptance. In a history class, you may need to explain why the atomic bomb was dropped during World War II and then argue that it should or should not have been used to end the war with Japan; in a business course, you may need to define inflation, explain how to combat it, and then go on to argue which combative strategy is the best. In an environmental science course, you may need to argue that the government should or should not sponsor legislation to address the causes of global warming or that individuals and "the market" are responsible for making the necessary changes.

Argumentation and persuasion are not frequently seen as a writing strategy in university and college textbooks because their emphasis is on an objective presentation of facts. When a controversy does surround an issue covered by a textbook, the author generally covers all sides of the issue even-handedly. However, at times, a text may include an opinion backed up with an element of argumentation or persuasion. Here is an example of such a passage, taken from the education textbook *Teachers, Schools, and Society* by Myra and David Sadker.

> There is an important difference between *teaching about* religion and *promoting* religion. Today's texts fail to discuss adequately many religious issues that are intellectually complex and socially controversial. Columnist Ellen Goodman suggests that as publishers retreat from controversy, they also retreat from many important lessons. Goodman points out that the strength of our nation, what children really need to learn, is that our history has not always had happy endings, and that we have not yet resolved all our differences. . . . The lesson to

be taught to children is that we can live together as a people and not agree on everything.

In this excerpt, the authors state the opinion that textbooks do not do a good job of discussing some religious issues, a view they support by quoting Ellen Goodman. When a textbook—or any other material—argues an opinion or attempts to persuade its audience, you must recognize the author's efforts to persuade you and accept or reject the idea advanced on the basis of its merit, how well it is argued, and your own reasoning.

Argumentation and persuasion are also frequently required in the workplace. For example, copywriters compose advertisements to persuade consumers to buy products. Lawyers write briefs to convince judges of the merits of their case. Public health officials draw on research to persuade people to improve their eating habits or to promote no-smoking legislation. Artists write proposals to convince arts councils to fund their projects. Contractors write project proposals to persuade builders to hire them. Managers write reports to convince co-workers and supervisors of many things: which phone service to purchase, which contract to accept, how to reorganize an office, what investment to make, which property to buy, and so forth. Employees in many sectors write proposals for special projects, perhaps for a fundraising drive to help a charitable organization.

Outside of the workplace and classroom, you will use argumentation and persuasion frequently in your personal writing, such as in a letter to the editor to persuade others to share your view on an issue important to you, an email to convince a friend to join you on a cross-country trip, a letter to a customer service representative to persuade a business to give you a refund for a faulty product, a grant proposal to convince the provincial arts council to fund a community theatre, or a speech to convince school board members to change a school bus route.

SUPPORTING DETAILS

Our system of logic was formulated by the ancient Greeks, who identified three elements of a successful argument: *logos, pathos,* and *ethos* (often called the Rhetorical Triangle or the Aristotelian Triad; see the illustration on page 380). **Logos** (from which our word *logical* derives) refers to the sound reasoning of the argument. It includes the evidence, facts, statistics, examples, authoritative statements, and so forth that you supply to back up your position. **Pathos** (from which our words *empathy* and *pathetic* derive) refers to the emotional component of language and its ability to appeal to the reader's feelings,

The Rhetorical Triangle or Aristotelian Triad

values, attitudes, and beliefs. Say you want to persuade your reader to buy a particular stock. If you said that failure to buy the stock could mean missing the opportunity of a lifetime, that part of your argument would use pathos because it appeals to the reader's fear of passing up an opportunity. However, if you explained that the stock was undervalued and part of a growing market sector, that part of your argument would use logos because it appealed to the reader's intellect. **Ethos** (from which our word *ethical* derives) refers to establishing your honesty, integrity, and reliability so your reader will trust you and, therefore, believe what you say. You must present yourself as knowledgeable and thoughtful, as one who carefully weighs all evidence before drawing conclusions. If your reader thinks you are impetuous, careless, or biased, he or she may not accept your position no matter how well argued it is.

Logos

To present your argument soundly, you must reason logically. Be careful, then, to avoid the errors in logic discussed on pages 9–12.

For the most part, your argumentative detail will be the evidence you have considered to come to your conclusions. Thus, if you want to convince your reader that the federal government should create daycare spaces for the children of working parents, you would give all the evidence that has suggested this position to you. Preliminary research might turn up the Organization for Economic Cooperation and Development's report "Early Childhood Education and Care Policy," which indicates that daycares that are run for profit have more poorly trained staff and invest less in teaching the children under their care. In contrast, the report indicates that national daycares in the U.K., Belgium, Denmark, and France have learning goals for children in daycares and standards for the training of staff. A more considered search of the library's holdings with the subject heading "daycare—Canada" would turn up a plethora of books. Seldom in your post-secondary career are you likely to have adequate personal experience and knowledge to write a solid argument.

To provide evidence or to suggest where your reader can find it, you can rely on a number of sources and strategies, including personal experience and observation, interviews, expert opinion, and facts and statistics. We present these here in the order of their soundness, from least effective to most effective. The patterns of development help you to consider the forms that evidence might take.

Draw on Personal Experience and Observation

Say that you are in favour of federally funded daycare, and you cite as one reason the fact that children of working parents do not always get satisfactory care without it. To back up this claim, you could rely on observation by telling your audience about your neighbour, who cannot afford decent care for her child while she is at work. As a consequence, her daughter is learning to fight with other children when she wants something because the daycare workers are too busy to teach children to negotiate and compromise. If your own experience as a working parent supports the point, you could also write about that experience to back up your claim.

Conduct Interviews

In the material on errors in logic (page 10) and again when we discussed cause-and-effect reasoning (page 319), we pointed out the danger of over-generalizing. When you draw conclusions based only on your own experience, you are in danger of committing this error by suggesting that the experience of a single individual is typical. You can address this problem by interviewing other people. Say that to argue for federally funded daycare you note that the daycare fees are too high for some individuals. To support this reason, you can interview the owners of local daycare centres to learn the cost of enrolment. You could then interview parents searching for daycare and report their thoughts on the enrolment fees you discovered.

Use Expert Opinion

A significant part of your early research will be devoted to discovering which individuals are considered by their fields to be knowledgeable and trustworthy. (See the section "Evaluating Print and Internet Sources" in Chapter 14, on page 503.) Once you have found reliable experts, quote them or paraphrase their ideas. On the issue of hate speech, for example, Canada's landmark decision to exempt it from the freedom of speech protected by the Charter of Rights and Freedoms was written by Chief Justice Dickson in his opinion in the Supreme Court Case of *R. v. Keegstra*. In an essay where you also argue that censoring hate speech doesn't violate the right to free speech, you could quote and paraphrase Chief Justice Dickson, who argues that two kinds of damage are done when we tolerate hate speech. The first kind of damage is harm done to individuals: "It is indisputable that the emotional damage caused by words may be of grave psychological and social consequence." The second kind of damage is done to "society at large," in the event that citizens might adopt the attitudes of the speaker and become less tolerant. If you do use quotations or paraphrases, be sure to follow the guidelines for documenting your sources given in Chapter 14.

The opinions of experts, while they remain *opinions*, are also those of *experts*, individuals who have carefully studied the sides of an issue and brought their own expertise to bear. While not as strong as facts and statistics, expert opinion is often more meaningful because it's based on the reasoned interpretation of data and information. In the essay "Predicting Addiction" (page 435) the authors use the data from a study of twins to attempt to understand how nature and nurture, genes and personal experience, both play a role in an individual's susceptibility to addiction. Twins, obviously, share many genes, so genetic differences between individuals are minimized but not altogether eliminated. It takes an expert, then, to interpret this data.

Use Facts and Statistics

Say that you want to convince your reader that drugs by themselves do not cause addiction. You could cite an article in the *Canadian Journal of Medicine* used by Gabor Maté in his book *In the Realm of Hungry Ghosts* (see page 422), which observed that after studying 6000 people who had been given narcotics for chronic pain, "there was no significant risk of addiction, a finding common to all studies that examine the relationship between addiction and the use of narcotics for pain relief" (Maté 133). If you do use facts and statistics from sources, be sure to document this information according to the conventions explained in Chapter 14.

Use the Patterns of Development

To suggest what kinds of evidence you might look for and give it shape in your essay, you can use any of the patterns discussed in this book. If, for instance, you want to convince your reader that free speech is crucial but has its limits, you could narrate a story about a friend who was deeply hurt by a racist remark, provide examples of expression (like racist slurs) that shouldn't be tolerated, consider what experts believe to be the effects of hate speech on the larger community, contrast examples of speech that should be tolerated with examples that need the censure of the community, and describe what legal authorities believe to be reasonable limits to freedom of speech.

Pathos

In addition to appealing to your reader's intellect with sound reasons, you can be convincing by appealing to your reader's emotions, needs, values, beliefs, and concerns. For example, to persuade your reader to support assisted suicide, you can move the reader to compassion by describing a patient who must linger in pain with no hope of recovery. Similarly, to convince your reader that the federal government should fund daycare, you can stir up the reader's emotions with a graphic explanation of the substandard care the child next door is getting. Persuasive detail, then, uses emotionally charged language to move a reader to a particular view or action.

For example, the essay "Predicting Addiction" (page 435) begins with a brief narrative of a woman who froze to death after a night of heavy drinking and tells of her previous repeated attempts at detoxification. This example solicits our interest in an essay that is otherwise quite scientific and looks at evidence that attempts to distinguish between environmental factors that cause addiction and genetic predispositions to a suite of "externalizing tendencies" that include taking risks and defying authority as well as substance abuse. "The Surprising Truth about Heroin and Addiction" (page 446), an essay that suggests the media overuse fear to get us excited about drug addiction (and make us buy their newspapers and magazines), begins with an example of inappropriate use of emotional appeal. You can learn much about the appropriate and inappropriate use of emotional appeal by noting when the writers in the following sections use it. You might also note when they *don't*.

Appealing to your reader's emotions is a valid technique, but do not overdo it. Emotional appeal should be restrained. It is fine to move your reader's emotions by arousing compassion for a homosexual couple who wants to marry, but it is unfair to charge that tens of thousands of people are despondent and totally unfulfilled because they cannot marry. Your reader will quickly guess that you are overgeneralizing and cease to trust you. (See the section on ethos, below.) Further, emotional appeals should appear *in addition* to logical reasons—not *instead of* them. Rely mostly on logical reasons, and supplement those reasons with emotional appeal when you are dealing with a very resistant audience or feel your essay is becoming dry and impersonal.

Nora Underwood's essay "The Teenage Brain" (page 327) indicates that when we're young we often "think" with our feelings. We usually start post-secondary education, not incidentally, at that point in our intellectual development when we begin to think by considering evidence. When we overload our essays with emotional appeal, we illustrate our own lack of knowledge and condescend to our audience, by suggesting they are willing to make important decisions or take stands based largely on their feelings.

Ethos

You can do a number of things to earn your reader's trust. Perhaps most importantly, you can present a well-reasoned argument based on solid evidence, restrained emotional appeals, and a logical progression of ideas.

While the issue of doing adequate research and finding appropriate experts was discussed above as part of logos, the evidence you find for your argument is a matter of ethos as well. If you want your readers to trust you, you need to convince them of your reliability, albeit implicitly, by using the most current information available and by depending on experts they can trust. If you have particular knowledge or experiences that make you authoritative on a relevant issue, mention them to establish your credentials. For example, if you are arguing that your community should update its zoning laws, note that you were on the zoning board for five years; if you are arguing for improved safety guidelines for playground equipment, mention that your child or sibling was injured on a piece of unsafe equipment.

Finally, you can present yourself as a thoughtful person who weighs all sides of an issue before forming an opinion. The best way to show your reader that you have done that is by raising and countering objections, a technique that is discussed on page 386.

How Logos, Pathos, and Ethos Relate to Purpose and Audience

When you craft an argument and write persuasively, you will usually use some combination of logos, pathos, and ethos. To determine the proportions of these elements, consider your purpose and audience. Of what do you want to persuade your reader? Do you want to convince your audience to think a particular way, perhaps agree that homosexuals should be protected from hate propaganda? Then you can emphasize sound reasons (logos) and your own trustworthiness (ethos). Or do you want your readers to take action and write members of Parliament to encourage them to vote for Hedy Fry's private member's bill adding cyber-bullying to the criminal code? That purpose may require the addition of emotional appeal (pathos), perhaps by moving your reader to anger over a particular instance of cyber-bullying and the way individuals were affected by it.

To determine the appropriate blend of logos, pathos, and ethos, assess your audience in light of your purpose to determine whether your reader is *supportive, wavering,* or *hostile.*

- A *supportive reader* is already on your side. This reader trusts you and shares some or all of your positions. If you were arguing for strengthening the sex education curriculum in local schools, a supportive audience would include members of Planned Parenthood. Although you will still use sound reasoning to support your argument, you can also draw on your trustworthiness to establish your bond with the reader and rely more heavily on emotional appeals to tap into shared beliefs, attitudes, and emotions and solidify support for your assertion. You will still need to use some elements of logos to remind the reader of certain facts and thereby reaffirm agreement. Alter your purpose, however, and the balance of appeals changes. For example, to convince members of Planned Parenthood to contribute to the campaign of a school board candidate, you will need to rely much more on sound reasoning—including information about the candidate's views, qualifications, and commitment to sex education. People generally don't act without being given solid reasons for doing so.
- A *wavering reader* can be brought to your side but is currently not committed to your assertion. Such a reader may be insufficiently informed about the issue, may not have made up his or her mind, or may not have a reason to care. If you were arguing for strengthening the sex education curriculum in local schools, a wavering audience might be parents with very young children, parents who have not yet turned their attention to this issue, or parents who are uncertain about what will be best for their children. For a wavering audience, you must draw on reliable evidence and sound reasoning to convince your readers of the validity of your position and of your own trustworthiness (perhaps as a parent yourself) to incline readers to trust what you say. Emotional appeals (pathos) can be used, but they must be very restrained, or you can alienate your readers by giving them the impression that you are trying to manipulate them.
- A *hostile reader* is the most difficult audience to persuade. This reader is strongly opposed to your assertion or difficult to reach for some other

reason—perhaps because of lack of interest, anger, or reluctance to considering opposing viewpoints. With a hostile audience, you must shape your purpose realistically. You may not have a chance of changing a reader's mind, but you may be able to soften that person's objection a bit or earn some respect for your assertion. For example, if your reader has strong moral beliefs that sex education belongs in the home and not in schools, you will not be able to convince that person to support a stronger sex education curriculum. However, you may be able to help that person see that sex education has some positive aspects. With a hostile reader, emphasize logos. Give your audience your best facts and reasoning and hope they have some impact.

RAISING AND COUNTERING OBJECTIONS

No matter what stand you take on an issue, some reasonable people will disagree with you, and those people will have valid points to support their view. Ignoring this opposition will weaken your argumentation or persuasion because you will not come across as someone who has carefully examined all sides before arriving at a position. Furthermore, even if you ignore the opposition, your reader will not. Your audience will be thinking about the points that work against your assertion, and if you do not deal with those points, you may fail to convince your reader. Thus, you must recognize the opposing arguments and find a way to make them less compelling. Recognizing and making opposition points less compelling is called *raising and countering objections.*

To raise and counter objections, you first acknowledge the objection to your stand by stating it. This is *raising the objection.* Then you make the objection less compelling. This is *countering the objection.* In general, you can raise and counter objections three ways, as illustrated below.

1. *State that the opposition has a point, but so do you.*

   Many people are concerned because federally funded daycare will raise taxes [*objection raised*]. However, children who are currently given substandard care because we lack a comprehensive, federally funded program will not thrive. Children who do not thrive fail to realize their potential or they develop problems, both of which end up costing society more money than daycare [*objection countered*].

   Many people believe that if drugs are decriminalized, they will be more widely available and more people will become addicted [*objection raised*]. Studies of Vietnam veterans and of patients who have used opioid pain relievers, however, indicate that once the external stress or the pain is relieved, the individual no longer craves or uses narcotic drugs [*objection countered*].

2. *State that the opposition has a point, but your point is better.*

Although some are concerned about the cost of federally funded daycare [*objection raised*], such costs are warranted by the benefits. Children who attend daycares with well-trained staff and appropriate learning goals are better prepared for kindergarten and thus have a more positive attitude toward school [*objection countered*].

Many people believe that if drugs are decriminalized, they will be more widely available, more people will become addicted, and the streets will be less safe for everyone [*objection raised*]. In truth, the artificially inflated price of black market drugs is what encourages addicts to steal, prostitute themselves, and become drug dealers in order to pay for their habit. Much drug-related crime, at both the local and international level, is the result of a black market that keeps the price of drugs inflated and makes pushing drugs profitable and thus attractive [*objection countered*].

3. *State that the opposition's point is untrue.*

There are those who maintain that we do not need federally funded daycare [*objection raised*]. However, the number of mothers who must work outside the home is very high, and many of these working mothers are the sole support of their children and could not stay home even if they wanted to. As a result, many parents are forced into substandard, or even downright dangerous, child-care arrangements [*objection countered*].

Some people believe that simply trying heroine or cocaine will turn you into an addict [*objection raised*]. Government statistics suggest, however, that our image of the substance abuser as a street person waiting to mug us to feed his or her habit is alarmist. "The National Household Survey on Drug Abuse indicates that about 3 million Americans have used heroine in their lifetimes; of them, 15 percent had used it in the last year, 4 percent in the last month. These numbers suggest that the vast majority of heroin users either never become addicted or, if they do, manage to give the drug up" (Sullum 449) [*objection countered*].

Raising and countering objections helps strengthen your case, but you need not deal with every opposition point. Instead, identify the most compelling objections and deal with those.

THE TOULMIN MODEL

In his book *The Uses of Argument* (1958), Stephen Toulmin identifies three parts of an argument. An adaptation of his division is given here. You may find it helpful as you analyze the arguments of others and write your own arguments.

In the Toulmin model, you can think of argumentation and persuasion as having three parts: the claim, the support, and the assumption.

The *claim* is the point you are arguing; it is what you are trying to convince your reader of. Here are some examples of claims.

CLAIM   This university should switch from its current quarter system
                    to the semester system.

CLAIM   Teachers should not be permitted to engage in labour strikes.

CLAIM   Canada's immigration policy creates many problems.

In argumentation and persuasion, the claim appears in the thesis.

The *support* is the ideas and information you include to convince the reader. The support can be evidence based on logical reasoning—statistics and facts, for example—or it can be appeals to emotions, values, and beliefs. Here are examples of both kinds of support.

CLAIM   This university should switch from its current quarter system to
                    the semester system.

SUPPORT   The administration says that the switch would save the university
(BASED ON   money because fewer terms would reduce the cost of registration
REASON)   and advisement.

SUPPORT   Semesters allow students to study subjects more in depth.
(APPEAL TO   (An appeal to the belief that it is better to have a chance to
BELIEF)   examine a topic in depth.)

In argumentation and persuasion, the support will be the supporting details.

The third part of argumentation and persuasion is the *assumption,* which is the inference or belief that connects the claim and the support. To see how the assumption connects the claim and support, study this example.

CLAIM   This university should switch from its current quarter system to
                    the semester system.

SUPPORT   The administration says that the switch would save the university
(REASON)   money because fewer terms would reduce the cost of registration
                    and advisement.

UNSTATED   The administration is trustworthy, so it can be believed when it
ASSUMPTIONS   says that money will be saved. Saving the administration money
                    is a good thing.

If the reader trusts the administration, the assumption is accepted and the support is convincing. However, if the reader does not trust the administration, then the assumption is not accepted and the support fails to convince. When a reader might not accept an assumption automatically, you must articulate and support the assumption to make it convincing.

STATED
ASSUMPTION
WITH SUPPORT

The administration says that the switch would save the university money because fewer terms would reduce the cost of registration and advisement. They arrived at this conclusion after surveying 200 schools that have switched from the quarter to the semester system.

Sometimes an assumption is a value or belief.

CLAIM

Teachers should not be allowed to engage in labour strikes.

SUPPORT

When teachers strike, they cause a great deal of harm.

ASSUMPTION

The need for students to have stable learning environments is more important than the need for teachers to be able to strike.

This example shows that the assumption is very much at the heart of an argument because it is what will or will not incline the reader to move from the support to accepting the claim. To prove that teachers should not strike, you would have to prove the assumption and show how teachers are different from others who strike: steelworkers, truck drivers, television writers, and so forth.

Sometimes the assumption is self-evident, so it need not be written out. Say, for example, that you want to argue that we should censor the Internet to protect children from predatory adults. The assumption that we do not want children harmed is so obvious that it need not be stated. Now say that you want to argue that teenagers who commit murder should be tried as adults. In this case, the assumption that some teenagers are emotionally and intellectually mature needs to be stated and proven. Otherwise, your reader may have difficulty moving from your support to accepting your claim.

INDUCTIVE AND DEDUCTIVE REASONING

Induction and deduction are two methods of reasoning especially helpful for supporting a claim.

Induction

Induction is a form of reasoning that moves from specific evidence to a general conclusion. That is, when you reason inductively, you examine specific facts, cases, examples, and other available evidence and then draw a reasonable conclusion based on that information. Induction is used all the time: A doctor ponders a patient's symptoms and test results and reasons inductively to reach a diagnosis; a jury considers the evidence presented at the trial and reasons inductively to reach a verdict; a police officer studies the crime scene, examines clues, and reasons inductively to establish a list of suspects.

When you write argumentation or persuasion, induction can serve you well. Assume, for example, that you wish to argue the need for a traffic light at the corner of First Street and Third Avenue. You can first present your specific evidence: In the last year, traffic accidents at that intersection have increased 80 percent; five people have died there, including two children; traffic at that intersection has increased since the shopping mall opened a mile away; the police force has said a traffic light there could reduce the number of accidents. After offering this evidence, you can present your view in the form of a generalization that follows from the evidence: We need a traffic light installed at the corner of First Street and Third Avenue. This generalization would be your thesis.

No matter how compelling your evidence seems to be, you cannot always be certain of the reliability of the generalization you conclude from it. Thus, it may well be true that a traffic light would solve the problem at First Street and Third Avenue, but it could also be true that the real problem is the speed limit and a better solution is to reduce it from 60 kph to 40 kph. Because the conclusion drawn in inductive reasoning is rarely certain beyond a doubt, that conclusion is called an *inference.* To increase the likelihood that your inferences are accurate, be sure that your evidence is sound. Be careful to supply enough evidence and to verify that the evidence is accurate, recent, specific, and representative. For help with supplying sound evidence, review the information on avoiding errors in logic on pages 9–12.

Deduction

In a broad sense, deduction involves reasoning from the general to the specific, but you should not think of deduction as the opposite of induction. Instead, **deduction** moves from a generalization (called a *major premise*) to a specific case (called a *minor premise*) and on to a conclusion, like this:

MAJOR PREMISE
(GENERALIZATION)   Because of compulsory attendance laws, a number of students who do not want to be in school disrupt the educational process.

MINOR PREMISE
(SPECIFIC CASE)   Many students in this province do not want to be in school, and they disrupt the educational process for those who do want to learn.

| CONCLUSION | If we abolish compulsory attendance laws in this province, students who do not want to be in school can leave and make it easier for others to learn. |

Recall that with inductive reasoning, the conclusion is an inference rather than a certainty. In deductive reasoning, however, if the two premises are accurate, then the conclusion will follow inescapably. If one or both of the premises are wrong, then the conclusion will not follow, as is the case in this example:

MAJOR PREMISE	All college students drink beer.
MINOR PREMISE	Chris is a college student.
CONCLUSION	Chris drinks beer.

In this example, the conclusion cannot be accepted because the major premise is an overgeneralization. (See page 10.) Not all college students drink beer; therefore, we cannot conclude inescapably that college-student Chris drinks beer. To be sure your major and minor premises meet the test of logic, refer to page 9 on avoiding errors in logic.

Deductive reasoning can provide a very useful frame work for argumentation and persuasion. You can set up your essay so that your supporting details present the evidence demonstrating the truth of each premise. With the premises proven, your reader will accept your thesis, which is the point you are arguing.

ORGANIZING ARGUMENTATION AND PERSUASION

The introduction to an essay using argumentation or persuasion can be handled many ways. Explaining why the issue is important can be effective because it helps the reader understand the seriousness of your purpose. Thus, if you are arguing that high schools should have daycare centres for teenage mothers, your introduction can note the large number of teen mothers who drop out of school because they have no child care. This figure should help your reader appreciate the urgency of the issue. If your reader needs certain background information in order to appreciate your argument, the introduction can be a good place to provide that information. Thus, if you are arguing the need to return to homogeneous groupings in classrooms, you should explain what a homogeneous grouping is if your reader is not likely to know. The introduction can also be a good place to establish your ethos. Thus, if you are arguing in favour of increasing the provincial sales tax, you can note that you have worked in the province's finance department for three years and can confirm the recent claims of shortfalls.

Your thesis, whether it appears in the opening paragraphs or elsewhere, should state the issue and your assertion about that issue, like one of the following:

> Canada desperately needs federally funded daycare. (*issue:* federally funded daycare; *stand:* in favour of it)

> Federally funded daycare would create more problems than it solves. (*issue:* federally funded daycare; *stand:* against it)

Be sure that the issue you are arguing is genuinely debatable. There is no reason to argue that parents should love their children because no one will disagree with you. Similarly, avoid matters of taste. For example, arguing that basketball is a better sport than football is not productive because the issue is a matter of personal preference.

In general, arranging your points in a progressive order (from least to most compelling) is effective. This way, you can save your most convincing arguments for the end so your reader leaves your essay with them fresh in mind. Or you can place your second strongest argument first for a strong, persuasive beginning, and your strongest argument last for a compelling conclusion. Remember, the points at the end of an essay are in the most emphatic position and therefore likely to have the biggest impact.

If you are reasoning inductively, you can place your thesis at the end of your essay, after you have presented all the specific evidence pointing to the inference that stands as your thesis. Placing the thesis at the end can work well for a hostile reader. You can build your case and then present your assertion about the issue. If you are reasoning deductively, you can first present the evidence to support your major premise, and then present the evidence to support your minor premise.

You will probably find topic sentences helpful when you structure argumentation or persuasion. You can place each reason for your thesis in its own topic sentence and follow each topic sentence with the appropriate support. Thus, an essay arguing that we should pay university athletes rather than give them scholarships could have these topic sentences:

> If we pay university athletes, the players can use the money for whatever they like—including tuition and books.

> If we pay university athletes, we can finally dispel the myth that the players are always students first.

Finally, once we pay university athletes, we can allow universities to openly acknowledge that they are farm clubs for professional teams.

If you raise and counter objections, you can do this throughout the essay, wherever a point to be countered logically emerges. However, if you are dealing with very few objections, you can raise and counter them together in one or two paragraphs at the beginning or end of the essay.

To conclude, you can reaffirm your assertion for emphasis, summarize your chief arguments if your reader is likely to appreciate the reminder, or present your most persuasive point. In addition, you can call your audience to action by explaining what you want your reader to do. Or you can recommend a particular solution to a problem. Finally, explaining what would happen if your thesis were or were not adopted can be an effective closing.

VISUALIZING AN ARGUMENTATION OR PERSUASION ESSAY

The chart on page 394 can help you visualize the structure for an argumentation or persuasion essay. Like all good models, however, this one can be altered as needed.

PROCESS GUIDELINES: STRATEGIES FOR WRITING ARGUMENTATION OR PERSUASION

1. **Selecting a Topic.** If you need help discovering a topic, try one of these strategies.
    - Review the essays in this book for ideas. Or review local and campus newspapers to learn about controversial issues of importance.
    - Fill in the blank in one of these sentences:
      It is unfair that _____.
      It makes me angry that _____.
      I disagree with people who believe that _____.

Troubleshooting Guide

Avoiding Errors in Logic
If you have trouble avoiding errors in logic, review pages 9–12 on "Detecting Errors in Logic." Being able to detect errors in the logic of others should help you, during revision, to avoid faulty reasoning in your own writing as well.

Introduction
• Creates interest in the essay, perhaps by explaining why the issue is important, providing background information, or establishing your reliability • States the thesis, which gives the debatable issue and your assertion

Body Paragraphs
• Give and explain the points to support your assertion, continuing until all points are made • May rely on logos, pathos, and /or ethos • May raise and counter objections • Rely on inductive or deductive reasoning • Arrange details in progressive order

Conclusion
• Can reaffirm your position or present your most persuasive point • Can call your reader to action or recommend a solution to a problem • Can explain what would happen if your thesis were or were not adopted

The quality of life in my community would be better if _____.

People of my generation would be more confident about our future if

_____.

Opportunities for children would be enhanced if _____.

2. **Determining Purpose and Assessing Audience**. Answer these questions:
    - Do you want to convince your reader to think a particular way about an issue? If so, what do you want your reader to think?
    - Do you want your reader to take a particular action? If so, what do you want your reader to do?
    - Is your reader supportive, wavering, or hostile? Is your purpose reasonable for such an audience?

3. **Generating Ideas.** Answering the following questions can help you generate ideas:
    - Based on your purpose and audience, how will you balance logos, pathos, and ethos?
    - Why is your issue important? To whom is it important?
    - What would happen if your thesis were adopted? If it were not adopted?
    - What are the chief objections to your thesis? How can you logically and constructively counter those objections?

- How can you appeal to your reader's emotions?
- How can you present yourself as trustworthy?

4. **Revising.** Ask two reliable readers to review your draft to be sure you have avoided errors in logic (see page 9) and that you have countered important objections.

✔ Checklist for Revising Argumentation or Persuasion

Be sure:

_____ Your thesis is genuinely debatable.

_____ Your introduction provides background, explains why your topic is important, or otherwise engages readers' interest.

_____ Your thesis notes the issue and your assertion.

_____ All your points are clarified and supported.

_____ Logos, pathos, and ethos are appropriately balanced.

_____ You have avoided "as any fool can see" phrasings.

_____ If necessary, you have stated and supported the assumptions that connect your claims and support.

_____ You have appealed to emotion, values, and beliefs with appropriate restraint.

_____ You have avoided problems with logic.

_____ You have raised and countered compelling objections.

_____ Paraphrases and quotations are documented according to the conventions given in Chapter 14.

_____ Your conclusion brings the essay to a satisfying close.

ANNOTATED STUDENT ESSAY

Student-author Hannah Scheels uses argumentation to convince readers that the Kansas attorney general's rejection of 1600 free CDs is a serious form of censorship. She also works to move readers to take action against this censorship. After you read the essay, you will have an opportunity to evaluate it.

Title
Notice the word play: "Cast Out" is a clever reference to OutKast.

Paragraph 1
This introductory paragraph gives background information— the details of the settlement. The thesis is the last sentence. The issue is the action of the Kansas attorney general; the assertion is that the action undermines the first amendment. Notice the use of quotation.

Paragraph 2
The topic sentence idea (library patrons are denied access to important music) is implied. The details establish that the rejected music is important, which helps support the idea that the attorney general did the wrong thing. Notice that the source of information is acknowledged.

Cast Out of Kansas: Music Censorship in Public Libraries

1   In the summer of 2004, Kansas was one of forty states nationwide to receive several thousand free compact disks as part of a settlement to resolve charges that the music industry had fixed prices for recordings. The disks were intended to be given, free of charge, to public libraries in these forty states, where they would be made available to anyone who wished to listen to them. However, library patrons in Kansas will not be able to listen to more than 1,600 of these recordings (out of a total 51,000) because the Kansas attorney general found that they "did not mesh with the values of a majority of Kansans" (CNN.com). This chilling example of state-sponsored censorship interferes with the ability of Kansas citizens—and their librarians—to determine their own "values" for themselves. Left unchallenged, the actions of the Kansas attorney general set a dangerous precedent that undermines First Amendment rights to free speech guaranteed to all by the U.S. Constitution.

2   According to an article on CNN.com, the rejected disks include works by the rap artists OutKast and Notorious B.I.G., the popular alternative rock bands Stone Temple Pilots and Rage Against the Machine, and classic alternative voices ranging from Lou Reed to Devo. All of these artists have well-earned reputations for the quality and expressiveness of their lyrics as well as their innovative music. Another quality these artists share is their status as "alternative." Even though many of these artists are Grammy winners (a testament to their popularity and the enormous sales of their music), they are more importantly critically acclaimed. Rap artists OutKast have merged funk, rhythm and blues, and hip-hop in a significantly creative fashion. At the same time, their music videos brilliantly send up stereotypical images of black musicians. Notorious B.I.G.'s lyrics capture the very real violence that defines the lives of so many urban Americans. Lou Reed's deadpan lyrics describe the alternative lifestyles of the 1960s and 1970s in unforgettable images. And both the Stone Temple Pilots and Rage Against the Machine evoke, in both their lyrics and their musical arrangements, the frustration and lack of opportunity felt by so many young people in an age of increasing cultural and economic conformity.

3   It is true that these artists, in their desire to tell the truth as they see it and express the realities they believe we should all at least acknowledge, often use explicit language and create images that can be disturbing. Sometimes, as in the work of OutKast, the sexual language and imagery can be pornographic. This is why the recording industry puts parental advisory stickers on disks that contain violent or explicit language, and why many artists (including OutKast) also release "clean" versions of their albums that digitally remove the potentially offensive language without interfering with the overall integrity of the music.

4   What is most disturbing about the decision of the Kansas attorney general is that he has made his decision based on "Internet databases of lyrics" (CNN.com). In other words, these artists are being censored as writers, not just as musicians. If these musicians published their lyrics as poetry or short stories instead of albums, this decision would seem to set a precedent that would allow a state attorney general to remove books from a library—or, as in this case, prevent some books from ever even reaching a library's shelves.

5   The actions of the Kansas attorney general also override the expertise, experience, and responsibilities of local librarians. Even though the executive director of the Kansas Library Association is quoted in the CNN. com article as saying that the attorney general "did libraries a big favor by selecting these CDs because there's no way libraries could have said what they wanted," the fact is that librarians had no say at all in this decision. Local librarians are trained to be sensitive to the needs and "values" of their particular neighborhoods and communities. By abdicating their responsibility to a state attorney general—an elected official with a political agenda—the librarians of Kansas have damaged the First Amendment rights of Kansas citizens. Further, they have violated the Code of Ethics of the American Library Association, which states that librarians must "uphold the principles of intellectual freedom and resist all efforts to censor library resources" (American Library Association).

6   Furthermore, this decision is grossly unfair to those citizens who either cannot afford to purchase CDs, or who wish to sample a recording before purchasing it (or allowing their children to purchase it). Paradoxically, in an age where major retailers such as Wal-Mart are themselves curtailing (based on "values") the kinds of music, DVDs, books, and magazines they make available to consumers, public libraries may in some communities be the *only* place people can turn to for a genuinely diverse and fair selection of media.

Paragraph 3
The topic sentence (the first sentence) presents an objection, and the rest of the paragraph counters that objection.

Paragraph 4
The topic sentence (the second sentence) gives the next reason supporting the assertion. The rest of the paragraph relies on sound reasoning (logos) for support. Notice that transition is achieved with the synonym "decision." Also notice the quotation, which is credited in parentheses.

Paragraph 5
The topic sentence (the first sentence) gives the next reason supporting the assertion. The rest of the paragraph relies on sound reasoning (logos) for support. Notice the quotation and that the source is given.

Paragraph 6
The topic sentence (the first sentence) gives the next reason supporting the assertion. The rest of the paragraph relies on sound reasoning (logos) for support. Notice the transition, "furthermore."

Paragraph 7
This is the conclusion. The essay ends with a call to action.

7   Patrons of libraries nationwide should actively protest what is happening in Kansas, unless they want their acquisitions and holdings to be managed by lawyers rather than librarians. The issue here is not about the "decency" of certain musicians, but about the freedom of Americans to determine their values for themselves.

Works Cited

Works cited
For information on how to document paraphrases and quotations, including how to write a works cited citation, see Chapter 14.

American Library Association. "Code of Ethics." ALA, 28 June 1995. Web. 12 Sept. 2004.

"'OutKast' Not Allowed in Kansas Libraries." *CNN.com*. Cable News Network, 6 Aug. 2004. Web. 12 Sept. 2004.

PEER REVIEW

Responding to "Cast Out of Kansas: Music Censorship in Public Libraries"
Evaluate "Cast Out of Kansas: Music Censorship in Public Libraries" by responding to these questions:

1. Is the essay persuasive? Why or why not?
2. Should the essay include more logos, ethos, or pathos? Explain.
3. Are significant objections raised and countered effectively? Explain.
4. Are there any problems with logic?
5. Do paraphrases and quotations help the writer achieve her persuasive purpose?
6. What do you like best about the essay?
7. What single change do you think would improve the essay?

READING SELECTIONS

How Can We Address the Issue of Climate Change?

The majority of Canadians identify "the environment" as an issue that needs to be addressed. But what do we mean by "the environment"? We probably make a connection between "global warming" and the price of gas; we've heard our leaders talk about revenue-neutral carbon taxes or a cap-and-trade system that allows some companies to go on creating CO_2 as long as it doesn't hurt their bottom line. But "the environment" is more complicated than this.

It's true that we are using non-renewable sources of energy (like coal to produce electricity and oil to drive our cars) and that a by-product of these is carbon dioxide. CO_2, in turn, is destroying the ozone layer, which acts as earth's sunscreen, causing climate change. We're seeing this effect in hotter summers, the melting of polar ice and permafrost, and in the wilder weather; we're also seeing it in rising skin cancer rates. It's also clear that we need to do something about this before our climates become inhospitable and coastal cities find themselves under water. But what do we do? Do we legislate a response to climate change by imposing penalties on companies that produce CO_2—something British Columbia has dared to do with its revenue-neutral carbon tax but the federal government avoids? Do we invest in alternative sources of renewable power, like wind or solar energy? Or do we put our hopes behind alternatives fuels for the car? Do we throw our support behind public transit? Do we all bicycle or walk to work? And how do we effect these changes, given that our cities have grown in a way that depends on the automobile, sprawling outward to the suburbs and resulting in commute times that too often exceed an hour, given the traffic jams? Do we stop eating meat, given that it takes 10 kilograms of grain to produce 1 kilogram of meat, and that livestock produces as much greenhouse gas as our cars and planes do?

But the ozone layer isn't the only problem. In many developing parts of the world, people are already fighting over limited resources like clean water. In others, farmers are burning forests that turn carbon dioxide into oxygen in exchange for poor soil that will allow them to farm for a few more years. In still others, we're changing the habitat of the grizzly or of wolves; Canada's talk, once again, of a pipeline, risks disrupting the migration of the caribou. Logging in Mexico is affecting the winter habitat of Monarch butterflies that spend their summers in Canada. Each time we destroy a species or disrupt its habitat, we're playing Russian roulette with the delicate balance of ecosystems.

How do we—and our political parties, which believe that being elected means a sound economy and the lowest possible taxes—balance our concern for the environment with their effects on our economy and our way of life? Because the planet is a very complex ecosystem and because economics, though it seems like a dispassionate and scientific discipline, is nevertheless subjective, we don't know how much it will cost to reduce our CO_2 emissions to a sustainable level. Yet we've certainly seen that the pocketbook speaks, given that rising gas prices have slowed the purchase of inefficient vehicles and prompted car manufacturers to explore more fuel-efficient engines and to work to create engines that can run on renewable energy sources. It's true that some solutions—like building nuclear reactors or retooling coal-fired power stations so the carbon can be captured and stored—might be costly. But the truth is that improving the insulation in our houses, driving fuel-efficient vehicles, keeping our houses a little warmer in the summer and a little cooler in the winter, using canvas bags when we shop, and not buying bottled water would effect a major change in CO_2 levels while saving us money.

Psychologists tell us that it's hard to change habits. It's easier to convince people to do something once, like buy a fuel-efficient car, than it is to ask them to change habits and consistently turn down the furnace every night before they go to bed or close windows and drapes during hot days and open them again in the cooler evenings. Psychologists have also noted, however, that two strategies are quite effective.

We need prompts that remind us to make those changes. And if those prompts are delivered by a real person, not an anonymous media campaign, they're likely to be even more effective. (See the research writing assignment on page 419 for more information.)

We also need to be connected to our world to realize what we're risking and what we're committing ourselves to. This is a different kind of connectedness than email, text messaging, or even Facebook. In fact, this means putting away your iPod and going for a walk, all your senses on high alert. What do you see? What do you hear and smell? What do you feel if you imagine that human beings two generations hence will live in a changed world that has more wars over scarce resources and that has destroyed the habitat of the birds you are hearing?

Background

Wayne Grady has written eight books of non-fiction about travel and natural history, including *Bringing Back the Dodo*, from which this selection is taken. He has won three Science in Society awards from the Canadian Science Writers' Association for his writing on nature. As freelance editor, he has gathered six literary anthologies. He is also a translator of French Canadian fiction into English, winning the Governor General's award for his translation of *On the Eighth Day* by Antoine Maillet. He's the former editor of *Harrowsmith*, and science editor of *Equinox*.

The Pattern and its Purposes

Wayne Grady's essay "On Walking" attempts to persuade us that there are rewards to putting down the remote control, getting out of cars and planes, and simply walking. Part of his persuasion comes in the form of examples of famous walkers: the pilgrims in Chaucer's *Canterbury Tales*, Bill Bryson, Henry David Thoreau, and Charles Wilkins who, in 2002, set out to walk from Thunder Bay to New York City and found walking transformed his relationship with time. Grady uses cause and effect hypothesis to consider why humans have evolved—though not perfectly—to walk and concludes that it's to get perspective. Though not an explicit argument for environmental change, Grady's peripatetic essay nevertheless encourages us to create a new relationship with the natural world— a crucial step in respecting and becoming stewards of that world.

On Walking

Wayne Grady

1   Late in the morning of April 27, 2002, Charles Wilkins set out from his home in Thunder Bay, Ontario, with the idea of walking to New York City. It wasn't a last-minute vanishing act; he did make some preparations. He got a cellphone. He bought some gear. He convinced a friend, George Morrissette, who is a poet, to "more or less keep pace" with him in a van. He threw a few necessities into the van—a laptop, some warm clothes, extra shoes, tins of sardines—and set off, with Morrissette driving on ahead to wait for him somewhere far, far down the road. He soon realized that there were a few things he hadn't done enough of. Training, for example.

> **As you read**
> Consider the way your usual mode of transportation influences your interactions with and perceptions of the world around you.

2   "On my first day out," he told me while still en route, "I walked twenty-five kilometres and was wobbly by the time I stopped. The next day my knee hurt so badly I had to finish my walking going backwards!" But the body, he said, "adjusts marvellously." It took only three weeks of walking for him to become "totally comfortable," during which time he upped his daily progress to thirty-five kilometres, dropped his weight to 150 pounds, gained two inches on his calves, hardened his buttocks, and shed a dozen layers of skin from his soles. "My feet," he reported, "have adjusted to the point where, when a layer of skin is ripped off, there's another waiting serviceably underneath, ready to go."

3   His motivation for taking the big walk, apart from "simple curiosity about this most ancient and fundamental means of transportation"—more than any other attribute, it is upright walking that distinguishes us from most other vertebrates: even birds,

though bipedal, walk with their spines parallel to the ground—was to prove to the, rest of us that we have become a sedentary species, or rather a species that, thanks to technology, moves incredibly fast while remaining physically and mentally in one place. "While jet travel and the Internet shrink the planet," he said, "walking expands it." By walking, he slowed the world down to a pace "at which noticing becomes not just possible but unavoidable."

4   Such a pace is too slow for most of us. As a rule, North Americans don't walk. I mean really walk, as Charles walked, or as they walked, say, in, Chaucer's England, when April with its sweet breath reportedly made everyone long to go on pilgrimages and talk one another's ears off. Even eighty years ago walking was more common than it is now. Walking tours were a commonplace, like today's bus tours. In 1927, the novelist V.S. Pritchett set off, on a whim and on his own, to walk across Spain. He wanted, as he recorded in his first book, *Marching Spain*, to know "the monotony of that burned-up country, the dumbness of its cottages and taverns. It would be unpleasant for my body," he shrugged, "but for the soul it would be ennobling."

> "We think nothing of driving an hour to see a movie but wouldn't dream of walking for an hour to see a friend."

5   Nowadays, as Wilkins noted, the car drive and the hard drive have yanked the legs out from under us. He might have added that, while motorized conveyances have brought distant places closer, they have also robbed us of the nearer destinations: we think nothing of driving an hour to see a movie but wouldn't dream of walking for an hour to see a friend. A study conducted recently at the University of California determined that the average American walks less than seventy-five miles a year, or about one thousand steps a day. As Bill Bryson, author of *A Walk in the Woods*, notes, "I rack up more mileage than that just looking for the channel changer."

6   Bryson's plan to test the level of wimpiness to which we have descended was to spend two summers racking up the better part of two thousand miles walking the Appalachian Trail from Virginia to Maine. About two thousand hikers attempt it each year, of whom fewer than two hundred make it all the way. Not to detract from their achievement, but completing the Appalachian Trail, or the Yellowstone-to-Yukon Trail, or the still-on-the-drawingboard Trans Canada Trail, is not walking but hiking, and hiking differs markedly from what Charles Wilkins did, which was closer to answering American naturalist John Muir's call to "throw a loaf of bread and a pound of tea in an old sack and jump over the back fence." A hike is more like a business trip than a vacation. It has that purposeful, heads-down, chalk-up-the-kilometres feel to it that walking lacks. Chaucer's pilgrims, though they walked with a purpose and many of them carried sticks, cannot be said to have been hiking. They told each other stories as they went. In fact, they told so many stories they never made it to Canterbury.

7   Thoreau would have said they were sauntering. In his essay "Walking," he traced the origin of the word *saunter* to pilgrims making their way to the Holy Land, the

Sainte-Terre and so were called "Sainte-terrers," which became saunterers. That is, of course, a wild conjecture—the OED admits the word's origin is "obscure" (an OED euphemism for anybody's guess, without acknowledging Thoreau's)—but it does catch the sense of a pilgrimage as something done more for the sake of walking than of getting anywhere.

8   Thoreau believed that walking freed the soul, allowed the mind to range as it could not when confined to a cabin, a cab, or a coach. "I think that I cannot preserve my health and spirits," he wrote, "unless I spend four hours a day at least—and it is commonly more than that—sauntering through the woods and over the hills and fields, absolutely free from all worldly engagements." His essay is a record of the many and varied and often unrelated thoughts that flitted through his mind as he walked, composing his own version of the *Canterbury Tales*. He never walked on roads, he said, and always instinctively headed west when he left his cabin, for "the West of which I speak is but another name for the Wild, and . . . in Wilderness is the preservation of the World." Humans require daily sustenance from nature: "Every tree sends its fibres forth in search of the Wild," and we should do likewise.

9   Although Bryson was hiking, he agreed with Thoreau. The restorative power of walking, he wrote, comes from the fact that, while doing it "you have no engagements, commitments, obligations, or duties; no special ambitions and only the smallest, least complicated of wants; you exist in a tranquil tedium, serenely beyond the reach of exasperation."

10   When Thoreau proclaimed himself a walker, he meant something a little more demanding than going for an after-dinner stroll. "If you are ready to leave father and mother," he wrote, "and brother and sister, and wife and child and friends, and never see them again, if you have paid your debts and made your will, and settled all your affairs, and are a free man, then you are ready for a walk." Was that how he prepared for the trip he described in *A Yankee in Canada*, published in 1866, for which he walked from Montreal to Quebec City, a distance of some three hundred kilometres, in a week? One suspects not. He made the journey in much the same way that walking-tourists today amble about the Italian or English countryside, sticking to the roads, light day-bags over their shoulders, and eyes sharply peeled for five-star inns. When a coach offered itself, Thoreau happily hopped aboard.

11   Getting up on our hind legs was, biologically speaking, an interesting posture to adopt. Evolutionists argue about what prompted it. There are as many theories as there are theorists. Even a brief rundown of them is illuminating (my objections to them are in brackets): walking upright made it easier to carry food and babies (all animals carry food and babies); it evolved from wading and swimming (then why didn't other aquatic attributes, such as webbed feet?); it allowed us to follow migratory herds across the savannahs (you mean, the way lions do?); it was more energy efficient than walking on four legs (then why don't more animals do it?); it exposed our bodies to less sun, thereby allowing us to colonize hotter habitats (so would smaller heads and

keeping our bodily hair, and some of us can't even keep the hair on our heads); it exposed the male genitalia, which was either attractive to females (!) or frightening to rival males (!!).

12   The one I like best, though it has been unpopular for two decades, holds that, as early hominids emerged from the forest onto the savannahs, they needed to stand upright in order to see above the tall grass. One may wonder why other grassland species—lions and hyenas and gazelles and such—remained staunchly quadrupedal, but perhaps having started out as tree-dwellers, we had become accustomed to seeing greater distances, to being able to situate ourselves with reference to a horizon, or a distant landmark, and that is what we missed when we sauntered out onto the prairie. Little knolls and the occasional shrub didn't do it for us. We needed perspective.

13   However we acquired bipedality, the benefits soon multiplied. Most evolutionists credit our large brains to the complex neurological demands imposed upon it by upright walking. Seeing farther meant seeing more; the brain had to deal with a vast increase in peripheral input, had constantly to assess the possible meaning of vaguely perceived movements and shapes. Our binocular vision sharpened, turning us into predators—usually a bigger-brained occupation than cud-chewing. (Predatory species, with the exception of some fish, are binocular; that is, with both eyes facing forward and thus providing depth perception. Prey species tend to have eyes on the sides of their heads, to see more of what's happening all around. Think of eagles and chickens, or wolves and sheep.) Standing upright also meant hearing more, which required extensive renovations to our auditory chambers.

14   Many dinosaurs were bipedal, particularly those that evolved into birds, without developing Mensa-sized brains. Why not? One possible answer is that they didn't have much in the way of front legs before they started walking on their hind legs. Most of the big bipedal carnivores, the *T. rexes* and their raptorial kin, had spindly little front legs that were so short they couldn't reach their gigantic mouths. It's hard to think what use they were. Too short for feeding, no good for balance, useless for holding down an opposite number during battles or sex. Such forelimbs hardly required a dinosaur to do much more thinking than it did when it was horizontal. But the forelimbs of primates were at least as long as their hindlimbs, and standing upright left those long front legs and hands free to develop into tool-holding appendages, which allowed the brain to devise splendid new uses for such things as sticks and rocks (with which materials we still make most of our houses). The palms of our hands became almost as sensitive as our tongues. Our brains swelled to accommodate all this new input from the five senses.

> "Walking on two legs is riskier than is riskier than walking on all four, just as riding on two wheels is wobblier than riding on four."

15   There were, however, trade-offs. Walking on two legs is riskier than walking on all four, just as riding on two wheels is wobblier than riding on four. John Napier, an

evolutionist who argues for the early development of bipedality in humankind (before larger brains), writes that "human walking is a unique activity during which the body, step by step, teeters on the edge of catastrophe." It may not be such a bad thing that we teeter on that edge for only 315 metres a day; couch potatoes may be the saviours of our species—unless, of course, we need an occasional dose of catastrophe in our lives, to keep the adrenalin flowing. There is much in history to suggest that that is the case.

16   If so, walking would do it. It's a nail-biting, bone-jarring activity. After 3.7 million years of near-disaster, we have arrived at a better bone structure for bipedalism, but we still haven't got it quite right, and there have been attendant disadvantages. We have widened our hip joints and brought our knees together (chimpanzees have narrow hips and bowed legs, which accounts for their awkward gait on land) and the pelvis, as Rebecca Solnit observes nice in *Wanderlust: A History of Walking,* "has tilted up to cradle the viscera and support the weight of the upright body, becoming a shallow vase from which the stem of the waist rises."

17   But, as physiotherapists know, wide hips and narrowed knees don't seem to work well together. The patellae, or kneecaps, wander around, slip sideways, tilt upward, and tendons and ligaments have a half-life of about twenty years, which is why knees are often the first things to go in athletes such as hockey players and skiers. By the age of fifty, most of us begin to stiffen up in the knees, and by the time we reach our allotted threescore years and ten, shoe inserts, knee and hip replacements, and patella manipulations are our common lot.

18   But the real adrenalin flows during childbirth. The brain of a human infant at birth is already as large as that of a fullgrown chimpanzee, and yet the birth canal in humans has become smaller over evolutionary time, a consequence of our upright stance, making childbirth—the thing animals are supposed to be best at—a difficult, painful, and sometimes fatal process for both mother and child. We gestate our children longer than other primates, because our big brains take longer to develop; but in doing so we jeopardize our chances of surviving birth. This seems a contradiction. Our large brains are both our liberation and our limitation.

19   We seem to thrive on contradiction. Charles Wilkins observes that walking gave us larger heads, which made us more intelligent, which allowed us to invent ways to avoid walking. Thoreau made his living as a surveyor, pacing out and parcelling up the land that he would have remain free and unencumbered. In "Walking," for all its Whitmanesque enthusiasm for wilderness—"I believe in the forest, and in the meadow, and in the night in which the corn grows"—he also suggested it was by taming the wilderness that humankind achieved its ultimate purpose: "I think that the farmer displaces the Indian even because he redeems the meadow, and so makes himself stronger and in some respects more natural." We don't normally think of Thoreau as a spin doctor for land development.

20   All of which goes to show that, while walking, the mind wanders with the feet, and both can be errant if they are so inclined. Many ancient and modern philosophers

walked in order to set their thoughts to roaming. Greece had its Peripatetic school of wandering scholars, whose loyalties were more to ideas than to city-states—"an attachment," Solnit notes, "that requires detachment." Thomas Hobbes carried a walking stick with a built-in inkwell, in case he had a brainstorm during his afternoon stroll. Einstein claimed to have done his best thinking while walking on a beach. Wordsworth and his fellow Romantic poets regularly stalked the Lake District, though they took the train to get there (Bill Bryson remarked sourly on his neighbours in New Hampshire who drove the few blocks from home to their exercise classes, and I have a friend, a carpenter, who recently worked on a house in which the occupants took an elevator up to the fourth floor, where they kept their StairMaster).

"Country people rarely walk, and those who do are noticed."

21   "I nauseate walking," William Congreve, the eighteenth-century playwright, has one of his characters opine. "'Tis a country diversion; I loathe the country." I live in the country, but I do not find walking a country diversion. Country people rarely walk, and those who do are noticed. A neighbour passes our house regularly and often stops to chat (and, I suspect, catch his breath); he has been ordered to walk three kilometres a day by his doctor. It isn't a walk then, it's a forced march. "But I enjoy it!" he says, surprised, as I imagine psychiatric patients might have said about cold baths.

22   I do most of my walking in the city, especially in unfamiliar cities. A few years ago, finding myself with four days' unexpected leisure in Buenos Aires, which is a very large city, I walked each day from early morning until after dark, crossing its extraordinarily wide *avenidas* and exploring its hidden *ruels* and passageways, making some of its secrets my own. I have done the same in dozens of cities: Beijing, London, Florence, Oslo, Helsinki. My wife, Merilyn, and I wore ourselves out walking in Paris, doing what Americans call rubber-necking," or taking in the sights. The philosopher of city walking, Walter Benjamin (who called Paris "the capital of the 19th century"), employed the term *flâneur* to impart the same sense of alert yet aimless wandering that Thoreau meant by "saunterer," and that's pretty much what I am in a strange city, a flannerer (to anglicize an old Norman form of the same verb). Baudelaire, in three poems dedicated to the exiled Victor Hugo ("The old Paris is gone / the form of a city / changes more quickly, alas, than a mortal's heart"), was writing as a flannerer. Paris was made for flannery, but any large city will do. Stephen Daedalus, the hero of James Joyce's *Ulysses*, was a Dublin flannerer—"Am I walking into eternity along Sandymount strand?" Apparently, one can flanner in a city one knows well. Why not? Thoreau could saunter in the same woods every day and always have a different string of thoughts, and I doubt that Einstein needed a new beach for each new equation. I have often wondered at my disinclination to saunter in the country, given my propensity to flanner in the city. Driving to the city in order to go walking seems like a contradiction to me, like taking an elevator up to the StairMaster.

23   Contradictions, however, are the fertile ground from which decisions arise, and as V.S. Pritchett remarked, "All the great decisions in life are made by the legs." A

return to walking may be the greatest decision we can make, the best way most of us have of slowing down our lives and falling into step with the natural rhythms of nature. Charles Wilkins hoped to get to New York in September or October, before it became too cold, but he wasn't worried about it particularly. New York wasn't what he was looking for. "One thing I have noticed," he said as he strolled past Sault Ste. Marie, "is the way in which time seems almost to have been created for me, to have been returned to me, as I walk."

24   That's a better discovery than New York.

Reading Closely and Thinking Critically

1. How well do you know the houses, streets, gardens, and parks around you? What might be the connection between knowing your environment and deciding to change your behaviour in order to protect it?
2. Grady pauses his consideration of famous walkers to explore why humans walk upright. He has no solid theories, only hypotheses—some of which he himself considers fanciful. Why has he included this discussion? What does it contribute to the essay?
3. How does walking change the perspective of Charles Wilkins?
4. Describe the *flâneur.* What different kind of knowledge is gained by walking in the city rather than the country? Many famous and successful writers have been *flâneurs.* What might they learn as they walk the city streets and sit at outdoor cafés?

Examining Structure and Strategy

1. Consider Grady's examples carefully. What does each of them contribute to the portrait of walking Grady is sketching for us here?
2. This essay, like walking around one's neighbourhood, takes a rather circuitous route. It begins and ends by telling us of Wilkins's experience, but takes many detours in between. In what way is the essay's structure described by Grady's observation that "while walking, the mind wanders with the feet, and both can be errant if they are so inclined"? Is this an effective structure? Why or why not?

Considering Language and Style

1. With respect to the structure of Grady's essay, explain the elements of style that make you willing to follow him, in spite of not knowing where he's going.
2. What's the connection, raised in paragraphs 17, 18, and 19, between walking and contradiction?
3. How would you characterize Grady's use of language? Normally writers use vocabulary that is similar in its relative formality or informality. Yet Grady uses the rather formal "motorized conveyances" in paragraph 5 and the informal if not slangy "wimpiness" in paragraph 6. Do these changes in register work? What do they tell you about Grady's attitudes and purpose?
4. What's the difference between walking, sauntering, and hiking? How are these distinctions important?

For writing assignments based on this essay, see page 418.

Background

Gary Mason has worked as a journalist since 1981, writing for the *Victoria Times-Colonist* and the *Vancouver Sun* in a number of roles, including legislative bureau chief, city editor, and deputy managing editor. He joined *The Globe and Mail* in 2005, writing a national column on British Columbia. He has twice received the Jack Webster Award, the highest honour given to a British Columbia journalist, and has been nominated three times for the National Newspaper Awards, winning twice for his sportswriting. His latest best-selling book is *Oldtimers: On the Road with the Legends of Hockey* (2003).

Combined Patterns and Their Purposes

Mason uses examples of institutions, cities, and countries that have addressed their need to conserve energy in order to suggest that we can reduce our carbon footprint by thinking small, not big.

Call Me an Optimist, but if Denmark Can Go Green, Canada Can Too

Gary Mason

As you read

Think about the relationship between leadership and our collective response to global warming. What characterizes the most successful leadership?

1   In a recent column in The New York Times, Thomas Friedman writes about a stay at the Hotel Arctic in Ilulissat, Greenland. He was floored by the experience.

2   It wasn't the service that impressed Mr. Friedman, although by all accounts it was terrific, but rather some of the energy-saving technologies the hotel featured. Dimly lit hallways brightened when guests walked down them. Toilets had highly advanced and efficient flushing systems. Measures being taken by the hotel allow it to use 20 per cent less electricity, 25 per cent less energy for heating and 27 per cent less water per guest than most hotels in North America.

3   This at a place located 250 kilometres north of the Arctic Circle.

4   What Mr. Friedman found at the Hotel Arctic was representative of what he would discover throughout Denmark, which has become one of the most energy-smart countries in the world. But Denmark didn't become green in response to growing concerns over climate change or the soaring price of crude oil. No, it began its energy transformation more than 30 years ago, when the Arab oil embargo badly battered the Danish economy.

5   Never again, the Danes vowed. And off the country went to explore ways of solving its oil-dependency problem.

6   I mention this because I believe a similar transformation can occur here in Canada. In fact, if you look closely, it's already under way.

7   Away from the loud and often sad and petty debate that surrounds green-inspired measures such as carbon taxes and cap-and-trade systems, local governments are quietly considering and implementing innovative approaches to meet their energy needs in the most environmentally friendly and cost-effective way possible.

8   In the municipality of Delta, where I live, council is considering producing its own electricity by installing solar panels atop many of its facilities. (Delta gets up to 25-per-cent more sunshine than other parts of Greater Vancouver.) The collected energy would be sent to a new power station, converted to electricity, and then sent back to light up many of the facilities and buildings within the district, including city hall.

9   It's an idea whose time has come.

10   Other municipalities in Greater Vancouver have been thinking along these lines for a while. A few years ago, the City of North Vancouver established Lonsdale Energy Corp., which provides power through a network of boiler mini-plants that circulate hot water through underground pipes to heat buildings connected to the system. It is an idea that is not only cost-effective but self-sustaining.

11   The City of Vancouver is doing its bit.

12   A new neighbourhood that is going up on the south side of False Creek—where the Olympic village will be for the 2010 Winter Games—will have an energy system that will be so efficient it will produce 50- to 65-per-cent fewer heating-related greenhouse gas emissions than it would if built using conventional methods.

13   Methane captured at the Vancouver landfill is being used to generate heat and electricity. The city's initiatives to promote alternatives to driving have resulted in a 180-per-cent increase in the number of bike trips since the late 1990s and a 20-per-cent increase in transit use, according to the city.

14   It may not seem like a lot in the grand scheme of things, but it is.

15   To break our dependence on oil, to reduce greenhouse gas emissions, to bring some sanity and reliability to energy costs, we need to think small, not big. By that I mean that thinking about how we're going to solve the world's energy problems can seem overwhelming and hopeless. But if we focus on solving problems in and around our own little patch of earth first, it will be a more satisfying, and ultimately more practical, way to go.

16   Call me an optimist—it wouldn't be the first time—but I think we in North America are going to find ways to beat our dependency on foreign oil once and for all. Brain power will ultimately produce new forms of electrical power that will fuel our cars and light our cities.

17   It won't be easy and it won't be without some pain along the way. (And it will certainly take some courageous political leadership.) But I believe it can and will be done.

18   Look at Demark. In 1973, the year of the Arab oil embargo that sent the Danish economy into a historic tailspin, the tiny country got 99 per cent of its energy from the Middle East.

19   Today that is zero.

Reading Closely and Thinking Critically

1. What's the relationship between our use of non-renewable resources like oil and coal to keep us warm and move us from place to place and our carbon footprint? Why do we need to release less carbon into our atmosphere? You may have to do some research on these questions, but they're crucial to understanding this essay and others in this section.

2. Why is the debate about carbon taxes and cap-and-trade systems "loud"? This is the debate going on at the federal level. Have you paid much attention to it? Has it been a hot topic of conversation among your family and friends? What environmental issues or strategies do people talk about? What does this say about how and how much we are thinking about the environment?

3. Why is innovating easier in smaller groups? What does this say about leadership and the limits of leadership?

4. How is this essay an example of inductive reasoning? Can you follow Mason's logic?

Examining Structure and Strategy

1. Mason uses three examples of groups who have reduced their dependency on oil specifically and on non-renewable resources in particular. Are three brief examples more effective than a single, longer example? Why or why not?

2. Why has Mason included examples of single institutions—the hotel in Greenland, a municipality, and a country? What does this scope of examples help him accomplish?

3. Both the title and paragraph 16 refer to Mason's optimism. Why does he highlight this attitude? What other attitudes about climate change circulate around us? Which do you find most effective and why?

Considering Language and Style

Newspaper articles are frequently written in short paragraphs, partly because long paragraphs split into narrow columns are difficult to read, but also partly because newspaper style is brief and factual. Even within that context, however, Mason uses one-sentence paragraphs. What does he accomplish by using them?

For writing assignments based on this essay, see page 418.

Background

Tim Falconer is the author of *Watchdogs and Gadflies: Activism from Marginal to Mainstream* (2001) and *Drive: A Road Trip through our Complicated Affair with the Automobile* (2008). He teaches magazine writing at Ryerson University and lives in Toronto with his wife.

Combined Patterns and Their Purposes

Tim Falconer opens his analysis of the car's role in our lives by narrating the story of a typical drive to the cottage. His delight in speed and freedom is mixed with his awareness that he is contributing to the greenhouse gases threatening our environment and to the gridlock blocking up our streets. In the course of the essay, he uses several other narratives: the story of his finally learning how to drive and the story of Jane Jacobs's crusade against an expressway that would have spoiled Toronto's neighbourhoods. He uses cause and effect to consider how the car has become so important in our culture and what it has done to our cities and threatens to do to our way of life.

Toronto Cars. Can't Live with 'Em, Can't Live without 'Em
Tim Falconer

1   Even though I left early to avoid the worst of the Friday afternoon snarl, the city roads are thick with cars and I don't reach the highway as quickly as I'd hoped. Once I do, three lanes of high-speed congestion surround my car. I'm heading north to a cottage for the weekend, but suburban sprawl mars the landscape for most of the next hour; the subdivisions seem to creep a little farther every time I drive up here and I feel old remembering how all this land was nothing but fields when I was a kid. As soon as the traffic eases and I hit open road, and the dispiriting tract housing gives way to lush farms and dense forest, I sit back, crank the tunes a little louder and step on the gas. Within an hour, I will be lakeside, far from the smog, a cold beer in my hand   though it's not just my destination that makes me happy. My car is not a convertible, but as I rejoice in the speed, the power and the freedom it offers, I imagine the sun on my face and the wind in my thinning hair. I press the pedal a little harder. I feel exhilarated.

> **As you read**
> Think about your own relationship with the car. Why has driving become such an unexamined, automatic part of our lives?

2   That doesn't mean I don't feel guilty. I do. After all, I'm contributing to the traffic I curse, I'm spewing greenhouse gases and other harmful emissions and I'm part of the reason we build cities for cars instead of people (not that we're doing even that well). Most North Americans, and increasingly those in other countries, have convinced themselves that a car is a necessity. I'm not that addicted, but my relationship to the automobile—a complicated mix of desire and disgust—is still a powerful one. While car lovers can make a passionate case for the object of their affection and car haters can marshal the facts against it, most of us are conflicted: the more we've allowed ourselves to be sucked into the car's considerable charms, the more brutal and complete our subjugation to it has become. If intelligent life forms on a distant planet ever bothered to study our civilization, they would surely conclude that the vehicles were

the dominant creatures while the humans, who build roads, provide warm, dry spots to park and do the cleaning and fixing, were the servants.

3   The closer the aliens looked, the more baffled they would become. Even as road engineering and automobile safety have improved dramatically, the death toll remains ludicrously high: 1.2 million people die on the world's roads each year. The thirst for oil has led to many conflicts around the world, including two wars in the Persian Gulf and civil unrest in Nigeria, and it threatens environmentally sensitive habitats. All the while, the humans fret about their tailpipe toxins, lament the lost hours spent stuck in traffic and cluck at the urban sprawl that makes no economic, environmental or aesthetic sense.

> "1.2 million people die on the world's roads each year."

4   Beyond its pivotal role in our day-to-day lives, the automobile has worked its way into our psyches. From the sunny California of the Beach Boys to the darker New Jersey of Bruce Springsteen, the car is a central image in American music. And from the chicken run in *Rebel Without a Cause* to the main-street cruising in *American Graffiti* to every road trip movie ever made, the car plays an essential role in film. It's not just that the automobile is a handy device for storytelling. Through music, movies, television and literature—and advertising—vehicles have become metaphors for freedom and symbols of status and success.

5   Though it started developing earlier, the iconography of the car generated by movies and music really took hold in the 1950s and 1960s, when the automobile posed no pressing problems. With the building of the interstate highway system in the 1950s, the American economy boomed. People moved around easily and trucking quickly became the preferred shipping method. But it didn't take long for the true cost of these freeways to surface: bypassed towns slowly withered and died while inner-city neighbourhoods succumbed to a similar fate quickly because of expressway construction. That led to a flight to the suburbs, exacerbating the urban sprawl the highways had already spurred. Today, it's no stretch to live without a car in a few cities—and in Manhattan, it's actually advisable—but I wouldn't want to try it in Atlanta or Houston.

6   And yet, for some people, a car is still an *objet d'art* to be collected and fawned over, though perhaps seldom driven. Talk show host Jay Leno has more than 150 cars, trucks and motorcycles, and a full-time staff to keep them running. No doubt buying and maintaining a fleet of collectible cars puts little strain on Leno's fortune, but for most regular folk, a vehicle is the second-most expensive purchase they'll ever make. And between loan payments, insurance, gas, maintenance, parking and other costs, some people spend more each month to keep their car going than they do on their rent or their mortgage. That's even more likely for those with more than one set of wheels: so many families insist on owning several—they should be thankful they don't live in Bermuda, where automobile ownership is limited to one per household—that

the United States now has more vehicles than drivers. Americans, who represent just 5 percent of the global population, own 200 million of the more than 520 million cars in the world.

7   This proliferation has shaped where and how we live. Many businesses, from drive-in cinemas to drive-thru banks, cater to those behind the wheel (and often exclude those on foot). No wonder people say we either love cars or we need them. Even some activists dedicated to protesting against the auto and oil industries and to promoting environmental awareness find they have no choice but to own what they hate—or at least take a lot of taxis.

8   City dwellers come in three categories: drivers (and passengers), cyclists and pedestrians. Each one can't stand the other two. Drivers have nothing but contempt for pedestrians who jaywalk or, even when crossing the street legally, take too long, and they detest cyclists who sneer at the rules of the road. Cyclists despise drivers because too many of them refuse to admit bike riders have a right to be on the road and they hate pedestrians the way a bully hates the smallest kid in the playground. Pedestrians fear and loathe aggressive and distracted drivers, especially the ones who prefer yakking on a cell phone to paying attention, and they dread and abhor cyclists who won't obey stop signs and seem to take joy in running down people on sidewalks.

9   I am a pedestrian.

10   My first choice has long been to walk whenever possible, but I always intended to get my licence. Someday. Owning a set of wheels isn't essential where I live, so I was able to avoid getting a driver's licence until I was in my late thirties. Finally, a friend who was a magazine editor asked me if I wanted to rent an RV for two weeks and write about it. Turning down such a fun assignment was so painful—and felt so pathetic—that I decided it was finally time to grow up. Driving *seemed* like the adult thing to do. And so I joined the ranks of the drivers, and then, a few years later, the owners.

11   When I finally did, I regretted having waited so long. True, my 1991 Nissan Maxima, my first—and so far, only—automobile, is no aficionado's idea of a sweet ride. Light blue (or Silver Blue, according to the manufacturer), the body is still in good shape, but it's old, and even when it was new, it wasn't the most stylish car on the road. The horsepower isn't impressive, and I don't spend any time tinkering with it, let alone tricking it out. I don't even use it that much. In the summer, I love to escape the city without cadging a ride from friends, but in the winter, it just sits on the street for days until I throw two sticks and a big equipment bag in to the back seat and drive to a hockey arena. Since 1999, I've added just sixty thousand kilometres to the hundred thousand that were already on the odometer. I certainly could live without a car, and I know I should, but I don't want to give it up.

12   The street where I park my car is a short, leafy cul-de-sac in midtown Toronto. In most American cities, my street, which is just a block from a six-lane north-south

arterial road, would be no place for single-family homes. Fortunately, my city never suffered an exodus to the suburbs. The evacuation that killed the central core of too many cities didn't happen here because a group of citizens killed a highway.

13   The Spadina Expressway—which would take suburbanites from the northwest corner of the city into downtown in the morning, and then out again in the evening—was all part of a master plan that featured five expressways. Plenty of putative experts thought the scheme was an excellent one; after all, the great American cities were doing it. And in the 1960s, Toronto was anything but a great city: it was puritanical, placid and parochial. A good time was hard to find. My parents, like a lot of people who lived here back then, drove to Buffalo or Detroit to shop and enjoy some night-life. Today, that seems laughable because those places are decaying cities with dead downtowns, while Toronto is now a vibrant place. It will never have the energy of Manhattan, the joie de vivre of Montreal or the architecture of Chicago (a town Toronto looks up to the way a kid reveres his big brother), but to most objective observers, the city is largely a success. True, the place is still a bit uptight, developers seem to take pride in throwing up unremarkable buildings and the wasted opportunity of the waterfront is a disgrace, but it is also dynamic, tolerant, wealthy, safe and among the most livable cities in the world.

14   Some good decisions and a huge dollop of luck helped make this possible, but stopping the Spadina Expressway was crucial. In 1971, the road was already under construction. Suburbanites were all for it; downtowners, not so much. They knew the highway would mean the end for central neighbourhoods. Some of the most vocal opponents were from the Annex, which was right on the path of the planned construction. Annex resident Jane Jacobs led the activists who stopped Spadina. Born in Scranton, Pennsylvania, she moved to New York City, where she took on Robert Moses, the autocratic master builder who was, for more than four decades, one of the most powerful people in New York. Though he never learned to drive, he favoured highways over public transit, suburbs over cities and grand projects over neighbourhoods. His plan for the Lower Manhattan Expressway would have destroyed Greenwich Village and SoHo. Jacobs and her first book, *The Death and Life of Great American Cities*, galvanized opposition to the proposed road. After that defeat, Moses lost much of his influence in New York, but by then his ideas had infected other cities across the continent.

15   A few years after helping to save it, Jacobs left the West Village. Appalled that their taxes were being used to fight the Vietnam War—and with two sons eligible for the draft—she and her architect husband moved to Toronto and settled in the Annex. She stayed until she died in April 2006, just a few days shy of her ninetieth birthday. In the rest of the world, she'll be best remembered for *The Death and Life of Great American Cities*, but in many ways her legacy is modern Toronto. Along with leading the crusade against Spadina, she was prominent in many other fights (for public housing, for intensification) and was a mentor to some of our better municipal politicians. The central plan that shaped Toronto from 1975 to 2000 incorporated many of her ideas.

16   The Annex became one of the most desirable parts of the city. John Barber, the city columnist for *The Globe and Mail*, lives there—on a street where his great-grandparents bought their first house in 1880. Though he and his wife ride their bikes to work, he loves American V8s and is the proud owner of a 1998 Mercury Grand Marquis LS, which he calls the Grand Monkey. I had lunch with him two weeks before Jacobs died, and when, inevitably, the subject of the Spadina Expressway came up, he pointed out that many people who complain about the traffic in the city still argue that the big mistake was not building Spadina. I stated the obvious: "You wouldn't live where you live if it had gone through."

17   "I'd be living on an off-ramp," he agreed.

18   Other residential areas—including mine—would likely have been collateral damage. Some of the highway's opponents may have been motivated more by NIMBYism than anything else, but when the provincial government finally agreed to kill the project—along with three of the other proposed inner-city expressways—it not only saved the Annex but also changed the way the city thought about its neighbourhoods. (The fifth highway, the Don Valley Parkway, had already been built in a bosky river valley. Environmentalists would never let that happen these days, but it did mean that fewer homes were destroyed. And though it usually seems closer to a parking lot than a parkway, it does offer a lovely, winding and tree-lined drive into Toronto and an impressive view of downtown.) With the scrapping of the planned inner-city highways, Toronto became a city of neighbourhoods—and, more important, a city that valued them. Aside from meaning fewer people fled to the suburbs, that mindset was also an ideal fit with the waves of immigration that would, over the next couple of decades, transform Toronto from a sleepy regional town full of dull, white Protestants to the most multicultural place on the planet.

> "Toronto became a city of neighbourhoods—and,
> more important, a city that valued them."

19   While much of downtown Detroit remains a no-go zone, the American cities having the most success revitalizing their downtowns—San Francisco, Portland and Washington, D.C., for example—boast extensive, if often aging, transit systems. So Toronto is fortunate it didn't tear up all of its streetcar tracks and for a while built subways, but the transit system is now underfunded, overcrowded and struggling to keep riders happy. For downtowners at least, it offers an alternative to driving, though apparently I'm not alone in thinking that walking is an even better option. After a study found that 45 percent of people who live close to the waterfront walk to work, Rod McPhail, the city's director of transportation planning, told the *Toronto Star* in October 2004, "What we found, it blew me away."

20   Inner-city success couldn't stop the surrounding suburbs from sprawling, but the vigour of the downtown made the region a magnet for newcomers from across Canada and around the world. The city now has a population of almost 2.5 million and a healthy density greater than 10,000 people per square mile, but the Greater

Toronto Area has more than 5 million residents, most mired in car dependency and poorly served by public transit. Many of those people commute to Toronto for work, but only 20 percent take public transit. Solo drivers account for 67 percent of the trips into the city each morning, and since the road infrastructure hasn't kept pace with the growth, travel times continue to rise.

21   I've always thought Hogtown, as we call it, was akin to older East Coast American cities that have grown in a radial pattern around a downtown core, and I was surprised to hear that many American urban planners see Toronto as closer to the polycentric cities of the American West. Perhaps it has a chance to combine the best of both. Or it could become everything it fears. Eric Miller, a professor at the University of Toronto's Department of Civil Engineering Joint Program in Transportation, worries the city has been dining out on some good choices, such as killing Spadina, that are now decades old. "I don't think we've made any smart decisions since," he told me, citing the failure to continue building subways and the sprawling suburbs as examples. "We lost control over the situation and we lost our will to make decisions and to see the vision through. We still talk about it but we don't really do it and we haven't done it for a long time and now we have a lot of catching up to do. We're resting on our laurels."

22   Unfortunately, now is the worst time to be coasting. The city's population is growing rapidly, and already 49 percent of the people who live in Toronto were born in another country and 43 percent of the population are part of a visible minority. This is our great experiment, and so far the results have been encouraging. If it is a success, that diversity will be our greatest strength and could turn Toronto into a model of multicultural urban living for the rest of the world. But pulling it off won't mean a thing if we don't solve the problem of the car.

23   My hometown isn't the only place facing this challenge: as a society, we can't live with the car and we can't live without it. Although the suburbs promise more space and relief from inner-city woes, they are too often dismal, wasteful and unhealthy communities filled with soulless shopping malls, drive-thru fast-food joints and clogged roads. And we've now sprawled so much that commutes of over an hour—once unthinkable—are now commonplace. And that's on a day without lane-closing crashes. All that time in the car is not good for us. Traffic tie-ups are costly in terms of wasted fuel and productivity—and human health and sanity. Many suburbanites suffer from frazzled nerves and neck and back problems brought on by long commutes, and because they must get in a car just to pick up a litre of milk, they are less fit and more likely to be overweight or obese than their inner-city counterparts. Even if governments could afford to build as many highways as they wanted, they'd never get ahead of demand: more roads beget more cars. And although most politicians prefer subsidizing roads to public transit, many highways are in disrepair. So no one's happy.

"All that time in the car is not good for us."

24   More worrisome is the prospect of people in other countries joining in. So far, the obsession with the automobile has been most acute in North America. Europeans love

their cars, but their societies don't revolve so completely around the automobile: the vehicles are smaller, the gas more expensive, the transit systems better, the urban densities greater and the distances people travel shorter. Nevertheless, traffic in London was so bad that the city introduced a congestion charge for cars entering the central core. Worse, as emerging economic powerhouses such as China and India—where automobile ownership is 10 percent but growing rapidly—fall in love with the car the way we have, we're headed for deeper trouble. Mexico City gives us a hint of what could happen: the streets are so overwhelmed with cars that it takes several hours to drive across town, while the pollution is so bad that many visitors cannot even wear their contact lenses. And all those cars don't necessarily mean a vibrant economy: the most car-dependent cities are the least efficient.

25   As always, though, there is some hope. Many companies, trumpeting a variety of technologies, work feverishly to find the alternative fuel that will be clean enough, efficient enough and cheap enough to make future generations wonder what the hell a gas-guzzler was. And despite the disappointing results of experiments such as New Urbanism, planners can take comfort in the knowledge that many North Americans actually want to live downtown again.

26   The glory days of the automobile, extended beyond all good sense by twenty-five years of cheap gasoline, are finally over. Despite what the auto industry and the oil industry and the politicians in their pockets would have us believe, we won't survive our current addiction—yet the Utopians calling for a ban on all cars are equally deluded. A carless future won't happen anytime soon because we couldn't go cold turkey even if we wanted to. Before I could consider solutions in between those two extremes, I knew I had to develop a better understanding of our peculiar love–hate relationship with our wheels. And the best way to do that, I figured, was to take a road trip to the heart of car culture: Los Angeles, California.

Reading Closely and Thinking Critically

1. Falconer both comments on and embodies ambivalence toward the car. Discuss your attitude toward the car and that of those about you. Is this attitude changing with the increasing price of gas and longer commutes?

2. In paragraph 3, Falconer presents the following facts: "1.2 million people die on the world's roads each year. The thirst for oil has led to many conflicts around the world, including two wars in the Persian Gulf and civil unrest in Nigeria, and it threatens environmentally sensitive habitats. All the while the humans fret about their tailpipe toxins, lament the lost hours spent stuck in traffic, and cluck at the urban sprawl that makes no economic environmental or aesthetic sense." Were you aware, for example, of the number of deaths and wars associated with oil? Why or why not? In the face of these negative effects on our lives, why do we continue to drive?

3. Falconer observes that "City dwellers come in three categories: drivers (and passengers), cyclists and pedestrians." How does your city mediate the relationships between these three groups—both through its infrastructure and through the unwritten code? (In London, England, for example, the unwritten code dictates that pedestrians are almost treated like targets by drivers in a hurry. Regina, on the other hand, has an extensive system of bicycle trails and bike lanes for some major streets.)

4. What role does the car play in popular culture? How does this shape our attitudes?
5. What role does mass transit play in popular culture? How does this shape our attitudes?

Examining Structure and Strategy

1. Why does Falconer begin his essay with the brief narrative of his drive to the cottage?
2. What's the point of Falconer's narrative about how he learned to drive and how he now uses his car (paragraphs 10 and 11)?
3. Falconer is suggesting that we examine something that is pretty basic to our daily lives: how we use the car for transportation and pleasure. Because of his purpose, he must create a friendly relationship with his audience. How does he do this? What do you know about him as an individual that's not central to his argument but that prompts you to like and trust him?
4. Map out the causal chain of events between Toronto's decision not to put in the Spadina Expressway and the resulting shape and ethos of Toronto.

Considering Language and Style

1. In paragraphs 2 and 3, Falconer describes what our cities and lives would look like to an alien from outer space. What's he trying to accomplish with this rather whimsical description?
2. Consider the language Falconer uses to describe Toronto. Is it persuasive—particularly if you live somewhere other than Toronto?
3. What's NIMBYism? Is this a useful choice of words?
4. Why does Falconer tell you about a conversation between himself and John Barber? What does it contribute to the essay? Is it part of logos, pathos, or ethos—or some combination?

Assignments for Discussion and Writing

"On Walking," "Call Me an Optimist, but if Denmark Can Go Green, Canada Can Too," and "Toronto Cars. Can't Live with 'Em, Can't Live without 'Em"

1. **For discussion in class or online.** Discuss what steps you as an individual are or might easily take to minimize climate change. If your instructor so directs, post your responses on your class Web site.
2. **In your journal.** You need some kind of emotional commitment to a purpose beyond yourself to make some of the sacrifices of money or convenience necessitated by being a good global citizen. What makes you willing to make those sacrifices? Fear? The thought of grandchildren? The well-being of a community? Write about that principle that underlies your willingness—or unwillingness.
3. **Using argumentation and persuasion for a purpose.** The purposes in the assignments are possibilities. You may establish whatever purposes you like, within your instructor's guidelines.
    *   To express feelings and persuade your reader, describe your attachment to a place that might be threatened by spreading suburbs, logging, road construction, or other human activity. Then argue why this should not happen. Try to generalize that argument to address the need to be much more careful about the space humans take up on this planet.
    *   To entertain and persuade your reader, describe the joys of water—the nighttime swish of sprinklers, the crisp exhilaration or giddy laughter of public swimming pools, the threads of warm and cool water that wind around your legs in stream-fed lakes. Then talk about what will happen if Canada experiences a water shortage like those occurring elsewhere.
    *   To entertain and persuade your reader, write about something humans do or make or own or throw away from the point of view of an alien archaeologist or anthropologist visiting earth 200 years from now. For example, Falconer gives us an alien's view of our relationship with our cars. Choose something that we really don't need and allow the alien's eye view to reveal how unnecessary it is

- To inform and persuade, write about the efforts to go green made at the local level where you live. These need not be citywide; they can refer to what your campus or the company you work for is doing. Are there showers for people who bike to work? Is your bookstore giving away cloth bags and encouraging you to re-use them? Do the buildings you frequent have drinking fountains that are easily accessible? Then discuss what else your community might do.
- On April 25, 2006, Douglas Martin wrote in *The New York Times,* "At a time when both common and inspired wisdom called for bulldozing slums and opening up city space, Ms. Jacobs's prescription was ever more diversity, density and dynamism—in effect, to crowd people and activities together in a jumping, joyous urban jumble." Where in your community do you find such street life? Describe how being part of that street life makes you feel about your community and, in turn, about the well-being of the planet.

4. **Connecting the readings.**
   - In "A Sleuth of Bears" (page 128), Brian Payton talks about our need to step beyond what we know. Discuss how this attitude can help the environmental movement, making an argument to teach environmentalism in the schools.
   - In Bruce Mau's "Imagining the Future" (page 338), he suggests that cynicism has an effect on what we believe we can accomplish. Discuss the role cynicism plays in our willingness to turn over the global thermostat to someone else. What kind of leadership do we need to change this response?

5. **Drawing on sources.**
   - Falconer mentions Jane Jacobs' *Death and Life of Great American Cities.* Read this work, or read about it, and discuss how your city or town conforms to some of the problems she identifies. Then propose solutions. (A good start might be *Jane Jacobs: Ideas that Matter,* a book that came out of a conference dedicated to her ideas in Toronto in 1997. Jacobs' argument is both enduring and dated; it has been the inspiration for quite a number of other people who have made it more relevant to the present time. Thus, while students should ordinarily go to the original primary text, it would be fine in this case to simply read work inspired by it.)
   - Psychologists tell us that campaigns to persuade people to change their habits are not always effective. It's easier to do something once (like buying an energy-efficient car or furnace) than it is to do something repeatedly (like bike to work or turn down the furnace at night). The best ways of shaping effective campaigns identify the barriers to the habit or practice, address these, build in prompts or reminders, and deliver these personally. Look at the psychological literature on this issue and devise an effective campaign to change one habit of a group of people. A good place to start would be "Fostering Sustainable Behaviour through Community-Based Social Marketing" by Doug McKenzie-Mohr, who teaches at St. Thomas University in Fredericton. It was published in May 2000 in *American Psychologist*, 531–537.

What Causes Substance Abuse and What Are the Best Ways of Responding to It?

The substance of the debate about how best to address the damage to individuals and to society from the abuse of licit and illicit drugs focuses on two questions: Are illicit drugs inherently addictive or are some individuals particularly vulnerable to addiction? And is drug use a criminal justice issue or a health issue?

Those who view drug use as criminal activity believe that there are two ways of most effectively minimizing that damage. One is prevention campaigns to discourage drug use, though the effectiveness of these is not clear. The other is the provisions of the criminal justice system that focus on law enforcement measures that target users and dealers. As a consequence of this emphasis, 80 percent of the prison population in Canada consists of drug users or people arrested for crimes they committed to pay for their drugs. Canada spent, as of October 2007, $245 million a year on the drug problem. Three-quarters of that money went to law enforcement, 14 percent to treatment, 7 percent to research, and 3 percent each to prevention and harm reduction, according to Anne McIlroy, Rod Mickleburg, and Gloria Galloway, science writers for *The Globe and Mail* (1 October 2007, A-4, and 15 January 2007, A-1). The Le Dain Commission's study of drug use, written between 1969 and 1972, found that prohibition of drugs was ineffective; no commission since has overturned Gerald Le Dain's findings. Although we readily acknowledge that the prohibition of alcohol in Canada was unsuccessful, we assume it will work with other consciousness-altering substances.

The other side of the debate views drug use as a health issue, one that is most effectively addressed through attempts to reduce the harm done by drugs. Basing their views on programs in countries such as Holland and Great Britain, advocates of the health response argue that criminalizing drug use victimizes individuals who are already society's vulnerable by casting them even farther outside their communities. They argue that decriminalizing drug use (which is not the same as making drugs legal) brings addicts back into the community, thus providing individuals with the social supports necessary to kick or control their habits. This approach, they contend, also has the additional benefit of minimizing the criminal activities of pushers and users, thus making our communities safer.

This debate has been rekindled recently in Canada by the decision of the Supreme Court of British Columbia stipulating that drug use is a health issue and as such is subject to the laws of the province, not the federal government. This decision was prompted by attempts to protect Insite, the only safe injection site in North America, from being closed by the federal government. As of August 2008, the current federal government plans to appeal this decision.

In Chapter 10, we make the point that causes and effects are often complex, that it is often difficult to distinguish between correlations and causes, that immediate and distant causes need to be considered, that writers need to distinguish between necessary and contributory causes. Nowhere is this problem of causes and effects more fraught than in the discussion of substance abuse and addiction. Are individuals, once they have tried the forbidden substance, helpless to say no to continued use? Why can some individuals abuse heroin, cocaine, or alcohol for a brief period and then decide to stop? Does personal history shape one's response to consciousness-altering substances, or does brain chemistry play an important role? Are some individuals, by virtue of their genetic makeup, destined to become addicts? How can society and society's response to addicts and addiction contribute to or prevent the problem of addiction? Does the illegality of substance abuse deter some individuals or does it cast the addict into the role of society's undesirable and outsider?

Maté, here and in the essay appearing in Chapter 6 on exemplification, argues that addicts self-medicate for depression, anxiety, post-traumatic stress disorder, attention deficit hyperactivity disorder, and above all for the pain that they have experienced. As a doctor, Maté also observes that drug addiction disrupts the body's dopamine circuits. Your body gives you a dopamine "hit" when you ace an exam, run for half an hour, cuddle with your dog or cat, eat a chocolate bar, or even when you go in search of your "drug of choice"—a new CD or pair of shoes. Dopamine is also implicated in reinforcing behaviours; the pleasurable dopamine "hit" you get from doing well on an assignment or exercising encourages you to work hard and exercise. Addicts' dopamine circuits may be faulty from childhood; certainly addiction disrupts those circuits, Maté argues, so that the simple things that bring us pleasure or that reinforce adaptive behaviours aren't adequate to assuaging emptiness, despair, or anxiety that the addict feels.

The other two essays, "Predicting Addiction" by LeGrand, Iacono, and McGue and "The Surprising Truth about Heroin and Addiction," come from *Taking Sides: Clashing Views in Drugs and Society.* They consider, from different viewpoints, what we know about addiction in order to answer the question, should drug addiction be considered a disease? In "Predicting Addiction," the authors have gathered data from a study of twins to come to the conclusion that a genetic predisposition to "externalizing tendencies," a cluster of behaviours that include rebellion against authority, thrill-seeking, and lack of self-control, plays a significant role in an individual's chances of becoming an addict. At the same time, however, they recognize that familial and social context plays an equally powerful role. Sullum, in contrast, argues in "The Surprising Truth about Heroin and Addiction" that the media tends to view drugs as causing addiction, whereas anecdotal and statistical evidence illustrates the fact that many individuals who use drugs also quit on their own.

Human use of substances that alter consciousness goes back to the beginnings of human history, sometimes as part of religious or ceremonial occasions. As a society, we decide to legalize certain drugs that alter consciousness, like alcohol and tobacco, in spite of the harm these substances can do to our health if we are addicted to them.

What is addiction? The World Health Organization defines addiction as

the repeated use of a psychoactive substance or substances, to the extent that the user (referred to as an addict) is periodically or chronically intoxicated, shows a compulsion to take the preferred substance (or substances), has great difficulty in voluntarily ceasing or modifying substance use, and exhibits determination to obtain psychoactive substances by almost any means. Typically, tolerance is prominent and a withdrawal syndrome frequently occurs when substance use is interrupted. The life of the addict may be dominated by substance use to the virtual exclusion of all other activities and responsibilities.

The New Brunswick Department of Health defines addiction to include behaviours besides substance abuse:

Addiction can take many forms. The most common addictions are substance abuse and repetitive, damaging behaviors. Substance abuse is a dependence on alcohol, narcotics, and/or prescription drugs. Problem gambling is a repetitive behavior which leads one to spending money on lottery tickets, video lottery terminals, slot machines, and other betting schemes. Dependences can result in serious health risks, legal and financial problems, as well as family disturbance.

There is a difference between a habit and an addiction. Habits shape our personalities and enrich our lives, but when they become obsessive and harmful, they turn into addictions.

How long can you stand to turn off your cellphone? How long could you live without the Internet, instant messaging, the TV, or fast food? Do you or your friends find it easy to quit smoking or improve their diets? Are these habits or obsessions?

Background

Gabor Maté is the author or co-author of numerous books, including *Scattered Minds*, on attention deficit disorder, and *When the Body Says No,* on the effects of stress. He frequently writes for *The Vancouver Sun* and *The Globe and Mail*. Born in Hungary, he emigrated to Canada when he was 13. He spent several years as a high school English teacher, then returned to university to train as a doctor. Currently he is the staff physician at the Portland Hotel, a residence and resource centre for the people of Vancouver's Downtown Eastside. Many of his patients suffer from mental illness, drug addiction, and HIV, or all three.

Combined Patterns and Their Purposes

In his book *In the Realm of Hungry Ghosts,* Maté provides an understanding of addiction from numerous perspectives. He considers what neuroscientists have to say about why the brain craves drugs, how it responds to drugs, and how drugs disrupt the brain's usual way of experiencing pleasure and joy. He describes the social causes of addiction, and the ways the developing child's environment shape him or her to need the mind-altering effect of drugs. "Like patterns in a tapestry, recurring themes emerge in my interviews with addicts: the drug as emotional anaesthetic; as an antidote to a frightful feeling of emptiness; as a tonic against fatigue, boredom, alienation and a sense of personal inadequacy; as stress reliever and social lubricant" (32). He argues that addiction needs a more compassionate response from Canadian society.

Imagining an Enlightened Social Policy on Drugs
Gabor Maté

As you read
Maté suggests that "moralizing displaces compassion" in our response to drug addicts. Think about your own responses people who are addicted.

1   I'll start from the assumption that we want to redeem people trapped in drug addiction—and that redemption can be something other than an addict's complete abstinence from addictive chemicals, a goal that's not always realistic. Under current conditions it hardly ever is for most hardcore substance users, although I believe our success rate could be much higher if we abandoned our present intolerant and self-defeating social attitudes toward addiction and the care of addicted people. Even in cases where abstinence is not achieved, redemption would mean the reintegration of the user into the larger community and the restoration of his value as a person in his own eyes.

2   In the next pages, I'll outline what I believe would be a rational and humane stance toward drug users, along with the policies that would flow from it. I do not expect such ideas to be embraced by society any time soon; an informed approach may be, for now, no more than a dream. In a culture that projects its darkest features onto the addict and makes addicted people into scapegoats for its shortcomings, insight and knowledge are almost entirely absent from public discourse concerning drug policies. Moralizing displaces compassion and prejudice substitutes for inquiry. The evidence accumulated by decades of scientific research into the psychology of addiction, brain development, child rearing and the social origins of addictive drives rarely enters into the discussion of how to tackle the persisting problem of drug addiction. Indeed, as this book goes to press, the *Globe and Mail* reports that Canada's assault on drug addicts is about to escalate. According to the *Globe*, "the federal

Conservative government [is preparing] to unveil a strategy that cracks down on illicit drug users," with harsher penalties for users of illicit substances. The mountain of evidence showing the worthlessness of this get-tough approach is, once more, ignored.[1]

3   The scarcity of scientific thought informing public debates on addiction is mirrored in the academic and medical arenas. In this era of sub-sub-specialization, each discipline appears to work in isolation from knowledge gathered by other researchers in closely related fields. We need far more integration of knowledge both in the professional realm and among laypeople.

4   Why does medical practice appear to be so opaque to the light of new findings? "I've thought about this a lot," child psychiatrist and researcher Dr. Bruce Perry said when I interviewed him, "because I've been involved in several public education campaigns. What we found is that the groups that have the greatest vested interest in the old beliefs are the last to absorb new content. As such, medicine has been the most resistant professional group to absorb and integrate the emerging findings about brain development and the importance of early childhood."

5   I don't believe that the "vested interests" of medical professionals are, in this case, consciously selfish or motivated by material considerations; they are the investment we have in maintaining that our way of thinking is right, that the principles and methods we have practised are sound and that approaches outside our emotional or intellectual comfort zones are not worth investigating. Institutions such as professional bodies, medical schools and scientific associations tend to be deeply conservative, even if in some ways they are at the forefront of bold exploration. They mistrust new paradigms and resist moving outside the boundaries of a narrowly defined science-ideology that separates mind from body, human beings from their lifetime environments.

6   Similarly, most political leaders and policymakers seem unaware of the abundance of facts and experience refuting the theory and practices of the War on Drugs or they lack the will to act on the evidence. In the worst-case scenario some may be too blinded by a moralistic and judgment-ridden ideology to act according to the Christian principles they profess. Hence the need to imagine a humane reality that we could create if we chose to honour what science, insight and the precepts of our ethical and spiritual traditions teach us.

7   "The current set of public beliefs and institutional beliefs about substance abuse are impediments to the application of high-quality successful intervention," says Dr. Perry. "The more we dehumanize and vilify substance abusers, the more it is impossible to put in place the kind of interventions that will help them."

8   In other words, we need to get outside the box. The system we have doesn't work—not for the addict and not for society. This system cannot be improved; it needs to be transformed.

---

[1]Anne McIlroy, "Get-tough policy on drugs doomed, experts say." *The Globe and Mail*, October 1, 2007, p. A-4.

9   I don't claim that what I will propose is without potential pitfalls, or that I could possibly have got all the details right. But for this discussion the details are not the issue. The issue is the relationship society creates between itself and its drug-addicted citizens; the fundamental question is whether or not we recognize these people as human beings who are legitimately part of the social fabric, deserving compassion and respect. "Action has meaning only in relationship," said the spiritual teacher Jiddu Krishnamurti, "and without understanding relationship, action on any level will only breed conflict. The understanding of relationship is infinitely more important than the search for any plan of action."[2] It's not the particulars of a social policy that matter most, but the relationship between those who influence policy and those who are affected by it.

10   People may well disagree with what is suggested in this chapter, but we cannot afford to ignore Krishnamurti's teaching on the precedence of relationship over action.

11   First, we need to take stock of ourselves and give up any hint of moral superiority and judgment toward the addict. Judging others clouds our eyes not only to their needs but to our own as well. Going back to the words of Jesus, *"first take the plank out of your own eye, and then you will see clearly to take the splinter out of your brother's eye."* We cannot help people when we put ourselves in a position of judgment. Addicts, all but the very few completely sociopathic ones, are deeply self-critical and harsh with themselves. They are keenly sensitive to judgmental tones in others and respond with withdrawal or defensive denial.

12   Second, any rational approach to the problem of addiction has to be grounded in an appreciation of the interactive psychology and brain physiology of addiction. "An understanding of emotions should not be separated from neuroscience," Dr. Jaak Panksepp told me. "If you don't recognize that the brain creates psychological responses, then neuroscience becomes a highly impoverished discipline. And that's where the battle is right now. Many neuroscientists believe that mental states are irrelevant for what the brain does. This is a Galileo-type battle and it will not be won very easily because you have generations and generations of scholars, even in psychology, who have swallowed hook, line and sinker the notion—the Skinnerian notion—that mentality is irrelevant in the control of behavior."[3]

13   Dr. Panksepp is not tilting at windmills. Narrow behaviourist thinking permeates political and social policy and medical practice, the childrearing advice dispensed by "parenting experts" and academic discourse. We keep trying to change people's behaviours without a full understanding of how and why those behaviours arise.

---

[2]Jiddu Krishnamurti, *On Relationship* (San Francisco: HarperOne, 1992).
[3]B.F. Skinner of Indiana University is considered the founder of the hugely influential behaviourist school of psychology, which focuses only on behaviours, excluding "invisible" factors like emotions from its analysis of human conduct and relationships.

"Inner causes are not the proper domain of psychology," writes Roy Wise, an expert on the psychology of addiction, and a prominent investigator in the National Institute on Drug Abuse in the U.S.A.[4] This statement seems astonishing, coming from a psychologist. In reality, there can be no understanding of human beings, let alone of addicted human beings, without looking at "inner causes," tricky as those causes can be to pin down at times. Behaviours, especially compulsive behaviours, are often the active representations of emotional states and of special kinds of brain functioning.

14   As we have seen, the dominant emotional states and the brain patterns of human beings are shaped by their early environment. Throughout their lifetimes, they are in dynamic interaction with various social and emotional milieus. If we are to help addicts, we must strive to change not them but their environments. These are the only things we *can* change. Transformation of the addict must come from within and the best we can do is to encourage it. Fortunately, there is much that we can do.

15   In the previous chapter I presented evidence that addictive habits, generally speaking, are too deeply entrenched in the brain of the hardcore substance user to be overcome by a simple act of will. As Jaak Panksepp put it: "Those habit structures are so incredibly robust, and once they are laid into a nervous system they will guide behaviour without free choice." My discussion with Professor Panksepp did not end there. We went on to consider what support addicts would need to overcome the powerful drives imprinted by their painful experiences. "The only way they can escape drug addictions is if their pain is alleviated, their emotions are brought back toward healthy balance, so they have a chance to think about it," Dr. Panksepp said, echoing both what brain research has told us about mental freedom and what human experience has confirmed. "Free choice only comes from thinking, it doesn't come from emotions. *It emerges from the capacity to think about your emotions.* When you're operating in the habit mode you are feeling, but those feelings are not being reflected upon. They are too powerful, they are too habitual. So, the treatment of addiction requires the island of relief where a need to soothe pain does not constantly drive a person's motivation. It requires a complex and supportive social environment."

16   How to create that island of relief is the core issue in projecting a humane policy toward addiction. The work of the Portland Hotel Society is an isolated, flawed but worthy attempt at offering the respite from anguish and anxiety that Dr. Panksepp suggests. Although the PHS has grown from an initial grant of $23,000 back in 1991 to a current annual operating budget of over $11 million—most of it for housing—the services it can provide are no more than a drop in the bucket compared with the needs of the community it serves in the Downtown Eastside.

17   Addicts are locked into addiction not only by their painful past and distressing present, but equally by their bleak view of the future. They cannot envision the real

[4]Roy A. Wise, "The Neurobiology of Craving: Implications for the Understanding and Treatment of Addiction," *Journal of Abnormal Psychology* 97(2) (1998): 118–32.

possibility of sobriety, of a life governed by values rather than by immediate survival needs and by desperation to escape physical and mental suffering. They are unable to develop compassion toward themselves and their bodies while they are regarded as outcasts, hunted as enemies and treated like human refuse.

18   As we have seen, a major factor in addiction that medical and social policies must take into account is stress. If we want to support people's potential for healthy transformation, we must cease to impose debilitating stress on their already burdened existence. Recall that uncertainty, isolation, loss of control and conflict are the major triggers for stress and that stress is the most predictable factor in maintaining addiction and triggering relapse. These are also precisely the conditions that the demonization of addiction and the War on Drugs (deliberately!) impose on hardcore substance users.

19   I have quoted a report in the *Journal of the American Medical Association*, which showed that a history of childhood abuse increases physiological stress reactivity for a lifetime, a reactivity "which is further enhanced when additional trauma is experienced in adulthood."[5] The addict is re-traumatized over and over again by ostracism, harassment, dire poverty, the spread of disease, the frantic hunt for a source of the substance of dependence, the violence of the underground drug world and harsh chastisement at the hands of the law—all inevitable consequences of the War on Drugs.

20   Studies on primates and other animals have also shown that low social status and being dominated enhance the risk of drug use, with negative effects on dopamine receptors. By contrast, after being housed with more subordinate animals, dominant monkeys had an *increase* of over 20 per cent of their dopamine receptors and less tendency to use cocaine.[6] The findings of stress research suggest that the issue is not control over others, but whether one is free to exercise control in one's own life. Yet the practices of the social welfare, legal and medical systems subject the addict to domination in many ways and deprive her of control, even if unwittingly.

21   In relegating the addict to the bottom of the social and moral scales and in our contemptuous rejection of her as a *person*, we have created the exact circumstances that are most likely to keep her trapped in pathological dependence on drugs. There is no island of relief, only oceanic despair.

22   "The War on Drugs is cultural schizophrenia," says Jaak Panksepp. I agree. The War on Drugs expresses a split mindset in two ways: we want to eradicate or limit

---

[5]C. Heim et al., "Pituitary-Adrenal and Autonomic Responses to Stress in Women after Sexual and Physical Abuse in Childhood," *JAMA* 284(5) (2 August 2000): 592–97.

[6]D. Morgan et al., "Social Dominance in Monkeys: Dopamine D2 Receptors and Cocaine Self-administration," *Neuroscience* 5(2) (2002): 169–74; S. P. Martin et al., "Effects of Dominance Rank on d-Amphetamine-Induced Increases in Aggression," *Pharmacology, Biochemistry & Behavior* 37 (1990): 493–96.

addiction, yet our social policies are best suited to promote it, and we condemn the addict for qualities we dare not acknowledge in ourselves. Rather than exhort the addict to be other than the way she is, we need to find the strength to admit that we have greatly exacerbated her distress and perhaps our own. If we want to help people seek the possibility of transformation within themselves, we first have to transform our own view of our relationship to them.

23   That our current approach is a dead end has been acknowledged in Canada, in the U.S. and internationally by many people whose political and ideological starting point was not anywhere close to embracing the decriminalization of drugs. Today, November 17, 2006, as I'm writing this chapter, the *Globe and Mail* reports that the B.C. Progress Board, a blue-ribbon panel made up of businesspeople and academics appointed by the British Columbia government to offer advice on economic and social issues, has proposed that drugs either be decriminalized or that the War on Drugs be stepped up so as to completely eliminate the drug trade in this province. One or the other. The status quo is "clearly unacceptable if we seek truly to reduce the rates of crime and victimization in the province," the Progress Board stated.[7]

24   The panel warns, in the words of the *Globe* report, that "a crackdown on the drug trade would mean more police, tougher penalties for drug-related crimes and more jails to accommodate the dramatically increased demand for secure facilities." In effect, the recommendations are a barely camouflaged call for decriminalization. The so called other "option," the elimination of drug trafficking and use, is no option at all—only a chimera that even the most Draconian measures have failed to conjure into reality anywhere in the world. Unless we are willing to see our society metamorphose into a brutal police state, no coercive policy will come close to even limiting drug use, let alone eliminating it.

25   Once we understand that the current assault on addicts creates greater insecurity for everyone and severe hardship for users, once we understand that stressing people chronically and mercilessly can in no way promote their capacity for healthy transformation, it becomes a straightforward matter to envision approaches that rely not on moralizing but on science and humane values.

26   The indispensable foundation of a rational stance toward drug addiction would be the decriminalization of all substance dependence and the provision of such substances to confirmed users under safely controlled conditions. It's important to note that *decriminalization does not mean legalization*. Legalization would make manufacturing and selling drugs legal, acceptable commercial activities. Decriminalization refers only to removing from the penal code the possession of drugs for personal use. It would create the possibility of medically supervised dispensing when necessary. The

[7]Robert Matas, "Consider Legalizing Drug Use, Panel Says," *The Globe and Mail,* 17 November 2006, S-6.

fear that easier access to drugs would fuel addiction is unfounded: drugs, we have seen, are not the cause of addiction. Despite the fact that cannabis is openly available in Holland, for instance, Dutch per-capita use of marijuana is half that in the United States. And no one is advocating the open availability of hard drugs.

27   Decriminalization also does not mean that addicts will be able to walk into any pharmacy to get a prescription of cocaine. Their drugs of dependence should be dispensed under public authority and under medical supervision, in pure form, not adulterated by unscrupulous dealers. Addicts also ought to be offered the information, the facilities and the instruments they need to use drugs as safely as possible. The health benefits of such an approach are self-evident: greatly reduced risk of infection and disease transmission, much less risk of overdose and, very importantly, comfortable and regular access to medical care.

28   Not having to spend exorbitant amounts on drugs that, in themselves, are inexpensive to prepare, addicts would not be forced into violence, prostitution or poverty to pay for their habits. They would not have to decide between eating or drug use, or to scrounge for food in garbage cans or pick cigarette butts out of sidewalk puddles. They would no longer need to suffer malnutrition.

29   I admit I am ambivalent about the decriminalization of certain drugs, particularly crystal meth, and I understand why some people would resist even discussing the possibility. But if it seems bizarre to suggest that such a potentially brain-toxic drug be legally administered to addicts, consider that the street products currently available are full of impurities, mixed with noxious chemicals that magnify the damage from the stimulant itself. By bringing the crystal meth addict into a therapeutic interaction with the health care system, we would be fostering the possibility of use and gradual detoxification and withdrawal under relatively safe circumstances—*relatively*, because there is no safe way to use crystal meth. Above all, such an approach would create a basis for gently shepherding the addict toward rehabilitation. It would provide an opportunity to create a healing relationship with users who are currently relegated to streets and back alleys. Further, if many users no longer had to turn to illicit drug labs and dealers for their substance, the underground economy of crystal meth would be deprived of much of its profit and allure. Not an ideal situation, but a vast mitigation of the present dismal scenario.

30   And, very much to the point, most young people who become hooked on crystal meth are self-medicating for other conditions: most commonly ADHD, but also depression, post-traumatic stress disorder or the effects of emotional and social dislocation. As we discussed in Chapter 3, some young street people who use crystal meth see it as a way of survival. If the necessary physical, psychological and social supports were provided, I believe it would not take long to diminish the appeal of methamphetamine and to wean the vast majority of stimulant addicts away from this harmful chemical.

31   Many people fear that decriminalization and the controlled dispensing of drugs will lead to widespread substance use among people who are now deterred from becoming addicts only by existing legal prohibitions. Like other tenets of the War on Drugs, this view entirely lacks supporting evidence. Any data on the subject points to the opposite prediction. For example, for many decades in the United Kingdom, heroin has been dispensed, under legal supervision, to addicts. The same type of program has been offered on a limited basis in other countries as well, and nowhere has it been found that this measure served in any way to entice unaddicted people into addiction. That is not surprising, given that addiction is a response to life experience, not simply to a drug. People who do not suffer the searing emotional pain that drives hardcore drug addiction will rarely fall into dependency on chemicals, even if these were more readily available—and, once more, public access to habit-forming substances is not being proposed. The call for the decriminalization of drugs for personal use does not imply legal acceptance of drug dealing.

32   Criminalization and prevention are not identical—if anything, the first undermines the other. Paradoxical though it may seem, current drug laws against possession make drugs more readily available to potential new users than decriminalization would. Only the War on Drugs creates the *raison d'être* of the international trafficking industry, most of whose wealth is based on satisfying the cravings of established drug addicts. Without the exorbitant profits yielded by supplying to addicted users desperate for their substances, the illegal market would shrink to a fragment of its present size. Further, much of the street-level front-line sales force of the illicit drug trade consists of users raising money to support their habit. With the decriminalization of possession for personal use and the medically supervised distribution of drugs, the incentive to sell to new "customers," including young kids, would largely evaporate. Policing resources could then be concentrated on the remaining large-scale traffickers—if any.

33   Addicts should not be coerced into treatment, since in the long term coercion creates more problems than it solves. On the other hand, for those addicts who opt for treatment, there must be a system of publicly funded recovery facilities with clean rooms, nutritious food and access to outdoors and nature. Well-trained professional staff need to provide medical care, counselling, skills training and emotional support. Our current nonsystem is utterly inadequate, with its patchwork of recovery homes run on private contracts and, here and there, a few upscale addiction treatment spas for the wealthy. No matter how committed their staff and how helpful their services may be, they are a drop in comparison to the ocean of vast need. In the absence of a coordinated rehabilitation system, the efforts of individual recovery homes are limited and occur in a vacuum, with no follow-up.

34   It may be thought that the cost of such a drug rehabilitation and treatment system would be exorbitant. No doubt the financial expenses would be great—but surely less than the funds now freely squandered on the War on Drugs, to say nothing of the

savings from the cessation of drug-related criminal activity and the diminished burden on the health care system.

35   To expect an addict to give up her drug is like asking the average person to imagine living without all her social skills, support networks, emotional stability and sense of physical and psychological comfort. Those are the qualities that, in their illusory and evanescent way, drugs give the addict. People like Serena and Celia and the others whose portraits have appeared in this book perceive their drugs as their "rock and salvation." Thus, for all the valid reasons we have for wanting the addict to "just say no," we first need to offer her something to which she can say "yes." We must provide an island of relief. We have to demonstrate that esteem, acceptance, love and humane interaction are realities in this world, contrary to what she, the addict, has learned all her life. It is impossible to create that island for people unless they can feel secure that their substance dependency will be satisfied as long as they need it.

36   One of the greatest difficulties we human beings seem to have is to relinquish long-held ideas. Many of us are addicted to being right, even if facts do not support us. One fixed image we cling to, as iconic in today's culture as the devil was in previous ages, is that of the addict as an unsavoury and shadowy character, given to criminal activity. What we don't see is how we've contributed to making him a criminal.

37   There is nothing more intrinsically criminal in the average drug user than in the average cigarette smoker or alcohol addict. The drugs they inject or inhale do not themselves induce criminal activity by their pharmacological effect, except perhaps in the way that alcohol can also fuel a person's pent-up aggression and remove the mental inhibitions that thwart violence. Stimulant drugs may have that effect on some users, but narcotics like heroin do not; on the contrary, they tend to calm people down. It is withdrawal from opiates that makes people physically ill, irritable and more likely to act violently—mostly out of desperation to replenish their supply.

38   The criminality associated with addiction follows directly from the need to raise money to purchase drugs at prices that are artificially inflated owing to their illegality. The addict shoplifts, steals and robs because it's the only way she can obtain the funds to pay the dealer. History has demonstrated many times over that people will transgress laws and resist coercion when it comes to struggling for their basic needs—or what they perceive as such. Sam Sullivan, Vancouver's quadriplegic mayor, told a conference on drug addiction once that if wheelchairs were illegal, he would do anything to get one, no matter what laws he had to break. It was an apt comparison: the hardcore addict feels equally handicapped without his substances. As we have seen, many addicts who deal in drugs do so exclusively to finance their habit. There is no profit in it for them.

39   As with petty drug pushing, so with prostitution. As this book is being completed, the disturbing details of the serial murder case against pig farmer Robert Pickton are emerging in a British Columbia courtroom. If convicted, Pickton will be counted among the most prolific and most sadistic killers of women in North American history. I

believe that as a society we are unwitting accomplices in the deaths of the Downtown Eastside women who allegedly became Pickton's victims because our criminalization of drug use drove those women into prostitution and into the underground street life that led to their deaths. If an evidence-based policy had been in operation in this country, these dozens of women—and their many counterparts elsewhere—might still be alive.

40   Society would have much to gain from decriminalization. On the immediate practical level, we would feel safer in our homes and on our streets and much less concerned about the danger of our cars being burgled. In cities like Vancouver such crimes are often committed for the sake of obtaining drug money. More significantly perhaps, by exorcising this menacing devil of our own creation, we would automatically give up a lot of unnecessary fear. We could all breathe more freely.

41   Many addicts could work at productive jobs if the imperative of seeking illegal drugs did not keep them constantly on the street. It's interesting to learn that before the War on Drugs mentality took hold in the early twentieth century, a prominent individual such as Dr. William Stewart Halsted, a pioneer of modern surgical practice, was an opiate addict for over forty years. During those decades he did stellar and innovative work at Johns Hopkins University, where he was one of the four founding physicians. He was the first, for example, to insist that members of his surgical team wear rubber gloves—a major advance in eradicating post-operative infections. Throughout his career, however, he never got by with less than 180 milligrams of morphine a day. "On this," said his colleague, the world-renowned Canadian physician Sir William Osler, "he could do his work comfortably and maintain his excellent vigor." As noted at the Common Sense for Drug Policy website:

> Halsted's story is revealing not only because it shows that with a morphine addiction the proper maintenance dose can be productive. It also illustrates the incredible power of the drug in question. Here was a man with almost unlimited resources—moral, physical, financial, medical—who tried everything he could think of and he was hooked until the day he died. Today we would send a man like that to prison. Instead he became the father of modern surgery.[8]

42   Most hardcore addicts could not function at such a high level, given the social and psychological adversity of their life histories. But surely, if their substance needs were met, they would have much greater opportunity to realize their potential to be creative and contributing members of society. At the very least, they would be a lesser burden. Decriminalization of drug use would establish the possibility of integrating addicts into the larger community, an essential step if they are to be rehabilitated in any large numbers.

---

[8]http://www.csdp.org/publicservice/halsted.pdf

43   In Chapter 1 I introduced Stan, a Native Canadian man, an addict and street dweller just out of jail. On chilly nights Stan should not be sleeping on stone steps under an archway in the Downtown Eastside. Without having to steal to support his drug habit, he would not have lived in prison the past eighteen months but in a recovery home or, if still needing to use, in a decent housing facility. He ought to be receiving remedial training for his learning disabilities and counselling to help him overcome the emotional defensiveness and impulsive reactivity that has so often landed him in trouble. Such support would help prepare him to join normal society.

44   Seeking insight into my First Nations patients, I spoke with psychiatrist Lewis Mehl-Madrona, author of *Coyote Medicine: Lessons from Native American Healing* and Associate Professor of Family Medicine and Psychiatry at the University of Saskatchewan. "People fall into these communities of substance, centred around drugs," Dr. Mehl-Madrona pointed out. "You can fall into communities around alcohol or cocaine and whatever. Everyone has a need to belong. Unless people have another community, an alternative community that provides them with more belonging, being wanted, and purpose, the so-called treatment always fails. What seems to work here for aboriginal people is to switch their allegiance to an alternative community, modern but honouring traditional values. As long as they can maintain their position in that non-using community, they are not using substances."

45   Lewis Mehl-Madrona's insights apply not only to Native people, but to all the marginalized addicts who, like Stan, haunt the streets and alleys in the vicinity of the Portland Hotel. They need to be invited into communities that can offer them acceptance, belonging and value. At least transitionally, such communities have to be founded and maintained with public support until, step by step, former users are fully able to join society at large. Those unable to give up their habits ought not to be ostracized, nor should their voices be excluded from social discourse. If we understood the sources of their dysfunction, we would want to reduce their suffering, whether or not they continue to use.

46   "Drug addiction has to be de-vilified," Bruce Perry said during our interview. "If we create environments that are safe and predictable and relationally enriched, then all of the other factors involved in substance abuse and dependence will be so much easier to dissolve away. Our challenge is to figure out how to create these environments.

47   "We really need . . . and I know it sounds kind of corny . . . we need to be very loving, very accepting, and very patient with people who have these problems. And if we are, they will have a much higher probability of getting better."

48   We need to absorb in our minds and guts the utter futility of what we are doing now. We need to wake to the reality that our present system actively generates misery for users and nonusers alike and places intolerable burdens on society. More of the same will only cause more of the same.

49   A 2007 study by physicians and researchers at the B.C. Centre for Excellence in HIV/AIDS stated that "the federal government continues to invest heavily in policies

and practices that have been repeatedly shown in the scientific literature to be ineffective or harmful." According to a front-page report in the *Globe and Mail*, the study found that "law enforcement consumed by far the largest chunk (73 per cent) of the [national] drug strategy's annual $245 million budget, with no demonstrated impact on curbing the use of illegal drugs. At the same time, 14 per cent is spent on treatment, 7 per cent on research, and 3 per cent each for addiction prevention and harm reduction."[9]

50   "I'm paid to treat disease," said one of the authors, Dr. Thomas Kerr, "and I don't like what I'm seeing. Canada simply does not have an evidence-based drug strategy. There's way too much ideology and politics, and not enough science and principle."

51   On the same morning that this new study was reported, my last patient was Serena, the young Native woman from Kelowna whose life story is described in Chapter 4. She came late, panting into my office with a high fever and a strangulating cough. Her pneumonia had begun several days before that, when she woke up after one of Vancouver's heavy windstorms to find that the windows of her hotel room had been shattered during the night and the water in her sink was frozen solid.

52   In a commentary published in the *Globe*'s web edition I summarized Serena's history and explained that she deals drugs only to support her own cocaine habit. "Proper nutrition, shelter, the controlled provision of their substances of dependence, counselling, and compassionate caring are what most addicts need if we are to help wean them from their debilitating habits," I wrote.

53   The piece ignited a lively set of exchanges at the newspaper's website, indicating how deeply felt are the views of many people on the issue of drug addiction. I was encouraged by the discourse. Many participants seemed interested in basing social policies not on subjective emotional responses toward addicts, but on facts and compassionate principle. "This is an excellent discussion that shows the complexity of the issue and the lack of perfect solutions," wrote one of the contributors.

> Few harm-reductionists who know their stuff recommend a market-led free-for-all in drugs like heroin and cocaine and the amphetamine stimulants. But there is now an undisputable body of evidence that demonstrates that developing mechanisms to make safer forms of these drugs available to those with an intractable need brings enormous benefits to both the drug user and the society around them. Thus both Holland and Switzerland and parts of Germany, have changed policies and seen an enormous drop in the levels of drug related crime. The average age of hard drug users is rising there, indicated that fewer young people are taking up such an activity. The real obscenity here is the shocking lack of funding for treatment and care and

[9]Rod Mickleburgh and Gloria Galloway, "Storm Brews over Drug Strategy," *The Globe and Mail*, 15 January 2007.

harm reduction initiatives that have been shown to work. The UK National Treatment Outcome Survey (known as NTROS) showed that for every 1 pound invested in treatment and care, 3 pounds came back in health care and enforcement savings. If such a return was available in the financial markets, we'd all rush to take advantage.

54   Would the decriminalization of drug use and the controlled distribution of drugs bring up a new set of problems? No doubt they would. Innumerable practical issues would need to be resolved, some extremely complicated, and there would be risks. Around drug addiction there are no easy, risk-free solutions to be found. But for every fresh difficulty there would be new benefits that would weigh far more in the balance. No foreseeable risk can to any degree resemble the tremendous harm currently being done.

Reading Closely and Thinking Critically

1. What are the basic components of Maté's "enlightened social policy"? Considering his policy as a cause, what effects does he suggest it will it generate?
2. What causes individuals to need mind-altering drugs? What are the effects of that use, and how would Maté's policy counter those effects?
3. What view of the user of illicit drugs is implicit in Maté's proposals?
4. What's the difference between *decriminalizing* illicit drugs and *legalizing* illicit drugs? Do you think Maté is "splitting hairs"?

Examining Structure and Strategy

1. What objections does Maté acknowledge there might be to his proposals? How does he counter them?
2. Maté knows that our current government's approach to the war on drugs is taken for granted. Maté's argument emphasizes, understandably, our *knowledge* about addiction. How does he combine information with *pathos*?
3. What part does the appeal to other experts or to respected individuals play in Maté's strategy?
4. Look again at the discussion of ways to address the concerns of hostile, wavering, or supportive readers, particularly with respect to the use of *logos, pathos,* and *ethos* (page 379). How does Maté use these resources and does he balance them? What kind of reader do you think he's writing for?
5. In paragraph 41, Maté tells the story of opium addict and surgeon Dr. William Stewart Halsted. What role does that story play in his attempts to persuade us?

Considering Language and Style

1. In paragraphs 9, 10, and 11, Maté, a Jew originally from Hungary, refers to the teachings of Jiddu Krishnamurti and Jesus. (Google these two teachers if necessary.) What do these references contribute to his argument? Are they a matter of *logos, ethos, or pathos,* or some combination?
2. How does Maté's language mediate between logos and pathos? Can you find a couple of passages that are particularly effective?

For writing assignments based on this essay, see page 457.

Background

Lisa LeGrand, William G. Iacono, and Matt McGue all work at the University of Minnesota. LeGrand and McGue are both associated with the Minnesota Centre for Twin and Family Research, which provides scholars with access to this important study. The study of twins allows researchers to consider the extent to which genetics plays a dominant role in individuals' lives. Dr. Iacono is a Distinguished McKnight University Professor. This essay first appeared in *American Scientist*, a magazine for general readers that publishes the work of leading researchers whose findings have been peer-reviewed in other contexts. In other words, the articles are written for a general reader, but the research has been validated by the writers' colleagues.

The Patterns and Their Purposes

The authors begin their essay with the narrative of Terry McGovern's death to make the need to intervene in the lives of addicts less theoretical. They then depend on research that contrasts and compares the addiction of twins to more scientifically explore the way individuals might be genetically predisposed to addiction. They also define "externalizing tendencies" to explore the behavioural patterns of young people who are particularly vulnerable to addiction.

Predicting Addiction

Lisa Legrand, William G. Iacono, and Matt McGue

1   In 1994, the 45-year-old daughter of Senator and former presidential nominee George McGovern froze to death outside a bar in Madison, Wisconsin. Terry McGovern's death followed a night of heavy drinking and a lifetime of battling alcohol addiction. The Senator's middle child had been talented and charismatic, but also rebellious. She started drinking at 13, became pregnant at 15 and experimented with marijuana and LSD in high school. She was sober during much of her 30s but eventually relapsed. By the time she died, Terry had been through many treatment programs and more than 60 detoxifications.

> *As you read*
> Think about the assumptions you have made about the causes of addiction and note in the writing where those assumptions are challenged.

2   Her story is not unique. Even with strong family support, failure to overcome an addiction is common. Success rates vary by treatment type, severity of the condition and the criteria for success. But typically, fewer than a third of alcoholics are recovered a year or two after treatment. Thus, addiction may be thought of as a chronic, relapsing illness. Like other serious psychiatric conditions, it can cause a lifetime of recurrent episodes and treatments.

3   Given these somber prospects, the best strategy for fighting addiction may be to prevent it in the first place. But warning young people about the dangers of addiction carries little force when many adults drink openly without apparent consequences. Would specific warnings for individuals with a strong genetic vulnerability to alcoholism be more effective? Senator McGovern became convinced that his daughter possessed such a vulnerability, as other family members also struggled with dependency. Perhaps Terry would have taken a different approach to alcohol, or avoided it altogether, if she had known that something about her biology made drinking particularly dangerous for her.

4   How can we identify people—at a young enough age to intervene—who have a high, inherent risk of becoming addicted? Does unusual susceptibility arise from differences at the biochemical level? And what social or environmental factors might tip the scales for kids at greatest risk? That is, what kind of parenting, or peer group, or neighbourhood conditions might encourage—or inhibit—the expression of "addiction" genes? These questions are the focus of our research.

MINNESOTA TWINS

5   We have been able to answer some of these questions by examining the life histories of almost 1,400 pairs of twins. Our study of addictive behavior is part of a larger project, the Minnesota Center for Twin Family Research (MCTFR), which has studied the health and development of twins from their pre-teen years through adolescence and into adulthood. Beginning at age 11 (or 17 for a second group), the participants and their parents cooperated with a barrage of questionnaires, interviews, brainwave analyses and blood tests every three years. The twin cohorts are now 23 and 29, respectively, so we have been able to observe them as children before exposure to addictive substances, as teenagers who were often experimenting and as young adults who had passed through the stage of greatest risk for addiction.

6   Studies of twins are particularly useful for analyzing the origins of a behavior like addiction. Our twin pairs have grown up in the same family environment but have different degrees of genetic similarity. Monozygotic or identical twins have identical genes, but dizygotic or fraternal twins share on average only half of their segregating genes. If the two types of twins are equally similar for a trait, we know that genes are unimportant for that trait. But when monozygotic twins are more similar than dizygotic twins, we conclude that genes have an effect.

7   This article reviews some of what we know about the development of addiction, including some recent findings from the MCTFR about early substance abuse. Several established markers can predict later addiction and, together with recent research, suggest a provocative conclusion: that addiction may be only one of many related behaviors that stem from the same genetic root. In other words, much of the heritable risk may be nonspecific. Instead, what is passed from parent to child is a tendency toward a group of behaviors, of which addiction is only one of several possible outcomes.

MARKERS OF RISK

Personality

8   Psychologists can distinguish at-risk youth by their personality, family history, brainwave patterns and behavior. For example, certain personality traits do not distribute equally among addicts and nonaddicts: The addiction vulnerable tend to be more impulsive, unruly and easily bored. They're generally outgoing, sociable, expressive

and rebellious, and they enjoy taking risks. They are more likely to question authority and challenge tradition.

9   Some addicts defy these categories, and having a certain personality type doesn't doom one to addiction. But such traits do place individuals at elevated risk. For reasons not completely understood, they accompany addiction much more frequently than the traits of being shy, cautious and conventional.

10   Although these characteristics do not directly cause addiction, neither are they simply the consequences of addiction. In fact, teachers' impressions of their 11-year-old students predicted alcohol problems 16 years later, according to a Swedish study led by C. Robert Cloninger (now at Washington University in St. Louis). Boys low in "harm avoidance" (ones who lacked fear and inhibition) and high in "novelty seeking" (in other words, impulsive, disorderly, easily bored and distracted) were almost 20 times more likely to have future alcohol problems than boys without these traits. Other studies of children in separate countries at different ages confirm that personality is predictive.

Family Background

11   Having a parent with a substance-abuse disorder is another established predictor of a child's future addiction. One recent and intriguing discovery from the MCTFR is that assessing this risk can be surprisingly straightforward, particularly for alcoholism. The father's answer to "What is the largest amount of alcohol you ever consumed in a 24-hour period?" is highly informative: The greater the amount, the greater his children's risk. More than 24 drinks in 24 hours places his children in an especially risky category.

12   How can one simple question be so predictive? Its answer is laden with information, including tolerance—the ability, typically developed over many drinking episodes, to consume larger quantities of alcohol before becoming intoxicated—and the loss of control that mark problematic drinking. It is also possible that a father, who equivocates on other questions that can formally diagnose alcoholism—such as whether he has been unsuccessful at cutting down his drinking or whether his drinking has affected family and work—may give a frank answer to this question. In our society, episodes of binge drinking, and being able to "hold your liquor," are sometimes a source of male pride.

Brainwaves

13   A third predictor comes directly from the brain itself. By using scalp electrodes to detect the electrical signals of groups of neurons, we can record characteristic patterns of brain activity generated by specific visual stimuli. In the complex squiggle of evoked brainwaves, the relative size of one peak, called P300, indicates addiction risk. Having a smaller P300 at age 17 predicts the development of an alcohol or drug problem by age 20. Prior differences in consumption don't explain this observation, as the

reduced-amplitude P300 (P3-AR) is not a consequence of alcohol or drug ingestion. Rather, genes strongly influence this trait: P3-AR is often detectable in the children of fathers with substance-use disorders even before these problems emerge in the off-spring. The physiological nature of P300 makes it an especially interesting marker, as it may originate from "addiction" genes more directly than any behavior.

Precocious Experimentation

14   Lastly, at-risk youth are distinguished by the young age at which they first try alcohol without parental permission. Although the vast majority of people try alcohol at some point during their life, it's relatively unusual to try alcohol *before* the age of 15. In the MCTFR sample of over 2,600 parents who had tried alcohol, only 12 percent of the mothers and 22 percent of the fathers did so before the age of 15. In this subset, 52 percent of the men and 25 percent of the women were alcoholics. For parents who first tried alcohol after age 19, the comparable rates were 13 percent and 2 percent, respectively. So, what distinguishes alcoholism risk is not *whether* a person tries alcohol during their teen years, but *when* they try it.

15   In light of these data, we cannot regard very early experimentation with alcohol as simply a normal rite of passage. Moreover drinking at a young age often co-occurs with sex, the use of tobacco and illicit drugs, and rule-breaking behaviors. This precocious experimentation could indicate that the individual has inherited the type of freewheeling, impulsive personality that elevates the risk of addiction. But early experimentation may be a problem all by itself. It, and the behaviors that tend to co-occur with it, decrease the likelihood of sobriety-encouraging experiences and increase the chances of mixing with troubled peers and clashing with authority figures.

A GENERAL, INHERITED RISK

16   Some of these hallmarks of risk are unsurprising. Most people know that addiction runs in families, and they may intuit that certain brain functions could differ in addiction-prone individuals. But how can people's gregariousness or their loathing of dull tasks or the age at which they first had sex show a vulnerability to addiction? The answer seems to be that although addiction risk is strongly heritable, the inheritance is fairly nonspecific. The inherited risk corresponds to a certain temperament or disposition that goes along with so-called *externalizing* tendencies. Addiction is only one of several ways this disposition may be expressed.

17   Externalizing behaviors include substance abuse, but also "acting out" and other indicators of behavioral under control or disinhibition. In childhood, externalizing traits include hyperactivity, "oppositionality" (negative and defiant behavior) and anti-social behavior, which breaks institutional and social rules. An antisocial child may lie, get in fights, steal, vandalize or skip school. In adulthood, externalizing tendencies may lead to a personality marked by low constraint, drug or alcohol abuse, and

antisocial behaviors, including irresponsibility, dishonesty, impulsivity, lawlessness and aggression. Antisociality, like most traits, falls on a continuum. A moderately antisocial person may never intentionally hurt someone, but he might make impulsive decisions, take physical and financial risks or shirk responsibility.

18   It's worth reiterating that an externalizing disposition simply increases the risk of demonstrating problematic behavior. An individual with such tendencies could express them in ways that are not harmful to themselves and actually help society: Fire fighters, rescue workers, test pilots, surgeons and entrepreneurs are often gregarious, relatively uninhibited sensation-seekers—that is, moderate externalizers.

19   So a genetic inclination for externalizing can lead to addiction, hyperactivity, acting-out behavior, criminality, a sensation-seeking personality or *all* of these things. Although the contents of this list may seem haphazard, psychologists combine them into a single group because they all stem from the same *latent factor*. Latent factors are hypothesized constructs that help explain the observed correlations between various traits or behaviors.

20   For example, grades in school generally correlate with one another. People who do well in English tend to get good marks in art history, algebra and geology. Why? Because academic ability affects grades, regardless of the subject matter. In statistical lingo, academic ability is the "general, latent factor" and the course grades are the "observed indicators" of that factor. Academic ability is latent because it is not directly measured; rather, the statistician concludes that it exists and causes the grades to vary systematically between people.

21   Statistical analyses consistently show that externalizing is a general latent factor—a common denominator—for a suite of behaviors that includes addiction. Furthermore, the various markers of risk support this conclusion. Childhood characteristics that indicate later problems with alcohol also point to the full spectrum of externalizing behaviors and traits. Thus, drinking alcohol before 15 doesn't just predict future alcohol and drug problems, but also future antisocial behavior. A parent with a history of excessive binge drinking is apt to have children not only with substance-use problems, but with behavioral problems as well. And a reduced-amplitude P300 not only appears in children with a familial risk for alcoholism, but in kids with a familial risk for hyperactivity, antisocial behavior or illicit drug disorders.

22   The associations between externalizing behaviors aren't surprising to clinicians. Comorbidity—the increased chance of having other disorders if you have one of them—is the norm, not the exception, for individuals and families. A father with a cocaine habit is more likely to find that his daughter is getting into trouble for stealing or breaking school rules. At first glance, the child's behavioral problems look like products of the stress, conflict and dysfunction that go with having addict in the family. These are certainly aggravating factors. However, the familial and genetically informative MCTFR data have allowed us to piece together a more precise explanation.

23   Environment has a strong influence on a child's behavior—living with an addict is rife with challenges—but genes also play a substantial role. Estimates of the genetic effect on externalizing behaviors vary by indicator and age, but among older adolescents and adults, well over half of the differences between people's externalizing tendencies result from inheriting different genes.

24   Our analysis of the MCTFR data indicates that children inherit the general latent factor of externalizing rather than specific behavioral factors, Thus, an antisocial mother does not pass on genes that code simply for antisocial behavior, but they do confer vulnerability to a range of adolescent disorders and behaviors. Instead of encounters with the law, her adolescent son may have problems with alcohol or drugs. The outcomes are different, but the same genes—expressed differently under different environmental conditions—predispose them both.

THE ROLE OF THE ENVIRONMENT

25   Even traits with a strong genetic component may be influenced by environmental factors. Monozygotic twins exemplify this principle. Despite their matching DNA, their height, need for glasses, disease susceptibility or personality (just to name a few) may differ.

26   When one member of a monozygptic pair is alcoholic, the likelihood of alcoholism in the other is only about 50 percent. The high heritability of externalizing behaviors suggests that the second twin, if not alcoholic, may be antisocial or dependent on another substance. But sometimes the second twin is problem free. DNA is never destiny.

27   Behavioral geneticists have worked to quantify the role of the environment in addiction, but as a group we have done much less to specify it. Although we know that 50 percent of the variance in alcohol dependence comes from the environment, we are still in the early stages of determining what those environmental factors are. This ignorance may seem surprising, as scientists have spent decades identifying the environmental precursors to addiction and antisocial behavior. But only a small percentage of that research incorporated genetic controls.

28   Instead, many studies simply related environmental variation to children's eventual problems or accomplishments. A classic example of this failure to consider genetic influence is the repeated observation that children who grow up with lots of books in their home tend to do better in school. But concluding that books create an academic child assumes (falsely) that children are born randomly into families—that parent-child resemblance is purely social. Of course, parents actually contribute to their children's environment *and* their genes. Moreover, parents tend to provide environments that complement their children's genotypes: Smart parents often deliver both "smart" genes and an enriched environment. Athletic parents usually provide "athletic" genes and many opportunities to express them. And, unfortunately, parents with addiction

problems tend to provide a genetic vulnerability coupled with a home in which alcohol or drugs are available and abusing them is normal.

29   To understand the true experiential origins of a behavior, one must first disentangle the influence of genes. By using genetically informative samples, we can subtract genetic influences and conclude with greater confidence that a particular environmental factor affects behavior. Using this approach, our data suggest that deviant peers and poor parent-child relationships exert true environmental influences that promote substance use and externalizing behaviors during early adolescence.

30   When considering the effect of environment on behavior, or any complex trait, it's helpful to imagine a continuum of liability. Inherited vulnerability determines where a person begins on the continuum (high versus low risk). From that point, psychosocial or environmental stressors such as peer pressure or excessive conflict with parents can push an individual along the continuum and over a disease threshold.

31   However, sometimes the environment actually modifies gene expression. In other words, the relative influence of genes on a behavior can vary by setting. We see this context-dependent gene expression in recent, unpublished work comparing study participants from rural areas (population less than 10,000) with those from more urban settings. Within cities of 10,000 or more, genes substantially influence which adolescents use illicit substances or show other aspects of the externalizing continuum—just as earlier research indicated. But in very rural areas, environmental (rather than genetic) factors overwhelmingly account for differences in externalizing behavior.

32   One way to interpret this finding is that urban environments, with their wider variety of social niches, allow for a more complete expression of genetically influenced traits. Whether a person's genes nudge her to substance use and rule-breaking, or abstinence and obedience, the city may offer more opportunities to follow those urges. At the same time, finite social prospects in the country may allow more rural parents to monitor and control their adolescents' activities and peer-group selection, thereby minimizing the impact of genes. This rural-urban difference is especially interesting because it represents a gene-by-environment interaction. The genes that are important determinants of behavior in one group of people are just not as important in another.

THE FUTURE OF ADDICTION RESEARCH

33   This complex interplay of genes and environments makes progress slow. But investigators have the data and statistical tools to answer many important addiction-related questions. Moreover, the tempo of discovery will increase with advances in molecular genetics.

34   In the last fifteen years, geneticists have identified a handful of specific genes related to alcohol metabolism and synapse function that occur more often in

alcoholics. But the task of accumulating the entire list of contributing genes is daunting. Many genes influence behavior, and the relative importance of a single gene may differ across ethnic or racial populations. As a result, alcoholism-associated genes in one population may not exert a measurable influence in a different group, even in well-controlled studies. There are also different pathways to addiction, and some people's alcoholism may be more environmental than genetic in origin. Consequently, not only is any one gene apt to have small effects on behavior, but that gene may be absent in a substantial number of addicts.

35   Nonetheless, some day scientists should be able to estimate risk by reading the sequence of a person's DNA. Setting aside the possibility of a futuristic dystopia, this advance will usher in a new type of psychology. Investigators will be able to observe those individuals with especially high (or low) genetic risks for externalizing as they respond, over a lifetime, to different types of environmental stressors.

36   This type of research is already beginning. Avshalom Caspi, now at the University of Wisconsin, and his colleagues divided a large group of males from New Zealand based on the expression level of a gene that encodes a neurotransmitter-metabolizing enzyme, monoamine oxidase A or MAOA. In combination with the life histories of these men, the investigators demonstrated that the consequences of an abusive home varied by genotype. The gene associated with high levels of MAOA was protective—those men were less likely to show antisocial behaviors after childhood maltreatment than the low-MAOA group.

37   Further advances in molecular genetics will bring opportunities for more studies of this type. When investigators can accurately rank experimental participants by their genetic liability to externalizing, they will gain insight into the complexities of gene-environment interplay and answer several intriguing questions: What type of family environments are most at-risk children born into? When children with different genetic risks grow up in the same family, do they create unique environments by seeking distinct friends and experiences? Do they elicit different parenting styles from the same parents? Could a low-risk sibling keep a high-risk child from trouble if they share a close friendship? Is one type of psychosocial stressor more apt to lead to substance use while another leads to antisocial behavior?

38   Molecular genetics will eventually deepen our understanding of the biochemistry and biosocial genesis of addiction. In the interim, quantitative geneticists such as ourselves continue to characterize the development of behavior in ways that will assist molecular geneticists in their work. For example, if there is genetic overlap between alcoholism, drug dependence and antisocial behavior—as the MCTFR data suggest—then it may help to examine extreme externalizers, rather than simply alcoholics, when searching for the genes that produce alcoholism vulnerability.

MUCH LEFT TO LEARN

39   Although the MCTFR data have resolved some addiction-related questions, many others remain, and our team has just begun to scratch the surface of possible research. Our work with teenagers indicates that externalizing is a key factor in early-onset substance-use problems, but the path to later-life addiction may be distinct. Some evidence suggests that genes play a lesser role in later-onset addiction. Moreover, the markers of risk may vary. Being prone to worry, becoming upset easily and tending toward negative moods may, with age, become more important indicators. We don't yet know. However, the MCTFR continues to gather information about its participants as they approach their 30s, and we hope to keep following this group into their 40s and beyond.

40   Meanwhile, the evidence suggests that for early-onset addiction, most relevant genes are not specific to alcoholism or drug dependence. Instead, the same genes predispose an overlapping set of disorders within the externalizing spectrum. This conclusion has significant implications for prevention: Some impulsive risk-takers, frequent rule-breakers and oppositional children may be just as much at risk as early users.

41   At the same time, many kids with a genetic risk for externalizing don't seem to require any sort of special intervention; as it is, they turn out just fine. DNA may nudge someone in a certain direction, but it doesn't force them to go there.

BIBLIOGRAPHY

Burt, S. A., M. McGue, R. F. Krueger and W. G. Iacono. 2005. How are parent-child conflict and childhood externalizing symptoms related over time? Results from a genetically informative cross-tagged study. *Development and Psychopathology* 17:1–21.

Caspi, A., J. McClay, T. E. Moffitt, J. Mill, J. Martin, I. W. Craig, A. Taylor and R. Poulton. 2002. Role of genotype in the cycle of violence in maltreated children. *Science* 297:851–854.

Cloninger, C. R., S. Sigvardsson and M. Bohman. 1988. Childhood personality predicts alcohol abuse in young adults. *Alcoholism: Clinical and Experimental Research* 12:494–505.

Hicks, B. M., R. F. Krueger, W. G. Iacono, M. McGue and C. J. Patrick. 2004. Family transmission and heritability of externalizing disorders: A twin-family study. *Archives of General Psychiatry* 61:922–928.

Iacono, W. G., S. M. Malone and M. McGue. 2003. Substance use disorders, externalizing psychopathology, and P300 event-related potential amplitude. *International Journal of Psychophysiology* 48:147–178.

Krueger, R. F., B. M. Hicks, C. J. Patrick, S. R. Carlson, W. G. Iacono and M. McGue 2002. Etiologic connections among substance dependence, antisocial behavior, and personality: Modeling the externalizing spectrum. *Journal of Abnormal Psychology* 111:411–424.

Malone, S. M., W. G. Iacono and M. McGue. 2002. Drinks of the father: Father's maximum number of drinks consumed predicts externalizing disorders, substance use, and substance use disorders in preadolescent and adolescent offspring. *Alcoholism: Clinical and Experimental Research* 26:1823–1832.

McGovern, G. 1996. *Terry. My Daughter's Life-and-Death Struggle With Alcoholism.* New York: Random House.

McGue, M., W. G. Iacono, L. N. LeGrand, S. Malone and I. Elkins. 2001. The origins and consequences of age at first drink. I. Associations with substance-abuse disorders, disinhibitory behavior and psychopathology, and P3 amplitude. *Alcoholism: Clinical and Experimental Research* 25:1156–1165.

Porjesz, B., and H. Begleiter. 2003. Alcoholism and human electrophysiology. *Alcohol Research & Health* 27:153–166.

Turkheimer, E., H. H. Goldsmith and I.I. Gottesman. 1995. Some conceptual deficiencies in "developmental" behavioral genetics: Comment. *Human Development* 38:142–153.

Walden, B., M. McGue, W. G. Iacono, S. A. Burt and I. Elkins. 2004. Identifying shared environmental contributions to early substance use: The respective roles of peers and parents. *Journal of Abnormal Psychology* 113:440–450.

Reading Closely and Thinking Critically

1. What are the authors trying to accomplish with their research? Why does studying twins help them to accomplish this?
2. In the section "Markers of Risk," the authors examine personality, family background, brainwaves, and precocious experimentation. Are these causes of addiction, or do these markers *correlate* with addiction? What's the difference? Why is this difference important?
3. How do the authors view the role genes play in addiction? How do they view the role of the family and social environment?
4. Do the authors come to any conclusion about the causes of addiction? Why or why not?
5. How do the closing paragraphs influence the reader's trust in the authors' observations?

Examining Structure and Strategy

1. Which of the three elements of argument and persuasion—logos, pathos, or ethos—dominate here? Why? Identify examples of each in the essay.
2. In paragraphs 16, 17, and 18 the authors define "externalizing tendencies." In paragraphs 19 and 20, they define "latent factors" and in paragraph 22 they define "comorbidity." What do these definitions tell you about how the writers view their audience?

3. Many writing instructors prefer students not to use headings like those employed by LeGrand, Iacono, and McGue. Why? What problems with an essay's structure might headings mask? In this essay, are they helpful or distracting? Why?

4. Discuss the way in which paragraphs 30, 31, and 32 constitute the authors' real conclusion. Why is it placed where it is?

Considering Language and Style

1. What is the tone of the essay? What relationship with readers are the authors trying to create?

2. In light of the essay's tone, why does the essay begin with the anecdote of the death of a presidential candidate's daughter? What element of persuasion do the authors introduce here?

3. What do the authors mean by the first two sentences of paragraph 30: "When considering the effect of environment on behavior, or any complex trait, it's helpful to imagine a continuum of liability. Inherited vulnerability determines where a person begins on the continuum (high versus low risk)." Why is the concept of a "continuum of liability" important?

4. Look at the essay's final sentence. How does it function as a secondary conclusion?

For writing assignments based on this essay, see page 457.

Background

Jacob Sullum is a syndicated newspaper columnist and senior editor at *Reason*, the monthly magazine in which this essay first appeared. *Reason* is published by the Reason Foundation, a not-for-profit think tank based in Los Angeles whose values can generally be described as libertarian, the belief that that individual liberty and free markets produce the best societies. *Reason* has a circulation of around 60 000 and has won numerous awards, including being named one of the 50 best magazines by the *Chicago Tribune* twice. As is common in magazine articles, there are no footnotes or bibliography. How does this fact influence your reading of the essay?

The Patterns and Their Purposes

Sullum uses examples to argue that the image of addiction as a complete loss of control to a drug is a false one. He also uses facts and statistics to point out that the number of heroin addicts is relatively small. He questions the definition of addiction as a way of countering the common belief that certain substances are inherently addictive.

The Surprising Truth about Heroin and Addiction
Jacob Sullum

As you read
Think again about your assumptions about addicts and addiction and note those points that challenge your assumptions.

1   In 1992, *The New York Times* carried a front-page story about a successful businessman who happened to be a regular heroin user. It began: "He is an executive in a company in New York, lives in a condo on the Upper East Side of Manhattan, drives an expensive car, plays tennis in the Hamptons and vacations with his wife in Europe and the Caribbean. But unknown to office colleagues, friends, and most of his family, the man is also a longtime heroin user. He says he finds heroin relaxing and pleasurable and has seen no reason to stop using it until the woman he recently married insisted that he do so. "The drug is an enhancement of my life," he said. "I see it as similar to a guy coming home and having a drink of alcohol. Only alcohol has never done it for me."

2   *The Times* noted that "nearly everything about the 44-year-old executive . . . seems to fly in the face of widely held perceptions about heroin users." The reporter who wrote the story and his editors seemed uncomfortable with contradicting official anti-drug propaganda, which depicts heroin use as incompatible with a satisfying, productive life. The headline read, "Executive's Secret Struggle With Heroin's Powerful Grip," which sounds more like a cautionary tale than a success story. And *The Times* hastened to add that heroin users "are flirting with disaster." It conceded that "heroin does not damage the organs as, for instance, heavy alcohol use does." But it cited the risk of arrest, overdose, AIDS, and hepatitis—without noting that all of these risks are created or exacerbated by prohibition.

3   The general thrust of the piece was: Here is a privileged man who is tempting fate by messing around with a very dangerous drug. He may have escaped disaster so far, but unless he quits he will probably end up dead or in prison.

4   That is not the way the businessman saw his situation. He said he had decided to give up heroin only because his wife did not approve of the habit. "In my heart," he said, "I really don't feel there's anything wrong with using heroin. But there doesn't seem to be any way in the world I can persuade my wife to grant me this space in our relationship. I don't want to lose her, so I'm making this effort."

5   Judging from the "widely held perceptions about heroin users" mentioned by *The Times*, that effort was bound to fail. The conventional view of heroin, which powerfully shapes the popular understanding of addiction, is nicely summed up in the journalist Martin Booth's 1996 history of opium. "Addiction is the compulsive taking of drugs which have such a hold over the addict he or she cannot stop using them without suffering severe symptoms and even death," he writes. "Opiate dependence . . . is as fundamental to an addict's existence as food and water, a physio-chemical fact: an addict's body is chemically reliant upon its drug for opiates actually alter the body's chemistry so it cannot function properly without being periodically primed. A hunger for the drug forms when the quantity in the bloodstream falls below a certain level. . . . Fail to feed the body and it deteriorates and may die from drug starvation." Booth also declares that "everyone . . . is a potential addict"; that "addiction can start with the very first dose"; and that "with continued use addiction is a certainty."

6   Booth's description is wrong or grossly misleading in every particular. To understand why is to recognize the fallacies underlying a reductionist, drug-centered view of addiction in which chemicals force themselves on people—a view that skeptics such as the maverick psychiatrist Thomas Szasz and the psychologist Stanton Peele have long questioned. The idea that a drug can compel the person who consumes it to continue consuming it is one of the most important beliefs underlying the war on drugs, because this power makes possible all the other evils to which drug use supposedly leads.

7   When Martin Booth tells us that anyone can be addicted to heroin, that it may take just one dose, and that it will certainly happen to you if you're foolish enough to repeat the experiment, he is drawing on a long tradition of anti-drug propaganda. As the sociologist Harry G. Levine has shown, the original model for such warnings was not heroin or opium but alcohol. "The idea that drugs are inherently addicting," Levine wrote in 1978, "was first systematically worked out for alcohol and then extended to other substances. Long before opium was popularly accepted as addicting, alcohol was so regarded." The dry crusaders of the 19th and early 20th centuries taught that every tippler was a potential drunkard, that a glass of beer was the first step on the road to ruin, and that repeated use of distilled spirits made addiction virtually inevitable. Today, when a kitchen wrecked by a skinny model wielding a frying pan is supposed to symbolize the havoc caused by a snort of heroin, similar assumptions about opiates are even more widely held, and they likewise are based more on faith than facts.

WITHDRAWAL PENALTY

8   Beginning early in the 20th century, Stanton Peele notes, heroin "came to be seen in American society as the nonpareil drug of addiction—as leading inescapably from even the most casual contact to an intractable dependence, withdrawal from which was traumatic and unthinkable for the addict." According to this view, reflected in Booth's gloss and other popular portrayals, the potentially fatal agony of withdrawal is the gun that heroin holds to the addict's head. These accounts greatly exaggerate both the severity and the importance of withdrawal symptoms.

9   Heroin addicts who abruptly stop using the drug commonly report flu-like symptoms, which may include chills, sweating, runny nose and eyes, muscular aches, stomach cramps, nausea, diarrhea, or headaches. While certainly unpleasant, the experience is not life threatening. Indeed, addicts who have developed tolerance (needing higher doses to achieve the same effect) often voluntarily undergo withdrawal so they can begin using heroin again at a lower dose, thereby reducing the cost of their habit. Another sign that fear of withdrawal symptoms is not the essence of addiction is the fact that heroin users commonly drift in and out of their habits, going through periods of abstinence and returning to the drug long after any physical discomfort has faded away. Indeed, the observation that detoxification is not tantamount to overcoming an addiction, that addicts typically will try repeatedly before successfully kicking the habit, is a commonplace of drug treatment.

10   More evidence that withdrawal has been overemphasized as a motivation for using opiates comes from patients who take narcotic painkillers over extended periods of time. Like heroin addicts, they develop "physical dependence" and experience withdrawal symptoms when they stop taking the drugs. But studies conducted during the last two decades have consistently found that patients in pain who receive opioids (opiates or synthetics with similar effects) rarely become addicted.

11   Pain experts emphasize that physical dependence should not be confused with addiction, which requires a psychological component: a persistent desire to use the substance for its mood-altering effects. Critics have long complained that unreasonable fears about narcotic addiction discourage adequate pain treatment. In 1989, Charles Schuster, then director of the National Institute on Drug Abuse, confessed, "We have been so effective in warning the medical establishment and the public in general about the inappropriate use of opiates that we have endowed these drugs with a mysterious power to enslave that is overrated."

12   Although popular perceptions lag behind, the point made by pain specialists—that "physical dependence" is not the same as addiction—is now widely accepted by professionals who deal with drug problems. But under the heroin-based model that prevailed until the 1970s, tolerance and withdrawal symptoms were considered the hallmarks of addiction. By this standard, drugs such as nicotine and cocaine were not truly addictive; they were merely "habituating." That distinction proved untenable,

given the difficulty that people often had in giving up substances that were not considered addictive.

13   Having hijacked the term addiction, which in its original sense referred to any strong habit, psychiatrists ultimately abandoned it in favor of substance dependence. "The essential feature of Substance Dependence," according to the American Psychiatric Association, "is a cluster of cognitive, behavioral, and physiological symptoms indicating that the individual continues use of the substance despite significant substance-related problems. . . . Neither tolerance nor withdrawal is necessary or sufficient for a diagnosis of Substance Dependence." Instead, the condition is defined as "a maladaptive pattern of substance use" involving at least three of seven features. In addition to tolerance and withdrawal, these include using more of the drug than intended; trying unsuccessfully to cut back; spending a lot of time getting the drug, using it, and recovering from its effects; giving up or reducing important social, occupational, or recreational activities because of drug use; and continuing use even while recognizing drug-related psychological or physical problems.

14   One can quibble with these criteria, especially since they are meant to be applied not by the drug user himself but by a government-licensed expert with whose judgment he may disagree. The possibility of such a conflict is all the more troubling because the evaluation may be involuntary (the result of an arrest, for example) and may have implications for the drug user's freedom. More fundamentally, classifying substance dependence as a "mental disorder" to be treated by medical doctors suggests that drug abuse is a disease, something that happens to people rather than something that people do. Yet it is clear from the description that we are talking about a pattern of behavior. Addiction is not simply a matter of introducing a chemical into someone's body, even if it is done often enough to create tolerance and withdrawal symptoms. Conversely, someone who takes a steady dose of a drug and who can stop using without physical distress may still be addicted to it.

SIMPLY IRRESISTIBLE?

15   Even if addiction is not a physical compulsion, perhaps some drug experiences are so alluring that people find it impossible to resist them. Certainly that is heroin's reputation, encapsulated in the title of a 1972 book: *It's So Good, Don't Even Try It Once*.

16   The fact that heroin use is so rare—involving, according to the government's data, something like 0.2 percent of the U.S. population in 2001—suggests that its appeal is much more limited than we've been led to believe. If heroin really is "so good," why does it have such a tiny share of the illegal drug market? Marijuana is more than 45 times as popular. The National Household Survey on Drug Abuse indicates that about 3 million Americans have used heroin in their lifetimes; of them, 15 percent had used it in the last year, 4 percent in the last month. These numbers suggest that the vast majority of heroin users either never become addicted or, if they do, manage to give

the drug up. A survey of high school seniors found that 1 percent had used heroin in the previous year, while 0.1 percent had used it on 20 or more days in the previous month. Assuming that daily use is a reasonable proxy for opiate addiction, one in 10 of the students who had taken heroin in the last year might have qualified as addicts. These are not the sort of numbers you'd expect for a drug that's irresistible.

17   True, these surveys exclude certain groups in which heroin use is more common and in which a larger percentage of users probably could be described as addicts. The household survey misses people living on the street, in prisons, and in residential drug treatment programs, while the high school survey leaves out truants and dropouts. But even for the entire population of heroin users, the estimated addiction rates do not come close to matching heroin's reputation. A 1976 study by the drug researchers Leon G. Hunt and Carl D. Chambers estimated there were 3 or 4 million heroin users in the United States, perhaps 10 percent of them addicts. "Of all active heroin users," Hunt and Chambers wrote, "a large majority are not addicts: they are not physically or socially dysfunctional; they are not daily users and they do not seem to require treatment." A 1994 study based on data from the National Comorbidity Survey estimated that 23 percent of heroin users never experience substance dependence.

18   The comparable rate for alcohol in that study was 15 percent, which seems to support the idea that heroin is more addictive: A larger percentage of the people who try it become heavy users, even though it's harder to get. At the same time, the fact that using heroin is illegal, expensive, risky, inconvenient, and almost universally condemned means that the people who nevertheless choose to do it repeatedly will tend to differ from people who choose to drink. They will be especially attracted to heroin's effects, the associated lifestyle, or both. In other words, heroin users are a self-selected group, less representative of the general population than alcohol users are, and they may be more inclined from the outset to form strong attachments to the drug.

19   The same study found that 32 percent of tobacco users had experienced substance dependence. Figures like that one are the basis for the claim that nicotine is "more addictive than heroin." After all, cigarette smokers typically go through a pack or so a day, so they're under the influence of nicotine every waking moment. Heroin users typically do not use their drug even once a day. Smokers offended by this comparison are quick to point out that they function fine, meeting their responsibilities at work and homey [sic] despite their habit. This, they assume, is impossible for heroin users. Examples like the businessman described by The New York Times indicate otherwise.

20   Still, it's true that nicotine's psychoactive effects are easier to reconcile with the requirements of everyday life than heroin's are. Indeed, nicotine can enhance concentration and improve performance on certain tasks. So one important reason why most cigarette smokers consume their drug throughout the day is that they can do so without running into trouble. And because they're used to smoking in so many different settings, they may find nicotine harder to give up than a drug they use only with

certain people in secret. In one survey, 57 percent of drug users entering a Canadian treatment program said giving up their problem substance (not necessarily heroin) would be easier than giving up cigarettes. In another survey, 36 heroin users entering treatment were asked to compare their strongest cigarette urge to their strongest heroin urge. Most said the heroin urge was stronger, but two said the cigarette urge was, and 11 rated the two urges about the same.

21   In a sense, nicotine's compatibility with a wide range of tasks makes it more addictive than alcohol or heroin. But this is not the sort of thing people usually have in mind when they worry about addiction. Indeed, if it weren't for the health effects of smoking (and the complaints of bystanders exposed to the smoke), nicotine addiction probably would be seen as no big deal, just as caffeine addiction is. As alternative sources of nicotine that do not involve smoking (gum, patches, inhalers, beverages, lozenges, oral snuff) become popular not just as aids in quitting but as long-term, replacements, it will be interesting to see whether they will be socially accepted. Once the health risks are dramatically reduced or eliminated, will daily consumption of nicotine still be viewed as shameful and declasse, as a disease to be treated or a problem to be overcome? Perhaps so, if addiction per se is the issue. But not if it's the medical, social, and psychological consequences of addiction that really matter.

THE NEEDLE AND THE DAMAGE DONE

22   To a large extent, regular heroin use also can be separated from the terrible consequences that have come to be associated with it. Because of prohibition, users face the risk of arrest and imprisonment, the handicap of a criminal record, and the violence associated with the black market. The artificially high price of heroin, perhaps 40 or 50 times what it would otherwise cost, may lead to heavy debts, housing problems, poor nutrition, and theft. The inflated cost also encourages users to inject the drug, a more efficient but riskier mode of administration. The legal treatment of injection equipment, including restrictions on distribution and penalties for possession, encourages needle sharing which spreads diseases such as AIDS and hepatitis. The unreliable quality and unpredictable purity associated with the black market can lead to poisoning and accidental overdoses.

23   Without prohibition, then, a daily heroin habit would be far less burdensome and hazardous. Heroin itself is much less likely to kill a user than the reckless combination of heroin with other depressants, such as alcohol or barbiturates. The federal government's Drug Abuse Warning Network counted 4,820 mentions of heroin or morphine (which are indistinguishable in the blood) by medical examiners in 1999. Only 438 of these deaths (9 percent) were listed as directly caused by an overdose of the opiate. Three-quarters of the deaths were caused by heroin/morphine in combination with other drugs. Provided the user avoids such mixtures, has access to a supply of reliable purity, and follows sanitary injection procedures, the health risks of long-term opiate consumption are minimal.

24   The comparison between heroin and nicotine is also instructive when it comes to the role of drug treatment. Although many smokers have a hard time quitting, those who succeed generally do so on their own. Surprisingly, the same may be true of heroin addicts. In the early 1960s, based on records kept by the Federal Bureau of Narcotics, sociologist Charles Winick concluded that narcotic addicts tend to "mature out" of the habit in their 30s. He suggested that "addiction may be a self limiting process for perhaps two-thirds of addicts." Subsequent researchers have questioned Winick's assumptions, and other studies have come up with lower estimates. But it's clear that "natural recovery" is much more common than the public has been led to believe.

25   In a 1974 study of Vietnam veterans, only 12 percent of those who were addicted to heroin in Vietnam took up the habit again during the three years after their return to the United States. (This was not because they couldn't find heroin; half of them used it at least once after their return, generally without becoming addicted again.) Those who had undergone treatment (half of the group) were just as likely to be re-addicted as those who had not. Since those with stronger addictions were more likely to receive treatment, this does not necessarily mean that treatment was useless, but it clearly was not a prerequisite for giving up heroin.

26   Despite its reputation, then, heroin is neither irresistible nor inescapable. Only a very small share of the population ever uses it, and a large majority of those who do never become addicted. Even within the minority who develop a daily habit, most manage to stop using heroin, often without professional intervention. Yet heroin is still perceived as the paradigmatic voodoo drug, ineluctably turning its users into zombies who must obey its commands.

HEROIN IN MODERATION

27   The idea that drugs cause addiction was rejected in the case of alcohol because it was so clearly at odds with everyday experience, which showed that the typical drinker was not an alcoholic. But what the psychologist Bruce Alexander calls "the myth of drug-induced addiction" is still widely accepted in the case of heroin—and, by extension, the drugs compared to it—because moderate opiate users are hard to find. That does not mean they don't exist; indeed, judging from the government's survey results, they are a lot more common than addicts. It's just that people who use opiates in a controlled way are inconspicuous by definition, and keen to remain so.

28   In the early 1960s, however, researchers began to tentatively identify users of heroin and other opiates who were not addicts. "Surprisingly enough," a Northwestern University psychiatrist wrote in 1961, "in some cases at least, narcotic use may be confined to weekends or parties and the users may be able to continue in gainful employment for some time. Although this pattern often deteriorates and the rate of use increases, several cases have been observed in which relatively gainful and steady

employment has been maintained for two to three years while the user was on what might be called a regulated or controlled habit."

29   A few years later, Harvard psychiatrist Norman Zinberg and David C. Lewis, then a medical resident, described five categories of narcotic users, including "people who use narcotics regularly but who develop little or no tolerance for them and do not suffer withdrawal symptoms." They explained that "such people are usually able to work regularly and productively. They value the relaxation and the 'kick' obtained from the drug, but their fear of needing more and more of the drug to get the same kick causes them to impose rigorous controls on themselves."

30   The example offered by Zinberg and Lewis was a 47-year-old physician with a successful practice who had been injecting morphine four times a day, except weekends, for 12 years. He experienced modest discomfort on Saturdays and Sundays, when he abstained, but he stuck to his schedule and did not raise his dose except on occasions when he was especially busy or tense. Zinberg and Lewis's account suggests that morphine's main function for him was stress relief: "Somewhat facetiously, when describing his intolerance of people making emotional demands on him he said that he took 1 shot for his patients, 1 for his mistress, 1 for his family and 1 to sleep. He expressed no guilt about his drug taking, and made it clear that he had no intention of stopping."

31   Zinberg eventually interviewed 61 controlled opiate users. His criteria excluded both dabblers (the largest group of people who have used heroin) and daily users. One subject was a 41-year-old carpenter who had used heroin on weekends for a decade. Married 16 years, he lived with his wife and three children in a middle-class suburb. Another was a 27-year-old college student studying special education. He had used heroin two or three times a month for three years, then once a week for a year. The controlled users said they liked "the 'rush' (glow or warmth), the sense of distance from their problems, and the tranquilizing powers of the drug." Opiate use was generally seen as a social activity, and was often combined with other forms of recreation. Summing up the lessons he learned from his research, Zinberg emphasized the importance of self-imposed rules dictating when, where, and with whom the drug would be used. More broadly, he concluded that "set and setting"—expectations and environment—play crucial roles in shaping a drug user's experience.

32   Other researchers have reported similar findings. After interviewing 12 occasional heroin users in the early 1970s, a Harvard researcher concluded that "it seems possible for young people from a number of different backgrounds, family patterns, and educational abilities to use heroin occasionally without becoming addicted." The subjects typically took heroin with one or more friends, and the most frequently reported benefit was relaxation. One subject, a 23-year-old graduate student, said it was "like taking a vacation from yourself . . . When things get to you, it's a way of getting away without getting away." These occasional users were unanimous in rejecting addiction

as inconsistent with their self-images. A 1983 British study of 51 opiate users likewise found that distaste for the junkie lifestyle was an important deterrent to excessive use.

33   While these studies show that controlled opiate use is possible, the 1974 Vietnam veterans study gives us some idea of how common it is. "Only one-quarter of those who used heroin in the last two years used it daily at all," the researchers reported. Likewise, only a quarter said they had felt dependent, and only a quarter said heroin use had interfered with their lives. Regular heroin use (more than once a week for more than a month) was associated with a significant increase in "social adjustment problems," but occasional use was not.

34   Many of these occasional users had been addicted in Vietnam, so they knew what it was like. Paradoxically, a drug's attractiveness, whether experienced directly or observed secondhand, can reinforce the user's determination to remain in control. (Presumably, that is the theory behind all the propaganda warning how wonderful certain drug experiences are, except that the aim of those messages is to stop people from experimenting at all.) A neuroscientist in his late 20s who smoked heroin a couple of times told me it was "nothing dramatic, just the feeling that everything was OK for about six hours, and I wasn't really motivated to do anything." Having observed several friends who were addicted to heroin at one time or another, he understood that the experience could be seductive, but "that kind of seduction . . . kind of repulsed me. That was exactly the kind of thing that I was trying to avoid in my life."

35   Similarly, a horticulturist in his 40s who first snorted heroin in the mid-1980s said, "It was too nice." As he described it, "you're sort of not awake and you're not asleep, and you feel sort of like a baby in the cradle, with no worries, just floating in a comfortable cocoon. That's an interesting place to be if you don't have anything else to do. That's Sunday-afternoon-on-the-couch material." He did have other things to do, and after that first experience he used heroin only "once in a blue moon." But he managed to incorporate the regular use of another opiate, morphine pills, into a busy, productive life. For years he had been taking them once a week, as a way of unwinding and reliving the aches and pains from the hard manual labor required by his landscaping business. "We use it as a reward system," he said. "On a Friday, if we've been working really hard and we're sore and it's available, it's a reward. It's like, 'We've worked hard today. We've earned our money, we paid our bills, but we're sore so let's do this. It's medicine.'"

BETTER HOMES & GARDENS

36   Evelyn Schwartz learned to use heroin in a similar way: as a complement to rest and relaxation rather than a means of suppressing unpleasant emotions. A social worker in her 50s, she injected heroin every day for years but was using it intermittently when I interviewed her a few years ago. Schwartz (a pseudonym) originally became addicted after leaving home at 14 because of conflict with her mother. "As I felt more and more alienated from my family, more and more alone, more and more

depressed," she said, "I started to use [heroin] not in a recreational fashion but as a coping mechanism, to get rid of feelings, to feel OK. . . . I was very unhappy . . . and just hopeless about life, and I was just trying to survive day by day for many years."

37   But after Schwartz found work that she loved and started feeling good about her life, she was able to use heroin in a different way. "I try not to use as a coping mechanism," she said. "I try very hard not to use when I'm miserable, because that's what gets me into trouble. It's set and setting. It's not the drug, because I can use this drug in a very controlled way, and I can also go out of control." To stay in control, "I try to use when I'm feeling good," such as on vacation with friends, listening to music, or before a walk on a beautiful spring day. "If I need to clean the house, I do a little heroin, and I can clean the house, and it just makes me feel so good."

38   Many people are shocked by the idea of using heroin so casually, which helps explain the controversy surrounding a 2001 BBC documentary that explored why people use drugs. "Heroin is my drug of choice over alcohol or cocaine," said one user interviewed for the program. "I take it at weekends in small doses, and do the gardening." It may be unconventional, but using heroin to enliven housework or gardening is surely wiser than using it to a alleviate grief, dissatisfaction, or loneliness. It's when drugs are used for emotional management that a destructive habit is apt to develop.

39   Even daily opiate use is not necessarily inconsistent with a productive life. One famous example is the pioneering surgeon William Halsted, who led a brilliant career while secretly addicted to morphine. On a more modest level, Schwartz said that even during her years as a self-described junkie she always held a job, always paid the rent, and was able to conceal her drug use from people who would have been alarmed by it. "I was always one of the best secretaries at work, and no one ever knew because I learned how to titrate my doses," she said. She would generally take three or four doses a day: when she got up in the morning, at lunchtime, when she came home from work, and perhaps before going to sleep. The doses she took during the day were small enough so that she could get her work done. "Aside from the fact that I was a junkie" she said, "I was raised to be a really good girl and do what I'm supposed to do, and I did."

40   Schwartz, a warm, smart, hard-working woman, is quite different from the heroin users portrayed by government propaganda. Even when she was taking heroin every day, her worst crime was shoplifting a raincoat for a job interview. "I never robbed," she said. "I never did anything like that. I never hurt a human being. I could never do that . . . I'm not going to hit anybody over the head. . . . I went sick a lot as a con-sequence. When other junkies would commit crimes, get money, and tighten up, I would be sick. Everyone used to say: 'You're terrible at being a junkie.'"

Reading Closely and Thinking Critically

1. Sullum frequently uses examples of individuals who have managed their relationship to addiction. First, describe his conclusions about what makes the management of heroin use possible. Second, consider whether you think he is overgeneralizing from his examples, When does he provide other data to back up the conclusions he draws from his examples?

2. In paragraph 7, Sullum writes that "The idea that a drug can compel the person who consumes it to continue consuming it is one of the most important beliefs underlying the war on drugs, because this power makes possible all the other evils to which drug use supposedly leads." What other evils is he speaking of?

3. The "war on drugs" refers to the North American practice of using mainly a law and order approach to the problem of addiction and the problems caused by addiction. Why does such a war depend on the belief that drugs are inherently addicting? Given this essay and your previous reading, is this strategy effective? What issues does such a war oversimplify?

4. Sullum makes a distinction between a drug user's addiction, the user's growing tolerance for the drug, and the user's experience of withdrawal. Why? Is this a valid distinction? Does he have any sources to support his conclusion?

5. In paragraph 16, Sullum draws some conclusions from the data provided by a National Household Survey on Drug Abuse. Are these legitimate conclusions? Does he have other ways of backing up these conclusions?

6. Is it possible to agree with Sullum's conclusions and argue with his strategy for reaching them? Why or why not? You can bring to bear the other reading you have done on this issue.

Examining Structure and Strategy

1. Once again, consider the balance of logos, pathos, and ethos in this essay. How does this balance influence your trust in the writer's conclusions?

2. When do you know the writer's opinion of the effectiveness of drug prohibition? Is this an effective placement of that opinion?

3. Sullum, like the authors of "Predicting Addiction," uses headings. Are they necessary in this essay? Are they distracting? Explain your answer.

4. Although this essay uses magazine style and doesn't site sources, Sullum frequently tells you in the text itself what report or author he is quoting. When do you trust his sources and when don't you? Consult the material in Chapter 14 for evaluating sources and consider which of his sources you trust the most.

Considering Language and Style

1. What's the tone of this essay? What relationship with the reader is Sullum trying to create? What relationship to other researchers is implied by Sullum's tone?

2. At the end of paragraph 7, Sullum writes, "Today, when a kitchen wrecked by a skinny model wielding a frying pan is supposed to symbolize the havoc caused by a snort of heroin, similar assumptions about opiates are even more widely held, and they likewise are based more on faith than facts." Is Sullum's strategy different from those of the general media? To what extent is his argument based more on "faith than facts"? To answer this, you might want to consider the website of the Reason Foundation.

3. Consider Sullum's final example. Is this an effective conclusion to the essay?

Assignments for Discussion and Writing
"Imagining an Enlightened Social Policy on Drugs," "Predicting Addiction,"
and "The Surprising Truth about Heroin and Addiction."

1. **For discussion in class or online:** What kinds of assumptions do we have about people who are addicted to illegal substances? What kinds of assumptions do we have about people who cannot give up alcohol or cigarettes? Why are these assumptions different? Where do they come from? Are they helpful? If your instructor so directs, post your responses on your class Web site.

2. **In your journal.** What are you addicted to? Chocolate? VLT's? Work? How does your addiction shape your life? When are your needs particularly strong?

3. **Using argumentation/persuasion for a purpose.** The purposes in the assignments are possibilities. You may establish whatever purposes you like, within your instructor's guidelines.
   - To entertain and persuade your reader, describe the experience of you or someone you know well who coped with an addiction. Use your description or narrative as the springboard to persuade your reader that seeing the similarities between addicts and ourselves is both more accurate and more useful, with respect to our hope of challenging addiction.
   - Both Maté and Sullum argue that there is little difference, particularly with respect to the damage done to our bodies, between being addicted to licit substances like tobacco and alcohol and being addicted to illicit drugs. Take a stand on one side of this issue and explain your reasoning.
   - Choose one aspect of the North American approach to drug addiction—discussion of abstinence in high schools or provincial drug courts that encourage addicts to accept treatment in return for not going to jail, and discuss the extent to which it is an over-simplification of the real problem or a response to the complexity of the problem.

4. **Combining patterns.** Drawing on several definitions of addiction, create an extended definition that persuades people to look at addiction in a different light.

5. **Connecting the readings.** In the definition chapter (Chapter 7), Mark Kingwell talks about our common ideas of the good life: that we have more money and more prestige than the other people in our circles. Maté suggests that such attitudes create fertile grounds for addictions insofar as they create hungers that can never be sated. Discuss the relationship between our misconceptions about the good life and addiction.

6. **Drawing on sources.** Research the addiction rates in European countries that have decriminalized drug use. Contrast or compare rates in those jurisdictions with rates in your community. Base an argument either for change or the status quo on your findings.

Chapter 13

Combining Patterns of Development

Words—so innocent and powerless as they are, as standing in a dictionary, how potent for good and evil they become in the hands of one who knows how to combine them.

— Nathaniel Hawthorne

All the interests of my reason, speculative as well as practical, combine in the three following questions: 1) What can I know? 2) What ought I to do? 3) What may I hope?

— Immanuel Kant

PATTERNS FOR A PURPOSE

An important focus of this book is to demonstrate how you can use the patterns of development to achieve your purpose for writing. In fact, this focus is so important that it gives this book its title, *Patterns for a Purpose*.

You have probably noticed that in addition to demonstrating how individual patterns of development can help you achieve your writing purpose, *Patterns for a Purpose* also demonstrates how you can *combine* two or more patterns to achieve your purpose:

- Many readings in the book combine patterns.
- Pre-reading headnotes labelled "Combined Patterns and Their Purpose(s)" signal when and why patterns are combined.
- Post-reading questions labelled "Noting Combined Patterns" help you study strategies for combining patterns.
- Writing assignments labelled "Combining Patterns" give you experience combining patterns in a single essay.

To emphasize further that you can combine patterns to achieve your writing purpose, this chapter includes six additional readings that combine patterns to achieve a range of purposes.

USING THE PATTERNS OF DEVELOPMENT IN YOUR WRITING

How do you know if your writing is successful? The best indicator of success is whether your writing achieves its purpose with its target audience. Sometimes you can achieve your purpose using a single pattern of development, and sometimes you need to combine two or more patterns. For example, assume that at work you are the editor of the company newsletter and must write an article to inform new employees about vacation and sick leave policies. For this target audience, a single pattern—process analysis—may be sufficient to explain how the policies work. However, if your audience is long-term employees and your purpose is to inform them of changes in vacation and sick leave policies, you may need two patterns—process analysis to explain how the new policies work and comparison-contrast to make sure long-term employees understand how the new policies differ from the old.

Sometimes you need more than two patterns to achieve your purpose. Let's say that in another edition of the newsletter you profile the employee-of-the-month to inspire other employees to strive for the same award. To achieve this purpose, you might use exemplification to give examples of the employee's accomplishments, narration to tell a story about a time the employee did something extraordinary, and cause-and-effect analysis to explain how the employee affects the success of the company.

When you combine patterns to achieve your writing purpose, you often draw on one pattern more heavily than the others. That is, you will have primary and secondary patterns. For example, an essay about your favourite vacation spot can rely heavily on description. However, in a paragraph or two, you might also narrate a story about something enjoyable that happened when you last visited the spot. Then, description would be your *primary pattern*, and narration would be your *secondary pattern*. Or to convince readers to practise meditation, you might use exemplification as a primary pattern to illustrate the benefits of meditation, and process analysis and classification as secondary patterns to explain how meditation works and to explain the kinds of meditation, to help readers decide which kind is best for them.

Whenever you write—in post-secondary institutions, at work, in the community—be open to the possibility of combining patterns to achieve your purpose. Combining patterns often strengthens your writing and makes it more interesting and more likely to appeal to your audience.

PROCESS GUIDELINES: STRATEGIES FOR COMBINING PATTERNS

1. **Selecting a Topic.** If your topic has been assigned, look for combinations of patterns suggested by that topic. For example, the essay topic "What is media bias and how common is it?" suggests that you will combine a definition of media bias with examples of its occurrence. Or if you have to write about media bias and have trouble narrowing your topic, call on the patterns to help you. Exemplification will focus your topic on examples of media bias; cause-and-effect analysis will narrow your topic to discuss the reasons for and consequences of media bias; classification will narrow the topic to types of media bias; definition will guide you toward explaining the meaning of media bias. Looking at your topic through the lens of the patterns can help you bring your ideas into focus.

2. **Achieving Your Purpose and Assessing Your Audience.** Ask yourself how multiple patterns can help you achieve your purpose with your target audience. The answer may suggest ways to combine patterns to heighten your essay's appeal.

3. **Generating Ideas.** If you have trouble discovering ideas for developing your writing topic, use the patterns. They help you generate ideas by looking at your topic from different angles. To generate ideas for a newsletter article about the employee-of-the-month, for instance, consider each pattern and the detail it can provide. Ask, "What can I describe?" and you might answer, "the employee's desk—for humour." Ask, "What can I narrate?" and you might answer, "the time the employee administered CPR to another worker."

4. **Organizing Details.** Consider whether your pattern combination suggests combining certain organizational schemes. For example, if you combine process analysis and cause-and-effect analysis, you may need to order your details with a combination of chronological and progressive orders.

5. **Revising.** For help revising an essay with multiple patterns, you can consult the revising checklists in Chapters 4–11. These checklists note the revision concerns for each pattern of development.

Troubleshooting Guide

Using Transitions and Other Coherence Devices

If you have trouble signalling the relationships among the ideas you express with combined patterns, consult the transition chart on page 75. The transitions in this chart, along with the other coherence devices explained on pages 76–77, can also help you move smoothly from pattern to pattern.

ANNOTATED STUDENT ESSAY

In the following essay, student writer Mary Ann Bevilacqua combines comparison-contrast, exemplification, and cause-and-effect analysis to explain to parents of teenagers the attraction—and danger—associated with instant messaging (IM). Consider the way Mary Ann's points might apply, now, to Facebook, Twitter, and smartphones. After you read, you will have an opportunity to evaluate this essay.

The Telephone Is Out; IM Is In

1   In the not-too-distant past, parents could not get their teenagers off the telephone. So permanently was the phone glued to their teens' ears that parents, desperate for their own access to the phone, often added a second phone line exclusively for their teenagers' use. Today, teens are still chatting incessantly, but now they are using AOL Instant Messenger, America Online's chat network that enables users to "talk" to others in real time at the touch of a computer keyboard. AOL Instant Messenger (IM for short) is rapidly becoming indispensable to teenagers and young adults. As a result, parents are less likely to ask, "What can they possibly be talking about on that phone for so long?" and more likely to wonder, "What in the world are they doing on that computer for so long?" Parents, let me explain the attraction.

Paragraph 1
This introduction gives background information. The thesis is the last sentence. It identifies the audience as parents of teenagers and states the informational purpose: The essay will explain why IM is so appealing to teenagers.

2   Instant Messenger has advantages over the telephone. Unlike the telephone, IM allows your teenager to chat with people all over the world without creating exorbitant bills. Your teen can talk to the Japanese exchange student who returned to Tokyo just as easily, immediately, and cheaply as to Tiffany down the street. Further, IM eliminates the need for time-consuming small talk. For example, to invite a friend to meet for dinner at six o'clock using the telephone, your teen would first have to say "hello," then inquire how the friend was doing, perhaps listen to complaints about the awful calculus quiz for fifteen minutes, and only then be able to propose dinner. With Instant Messenger, on the other hand, your teen would simply type three things: Dinner @ 6. Also unlike with the telephone, more than two people can talk at once, without arranging complicated conference calls that require special equipment and services. In fact, there is really no limit to the number of people who can participate in an IM conversation, so teens have access to all their friends at once, as long as they are all online at the same time. Imagine the possibilities in the world of incessant teenage chatter.

Paragraph 2
To fulfill the informational purpose, this paragraph contrasts IM with something parents understand better: the telephone. The contrast also includes clarifying examples.

3   Another draw of IM is the "accessorizing" it offers. In particular, IM allows users to convey emotions much more simply and precisely than with any telephone. Volatile teens can "scream" over the Internet by using Caps Lock, Bold font, or a stream of exclamation points. Using emoticons, IM users can clearly indicate happiness (:->), sadness (:-<), anger (>:-/), shock (:-o), sleepiness (‡ o), boredom, (o :-I), and confusion

Paragraph 3
This paragraph relies heavily on exemplification to illustrate an important attraction of IM to help parents understand why teens are drawn to it.

(:-?). IM also allows teens to hide emotions, which is not so easily done on the phone. Imagine a person on the phone trying to play it cool with his or her latest crush while a quivering voice and nervous attempts at clever conversation constantly betray true emotions. In contrast, Instant Messenger and emoticons allow your teen to retain some dignity while being unceremoniously cyber-dumped ("Of course, we can still be friends ☺").

Paragraph 4
This paragraph combines comparison-contrast and exemplification to further explain the attraction and a drawback of IM (when it affords and does not afford privacy).

4   While the telephone does not offer privacy when others are within earshot, IM affords privacy as long as no one is peeking over the typist's shoulder. During my first year of college, I lived in a quad with three other girls, and there was no privacy at all. If I wanted to discuss with Roommate A an issue I was having with Roommate B, our cramped quarters made it very difficult to do so. Fortunately, Instant Messenger came to the rescue and gave new meaning to the term "talking behind one's back." Often, while the four of us were at our desks attempting to write five-page papers for our various intro courses, Lizzie and I would secretly type each other messages over Instant Messenger—Can you **BELIEVE** what Abby said to me?!?!

Paragraph 5
This paragraph combines cause-and-effect analysis, and exemplification to explain a drawback of IM, so parents have a more complete understanding of the technology.

5   Instant messaging is not without its problems, however. So addictive is the technology that otherwise sane people carry their laptops everywhere because they cannot bear to be cut off from their IM buddies. Checking "away messages" can quickly turn into a dangerously obsessive pastime. While it may be useful to know that IcePrincess502 is planning a trip to the mall later in the evening, checking every fifteen minutes to learn what she is up to may be regarded as slightly unhealthy behaviour. When the Instant Messenger service is down, the body of the addicted teen experiences a host of withdrawal symptoms such as depression, anxiety, moodiness, and itchy fingers.

Paragraph 6
The conclusion is a restatement.

6   Instant Messenger is an important, useful addition to the canon of modern communication, and for many teenagers it has replaced the telephone. Parents should respect the importance of IM to their teens, but they should also be aware of its addictive potential. Like all technology, IM has its dark side.

PEER REVIEW

Responding to "The Telephone Is Out; IM Is In"
Evaluate "The Telephone Is Out; IM Is In" by responding to these questions:

1. Does the essay hold your interest? Why or why not?
2. Could the author have achieved her purpose if she used only one pattern? Explain.
3. Are all the author's points adequately supported? Explain.
4. What do you like best about the essay? Why?
5. What change do you think would improve the essay? Why?

READING SELECTIONS

Background

Thomas King is of Cherokee, Greek, and German descent. He grew up in Northern California and received his PhD at the University of Utah in 1986. He was the chair of the American Indian Studies Program at the University of Minnesota before coming to Canada to teach at the University of Lethbridge. He currently teaches creative writing and Native literature at the University of Guelph. He has written numerous books that are characterized by a sense of humour combined with trenchant criticism of North American society. These include *Medicine River* (2005); *Green Grass, Running Water* (1993), which was nominated for a Governor General's Award; *One Good Story, That One* (1999), a collection of short stories; *Truth and Bright Water* (2000); and *Coyote's New Suit* (2004). In 2003, Thomas King delivered the prestigious Massey Lectures at the University of Toronto, the first Aboriginal person to do so.

Combined Patterns and Their Purpose

In the following pages, King uses a variety of examples of narratives to illustrate the way we are our stories. Some of these stories influence us as individuals; other stories shape our cultures. Later in the essay, King contrasts a Native creation myth with the Judeo-Christian to examine how the stories we tell have an effect on the people and societies we become.

"You'll Never Believe What Happened" Is Always a Great Way to Start

Thomas King

1   There is a story I know. It's about the earth and how it floats in space on the back of a turtle. I've heard this story many times, and each time someone tells the story, it changes. Sometimes the change is simply in the voice of the storyteller. Sometimes the change is in the details. Sometimes in the order of events. Other times it's the dialogue or the response of the audience. But in all the tellings of all the tellers, the world never leaves the turtle's back. And the turtle never swims away.

As you read
Think about your own family stories and how they have shaped your view of yourself and of the world.

2   One time, it was in Prince Rupert I think, a young girl in the audience asked about the turtle and the earth. If the earth was on the back of a turtle, what was below the turtle? Another turtle, the storyteller told her. And below that turtle? Another turtle. And below that? Another turtle.

3   The girl began to laugh, enjoying the game, I imagine. So how many turtles are there? she wanted to know. The storyteller shrugged. No one knows for sure, he told her, but it's turtles all the way down.

4   The truth about stories is that that's all we are. The Okanagan storyteller Jeannette Armstrong tells us that "Through my language I understand I am being spoken to, I'm not the one speaking. The words are coming from many tongues and mouths of Okanagan people and the land around them. I am a listener to the language's

stories, and when my words form I am merely retelling the same stories in different patterns."[1]

5   When I was a kid, I was partial to stories about other worlds and interplanetary travel. I used to imagine that I could just gaze off into space and be whisked to another planet, much like John Carter in Edgar Rice Burroughs's Mars series. I'd like to tell you that I was interested in outer space or that the stars fascinated me or that I was curious about the shape and nature of the universe. Fact of the matter was I just wanted to get out of town. Wanted to get as far away from where I was as I could. At fifteen, Pluto looked good. Tiny, cold, lonely. As far from the sun as you could get.

6   I'm sure part of it was teenage angst, and part of it was being poor in a rich country, and part of it was knowing that white was more than just a colour. And part of it was seeing the world through my mother's eyes.

7   My mother raised my brother and me by herself, in an era when women were not welcome in the workforce, when their proper place was out of sight in the home. It was supposed to be a luxury granted women by men. But having misplaced her man, or more properly having had him misplace himself, she had no such luxury and was caught between what she was supposed to be—invisible and female—and what circumstances dictated she become—visible and, well, not male. Self-supporting perhaps. That was it. Visible and self-supporting.

8   As a child and as a young man, I watched her make her way from doing hair in a converted garage to designing tools for the aerospace industry It was a long, slow journey. At Aerojet in California, she began as a filing clerk. By the end of the first year, she was doing drafting work, though she was still classified and paid as a filing clerk. By the end of the second year, with night school stuffed into the cracks, she was doing numerical-control engineering and was still classified and paid as a filing clerk.

9   It was, after all, a man's world, and each step she took had to be made as quietly as possible, each movement camouflaged against complaint. For over thirty years, she held to the shadows, stayed in the shade.

10   I knew the men she worked with. They were our neighbours and our friends. I listened to their stories about work and play, about their dreams and their disappointments. Your mother, they liked to tell me, is just one of the boys. But she wasn't. I knew it. She knew it better.

11   In 1963, my mother and five of her colleagues were recruited by the Boeing Company to come to Seattle, Washington, as part of a numerical-control team. Everyone was promised equal status, which, for my mother, meant being brought into Boeing as a fully fledged, salaried engineer.

---

[1]Jeanette Armstrong, *Speaking for the Generations: Native Writers on Writing*, Ed. Simon Ortiz (Tucson: University of Arizona Press, 1998), 181.

12   So she went. It was more money, more prestige. And when she got there, she was told that, while everyone else would be salaried and would have engineer status, she would be an hourly employee and would have the same status as the other two women in the department, who were production assistants. So after selling everything in order to make the move, she found herself in a job where she made considerably less than the other members of the team, where she had to punch a time clock, and where she wasn't even eligible for benefits or a pension.

13   She objected. That wasn't the promise, she told her supervisor. You brought everyone else in as equals, why not me?

14   She didn't really have to ask that question. She knew the answer. You probably know it, too. The other five members of the team were men. She was the only woman. Don't worry she was told, if your work is good, you'll get promoted at the end of the first year.

15   So she waited. There wasn't much she could do about it. And at the end of the first year, when the review of her work came back satisfactory, she was told she would have to wait another year. And when that year was up . . .

16   I told her she was crazy to allow people to treat her like that. But she knew the nature of the world in which she lived, and I did not. And yet she has lived her life with an optimism of the intellect and an optimism of the will. She understands the world as a good place where good deeds should beget good rewards. At eighty-one, she still believes that that world is possible, even though she will now admit she never found it, never even caught a glimpse of it.

17   My father is a different story. I didn't know him. He left when I was three or four. I have one memory of a man who took me to a small café that had wooden booths with high backs and a green parrot that pulled at my hair. I don't think this was my father. But it might have been.

18   For a long time I told my friends that my father had died, which was easier than explaining that he had left us. Then when I was nine, I think, my mother got a call from him asking if he could come home and start over. My mother said okay. I'll be home in three days, he told her.

19   And that was the last we ever heard from him.

20   My mother was sure that something had happened to him. Somewhere between Chicago and California. No one would call to say they were coming home and then not show up, unless they had been injured or killed. So she waited for him. So did I.

21   And then when I was fifty-six or fifty-seven, my brother called me. Sit down, Christopher said, I've got some news. I was living in Ontario, and I figured that if my brother was calling me all the way from California, telling me to sit down, it had to be bad news, something to do with my mother.

22   But it wasn't.

23   You'll never believe what happened, my brother said.

24   That's always a good way to start a story, you know: you'll never believe what happened.

25   And he was right.

26   We found our father. That's exactly what he said. We found our father.

27   I had dreamed about such an occurrence. Finding my father. Not as a child, but as a grown man. One of my more persistent fictions was to catch up with him in a bar, sitting on a stool, having a beer. A dark, dank bar, stinking of sorrow, a bar where men who had deserted their families went to drink and die.

28   He wouldn't recognize me. I'd sit next to him, and after a while the two of us would strike up a conversation.

29   What do you do for a living? How do you like the new Ford? You believe those Blue Jays?

30   Guy talk. Short sentences. Lots of nodding.

31   You married? Any kids?

32   And then I'd give him a good look at me. A good, long look. And just as he began to remember, just as he began to realize who I might be, I'd leave. *Hasta la vista.* Toodle-oo. See you around. I wouldn't tell him about my life or what I had been able to accomplish, or how many grandchildren he had or how much I had missed not having a father in my life.

33   Screw him. I had better things to do than sit around with some old bastard and talk about life and responsibility.

34   So when my brother called to tell me that we had found our father, I ran through the bar scene one more time. So I'd be ready.

35   Here's what had happened. My father had two sisters. We didn't know them very well, and, when my father disappeared, we lost track of that side of the family. So we had no way of knowing that when my father left us, he vanished from his sisters' lives as well. I suppose they thought he was dead, too. But evidently his oldest sister wasn't sure, and, after she had retired and was getting on in years, she decided to make one last attempt to find out what had happened to him.

36   She was not a rich woman, but she spotted an advertisement in a local newspaper that offered the services of a detective who would find lost or missing relatives for $75. Flat rate. Satisfaction guaranteed.

37   My brother took a long time in telling this story, drawing out the details, repeating the good parts, making me wait.

38   The detective, it turned out, was a retired railroad employee who knew how to use a computer and a phone book. If Robert King was alive and if he hadn't changed his name, he'd have a phone and an address. If he was dead, there should be a death

certificate floating around somewhere. The detective's name was Fred or George, I don't remember, and he was a bulldog.

39   It took him two days. Robert King was alive and well, in Illinois.

40   Christopher stopped at this point in the story to let me catch my breath. I was already making reservations to fly to Chicago, to rent a car, to find that bar.

41   That's the good news, my brother told me.

42   One of the tricks to storytelling is, never to tell everything at once, to make your audience wait, to keep everyone in suspense.

43   My father had married two more times. Christopher had all the details. Seven other children. Seven brothers and sisters we had never known about. Barbara, Robert, Kelly.

44   What's the bad news? I wanted to know.

45   Oh, that, said my brother. The bad news is he's dead.

46   Evidently, just after the railroad detective found him, my father slipped in a river, hit his head on a rock, and died in a hospital. My aunt, the one who had hired the detective, went to Illinois for the funeral and to meet her brother's other families for the first time.

47   You're going to like the next part, my brother told me.

48   I should warn you that my brother has a particular fondness for irony.

49   When my aunt got to the funeral, the oldest boy, Robert King Jr., evidently began a sentence with "I guess as the oldest boy . . ." Whereupon my aunt told the family about Christopher and me.

50   They knew about each other. The two families. Were actually close, but they had never heard about us. My father had never mentioned us. It was as though he had disposed of us somewhere along the way, dropped us in a trash can by the side of the road.

51   That's my family. These are their stories.

52   So what? I've heard worse stories. So have you. Open today's paper and you'll find two or three that make mine sound like a Disney trailer. Starvation. Land mines. Suicide bombings. Sectarian violence. Sexual abuse. Children stacked up like cordwood in refugee camps around the globe. So what makes my mother's sacrifice special? What makes my father's desertion unusual?

53   Absolutely nothing.

54   Matter of fact, the only people who have any interest in either of these stories are my brother and me. I tell the stories not to play on your sympathies but to suggest how stories can control our lives, for there is a part of me that has never been able to move past these stories, a part of me that will be chained to these stories as long as I live.

55   Stories are wondrous things. And they are dangerous. The Native novelist Leslie Silko, in her book *Ceremony*, tells how evil came into the world. It was witch people. Not Whites or Indians or Blacks or Asians or Hispanics. Witch people. Witch people from all over the world, way back when, and they all came together for a witches' conference. In a cave. Having a good time. A contest, actually. To see who could come up with the scariest thing. Some of them brewed up potions in pots. Some of them jumped in and out of animal skins. Some of them thought up charms and spells.

56   It must have been fun to watch.

57   Until finally there was only one witch left who hadn't done anything. No one knew where this witch came from or if the witch was male or female. And all this witch had was a story.

58   Unfortunately the story this witch told was an awful thing full of fear and slaughter, disease and blood. A story of murderous mischief. And when the telling was done, the other witches quickly agreed that this witch had won the prize.

59   "Okay you win," they said. "[B]ut what you said just now—it isn't so funny. It doesn't sound so good. We are doing okay without it. We can get along without that kind of thing. Take it back. Call that story back."[2]

60   But, of course, it was too late. For once a story is told, it cannot be called back. Once told, it is loose in the world.

61   So you have to be careful with the stories you tell. And you have to watch out for the stories that you are told. But if I ever get to Pluto, that's how I would like to begin. With a story. Maybe I'd tell the inhabitants of Pluto one of the stories I know. Maybe they'd tell me one of theirs. It wouldn't matter who went first. But which story? That's the real question. Personally, I'd want to hear a creation story, a story that recounts how the world was formed, how things came to be, for contained within creation stories are relationships that help to define the nature of the universe and how cultures understand the world in which they exist.

62   And, as luck would have it, I happen to know a few. But I have a favourite. It's about a woman who fell from the sky. And it goes like this.

63   Back at the beginning of imagination, the world we know as earth was nothing but water, while above the earth, somewhere in space, was a larger, more ancient world. And on that world was a woman.

64   A crazy woman.

65   Well, she wasn't exactly crazy. She was more nosy. Curious. The kind of curious that doesn't give up. The kind that follows you around. Now, we all know that being curious is healthy, but being *curious* can get you into trouble.

_____

[2]Leslie Silko, *Ceremony* (New York: Viking, 1977), 138.

66   Don't be too curious, the Birds told her.

67   Okay, she said, I won't.

68   But you know what? That's right. She kept on being curious.

69   One day while she was bathing in the river, she happened to look at her feet and discovered that she had five toes on each foot. One big one and four smaller ones. They had been there all along, of course, but now that the woman noticed them for the first time, she wondered why she had five toes instead of three. Or eight. And she wondered if more toes were better than fewer toes.

70   So she asked her Toes. Hey, she said, how come there are only five of you?

71   You're being curious again, said her Toes.

72   Another day, the woman was walking through the forest and found a moose relaxing in the shade by a lake.

73   Hello, said the Moose. Aren't you that nosy woman?

74   Yes, I am, said the woman, and what I want to know is why you are so much larger than me.

75   That's easy, said the Moose, and he walked into the lake and disappeared.

76   Don't you love cryptic stories? I certainly do.

77   Now before we go any further, we should give this woman a name so we don't have to keep calling her "the woman." How about Blanche? Catherine? Thelma? Okay, I know expressing an opinion can be embarrassing. So let's do it the way we always do it and let someone else make the decision for us. Someone we trust. Someone who will promise to lower taxes. Someone like me.

78   I say we call her Charm. Don't worry. We can change it later on if we want to.

79   So one day the woman we've decided to call Charm went looking for something good to eat. She looked at the fish, but she was not in the mood for fish. She looked at the rabbit, but she didn't feel like eating rabbit either.

80   I've got this craving, said Charm.

81   What kind of craving? said Fish.

82   I want to eat something, but I don't know what it is.

83   Maybe you're pregnant, said Rabbit. Whenever I get pregnant, I get cravings.

84   Hmmmm, said Charm, maybe I am.

85   And you know what? She was.

86   What you need, Fish and Rabbit told Charm, is some Red Fern Foot.

87   Yes, said Charm, that sounds delicious. What is it?

88   It's a root, said Fish, and it only grows under the oldest trees. And it's the perfect thing for pregnant humans.

89   Now, you're probably thinking that this is getting pretty silly, what with chatty fish and friendly rabbits, with moose disappearing into lakes and talking toes. And you're probably wondering how in the world I expect you to believe any of this, given the fact that we live in a predominantly scientific, capitalistic, Judeo-Christian world governed by physical laws, economic imperatives, and spiritual precepts.

90   Is that what you're thinking?

91   It's okay. You won't hurt my feelings.

92   So Charm went looking for some Red Fern Foot. She dug around this tree and she dug around that tree, but she couldn't find any. Finally she came to the oldest tree in the forest and she began digging around its base. By now she was very hungry, and she was very keen on some Red Fern Foot, so she really got into the digging. And before long she had dug a rather deep hole.

93   Don't dig too deep, Badger told her.

94   Mind your own business, Charm told him.

95   Okay, said Badger, but don't blame me if you make a mistake.

96   You can probably guess what happened. That's right, Charm dug right through to the other side of the world.

97   That's curious, said Charm, and she stuck her head into that hole so she could get a better view.

98   That's very curious, she said again, and she stuck her head even farther into the hole.

99   Sometimes when I tell this story to children, I slow it down and have Charm stick her head into that hole by degrees. But most of you are adults and have already figured out that Charm is going to stick her head into that hole so far that she's either going to get stuck or she's going to fall through.

100   And sure enough, she fell through. Right through that hole and into the sky.

101   Uh-oh, Charm thought to herself. That wasn't too smart.

102   But she couldn't do much about it now. And she began to tumble through the sky, began to fall and fall and fall and fall. Spinning and turning, floating through the vast expanse of space.

103   And off in the distance, just on the edge of sight, was a small blue dot floating in the heavens. And as Charm tumbled down through the black sky, the dot got bigger and bigger.

104   You've probably figured this part out, too, but just so there's no question, this blue dot is the earth. Well, sort of. It's the earth when it was young. When there was nothing but water. When it was simply a water world.

105   And Charm was heading right for it.

106   In the meantime, on this water world, on earth, a bunch of water animals were swimming and floating around and diving and talking about how much fun water is.

107   Water, water, water, said the Ducks. There's nothing like water.

108   Yes, said the Muskrats, we certainly like being wet.

109   It's even better when you're under water, said the Sunfish.

110   Try jumping into it, said the Dolphins. And just as the Dolphins said this, they looked up into the sky.

111   Uh-oh, said the Dolphins, and everyone looked up in time to see Charm falling toward them. And as she came around the moon, the water animals were suddenly faced with four variables—mass, velocity, compression, and displacement—and with two problems.

112   The Ducks, who have great eyesight, could see that Charm weighed in at about 150 pounds, And the Beavers, who have a head for physics and math, knew that she was coming in fast. Accelerating at thirty-two feet per second per second to be precise (give or take a little for drag and atmospheric friction). And the Whales knew from many years of study that water does not compress, while the Dolphins could tell anyone who asked that while it won't compress, water will displace.

113   Which brought the animals to the first of the two problems. If Charm hit the water at full speed, it was going to create one very large tidal wave and ruin everyone's day.

114   So quick as they could, all the water birds flew up and formed a net with their bodies, and, as Charm came streaking down, the birds caught her, broke her fall, and brought her gently to the surface of the water.

115   Just in time.

116   To deal with the second of the two problems. Where to put her.

117   They could just dump her in the water, but it didn't take a pelican to see that Charm was not a water creature.

118   Can you swim? asked the Sharks.

119   Not very well, said Charm.

120   How about holding your breath for a long time? asked the Sea Horses.

121   Maybe for a minute or two, said Charm.

122   Floating? said the Seals. Can you float?

123   I don't know, said Charm. I never really tried floating.

124   So what are we going to do with you? said the Lobsters.

125   Hurry up, said the Birds, flapping their wings as hard as they could.

126   Perhaps you could put me on something large and flat, Charm told the water animals.

127   Well, as it turns out, the only place in this water world that was large and flat was the back of the Turtle.

128   Oh, okay, said Turtle. But if anyone else falls out of the sky, she's on her own.

129   So the water animals put Charm on the back of the Turtle, and everyone was happy. Well, at least for the next month or so. Until the animals noticed that Charm was going to have a baby.

130   It's going to get a little crowded, said the Muskrats.

131   What are we going to do? said the Geese.

132   It wouldn't be so crowded, Charm told the water animals, if we had some dry land.

133   Sure, agreed the water animals, even though they had no idea what dry land was.

134   Charm looked over the side of the Turtle, down into the water, and then she turned to the water animals.

135   Who's the best diver? she asked.

136   A contest! screamed the Ducks.

137   All right! shouted the Muskrats.

138   What do we have to do? asked the Eels.

139   It's easy, said Charm. One of you has to dive down to the bottom of the water and bring up some mud.

140   Sure, said all the water animals, even though they had no idea what mud was.

141   So, said Charm, who wants to try first?

142   Me! said Pelican, and he flew into the sky as high as he could and then dropped like a knife into the water. And he was gone for a long time. But when he floated to the surface, out of breath, he didn't have any mud.

143   It was real dark down there, said Pelican, and cold.

144   The next animal to try was Walrus. Sorry.

145   I don't mind the dark, said Walrus, and my blubber, will keep me warm. So down she went, and she was gone for much longer than Pelican, but when she came to the surface coughing up water, she didn't have any mud, either.

146   I don't think the water has a bottom, said Walrus. Sorry.

147   I'm sure you're beginning to wonder if there's a point to this story or if I'm just going to work my way through all the water animals one by one.

148   So one by one all the water animals tried to find the mud at the bottom of the ocean, and all of them failed until the only animal left was Otter. Otter, however, wasn't particularly interested in finding mud.

149   Is it fun to play with? asked Otter.

150   Not really, said Charm.

151   Is it good to eat? asked Otter.

152   Not really, said Charm.

153   Then why do you want to find it? said Otter.

154   For the magic, said Charm.

155   Oh, said Otter. I like magic.

156   So Otter took a deep breath and dove into the water. And she didn't come up. Day after day, Charm and the animals waited for Otter to come to the surface. Finally, on the morning of the fourth day, just as the sun was rising, Otter's body floated up out of the depths.

157   Oh, no, said all the animals, Otter has drowned trying to find the mud. And they hoisted Otter's body onto the back of the Turtle.

158   Now, when they hoisted Otter's body onto the back of the Turtle, they noticed that her little paws were clenched shut, and when they opened her paws, they discovered something dark and gooey that wasn't water.

159   Is this mud? asked the Ducks.

160   Yes, it is, said Charm. Otter has found the mud.

161   Of course I found the mud, whispered Otter, who wasn't so much dead as she was tired and out of breath. This magic better be worth it.

162   Charm set the lump of mud on the back of the Turtle, and she sang and she danced, and the animals sang and danced with her, and very slowly the lump of mud began to grow. It grew and grew and grew into a world, part water, part mud. That was a good trick, said the water animals. But now there's not enough room for all of us in the water. Some of us are going to have to live on land.

163   Not that anyone wanted to live on the land. It was nothing but mud. Mud as far as the eye could see. Great jumbled lumps of mud.

164   But before the animals could decide who was going to live where or what to do about the mud-lump world, Charm had her baby.

165   Or rather, she had her babies.

166   Twins.

167   A boy and a girl. One light, one dark. One right-handed, one left-handed.

168   Nice-looking babies, said the Cormorants. Hope they like mud.

169   And as it turned out, they did. The right-handed Twin smoothed all the mud lumps until the land was absolutely flat.

170   Wow! said all the animals. That was pretty clever. Now we can see in all directions.

171 But before the animals could get used to all the nice flat land, the left-handed Twin stomped around in the mud, piled it up, and created deep valleys and tall mountains.

172 Okay, said the animals, that could work.

173 And while the animals were admiring the new landscape, the Twins really got busy. The right-handed Twin dug nice straight trenches and filled them with water.

174 These are rivers, he told the animals, and I've made the water flow in both directions so that it'll be easy to come and go as you please.

175 That's handy, said the animals.

176 But as soon as her brother had finished, the left-handed Twin made the rivers crooked and put rocks in the water and made it flow in only one direction.

177 This is much more exciting, she told the animals.

178 Could you put in some waterfalls? said the animals. Everyone likes waterfalls.

179 Sure, said the left-handed Twin. And she did.

180 The right-handed Twin created forests with all the trees lined up so you could go into the woods and not get lost. The left-handed Twin came along and moved the trees around, so that some of the forest was dense and difficult, and other parts were open and easy.

181 How about some trees with nuts and fruit? said the animals. In case we get hungry.

182 That's a good idea, said the right-handed Twin. And he did.

183 The right-handed Twin created roses. The left-handed Twin put thorns on the stems. The right-handed Twin created summer. The left-handed Twin created winter. The right-handed Twin created sunshine. The left-handed Twin created shadows.

184 Have we forgotten anything? the Twins asked the animals.

185 What about human beings? said the animals. Do you think we need human beings?

186 Why not? said the Twins. And quick as they could the right-handed Twin created women, and the left-handed Twin created men.

187 They don't look too bright, said the animals. We hope they won't be a problem.

188 Don't worry, said the Twins, you guys are going to get along just fine.

189 The animals and the humans and the Twins and Charm looked around at the world that they had created. Boy, they said, this is as good as it gets. This is one beautiful world.

190 It's a neat story, isn't it? A little long, but different. Maybe even a little exotic. Sort of like the manure-fired pots or the hand-painted plates or the woven palm hats or

the coconuts carved to look like monkey faces or the colourful T-shirts that we buy on vacation.

191   Souvenirs. Snapshots of a moment. And when the moment has passed, the hats are tossed into closets, the T-shirts are stuffed into drawers, the pots and plates and coconuts are left to gather dust on shelves. Eventually everything is shipped off to a garage sale or slipped into the trash.

192   As for stories such as the Woman Who Fell from the Sky, well, we listen to them and then we forget them, for amidst the thunder of Christian monologues, they have neither purchase nor place. After all, within the North American paradigm we have a perfectly serviceable creation story.

193   And it goes like this.

194   In the beginning God created the heaven and the earth. And the earth was without form, and void and darkness was upon the face of the deep. And the Spirit of God moved upon the face of the waters. And God said, let there be light, and there was light.

195   You can't beat the King James version of the Bible for the beauty of the language. But it's the story that captures the imagination. God creates night and day, the sun and the moon, all the creatures of the world, and finally, toward the end of his labours, he creates humans. Man first and then woman. Adam and Eve. And he places everything and everyone in a garden, a perfect world. No sickness, no death, no hate, no hunger.

196   And there's only one rule.

197   Of every tree of the garden thou mayest freely eat. But of the tree of the knowledge of good and evil, thou shalt not eat of it, for in the day that thou eatest thereof thou shalt surely die.

198   One rule. Don't break it.

199   But that's exactly what happens. Adam and Eve break the rule. Doesn't matter how it happens. If you like the orthodox version, you can blame Eve. She eats the apple and brings it back to Adam. Not that Adam says no. A less misogynist reading would blame them both, would chalk up the debacle that followed as an unavoidable mistake. A wrong step. Youthful enthusiasm. A misunderstanding. Wilfulness.

200   But whatever you wish to call it, the rule has been broken, and that is the end of the garden. God seals it off and places an angel with a fiery sword at the entrance and tosses Adam and Eve into a howling wilderness to fend for themselves, a wilderness in which sickness and death, hate and hunger are their constant companions.

201   Okay. Two creation stories. One Native, one Christian. The first thing you probably noticed was that I spent more time with the Woman Who Fell from the Sky than I did with Genesis. I'm assuming that most of you have heard of Adam and Eve, but few, I imagine, have ever met Charm. I also used different strategies in the telling of these stories. In the Native story, I tried to recreate an oral storytelling voice and craft

the story in terms of a performance for a general audience. In the Christian story, I tried to maintain a sense of rhetorical distance and decorum while organizing the story for a knowledgeable gathering. These strategies colour the stories and suggest values that may be neither inherent nor warranted. In the Native story, the conversational voice tends to highlight the exuberance of the story but diminishes its authority, while the sober voice in the Christian story makes for a formal recitation but creates a sense of veracity.

202 Basil Johnston, the Anishinabe storyteller, in his essay "How Do We Learn Language?" describes the role of comedy and laughter in stories by reminding us that Native peoples have always loved to laugh: "It is precisely because our tribal stories are comical and evoke laughter that they have never been taken seriously outside the tribe. . . . But behind and beneath the comic characters and the comic situations exists the real meaning of the story . . . what the tribe understood about human growth and development."[3]

203 Of course, none of you would make the mistake of confusing storytelling strategies with the value or sophistication of a story. And we know enough about the complexities of cultures to avoid the error of imagining animism and polytheism to be no more than primitive versions of monotheism. Don't we?

204 Nonetheless, the talking animals are a problem.

205 A theologian might argue that these two creation stories are essentially the same. Each tells about the creation of the world and the appearance of human beings. But a storyteller would tell you that these two stories are quite different, for whether you read the Bible as sacred text or secular metaphor, the elements in Genesis create a particular universe governed by a series of hierarchies—God, man, animals, plants—that celebrate law, order, and good government, while in our Native story, the universe is governed by a series of co-operations—Charm, the Twins, animals, humans—that celebrate equality, and balance.

206 In Genesis all creative power is vested in a single deity who is omnipotent, omniscient, and omnipresent. The universe begins with his thought, and it is through his actions and only his actions that it comes into being. In the Earth Diver story, and in many other Native creation stories for that matter, deities are generally figures of limited power and persuasion, and the acts of creation and the decisions that affect the world are shared with other characters in the drama.

207 In Genesis, we begin with a perfect world, but after the Fall, while we gain knowledge, we lose the harmony and safety of the garden and are forced into a chaotic world of harsh landscapes and dangerous shadows.

---

[3]Basil Johnston, "How Do We learn Language?" *Talking on the Page: Editing Aboriginal Oral Texts*, Ed. Laura Murray and Keren Rice (Toronto: University of Toronto Press, 1999), 14.

208 In our Native story, we begin with water and mud, and, through the good offices of Charm, her twins, and the animals, move by degrees and adjustments from a form-less, featureless world to a world that is rich in its diversity, a world that is complex and complete.

209 Finally, in Genesis the post-garden world we inherit is decidedly martial in nature, a world at war—God vs. the Devil, humans vs. the elements. Or to put things into corporate parlance, competitive. In our Native story, the world is at peace, and the pivotal concern is not with the ascendancy of good over evil but with the issue of balance.

210 So here are our choices: a world in which creation is a solitary, individual act or a world in which creation is a shared activity, a world that begins in harmony and slides toward chaos or a world that begins in chaos and moves toward harmony; a world marked by competition or a world determined by co-operation.

211 And there's the problem.

212 If we see the world through Adam's eyes, we are necessarily blind to the world that Charm and the Twins and the animals help to create. If we believe one story to be sacred, we must see the other as secular.

213 You'll recognize this pairing as a dichotomy, the elemental structure of Western society. And cranky old Jacques Derrida notwithstanding, we do love our dichoto-mies. Rich/poor, white/black, strong/weak, right/wrong, culture/nature, male/female, written/oral, civilized/barbaric, success/failure, individual/communal. We trust easy oppositions. We are suspicious of complexities, distrustful of contradictions, fearful of enigmas.

214 Enigmas like my father.

215 I have a couple of old black-and-white pictures of him holding a baby with my mother looking on. He looks young in those photos. And happy. I'm sure he didn't leave because he hated me, just as I'm sure that my mother didn't stay because she loved me. Yet this is the story I continue to tell myself, because it's easy and contains all my anger, and because, in all the years, in all the tellings, I've honed it sharp enough to cut bone.

216 If we had to have a patron story for North America, we could do worse than the one about Alexander the Great, who, when faced with the puzzle of the Gordian knot, solved that problem with nothing more than a strong arm and a sharp sword.

217 Perhaps this is why we delight in telling stories about heroes battling the odds and the elements, rather than about the magic of seasonal change. Why we relish stories that lionize individuals who start at the bottom and fight their way to the top, rather than stories that frame these forms of competition as varying degrees of insanity. Why we tell our children that life is hard, when we could just as easily tell them that it is sweet.

218   Is it our nature? Do the stories we tell reflect the world as it truly is, or did we simply start off with the wrong story? Like Silko's witches in the cave conjuring up things to impress each other.

219   Making magic.

220   Making faces.

221   Making mistakes.

222   I'm dying to remind myself that the basis of Christian doctrine is rectitude and reward, crime and punishment, even though my partner has warned me that this is probably not a good idea. Tell a story, she told me. Don't preach. Don't try to sound profound. It's unbecoming, and you do it poorly. Don't show them your mind. Show them your imagination.

223   So am I such an ass as to disregard this good advice and suggest that the stories contained within the matrix of Christianity and the complex of nationalism are responsible for the social, political, and economic problems we face? Am I really arguing that the martial and hierarchical nature of Western religion and Western privilege has fostered stories that encourage egotism and self-interest? Am I suggesting that, if we hope to create a truly civil society, we must first burn all the flags and kill all the gods, because in such a world we could no longer tolerate such weapons of mass destruction?

224   No, I wouldn't do that.

225   Though certainly we understand that we clear-cut forests not to enrich the lives of animals but to make profit. We know that we dam(n) rivers not to improve water quality but to create electricity and protect private property. We make race and gender discriminatory markers for no other reason than that we can. And we maintain and tolerate poverty not because we believe adversity makes you strong, but because we're unwilling to share.

226   Ah. You've heard all this before, haven't you.

227   You may have already leaned over to a friend and whispered, Platitude. Platitude, platitude, platitude. Thomas King the duck-billed platitude.

228   But give this a thought. What if the creation story in Genesis had featured a flawed deity who was understanding and sympathetic rather than autocratic and rigid? Someone who, in the process of creation, found herself lost from time to time and in need of advice, someone who was willing to accept a little help with the more difficult decisions?

229   What if the animals had decided on their own names? What if Adam and Eve had simply been admonished for their foolishness?

230   I love you, God could have said, but I'm not happy with your behaviour. Let's talk this over. Try to do better next time.

231 What kind of a world might we have created with that kind of story?

232 Unfortunately, by the time we arrived in the wilderness, broke and homeless, the story of being made in God's image, of living in paradise, of naming the animals must have gone to our heads, for while we weren't the strongest or the fastest or the fiercest creatures on the planet, we were, certainly, as it turned out, the most arrogant.

233 God's Chosen People. The Alpha and the Omega. Masters of the Universe.

234 It is this conceit we continue to elaborate as we fill up our tanks at the gas station, the myth we embrace as we bolt our doors at night, the romance we pursue as we search our guidebooks for just the right phrase. The lie we dangle in front of our appetites as we chase progress to the grave.

235 Or as Linda McQuaig so delightfully puts it in her book *All You Can Eat: Greed, Lust and the New Capitalism*, "The central character in economics is Homo Economicus, the human prototype, who is pretty much just a walking set of insatiable material desires. He uses his rational abilities to ensure the satisfaction of all his wants, which are the key to his motivation. And he isn't considered some weirdo; the whole point of him is that he represents traits basic to all of us—Homo Economicus 'R' Us, as it were."[4]

236 It was Sir Isaac Newton who said, "To every action there is always opposed an equal reaction." Had he been a writer, he might have simply said, "To every action there is a story."

237 Take Charm's story, for instance. It's yours. Do with it what you will. Tell it to friends. Turn it into a television movie. Forget it. But don't say in the years to come that you would have lived your life differently if only you had heard this story.

238 You've heard it now.

---

[4]Linda McQuaig, *All You Can Eat: Greed, Lust, and the New Capitalism* (Toronto: Viking, 2001), 12.

Reading Closely and Thinking Critically

1. "The truth about stories is that that's all we are," King boldly announces in his fourth paragraph. *All* cultures, no matter how various their other customs with respect to work, religion, or relationships, tell stories. But King seems to be making an even larger claim about stories. How do our stories express what is most important to us—our beliefs, our worldviews, our dreams and desires, our joys?
2. What advice does King give you about how to tell good stories? What do his narratives themselves suggest about good storytelling strategies?
3. What's the relationship between the story that brings evil into the world and the stories that King tells of his own life?
4. Why, once a story is loosed in the world, can't it be taken back? What does this say about our relationship with stories?

5. Why would King hypothetically begin a visit to Pluto with a story? Connect your thoughts about this to the quotation from Kwame Anthony Appiah that begins Chapter 5, on narrative.
6. What stories dominate our culture? Do the people around you—families and friends and fellow students—believe their stories are important? Why or why not? What happens in a culture (or a subset of a culture) when people don't believe their own stories are important?

Examining Structure and Strategy

1. Frequently, King addresses his audience. For instance, he suggests that we know why his mother didn't really need someone to explain why she wasn't being treated as an equal, or he assumes that we've heard stories like the one he tells, or that we know how a good story begins. What is he trying to accomplish by addressing us? What relationship is he creating with us?
2. This essay isn't a single story, but a group of stories that function as examples. What do they have in common? How do they work together?
3. Why does King choose to cite Jeannette Armstrong and Leslie Marmon Silko as experts on storytelling?
4. Why does King spend so much more time telling the myth of Charm than relating the Judeo-Christian myth of the creation? Is this simply because one story is unfamiliar while the other is relatively well known? Or does it have something to do with the freedom to play and embellish implied by an oral tradition? Connect your ideas here to the opening example of a well-known story and the child's delight in the punchline: "It's turtles all the way down."
5. In paragraph 112, King brings up the laws of physics. Yet earlier, in paragraph 89, he suggests his story didn't take place in a world of "physical laws, economic imperatives, and spiritual precepts." What do you make of this contradiction?
6. In paragraph 147, King suggests we might not think there's a point to his story. Why is this the last thing on a reader's or listener's mind?
7. In paragraph 214, King brings up his father again. How are his feelings about his father different in this new context? How has his analysis of the significance of the stories of Genesis and Charm changed the way he looks at his father's story?
8. Why does King ask questions in paragraph 218 that he assumes his listener knows the answer to? What do these questions have to do with the question he poses in paragraphs 228, 229, and 231 about the stories we choose to tell our culture? How is he preparing us to consider his criticism of the Judeo-Christian narrative about the creation of the earth?

Noting Combined Patterns

1. What is King's primary pattern of development?
2. How does King's use of numerous examples facilitate his causal analysis of the effects of stories on our identities or our cultures?
3. What do the descriptive paragraphs add to the effectiveness of the essay?
4. King contrasts the aboriginal creation myth of Charm with that of Genesis. In what way does this comparison illuminate the contrast between his stories about his mother's and his father's lives?

Considering Language and Style

1. The Massey Lectures are a formal occasion. Established in 1961 to honour Vincent Massey, the Governor General of Canada, they are given by scholars of international importance like Northrop Frye, Noam Chomsky, John Ralston Saul, and even Martin Luther King. Yet for all their prestige and formality, King uses quite an informal style. Why?
2. In paragraph 7, King seems to be finding his words as he goes along, as if he's not sure what he will say. Why does he do this?

3. Why does he use the word "camouflaged" in paragraph 9 to describe the way his mother must make her progress through the ranks at Aerojet? Why does he say, "She held to the shadows, stayed in the shade"? Why are visual images important here?
4. Why does King compare the story of Charm to the souvenirs we pick up on holidays and then pack away and forget?
5. Why does King call himself a "duck-billed platitude" in paragraph 227?

For Discussion in Class or Online

Kwame Anthony Appiah, a philosopher at Princeton, argues that one way we can understand cultural differences is to share our stories. Which stories have brought you sudden insight into something or someone you didn't understand? Were they stories that a culture shared widely, in the news or in movies? Or were they private stories told by one person to another? Share your conclusions with your classmates, and if your instructor directs, post them to your class Web site.

Writing Assignments

1. **In your journal.** If you could tell a friend one story that would explain the person you have become, what would it be? (Narration; cause and effect)
2. **Combining patterns for a purpose.** The purposes in the assignments are possibilities. You may establish whatever purposes you like, within your instructor's guidelines.
   - Use two narratives to define a human quality or experience like hope, heroism, or tragedy. Contrast the narratives to show how there are different paths to the same insights.
   - Use a narrative and contrast-comparison patterns to persuade your readers that someone or something that intimidates or frightens them is actually familiar.
3. **Connecting the readings.** In "Once More to the Lake" (page 491), "In the Kitchen" (page 273), and "'You'll Never Believe What Happened' Is Always a Great Way to Start," the authors explore how events and traditions from their childhood continue to influence their lives. Use two narratives, one from your childhood and one relatively recent, to explore how events occurring in our youth form us, allowing us to hear their echoes throughout our lives.
4. **Drawing on sources.** Scholars have long been interested in the relationship between myths and culture, often arguing that while these stories have different details, there are common elements that vary little from culture to culture. In Jungian psychology, these elements are called archetypes. Look at a book such as Joseph Campbell's *Hero of a Thousand Faces* to learn about the archetype of the hero. Or find multiple variants of a basic fairy tale. You could also explore the way a single figure like the trickster is translated from culture to culture. How does this knowledge help you see the connection between the story with which King opens and the stories of his life?

Background

When Brad Whetstine wrote "Augustinian Influences," he was a senior majoring in English at Indiana University. The essay was published in *The College*, which is a publication of the Indiana University Alumni Association, in its winter, 2003–2004 edition.

Combined Patterns and Their Purposes

Brad Whetstine combines narration, cause-and-effect analysis, comparison-contrast, and description to explain why he left welding to become a college student. He relates his experience and expresses his feelings. However, *The College*, which published Whetstine's essay, gives its purpose as encouraging "alumni interest in and support for Indiana University," so the essay also has a persuasive purpose.

Augustinian Influences
Brad Whetstine

As you read
Ask yourself why this essay was published in Indiana University's alumni magazine.

1   Known for its sweet corn and community fish fries, my hometown was a farming community built along a glacial boundary where the rumpled landscape matched that of a blanket on an unmade bed. The schools in this area were small, consolidated, and known more so for their athletics than their academics. Students like me who weren't on the honor roll or the ball team soon found themselves in the vocational tracks learning a trade, and it was here I took my first welding class.

2   Welders were heroes in my hometown: They fixed machinery and kept the farmers farming. It was a vocation few knew well enough to master, but I was fortunate to learn the science of welding through my high school classes and to be one of two students chosen to expand our skills at a larger vocational school. The skills I acquired there landed me a job in sheet metal fabrication, where I welded for 10 years.

"Welders were heroes in my hometown."

3   The economy was up then. The shop I worked in was a small, privately owned business committed to quality rather than quantity. The hours were plentiful; the days were long; overtime was not a problem. They were days of cutting, fitting, and fusing—days of hundred-degree heat that felt clean and refreshing once I was out of the mask and heavy leathers worn to protect my face, arms, hands, and torso from hot slag, sharp sparks, and blinding light. The well-oiled steel smelled of freshly laid asphalt when heated, and the smoke that rose with the temperature proved just as black. This same blackness I washed from my hair, blew from my nose, and coughed up each night after work. Though the conditions were not the best, at the time, I still thought they fared better than farming. One evening after work while couched on the sofa, eating left-over Hamburger Helper and worn out from another 10-hour day, I began to listen carefully to the film playing on television.

4   Larry McMurtry's epic western *Lonesome Dove* was a story of chance and change, and as I listened to the retired Texas Rangers Augustus McCrae and Woodrow Call

discuss leaving the dust-laden corrals of southwest Texas for a lush new ranch in northern Montana, I, too, began to wonder what life outside of welding was like. I selected portions of their discussion and cut them away as I would a piece of steel.

5   Call had heard of Montana's rolling terrain and grassy valleys where the grazing was good and the water pure, and he longed to see it. And after a decade of working in the same place at the same trade I, too, wondered after each work-day, staring into my handkerchief of black, if there was something better out there—a faraway land where to believe such a place existed meant going there and seeing it for myself.

6   As Call and McCrae rounded up hundreds of cattle and horses for the big drive north, I began rounding up the pieces I had cut from their conversation and equating the moving of the stock with reasons for trying something new. Suddenly, I had hundreds of reasons cut and fitted together.

7   The most influential scene—the scene that helped me fuse it all together—was when Augustus suddenly abandoned the herd right outside of Lonesome Dove to sit, lotus style, along a little stream and cry softly into a bandanna.

8   Augustus adored this spot. He had shared, loved, proposed, and quarreled here. In all his life this place, where he once picnicked with a woman long ago, was the one place where he was the happiest. After Woodrow rode up to the stream, Augustus asked him where in his life he was the happiest. Woodrow, being Woodrow, ignored the question. But I didn't.

"I realized that welding was keeping me from something more."

9   These pieces of thought I had cut, fitted, and fused formed another thought: Would I, one day, be able to recount a spot in my life where I could say I was the happiest? Choosing to live as an Augustus rather than a Woodrow, I realized that welding was keeping me from something more, reasoning that the same cutting, fitting, and fusing I had done in welding could apply to other things, mainly ideas. To one day tell a friend that out of all my life, here, where I stand, was where I was the happiest is a venture that will require many years and many moves. But I am happy with the moves I have made thus far, beginning with the move to higher education. Like welding, education offers promise and a way out, and I suspect it will take me places, as welding and a retired Texas Ranger once did.

Reading Closely and Thinking Critically

1. How did Whetstine feel about welding during most of the time he was a welder?
2. Explain how *Lonesome Dove* affected Whetstine. Why do you think the movie affected him that way?
3. What does Whetstine mean when he says in paragraph 9 that he chose to "live as an Augustus rather than a Woodrow"?
4. "Augustinian Influences" appeared in an Indiana University magazine, whose purpose is to encourage "alumni interest in and support for Indiana University." How does the essay help the magazine fulfill its persuasive purpose?

Examining Structure and Strategy

1. Why does Whetstine open his essay with a description of his hometown, the schools, and himself as a student?
2. How does Whetstine achieve transition from paragraph 1 to paragraph 2? From paragraph 2 to paragraph 3? From paragraph 3 to paragraph 4?
3. How does the final sentence tie everything together for satisfying closure?

Noting Combined Patterns

1. Stories are usually told to make a particular point. What point does Whetstine's narration make?
2. How does Whetstine use cause-and-effect analysis?
3. How does the description in paragraphs 1 and 3 help the author achieve his writing purpose?
4. What comparisons does Whetstine make in paragraphs 5 and 6? In paragraph 9?
5. Which of the patterns that Whetstine uses are primary, and which are secondary?

Considering Language and Style

1. Identify the metaphor in paragraph 1 and the simile in paragraph 4. What do you think of them? (Metaphors and similes are explained on page 116.)
2. Consult a dictionary if you do not know the meaning of *fabrication* (paragraph 2).

For Discussion in Class or Online

Whetstine began college after working as a welder for 10 years. Do you think people should delay college or university for a year or more after high school and get some life experiences before returning to school? If you instructor so directs, post your response to your class Web site.

Writing Assignments

1. **In your journal.** For Whetstine, education "offers promise and a way out" (paragraph 9). What does education offer you? Respond in a page or two.
2. **Combining patterns for a purpose.** The purposes in the assignments are possibilities. You may establish whatever purposes you like, within your instructor's guidelines.
   - *Classification and description.* In paragraph 1, Whetstine refers to "students like me." To inform, relate your experience, and express your feelings, classify types of students, note which classification you fit into, and describe students like you.
   - *Narration and cause-and-effect analysis.* Like Whetstine, narrate an account of an event that marked a turning point for you in order to relate your experience and express your feelings. Explain how you were affected by the event.
   - *Comparison-contrast and description.* Whetstine compares welding to writing. To relate experience, express feelings, and inform, explain what writing is similar to for you.
   - *Narration and cause-and-effect analysis.* Combine narration and cause-and-effect analysis to tell a story about a time a book, movie, television program, play, article, or song influenced you and to explain how it influenced you.
3. **Connecting the readings.** *Lonesome Dove* helped Whetstine realize that there other ways his life could be lived. The same realization is one of the points in "'You'll Never Believe What Happened' Is Always a Great Way to Start" (page 463), where King realizes that he can continue to be angry about his father's abandonment, or he can find more positive stories to frame his life. Using the ideas in these selections, along with your own experience and observation, discuss the tensions that exist between a satisfactory but not entirely satisfying life you might drift into and the extra effort you would have to make to live a life that is closer to your ideal.

4. **Drawing on sources.**
   - The movie *Lonesome Dove* is an adaptation of the novel with the same name written by Larry McMurtry. Look up reviews of the novel using *Book Review Digest* in your library's reference room, or type "Lonesome Dove book review" into your favourite search engine. In an essay, summarize three of the reviews and go on to indicate whether you would be interested in reading the novel and why. If you have already read it, summarize the reviews and explain whether or not you agree with them and why.
   - The television miniseries version of *Lonesome Dove,* starring Robert Duvall and Tommy Lee Jones, is available on video. Watch the video and write a summary and response.

Background

Born in 1944 in San Francisco, Richard Rodriguez is a first-generation Mexican American who spoke only Spanish until he was six years old. He is an editor at Pacific News Service and a contributing editor for *Harper's Magazine, U.S. News & World Report,* and the Sunday "Opinion" section of the *Los Angeles Times.* A prolific author who frequently writes of his heritage, Rodriguez has published numerous articles in the *New York Times, The Wall Street Journal, The American Scholar, Time, Mother Jones,* and *The New Republic,* as well as other publications. His three autobiographical books are *Hunger of Memory* (1981), from which "Complexion" is taken, *Days of Obligation: An Argument with My Mexican Father* (1992), and *Brown: The Last Discovery of America* (2002). In 1997, Rodriguez earned the prestigious George Foster Peabody Award for his essays on American life for the PBS series *The News Hour with Jim Lehrer.* He has also received the Frankel Medal from the National Endowment for the Humanities and the International Journalism Award from the World Affairs Council of California.

Combined Patterns and Their Purposes

In "Complexion," Richard Rodriguez expresses his feelings and relates his experience by combining contrast, narration, and description with his discussion of the effects his skin colour had on his self-concept. In doing so, he also informs his audience about the Mexican-American experience and reminds the reader of the adolescent struggle to feel at ease with one's physical appearance.

Complexion
Richard Rodriguez

As you read
Consider how the author defines masculinity.

1   Complexion. My first conscious experience of sexual excitement concerns my complexion. One summer weekend, when I was around seven years old, I was at a public swimming pool with the whole family. I remember sitting on the damp pavement next to the pool and seeing my mother, in the spectator's bleachers, holding my younger sister on her lap. My mother, I noticed, was watching my father as he stood on a diving board, waving to her. I watched her wave back. Then saw her radiant, bashful, astonishing smile. In that second I sensed that my mother and father had a relationship I knew nothing about. A nervous excitement encircled my stomach as I saw my mother's eyes follow my father's figure curving into the water. A second or two later, he emerged. I heard him call out. Smiling, his voice sounded, buoyant, calling me to swim to him. But turning to see him, I caught my mother's eye. I heard her shout over to me. In Spanish she called through the crowd: "Put a towel on over your shoulders." In public, she didn't want to say why. I knew.

2   That incident anticipates the shame and sexual inferiority I was to feel in later years because of my dark complexion. I was to grow up an ugly child. Or one who thought himself ugly. (*Feo.*) One night when I was eleven or twelve years old, I locked myself in the bathroom and carefully regarded my reflection in the mirror over the sink. Without any pleasure I studied my skin. I turned on the faucet. (In my mind I heard the swirling voices of aunts, and even my mother's voice, whispering, whispering incessantly about lemon juice solutions and dark, *feo* children.) With a bar of soap,

I fashioned a thick ball of lather. I began soaping my arms. I took my father's straight razor out of the medicine cabinet. Slowly, with steady deliberateness, I put the blade against my flesh, pressed it as close as I could without cutting, and moved it up and down across my skin to see if I could get out, somehow lessen, the dark. All I succeeded in doing, however, was in shaving my arms bare of their hair. For as I noted with disappointment, the dark would not come out. It remained. Trapped. Deep in the cells of my skin.

3   Throughout adolescence, I felt myself mysteriously marked. Nothing else about my appearance would concern me so much as the fact that my complexion was dark. My mother would say how sorry she was that there was not money enough to get braces to straighten my teeth. But I never bothered about my teeth. In three-way mirrors at department stores, I'd see my profile dramatically defined by a long nose, but it was really only the color of my skin that caught my attention.

4   I wasn't afraid that I would become a menial laborer because of my skin. Nor did my complexion make me feel especially vulnerable to racial abuse. (I didn't really consider my dark skin to be a racial characteristic. I would have been only too happy to look as Mexican as my light-skinned older brother.) Simply, I judged myself ugly. And, since the women in my family had been the ones who discussed it in such worried tones, I felt my dark skin made me unattractive to women.

5   Thirteen years old. Fourteen. In a grammar school art class, when the assignment was to draw a self-portrait, I tried but could not bring myself to shade in the face on the paper to anything like my actual tone. With disgust then I would come face to face with myself in mirrors. With disappointment I located myself in class photographs— my dark face undefined by the camera which had clearly described the white faces of classmates. Or I'd see my dark wrist against my long-sleeved white shirt.

6   I grew divorced from my body. Insecure, overweight, listless. On hot summer days when my rubber-soled shoes soaked up the heat from the sidewalk, I kept my head down. Or walked in the shade. My mother didn't need anymore to tell me to watch out for the sun. I denied myself a sensational life. The normal, extraordinary, animal excitement of feeling my body alive —riding shirtless on a bicycle in the warm wind created by furious self-propelled motion—the sensations that first had excited in me a sense of my maleness, I denied. I was too ashamed of my body. I wanted to forget that I had a body because I had a brown body. I was grateful that none of my classmates ever mentioned the fact.

7   I continued to see the *braceros*,[1] those men I resembled in one way and, in another way, didn't resemble at all. On the watery horizon of a Valley afternoon, I'd see them. And though I feared looking like them, it was with silent envy that I

_____

[1]Mexican labourers admitted into the U.S. temporarily to do seasonal work, such as harvesting crops.

regarded them still. I envied them their physical lives, their freedom to violate the taboo of the sun. Closer to home I would notice the shirtless construction workers, the roofers, the sweating men tarring the street in front of the house. And I'd see the Mexican gardeners. I was unwilling to admit the attraction of their lives. I tried to deny it by looking away. But what was denied became strongly desired.

8   In high school physical education classes, I withdrew, in the regular company of five or six classmates, to a distant corner of a football field where we smoked and talked. Our company was composed of bodies too short or too tall, all graceless and all—except mine—pale. Our conversation was usually witty. (In fact we were intelligent.) If we referred to the athletic contests around us, it was with sarcasm. With savage scorn I'd refer to the "animals" playing football or baseball. It would have been important for me to have joined them. Or for me to have taken off my shirt, to have let the sun burn dark on my skin, and to have run barefoot on the warm wet grass. It would have been very important. Too important. It would have been too telling a gesture—to admit the desire for sensation, the body, my body.

9   Fifteen, sixteen. I was a teenager shy in the presence of girls. Never dated. Barely could talk to a girl without stammering. In high school I went to several dances, but I never managed to ask a girl to dance. So I stopped going. I cannot remember high school years now with the parade of typical images: bright drive-ins or gliding blue shadows of a Junior Prom. At home most weekend nights, I would pass evenings reading. Like those hidden, precocious adolescents who have no real-life sexual experiences, I read a great deal of romantic fiction. "You won't find it in your books," my brother would playfully taunt me as he prepared to go to a party by freezing the crest of the wave in his hair with sticky pomade. Through my reading, however, I developed a fabulous and sophisticated sexual imagination. At seventeen, I may not have known how to engage a girl in small talk, but I had read *Lady Chatterley's Lover.*

10   It annoyed me to hear my father's teasing: that I would never know what "real work" is: that my hands were so soft. I think I knew it was his way of admitting pleasure and pride in my academic success. But I didn't smile. My mother said she was glad her children were getting their educations and would not be pushed around like *los pobres.*[2] I heard the remark ironically as a reminder of my separation from *los braceros.* At such times I suspected that education was making me effeminate. The odd thing, however, was that I did not judge my classmates so harshly. Nor did I consider my male teachers in high school effeminate. It was only myself I judged against some shadowy, mythical Mexican laborer—dark like me, yet very different.

---

[2] The poor.

Reading Closely and Thinking Critically

1. What effects did the colour of Rodriguez's complexion have on him?
2. In what ways did the women in Rodriguez's family make him feel self-conscious and inferior?
3. Why do you think that Rodriguez was so attracted to the lives of the Mexican gardeners and construction workers?
4. Using the information in the essay for clues, explain the author's idea of masculinity.
5. Why did Rodriguez read so much? Why do you think he was afraid that reading and education would make him effeminate?
6. "Complexion" came from Rodriguez's autobiographical *Hunger of Memory*. What kind of reader do you think would enjoy reading about Rodriguez's life?

Examining Structure and Strategy

1. In which paragraph does Rodriguez indicate what is *not* an effect of his reaction to his complexion?
2. In what order are the effects of Rodriguez's skin colour arranged? What are the clues to this arrangement?
3. If the first paragraph omitted the initial fragment, "Complexion" and began instead with the sentence that follows, "My first conscious experience of sexual excitement concerns my complexion," how would the emphasis shift?

Noting Combined Patterns

1. What is Rodriguez's primary pattern of development? How does he use that pattern?
2. In which paragraph does Rodriguez use narration to help develop the cause-and-effect relationship?
3. With what people does Rodriguez contrast himself? How does that element of contrast help the author achieve his purpose?
4. Cite an example of descriptive language and explain how the description helps the author achieve his purpose.

Considering Language and Style

1. Rodriguez uses sentence fragments intentionally in paragraphs 1, 2, 5, 6, 8, and 9. Ordinarily, sentence fragments are an editing error. Here, the fragments serve a purpose. What is that purpose?
2. Rodriguez uses three Spanish words: *feo, braceros,* and *los pobres.* What does this use of Spanish contribute to his essay? Explain.
3. Consult a dictionary if you are unsure of the meaning of any of these words: *buoyant* (paragraph 1), *menial* (paragraph 4), *listless* (paragraph 6), *taboo* (paragraph 7), *precocious* (paragraph 9), *pomade* (paragraph 9).

For Discussion in Class or Online

With some classmates, consider the factors that shape a person's self-concept. Discuss the influence of family, friends, teachers, coaches, television, advertisements, and anything else you can think of. If your instructor directs you to do so, post your response to your class Web site.

Writing Assignments

1. **In your journal.** Rodriguez tells about feeling self-conscious because of his skin colour. Write about some aspect of your physical appearance that made you self-conscious as an adolescent and explain the reason for your feeling. As an alternative, write about some feature of your appearance that made you proud.

2. **Combining patterns for a purpose.** The purposes in the assignments are possibilities. You may establish whatever purposes you like, within your instructor's guidelines.

- *Description and cause-and-effect analysis.* Pick one aspect of your physical appearance, such as your height, weight, nose, or skin colour. To relate experience, express feelings, and inform, describe that feature of your appearance and explain the effect it has had on you. (The previous journal writing may give you some ideas.)
- *Classification and exemplification.* Rodriguez says he was shy as an adolescent and that he withdrew from the company of family and friends because of his insecurity. To inform, classify the kinds of behaviours adolescents exhibit in response to how they feel about their looks. Give examples for each category in your classification. Then, use your classification as a basis for arguing whether or not schools should institute courses to help students feel comfortable with their looks or improve their looks.
- *Definition and classification.* To inform, write an extended definition of *body image* and classify the most common kinds.
- *Narration and comparison-contrast.* In paragraph 1, Rodriguez tells about his realization that his parents had a sexual relationship. Tell about a time when you came to understand something about one or both or your parents or other caregiver. To relate experience and express feelings, contrast your feelings and understanding before and after the realization. If you prefer, write about another adult in your life, such as a coach, clergy member, teacher, or grandparent.

3. **Connecting the readings.** School has a significant impact on the self-concepts of young people. Explain school's potential to affect the way we view ourselves. You might get some ideas from rereading "Ring Leader" (page 166).

4. **Drawing on sources.** Ask 10 men and 10 women this question: "If you could get free plastic surgery on one part of your body, what would you change and why?" Report your findings and discuss any conclusions you can draw from them.

Background

A superb essayist whose literary accomplishments won him the U.S. Presidential Medal of Freedom in 1963, Elwyn Brooks White (1899–1985) was a reporter for the *Seattle Times* before moving to New York to become an advertising copywriter. He went on to write for *The New Yorker* for 50 years and helped establish its reputation for excellence with his "Talk of the Town" column. He soon became known for his prose style and his personal essays, which often display an ironic view of the world. White also wrote the "One Man's Meat" column for *Harper's*, where "Once More to the Lake" first appeared in 1941. You may know White as the author of the popular children's book *Charlotte's Web* (1952) or as the author, with William Strunk, Jr., of the popular and enduring writer's guide, *The Elements of Style* (1959), a reference often checked by students and professional writers alike.

Combined Patterns and Their Purposes

In "Once More to the Lake," White uses description to relate the experience of his visits to a family vacation spot in Maine, visits he made both as a child and as an adult. Using narration, White recounts a visit that he made with his son. Using comparison-contrast, he reveals that the spot is, at once, the same and different after the passing of years. Be sure to notice that his description allows White to express his feelings about the vacation spot. Notice, too, how it leads the author to an unnerving conclusion.

Once More to the Lake
E. B. White

1   One summer, along about 1904, my father rented a camp on a lake in Maine and took us all there for the month of August. We all got ringworm from some kittens and had to rub Pond's Extract on our arms and legs night and morning, and my father rolled over in a canoe with all his clothes on; but outside of that the vacation was a success and from then on none of us ever thought there was any place in the world like that lake in Maine. We returned summer after summer—always on August 1 for one month. I have since become a salt-water man, but sometimes in summer there are days when the restlessness of the tides and the fearful cold of the sea water and the incessant wind that blows across the afternoon and into the evening make me wish for the placidity of a lake in the woods. A few weeks ago this feeling got so strong I bought myself a couple of bass hooks and a spinner and returned to the lake where we used to go, for a week's fishing and to revisit old haunts.

> **As you read**
> Notice how the essay makes you feel. Do you find the essay upbeat or depressing?

> "I took along my son, who had never had any fresh water up his nose and who had seen lily pads only from train windows."

2   I took along my son, who had never had any fresh water up his nose and who had seen lily pads only from train windows. On the journey over to the lake I began to wonder what it would be like. I wondered how time would have marred this unique, this holy spot—the coves and streams, the hills that the sun set behind, the camps and the paths behind the camps. I was sure that the tarred road would have found it out, and I wondered in what other ways it would be desolated. It is strange how much

you can remember about places like that once you allow your mind to return into the grooves that lead back. You remember one thing, and that suddenly reminds you of another thing. I guess I remembered clearest of all the early mornings, when the lake was cool and motionless, remembered how the bedroom smelled of the lumber it was made of and of the wet woods whose scent entered through the screen. The partitions in the camp were thin and did not extend clear to the top of the rooms, and as I was always the first up I would dress softly so as not to wake the others, and sneak out into the sweet outdoors and start out in the canoe, keeping close along the shore in the long shadows of the pines. I remembered being very careful never to rub my paddle against the gunwale for fear of disturbing the stillness of the cathedral.

3   The lake had never been what you would call a wild lake. There were cottages sprinkled around the shores, and it was in farming country although the shores of the lake were quite heavily wooded. Some of the cottages were owned by nearby farmers, and you would live at the shore and eat your meals at the farmhouse. That's what our family did. But although it wasn't wild, it was a fairly large and undisturbed lake and there were places in it that, to a child at least, seemed infinitely remote and primeval.

4   I was right about the tar: It led to within half a mile of the shore. But when I got back there, with my boy, and we settled into a camp near a farmhouse and into the kind of summertime I had known, I could tell that it was going to be pretty much the same as it had been before—I knew it, lying in bed the first morning smelling the bedroom and hearing the boy sneak quietly out and go off along the shore in a boat. I began to sustain the illusion that he was I, and therefore, by simple transposition, that I was my father. This sensation persisted, kept cropping up all the time we were there. It was not an entirely new feeling, but in this setting it grew much stronger. I seemed to be living a dual existence. I would be in the middle of some simple act, I would be picking up a bait box or laying down a table fork, or I would be saying something and suddenly it would be not I but my father who was saying the words or making the gesture. It gave me a creepy sensation.

"I seemed to be living a dual existence."

5   We went fishing the first morning. I felt the same damp moss covering the worms in the bait can, and saw the dragonfly alight on the tip of my rod as it hovered a few inches from the surface of the water. It was the arrival of this fly that convinced me beyond any doubt that everything was as it always had been, that the years were a mirage and that there had been no years. The small waves were the same, chucking the rowboat under the chin as we fished at anchor, and the boat was the same boat, the same color green and the ribs broken in the same places, and under the floorboards the same fresh water leavings and debris—the dead hellgrammite, the wisps of moss, the rusty discarded fishhook, the dried blood from yesterday's catch. We stared silently at the tips of our rods, at the dragonflies that came and went. I lowered the tip of mine into the water, tentatively, pensively dislodging the fly, which darted two feet

away, poised, darted two feet back, and came to rest again a little farther up the rod. There had been no years between the ducking of this dragonfly and the other one— the one that was part of memory. I looked at the boy, who was silently watching his fly, and it was my hands that held his rod, my eyes watching. I felt dizzy and didn't know which rod I was at the end of.

6   We caught two bass, hauling them in briskly as though they were mackerel, pulling them over the side of the boat in a businesslike manner without any landing net, and stunning them with a blow on the back of the head. When we got back for a swim before lunch, the lake was exactly where we had left it, the same number of inches from the dock, and there was only the merest suggestion of a breeze. This seemed an utterly enchanted sea, this lake you could leave to its own devices for a few hours and come back to, and find that it had not stirred, this constant and trustworthy body of water. In the shallows, the dark, water-soaked sticks and twigs, smooth and old, were undulating in clusters on the bottom against the clean ribbed sand, and the track of the mussel was plain. A school of minnows swam by, each minnow with its small individual shadow, doubling the attendance, so clear and sharp in the sunlight. Some of the other campers were in swimming, along the shore, one of them with a cake of soap, and the water felt thin and clear and unsubstantial. Over the years there had been this person with the cake of soap, this cultist, and here he was. There had been no years.

7   Up to the farmhouse to dinner through the teeming dusty field, the road under our sneakers was only a two-track road. The middle track was missing, the one with the marks of the hooves and the splotches of dried, flaky manure. There had always been three tracks to choose from in choosing which track to walk in; now the choice was narrowed down to two. For a moment I missed terribly the middle alternative. But the way led past the tennis court, and something about the way it lay there in the sun reassured me; the tape had loosened along the backline, the alleys were green with plantains and other weeds, and the net (installed in June and removed in September) sagged in the dry noon, and the whole place steamed with midday heat and hunger and emptiness. There was a choice of pie for dessert, and one was blueberry and one was apple, and the waitresses were the same country girls, there having been no passage of time, only the illusion of it as in a dropped curtain—the waitresses were still fifteen; their hair had been washed, that was the only difference— they had been to the movies and seen the pretty girls with the clean hair.

> "There had always been three tracks to choose from in choosing which track to walk in; now the choice was narrowed down to two."

8   Summertime, oh, summertime, pattern of life indelible with fadeproof lake, the wood unshatterable, the pasture with the sweetfern and the juniper forever and ever, summer without end; this was the background, and the life along the shore was the design, the cottages with their innocent and tranquil design, their tiny docks with the flagpole and the American flag floating against the white clouds in the blue sky,

the little paths over the roots of the trees leading from camp to camp and the paths leading back to the outhouses and the can of lime for sprinkling, and at the souvenir counters at the store the miniature birch-bark canoes and the postcards that showed things looking a little better than they looked. This was the American family at play, escaping the city heat, wondering whether the newcomers in the camp at the head of the cove were "common" or "nice," wondering whether it was true that the people who drove up for Sunday dinner at the farmhouse were turned away because there wasn't enough chicken.

9   It seemed to me, as I kept remembering all this, that those times and those summers had been infinitely precious and worth saving. There had been jollity and peace and goodness. The arriving (at the beginning of August) had been so big a business in itself, at the railway station the farm wagon drawn up, the first smell of the pine-laden air, the first glimpse of the smiling farmer, and the great importance of the trunks and your father's enormous authority in such matters, and the feel of the wagon under you for the long ten-mile haul, and at the top of the last long hill catching the first view of the lake after eleven months of not seeing this cherished body of water. The shouts and cries of the other campers when they saw you, and the trunks to be unpacked, to give up their rich burden. (Arriving was less exciting nowadays, when you sneaked up in your car and parked it under a tree near the camp and took out the bags and in five minutes it was all over, no fuss, no loud wonderful fuss about trunks.)

"The only thing that was wrong now, really, was the sound of the place."

10   Peace and goodness and jollity. The only thing that was wrong now, really, was the sound of the place, an unfamiliar nervous sound of the outboard motors. This was the note that jarred, the one thing that would sometimes break the illusion and set the years moving. In those other summer times all motors were inboard; and when they were at a little distance, the noise they made was a sedative, an ingredient of summer sleep. They were one-cylinder and two-cylinder engines, and some were make-and-break and some were jump-spark, but they all made a sleepy sound across the lake. The one-lungers throbbed and fluttered, and the twin-cylinder ones purred and purred, and that was a quiet sound, too. But now the campers all had out-boards. In the daytime, in the hot mornings, these motors made a petulant, irritable sound; at night in the still evening when the afterglow lit the water, they whined about one's ears like mosquitoes. My boy loved our rented outboard, and his great desire was to achieve single-handed mastery over it, and authority, and he soon learned the trick of choking it a little (but not too much), and the adjustment of the needle valve. Watching him I would remember the things you could do with the old one-cylinder engine with the heavy flywheel, how you could have it eating out of your hand if you got really close to it spiritually. Motorboats in those days didn't have clutches, and you would make a landing by shutting off the motor at the proper time and coasting in with a dead rudder. But there was a way of reversing them, if you learned the trick, by cutting the switch and putting it on again exactly on the final dying revolution of

the flywheel, so that it would kick back against compression and begin reversing. Approaching a dock in a strong following breeze, it was difficult to slow up sufficiently by the ordinary coasting method, and if a boy felt he had complete mastery over his motor, he was tempted to keep it running beyond its time and then reverse it a few feet from the dock. It took a cool nerve, because if you threw the switch a twentieth of a second too soon you would catch the flywheel when it still had speed enough to go up past center, and the boat would leap ahead, charging bull-fashion at the dock.

11 We had a good week at the camp. The bass were biting well and the sun shone endlessly, day after day. We would be tired at night and lie down in the accumulated heat of the little bedrooms after the long hot day and the breeze would stir almost imperceptibly outside and the smell of the swamp drift in through the rusty screens. Sleep would come easily and in the morning the red squirrel would be on the roof, tapping out his gay routine. I kept remembering everything, lying in bed in the mornings—the small steamboat that had a long rounded stern like the lip of a Ubangi, and how quietly she ran on the moonlight sails, when the older boys played their mandolins and the girls sang and we ate doughnuts dipped in sugar, and how sweet the music was on the water in the shining night, and what it had felt like to think about

girls then. After breakfast we would go up to the store and the things were in the same place— the minnows in a bottle, the plugs and spinners disarranged and pawed over by the youngsters from the boys' camp, the Fig Newtons and the Beeman's gum. Outside, the road was tarred and cars stood in front of the store. Inside, all was just as it had always been, except there was more Coca-Cola and not so much Moxie and root beer and birch beer and sarsaparilla. We would walk out with the bottle of pop apiece and sometimes the pop would backfire up our noses and hurt. We explored the streams, quietly, where the turtles slid off the sunny logs and dug their way into the soft bottom; and we lay on the town wharf and fed worms to the tame bass. Everywhere we went I had trouble making out which was I, the one walking at my side, the one walking in my pants.

> "We would walk out with the bottle of pop apiece and sometimes the pop would backfire up our noses and hurt."

12   One afternoon while we were at that lake a thunderstorm came up. It was like the revival of an old melodrama that I had seen long ago with childish awe. The second-act climax of the drama of the electrical disturbance over a lake in America had not changed in any important respect. This was the big scene, still the big scene. The whole thing was so familiar, the first feeling of oppression and heat and a general air around camp of not wanting to go very far away. In midafternoon (it was all the same) a curious darkening of the sky, and a lull in everything that had made life tick; and then the way the boats suddenly swung the other way at their moorings with the coming of a breeze out of the new quarter, and the premonitory rumble. Then the kettle drum, then the snare, then the bass drum and cymbals, then crackling light against the dark, and the gods grinning and licking their chops in the hills. Afterward the calm, the rain steadily rustling in the calm lake, the return of light and hope and spirits, and the campers running out in joy and relief to go swimming in the rain, their bright cries perpetuating the deathless joke about how they were getting simply drenched, and the children screaming with delight at the new sensation of bathing in the rain, and the joke about getting drenched linking the generations in a strong inde-structible chain. And the comedian who waded in carrying an umbrella.

13   When the others went swimming my son said he was going in, too. He pulled his dripping trunks from the line where they had hung all through the shower and wrung them out. Languidly, and with no thought of going in, I watched him, his hard little body, skinny and bare, saw him wince slightly as he pulled up around his vitals the small, soggy, icy garment. As he buckled the swollen belt, suddenly my groin felt the chill of death.

Reading Closely and Thinking Critically

1. Why does White return to the lake after an absence of 40 years? Do you think the reasons the author gives are the only ones? Explain.
2. What do you think White's dominant impression of the lake is as an adult?
3. What conclusion does White draw about the passage of time? Where is that conclusion best expressed?
4. White mentions several times that he has trouble distinguishing himself from his son and that he has trouble distinguishing the present from the past. Why do you think he experiences this blurring of identities and time?
5. White believes that his past summers at the lake were "infinitely precious and worth saving" (paragraph 9). Why?
6. If White had visited the lake more regularly over the past 40 years, do you think the visit narrated and described in the essay would have prompted the same feelings and realizations? Explain.
7. Is "Once More to the Lake" upbeat or depressing? Explain.

Examining Structure and Strategy

1. To make the essay vivid, White appeals to the sense of smell, touch, and sound in addition to the sense of sight. Mention one example each of a description that appeals to smell, touch, and sound. Underline the specific words that appeal to the senses.
2. Cite two other descriptions that you find particularly appealing. Underline the specific words.
3. White does not refer to his son by name, nor does he describe the boy very much. Why does he not give his son more identifying characteristics?

Noting Combined Patterns

1. Without White's vivid description, much of the essay's joy would be lost. What else would be lost? Is description a primary or secondary pattern?
2. What narration does White include? How does the narration help him achieve his purpose for writing? Is narration a primary or secondary pattern?
3. In what way does White compare and contrast? How does the comparison-contrast help White achieve his purpose for writing? Is comparison-contrast a primary or secondary pattern?

Considering Language and Style

1. Look up the meaning of *paean* in a dictionary; then read paragraph 8 aloud. How is that paragraph similar to a paean?
2. What metaphor (see page 118) does White include in paragraph 2? In paragraph 12? What do these metaphors contribute?
3. Consult a dictionary if you are unsure of the meaning of any of these words: *incessant* (paragraph 1), *gunwale* (paragraph 2), *primeval* (paragraph 3), *helgrammite* (paragraph 5), *pensively* (paragraph5), *indelible* (paragraph8), *petulant* (paragraph10), *Ubangi* (paragraph 11), *premonitory* (paragraph 12), *languidly* (paragraph 13).

For Discussion in Class or Online

"Once More to the Lake" deals with issues of youth and age. With your classmates, discuss the extent to which we are concerned with issues of youth and age in our culture. Cite specific examples to support your view. If your instructor so directs, post your responses to your class Web site.

Writing Assignments

1. **In your journal.** In paragraph 12, when he writes of the thunderstorm, White notes that "the joke about getting drenched [links] the generations in a strong indestructible chain." What events, experiences, and circumstances link the generations in your family or in your locale? Explain in a page or two.

2. **Combining patterns for a purpose.** The purposes in the assignments are possibilities. You may establish whatever purposes you like, within your instructor's guidelines.

   - *Description and process analysis.* Paragraph 12 describes a thunderstorm. To entertain and inform your reader, write your own description of a thunderstorm or other weather event as it develops, peaks, and wanes.

   - *Description and comparison-contrast.* If you have ever returned to a place after being gone for a while, compare and contrast by describing how the place was when you returned and how it was at the earlier time. For example, you could describe your first trip home after being away at school for several months or your elementary school after seeing it for the first time as an adult. Your purpose is to relate your experience and express your feelings.

   - *Narration and description.* Narrate a story about a place that holds special significance for you, and describe that place in a way that helps the reader understand why the place is important to you. Your purpose is to express your feelings and perhaps relate experience.

   - *Narration and cause-and-effect analysis.* In the essay, White recognizes his own mortality. Tell about an event that caused you to recognize your mortality—or at least your inability to control something. To relate experience and express feelings, narrate what happened and use cause-and-effect to explain how you were affected.

3. **Connecting the readings.**

   - In "Once More to the Lake," White's description of the natural world indicates that he has had both the time and inclination to observe carefully. In "On Walking" (page 401), Wayne Grady writes about people's engagement with the world when they are walking. Contrast or compare the attitudes toward nature and time of White's narrator with that of any of the numerous individuals Grady quotes. What is it about being in the natural world that takes us out of time?

   - In Brian Payton's "A Sleuth of Bears" (page 128), the author observes the landscape carefully because it's threatened. Contrast or compare that motive to the sense of mortality White experiences in "Once More to the Lake."

4. **Drawing on sources.** Advertisers are often accused of targeting youthful populations at the expense of older ones. Decide for yourself whether this allegation is true by going to the source: Watch television commercials for at least three popular programs and review recent magazine advertisements from at least three mainstream publications: *Maclean's, Time,* or *Newsweek,* for example. Then write an essay arguing that advertisers either do or do not target the younger consumers and neglect older ones. Be sure to back up your points with descriptions of specific commercials and advertisements.

Chapter 14

Locating, Evaluating, and Drawing on Sources

Research is formalized curiosity. It is poking and prying with a purpose.

— Zora Neale Hurston

Research serves to make building stones out of stumbling blocks.

— Arthur D. Little

USING SOURCES

You can think about Canadian society as a lot of ad hoc conversations going on at once. A filmmaker observes several skateboarders outside his favourite coffee shop and decides to make a documentary about them. In all likelihood, the film he makes is shaped by his conversations with his subjects and with other people who are helping him make it. When the film comes out, reviewers react to it in newspapers and magazines; on the basis of those reviews you decide to see it, though this also involves a conversation with your girlfriend or boyfriend about whether this is what you want to do tonight. When you leave the movie theatre, you go for coffee or beer and talk about whether the documentary gave an accurate view of skateboarders, about whether it was well made, about whether you just wasted your time and money or decided to get out your old skateboard.

Similarly, post-secondary institutions involve avid conversations between people who do research, many of them instructors and professors, many of them students like you. Writers frequently draw on the work of other writers. For example, you may use an idea from an essay in this book to back up one of your points, or another writer's idea may prompt you to write an essay of your own. That is one of the exciting things about writing—writers engage in an ongoing conversation by responding to each other's ideas and using them for support or departure points. In addition, when they take in-depth looks at subjects, writers often produce research papers that bring together authoritative facts, opinions, and speculation. But as you know, the good ideas that find their way into our writing are the result of considerable thought, hard work, and personal perspectives. Naturally, then, you don't want someone to claim your ideas as their own. And you don't present other people's ideas as if they were yours. As a consequence, the conversations going on in the academy have some ground rules. To be part of the ongoing conversation and to produce credible research papers, you must learn both how to locate relevant, reliable sources and how to credit them fairly and responsibly.

LOCATING SOURCES

The amount of material currently available to researchers is both thrilling and daunting, which is why there are two keys to a successful research paper: a topic that captures your imagination, your curiosity, or your passion; and an early start. While some of the material you seek may be online, do not give yourself so little time that you find it impossible to find or recall relevant books or even use interlibrary loans. While magazines, newspapers, and journals often provide the most up-to-date information, books, by virtue of the financial investment publishers make in an author's work, may bring you the most considered views and ideas. While articles provide an up-to-date "slice" of your topic, books probably give you the wider view.

To locate material in the midst of the information explosion, you need efficient strategies, like the ones explained next.

- **Take a tour of your campus library to learn about its resources, where they are located, and how to use them.** You may be tempted to rely solely on Internet research, but your campus library houses a considerable amount of information unavailable on the Internet. Many libraries offer self-guided tours to take at your convenience; others have regularly scheduled tours or workshops given by staff members.
- **Decide on the kind of information you need.** Perhaps you are in the earliest stages of a writing project and need an overview of a topic such as gun control in order to narrow your topic. Or perhaps you already have your topic and need a sense of the most compelling arguments for and against the registration of long guns. Or you may need a single piece of specific information, such as the number of registered hand guns in the country. Knowing what you want helps your research go more quickly and efficiently.
- **Consult your librarian.** Reference librarians who staff your library's reference desk can direct you to print and electronic resources that will save you

time. They are among the friendliest and most helpful people in the world, and their expertise—of which they are rightfully proud—is helping students and scholars find relevant material. Also, if you need materials unavailable in your library, the librarian can assist you in obtaining them through interlibrary loan.

- **Use general references, most of which are now found online.**

  a. While scholars continue to have reservations about *Wikipedia*, a recent study indicated it had no more errors than the paper copy of the *Encyclopedia Britannica*. Nevertheless, because it can be written and edited by anyone, use it mainly to get an overview of your topic.

  b. Specialty encyclopedias, like *Encyclopedia of Education* and *Encyclopedia of Crime and Justice*, give more in-depth information in a specific subject area. Your library probably has a distinct protocol for finding special encyclopedias, many of which are available online. Many libraries allow you to query a subject area combined with the capitalized word "AND" and the word "encyclopedia" with either a question mark or an asterisk (*). You might, for example, type in "literature AND encyclopedia?" and be given a list of the encyclopedias available for that discipline.

  c. Find discipline- or genre-specific works, such as *The Oxford Companion to Art, A Political Handbook of the World,* and *The Oxford Companion to Canadian Literature*. Your library might subscribe to *Oxford Reference Online,* a database of Oxford dictionaries, encyclopedias, and guides that are available online. Search your library's databases for "Oxford Reference Online." Their home page will allow you to choose from a list of subject categories such as Art and Architecture, Biological Sciences, Earth and Environmental Sciences, or Military History. Click on the relevant link, and you will find yourself with a list of possible Oxford resources available for that subject area.

  d. Almanacs and yearbooks, such as *Canadian Almanac, Scott's Canadian Sourcebook, World Almanac, Information Please Almanac,* and *Facts on File,* provide statistics and information on current events. Your library may subscribe to online versions of some of these references.

- **Locate books through the catalogue.** The computerized catalogue includes information on every book in the library. This information can be accessed by author, title, and subject. There are two ways to find information on a subject. If your subject, say "gambling," is fairly general and straightforward, you can do a keyword search and type in "gambling." You may, however, get way too many references (we found over 500), and so want to narrow your search by time and place, as well as by a particular kind of gambling—say poker. Here you may get a reasonable number—we found

23—but as we looked through the list, we saw an intriguing new book, published in 2006, called *Gambling on Campus*. You can do two things to find works with a similar and perhaps more interesting focus. One is to turn to the three-volume Library of Congress Subject Headings, which will probably be located near the computer terminals. This work lists the precise subject headings used in your institution's catalogue, so you can be sure you are looking up your subject using the appropriate key words. The other is to look at the record for *Gambling on Campus* and find the subject headings listed there—in this case "gambling" and "students—social life and customs."

- **Locate magazines, journals, and newspapers with indexes.** Because they are published at regular intervals, periodicals (magazines, journals, and newspapers) offer the most up-to-date information. Be sure to distinguish, however, between magazines—which are written for a popular audience, and journals—which are published for scholars. Magazines will seldom point you to other references, and while their content might be timely, no one from the particular discipline an article or essay falls into has approved the content. Journals, on the other hand, have the approval of other scholars and will always contain a bibliography that helps you find more resources. To discover useful periodicals, look up your subject in an online database. Some useful general databases for Canadian students and scholars are

  Expanded Academic ASAP
  CPI.Q—Canadian Periodical Index
  General OneFile
  Canadian Business and Current Affairs Complete (CBCA)

  — More scholarly databases include

  JSTOR
  Project Muse
  Periodicals Archive Online

  — In addition, some publishers have databases of the journals they publish. Examples include

  Cambridge Journals Online
  Oxford Journals Online
  Sage Journals Online

  — A university in Sweden has organized a *Directory of Open Access Journals*. These can be accessed from anywhere by going to www.doaj.org.

    Some publications, like the *New York Times*, are available from *Freely Accessible Journals*, Canadian newspapers like *The Globe and Mail* and the

National Post may be available to your library online, though you may not be able to access the most recent issues.

— If your library subscribes to *FirstSearch*, you will have access to *ArticleFirst*, which gives you access to over 12,000 journals in the fields of science, technology, medicine, social sciences, business, humanities, and popular culture.

- **Use Internet search engines.** While there have been many attempts to improve on Google (www.google.com), it remains one of the most useful search engines.

  For a more academically focused search, try Google scholar at scholar. google.com. Don't be seduced by the ease of finding material on the Internet, however. While Internet resources are part of a good *mix*, they should be complemented by books and periodicals.

EVALUATING PRINT AND INTERNET SOURCES

After locating sources, you must evaluate the quality and suitability of those sources by answering the questions given here.

Questions for Print Sources

- **Is the source recent enough?** Your topic will determine how current the information needs to be. For example, a historic topic such as the strategies used during the Battle of the Plains of Abraham will not be as time sensitive as an examination of new treatments for AIDS.
- **Is the source detailed enough to meet your needs?** Evaluate whether the material is written for students (elementary, secondary, post-secondary), professionals, technical experts, or the general public. Avoid material that is too simplistic, and let your purpose dictate whether to use a source aimed at a general audience or one aimed at readers with technical knowledge.
- **Is the author reliable?** Check the source or type the author's name into a search engine to learn the author's credentials. What are the person's publications, degrees, and professional affiliations? Has the author received any awards or professional acknowledgment? What professional experiences has the author had?
- **Is the author or publisher associated with a particular point of view?** For example, if you are researching gun control and encounter a piece published by the National Firearms Association, you can assume a particular point of view.
- **Can you understand the material?** If the material is too technical or specialized for you, it is not helpful.

Questions for Internet Sources

- Have you answered the relevant questions for print sources given above? These questions are also important for evaluating Internet sources.
- **Who is sponsoring the page?** A page sponsored by a university or research foundation may be more reliable than one sponsored by a for-profit company. Pages affiliated with major news and media organizations are also generally credible.
- **When was the site last updated?** For many topics, you will need current information.
- **Can the information be verified elsewhere?** Check other sites, reference works, books or periodicals to be sure any surprising or questionable information can be corroborated. Information that cannot be verified may not be false, but it should be scrutinized carefully. Consult with your instructor if you are unsure about a site.
- **Are there links to other credible sites?** Credible sites link to other sites that look professional (see below) and that are sponsored by news agencies, educational organizations, government agencies, non-profit groups and other trustworthy organizations.
- **Does the page look professional?** Is it free of grammatical and spelling errors; is it attractively designed?

You will find further suggestions for evaluating Web sites at the following tutorial, maintained by the University of California, Berkeley:

www.lib.berkeley.edu/TeachingLib/Guides/Internet/Evaluate.html

DRAWING ON SOURCES: PARAPHRASING AND QUOTING

At the beginning of this chapter, research was likened to a series of conversations. One of the first conversations you will have is between the topic as you have conceived it and the abundance—or lack—of material you find on the same subject. Consequently, you may find yourself changing or refocusing your topic slightly to make use of the knowledge you gain as you read. But after you've settled on your topic, you have some decisions to make about how to gather your research materials efficiently and effectively. Some of this material will be directly pertinent to your topic, succinctly expressed, and ready to be quoted in one of your paragraphs. Some of the material, while pertinent, may go into far greater detail than you want. Other information may be useful, but only some of it and only peripherally. In these latter two cases, you will want to paraphrase the writer's point. To incorporate source material into your writing, you need to learn the academy's conventions for paraphrasing or using a direct quotation.

Paraphrasing

To **paraphrase,** you restate another author's ideas, using your own writing style and wording. As suggested above, you will often paraphrase when a writer goes into more detail than you need, when the writer's wording doesn't suit the context you've created, or when the writer's perspective or purpose doesn't quite mesh with yours. One of the key qualities of a successful paraphrase is that it mediates honestly and accurately between the author's perspective and purpose and your own.

Paraphrasing is also useful because it helps you incorporate brief excerpts from different sources into your essays to support your own ideas. (See the discussion of how to synthesize information on page 8.)

When you paraphrase you should

- Use your own wording and style, not the wording and style in the source.
- Use quotation marks for key words and phrases that are the author's distinctive expression.
- Avoid adding meaning.
- Avoid changing meaning.

Here is an example of an acceptable paraphrase and unacceptable paraphrase of "Toronto Cars. Can't Live with 'Em, Can't Live without 'Em," by Tim Falconer, found on page 411. Notice that the acceptable paraphrase places the author's distinctive phrasing in quotation marks. The unacceptable paraphrase fails to alter style and wording enough. The examples here and throughout the chapter follow the Modern Language Association's (MLA) rules for in-text, parenthetical citations. You will find the original references for these sources in the section on documenting sources, below.

SOURCE   Even as road engineering and automobile safety have improved dramatically, the death toll remains ludicrously high: 1.2 million people die on the world's roads each year. The thirst for oil has led to many conflicts around the world, including two wars in the Persian Gulf and civil unrest in Nigeria, and it threatens environmentally sensitive habitats. All the while, the humans fret about their tailpipe toxins, lament the lost hours spent stuck in traffic and cluck at the urban sprawl that makes no economic, environmental or aesthetic sense (2).

UNACCEPTABLE   Falconer suggests that there are compelling reasons for people to consider ways to reduce their dependence on cars. Over a million people die on the roads around the world each year, and our need for oil has led to wars around the world, including the two conflicts in the Persian Gulf, as well as to a threat to sensitive habitats.

ACCEPTABLE   Falconer suggests that there are compelling reasons for people to consider ways to reduce their dependence on cars. Individually, we lose hours stuck in traffic jams and complain about "the urban sprawl that makes no economic, environmental or aesthetic sense" (2). But on a larger scale, there are more significant problems: millions of deaths on the roads each year, wars over natural resources, and the destruction of habitats.

When you write your paraphrases, avoid simply plugging in synonyms. If you merely substitute synonyms for words in the source, the paraphrase will lack your distinctive style. Furthermore, the result is often an awkward sounding sentence, as in the second sentence of the example above. Here is an example also using "Toronto Cars. Can't Live with 'Em, Can't Live without 'Em," as the source.

SOURCE   All that time in the car is not good for us. Traffic tie-ups are costly in terms of wasted fuel and productivity—and human health and sanity. Many suburbanites suffer from frazzled nerves and neck and back problems brought on by long commutes, and because they must get in a car just to pick up a litre of milk, they are less fit and more likely to be overweight or obese than their inner-city counterparts.

UNACCEPTABLE   All the time we spend in cars isn't good for our health. We waste fuel and people's time in traffic jams. Suburbanites suffer from stiff necks and back problems. Because they can't do anything— even pick up a loaf of bread—without getting into the car, they are less healthy and more overweight than people who live in the inner city.

ACCEPTABLE   While the suburbs promise the freedom of open spaces, they also contribute to an unhealthy culture that is dependent on a car. "All the time in the car is not good for us," argues Tim Falconer. We all know the feeling of helpless frustration we experience when we're trapped in a traffic jam, or the stiff necks and backs that come from being in a car too long. The suburban dependence on cars also contributes to obesity; without the diverse neighbourhoods proposed by Jane Jacobs, neighbourhoods with corner stores and local bakeries around the corner, there's not much we can do without getting in a car. In fact, many suburbs don't even have sidewalks—effectively discouraging walking.

Quoting

To use a **direct quotation,** reproduce the author's exact words within quotation marks. You should limit the number of quotations you use because using too many quotations obscures your distinctive style. As a general guide, limit your quoting to those times when something is so well expressed that you want to preserve the original wording.

A number of conventions govern the use of quotations. These are illustrated using material from "Imagining an Enlightened Social Policy on Drugs" (The parenthetical page numbers refer to the original book from which this essay was taken. You can find a citation for this book on page C-2.)

- Use ellipses (three spaced periods) to indicate that something has been left out of the original text. If the ellipsis comes at the grammatical end of a sentence, use a fourth period snug up against the final word to indicate this fact.

SOURCE	As we have seen, the dominant emotional states and the brain patterns of human beings are shaped by their early environment. Throughout their lifetimes, they are in dynamic interaction with various social and emotional milieus. If we are to help addicts, we must strive to change not them but their environments. These are the only things we *can* change (Maté 299).
QUOTATION	According to Dr. Maté, drug addicts are "shaped by their early environment. . . . If we are to help addicts, we must strive to change not them but their environments" (299).

- Use brackets to add clarification or to make changes to work the quotation into your sentence.

SOURCE	How to create that island of relief is the core issue in projecting a humane policy toward addiction. The work of the Portland Hotel Society is an isolated, flawed but worthy attempt at offering the respite from anguish and anxiety that Dr. Panksepp suggests.

QUOTATION   Offering addicts the supports they need to reduce the stresses in their lives is crucial to an effective response to addiction, argues Dr. Maté: "How to create that island of relief is the core issue in projecting a humane policy toward addiction. The work of the Portland Hotel Society [a non-profit organization founded in 1993 to provide housing and support for people with addiction or mental illness] is an . . . attempt at offering the respite from anguish and anxiety" needed by recovering addicts (299).

- Use single quotation marks for a quotation within a quotation.

SOURCE   The issue is the relationship society creates between itself and its drug-addicted citizens; the fundamental question is whether or not we recognize these people as human beings who are legitimately part of the social fabric, deserving compassion and respect. "Action has meaning only in relationship," said the spiritual teacher Jiddu Krishnamurti (Maté 297).

QUOTATION   "The issue is the relationship society creates between itself and its drug-addicted citizens; the fundamental question is whether or not we recognize these people as human beings who are legitimately part of the social fabric, deserving compassion and respect. 'Action has meaning only in relationship,' said the spiritual teacher Jiddu Krishnamurti" (Maté 297).

- When italics appear in your source, either carefully maintain the italics, or if that is not possible, underline the words that appeared in italics.

SOURCE   By contrast, after being housed with more subordinate animals, dominant monkeys had an *increase* of over 20 per cent of their dopamine receptors and less tendency to use cocaine (Maté 300).

QUOTATION   Research on primates illustrates that individuals who are accorded little respect or agency from their social group and who were inclined to use cocaine "had an increase of over 20 per cent of their dopamine receptors and less tendency to use cocaine" when they were moved into groups where they gained status. (Maté 300).

- Set off long quotations (five or more lines in your paper) by introducing it with *a main clause*, followed by a colon, and indenting it five spaces to the right of your normal margin.

SOURCE   As we have seen, the dominant emotional states and the brain patterns of human beings are shaped by their early environment. Throughout their lifetimes, they are in dynamic interaction with various social and emotional milieus. If we are to help addicts, we must strive to change not them but their environments. These are the only things we *can* change (Maté 299).

QUOTATION   Dr. Maté argues that we cannot help addicts manage or give up their addictions without addressing the way their environment influences the amount of stress they are experiencing:

> As we have seen, the dominant emotional states and the brain patterns of human beings are shaped by their early environment. Throughout their lifetimes, they are in dynamic interaction with various social and emotional milieus. If we are to help addicts, we must strive to change not them but their environments. These are the only things we *can* change. (Maté 299)

Do not write simply "Dr. Maté argues:" Doing so violates the rules for using colons. See the textbox below.

Troubleshooting Guide

Using Colons

You often use colons to introduce quotations, but you should do so only after a main clause—a grammatically complete thought. At the simplest level, you do not write, "I believe: we need to consider how we are going to protect the limited amount of potable water on the planet." You should therefore avoid introducing a quotation with a subject and a transitive verb—one that needs a direct object to make sense. Thus you do not introduce a quotation in the following ways:

The author argues:

The writer observes:

Rather, you might say,

The author argues against that strategy:

The writer observes that there isn't enough social support for addicts:

Both of these introductions are main clauses, and thus obey the rules for using a colon.

INTEGRATING PARAPHRASES AND QUOTATIONS

The following strategies will help you work paraphrases and quotations into your paper smoothly so your paper reads well, so your reader can tell that you are paraphrasing or quoting, and so your reader understands how you are using the source material.

- **Use sources to help you fulfill your writing purpose.** Avoid letting your sources drive the content and organization of your writing, and avoid stringing together quotations and paraphrases, one after another. Instead, use source material for a reason, such as to establish a point, support an argument, explain an idea, or illustrate a concept.

- **Include the author and/or source with the paraphrase or quotation.** Most often, that information comes before the quotation or paraphrase, but it can also come in the middle or at the end, as in these examples from Jill Boettger's essay "Inner City" (found on page 124) where we've underlined the source information.

AT THE BEGINNING	<u>Jill Boettger observes that</u> "In Calgary's inner city it seems another rooming house comes down every week. Or a hospital, or a school" (124).
IN THE MIDDLE	"In Calgary's inner city it seems another rooming house comes down every week," <u>observes Jill Boettger</u>. "Or a hospital, or a school" (124).
AT THE END	"In Calgary's inner city it seems another rooming house comes down every week. Or a hospital, or a school," <u>observes Jill Boettger</u> (124).

- **Vary the present tense verbs you use to work in the paraphrase or quotation.** Rather than repeating clauses such as "Collier says," try other verbs, including

acknowledges	implies	questions
argues	insists	replies
asserts	maintains	reveals
believes	notes	suggests
contends	points out	wonders

- **Indicate the purpose of each paraphrase and quotation by choosing verbs and including language to demonstrate how the source material relates to the ideas before or after.** Here is an example using

"The Surprising Truth about Heroin and Addiction," by Jacob Sullum, and "Imagining an Enlightened Social Policy on Drugs," by Gabor Maté. (The underlined transitional words help you see how the paragraph is constructed.)

Why do people use drugs despite the threat of legal sanction, the medical complications, and the difficulty of obtaining them? In "The Keys of Paradise," Dr. Gabor Maté <u>argues</u> that drug use is "far more than a quest for pleasure"; rather "chronic substance abuse is the addict's attempt to escape distress" (33). He <u>observes</u> that the addicts in his care are "trying to fill a void" that they can neither explain nor deal with. <u>Maintaining</u> that the research is "unequivocal: most hard-core substance abusers come from abusive homes," Maté <u>believes</u> that "The question is never 'why the addiction?' but 'Why the pain?'" (34). In "The Surprising Truth about Heroin and Addiction," Jacob Sullum <u>comes to the opposite conclusion</u>. As part of his strategy to promote the idea that drugs are not inherently addicting, Sullum <u>refers</u> to research that indicates heroine users tend to "'mature out' of the habit in their 30s" (157). His examples are drawn from a group of people who find heroine use relaxing, a way to unwind at the end of the day: it's "like taking a vacation from yourself . . . When things get to you, it's a way of getting away without getting away" (159). <u>The differences</u> between these two conclusions might come from the populations both authors are examining. Maté works in the Portland Hotel Project; his patients are often street people or the unemployed who are living in public housing. Sullum admits that his statistics are drawn from a "household survey [which] misses people living on the street, in prisons, and in residential drug treatment programs, while the high school survey leaves out truants and dropouts" (155). But because an effective national strategy for dealing with substance abuse needs to be based on the reason people use drugs, we need to find more sophisticated ways of collecting and analyzing data that will let us understand the full spectrum of reasons people turn to illicit drugs.

The reader can tell from the fifth sentence of the paragraph that the paraphrase and quotation of Sullum presents a view that contrasts with the view expressed in the Maté quotation. Take out the introductory sentences that provide the reader with context, as well as the language that shows how the borrowed material relates to other ideas, and the reader has a more difficult time connecting the two ideas:

In "The Keys to Paradise," Dr. Gabor Maté <u>argues</u> that drug use is "far more than a quest for pleasure"; rather "chronic substance abuse is the addict's attempt to escape distress" (33). He <u>observes</u> that the addicts in his care are "trying to fill a void" that they can neither explain nor deal with. <u>Maintaining</u> that the research is "unequivocal: most hard-core substance abusers come from abusive homes," Maté <u>believes</u> that "The question is never 'why the addiction?' but 'Why the pain?'" (34). As part of Jacob Sullum's strategy to promote the idea that drugs are not inherently addicting, he <u>refers</u> to research that indicates heroine users tend to "'mature out' of the habit in their 30s" (157). His examples are drawn from a group of people who find heroine use relaxing, a way to unwind at the end of the day: it's "like taking a vacation from yourself . . . When things get to you, it's a way of getting away without getting away" (159). Maté works in the Portland Hotel Project; his patients are often street people or the unemployed who are living in public housing. Sullum admits that his statistics are drawn from a "household survey [which] misses people living on the street, in prisons, and in residential drug treatment programs, while the high school survey leaves out truants and dropouts" (155). But because an effective national strategy for dealing with substance abuse needs to be based on the reason people use drugs, we need to find more sophisticated ways of collecting and analyzing data that will let us understand the full spectrum of reasons people turn to illicit drugs.

There are four other things to note about the first example. First, the quotations fit snugly into the syntax of the sentences that include them. To ensure that your quotations are carefully incorporated, *mentally* remove the quotation marks and ensure that your sentence is clear and your syntax uncompromised by the inclusion of someone else's words. Second, note that punctuation marks go inside quotation marks, except in the case of the

---

Troubleshooting Guide

Using the Present Tense with Paraphrases and Quotations

If you have trouble knowing what tense to use when you integrate paraphrases and quotations, remember that the present tense is conventional. This *present tense convention* is used because printed words—even ones written long ago—exist in the present.

YES   **While Maté agrees on the failure of the "war on drugs," he also questions the success of attempts to coerce addicts to change their lives.**

NO   **While Maté agreed on the failure of the "war on drugs," he also questioned the success of attempts to coerce addicts to change their lives.**

semicolon (;) in the second sentence. This is because the semicolon belongs to the structure of the sentence, never to the quotation itself. Third, in the first example the student's topic sentence indicates that she is in control of these ideas. *Never* begin a paragraph with a quotation; when you do, you are letting someone else's words set the agenda for your paragraph. Finally, the earlier example is a coherent paragraph. Coherence in the paragraph moves beyond simply staying on topic; coherence refers to the ways you use transitions to help your readers follow the precise shape of your thought.

AVOIDING PLAGIARISM

Plagiarism is theft. If you use another person's ideas, words, manner of expression, or research and pass that material off as your own, you are guilty of plagiarism. Whether intentional or unintentional, plagiarism can result in serious penalties, including failing an assignment, failing a course, or expulsion.

To avoid plagiarism, remember the following.

- **Never hand in another person's work as your own.** Knowingly submitting another person's work as your own—including a paper you buy on the Internet or elsewhere—is the most blatant form of intentional plagiarism.
- **Never copy material from the library and use it in a paper as if it were your own ideas.** Unless the information is common knowledge (see below on common knowledge), material taken from any library source must be credited according to the documentation conventions explained in the next section.
- **Never download material from the Internet, paste it into your paper, and use it as if it were your own.** Copying from the Internet into your paper is easily accomplished, but doing so amounts to theft of intellectual property if you do not cite the source according to the documentation conventions explained in the next section.
- **Give credit for all ideas, facts, opinions, and statistics that are not common knowledge.** Material that is common knowledge does not have to be cited. Common knowledge includes well-known facts (on the Celsius scale, 0 degrees is the freezing point), undisputed historical events (Germany was defeated in World War II), common sayings (It's always darkest before the dawn), and generally agreed upon information. If you are unsure whether something is common knowledge, consult with your instructor or err on the side of caution and credit the material according to the conventions explained in the next section.

- **Take notes carefully.** Before you even begin to take notes, write down the information you will need for your Works Cited page or your bibliography, preferably in the form it will take on that page. (Too many of us type up our Works Cited at about 3 A.M., and it's a lot less confusing if your references are already in the proper format.) As you take notes, be sure to distinguish between your own ideas and words or ideas you take from sources. Unintentional plagiarism can occur if you forget that you took something from a source and include it in a paper as if it were your own. It's a good idea, even in your notes, to put quotation marks around passages you copy word for word.
- **Always credit the source and use quotation marks around someone else's words.** Even if you only use one or two words, if they are another person's distinctive phrasing, place that phrasing in quotation marks and credit it according to the conventions explained in the next section.
- **Quote accurately.** Do not change the wording of a direct quotation without using ellipses for omissions and brackets for additions, as explained on page 507.
- **Credit all of your paraphrases and quotations according to the appropriate documentation conventions.** In the next section, we will cover two commonly used documentation conventions, that of the Modern Language Association and the American Psychological Association.

DOCUMENTING SOURCES

For proper **documentation,** you must show your reader the source of your paraphrases and quotations. Each discipline has its own conventions for documentation, conventions that reflect the needs of the discipline's scholars. Two documentation conventions are given in this book. First, we'll show you how to use the seventh edition of the *Handbook for Writers of Research Papers,* published by the Modern Language Association (called MLA style); these conventions are used in English classes. Then we'll illustrate the conventions of the *Publication Manual of the American Psychological Association* (also called APA style). These conventions are used by psychologists and other social scientists. Other disciplines have their own distinctive conventions; for example, mathematicians use the *AMS* [American Mathematical Society] *Author Handbook.* When in doubt, check with your instructor to learn the conventions you should follow; he or she will be impressed by your careful attention to detail!

MLA conventions have been streamlined; the main purpose of your parenthetical citation is to allow your reader to find the source on your works cited list and to ultimately find the passage if necessary. Thus, if you mention the name of the author in your text, you do not need to include it in the parenthetical citation. To document according to MLA conventions, do the following:

- **The first time you use a source, introduce it with the author's full name and the title of the source.**

  In "Imagining an Enlightened Social Policy on Drugs," Dr. Gabor Maté argues that our culture "projects its darkest features onto the addict and makes addicted people into scapegoats for its shortcomings" (295).

- **Subsequent times you use a source, you can introduce with either the author's last name or the title of the source; you do not need both.**

  Maté also suggests that with such attitudes "moralizing displaces compassion and prejudice substitutes for inquiry" (295).

- **Follow the paraphrase or quotation with a parenthetical text citation that gives the page number where the borrowed information or wording can be found.** If the introduction does not include the author's name, the parenthetical citation should note the name along with the page number. Otherwise, only the page number is needed. For sources that do not use page numbers, give another identifier such as paragraph number (e.g., *par. 26*) or section number (e.g., *sec. 4*), if available.

  For Maté, a successful drug policy addresses the way in which the addict's environment contributes to the need for drugs: "If we are to help addicts, we must strive to change not them but their environments (299).

  One researcher believes a successful drug policy addresses the way in which the addict's environment contributes to the need for drugs: "If we are to help addicts, we must strive to change not them but their environments (Maté 299).

- **For electronic sources that do not have page numbers, or for a reference to an entire work, place the author's name in parentheses. If the author's name is not given, place the title in parentheses.**

  Research shows that boys living with their mothers experience more hostility than girls do, both immediately after the divorce and far beyond (Linaman).

- **If you quote or paraphrase a source that is cited in a second source, note the secondhand nature of the borrowing with qtd. (meaning "quoted") in the parenthetical citation.**

  Justice John Marshall Harlan best described the relative nature of profanity when he said, "'One man's vulgarity is another's lyric'" (qtd. in Wasserman 628).

- **Follow your writing with a Works Cited page.** A "Works Cited" page is a listing of your sources alphabetized by author. (For an example of a Works Cited page, see page 525.) It includes full bibliographic information on each source from which you quoted or paraphrased. For the correct works cited forms, consult the next section.

MLA STYLE

For correct MLA documentation, the entries on your works cited page should follow the models given below. Regard these sample entries as recipes for you to follow. Pay particular attention to the order in which information is presented and to punctuation. Alphabetize your entries as you type. If you use sources that do not fit these models, consult a handbook or a research paper guide, or visit Purdue University's Online Writing Lab (OWL) at http://owl.english.purdue.edu/owl/.

Print Books

Book by One Author

Maté, Gabor. *In the Realm of Hungry Ghosts*. Toronto: Knopf Canada, 2008. Print.

Book by Two or more Authors

Walker, Gabrielle, and Sir David King. *The Hot Topic*. Toronto: Douglas & McIntyre, 2008. Print.

Chapter in a Book

Kearns, J. M. "How Men Choose Women." *What I Meant to Say*. Ed. Ian Brown. Toronto: Thomas Allen. 83-93. Print.

Revised Edition of a Book

Miller, Casey, and Kate Swift. *The Handbook of Nonsexist Writing*. 2nd ed. New York: Harper, 1988. Print.

A Book with an Editor

Marshall, Sam. A., ed. *1990 Photographer's Market*. Cincinnati, OH: Writer's Digest, 1989. Print.

Encyclopedia Article

"Terrorism." Encyclopedia Britannica. 2001 ed. Print.

More Than One Book by the Same Author

Tannen, Deborah. *I Only Say This Because I Love You: How the Way We Talk Can Make or Break Family Relationships throughout Our Lives*. New York: Random House, 2006. Print.

---. *You Just Don't Understand: Women and Men in Conversation.* New York: Ballantine, 1990. Print.

When you cite Tannen in your essay, place a short version of the title and the page numbers in parentheses: (Tannen, *I Only Say This* 33).

Print Periodicals

Article from a Weekly or Biweekly Magazine

Klein, Joe. "The Trouble with Polls and Focus Groups." *Time* 4 Oct. 2004: 29. Print.

Article from a Monthly or Bimonthly Magazine

Callwood, June. "Forgiveness." *The Walrus* June 2007: 36-37. Print.

Newspaper Article

Mason, Gary. "Call Me an Optimist, but if Denmark Can Go Green, Canada Can Too." *The Globe and Mail* 12 Aug. 2008: A6. Print.

Article from a Scholarly Journal with Volume and Issue Numbers

Tisseron, Serge. "The Mirror of the Internet." *Queen's Quarterly* 109.3 (2002): 329-334. Print.

Article from a Scholarly Journal with Only Issue Number

Luhmann, Susanne. "Ill-Fated Lessons: History, Remembrance, Trauma and Memory in Ann-Marie MacDonald's *The Way the Crow Flies*." *Topia: Canadian Journal of Cultural Studies* 16 (2006): 109-27. Print.

Online Sources

Online sources are varied. In general, your citation should include, in the following order, the author's name, the title of the work, the title of the online site (in italics), the publisher or sponsor of the site, the date of publication, the medium of publication (*Web*), and the date you consulted the source. Include the address (URL) at the very end of the entry, in angle brackets (< >), only if the source would be hard to find without it or your instructor requires it. When some of this information is unavailable, give as complete a citation as you can, but use the order given above.

Material from a News Site

"Canada's Munro Wins International Booker Prize." *CBC.ca*. Canadian Broadcasting
    Corporation, 26 Apr. 2009. Web. 21 May 2009.

Note: The second date refers to date of access.

Article in a Reference Database

"Abbott, Berenice." *Encyclopaedia Britannica Online*. Encyclopaedia Britannica, 2009.
    Web. 21 May 2009.

Magazine Article

Leo, John. "Self-Inflicted Wounds." *USNews.com*. U.S. News & World Report, 11 Oct. 2004.
    Web. 14 Oct. 2004.

Journal Article

Goleman, Judith. "An 'Immensely Simplified Task': Form in Modern Composition-
    Rhetoric." *College Composition and Communication* 56.1 (2004): 51-71. Web.
    20 May 2009.

Note: The information included is the same as for the print version except for
the medium of publication (*Web* instead of *Print*) and the date of access. If
you found the article on an online database, put the database name in italics
before *Web*.

Material from a Scholarly Site

Representative Poetry Online. University of Toronto, 2008. Web. 7 Oct. 2008 <http://
    rpo.library.utoronto.ca/display/>.

Online Posting to a Listserv, Newsgroup, or Forum

Quinlan, Rob. "Biocultural Evolution." Online posting. *Anthro-I: The General Anthropology
    Bulletin Board,* 19 Sept. 1995. Web. 30 Apr. 1998.

Note: The second date is the date the material was accessed.

Other Sources

Radio or Television Program

Moyers, Bill, and Robert Bly. *A Gathering of Men*. PBS. WNET, New York. 8 Jan. 1990.
    Radio.

Personal Interview

DeSalvo, Joy. Personal interview. 30 Sept. 1996.

A Sound Recording

Brooks, Mel. *The Producers*. Orch. Doug Besterman, Perf. Nathan Lane, Matthew Broderick, and Gary Beach. Sony Classical, 2001. CD.

Image of a Painting, Photograph, or Other Artwork from a Print Source

Remington, Frederic. *A Dash for the Timber, 1889*. Amon Carter Museum, Fort Worth. *American Art: History and Culture*. By Wayne Craven. New York: McGraw, 1994. 387. Print.

Note: Provide the institution or owner and the city, as well as publication information for the source in which the painting or photograph appears.

Image of a Painting, Photograph, or Other Artwork from an Electronic Source

Cézanne, Paul. *The Bather*. 1885. Museum of Mod. Art, New York. *The Collection*. Web. 14 June 2004.

APA STYLE

When you use APA style, the basic elements of a parenthetical citation are the author's last name, the year of publication, and the page number if you are referring to a specific passage in the source. If you use the author's name in your text to introduce a quotation, give the date alone or date and page numbers if you are referring to a particular passage.

The major differences between MLA and APA reflect the discipline. Literary scholars always want to be able to find the passage you are referring to, so MLA style always requires a page number. Obviously, the date of the research is of primary interest to those in the social sciences, so APA citations must always include the year.

While MLA style doesn't use any punctuation in parenthetical citations, APA uses commas to separate the elements and a period after the "p" or "pp" used to indicate page numbers. You can refer to the same examples above, on page 507, to see the differences between MLA and APA citations.

> For Maté (2008), a successful drug policy addresses the way in which the addict's environment contributes to the need for drugs: "If we are to help addicts, we must strive to change not them but their environments" (p. 299).

One researcher believes a successful drug policy addresses the way in which the addict's environment contributes to the need for drugs: "If we are to help addicts, we must strive to change not them but their environments (Maté, 2008, p. 299).

For correct APA documentation, the entries in your references should follow the models given below. Regard these sample entries as recipes for you to follow. Note that there are two major differences between MLA and APA. The latter uses only the initials of authors' first names. The date of publication comes right after the name. Only the first word of titles is capitalized. Also pay attention to the order in which other information is presented and to punctuation. Alphabetize your entries as you type. If you use sources that do not fit these models, consult a handbook or a research paper guide, or visit the Research and Citation link at Purdue University's Online Writing Lab (OWL) at http://owl.english.purdue.edu/owl/.

Books

Book by One Author

Maté , G. (2008). *In the realm of hungry ghosts*. Toronto: Knopf Canada.

Book by Two or More Authors

Walker, G., & King, D. (2008). *The hot topic*. Toronto: Douglas & McIntyre.

Note: An ampersand is used rather than "and" to join the names of the authors. Include the names of all the authors.

Chapter in a Book

Kearns, J. M. (2005). How men choose women. In Ian Brown (Ed.), *What I meant to say* (pp. 83–93). Toronto: Thomas Allen.

Revised Edition of a Book

Miller, C., & Swift, K. (1988). *Handbook of nonsexist writing* (2nd ed.). New York: Harper.

A Book with an Editor

Marshall, S. A. (Ed.). (1989). *1990 photographer's market*. Cincinnati, OH: Writer's Digest.

Encyclopedia or Dictionary

Robbins, J. E. (Ed.). (1970). *Encyclopedia Canadiana*. Toronto: Grolier.

More Than One Book by the Same Author

Tannen, D. (1990). *You just don't understand: Women and men in conversation.* New York: Ballantine,.

Tannen, D. (2006). *I only say this because I love you: How the way we talk can make or break family relationships throughout our lives.* New York: Random House.

Place the works in chronological order. Because your parenthetical citations always include the year, your reader will know which work of Tannen's you were referring to. If two books or articles by the same author are published in the same year, alphabetize the titles and include a letter with the date: the first work would be (2006a) and the second (2006b). Use those letters along with the date in your parenthetical citation.

Periodicals

In APA style you italicize both the names of journals and magazines and the volume number. You do not put quotation marks around the titles of articles appearing in them.

Magazine Article

Callwood, J. (2007, June). "Forgiveness." *The Walrus, 2007,* 36–37.

Newspaper Article

Mason, G. (2008, August 12). Call me an optimist, but if Denmark can go green, Canada can too. *The Globe and Mail,* p. A6.

Article from a Scholarly Journal with Continuous Pagination

Tisseron, S. (2002). The mirror in the Internet. *Queen's Quarterly, 109,* 329–334.

Article from a Scholarly Journal with Separate Pagination

Pierrous, P. (2003). Communicating in art museums: Language and concepts in art education. *Journal of Museum Education, 28*(1). 3–7.

Online Sources

Online sources are varied. In general, your citation should include the document title or description, a date (both the date of publication and the date you retrieved the information) and an Internet address that works. Whenever possible include the authors' names as well.

Magazine Article from a Print Source

Leo, J. (2004, October 11). Self-inflicted wounds. *U.S. News and World Report*. Retrieved October 14, 2004, from http://www.usnews.com/usnews/issue/041011/opinion/ 11john.htm

Note: The second date is the date the material was accessed.

Journal Article

Goleman, J. (2004, September). An "immensely simplified task": Form in modern composition-rhetoric. *College Composition and Communication.* Retrieved October 12, 2004, from http://www.ncte.org/library/files/Publications/Journals/ccc/0561-sept04/ CO0561Immensely.pdf

ANNOTATED STUDENT ESSAY

The following student paper illustrates how writers can combine their own ideas with research material in an essay. The notations in the margin call your attention to some of the essay's features, including its use of MLA conventions. (For other examples of student essays that incorporate sources, see pages 295 and 396.)

David 1

Florence David
Professor Dietz
English 551 14
November 2004

Divorce as a Violation of Trust

1   "The View of Me from Mars" by Lee K. Abbott is about trust, the trust between a husband and wife and the trust between a parent and child. Husbands and wives trust each other to be honest, and children trust their parents to tell the truth. However, as both the story and the story-within-a story illustrate, that trust is sometimes betrayed, and when it is, something important is lost. As I read the short story, I was at first reminded of the high divorce rate in this country, perhaps because of the main character's infidelity. Eventually, though, I realized that the theme of trust triggered my thinking about divorce because one of the most serious violations of trust occurs when spouses divorce, and children are left feeling frightened and insecure. Children trust their parents to love each other and take care of them as a unit. When parents divorce, they violate that trust and children suffer.

2   According to Nancy Dreger in "Divorce and the American Family," United States Census Bureau statistics show that in 1960, fifty-three percent of families consisted of a father, mother, and at least one child. In 1995, the percentage dropped about twenty percent and is still falling (2). Just in 1995 alone there were 1.2 million divorces, says Barry Frieman in "Two Parents-Two Homes" (5). The number of children affected by those divorces is staggering: over a million according to James Hopper in *The Effects of Divorce on Children* (3). The effects of these divorces are serious. In fact, they are so serious that I think couples should consider staying married for the sake of their children.

3   When our trust is violated, we feel stress, and children of divorce are no different. A study done on 700 junior-high students, reported by Karl Zinsmeister in "Divorce's Toll on Children," reveals that the stress of divorce ranks right beneath the stress of the death of a parent or close family member (19). The stress can lead to emotional and behavioral

Paragraphs 1 and 2 are the introduction. The thesis is the last sentence of paragraph 2.

Paragraph 2 synthesizes paraphrases from three sources to show the prevalence of divorce and the number of children affected. The writer uses parenthetical citations.

Paragraph 3 begins with a topic sentence. The paragraph combines three paraphrases with the author's own experience to show the effects of the stress of divorce. Notice that sentences with paraphrases include words to show the source and a parenthetical citation.

David 2

problems, says Hopper (3). When my parents divorced when I was twelve, for example, I became so nervous that I began to use drugs. That led to skipping school and finally getting arrested for shoplifting. I had never been in trouble before the divorce, at least not trouble that serious. Apparently my reaction is not uncommon because Zinsmeister reports that teenagers of divorced parents often abuse drugs and commit violent acts (21).

<table>
<tr>
<td>

Paragraph 4 combines paraphrase and quotation. Notice that the author adds her own sentences to connect the borrowings and show how they relate to each other.

</td>
<td>

4   Some girls whose parents divorce become promiscuous because their self-esteem is lowered. Zinsmeister calls this the "sleeper effect" of divorce (21). Boys can face a different problem, especially when they live with their mothers, because they lack a role model. As Robert Bly notes in "The Pillow and the Key," "When women, even women with the best intentions, bring up a boy alone, he may in some way have no male face, or he may have no face at all" (476). In "The Effects of Divorce on Children and Families," marriage and family therapist Todd E. Linaman reports one effect of the loss of the father figure. He says that boys living with their mothers experience more hostility than girls do, both immediately after the divorce and far beyond (Linaman). Imagine what it must be like for a young boy whose father is not on the scene. He can't help but feel hostile about the loss of trust in the dependability of his male parent.

</td>
</tr>
<tr>
<td>

Paragraph 5 opens with a topic sentence that is supported with three paraphrases and the author's own thinking.

</td>
<td>

5   After divorce, a family's finances may suffer, which can compound the feelings of loss of trust for children. As Linaman explains, women and children can be particularly hard hit because half of divorced men required to pay child support do not do so regularly; of the remaining half, a quarter make none of their payments, and a quarter pay less than the required amount (Linaman). A study by Jennifer Gerner and Dean Lillard, reported in "The Hidden Costs of Divorce" by Mike Powers, shows that even those who graduate from high school are less likely to go to college because of financial problems (25). In fact, according to Linaman, 60 percent fewer children of divorce attend college than children of intact families (Linaman). Again, children whose standard of living is reduced or whose college plans are sidetracked are likely to feel a threat to their basic security and a loss of trust in the ability of their parents to fulfill their responsibility to care for them.

</td>
</tr>
<tr>
<td>

Paragraph 6 In this paragraph, the author raises and counters some objections and suggests circumstances in which divorce may be the best option, but she also uses a source to point out that most divorces do not involve these circumstances. Notice the long quotation.

</td>
<td>

6   Of course, to suggest that all unhappy spouses should stay married when children are involved or that all divorces are harmful to children makes no sense. Mel Krantzler, in *Creative Divorce,* says that children are resilient and can come through a divorce just fine (192), and Linaman concedes that children in "high conflict" marriages, in which the couple "engages in hostile, aggressive and destructive fighting" may be better off

</td>
</tr>
</table>

David 3

if the parents do divorce (Linaman). However, Linaman also contends that most marriages ending in divorce are high conflict. He states:

> It is estimated that only 30% of divorces occur under these circumstances. Approximately 70% of all divorces end "low conflict" marriages. Many experts believe that these are marriages that could potentially be saved, and that continuing the marriage would not produce more negative stress for the child than would ending the relationship. (Linaman)

7   When trust is at stake, saving a marriage helps protect children. With very young children, the effects of loss of trust that divorce entails may be worse than they are for older children, who at least understand some of what is happening. Young children may not understand why one parent is gone and why the family unit is destroyed. In this case, the loss of trust can affect the child's security and ability to relate to people for all time. This is the child who may be afraid to get close to anyone for fear that the person will leave, or the child who thinks he or she is to blame for the divorce and is filled with guilt or self-loathing. The loss of trust a child of divorce experiences harms the child, and it may last a lifetime. Thus, couples with children should think carefully before divorcing.

Paragraph 7 is the conclusion. The author draws her points together and restates her thesis.

Works Cited

Bly, Robert. "The Pillow and the Key." *Writing about Diversity: An Argument Reader and Guide*. Ed. Irene L. Clark. 2nd ed. Fort Worth: Harcourt, 1997. 465–484. Print.

Dreger, Nancy. "Divorce and the American Family." *Current Health* 2 Nov. 1996: 6–12. Print.

Frieman, Barry B. "Two Parents-Two Homes." *Educational Leadership* Apr. 1997: 23–25. Print.

Hopper, James A. *The Effects of Divorce on Children: A Review of the Literature*. Maryland: ERIC Clearinghouse, 1997. ERIC NO-408539. Print.

Krantzler, Mel. *Creative Divorce: A New Opportunity for Personal Growth*. New York: M. Evans, 1974. Print.

Linaman, Todd E. "The Effects of Divorce on Children and Families." *Family Life Facts*. 9 Sept. 2004. Web. 8 Nov. 2008.

Powers, Mike. "The Hidden Costs of Divorce." *Human Ecology Forum* 25.1 (Winter 1997): 4–7. Print.

Zinsmeister, Karl. "Divorce's Toll on Children." *Current Health* Feb. 1997, 29–33. Print.

Literary Credits

Adams, Michael, and Neuman, Keith. "It's Not Easy Being Green" from *The Globe and Mail*, Oct. 20, 2006. Reprinted by permission of Environics Research Group.

Adler, Mortimer. "How to Mark a Book," originally published in the *Saturday Review*, 1940. Reprinted by permission of the Estate of Mortimer Adler.

Appiah, Kwame Anthony. From *Cosmopolitanism: Ethics in a World of Strangers* by Kwame Anthony Appiah. Copyright © 2006 by Kwame Anthony Appiah. Used by permission of W. W. Norton. & Company, Inc.

Boetgger, Jill. "Inner City." Originally published in *Geist* 64, Spring 2007.

Bok, Sissela. "White Lies" from *Lying* by Sissela Bok. Copyright © 1978 by Sissela Bok. Used by permission of Pantheon Books, a division of Random House, Inc.

Borson, Roo. "Gray Glove." Reprinted by permission of the author.

Brady, Judy. "I Want a Wife" by Judy Brady. Copyright © 1970 by Judy Brady. Reprinted by permission of the author.

Britt, Suzanne. "Neat People vs. Sloppy People" from *Show and Tell* by Suzanne Britt. Copyright © 1982 by Suzanne Britt. Reprinted by permission of the author.

Byfield, Joanne. "The Men from the Boys: Bull-riding Is Dangerous, Irrelevant, and a Rare Expression of Old-Style Masculinity.: First published in *The Report Newsmagazine*, Dec. 3, 2001. Reprinted with permission of the author.

Callwood, June. "Forgiveness." Originally published in *The Walrus*, June 2007.

Choy, Wayson. "The Ten Thousand Things." Copyright © 1997 by Wayson Choy. First published in Canada in *Writing Home: A PEN Canada Anthology.* Reprinted by permission of the author.

Connell, R. W. From *Masculinities* by R.W. Connell. Reprinted with permission by RightsLink.

Cole, Diane. "Don't Just Stand There" by Diane Cole originally published in *The New York Times,* April 16, 1989. Reprinted by permission of the author.

Dillard, Annie. "The Deer at Providencia" from *Teaching a Stone to Talk* by Annie Dillard. Copyright © 1982 by Annie Dillard. Reprinted by permission of HarperCollins Publishers Inc.

Ehrenreich, Barbara. "What I've Learned from Men: Lessons for a Full-Grown Feminist." Reprinted by permission of International Creative Management, Inc. Copyright © 1985 by Barbara Ehrenreich.

Falconer, Tim. "Toronto Cars. Can't Live with 'Em, Can't Live without 'Em." From *Drive* by Tim Falconer. Copyright © Tim Falconer, 2008. Reprinted by permission of Penguin Group (Canada), a division of Pearson Canada Inc.

Finkel, Alvin, and Margaret Conrad. From *History of the Canadian Peoples: Beginnings to 1867* by Alvin Finkel and Margaret Conrad, p. xv–xvi. Copyright © 2008 Pearson Education Canada. Reprinted with permission by Pearson Education Canada Inc.

Fowke, Edith. From *Canadian Folklore* by Edith Fowke. Reprinted with permission of The Writers' Union of Canada.

Gates, Henry Louis, Jr. "In the Kitchen" from *Colored People: A Memoir* by Henry

Glossary

This glossary provides definitions of the terms set in boldface throughout the text and gives the pages where the terms are first used. Words in small capital letters are defined elsewhere in the glossary.

alternating pattern In COMPARISON-CONTRAST, the arrangement of detail whereby a point is made for one subject, and then the corresponding point is made for the other subject. This arrangement continues until all points are made for both subjects.   page 290 (See also BLOCK PATTERN.)

analogy A comparison of two elements from different categories in order to shed light on one or both elements. For example, comparing marriage to a roller-coaster ride is an analogy, as is comparing divorce to a medieval siege.   page 286

anecdote A brief NARRATION often used as an example.   page 142

argumentation The use of reason and logic to persuade a reader to think or act a particular way. Argumentation employs compelling evidence and counters significant objections to the writer's view to earn the reader's agreement.   page 376 (See also PERSUASION.)

audience The readers for a particular piece of writing. For example, the audience for your campus newspaper is the students, faculty, staff, and administration of your college or university. Different audiences have different characteristics, and writers must be aware of those characteristics to meet the needs of their readers.   page 36

block pattern In COMPARISON-CONTRAST, the arrangement of detail by first presenting all the points about one subject and then all the points about the second subject.   page 289 (See also ALTERNATING PATTERN.)

body paragraph A paragraph composed of a TOPIC SENTENCE that gives a main idea and SUPPORTING DETAILS that develop that idea. A body paragraph helps support the THESIS.   page 69

causal chain In CAUSE-AND-EFFECT ANALYSIS, a sequence that occurs when a cause leads to an effect, and that effect becomes a cause leading to another effect, and so on.   page 318

cause-and-effect analysis A pattern of essay development that examines the reasons for an event (causes), the results of an event (effects), or both.   page 314

chronological order The arrangement of details in an essay according to a time sequence, usually beginning with the first event and proceeding to the second and subsequent events.   page 118 (See also FLASHBACK.)

classification A pattern of essay development that groups items into related categories according to a specific principle. In classification, items that share characteristics are grouped together.   page 350 (See also DIVISON.)

coherence The smooth connection of SUPPORTING DETAILS and BODY PARAGRAPHS in a clear, understandable way. To achieve coherence, writers use transitions, logical ordering of ideas, and repetition of keywords and ideas to show how ideas relate to each other.   page 75

comparison-contrast A pattern of essay development that notes the similarities and/or differences between two subjects. Comparison notes similarities, and contrast notes differences.   page 282

conclusion The final sentences or paragraph of an essay, meant to provide resolution and closure. An effective conclusion creates a satisfying ending and does not close abruptly.   page 79

context See WRITING CONTEXT.

deduction A form of reasoning that moves from the general to the specific, from a GENERALIZATION (the major premise) to a specific case (the minor premise) to a conclusion.   page 390 (See also INDUCTION.)

definition A pattern of essay development that gives the meaning of a term.   page 211 (See also EXTENDED DEFINITION, FORMAL DEFINITION, NEGATIVE DEFINITION, and STIPULATIVE DEFINITION.)

description A pattern of essay development that uses words to create mental images for the reader.   page 108 (See also EXPRESSIVE DETAILS and OBJECTIVE DETAILS.)

direct quotation The reproduction of exact spoken or written words.   pages 146 and 507

directional process analysis A form of PROCESS ANALYSIS that gives the steps in a procedure so the reader can perform it.   page 242 (See also EXPLANATORY PROCESS ANALYSIS.)

division A pattern of essay development that breaks an entity down into its parts.   page 350 (See also CLASSIFICATION.)

documentation The formal crediting of borrowed material (PARAPHRASE and DIRECT QUOTATION) by noting the source of the borrowing according to conventions of a particular discipline. Papers written in a literature or composition class are often documented according to the conventions of the Modern Language Association (MLA).   page 514

dominant impression In DESCRIPTION, the quality the descriptive details are meant to convey.   page 112

editing The process of finding and correcting errors in grammar, usage, punctuation, capitalization, and spelling.   page 90

errors in logic See LOGIC, ERRORS IN.

ethos One of three elements of a successful argument. (The other two elements are LOGOS and PATHOS.) Ethos refers to establishing the reliability and trustworthiness of the writer of an argument.   page 380

exemplification A pattern of essay development that uses specific instances (examples) to clarify a point, to add interest, or to persuade.   page 174 (See also HYPOTHETICAL EXAMPLE.)

explanatory process analysis A form of PROCESS ANALYSIS that explains how something works, how it is made, or how it is done. The procedure explained is not meant to be carried out by the reader.   page 243 (See also DIRECTIONAL PROCESS ANALYSIS.)

expressive details In DESCRIPTION, points that give a subjective or emotional view of what is being described.   page 112 (See also OBJECTIVE DETAILS.)

extended definition A form of DEFINITION in which the writer goes beyond the literal meaning of a word to give the significance, private meanings, and personal experiences associated with that word.   page 214 (See also FORMAL DEFINITION, NEGATIVE DEFINITION, and STIPULATIVE DEFINITION.)

fact A statement that can be proven or that has been proven. For example, it is a fact that plants manufacture oxygen from carbon dioxide.   page 6 (See also OPINION.)

first draft A writer's initial effort to get ideas down in essay form. A first draft is usually very rough and in need of REVISION.   page 65

flashback A form of CHRONOLOGICAL ORDER that involves moving from one point in time to a more distant point in the past and back again.   page 148

formal definition A DEFINITION that states the term to be defined, its class, and how it differs from other members of the class: An antibiotic is a type of drug that attacks bacteria.   page 211 (See also EXTENDED DEFINITION, NEGATIVE DEFINITION, and STIPULATIVE DEFINITION.)

generalization A broad statement that asserts that something is true in most cases or in every case.   page 70 (See also DEDUCTION.)

hypothetical example An illustration based on something that *could* happen.   page 178 (See also EXEMPLIFICATION.)

induction A form of reasoning that moves from specific evidence to a general conclusion.   page 389 (See also DEDUCTION and INFERENCE.)

inference A conclusion drawn on the basis of what a speaker or writer suggests, rather than what is specifically stated. In INDUCTION, an inference is the conclusion drawn; it is usually not certain beyond a doubt.   pages 7 and 390

introduction One or more paragraphs that open an essay. The introduction is meant to engage a reader's interest; many times the introduction also presents the THESIS.   page 66

journalist's questions Who? What? When? Where? Why? How? In NARRATION, the answers form much of the supporting detail.   page 144

logic, errors in Forms of faulty reasoning that lead a person to a false conclusion.   page 9

logos One of the three elements of a successful argument. (The other elements are ETHOS and PATHOS.) Logos refers to sound reasoning, facts, evidence, statistics, and authoritative statements used to back up an assertion.   page 379 (See also LOGIC, ERRORS IN.)

metaphor An implied comparison made without using the words *like* or *as*: "The play's opening act was a train wreck."   page 118

narration A pattern of essay development that involves telling a story.   page 141

negative definition A form of DEFINITION that draws the reader's attention to what the term or concept is not. Frequently brief, it often qualifies the term or challenges common assumptions. The following is an example: "Friendship is not just two people getting together so one can talk and the other can listen."   page 105 (See also EXTENDED DEFINITION, FORMAL DEFINITION, and STIPULATIVE DEFINITION.)

objective details In DESCRIPTION, points that give a factual, unemotional picture of what is described.   page 112 (See also EXPRESSIVE DETAILS.)

opinion A statement of a person's judgment, interpretation, or belief. Unlike a FACT, an opinion cannot be proven. For example, it is an opinion that the current movie rating system is inadequate.   page 6

paraphrase The restatement of an author's written ideas in your own words and style. Paraphrases are used in essays and research papers that draw on sources.   page 505

pathos One of the three elements of a successful argument. (The other elements are LOGOS and ETHOS.) Pathos refers to the appeal to emotions, attitudes, beliefs, and values.   page 379

persuasion Uses appeals to emotions, values, and beliefs to convince a reader to think or act a particular way.   page 376 (See also ARGUMENTATION.)

plagiarism A form of academic dishonesty that occurs when a person submits another's words, ideas, or work as his or her own, or when a person fails to provide DOCUMENTATION of borrowed material. page 513

process analysis A pattern of essay development that explains how something is made, how something is done, or how something works.   page 242 (See also DIRECTIONAL PROCESS ANALYSIS and EXPLANATORY PROCESS ANALYSIS.)

progressive order The arrangement of details from the least important or compelling points to the most important or compelling points.   page 118

purpose The reason a person writes, the goal the writer hopes to achieve. A writer's purpose can be to entertain, to express feelings or relate experience, to inform, and/or to persuade.   page 35

quotation See DIRECT QUOTATION.

revising The process of evaluating and making changes in a draft's content, organization, and expression of ideas in order to improve it. The revision process can involve writing multiple drafts.   page 84

role The way the writer presents himself or herself. For example, a writer can assume the role of a student, parent, average reader, concerned citizen, voter, and so forth.   page 38

sensory details DESCRIPTION that appeals to any of the five senses (sight, sound, taste, smell, touch).   page 113 (See also EXPRESSIVE DETAILS and OBJECTIVE DETAILS.)

simile A comparison made using the word *like* or the word *as*: "The overheated radiator spewed water like a geyser." page 116

spatial order The arrangement of details across space, for example from top to bottom, near to far, front to back, or left to right.   page 118

stipulative definition Explains a special or unexpected way a term is used. The following is an example: "By spouse, I do not refer merely to the legally married partner. I also refer to a same-sex partner in a committed relationship."   page 214 (See also DEFINITION, EXTENDED DEFINITION, FORMAL DEFINITION, and NEGATIVE DEFINITION.)

summary The brief restatement of the main points of a piece of writing in one's own words and style, given without adding or altering meaning.   page 15

supporting details In a BODY PARAGRAPH, all the points made to prove or explain the TOPIC SENTENCE.   page 69

synthesis The process whereby a person relates new information to previously learned information.   page 8 Also, the bringing together of material from two or more sources.   page 17

thesis The central point or controlling idea of an essay, the idea that everything else in the essay relates to and that the BODY PARAGRAPHS support.   page 49

tone The writer's attitude or feeling about the reader or about the subject of the writing. Tone can be neutral, angry, sympathetic, annoyed, and so on.   page 77

topic sentence In a BODY PARAGRAPH, the sentence that expresses the main idea. A topic sentence can be stated or implied.   page 69

writing context The combination of the writer's PURPOSE, AUDIENCE, and ROLE. The writing context creates the situation within which a person writes.   page 35

Index